*The Victory Garden*

# The Victory Garden

## THE ESSENTIAL COMPANION

**THREE COMPLETE VOLUMES IN ONE:**

*Masters of the Victory Garden*
BY JIM WILSON

*The New Victory Garden*
BY BOB THOMSON

*The Victory Garden Landscape Guide*
BY THOMAS WIRTH

BLACK DOG & LEVENTHAL
NEW YORK

Originally published in three separate volumes as:

*Masters of The Victory Garden*
*The New Victory Garden*
*The Victory Garden Landscape Guide*

This edition published by arrangement with Little, Brown and Company (Inc.)

Published by Black Dog & Leventhal Publishers, Inc.
151 West 19th Street
New York, NY 10011

Distributed by Workman Publishing Company
708 Broadway
New York, NY 10003

Manufactured in the United States of America

j i h g f e d c b a

ISBN:1-884822-23-1


**Library of Congress Cataloging-in-Publication Data**

The Victory garden : the essential companion
        p.    cm.
Includes bibliographical references (p.          ) and index.
Contains: Masters of the Victory garden / by Jim Wilson, The new Victory garden / by
Bob Thomson, The Victory garden landscape guide / by Thomas Wirth.
ISBN 1-884822-23-1 (hard cover)
1. Gardening    2. Landscape gardening.    I. Wilson, James W. (James Wesley), 1925–
Masters of the Victory garden.    II. Thomson, Bob. New Victory garden.    III. Wirth,
Thomas. Victory garden landscape guide.    IV. Victory garden (Television program)
SB453.V5765    1995
635—dc20                                                            95-37537
                                                                    CIP

# Contents

# The Victory Garden Landscape Guide 533

# Introduction

Welcome to The Victory Garden and the ultimate book for the amateur and serious gardener alike. For the first time the best of the Victory Garden is compiled into one encyclopedic edition. This book contains three volumes originally published as *Masters of the Victory Garden, The New Victory Garden,* and *The Victory Garden Landscape Guide.*

The book is photographed and illustrated with instructions on seed germination, soil preparation, planting techniques, fertilizing methods, and required watering for a variety of flowers, vegetables, fruits, shrubs and trees. Designs are included for garden layouts and construction projects such as decks, tool sheds, bird feeders and baths, and cold frames for early planting. "Green" solutions to pests and diseases are covered extensively, as well as composting and extending the growing season.

This new compendium in addition to being the complete gardeners guide, includes a delightful array of home projects. Learn how to press your own apple cider from the right combination of varieties to make a safe, tasty version of this old fashion beverage. Use bits and pieces of dried foliage and waste otherwise headed for the compost heap, to create beautiful wreaths for gifts and decoration. Learn how to grow and maintain a live Christmas tree for years of pleasure while helping the environment. Cross pollinate your lillies and discover a new perennial of your own. Master techniques used to bonsai existing trees and shrubs and learn what varieties lend themselves particularly well to this ancient method of landscaping.

Whether you are a novice facing the challenges of a new garden, or a "Garden Master" with years of experience, you are sure to find this a welcome addition to your library. From cover to cover this monumental edition will encourage, as well as, help you to solve problems you've faced for years. Open this book and plant the seeds that will set you on your way to becoming a Master of the Victory Garden.

# *Masters of the Victory Garden*

# *Masters of the Victory Garden*

*Specialty Gardeners Share Their Expert Techniques*

Jim Wilson

*To my friends on the **Victory Garden** staff, WGBH-TV, and especially executive producer Russ Morash, who suggested that I write this book from our experiences on location*

# *Preface*

*O*ften, when we are on location taping segments for *The Victory Garden*, the Executive Producer, Russell Morash, will say to me, "There's a lesson here, Jim: tell home gardeners what it means to them."

That's how this book came about. Over the years, as we visited gardens large and small, a "big picture" emerged, much more significant than the thousands of lessons we created for viewers. The revelation slowly unfolded that gardening is a two-way street. The accepted concept is that gardeners shape gardens. We believe that, even more important, gardens shape gardeners; it changes their personalities and their lifestyles, and all to the good.

We call such committed gardeners "Masters of Gardening," for, indeed, they have mastered so many of the elements that day-to-day duties are completed almost automatically. They are left with more time to enjoy their hobby, and it shows in their good nature, self-confidence, and feeling of oneness with Nature.

At some time in their gardening careers, Masters of Gardening take up a specialty plant as a hobby, and come to know it so well that they become enthusiasts, missionaries for their hobby. Their enthusiasm is infectious; they willingly share information and plants with novices and bring them into their circle of friends, usually within a specialty plant society.

Over the years, *The Victory Garden* has introduced its audience to many Masters of Gardening. We not only admire what these gardeners have accomplished, but we also like them as warm and sharing human beings. Russell Morash felt that other gardeners could benefit by reading about how they got into their hobby plant; their challenges, triumphs, and disappointments; and how plants changed their lives.

Russell asked me to write this book, and I jumped at the chance. Garden writing isn't new to me (I sold my first garden magazine article in 1956), nor is interviewing home gardeners and commercial growers. But, I can tell you that I never before learned so much about gardening and gardeners in such a short time. It was a tremendously exciting and inspiring time in my life. I have written the names and addresses of these Masters of Gardening in my address book because there is not a one of them I would not want as a close friend.

My job of interviewing these gardeners and accumulating and validating much information about their specialty plants went easily because of the affection and loyalty accorded *The Victory Garden*. It all started with James Underwood Crockett, the original host of the show. His depth of information, natural enthusiasm, and warm ways helped many a first-time gardener feel the delight of biting into a home-grown, vine-ripened tomato. A tragic illness claimed Jim's life in 1979, and it is a tribute to this remarkable man that his memory is still strong among gardeners across this great country.

Jim tended a made-for-television garden in a corner of the parking lot behind the WGBH-TV studios in Boston. It was built around large existing crabapple trees and expanded to include vegetable and flower gardens, landscaped seating areas, and a small greenhouse. Viewing these shows was a personal experience, like coming right into Jim's own home and garden. But, Jim's death meant a change for the show.

A new host was brought in, a well-established nurseryman and keen home gardener, Bob Thomson. Bob was given the almost impossible task of taking over for someone who had won the hearts of viewers. In time he, too, became a trusted friend and adviser, through his honest and unpretentious ways and mastery of gardening. Bob brought to the show a passion for tasteful landscaping; it came at a time when gardeners seemed ready to extend their horizons beyond the vegetable patch.

At that time, the program was being broadcast nationally on Public Television but had a distinctly northeastern focus. This was due partly to Jim and Bob's down east and Boston accents and partly to the timing of gardening projects, set by New England weather. And, even though good garden culture travels well to most parts of the country, the time seemed right to develop regional gardens. Utilizing local hosts and regional plants, and timed for the seasons of each region, such gardens could add credibility and enhance loyalty.

I came on board at that time. *The Victory Garden* knew me from a guest spot I had done with Bob. So, when a regional garden was projected for Callaway Gardens in Pine Mountain, Georgia, I was asked to serve as host. I had been in home and commercial horticulture for nearly forty years, grew up in the South, and still talked "southern." My wife, Jane, and I operated an herb farm just over the border in South Carolina.

My first appearance in March of 1984 must have been painful for the crew because I knew nothing about being in front of a camera. What saved me, I think, was years of experience in public speaking and exposure to all sorts of plants around the world. With the help of the crew, good gardeners all, I began to give southern flower and vegetable gardens their due. When this old Mississippi boy praises turnip greens, okra, and purple hull peas, he has been there!

Since then, we've expanded the show's outreach to include Victory Garden West at Rogers' Garden Center near Newport Beach, California. Bob Smaus, Garden Editor for the *Los Angeles Times*, does a great job of introducing to western gardeners the amazing variety of plants that will thrive in their mild climates. Rogers' is open year round and is nationally known for its creative uses of unusual plants and planters.

Two changes were made in Massachusetts. The parking-lot garden was moved to the grounds of a marvelous retail nursery and garden center, Lexington Gardens, in the historic town of Lexington. Bob Thomson introduces all programs from the quarter-acre garden, open to the public spring through fall. Also, a new "Suburban Garden" was begun on the outskirts of Boston, where enough open space exists to demonstrate major garden construction projects from start to finish. Roger Swain, Science Editor for *Horticulture* magazine, joined the team in 1986 and serves there as host.

Often, Roger will end a show by delivering fresh vegetables from the garden to Marian Morash, a bona fide chef. She never fails to come up with wonderful ways to prepare them.

In addition to taping segments at regional Victory Gardens, the show travels extensively throughout North America, giving each of us a chance to see what other gardeners are up to. And in recent years, we've roamed the world with British plantsman Peter Seabrook. Peter does a masterful job of presenting some of the great gardens of the world, sending reports from Europe, Asia, New Zealand, and Australia. How times have changed on *The Victory Garden* since our parking-lot days of 1976!

The one constant throughout this long history of service to gardeners has been Russell Morash. *The Victory Garden* was his vision and, to this day, he continues to impart his creative genius, keen eye, and talent for gardening to the show. John Pelrine, who began as the manager of the greenhouse in Crockett's days, has advanced to Producer. Another veteran is the Director of Photography, Dick Holden, the only person I know who can back uphill while taping, following a twisting, rutted path, and never bobble his hand-held camera. He translates Russell's ideas into vivid images.

We've been blessed with a great crew that you never see on camera: Chip Adams, Derek Diggins, Nina Sing, Sally Cook, and the technical staff at the studio who, within forty-eight hours of receiving our raw tape, can uplink a finished program to a satellite and transmit it to nearly three hundred PBS stations nationwide.

If I look good on TV, credit it more to the WGBH-TV staff than to my talent, and especially to my associates at Callaway Gardens, Bob Hovey and David Chambers. They work in Victory Garden South every day of the year and keep all 9,500 square feet neat and shining for visitors. It is a major attraction at this great horticultural center and 2,500-acre resort.

I am blessed to be in a position to work with gardeners all over the country and to record for you the stories of some of the best. When I think of these newfound but fast friends, a line from a hymn I learned in Epworth League these many years ago comes to mind . . . "Blest be the tie that binds."

# *Acknowledgments*

*I*f this book entertains and enlightens you, it will be due more to the garden-ers I interviewed and horticulturists I asked to help, than to what I know about gardening. If it fails, it will be because I was unable to absorb the huge amount of information involved, or to translate it into the working language of gardeners.

Most gardeners are generalists, and that includes me. In my years of garden-ing, I rubbed up against all sorts of hobby plant specialists, both amateur and professional, but never absorbed a great deal of information about any given plant. I don't mind telling you that I had to hit the reference books, the tele-phone, and the U.S. mail to write in depth about the eleven hobby plants fea-tured in this book. I queried skilled amateurs, commercial producers, public garden curators, and plant societies in many states.

I am indebted to Christina Ward, my editor at Little, Brown, who would not let me stop short of delivering the best that was in me, and to my associates at *The Victory Garden*, who have unselfishly shared their rich experiences.

It is a marvel that the featured gardeners didn't run me off, or chase away the photographers—we took up so much of their time with interviews, correspon-dence, and phone calls. They gave us what we call in the South "a gracious plenty" of cooperation. Bless every one of them!

So many people helped on daylilies: Roy Klehm of Klehm Nursery, Van Sell-ers of Iron Gate Gardens, and John Elsley of Wayside Gardens, to name a few.

Susan P. Martin, Curator of Conifers of the U.S. National Arboretum, sent a list, compiled by Tom Dilatush, of conifer collections open to the public. Gwen Fawthrop, a fellow garden writer, advised me on collections in Ontario. Jeanette Windham of Greensboro, North Carolina, checked my hardiness data on dwarf conifers.

I would be remiss in not thanking my wife, Jane, for double-checking my memory on how herbs grow in the South, and our friend Tom DiBaggio of Earthworks, Arlington, Virginia, for information on rosemary, oregano, and lav-ender. The Executive Director of The Herb Society, Julie McSoud, and Bob Hovey, the Resident Gardener at Victory Garden South, kindly helped me.

Roy Klehm, Van Sellers, and John Elsley also helped me with hostas, as did Peter Ruh of the Homestead Division of Sunnybrook Farms. Gene Ellis of Talla-hassee Nurseries and Ken Chatham of Crabapple Nurseries, Roswell, Georgia, helped me pinpoint the southern adaptation of hostas.

Dorothy B. Schaefer of the American Lily Society put her twenty-five years of experience at my disposal.

Elsley and Klehm read my copy on peonies. My information on peppers came partly from Dr. Jean Andrews Smith's book, partly from David Chambers of Callaway Gardens, and partly from my special interest in them.

Adele Jones, of the American Rhododendron Society, started me off on the right foot, and Fred Galle, "Mr. Azalea" himself, read my copy.

A fellow garden writer, Maggie Oster, led me to the Jeremiases, where I did the rose story. Anne Reilly counseled me on miniature roses and my friend of many years, Bill Fike of Jackson & Perkins, on rose hardiness.

Nell Lewis of Greensboro, North Carolina, let me shoot photos in her superb woodland wildflower garden and introduced me to Dr. Elwood Fisher, who is every bit as knowledgeable about wildflowers as he is about antique fruit trees.

*Photo Credits*

*Half title:* John Pelrine
*Title page:* Russell Morash
*Preface:* Stephen Butera
*Introduction:* Stephen Butera
*Rhododendrons:* photos by Don Normark, except p. 21, by Erin Smith
*Hostas:* photos by Kim Kauffman, except pp. 33, 35 (both), 41 (top), by John Pelrine;
    p. 47 (all), by Jim Wilkins
*Daylilies:* photos by Roy Klehm
*Roses:* photos by Chuck Armour, except pp. 70, 76, 81 (left), by Russell Morash; p. 81
    (right), by Stephen Butera
*Antique Fruit Trees:* photos by Robert C. Simpson, except pp. 93, 97, by Jim Wilson; p.
    95, by Elwood Fisher
*Herbal Arts:* photos by Stephen Butera
*Dwarf Conifers:* photos by Ann Reilley, except p. 147 (all), by Jim Wilson
*Peonies:* photos by Roy Klehm
*Wildflowers:* photos by Beth Maynor, except p. 189 (bottom row), by Jim Wilson
*Lilies:* photos by John Croft
*Peppers:* photos by Larry Albee, except p. 229, by John Pelrine; p. 230 (top left and
    bottom left), by John Swan

# *Masters of the Victory Garden*

# *Masters of Gardening*

*I*t was my happy privilege, for the better part of a year, to travel across the U.S.A., interviewing some of the best gardeners I have ever met. By design, these were all hobby growers of specialty plants. Most were noncommercial and involved only in gardening. Others had taken up plant breeding in addition to gardening. A few sold enough plants to help support their hobbies. I chose to interview mostly noncommercial growers because a person's attitude toward plants can alter when he or she begins to sell them. Evaluation of plants can change from favoring the traits the gardener likes to those he or she feels the general public will like enough to cause them to purchase the plant. Some had been featured on *The Victory Garden* program; others are scheduled for future productions. For lack of a better name, we call them "Masters of the Victory Garden." None has the hubris to proclaim, "I am the best!" They flinch at the term "expert," and even grumble at being called an "authority."

You see, what these seasoned gardeners have discovered is that no individual ever completely masters gardening. Much of the fascination in one of this country's most popular hobbies is that one revelation leads to another, and another. Gardening is a lifelong voyage of discovery.

Early on, these Garden Masters confronted the fact that an enormous amount of information had to be absorbed before they could become knowledgeable about gardening. I think they reached that conclusion at about the time they became pretty good general gardeners, capable of raising vegetables and herbs, annual and perennial flowers, bulbs, roses, and a few basic trees and shrubs. They became frustrated, I believe, at the difficulty of advancing their knowledge of gardening on such a broad front.

The Garden Masters I interviewed enjoyed learning about one plant at a time, through reference books, discussions with fellow hobbyists, lectures by authorities, and actual experience in the garden. They felt "in control" of the situation, instead of vaguely uneasy about the impossibility of absorbing the vast amount of information on general gardening. They felt, and I agree, that it makes good sense to narrow the amount of data you need to absorb to succeed at growing.

I expect you know what they are talking about. Just the process of learning where to find gardening information and how to winnow relevant and reliable guidance from the mass of often specious "facts" on general gardening is bewildering. Translating all that information into action is enough to intimidate anyone and to paralyze a few.

Some of the Garden Masters worked their way, at least superficially, through one or more hobby plants on their way to their present specialty. Others, having reached a high degree of competence with one specialty plant, retained it but took on one or two others as well.

It seems to me that most gardeners sort of drift into a specialty plant. It often starts with an affinity with a plant they have bought or received as a gift. The plant "grows on them," and they begin looking for more cultivars in the same genus or species, building little families of related plants. They buy garden books about their specialty and usually join a plant society. Some grow mostly for the enjoyment of friends and family, others not only for the challenge of growing new plants but of doing it better than anyone else in their area. Some work all season long at growing, mostly for the thrill of entering their handiwork in shows.

One commonality in backgrounds of these Garden Masters fascinated me. I encountered it in the first of the interviews, and my initial impression was reinforced with each succeeding gardener I came to know. It seems that every good gardener has a role model, a "mentor." With some, it was a parent or a grandparent. With others, particularly those who took up a specialty plant in later years, it was an advanced specialty grower, one who cared and shared.

That revelation speaks to every specialty plant society, every garden club, every horticultural society. It says, "Make a real effort to be friendly and sharing with newcomers." There is much more to this than merely perpetuating the organization. If you are the advanced gardener who reaches out to educate and inspire a newcomer, you may be amazed at the impact of your sharing. Without intending it, you may become a mentor. Just read the experiences of these Garden Masters and you'll get an idea of the place role models play in gardening.

I found all of our Masters of the Victory Garden to be decent, likable, intelligent individuals, sometimes eccentric, but always fun-loving. None sees himself or herself as a "Creator" but as a willing apprentice in the natural order of things. Some are aware that they have become role models to other gardeners and are humbled by that realization.

Another commonality among these Garden Masters is the need to control their garden. Gone are the days when, faced with weather or other environmental problems, gardeners would capitulate. Now, they seek out and use many means and devices to moderate the impact of weather, plant diseases and insects, soil deficiencies, and even space restrictions. Certain of these Garden Masters have realized that, in order to progress in gardening, understanding the environment is vital. They have become "Stewards of the Earth" or, at least, of that small part upon which they pay taxes. Two or three have become effective environmentalists.

Let me share with you one more observation about these Garden Masters, which is admittedly subjective and colored by my own approach to gardening. I realize the subject of the motives behind gardening is sensitive, so let me assure you that this observation is meant to compliment anyone who recognizes his own leanings. . . .

Some gardeners, I believe, use gardening as outdoor theater, with themselves as directors. Some prefer the security of repeating a similar production year after year; they thrive on the praise heaped on their efforts. Others prefer the challenge of new tableaux each year; the thrill of learning about new plants and how to fit them into the gardening environment is what gives them satisfaction. Some, in order to understand the plants who are players, imbue them with human characteristics. They talk to them, praise them, interact with them, move them around the stage, change the lighting . . . but, ultimately, if they fail to perform, they reach for the stage hook.

My new friends would be the first to admit that I would not have gone wrong had I chosen some other Garden Master in their specialties. The woods are full of good hobby gardeners growing specialty plants. I chose to feature these particular Garden Masters to present a cross section of backgrounds, ages, lifestyles, aspirations, and climates. I believe you will agree that they are the kind of gardeners you would enjoy meeting and learning from, even emulating.

I know I will get letters from advocates of other specialty plants. They are no less important than the few that could be featured in depth within these covers. If fortune smiles on this small beginning, perhaps we can cover other specialties in future books.

It is my hope that, in reading about these diverse plants and skilled gardeners, you may find intriguing possibilities and even role models. You may think of yourself as a generalist or "plain dirt gardener," and be happy in your situation. Well and good; you are among the majority of gardeners. But, should the day come when you feel flat and burned out with gardening, pick up this book and read how these Garden Masters rise above disappointments to wring more out of every day in their gardens.

# Rhododendrons

*Jeanine and Rex Smith's passion for rhododendrons transforms a dense northwestern forest into a landscaped showplace.*

*(Left) Jeanine's artistic talent shows in this landscape arrangement of R. 'Ken Janek' with sweet woodruff,* Galium odoratum, *and London pride,* Saxifraga umbrosa, *around a weathered log.*

*F*ew other flowering plants have the visual impact of rhododendrons, not just in bloom, but in flower bud and new growth stages, summer foliage, and winter form. The flower buds remind me of a coiled spring, winding tighter and tighter, swelling and swelling until, on one happy day, they burst through their restraining bud scales to dazzle the eye and nourish the spirit. The flowers are anything but ephemeral; in cool climates they remain fresh and unfaded for many days. Through careful selection of cultivars, gardeners can enjoy rhododendrons in bloom over many months. After the flowers drop, and the plants have summoned a new burst of energy, colorful new shoots branch from vegetative buds to grow a new canopy of leathery, evergreen leaves. During the summer, rhododendron plants are like a corps de ballet . . . beautiful, but subordinate to the principal dancers of the season. During the winter, in forest underplantings, the persistent foliage, dark green, often glossy, shines against the background of bare trunks, branches, and fallen leaves.

The history of rhododendrons is replete with stories of great sacrifices by plant explorers who braved harsh winters, nearly impassable terrain, hostile villagers, and venal officials to bring back species to enrich our gardens. In the early days of plant exploration, all members of the genus were called "rhododendrons." Later, certain species, some deciduous, some evergreen, came to be known collectively as "azaleas." Thus, all azaleas are rhododendrons, but only a few rhododendrons are azaleas.

Any attempt at a concise, precise distinction between the plants we call rhododendrons and the ones we call azaleas is doomed to failure. Yet, most experienced gardeners can tell garden cultivars of azaleas from rhododendrons at a glance. Most garden azaleas are hybrids between species, and come under such classes as Indian hybrids, Glen Dale hybrids, Kurume hybrids, Ghent hybrids, Robin Hill hybrids, and Shammarello evergreen hybrids. Many azaleas are deciduous, particularly the native American species and hybrids between them. Individual azalea flowers are shaped like funnels, sometimes fragrant, and are relatively slender, as compared to the more bell-like individual flowers of rhododendrons. A typical cluster or "truss" of rhododendron flowers is larger and denser than one of azaleas, and typical rhododendron leaves are much larger, evergreen, and usually glossy.

Generally, the species and hybrids we call rhododendrons, and the evergreen azaleas, occur in mountain ranges where cooler temperatures and higher moisture levels are kind to broad-leaved evergreens. By far the greatest number of rhododendron species are native to Asia, where they are most numerous on mountains and foothills that receive abundant rainfall and, often, snow cover. However, the tropical species of rhododendrons grow as understory plants in jungles. The deciduous azalea species generally occur at lower elevations and can thrive on drier soil. The species rhododendrons are more demanding in their soil and climatic requirements than the hybrids, yet are the favorites of many rhododendron enthusiasts because of their simplicity and grace.

Only in recent years have rhododendrons emerged as a major landscaping plant in the United States. Forty years ago, rhododendrons had established a foothold in three regions that were ideally suited to their culture, with relatively cool summers, mild winters, abundant rainfall, and acid soils. On the West Coast, the fog-shrouded or rain-washed coastal plain from Santa Cruz north into British Columbia provided the ideal site for growing the spectacular semihardy hybrids. On the East Coast, the temperate bays, estuaries, or islands from Boston south to the DelMarVa peninsula pampered a then-new generation of rhododendron hybrids hardy to 5 degrees F. Further inland, along the uplands of the Appalachian chain, the old Ironclad hybrids, based partly on hardy American native

R. *'Bow Bells'*
*has rather small*
*leaves and pen-*
*dant flowers*
*(left). The pale*
*yellow blossoms*
*of* R. hanceanum
*contrast beauti-*
*fully with its*
*smooth, dark*
*green foliage.*

rhododendrons, endured great extremes in temperature and fluctuations in soil moisture and humidity. Wild stands of species rhododendrons could be found in roughly the same areas.

Rhododendrons held unimaginable potential for American gardeners, but it could not be realized without more adaptable hybrids, efficient production and marketing methods, and greater publicity. Around the country were immensely talented geneticists, taxonomists, nurserymen, and amateur specialists in rhododendrons, all working more or less independently. Largely, theirs was a work of love; no one made much money out of new cultivars and some producers went broke. No one knew much about propagating rhododendrons on a commercial scale, and plants could not be patented. It all began to come together with the formation of the American Rhododendron Society after World War II.

The early rhododendron hybridizers wanted significant improvements in cold tolerance and resistance to dry soil conditions. They wanted fuller plants, and greater variety in foliage and plant habit. Above all, they wanted new and clearer colors. Cherry and magenta reds abounded in hybrids, along with muddy pastels. Desirable colors were available in species rhododendrons, but thousands of crosses were necessary to develop desirable

*Landscaping for
a succession of
bloom: the white
R. 'Alf Bowman'
will be followed
by the coral R.
'Paprika Spiced'
and R. 'Lem's
Cameo', right.
The yellow is R.
'Golden Witt'.*

hybrids from them. Progress was slow because of confusion in nomenclature, duplication in naming, inadequate pedigrees on existing hybrids, and the need for a broader genetic base.

World War II had an unexpected and positive effect on rhododendron breeding. Servicemen sent back seeds of rhododendron species from the far corners of the earth, and these deepened the genetic pool. The Europeans, with their generally "softer" climate, had been ahead of us in rhododendron improvement for some time, but their hybrids weren't tough enough for our more variable climate. After the war, using new Asian blood and native American species, our breeders rapidly began developing hybrids that were hardy as a rock, and as beautiful as any of the temperamental hybrids from Europe. The hardy eastern *Rhododendron catawbiense* and *R. maximum* were their mainstays and the more tender western *R. macrophyllum*.

During the first flush of enthusiasm over improved rhododendrons, new hybrids flooded arboreta, parks, and estates. Years passed before the plants matured sufficiently that their form, endurance under stressful weather, and resistance to insects and diseases could be evaluated fully. Today, although some of the better old hybrids linger on, vastly improved cultivars are taking over the market, some from other parts of the world. Plants are being bred for attractive foliage and neat form as well. Leaves may be blue-green or silvery, or dusted with velvety tomentum, the undersides purple, rust-colored, or white. New growth can be bronzy red, or as pale and fuzzy as a bunny's ears.

Even before *glasnost,* the cultivar *R. luteum* 'Batumi Gold' reached the U.S. National Arboretum from Russia's Batumi Botanical Garden. Two outstanding breeders, David Leach and the late Ed Mezitt, took the obvious route of developing and evaluating new hybrids in severe winter areas and introduced new lines of compact hybrids for today's smaller gardens. The Leach Hybrids provide extended bloom along with more attractive foliage and crisp, clean colors.

The improvements in rhododendrons have greatly increased their adaptability to other regions of the country. Still, in all of North America, no area can match the Pacific Northwest, from southwestern British Columbia through western Oregon and Washington, for growing a wide range of rhododendron hybrids and species. A few rhododendrons are native to the mountains in this area. Particularly near water level, the climate is temperate, the air and soil are moist for several months of the year, and the soil is porous and acidic, due to the abundance of decomposing organic matter and the leaching action of winter rains.

At their hillside home in Woodinville, Washington, Rex and Jeanine Smith have capitalized on all these advantages to amass a spectacular collection of rhododendrons, not lined up like an ill-assorted guard, but tastefully blended into a stunning landscape.

*Under the high canopy of shade, rhododendrons line the winding lane to the Smiths' home.*

When I turned into the driveway of the Smiths' secluded home, I was struck by the abundance of color and variety of choice rhododendrons. Pastel colors predominated, with an occasional accent mark of dark or bright, or a highlight of cream, yellow, or white like a shaft of sunlight. Plants ranged in height from groundcovers to taller than my head. Although basically a rhododendron garden, the landscape included azaleas, groundcovers, and choice perennials. I parked some distance from the Smiths' house and walked in, so I could get an idea of the number of rhododendrons in their collection. There must have been a hundred rhododendrons or more in the front yard alone! Rex and Jeanine are still working on the back yard of their three-acre lot. Only a few months ago, loggers dropped and hauled away the last of the hundred-foot-high Douglas firs tagged for removal. The lot hasn't been stripped of trees; far from it—more than a hundred firs, western red cedars, and hemlocks were left standing both to provide the high canopy of shade that rhododendrons like and to block the view of homes beyond their back and side fences.

Along the back fence stand several head-high rhododendrons. Jeanine, the hybridizer and propagator in the Smith family, told me that these big plants date back to her earliest experiments in growing rhododendrons from seeds. She grew them from hybrid seeds brought to a Seattle Rhododendron Society meeting in 1971 by Dr. Ned Brockenbrough, an amateur hybridizer. Little did she dream that, out of the thirty-five plants which she grew to maturity, would come an award-winning cultivar, 'Apricot Fantasy'.

In 1987–1989, Jeanine served as president of the nearly 450-member Seattle chapter of the American Rhododendron Society. She has good reasons for feeling strongly that one of the most important obligations of experienced plant society members is to introduce novices to the joys of growing specialty plants. "It was at one of those first meetings," she related, "that I received the seeds from Dr. Brockenbrough and, following the instructions in David Leach's book *Rhododendrons of the World*, I filled a covered plastic shoebox with moist milled sphagnum moss, planted the seeds, and grew dozens of tiny rhododendron seedlings on the bright end of our kitchen counter, out of the direct sun.

"Succeeding at my first attempt at germinating rhododendron seeds was so exciting!" she said. "It started me collecting and propagating rhododendrons from cuttings and, over the next three years, hundreds of small plants filled our city lot. Rex and I began thinking about having a piece of property large enough to grow and display our collection of rhododendrons."

Then she laughed and said, "I didn't know it, but I was already a 'Rhodoholic.'" She passed me a short essay by Heidi Shelton, a member of the Seattle chapter of the ARS, entitled *"The Five Stages of Rhodoholism."*

1. Patient buys commonly available hybrids ('Elizabeth', 'Hon. Jean Marie de Montague', 'Scintillation', 'Gomer Waterer', 'Pink Pearl', etc.). Notices the pretty flowers and relatively easy care, goes on to stage 2.

2. Begins to comb more prestigious and out-of-the-way nurseries for more unusual varieties and smaller plants (keeping in mind that he/she will run out of garden space in the near future as this acquisitive habit continues unfettered). Throws out or gives away perfectly healthy plants (especially non-rhodies) to make room for more of his favorites. Buys every book on rhododendrons available. Plants trees whose sole purpose it is to provide just the right amount of dappled shade for rhodies. Begins to collect plants for showy foliage alone. Tries rooting some cuttings. Joins the Rhododendron Society. *The disease can be halted at this stage but not reversed.*

3. Starts to look at "real estates" (minimum three acres) in outlying areas because garden is at capacity. Builds a greenhouse and makes some crosses, "just to see what happens." Dreams about owning a rhododendron nursery. If financial and physical resources are adequate for realizing this dream, patient may live out his/her life growing, hybridizing, exhibiting and selling rhodies and sharing experiences with like-minded people. All the while he/she harbors the secret hope to be the hybridizer of the next 'Lem's Cameo', i.e., a plant that will take the rhody world by storm and bring if not fortune, at least fame to its creator. *Recovery at this stage is difficult if not impossible, due to the fact that the patient sees the disease as entirely benign, even pleasurable.*

4. Admiration for rhododendron species, which began late in stage 2 or early in stage 3, begins to take over now. Patients will travel long distances to seek out unusual plants. Beauty of flowers or even acquisition of plants matters less and less; rarity is what patient is after. May sell house and car to finance a trek to the Himalayas. *Patient's family, if still intact at this point, gives up on his/her sanity.*

5. Patient shaves his head, dons a yellow robe, and becomes a Tibetan monk to live among his beloved species. It is not known how females cope with this stage; possibly they disguise themselves as mountaineers, naturalists, or missionaries. *As no case of recovery from stage 5 is known in the literature, it is generally considered terminal.*

At this point, Rex was smiling broadly. He likes rhododendrons, too, but the malady has not progressed as far in his case.

Jeanine continued her story. "Rex was gone from home a great deal as a pilot with Northwest Airlines and, in the evenings, I would pore over the rhododendron literature, which always filled my nightstand. The breaks between Rex's flights give us the time to pursue our projects.

"In 1973 we purchased three acres of land, in what was then a rural area northwest of Seattle. In 1976 we completed our present home and moved in with our daughter, Erin, then eighteen months old, and our sons, Greg, nine, and Kirk, seven years old. Building and moving at that time was difficult and it derailed my rhododendron hobby. Nevertheless, when we moved to our new home, we brought along several favorite large plants and countless small 'rhodies' including, of course, my treasured seedlings. We planted these in nursery beds. After the house was made livable, we began to tackle the vast project of clearing trees and brush, burning stump piles, designing gardens, building decks, and preparing soil.

"Actually, before I caught the rhododendron bug," Jeanine said, "I was interested in gardening and in landscape design. I have a background in art, and would have liked to have spent more time painting, but found that, while raising three children, the uninterrupted blocks of time weren't available. However, I could garden with children around me, and arranging plants in pleasing landscape designs fulfilled my creative instincts. Rex trusts my judgment about landscaping and never complains if a rhody has to be moved. I couldn't ask for a more supportive partner, in all things. Rex worked long and hard to clear this land of salal, brambles, brush, and tree trimmings after the loggers left. He built the service building, greenhouses, and cold frames and is now installing a sprinkler system."

Rex looked a little embarrassed when she told the following story about his willingness to help. "When we were about to move into our first home in 1968, I wanted to take a course in landscape design but was very pregnant with our second son. I knew I wouldn't be able to finish the class before delivery. Rex went instead, took notes, and reviewed them with me after each session."

Asked if he does any hybridizing, Rex smiled and answered, "No. I know how to hybridize but Jeanine knows why. I get my kicks out of helping her succeed, but I also enjoy building and heavy gardening. I guess that growing up around farms in Montana accustomed me to it. I'll tell you one thing: when I get out of that cockpit and rest up a little to get over jet lag, I enjoy the relaxation I get from building and gardening. Jeanine and I like working together on my days at home."

I like the way the Smiths defer to each other's strengths. When Rex finished talking about his involvement, Jeanine took over to show me

*Rex and Jeanine mulch around a choice rhododendron hybrid that was grown from seed. This one has survived the evaluation process.*

the steps of propagating rhododendrons. She began by demonstrating how to take, root, and "grow-on" cuttings to a size that can safely be transplanted to a nursery bed or border.

Jeanine showed me that, with the aid of rooting hormones, potting soils, bottom heat, and cold frames, increasing rhododendrons by taking cuttings is easy and almost foolproof. Now that their space is filling up rapidly, she has little room for plants other than her own seedlings, and has virtually discontinued growing from cuttings. It is quite a sacrifice because, as Jeanine puts it, she "likes to put roots on things." Nevertheless, she won't turn down a cutting from a rare rhododendron, and she will clone her own hybrids by cuttings when required.

Space limitations are also forcing Jeanine to be very selective about hybridizing. Long past the learning stage of making random crosses, she directs each cross toward what she sees as attainable goals, mostly new colors and improved growth habits. Through her ARS connections, Jeanine can receive pollen from species and hybrids not in her collection, even from foreign countries. In return, she sends pollen from her plants on request. Records of crosses and pollen donations are kept in what she calls her "stud book."

Jeanine is particularly fond of the plant habit and foliage of hybrids based on *R. yakusimanum* and, along with other hybridizers, is incorporating this species into her breeding program. The species is low growing and its rather slender leaves with truncated ends clothe the plants densely. New growth is colorful. The undersides of leaves are felty and give a bicolor effect when they blow in the breeze. The lack of a wide range of natural colors doesn't bother Jeanine, because she can cross *R. yakusimanum* with other species to get the colors she wants. She is aiming for full yellow, apricot, or orange trusses on compact, low-growing plants with attractive foliage.

I was struck by Jeanine's confident approach to difficult hybridizing goals. She explained how she got started: "I was inspired to try hybridizing by a dear lady, Elsie Watson, who taught me the techniques of crossing and encouraged me to join the hybridizers group of the Seattle chapter. She was my role model and her lovely hybrids gave me the assurance that, with a little luck and a lot of hard work, I might do the same. Elsie has several of her creations in the commercial trade, but is still searching for the elusive 'true blue' rhododendron, with no trace of purple color in the flower."

She showed me her pollen bank. Nestled in dozens of neatly tagged gelatin capsules were anthers and pollen grains, not only from her garden but also mailed from elsewhere. Pollen must be gathered from unopened or freshly opened blossoms. Wind and insects can vector in foreign pollen soon after blossoms open and contaminate hybrids.

Jeanine prefers gelatin capsules because moisture can escape through them and be absorbed by the layer of calcium chloride desiccant in the bottom of the sealed storage jar. She cools fresh pollen for two or three weeks at 40 degrees F. before transferring it to the freezer. Rhododendron pollen can keep for about three years when frozen.

I learned that rhododendrons set prodigious numbers of seeds as fine as petunias. Jeanine germinates hybrid seeds in one-pint plastic freezer containers filled to within one inch of the top with moist milled sphagnum moss. She showed me her bank of three fluorescent light fixtures that illuminate a table with a surface area of sixteen square feet.

In this restricted space, she could grow plants in one hundred containers, without sunlight. Each container could hold fifty to one hundred seedlings, but there is no way her outside production and display area could absorb so many. So, Jeanine uses 75 percent of the lighted area for growing on transplanted seedlings of choice hybrids which she wishes to accelerate.

When the seedlings are ready to transplant, she transfers them to plastic flats filled with a mixture of peat, perlite, and finely ground fir bark. These are kept under fluorescent lights until time to transplant again, at which stage they are moved to their lean-to greenhouse. There, they are

*(Right) On the deck behind their home, Jeanine and Rex enjoy the fruits of their labors, surrounded by the variegated Japanese maple,* Acer palmatum *'Ukigomo', the pale yellow* R. *'Butterfly', a pink rhododendron the Smiths hope to identify, and the large coral* R. *'Fabia x bureauvii'.*

acclimated and transplanted to six-inch pots. The seedlings are fed periodically with a weak solution of water-soluble fertilizer.

Under such forcing, the seedlings can put on several flushes of growth and reach a height of six to eight inches the first year.

The first winter, the potted seedlings are protected in the greenhouse or cold frame. Root growth continues during the winter, and new top growth will begin the following spring. If a branched plant is desired, Jeanine will pinch or snap out the center bud to force side buds to develop. At each transplanting, Jeanine culls out the seedlings that show poor foliage.

"I can hardly wait to see the first blooms appear on my seedlings," Jeanine said. "By that time, at least two years will have passed since I started seeds of the hybrid under lights. Some seedlings will keep me waiting for as long as five years before they will bloom!

"First bloom is the moment of truth for hybrid seedlings. I have to be ruthless about eliminating those which are deficient in color or form: only about one out of one hundred seedlings makes it past this stage of evaluation. Even so, Rex has to condense the few survivors of trial rows to make room for new seedlings. As soon as they grow enough to take shape, I evaluate them for landscape potential. Perhaps one out of fifty may survive the second screening."

From the plants grown to this stage, Jeanine will choose the most promising for moving into a landscaped border for growing on to the next "go or no-go" stage. Each seedling is tagged with its heritage. Within a year or two, any shortcomings of the few surviving seedlings will be evident. It is painful to have to dig these up and give them to friends after a gestation period of up to ten years, but that's what happens to all but the crème de la crème. Jeanine asks her friends to grow her discards as "unnamed seedlings" and occasionally revisits them to double-check her judgment.

Jeanine's goal is to produce hybrid seedlings that are not just good, but distinct from and superior to both parents. That may qualify the seedling for registration with the ARS, provided no one else has beat her to the punch with a similar cross. Qualifying for registration is difficult; technically you could win a red, white, or blue ribbon in a prestigious show and still not have a cultivar worthy of introduction.

After this relentless scourging, only one out of one thousand hybrid seedlings may remain in the landscape border. At this stage comes the moment that Jeanine and Rex have been working toward; judgment of their work by their peers in rhododendron growing and hybridizing. They cut a large truss of blossoms, stick the stem in a bottle of water, and take it to the annual show of the Seattle chapter of the ARS. Every hybridizer's dream is to win a "Best New Hybrid" ribbon, for it can catch the attention of commercial growers. It is gratifying to develop a new

1)
2)
3)
4)
5)
6)

## Hybridizing Rhododendrons

Here, Jeanine takes me through the steps involved in hybridizing rhododendrons. To prevent self-pollination, the blossom of the female parent is (1) emasculated by removing the anthers. Anthers and pollen are stored in gelatin capsules (2) tagged with the name of the donor cultivar and the date of collection. The pollen is transferred (3) by inserting the receptive stigma into a gelatin capsule containing pollen from the male parent. Jeanine uses fluorescent light fixtures for germinating and growing rhododendron crosses and species from seeds (4). In the greenhouse (5), potted-up seedlings and cuttings are grown to sufficient size for transplanting. Rex covers overwintering young plants (6) with a poly "tunnel," which is removed when the weather warms in the spring. Root growth continues over the winter, with new top growth appearing in the spring. At least two full years will have passed before the seedlings' first bloom.

*Jeanine gathers rhododendron trusses for a show. Rear, left to right: R. augustinii, R. luteum, R. oreotrephes. Front, left to right: R. 'Hotei' x 'Tropicana' seedling, R. 'May Day', R. 'Hotei', R. 'Paprika Spiced'.*

seedling that tops all others in shows, but even more fulfilling to see it increased for many home gardeners to enjoy.

Jeanine is not discouraged that, after so many years of educating herself in hybridizing and showing, she has only one seedling that has been registered and has commercial potential. 'Apricot Fantasy' won the "Best New Hybrid" award in a Seattle chapter show and was increased for introduction on a limited basis for spring of 1989 planting. I understood the reason for her optimism when I saw some of the beautiful seedlings in her landscape borders. She has the touch!

While we toured the evaluation trials and borders in the back and side yards, Rex told me some of their secrets for growing rhododendrons in the landscape. "In our climate," he said, "proper soil conditioning and mulching can influence a rhododendron's ability to perform in full sun. I've tried several kinds of soil amendments and prefer to add pulverized fir bark when preparing the soil. I'm lucky to have a small diesel tractor with five chisel points on a drawbar. I can gear down and loosen the soil to a depth of twelve inches. Chiseling breaks up soil compacted by the log trucks, and drags out tree roots. I spread a three- to four-inch layer of bark and about four pounds of ammonium sulfate per one hundred square feet, and mix it into the soil with a tiller. The nitrogen speeds the conversion of the raw bark into humus.

"I work three other organic materials into the soil when I can get them: wood shavings, stable manure, and chipped wood from the power company and road maintenance crews. We supplement sawdust with nitrogen to avoid nitrogen drawdown. Sawdust breaks down quickly, but I think it is worth the effort of application. We have purchased topsoil occasionally, but it always seems to bring in weeds. Consequently, we prefer to amend the existing sandy soil with organic matter. Cheaper to do it that way, too!"

I like the setup Rex has for lining out hybrid seedlings in rows for first and second evaluations. He has installed a solid-set sprinkler irrigation system with 36-inch risers pinned against posts to hold them erect. Looking ahead to possible water conservation restrictions, he used water-conserving micro-sprinkler heads. Combined with organic mulches, the efficient sprinklers should minimize water use.

Rex feels that they are blessed with not having many insect or disease problems. Root weevils can become a nuisance but are controllable. Mildew sometimes appears on susceptible types, but he controls it quickly with mild fungicidal sprays.

I spent three days with Rex, Jeanine, their daughter, Erin, and the photographer, dodging in and out between rain showers. It was a

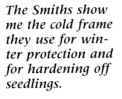

*The Smiths show me the cold frame they use for winter protection and for hardening off seedlings.*

delightful time because, with their cool spring weather, the rhododendron buds seemed to take forever to open. It gave me an opportunity to appreciate the great show that rhododendron buds can put on, and to enjoy the changing moods created by sun, shade, and showers.

Rex and Jeanine garden on a scale that would intimidate most gardeners. I asked how many hours Jeanine spent in the garden per week, on the average. "Oh, ten to fifteen hours a week," she answered; "more in the spring, less during the rainy winter season. Actually, I spend a lot of time in the garden just looking. I appreciate the principles of good garden design and have tried to express them in the front and side yards, and around the deck in the back. But, I believe the main purpose for a garden is to provide enjoyment for the owner, and should reflect his or her special interests. Good design can suffer when a person grows large numbers of a specialty plant. We've solved the old 'design versus plant collection' dilemma for now by locating our breeding and production grounds on the back of the property.

"I still have time," she said, "for my duties with the Seattle chapter of ARS. I feel I have benefited from the organization and should give something in return. We in the chapter are especially proud of our contribution to Meerkerk Rhododendron Gardens on Whidbey Island, near Seattle. It was given to the chapter a few years ago by Anne Meerkerk so that her large collection of rhododendrons and companion plants could be preserved. A hybrid test garden has been established for rating the performance of new hybrids in our climate. There are acres of woodland gardens for strolling and enjoying mature rhododendrons and towering forests. This large garden is open to the public during the spring and summer and should continue to improve with the work of the chapter."

Rex was less definite about how much time he spends in the garden. It was as if I had asked him which leg of his pants he pulls up first. He thought for a while and said, "I really can't say for sure. I'm usually home four days between trips and put most of my spare time to building and gardening. We have the opportunity to travel but, at this stage in our lives, most of our leisure time is spent gardening. We like it here. We've put a lot of ourselves into this home and garden."

He looked off into the distance and mused, "Then, again, Jeanine and I have talked about visiting the rhododendron gardens in Great Britain and perhaps New Zealand. . . ."

Something tells me that, in a few years, when Erin has flown the nest, Rex and Jeanine will be looking for a larger piece of property, nearer the water for frost protection. If only one of each one thousand hybrid seedlings she now has under way makes it to the landscape border, they will soon run out of space. It appears that Stage 4 of Rhodoholism is about to set in!

# More about Rhododendrons

To grow rhododendrons that remain beautiful and flower-filled from youth to old age requires more attention than growing, say, vegetables or herbs. Climate is the principal success factor, for without a hospitable balance of humidity, protection from intense sun and temperature extremes, and acid soil, even the hardy new cultivars will not flourish.

*Purchasing Rhododendrons*

To determine how rhododendrons will do in your area, make a few excursions to large home gardens in the vicinity, gardens with a few years behind them. Rhododendrons increase in beauty and stateliness with age. The garden owner can tell you if your climate is so fickle that it will damage or destroy rhododendrons periodically. Take note, especially, of his siting of rhododendrons in respect to shade, drainage, wind flow, and adjacent trees or shrubs.

If you are persuaded to go on, check out the better retail nurseries in your area at peak rhododendron time . . . early through late spring. Members of local ARS chapters can steer you to them. If the nursery offers only a few plants of rhododendrons and other acid-loving species such as pieris, leucothoe, and mountain laurel, it is a safe bet that rhododendrons are only marginally adapted to your area. At that point, you may decide either to find a mail-order source of hardy modern hybrids, or transfer your attention to the more ubiquitous azaleas.

Next, write to a few of the commercial rhododendron growers for catalogs. Most are located in prime rhododendron-growing areas and have retail stores as well. At first, patronize only those in your part of the country because they can offer you sound advice on adapted cultivars and species of rhododendrons and azaleas. They can tell you how to prepare the soil, using locally available materials. They will tell you how to control the few insect and disease problems of rhododendrons and will usually offer you a broader selection of cultivars than most general retail nurserymen.

On the other hand, if you live in an area where rhododendrons are popular, by all means start with your local nurseryman. Certain retail nurseries offer extraordinary assortments of rhododendrons.

I love to read rhododendron catalogs. As with most horticultural catalogs, they describe cultivars so compellingly that you find yourself condensing your wildly optimistic "want list" to a "need list" and finally to an "absolutely can't do without" list. But, at the core of descriptions is rock-solid information such as the relative hardiness of the cultivar, its average height and spread at ten years of age, foliage characteristics, and preference for protection or exposure in your climate zone. It is hard to fit all that on a plant tag in a retail nursery.

## Adaptability

Before you invest in the cultivars on your "absolutely must have" list, you might consider contacting the ARS to determine if a chapter is based anywhere near you. If not, the next best alternative is to visit the nearest botanical garden or arboretum. At the reception desk ask if they have plantings of rhododendrons, or literature on their culture. Another good information source is your local association of Master Gardeners, accessible through your County Extension Office.

## Site Selection

Next, consider the sites you have for planting rhododendrons. Here's what they like:

- High humidity to balance evaporation from their broad leaves. If summers are dry or hot in your area, plan on installing sprinklers.

- Protection from intense sun, either by fog or high, filtered shade. Only in favored areas can rhododendrons thrive in full sun. Hybrids vary in their tolerance for sun; as a rule, the smaller the leaf, the more sun the plant can tolerate. The small-leaved alpine types are exceptions; they are native to misty mountain ridges and can't tolerate hot, drying sun.

- Protection from rapid, drastic fluctuations in temperature, either by proximity to bodies of water or provision of a favorable microclimate, where drying winds are blocked off.

- Porous, well-drained, highly organic soil, pH 4.5 to 5.5.

## Soil and Planting

How you plant rhododendrons depends on whether you have sandy or clay soil. With clay or clay loam soils, till the soil and spread a 3-inch layer of coarse sphagnum peat moss, pulverized pine bark, or, in the West, composted sawmill waste. Work it into the soil.

Do not dig deep planting holes. Instead, make up a pile of planting mixture composed of equal parts of organic matter, sand, and garden soil pulverized by tilling. Set the new plant on top of the tilled soil. Tap it out of the container or, if the root ball is wrapped in burlap, remove the pins or ties and let it fall flat.

● Carefully scratch away the outer ½ to 1 inch of the root ball to expose root tips. This will help them grow into the surrounding planting mix rather than retreat into the old restricted root ball.

● Shovel the prepared planting mix around the root ball. Firm it down by hand. Be generous. Build up the soil level even with the top of the root ball, extending out at least 2 feet from the trunk. A skinny little cone of planter mixture will dry out quickly or wash away.

● Plant as described above if your soil is a shallow layer of sandy or loamy soil overlying clay. But, on deep sandy or gravelly, fast-draining soils a different approach is called for.

● Spread a 3- to 4-inch layer of organic matter over the soil and turn it under as deep as you can with a spade or tiller. Thoroughly mix it with the soil. Dig generous planting holes. Set the plant in place so that the top of the root ball stands 1 to 2 inches above the surrounding soil. Gently scarify all sides of the root ball to encourage rooting. Fill around the plant with the excavated soil and firm it down with your hands.

**Watering and Mulching**

Before mulching, set a sprinkler near the transplanted rhododendron and let it run at low pressure for an hour. Then, spread a 3-inch-deep mulch around the plant, extending out 2 or 3 feet. Finally, pull the mulch away from the trunk of the plant to eliminate the possibility of rotting.

You can select from many materials for mulching: pinestraw, shredded hardwood leaves, composted sawdust, woodchips, hardwood bark mulch, or forest floor leaf mold. Be sure to pile sawdust with a little manure or a sprinkling of ammonium sulfate and garden soil for a month or so before use. Wet the pile and cover loosely with plastic to hasten heating. Raw sawdust can cause recurring problems with nitrogen drawdown if not composted before mulching. Chipped green wood, pinestraw, shredded leaves, and bark mulches rarely induce nitrogen shortages.

Jeanine Smith advises, "Take care the first year that the newly transplanted rhododendron does not dry out. Until roots have spread out into the surrounding soil, the root ball is especially susceptible to drying out. When this happens, overhead watering can fail not only because the canopy of leaves tends to shed water but also because bone-dry soil can be difficult to rewet. You may need to lay a hose or a sprinkler directly on the root ball and allow it to run slowly until the dry soil is thoroughly moist."

**Fertilizing**

It is in feeding rhododendrons that many gardeners get into trouble; they apply too little or too much, too early or too late. Just remember that, in nature, rhododendrons get by with a low level of plant nutrients, mostly derived from rotting vegetation and ozone nitrogen from thunderstorms. Micronutrients are usually in good supply, due partly to the low soil pH in natural populations of rhododendrons. When the soil pH level begins to creep up, iron deficiency chlorosis can show up.

In most areas, two light applications of fertilizer per year are sufficient, but in coastal California, where there is little danger of cold-weather damage, three light applications may be made. Organic fertilizers such as cottonseed meal, soybean meal, or blood meal release nitrogen in the ammoniacal form preferred for rhododendrons. Or, you can use specially compounded azalea/rhododendron food. Application rates are one-third those for organic fertilizers: ⅛ cup for 18-inch plants; ¼ cup for 24-inch plants; and ½ cup for 36-inch rhododendrons. Top-dress around plants in early spring and again at blossom drop. In coastal California feed again just after fall rains begin.

The danger in feeding after midsummer comes from "tenderizing" the plants. They should go into the winter "hard," not growing rapidly.

The principal danger in overfeeding is the stimulation of overly long internodes, which results in lanky, sparsely leaved plants or, in extreme cases, failure to bloom. This can happen if organic fertilizers are applied in the spring when the soil is too cool for them to break down. The gardener sees no response to the fertilizer and applies more. Warm weather increases the soil temperature and the activity of organisms that decompose organic fertilizers. Suddenly, the plant is given a strong push into vegetative growth instead of a gentle, steady pull.

One of the most efficient feeding programs combines late fall mulching with an application of a slow-release plant food such as Osmocote 14-14-14 Controlled Release Fertilizer. Since Osmocote ceases releasing nutrients at soil temperatures below 40 degrees F., there is no danger of stimulating winter growth.

Spread Osmocote at the recommended rate and cover with 2 to 3 inches of organic mulch. Little or no nutrient release will take place until spring weather warms the mulch to the depth of the Osmocote. All the nutrients will be metered out within 90 to 120 days. The noted azalea enthusiast Fred Galle cautions that, because of the high percentage of nitrogen in the Osmocote formulation, application rates should be those recommended on the package for fertilizer-sensitive species.

You can opt to apply Osmocote at half the recommended rate and supplement with a top-dressing of organic fertilizer at half rate when the blossoms drop. The organic fertilizer should supply most of the micronutrients needed by rhododendrons except where the soil and water are limy or basic. There, chelated iron may be needed as well.

When it comes to mulching, you could do worse than to follow Rex Smith's example, but it is possible to overdo it. The idea is to simulate the layer of litter that carpets forest floors. If you lose plants to root rot, poor drainage and mulching may have to share the blame . . . for if you plant a rhododendron too deep, mulching will compound the problem.

**Housekeeping**    Ideally, you should aim for two flushes of new vegetative growth of moderate length followed by the formation of flower buds in late summer and fall.

When rhododendrons are small, and a dense, well-rounded form is preferred, the terminal buds can be pinched or snipped off to force more lateral buds to grow into shoots. Do this when new growth appears, or soon after blooming.

*Cutting back forces more compact, less leggy growth. New growth will come from the buds below the shears.*

Housekeeping should not be neglected; spent rhododendron blossoms should be picked up and composted and seed pods should be snapped off as they begin to form. With a little practice, you will learn to prune rhododendrons to produce more flushes of growth per season, thus shorter internodes and bushier, leafier plants.

**Pests and Diseases**

Rhododendrons have few serious insect and disease problems, but those need to be dealt with promptly and firmly. As with any broad-leaved evergreen, you don't want to risk allowing insects to disfigure leaves, because they are not replaced every year.

The rhododendron lace bug is probably the worst pest; the tiny nymphs suck plant juices and mottle the leaves, depositing unsightly black excreta on the undersides. You can't confuse their damage with that of the rhododendron bud moth; their grubs tunnel inside leaves, twigs, and the buds of flowers and new growth.

If you see sawdust around stems and breakage from the weakening, suspect the rhododendron borer; it is most troublesome in the East. Your State Cooperative Extension Service can suggest a spray program to control these and other local pests.

Diseases are relatively few; mildew on leaves is easily identifiable and dealt with. Root rots and the resulting wilting are symptomatic of poor drainage. Taking up and repositioning the plant may work, but usually comes too late to save the plants.

Once you have braved the mainstream of rhododendron growing, you may find yourself digging out, containerizing, and selling or giving away some of the more ornate rhododendron hybrids you acquired early in your hobby, to make room for less-formal species. A home garden can accommodate just so many prima donnas, each trying to upstage the other. But however your collection may evolve, the rewards will be gratifying.

# Hostas

*Jim and Jill Wilkins: a
Michigan physician's dexterity
and his wife's artistic eye team
up to create new vistas for
hostas.*

*Dainty, low-
growing, edging-
type hostas act as
a foil for tall iris.
H. 'Gold Drop'
lines the path; at
lower left is H.
'Princess Kara-
futo', backed by
Hosta longis-
sima; at right is
H. ventricosa
'Aureo-Margin-
ata'.*

How can it be possible? A foliage plant with only four basic leaf colors and unremarkable flowers has become the leading shade plant for American gardens. For the answer, all you have to do is see a well-grown collection of hostas. Plant breeders have achieved outstanding foliage color combinations in shades of green, gold, white, and blue-green, and fascinating leaf shapes. They have perfected plant sizes and growth habits for every garden situation.

Plant breeders understand that the true glory of the several species of the genus *Hosta* is in the size, shape, color, texture, and stance of the leaves, not necessarily in the flowers. You hardly notice that the basic foliage colors are rather ordinary because the variations are as endless as cloud formations on a June afternoon. The flower spikes of most hostas lack the visual impact of sun-loving flowers but are valuable because so few flower species will bloom in moderate shade.

Plant breeders are now working to increase the size and longevity of hosta flower spikes, and the range of colors. As they stand, today's simple hosta flowers, in shades of purple, lavender, or white, combine well with the strong foliage colors without clashing or competing for attention. Some hosta cultivars have a mild, pleasant fragrance, especially the hybrids derived from the white flowered *H. plantaginea*. When mature, hosta seed heads can be dried for use in winter bouquets and wreaths. Hostas begin flowering as early as June with some varieties, and flowering continues for several weeks.

One characteristic of hostas that varies dramatically is the "stance" of the plants . . . the angle at which stems and leaves are held. Some mature plants are tall, open, and airy. Others have huge, overlapping leaves that look like shingles on a roof and shed rain accordingly. Other leaves are like cupped hands; they hold enough water to attract birds for a sip. The visual density of plants is just as important as color and mature height and the little "added attractions" such as fancy leaf formations of certain cultivars.

Visitors to hosta collections are awed by the huge variation in plant sizes between cultivars. Some are man-high, with leaves as large as tobacco plants; others grow to a height of only two or three inches. The wee hostas such as *H. venusta* were so valued and jealously guarded in their Japanese homeland that introduction to the United States was delayed by many years.

We need only to look at the place of hostas in Japanese gardens today to predict a new use for them in this country. With little or no open garden space around homes, the Japanese long ago turned to growing hostas in containers. On the northern islands they move hostas indoors before cold weather comes, so that growth is not checked by a period of dormancy. The Japanese also chop and steam the petioles as we do asparagus, or sauté them. American gardeners may not be ready for hosta omelettes, however.

In this country, the popularity of hostas is greatest in the Midwest and lower New England, and decreases as you go south and west. Although they are valued for performance under conditions that would either kill or discourage most flowering species, they don't like hot, dry weather. They grow pretty well in the central and upper South and Northwest, but only a few rugged cultivars will survive in the deep South and dry, warm Southwest. Where adapted, hostas have the happy habit of quickly settling in and rounding into a colorful mound. A little plant in a four-inch pot can increase in size and beauty a dozen times over during the frost-free growing season. They look good from late spring into early fall; some cultivars are attractive when yellowed by fall cold but in hot, dry climates

*Stair-stepping hostas up a slope displays the shape and substance of each variety. The hostas are set off splendidly by companion plantings of* Hemerocallis 'Eenie Weenie,' *in the lower right corner;* Chamaecyparis obtusa nana, *and* Picea pungens 'Montgomery'.

merely look weatherbeaten. Hostas have few diseases and pests, except for slugs and snails. Hostas are very cold tolerant, yet can endure short periods of high heat and humidity such as occur during midwestern summers. They shade out weeds and require little maintenance. They give much but ask little from the gardener in return.

The dramatic increase in the popularity of hostas came late, in comparison with other perennials, and is largely due to enthusiastic promotion by the American Hosta Society. The United States boom actually began before the founding of the society in 1969. It may have been sparked by the need for more and better shade-tolerant plants. The many homes built during the decades following World War II are rapidly becoming shaded by trees planted by the new owners. As these trees grow, they complicate gardening with sun-loving shrubs, flowers, and food plants. Consequently, homeowners are looking for colorful, shade-tolerant plants. Potted hosta plants displayed in the shade plant sections of nurseries sell themselves.

The world of hostas is big, and can be bewildering to beginners. Hundreds of cultivars appear in catalogs of specialists, so many that commercial growers must drop obsolete varieties in order to add new ones. Still, the number of cultivars offered in catalogs is bound to increase substantially. It is rather sad that so many beginners plant their gardens with the limited selection of old varieties available from mass marketers because some are decades behind the times in plant density, color impact, and leaf elaboration.

To assist gardeners in learning about hostas, the American Hosta Society has divided the genus *Hosta* into four rather loose categories: "edgers": compact, rather upright; "groundcovers": low-growing, spreading mostly by rhizomes; "background": tall and rather massive; and "specimens": any size plant, but it must look exceptionally good when displayed alone.

No such categories existed when hostas first appeared in this country, probably in the early 1800s. No one knows for sure who had the honor of planting the first hosta garden in the United States. Plants and seeds came through Europe on their way here, but the genus is native to Japan, Korea, and China. Hosta plants are very long-lived and some eastern U.S.A. gardens could still be populated with descendants of the original imports. A second group arrived when the Japanese began trading with the occidental world.

Dormant hosta plants and seeds could be transported easily by settlers and, once established in their new homes on the frontier, could be divided and passed around. It is a testimony to the goodness of the human spirit that, amidst the confusion and apprehension of moving by wagon or riverboat to a hostile frontier, someone thought to bring starts of flowers.

A more significant avenue of entry for hostas opened during the nineteenth century, when advanced plant hobbyists brought improved selections here from England. "Hostamania" was epidemic there in Victorian days, not just among the wealthy, but among the inhabitants of cottages and row houses.

Today, hostas are second only to *Hemerocallis* (daylilies) in popularity among herbaceous perennials. Their fascinating diversity in the home landscape is abundantly demonstrated in the garden of Dr. James and Jill Wilkins.

*The Wilkinses gave me a tour of their elegantly landscaped hosta collection during taping for* The Victory Garden. *The Japanese painted fern,* Athyrium goeringanum, *right foreground, combines well with* Hosta 'Northern Halo,' *left front.*

*J*im and Jill Wilkins's large and lovely garden is the display area for their hobby of breeding and growing hostas, and for Jill's growing collection of dwarf conifers. The garden provides a serene setting for showing about twenty-five hundred plants of seven hundred hosta cultivars. It is one of five large private hosta gardens in the Jackson, Michigan, area that drew the twentieth annual convention of the American Hosta Society to their city in June 1988. About two hundred hosta enthusiasts trooped through the gardens to see their favorite plant in imaginative settings.

Visitors to the Wilkinses' garden enter through a path that meanders around hillocks, peninsulas, and islands, and offers new vistas at every turn. Large conifers, remnants of the forest that once clothed their property, have been thinned and limbed up to provide light shade for hostas. All the free-form display beds are of generous size to accommodate many groups of the smaller cultivars, individual specimen plants of massive hostas, and edgings of miniature cultivars. While all the hostas are stairstepped by height, groups of taller plants are occasionally brought forward to interrupt the regularity. Colors and variegations are placed for greatest total effect. The cultivars with more white or light yellow in the foliage variegations stand farther back in the shade of trees and the green or blue varieties are brought out toward stronger sunlight.

It must take great self-control to restrain a hosta enthusiast from planting display beds solidly with hostas. The Wilkinses leave enough room between groups of hostas to plant complementary perennials and groundcovers. These make the hostas stand out from the background, and separate the groups visually. Jill has taken a special interest in astilbes, epimediums, and primroses, shade-tolerant perennials that look good interplanted among hostas. Some of these bloom before and after the peak season for hostas. Jill has a good eye for color and avoids the jarring hues that would conflict with hosta foliage.

The garden slopes down from the house to a large grassy clearing in the back, then upward to meet a looming wall of dark, tall pine trees. Considerable forethought and work capitalized on the site and broke it into a number of intimate vistas, while maintaining flow and integrity.

Jim and Jill started by identifying the major "overlook" points into their garden. While one stood at an overlook, the other moved around the yard with a flag atop a tall pole for visibility. In this way, they identified the trees that had to be removed; the stand was so dense that nothing but moss would grow in the gloom. Once they completed thinning and limbing up the survivors to let more sun in, and to open up views, they used the flagpoles again to locate planting sites for choice trees or shrubs.

With the foundation of the garden established, they laid out a garden hose to outline "islands" beneath the shade of the large pine trees. They sprayed the area with a nonselective herbicide to kill broad-leaved perennial weeds and the invasive perennial quack grass. They had the soil tested, and spaded in the recommended nutrient sources and lots of organic matter. The islands became raised beds, 6 to 8 inches in height, which is just high enough to avoid their being flooded during thunderstorms.

To add interest, they sighted-in and laid out curving "berms," built-up hillocks that look perfectly natural. The berms serve to guide the numerous visitors into and through the back yard, and out the other side. They were major constructions and required severals loads of hauled-in topsoil to build them up to the desired height.

On the berms, they first applied a layer of chipped wood mulch to reduce soil erosion, then planted Jill's expanding collection of choice dwarf conifers. She placed the all-green types in full sun and the variegated, golden, and silver types where shade from afternoon sun would prevent browning and fading. Dwarf conifers are so appealing that you want to reach out and touch them; elevating them well above ground level lets you appreciate them fully. In sunny areas between islands and berms, a thick turf of bluegrass and fine-leaved fescue sets off the scene as would a pretty frame around a picture. Jim and Jill edge the turf with hoes, to keep it from encroaching on their ornamentals. Somehow, the natural line between turf and flower beds looks better than an artificial edging.

The Wilkinses have most of the heavy labor of garden construction behind them. After twelve years of work, their garden has expanded (to three acres), as has their enjoyment of it. They have added a service area well off from the side of the house, a large barn with an attached greenhouse, a new lath house for propagation, a food garden with numerous fruit trees, and a pen full of noisy "watch geese." Although each addition is functional, each is attractive, blends into the landscape, and agrees with the architecture of the home.

Both Jim and Jill came by gardening naturally. Born during World War II when money was scarce, Jim's birth was "paid for with gladiolus and Shasta daisies." In their Victory Garden, Jim's parents grew not only food for the war effort, but also flowers to cut and sell for extra income.

*(Above) A tri-color beech fills the space between the low hostas and the leggy pines. 'Gay-feather' and 'Curly Top' in the left foreground are backed by 'Golden Cascades'.*

*(Right) The highly popular and adaptable H. 'Frances Williams' is set off by the yellow-flowered perennial* Corydalis lutea.

Jill's parents were good gardeners. At their home in Ann Arbor, they followed the traditional division of food gardening for men and flower growing for women. Her mother's specialty is roses.

During Jim's long years in pre-med and med school, Jill completed two degrees, in zoology and education. While both were putting in long hours at school and living in a low-income housing development, they found time to beautify their little home with flowers and shrubs. Neighbors saw what they had accomplished and began to plant surrounding yards. Now, after more than twenty years and countless occupants, that little cluster of houses still boasts remarkably beautiful plantings. Their gardening had to be curtailed while Jim served his residency and completed a tour of duty in medicine with the U.S. army, but resumed in earnest upon his return to civilian life. Three daughters blessed the family; all are interested in gardening and environmental preservation.

Jim and Jill recall fondly the day they became interested in hostas. They were already good gardeners but their efforts lacked focus. Then, they visited the garden of a man who was to become their friend and mentor, Herb Benedict. He grows and breeds hostas at nearby Hillsdale, Michigan. "Herb gave us a start with numerous cultivars of hostas, convinced us to join the American Hosta Society, and showed me the elements of hybridization," said Jim.

"Hostas got us so fired up that we have persuaded a number of friends to take up gardening as a hobby and, in particular, with hostas. We are involved in several community projects, but bringing others into gardening may prove to be our most important contribution."

At Hosta Society meetings Jim listened closely to experienced hybridizers to learn their techniques and to get ideas on areas of hosta improvement that are within the reach of amateur plant breeders. Hosta breeding isn't a simple "A + B = C" proposition; the parentage of modern cultivars is so complex that it is impossible to predict what will come out of crosses. Success has a lot to do with the number of seedlings a breeder can grow and evaluate.

In selecting parent plants, breeders look for unusual color combinations and patterns, and graceful plants with an attractive ratio of leaf size to plant size. They lean toward hostas that emerge later in the spring and so avoid frost damage.

I asked Jim for some of the goals of hosta breeders. He said, "I think that more attention will be paid to hosta flowers and fragrance, which are now considered distinctly secondary to the colorful foliage. And, with the gardeners in the upper South using more hostas, I expect to see more sun-resistant cultivars. Not all cultivars are genetically stable and tend to revert to solid colors or throw color variations in the perimeter divisions taken from clumps. I think we will find ways to keep cultivars true to type. Now that we have learned from the Japanese how to keep hostas

*Jill grooms a dwarf Alberta spruce planted among the hostas. The variegated border plantings are* H. *'Louisa' and* H. *'Bold Ribbons'. At lower right is 'Gold Regal'; at far left,* H. *'Krossa Regal'.*

from going dormant, I think we will find ways to use them indoors during the winter as foliage plants. That is bound to have an effect on breeding programs. Certainly, we will see more hostas grown in containers, which will open up new applications for the small-framed cultivars."

Jim is by nature methodical and thorough; here's how he organized his hosta breeding program:

"First, I set up a system for record-keeping: good notes and labeling are essential. I use 4×6 cards to record crosses—one card for each plant. I also plan ahead which crosses I want to make, with a specific goal in mind.

"The night before I make the cross, I remove the petals from the pod parent's flower, that is, the flower that would be opening the next day. This prevents bees from being attracted to the flower and pollinating it instead of my doing it.

"The next morning, I remove stamens from the pollen parent and carry them to the pod parent. I hold the filament of the stamen like a paintbrush and literally paint the pollen from the anther onto the stigma, which is at the tip of the pistil. If the pistil is receptive, I can see the pollen stick to it and coat the tip.

"I use color-coded wire from telephone cable to mark the cross. When I have completed transferring the pollen, I loop a two-inch piece of colored wire around the stem (pedicel) below the flower. Then, I record the

## Starting Hostas from Seed

Jim Wilkins explains how he starts hostas from seeds. Seedlings are started in cell-packs (1) like the one shown here next to dried seed pods. Later, the tiny seedlings are transferred to book planters like this one (2), where their roots grow long and strong. The book planters allow Jim

1)

2)

3)

to transplant the young hostas with little or no root disturbance. Three stages of seedlings are shown here (3): just after sprouting, about one month old, and seven months old, ready for transplanting. After a winter under lights (4), the seedlings are transplanted to the lath house, where Jim can give them concentrated attention for the first year. Optimum fertilizer, moisture, and drainage maintain vigorous growth until the plants are large enough to be evaluated.

4)

color of the wire on the index card identifying the cross by pod parent and pollen parent.

"When the seed pods are ripe, the seeds will turn black. I harvest the hybridized pods then, put them into small paper bags, and label them with the parentage of the cross. The seed pods will split open in a few weeks. I clean them by rubbing gently and carefully blowing away the chaff.

"The seeds can be handled in three ways: if I have room under the fluorescent lights, I will plant them immediately. Or, if the soil is in condition for planting, I will plant them in short, labeled rows in the garden. If not, I will store them in a sealed jar with a desiccant until spring. I have heard that hosta seed is difficult to carry from season to season, but this has not been my experience."

Normally, a time span of two years from harvesting hybrid seeds is required to produce plants large enough for evaluation of foliage characteristics and plant habit. After a few years' experience with the slow process of growing new hybrid hostas from seeds, Jim decided to see what he could do to speed it up. He installed a battery of fluorescent light fixtures in the basement and experimented with burning the lights for various time spans. "Actually, I stumbled onto the answer," he said. "I forgot and left the lights burning day and night over my flats of hosta seedlings, instead of the usual fifteen to eighteen hours. To my surprise, I learned that, in the seedling stage, hostas grow faster under lights that burn twenty-four hours a day.

"The fixtures are on chains and can be lowered to no more than two inches above the tops of seed flats. The gentle warmth and intense radiant energy from the tubes keeps the surface of the potting medium at 70 to 75 degrees F., the preferred range for germinating hosta seeds. The twenty-four-hour lighting not only causes seedlings to grow faster but also to form superior root systems."

Jim uses a standard seed flat mixture of peat moss and vermiculite to start hosta seeds and covers them to about three times their diameter with potting medium. Seeds come up within ten to fourteen days with the fluorescent lights lowered to where they nearly touch the tops of the seed flats. "The intensity of the lights falls off drastically as the fixtures are raised," he explained. "As the seedlings grow, I raise the light fixtures a link or two at a time on the supporting chains, but never higher than two to three inches above the tops of plants."

Jim also experimented with various sizes and types of pots for growing on the seedlings he sprouted and grew in flats of soil. He settled on a plastic "book" planter that opens into mirror-image halves, hinged on one side. The book has long concavities that are filled with moist potting medium. The small, rooted seedlings from under the lights are pricked out from flats and positioned so that their tops protrude from the book when it is closed and snapped shut. The planted book is tipped up and stood on edge in holding trays, plants up, of course.

I asked Jim why he chose the book planters instead of standard pots. "The secret of the book planters," he replied, "is that the long, cylindrical root balls hold more soil than small pots of the same diameter, and give roots room to grow long and strong. When spring frost danger is past and hostas can be planted outside, the books can be popped open and the plants tipped out with little or no root disturbance. I feel that the long, strong root systems get my seedlings off to a faster start.

"I move the trays of plants in books out to the solar greenhouse in March, where I have black-painted drums of water against a reflecting wall. Even at that early date, the drums will have absorbed enough heat from the sun to protect plants from freezing at night. Ours is a south-facing, lean-to greenhouse with a slanted glass front. Nothing would be gained by moving plants there earlier because winter days are short and dark at our latitude. By April, hostas in the greenhouse begin responding to the increasing heat and longer, brighter days. I want them to grow rapidly and to be ready for transfer to the lath house or garden spots by late May. I wouldn't dare put hostas into an unheated greenhouse in March were it not for the tempering effect provided by five 55-gallon drums. They absorb daytime heat and radiate it at night to hold temperatures at 45 degrees Fahrenheit or higher. I have a backup gas heating system but have never had to use it."

As the last stage in accelerated propagation, Jim takes the now-sizable seedlings from the greenhouse and sets them in deep binlike planting beds of potting soil under shade in his lath house. He has one hundred square feet of these waist-high planting bins, space enough to plant three hundred hosta seedlings.

"The lath house is much more than a garden decoration," says Jim. "Beneath 50 percent shade from the lath, and protected on one side from wind, many seedlings will flower the first year. Controlled-release fertilizer, excellent drainage, and abundant moisure push the seedlings into optimum growth rates. I couldn't give my seedlings that kind of attention if they were scattered around the garden or lined out in nursery rows."

The end result of the accelerated propagation is a time span of only ten to twelve months from harvesting and planting hybrid seeds to producing plants large enough for evaluation of foliage characteristics and plant habit. The old method of propagation required two full years. Through the American Hosta Society, Jim published a technical paper on the subject: "Accelerated Growth of Hosta" in *The Hosta Journal* (No. 55).

The few seedlings that survive Jim's rigorous process of selection for color, variegation, vigor, and uniqueness are grown in the garden for

*(Above) Raised beds in the lath house are at a good height for evaluating hybrid seedlings.*

*(Below) Handsome hostas: the gold in the foreground is H. 'Ultraviolet Light', at the right edge is H. 'Fort Knox'. The green hostas are hybrid seedlings bred by Jim Wilkins and registered in 1989.*

another year to note their flower color, size, and fragrance, and to measure the height and spread of the mature plant. If any are felt to be sufficiently good, and distinct from existing cultivars, they will be named and their parentage registered with the American Hosta Society.

"Out of every thousand seedlings I grow from crosses," said Jim, "perhaps one plant will be sufficiently novel to justify introduction. But, I don't throw the others away; I plant the other 999 in the vegetable garden. Jill and I grow them to use as gifts for visitors, family, and friends. Every now and then, we'll get sentimental, dig up an unregistered hybrid seedling, and plant it in the hosta garden. It may not be unique, but it is one I just can't bear to part with."

I asked Jim what he feels lies ahead for hostas. "Bigeneric hybrids could be possible," he said, "and who knows what can be achieved with gene splicing? My hope would be the addition of the red/orange spectrum to foliage colors. Now, we are limited to shades of green and blue-green, plus gold, yellow, cream white, and silver.

"Above all," he continued, "I expect to see the Hosta Society institute tighter controls on registration to discourage the introduction of cultivars that are similar in many respects to existing hostas. There must be two thousand named cultivars, but even the experts have difficulty identifying hostas when they venture beyond the five hundred or so most popular cultivars."

Jim and Jill are concerned that beginners might be put off by the sheer numbers of hosta cultivars. They suggested this "starter list" to fit a cross-section of hostas into a small garden. In their list, the initial "H" indicates the genus *Hosta*, "Aureo-marginata" means simply "gold-edged," and "nebulosa" means "cloudlike."

- *H.* 'Hadspen Blue': Groundcover type; blue foliage.
- *H.* 'Wide Brim': Specimen type; blue-green leaves, irregularly margined with cream.
- *H.* 'Gayfeather': White-centered green.
- *H.* 'Aspen Gold': Medium height; gold, highly seersucked plant; lots of substance.
- *H. ventricosa* 'Aureo-marginata': Groundcover type; large green leaves with irregular margins of yellow to white.
- *H. tokudama* 'Aureo-nebulosa': Rare; textured green leaves with blue streaks; short stems.
- *H.* 'Blue Umbrellas': Large-leaved, blue, background type.
- *H.* 'Tot-Tot': Dwarf, with distinctive wedge-shaped dark green to blue-green leaves.
- *H. montana* 'Aureo-marginata': Large background type; huge glossy-green leaves with irregular margins; award winner.

- *H.* 'Gold Standard': Groundcover type; pale yellow-geen with green margins.
- *H.* 'Krossa Regal': A popular background type; blue-gray leaves and very tall flower spikes.

The Wilkinses caution beginners that only a few of these select cultivars will be available in retail garden centers, which tend to offer the old favorites.

As for Jill's striking combinations of dwarf conifers that set off the hostas in the Wilkinses' landscape, she recommends the following cultivars in her garden:

*Chamaecyparis* (false cypress)
  *C. obtusa* 'Filicoides'
  *C. obtusa* 'Corraliformis'
  *C. pisifera* 'Little Jamie'
  *C. pisifera* 'Snow'
  *C. pisifera* 'Filifera Nana'
*Microbiota decussata* (Siberian carpet cypress)
*Picea* (spruce)
  *P. abies* 'Little Gem'
  *P. abies* 'Pygmaea'
  *P. abies* 'Conica'
  *P. abies* 'Nidiformis'
  *P. abies* 'Gregoryiana Parsoni'
*Tsuga* (hemlock)
  *T. canadensis* 'Bennett'
  *T. canadensis* 'Gentsch White'
  *T. canadensis* 'Jacqueline Verkade'
  *T. canadensis* 'Lewisi'
  *T. canadensis* 'Sargenti'

She also added, "Hostas look good, as well, with *Buxus, Ilex, Kalmia, Rhododendron, Azalaea,* and, I suspect, *Pieris.*"

"Given no more hostas than we have today," says Jim, "a home gardener just beginning to collect hostas for landscaping will find a lifetime of fun and challenge. As for me, I can come home from a frustrating day at the office, feeling out of sorts with the world, and just ten minutes in my hosta garden will straighten me out. During the winter, I can unwind by inspecting the seedlings in the basement to see if that one-in-a-million breakthrough has finally occurred. It's a good life, and I recommend it to everyone!"

# *More about Hostas*

Climate has so much bearing on success with hostas that I called on friends who are commercial growers for advice, and asked the Wilkinses to put me through a short course on hosta growing.

**Sources**

Hosta plants lend themselves to both mail-order and retail sales. They can be shipped while dormant or grown in pots in greenhouses and sold as young plants. Local plant farms can dig up the hostas of your choice and sell them to you at any time during the growing season. Mail-order companies offer the newest cultivars, while retailers tend to offer mostly the old favorites, some of which are still highly rated.

Some producers grow plants in the field, others in greenhouses, still others by tissue culture. The advantages of tissue culture are that plants can be mass produced, thereby increasing availability and (eventually) lowering cost; systemic plant diseases such as virus can be eliminated, allowing healthy plants to reach their full potential. Someday, micropropagation may solve the problem of the color changes that come with age on some hosta cultivars: some take years to develop typical patterns, others tend to revert to the all-green color, especially in new growth coming from the margins of crowns. Tissue-culturing of hostas is now done mostly in the early increase stages of valuable new hybrids.

When ordering hostas, it is always a good idea to inquire if the varieties in which you are interested will perform well in your climate. While most cultivars are widely adapted, some, for reasons not clearly understood, have a distinct preference for certain areas of the country. One condition is universally liked by hostas, regardless of region: protection from wind. Windswept areas dry out rapidly and plants are subject to breakage of petioles.

**Plant Performance**

Experienced hosta growers know that catalogs should be used only as guides and that there is no such thing as a hard-and-fast description. For example:

Plant height and spread can vary considerably, due to the latitude of your area affecting day length, the amount and distribution of moisture, drainage, and the prevailing level of plant nutrients.

Flowering and foliage color can be affected by the degree and hours of shade. Beds in full sun and watered sparsely will flower more heavily and foliage colors will be richer, but there is always the chance of marginal scorch during extremely hot, dry, windy weather, especially on the lighter-colored cultivars.

The hostas with blue foliage prefer locations near a pool or on a streambank, where the high humidity keeps the air cooler. Some growers achieve this effect by modifying their soil highly with organic matter so that it can evaporate lots of moisture while retaining enough to meet the needs of plants' metabolism. In the South, growers employ sprinklers to keep the humidity high during hot, dry weather.

**Shade Quality**

The quality of sunlight and shade can differ from area to area. In some gardens, high humidity and or smog can cause refraction. Plants will perform differently in such locations than where the atmosphere is usually clear. The slope of the land can affect solar absorption. Fully exposed south- or west-facing slopes can stress hostas. Shade quality is determined largely by whether the shade comes in the morning or afternoon. In most climates, afternoon shade is preferred or, even better, high, filtered, daylong shade.

Considering the decided preference of many hosta species for high shade, you may want to limb up trees with low-hanging branches. You'll be surprised at not only the better growth of your hostas but also the brighter display provided by the stronger light.

## Fragrance

Fragrance may depend not only on the species (*H. plantaginea* and its crosses are the most fragrant) but also on dryness, wind, and the time of day.

## Soil Preparation

Take note of the advice in catalogs, or on packages, of the preferred site for the cultivar or cultivars you will be planting. Prepare the soil by mixing in a 1- to 2-inch layer of moist peat moss, pulverized pine bark, rotted sawdust or compost, and, if your soil is heavy clay, a similar amount of sharp sand as well. This will raise the level of the bed somewhat above the surrounding terrain. Hostas are not notably particular as to soil pH, but extremely acid soils should be limed to bring them up to about pH 6.0.

## Planting

Planting should be delayed until about ten days after the average frost-free date. Watch out for low-lying frost pockets; if you have an option, plant hostas where they can get good air drainage. In such favored locations, hostas push up tender growth from their strong crowns in mid-spring, after frost danger is past. However, where cold air collects, new growth can be hurt by late frost. The plants are rarely killed but development can be delayed a month or two.

When setting-in hostas, leave room between plants for them to spread out to full size. (Some of the large background hostas can spread to 3 to 5 feet across.) Hostas display better if the outer leaves of mature clumps just touch adjacent plants. Groundcover types can be planted closer together.

Before setting your plants in the garden, the Wilkinses advise, soak dormant plants for a few hours in warm water, and trim off dead roots. Loosen the root system and spread it out when planting. Position the "crown" or top of the rhizome level with the surface of the soil, or about 1 inch below it if your soil drains well. In very dry soil, fill the planting hole with water and let it soak in. Then, pull loose soil in around the plant and trickle water around it to settle the soil and eliminate air pockets. Careful planting and watering-in can make a critical difference to the plants' survival.

## Plant Care

Weeding is a problem only when hostas are young. As they mature, they crowd out, or shade out most weeds. Grass encroaching from turf pathways, or stoloniferus grass such as quack or Bermuda, can be controlled with edgings or spot treatment with a nonselective herbicide.

Water the new plants once or twice weekly until they are well established. After the plants have emerged, mulch around them. Once well rooted, hostas can go for two or three weeks without rain unless they are in soil that is invaded by tree roots. Experienced growers are careful about watering hostas.

1)

## Dividing Hostas

Hostas benefit from occasional division. Unlike many other perennials, hostas can, with care, be moved at any time the ground is not frozen, though the optimum time varies according to region. Here, a crowded clump is taken up with a spading fork (1). The soil is rinsed from the roots in a bucket of water to make division easier (2). Then the clump is cut or pulled apart (3). The divisions are ready for transplanting in soil modified with organic matter and fertilizer. Complete the process with a thorough watering. If you divide in the fall, after the foliage has been killed by frost, mulch the new plants so that they will root well before the ground freezes.

2)

3)

They follow the "occasional deep drink" principle. They try to water before noon, which gives the plants time to dry off before nightfall. Sun-baked beds of hostas, especially those with a southern or western exposure, may need weekly waterings.

Give hostas light applications of fertilizer. For example, each year, just after shoots emerge, the Wilkinses work a phosphate and magnesium source, "MagAmp," into their soil and add greensand to provide potassium. The decay of organic mulches provides sufficient nitrogen. Farther south and west, or on lighter soils, two or three applications of dry granular fertilizer per season may be needed.

Maintain tight control of slugs and snails: the Wilkinses' garden is surrounded by forest, and is infested with 2-inch long gray slugs. They use bran cereal or wheat bran from a feed store, sprinkled lightly with liquid metaldehyde, to control them. By making their own bait, slug-control cost is kept at only fifteen dollars per year. If they relax the slug-control program for even a short while, damage quickly gets out of hand, especially in years with average or above-average rainfall.

Inspect occasionally for bug damage. Hostas have very few insect or disease pests in the North. Black vine weevils may periodically notch hosta leaves, but they can be controlled with one spray application of Carbaryl.

## Division

Divide established hostas occasionally. While it is true that hosta plants can live for decades without being divided, certain clumps can grow too large for their sites. They can be taken up, divided, and replanted in soil modified with organic matter and fertilizer. In areas with severe winters, divide in late summer so that a strong root system can be established before the ground freezes. Hosta clumps are easy to pull or cut apart after soil has been rinsed off in a bucket of water. Unlike many other perennials, hostas can (with care) be moved at about any time the ground is not frozen. Therefore, they are not "set in concrete" and can be shifted around the garden to make just the right combinations of cultivars. Be sure to water divisions thoroughly after transplanting and to work rapidly to avoid their drying out during the process.

The admirable Graham Stuart Thomas in his book *Perennial Garden Plants* suggests a beautifully simple way for dividing large clumps of hostas. Quite correctly, he brings out the mixed feelings one has when approaching beautiful old specimens, with spade in hand. Rather than dig the entire plant up, cut out pie-shaped segments and use them as new starts. Fill in the hole with compost.

It has been my experience that you can take about half of a hosta crown in a single season without harming the established clump. I prefer to divide dormant plants in early spring. The growing season is so long in the Southeast where I live that hostas have plenty of time to establish themselves before hot weather. Up north, it seems that the new shoots begin popping up right after the soil has thawed and dried out. I hesitate to touch hostas then because the tender shoots can break so easily. If you divide in the fall, after the foliage has been killed by frost, you will need to mulch new plants to make sure they root strongly before the ground freezes.

In cold-winter areas where perennials are often damaged by heaving of soil, mulch established hostas after the soil has frozen and you have twisted off the dead tops. If you mulch too early, mice may invade the hosta beds and damage crowns.

## Hybridizing

Jim Wilkins encourages hobby gardeners, and they don't have to be experts, to try their hand at hybridizing hostas. The individual flower parts are large and visible enough to be easily reached. He offers the following advice about selecting hosta parents for hybridizing, based on his own experience:

"In general, hostas which have solid central or marginal color variegation will produce only solid-colored offspring. However, a plant that is 'streaked' or 'splashed' with contrasting colors will often produce variegated offspring when it is used as the female or 'pod' parent." (The trait for variegation is carried in the chloroplast of maternal cells.)

"The offspring from crosses using streaked or splashed cultivars as the pod parent may eventually form stable central or marginally variegated plants. They need to be watched for a few years to detect solid color reversions.

"The pod parents I have found most reliable for producing variegated offspring are *H*. 'Dorothy Benedict', *H*. 'Northern Mist', and *H*. 'Color Fantasy'. Pod parents that give good solid gold-colored offspring are *H*. 'Aspen Gold' and *H*. 'Gold Regal'. Pod parents that produce blue offspring are *H*. 'Dorset Blue' and *H*. 'Blue Moon'. For breeding toward beautiful blooms I use as pod parents *H. kikutii* (a species hosta) and *H*. 'Maruba Iwa'. And, to produce beautiful leaf shapes I use *H*. 'Holly's Honey' and *H*. 'Donahue Piecrust'.

"If the beginning hybridist stays with these cultivars, he or she will avoid the hostas that are sterile, such as *H*. 'Krossa Regal' and *H*. 'Birchwood Parky's Gold'. If any fertile hostas are incompatible in crosses, I am not aware of them. One hosta species, *H. ventricosa*, is 'apomictic,' and produces offspring almost always identical to itself, without genetic input by the pollen parent."

# *Daylilies*

*In nearly seventy years of service to humanity, Brother Charles Reckamp lets his light shine through his love for daylilies.*

*In all its glory: Brother Charles Reckamp's unnamed hybrid seedling 86-123 shows the multiple branching and high bud count desired by daylily enthusiasts. Note the prominent ruffling.*

*D*aylilies can be cast as the stars or the spear carriers of your garden grand opera. Massed in phalanxes or marshaled into small squads, they can back up or flank the stars on center stage. Like good troops, sturdy, adaptable daylilies can be moved about or dug in for a long occupation. Yet, among their ranks are individuals of such brilliance that they are destined to command attention. Daylilies are fast becoming the most popular herbaceous perennial in North America. Bright and bold, they require little care, can be planted at any time during the growing season, offer a broad variety of plant sizes, blossom colors, and conformations, can be tucked into niches in landscapes rather than requiring special beds, and thrive in containers.

Daylilies have long been beloved for their cheerful, sunny colors: yellow, gold, and orange. Plant breeders, however, were not content with such a limited palette and have added colors that, only a decade or two ago, would have seemed beyond the realm of possibility. Neither were the hybridists content with the rather brief shows of colors of the older cultivars, and they have significantly lengthened the duration of bloom. They have also stretched the season of bloom by developing early cultivars that bloom right after peonies, and late cultivars that bloom during the shortening days of late summer. They are introducing cultivars with remontant (repeat) blooming. They have increased the bud count to more than a hundred on well-established plants and have selected plants for precocious flowering. They have added peachy-coral pastels and somber dark hues, crystalline petal textures, broad petals, ruffled and waved.

If, when you hear the word "daylilies," you still think of the humble tawny daylilies that have naturalized along country roads over much of America, shake off this outdated stereotype. Today's cultivars are light-years removed from their country cousins. Entirely new colors and color patterns have been developed, entirely new classes of plants such as the miniatures and triploids have been introduced, the size and substance of blossoms have been improved, and the plants have been made more resistant to windstorms. If you have not recently visited a collection of modern daylilies at a public garden, you would hardly believe your eyes. You would recognize the new cultivars as daylilies—they still have the family resemblance—but what gorgeous creations they are. It would be hard to find another genus of plants so transformed in such a short time!

In no other plant specialty have amateur plant breeders contributed so much to the improvement of a hobby plant. (I'm counting as amateurs all who are not geneticists or who lack advanced education in the field of botany.) Back-yard plant breeders have contributed many of the twenty-five thousand or more cultivars developed during the past half century. The exciting part of daylily breeding is that much remains to be accomplished and that any reasonably intelligent, meticulous person might just be the one to make the next breakthrough.

Much of the potential for improvement lies in the deep genetic pool available to plant breeders. *Hortus III* lists about fifteen species within the genus *Hemerocallis*, all resembling typical daylilies enough to be easily identifiable. Even though there are differences in flower-head arrangement, foliage, and roots, the resemblance is strong between the species. Crosses between species, while difficult, are made with increasing frequency.

Long ago, civilized countries began planting daylilies for food rather than flowers. In their native China, gathered from the wild and eaten fresh or dried, daylilies were a staple in good times and a survival food during famines. Even now, dried daylily blossoms are exported in large quantities to be added to soups as thickeners or reconstituted to use as garnish. Curiously, it appears we are coming full circle: fine chefs in the U.S.A. are now using fresh daylily buds as an edible flower.

*The bicolored Reckamp hybrid seedling 84-42 shows the broad, ruffled petals and striping favored by Brother Charles.*

Daylilies deliver a lot of color for the small space they occupy and, during medieval days, were "naturals" to be taken from the wild and cultivated in the compact gardens of wealthy Chinese and Japanese. Early on, good plantsmen began making selections from the wild species. This caused considerable confusion among early plant explorers, who tended to assign a new name to every new acquisition if it differed from the norm for the species. Further confusing the issue was the tendency of daylily species to sport new forms in response to different environmental conditions.

It is believed that the first daylilies reached Europe in the middle of the sixteenth century. By the late sixteenth century, Dutch and English botanists were growing daylilies, but some of their early herbals posted confusing descriptions and inaccurate artwork. Little did the Europeans know that, because they were neither trusted nor respected in the Orient, the wealthy Chinese and Japanese held back their best developments and did not allow them out of their gardens.

The Western world didn't see the best daylilies from the Orient until Albert N. Steward, a botanist, and his wife, Celia B., taught there for many years and gained respect and trust. They sent to their friend, Dr. A. B. Stout, around fifty excellent cultivars and previously unknown species from private gardens on their travels in China. Their shipments set the stage for a quantum leap in daylily breeding. Perhaps the most important find of the Stewards was a seed-bearing plant of *Hemerocallis fulva:* previous introductions of this species were sterile and of little use in hybridizing.

Dr. A. B. Stout was one of the "greats" in horticulture, disciplined, insightful, and afire with a zeal for improving *Hemerocallis* and bringing order out of the chaos of daylily nomenclature. As director of the laboratories at the New York Botanical Garden and a colleague of many of the leading horticulturists between the two world wars, he was in the right place at the right time for his crusade. More than any other person, Dr. Stout set the course for daylilies and gave them a flying start to their present place as a bright star in the firmament of plants.

The very best cultivars developed by Stout were named and farmed out for increase. Some of his creations have stood the test of time and are still listed. He incorporated into new hybrids all but one of the traits he set up in his list of priorities: earliness, hardiness, higher bud count, showier (but not necessarily fancier) blossoms, new colors and variegations, greater extension of flower scapes above the foliage, and sturdy, blue-green leaves, not given to breakage or early yellowing. The one elusive dream? A pure white daylily: it remains to be found.

Since Dr. Stout's day, many hobby breeders of daylilies have upscaled to commercial production as they have developed an inventory of their own hybrid seedlings. They, along with less-advanced fanciers, keep track of the latest developments by visiting performance trials and by attending regional and national conferences of the American Hemerocallis Society. Just learning to recognize the thousands of cultivars by sight, and under different climate and soil conditions, requires several years of study. Fortunately, it is fun, and the advent of camcorders and videotape is accelerating the rate of recording and retaining information.

With most amateur daylily breeders, profit is a distinctly secondary consideration. Recognition from their peers in the daylily world is important, and a sense of contributing to the advancement of a plant they genuinely love. Brother Charles Reckamp is one of the world's foremost amateur breeders of daylilies, and is certainly not in it for profit. To see him at work evaluating his seedlings is to understand the satisfaction a person can realize from working to improve his chosen specialty plant.

*Many of Brother Charles's seedlings don't make the "first cut," his evaluation in first-year seedling rows.*

You may never be tempted to pick up a camel's-hair brush and transfer pollen from one flower to another. For some people, however, attempting to improve a species by hybridization is a natural step in learning about their chosen specialty plant. Some dabble in hybridization while maintaining large and beautiful gardens. Some become so wrapped up in plant improvement that they subordinate gardening to hybridizing and evaluating seedlings of their specialty plant.

If he chose to, Brother Charles Reckamp could grow the plants for a magnificent landscape. He has spent more days on the business end of a hoe than some of us enjoy on earth. But, more than fifty years ago, he made the choice to minimize gardening and maximize his efforts to improve daylilies through hybridization and selection. Long before I met Brother Charles, I had heard of his plant-breeding work. He, Dr. Robert A. Griesbach, and Nathan Rudolph are about the only survivors of the daylily specialists in the Chicago area who began revolutionizing the genus in the 1940s. Figuring that he had to be in his eighties, I expected to meet a frail, elderly man. When I arrived at the Society of the Divine Word U.S.A. headquarters in Techny, Illinois, I found how wrong preconceptions can be.

A brother at the residence pointed to a group of three men wrestling with transplanting a ten-foot-tall serviceberry tree. It had a root ball that must have weighed six hundred pounds. He said, "That's him over there, the one on the left." I went over and introduced myself to a bright-eyed, vigorous man who, while small in stature, was doing his share of the grunt work. Come to find out, he and an employee named Wally and a lay volunteer had transplanted several such trees in the heavy clay land around the campus. Wally and the layman appeared to be in their seventies. They courteously declined my offer to help, possibly because they considered me too old!

To understand Brother Charles's involvement in daylilies as a hobby plant, you need to know a little about his background. He came from a poor farm family who lived north of St. Louis, Missouri, near a town called Ethlyn. Times were hard and he never had a chance to attend high school, not unusual in those days. In 1927, as a young man, he was accepted as a working brother by the society, and, since then, has not ventured far from northern Illinois.

The Society of the Divine Word exists for educational and missionary work in some of the poorest districts of the poorest countries, as well as in the United States. Priests and brothers periodically rotate back to the headquarters for rest and medical treatment. Finally, when they grow too old to shoulder the load, they retire to the residence of the society at Techny.

Since its founding, the society has depended on working brothers to grow grain, livestock, vegetables, fruit, and bees to help feed the staff, visitors, and retirees. That was Brother Charles's first job but, soon, he became involved in growing nursery stock, garden plants, and flowers to cut and sell to the burgeoning suburban Chicago market. The society needed the income to augment that which they received from donations.

Among the flowers grown for cutting were gladiolus, peonies, and iris. At the time, Brother Charles was kept busy growing and harvesting and, during the winter, helping operate a large greenhouse for growing bedding plants. When I say "busy," you must understand that working brothers rise before dawn for devotions, labor hard through long days, and retire at dusk.

Two local men who went on to become legends in daylily breeding, Orville Fay and David Hall, took a liking to Brother Charles and showed him how to cross-pollinate and propagate iris from seed. At the time, Brother Charles had no idea that this newfound skill would lead to the second great love of his life. The mentor-friend relationship between him and established plant breeders opened the door to new opportunities and convinced this modest man that he, too, could make a success of plant breeding.

The good fortune then enjoyed by Brother Charles seemed almost inconceivable to him, but got even better. In the 1940s, Dr. Robert A. Griesbach began breeding "tetraploid" daylilies by treating seeds and seedlings with colchicine to double their chromosome number. He lived in the area and shared his techniques with Brother Charles. Also, James Marsh, a leading amateur plant breeder from Chicago, often came up to Techny. Concurrently, the developer of the famous 'Stella d'Oro' daylily, Walter Jablonski of Merrivale, Illinois, was making great strides in hybridization but was not part of Brother Charles's group.

Reckamp, Hall, Fay, Griesbach, and Marsh held long discussions on the improvements needed in daylilies, and how to go about achieving them. Even though Dr. A. B. Stout had made tremendous progress in improving the genus, he had only scratched the surface. The range of plant sizes, blossom colors and patterns, petal and sepal width and texture were still limited. Cultivars tended to hide their blossoms amidst the foliage, were rather shy bloomers, basically midsummer flowers.

It happens that daylilies are one of the easiest plants to hybridize; the reproductive parts are large and readily accessible. Anthers can be quickly removed from yet-to-open buds, and pollen transferred to the receptive stigma from a desirable pollen parent. Pollen from early bloomers can be dried and stored for crossing on later cultivars.

Brother Charles was still young and had the energy to keep up his food- and flower-growing duties while learning plant breeding. However, he decided to put iris breeding on the back burner because of his conviction that daylilies held greater potential for improvement, and greater possibilities as a landscape plant. He explained to me how daylilies came to be improved so greatly in a relatively short time span.

"It was the vast improvement in iris created by the introduction of tetraploids that convinced our little band of plant breeders to try the same approach on daylilies. When you double the number of chromosomes in a plant, a number of things can happen: its progeny can be dwarfed, with thicker stems, more massive flowers, and thicker petals. Hybrids between species are sometimes possible, when you work with tetraploid male and female parents.

"Dr. Griesbach had the scientific mind and equipment for the demanding task of experimenting with the powerful gene-altering drug, colchicine. He spent many hours in the lab at DePaul University, treating

*Daylilies have come a long way in two decades. Compare the modern tetraploid seedling BC 88-6, left, with the diploid 'Mission Moonlight', introduced by Brother Charles in 1967.*

newly germinated daylily seeds with various concentrations of colchicine to double the number of chromosomes within cells. The treatment is traumatic, very few seedlings survive, and those are slow to regain their natural fertility. All seedlings have to be grown to maturity in trials because many survivors will have the normal chromosome count but some will be crippled or deformed.

"Orville Fay worked closely with Dr. Griesbach, and they soon had a few tetraploid mutations that set marginally fertile seeds. It took several generations for the plants to regain full fertility. These tetraploids were hybridized to begin their daylily breeding program. It was like starting all over again; their tetraploid hybrids were like nothing we had ever seen before in daylilies.

"The price tag on the first tetraploid daylily introduced by Orville Fay was two hundred dollars per plant. It was the cultivar 'Crestwood Ann'. My superiors had confidence in me and purchased one plant as the start for a tetraploid gene pool of my own.

"I was fortunate to have working with me the young Brother Daniel Yunk. He had a good feel for daylilies and tried his luck with colchicine treatments. He succeeded in producing several nice tetraploids, which we restored to fertility and used in crosses with 'Crestwood Ann'. The resulting seedlings became the foundation stock for my future hybridizing. At this time, I also had access to valuable pollen from Orville Fay's collection, which included daylily cultivars I could not afford.

"During the 1950s, the five of us, while still friends, developed different goals in daylily breeding and began working independently. For example, Orville Fay was centering on wider petals and open-faced blossoms with ruffled edges. Griesbach was all wrapped up in creating new tetraploids, in which he did very well. One of his top achievements was a line of improved red daylilies with larger flowers, wider petals, and brighter, sunfast hues.

"I began finding extraordinary pastel shades amongst my hybrids and transferred the traits for ruffling and wider petals to them. My hybrids looked good and began to sell. I returned all the income to the society and they let me have a plot of farmland to evaluate my experimental seedlings.

"Gradually, my hybrids began to show a common 'signature'—a combination of wide petals and highly visible sepals. My latest hybrids show a tinge of gold around the ruffled edges. Most of my work has been with the creamy pastels, which, to me, seem richer than the straight pastels.

"For years I had searched for exceptional ruffling and found it in the hybrid I named 'Amen'. As a pollen parent, it passed on the ruffling to succeeding generations. Another turning point was the development of 'Milepost', a pastel pink. It became the source for an intensified pink blush color in my later hybrids.

*Brother Charles's "signature" of huge flowers, soft but clean colors, and broad, ruffled petals all show in his tetraploid seeding BC 86-42.*

"I've tried the red colors, but haven't produced anything to brag about. I haven't tried breeding miniature daylilies. Crosses between species are beyond my expertise in genetics. I haven't tried to pick up breeding lines from the evergreen *Hemerocallis*. I've stuck pretty close to the plants in the 20- to 36-inch class. Yet, there's still so much to be done in this category that I haven't felt at all limited."

In 1975, young Roy Klehm came over from nearby Barrington and offered to market all future Reckamp hybrids through the Klehm Nursery mail-order catalog. Brother Charles accepted; now, when you see the credit line of Reckamp-Klehm behind a cultivar name, you know it was introduced in or after 1975. Roy comes over to Brother Charles's plots, digs out most of the plants, and moves them to his own nursery for further evaluation and increase of promising lines. The only plants remaining are those Brother Charles tags to keep for use in his breeding work.

"At first," Brother Charles said, "Roy and I always saw eye-to-eye on the experimental hybrids. But now, thirteen years later, Roy has become more knowledgeable and a lot more critical. I like it because he makes

*Masters of the Victory Garden*

me defend my judgments. One thing we did agree on was to continue my practice of giving my introductions 'heavenly' names such as 'Amen' or 'Angel's Delight'. I don't consider myself any closer to the angels than anyone else, except perhaps due to my age, but 'heavenly' names come easily to me and I think they are memorable."

Brother Charles was experiencing long and dangerous delays in crossing busy Waukegan Road to reach the old daylily plots, so he moved his garden to a new location near the residence building. He showed me the new 85×125-foot trial garden. Klehm brought in a crew and large machines, and laid 900 feet of drain tile for it in a single day. After removing the sod from the garden plot, he hauled in an eight-inch layer of rotted leaves plus several loads of manure and turned them under with a chisel plow.

I think that Brother Charles has for so long given himself to serving others, that much of his life's pleasure comes from his ability to create beauty for others to enjoy. When asked what advice he could give to aspiring daylily growers, he said, "Visit demonstration gardens first, to find out which cultivars do well in your area, and which ones you like. Go on an early summer morning to catch most cultivars at their best. The hot, humid weather of late summer fades the colors quickly. The cultivars called 'rebloomers' offer a special advantage. When the first 'scapes,' or blossom sprays, have finished blooming, additional scapes develop to prolong the production of flowers.

"Unless you are making solid plantings of dwarf daylilies for groundcovers, plant them in groups of three or five of the same cultivar for best effect. Don't jumble up a bunch of different cultivars in the same bed; they will look like a hodgepodge. If you want to show several different cultivars in one bed, intersperse low-growing perennials between them, especially those with silvery leaves or blue flowers. Daylilies will take a half day of shade but the blossoms will face the sun. Keep that in mind when choosing a site for daylilies.

"Realize that individual daylily blossoms remain open only one day but are replaced by new flowers the following day. This is why planting a cultivar with a high bud count is so important. You may not be able to be home at ten A.M.; that is the best hour for freshness and color. Yet, some of the harsher colors look better to me when the afternoon sun has subdued them. Conversely, some of the dark colors lose a lot of character when faded by the sun. When evening comes, you will be glad for planting light-colored cultivars such as the creams and light yellows because they will show up better at dusk.

"If you can, plant daylilies in front of evergreens or deciduous shrubs. They display better with a green background. But, avoid planting them too near greedy, aggressive shrubs that will rob them of nutrients and water. Work organic matter deeply into the area to be used for planting,

*(Left) Brother Charles spaces his evaluation rows for easy cultivation with a small power tiller.*

and don't set crowns any deeper than they grew in the container or nursery bed.

"If you have a choice, plant daylilies in September. They will bloom the next year. Spring-planted daylilies often are shy about blooming the first season. Large, containerized plants get off to a fast start but, often, only the old standard varieties are offered in containers. Some mail-order sources offer young plants grown in pots.

"Your plants may occasionally have problems with spider mites and various leaf spots. Neither is terminal, but both will disfigure plants. I have a thirty-gallon power sprayer and use captan, Benlate and malathion, but only when I see outbreaks.

"In my rich soil modified with leaf mold, I feed only once a season, in spring with 5-10-5, worked in. Our deep soil seldom requires watering, except for newly transplanted seedlings, but I did have to turn on the sprinklers during the 1988 drought. I get color from late June through September, counting the rebloomers. Few other flowers can match that. Home gardeners can get color over such a long season, also, by choosing cultivars for season of bloom as well as for color and height.

"I like to divide daylilies more often than other specialists because the young plants are so vigorous, and because I need to grow several plants for proper evaluation of a new seedling. Every second year, I dig up old crowns with a spading fork, wash them off with a sharp spray of water, and use a sharp, stiff butcher knife to cut the crowns into four pie-shaped segments. I don't separate crowns into individual plants or 'fans' because some would not bloom until the second year. If I miss a crown and it grows large and dense, I do the first dividing with a sharp spade, and then pick up the knife.

"On the deciduous daylilies, which make up most of my collection, the tops shrivel to practically nothing after a hard winter. I leave them in place and twist them off during spring cleanup."

I asked Brother Charles for a starter list of daylilies for beginners—cultivars he really likes. After much hemming and hawing, which is typical for anyone who has seen thousands of cultivars, he offered this list:

- 'Priceless Pearl': A pale yellow tetraploid with a pink blush. The petals are edged with a golden yellow band, and have lacy, ruffled margins. Individual blossoms can reach 6 inches in diameter on 36-inch plants. *A late bloomer.*
- 'My Sunshine': These tetraploid plants are somewhat shorter than 'Priceless Pearl', with yellow blossoms up to 7 inches in diameter, suffused with pink and cream. Ivory midribs and deep golden, heavily ruffled petal margins add character to the large flowers. The recurved sepals that back up the three petals are blushed pink toward the centers. *Midseason.*

A subtle overlay
of yellow on a
cream base lights
up a garden. This
is BC 88-14, still
under evaluation.

● 'Heavenly Treasure': A most unusual tetraploid with a yellow-to-olive-green throat that sets off the apricot-melon petal color. The 36-inch-high plants sport blossoms of 6½-inch diameter. A thin yellow edge and tight, lacy ruffles dress up the petals. *Midseason.*

Brother Charles is a cheerful man who delights in recalling the many pleasant and humorous experiences he has enjoyed in daylily breeding. One of his favorite stories is the reaction of a fellow daylily breeder when he first saw the Reckamp cultivar 'Heavenly Treasure'. "Brother Charles," he said, "if this is what I can expect to see in heaven, I'm going to start leading a better life!"

If there is any connection between a hobby plant and one's reaching a serene, productive old age, I believe that Brother Charles has found it . . . in daylilies.

# More about Daylilies

My first recollection of daylilies was of a clump thrown on a pile of coal ashes and clinkers in an alley in Paducah, Kentucky. I was only five years old, but can recall how impressed I was at how that plant took root, grew, and bloomed in that impossible situation! I wouldn't recommend such severe treatment for any plant, but daylilies are one tough flower. They will thrive in all but the most severe climates and on a wide range of soil types. You need to pay attention to one of their peculiarities. Daylilies are separated into two major categories: deciduous and evergreen. The deciduous types are adapted all across the North, New England, and the upper South. The evergreen types are preferred for the Deep South and warm West. The two types look and are grown much alike but the evergreen types die back only partially or not at all during the winter, depending on minimum temperatures.

Treat daylilies as a sun-loving flower. In the South and West, light afternoon shade won't hurt but, up north, shade can cause plants to stretch and to flower sparsely. You can tell when plants are receiving more shade than they like; flowering will be delayed and sparse.

**Planting and Division**

You can plant new daylilies or divide old crowns at any time after flowering. Containerized plants can be set in the ground in full bloom. Observe one precaution . . . up north, plant them by late summer. The crowns need several weeks to send out the anchor roots that keep them from being heaved out of the ground by frost. That complicates the dividing of late bloomers because some of them are still showing color in September. Wait out the blooming, and mulch the divided plants heavily to keep the ground warm enough for root formation well into the fall season.

Daylilies require dividing about every five years. First, cut off the top growth about 6 to 8 inches above the ground. Use two spading forks for dividing. Shove them deep into the middle of the crown, back to back and touching. Lever the handles to split the crowns, pull the spading forks out, and repeat the process crosswise to make four divisions. Uproot the crown with the spading forks, invert the segments, and blast off the soil with a sharp spray of water to expose the roots. You can strip individual plants, called "fans," from the segments but most gardeners prefer to plant the entire segment to get abundant color, and faster.

You can transplant crown segments or fans, water them in, and do nothing else . . . they will eventually get over the shock and regrow. The cut-back plants will bleach from the sun and suffer in silence. You can ease the adjustment and hasten recovery by mulching transplants with a light scattering of straw to cast shade and reduce evaporation. Common sense will tell you to water transplants well and frequently for several days.

I try to rotate daylily planting every four or five years when I divide the crowns. I plant the new crowns in soil that has been fortified with organic matter by tilling in green manure crops such as winter rye. Mulches of compost, rotted sawdust, or chopped straw help to maintain a high level of organic matter, which encourages beneficial predatory nematodes and predatory bacteria. I

*Note the strong root system on these year-old hybrid daylily seedlings grown from seeds started indoors in late winter.*

use organic fertilizers or concentrated manures to replace all but liquid fertilizers. This approach is too new to claim complete control, but it looks promising.

Rotating daylily beds in small gardens is, of course, impractical. There, the best approach, when daylilies begin to decline, is to dig up the crowns, divide them, and incorporate generous amounts of organic matter and organic fertilizers before replanting. Organic fertilizers are safer to use at planting time than dry granular chemical fertilizers.

## Soil and Fertilizer

Despite the tolerance of daylilies for a wide range of soils, you need to add organic matter to the soil to get new plants or divisions off to a fast start and to get an acceptable show of color the first season after planting.

Add and mix in enough organic matter to build the beds up for good drainage in heavy soil, and to improve water-holding capacity in sandy soil: a layer of organic matter about 2 inches deep should be sufficient. Add and work in pelleted dolomitic limestone, if needed, to bring the soil pH into the 6.0 to 7.5 range. When planting, dig generous holes and make a mound of loose soil in the bottom of each. Spread out the roots of fans or segments and add or remove soil from the mound to position the crown level with the surrounding soil.

Don't add any fertilizer at planting time, except for a phosphate source. Young plants need to generate a new feeder-root system before they can take plant nutrients. Usually, two applications of balanced granular fertilizer per year will suffice for established plants: one in late spring and another just after blooming. You be the judge; if the foliage color begins to lighten (and it well might on poor, sandy soil), make a third application. Southern and western growers often make one or two applications of liquid fertilizer in addition to the granular feedings because of the length of their growing seasons. Be careful not to feed in the fall where winters are severe. Late fertilization can force plants to continue to grow later than they should, and delay the onset of dormancy. This makes plants vulnerable to injury from winter cold.

*Hybridizing*  Should you wish to cross daylilies to get a new seedling you can call your own, have at it. The odds of your finding a distinctive, different, and deserving seedling in the progeny of random crosses are about 1,000 to 1, but you wouldn't be ashamed to give any of the remaining 999 to your mother.

Start with valuable modern hybrids or tetraploids that differ considerably in color, blossom conformation, but that bloom at the same time. You can minimize seed sterility problems by crossing diploids with diploids and tetraploids with tetraploids. The flower parts are easy to reach and work with. I watched Brother Charles do it; here's how:

1. Select a female parent. Slit a flower bud that is about a day away from opening and trim off the petals so you can see the reproductive parts. Remove the pollen-bearing anthers. They are on long, translucent filaments that can be pinched off or tweaked off with tweezers. Tear off a square of aluminum foil and fold it to about half the size of your hand. Crimp it over the entire emasculated flower to exclude foreign pollen.

2. Within twelve to twenty-four hours, inspect the stigma of the covered blossom. If it feels sticky to the touch, it is receptive to pollen, ready for hybridization.

3. Select a male parent that is shedding pollen. Tap it into a small container such as a pillbox and transfer the pollen to the sticky stigma with a camel's-hair brush or a frayed toothpick. Pollen is large enough to be seen clearly; it should cling to the stigma.

4. Carefully cover the pollinated stigma to keep out insects, which could carry pollen from other daylily blossoms. If your timing was right, fertilization should take place and seeds should form. The first sign of success is a swelling of the ovary, behind the stigma. Label the cross in permanent ink with the names of the male and female parents and the date of the cross.

5. Watch the ripening seed pods. When they begin to turn brown, but before they split, gather them and put them in a warm, dry place to ripen. When the seeds are dry, shell them out and store them in a sealed bottle in the refrigerator until early the following spring.

6. Sow the seeds in vermiculite or in a special seed flat mixture and sprout and grow them under fluorescent lights. When the seedlings have four to six true leaves, transplant them to individual 2½-inch pots and grow them to a size large enough to move into the garden.

7. In late spring, harden off the seedlings and transplant them into a garden row, about 6 inches apart. Label the row with the parentage of the cross, date made, and date transplanted.

8. Although a few vigorous seedlings might form late-season blooms the same year, you won't be able to evaluate them properly until the second or third year. Discard or give away inferior seedlings or those which closely resemble either of the parents. Transplant any promising-looking seedlings to a flower border and invite a knowledgeable *Hemerocallis* specialist to see them in full bloom. They will probably tell you, "Close, but no cigar!" Don't be disappointed; beauty is in the eye of the beholder.

1)

2)

3)

4)

5)

## Hybridizing Daylilies

Brother Charles's hybridizing process begins with these simple tools of the trade: cotton swabs, aluminum foil, scissors, scalpels, tags and marking pens, and envelopes for collecting pollen (1). The female parent is selected and tagged (2). Pollen-laden anthers and stigma of the female parent are visible in this photo of tetraploid seedling BC 87-15 (3). The anthers are removed and the flower protected from foreign pollen with a square of aluminum foil. When the stigma of the covered blossom feels sticky to the touch — within twelve to twenty-four hours — it is ready for hybridization. Pollen is applied from the male parent, and the cross is indicated on the tags (4), shown with these developing seed pods. The ripe seed pods of this tetraploid *Hemerocallis* (5) are at the prime stage for picking.

*Weeding*     Put away your chopping hoe when it comes time to weed around daylily plants. Daylily roots are shallow and deep cultivation can injure them. I prefer to use a push-pull scuffle hoe for weeding between plants and to hand-pull the weeds growing close to daylily clumps. Scuffle hoes slide just beneath the surface to stir the soil and uproot weeds without disturbing the roots of adjacent ornamentals. Mulching with pinestraw, composted pine bark, wood chips, or saltmarsh hay can greatly reduce the frequency of weeding.

*Pests and Diseases*     I haven't seen many insects on daylilies at the regional Victory Gardens. Occasionally, thrips or aphids will jump on weak cultivars as they begin to set blooms, but they are easy to control with botanical insecticides such as pyrethrum, or with insecticidal soap. Southern and western gardens occasionally suffer outbreaks of spider mites during hot, dry weather. Sharp sprays of water directed at the undersides of leaves will blast off many insects and mites, and a program of spraying with insecticidal soap should get rid of the rest. The important thing is to prevent small outbreaks of spider mites from spreading throughout your garden.

A serious problem with daylilies in the South and Southwest is with nematodes, especially on dry, sandy soils. The usual method of control is periodic fumigation of the soil with a chemical such as methyl bromide. I find that such drastic measures are self-defeating. A better approach seems to be using organic amendments and natural fertilizers to keep nematode populations at levels that create little or no injury to plants. Nematodes have always been present in warm-climate soils. They always will be and, in order to eliminate them, you have to kill every living thing in the soil.

Other than a few leaf spots, I have seen few diseases on daylilies. Good sanitation every spring, gathering and composting old leaves from deciduous species, seems to keep diseases in check.

*Landscaping with Daylilies*     Arranging daylilies in landscapes is not complicated. Heights range from about 12 to 48 inches at maturity; catalog listings are usually reliable. Your first consideration should be to place daylilies where they won't tower over plants growing behind them. Your second consideration should be toward selecting a range of blooming dates in cultivars to extend the season of color. Finally, look at colors, patterns, and fancy frills; lean toward the yellows and pastels, with just enough dark colors for a bit of variety. Too many dark hues can deaden a color scheme.

If you buy plants from a local grower or a mail-order source in your geographical region, you can count on getting adapted cultivars. Northern and midwestern growers will sell only hardy deciduous cultivars; southern and western growers will specialize in evergreen types.

A single, well-grown, mature plant of a tall daylily cultivar can make an impressive specimen. However, most daylily specialists prefer to plant individual cultivars in groups. If you have a large garden, you can plant three to five fans of the same cultivar in a circle about three feet across. In a small garden, where the impulse is to cram more variety into a given area, you can make up the group from different cultivars having related colors. Plants within groups should bloom together for impact; make up other groups from earlier or later cultivars to extend the season of color.

There must be more to this landscaping approach than the numerological significance of threes and fives. I see variations of such groupings used in many gardens. Grouping the same or related colors in threes or fives looks so much better than jumbling colors in a pastiche that gives the eye no rest and the stress-ridden mind no solace.

## Miniatures and Dwarfs

You may want to try your hand at hybridizing "miniature" daylilies. They have been the center of the latest flurry of activity in daylily breeding, and interest is continuing to grow. Miniatures are distinct from dwarf daylilies. Surprisingly, the term "miniature," as applied to daylilies, doesn't necessarily pertain to the size of the plant. The American Hemerocallis Society classifies a miniature daylily as one having a flower of 3-inch diameter or less, with no mention of plant height.

If short daylily plants with flowers larger than 3 inches are not miniatures, what are they? They are dwarfs. You can buy dwarf species daylilies, dwarf diploid (normal) hybrids, and dwarf tetraploids.

The increase in interest in container growing has helped to further advances in miniature and dwarf daylilies. Full-size clumps, with crowns a foot or more across, can be grown in 5- to 7-gallon tubs. Plants a year or two old can be accommodated in a 3-gallon can. The dwarf miniatures can also serve as edgings, giving a welcome change from liriope as an edging in the South. The most rugged miniatures are in the 12- to 18-inch height range, which makes them practical for edging taller daylilies or perennials.

As with all gardeners, I have my own set of preferences and biases. In daylilies, I like the bright or light colors that can be seen from a distance, rather than the darker hues that seem to disappear when the sun is low in the sky. I like a little frilling and waving on the petals but not so much doubling that the blossoms look clunky. Nothing pleases me so much, however, as a high flower bud count, which tells me I can expect fresh flowers to open every day for weeks. My great expectations for daylilies are seldom disappointed.

# Roses

*Charles and Lee Jeremias's life is filled with roses: growing, showing, and sharing them with others.*

*(Left) A view of the Jeremiases' front verandah evokes the time-less appeal of roses. The poly-antha roses in the foreground are, left to right: the red-orange 'Golden Salmon', the white 'Clo-tilde Soupert', and the pink 'La Marne'.*

*D*eep within the subconscious of every man or woman is a rose. What else could trigger instantaneous comparisons between freighted stimuli: fragrances, textures, forms—and roses. Where would we be without the simile "like a rose"?

Man never was good at leaving well enough alone. Despite the beauty, fragrance, and ruggedness of wild roses, man began domesticating and improving them long before the dawn of systematic botany. Rose culture had to be the province of the wealthy or educated because common man was busy dawn to dusk, wresting a living from the soil or the sea. But we can believe that he, too, responded to the beauty of the roses of the field. Perhaps it was this common experience that planted an archetypal rose in the soul of each of us.

Long ago, rose culture expanded beyond the great gardens of the wealthy and the few public gardens, into the gardens of less-favored people. Along the way, roses collected champions: military, clerical, scholarly, and purely commercial. Collectively, these friends of the rose raised the level of awareness of their favorite and improved the genus *Rosa* tremendously. The name "rosarian" became attached to one who knew enough about roses to be regarded as an "authority" by his or her peers.

Over the centuries, rosarians have developed arbitrary divisions for the huge genus *Rosa*, dividing it more by form and function than by species. Without being divided into categories, the genus would be incomprehensible. Novices would be so bewildered by the thousands of cultivars in commerce that they would not know where or how to begin learning about roses.

Since the turn of the century, rosarians have evolved tight standards for naming, recording, showing, and judging roses. Gradually, they are resolving differences in international standards and are attempting to coordinate research to make rose growing easier and more gratifying for everyone. Progress has been rapid since World War II. Prior to that time, when German was the accepted scientific language, international communications were mostly limited to scientists and the few multilingual European nurserymen. With the coming of English as the major language of commerce, scientists, nurserymen, and amateur rose enthusiasts worldwide can work together more readily at international rose conferences.

Generally, the United States rose trade is a bit looser about divisions than the European. You will doubtless recognize some of the standard divisions that appear in American catalogs: hybrid teas, floribundas, grandifloras, climbers, miniatures, shrub roses, old garden roses, and polyanthas. (These are discussed in greater depth in the section "More about Roses" at the end of this chapter.) Of these divisions, "old garden roses" is the most heterogeneous. Any rose introduced before 1867 is automatically in this category.

Botanical historians have exhaustively studied geological and archaeological findings to trace when roses first appeared in fossils and artifacts. Fossils can validate origins that might otherwise be obscured by introduced plant material. Botanical artifacts—paintings, sculptures, medallions, carvings—can augment written records of man's wanderings, systematic exploration, war- or famine-induced migrations, or territorial expansion.

*(Right) An artful arrangement of old roses by Lee Jeremias: (clockwise from bottom) 'Sombreuil', 'Belle de Crecy', R. rugosa 'Alba'. Top: 'Salet', 'Shailer's Provence'; center, 'Paquerette'.*

Asia is believed to be the home of the greatest number of rose species of proven value. Reverence for roses was evident in early Chinese writings and, not much later, in poetry from India, Persia, and Southeast Asia. Always, roses were the stuff of romance, redemption, spirituality, grace, and surpassing beauty.

Rose species and "sports" (natural mutations) were collected, traded, bestowed as gifts, and transported over increasingly long distances as early centers of civilization expanded and coalesced. Long-distance transfers of plants were rare before the Crusades. Until that time, rose gardens were

filled with improved wild roses collected within the short range of trading ships, caravans, and limited military expeditions. Thus, each major center of civilization had its own set of rose species.

Roses, like tulips at a later date in Holland, were at times revered, exalted, and pursued to the point of irrationality. Blossoms, petals, oils, attars, and extracts were used prodigiously in festivals, anointments, funerals, and bacchanals. The numerous nurseries needed to produce fresh and dried rose blossoms for imperial Rome, at the expense of food production, were typical of the excesses and indulgences that toppled the empire.

The poignant effects of poverty, not only of the pocketbook but also of the mind, were typified in the decline and metamorphosis of rose culture during the Dark Ages. Cultivation persisted mostly around monasteries, where roses were grown more for medicinal uses than for landscaping or cut flowers. Commercial nurseries and royal gardens disappeared.

But, it would be a mistake to see the rose as a product of Christian endeavor. Islamic incursions into Europe—the Moors into North Africa and Spain, the sultans through the Balkans all the way to Austria—introduced Eastern species and highly refined landscape applications.

It was the spice trade that gave Renaissance scholars and gardeners access to the vast range of rose species from China, Southeast Asia, and, later, Japan. But it was not until the time of Josef Gottlieb Koelreuter in the mid-1700s that much progress was made in rose breeding. Well before Mendel, while working in the royal park at Karlsruhe, Germany, Koelreuter described the flower parts of roses and their functions.

Leadership in rose breeding moved around from France, Holland, and Germany to England and back, depending on the fortunes of royal or commercial underwriters of great gardens, and on freedom from the ravages of war. Competent and ethical nurseries developed to supply the demand for improved roses, including those from the Colonies.

The nineteenth century was the heyday of plant explorers from Europe and the United States. They descended on Afghanistan, China, Japan, India, Korea, and Burma. They were not always welcome and sometimes had to work through trusted, English-speaking native entrepreneurs. Some of the species roses in these areas are now threatened by agricultural expansion; these collectors may have saved certain wild roses from extinction.

North America is the home of several species of wild roses, but not until later years were these incorporated into the bloodlines used by plant breeders. For example, the first rose cultivar developed in the U.S.A. was produced from parental lines from Europe. This was 'Noisette', bred by John Champney of Charleston, South Carolina, in 1815.

Appreciation of roses in the United States is just as strong as in Europe. Roses are a bit more difficult to grow in many sections of the country, but easier in favored climates such as the West Coast. Some cultivars perform well in certain areas, but not in others. The trying winters across the North, and the heat and humidity of the South have necessitated the creation of American Rose Society Rose Testing Panels to evaluate the regional performance of new hybrids. Rose enthusiasts innovate new ways to grow, feed, water, prune, and spray roses to maximize performance under their particular conditions. While some cultural practices are common across the country, others vary widely.

The garden I visited is in South Carolina, on the northern edge of climate zone 7. It is large by any standard, with an old-fashioned, informal look. The dozens of beds are separated by broad turf paths. Neatly pruned modern and miniature roses are placed up front, with the huge, mounded plants of old-fashioned and shrub roses to the back and side of the property. Roses run up fences and over arches, mark boundary lines, and guide you from one section of the garden to another.

Mother's Day attracts visitors from all over the upstate of South Carolina to the rose garden of Charles and Lephon Jeremias in the historic town of Newberry. Families bring their mothers to see and smell the roses: some wear white roses to honor a mother who has passed on. Everybody calls Charles "Doctor" because he headed the chemistry department at Newberry College and holds a Ph.D. Lephon is known as "Lee," and hosts a local radio program, "Coffee with Lee," over station WKDK, Newberry.

*The Jeremiases often grow old roses for identification. This tea rose grew from a cutting taken in an old cemetery; they are still trying to identify it.*

*O*ne look at the rose garden of Charles and Lee Jeremias and you know it is a full-time activity. A closer look will reveal a few sensible concessions. When you learn the extent of the Jeremiases' involvement in the American Rose Society, rose shows, and community activities, you have to marvel at how they manage to keep their roses weeded, pruned, fed, and trained. Somehow they find time to care for nearly a thousand bushes, perhaps because they have sectioned off their garden and have planted each section with roses that require similar culture. Special areas are provided for old roses, miniatures, shrub roses, and modern hybrids such as grandifloras, multifloras, and hybrid teas. More than six hundred visitors showed up on Mother's Day the year the Jeremiases' garden was featured on *The Victory Garden*. Another six hundred or so trickle through the garden throughout the balance of the major bloom season, which, in an average year, can last into June. Every visitor is made welcome and headed out on a self-guided tour. Many visitors come especially to see the Jeremiases' collection of about six hundred old roses. Gradually, the Jeremiases are focusing on old roses because of their nostalgic charm and because the state of South Carolina has proved a good hunting ground for roses planted prior to the War Between the States.

It is obvious to visitors that Charles and Lee Jeremias are excellent rose growers and that they have an outstanding collection of old, modern, and miniature roses on their one-acre lot. What isn't obvious, and the Jeremiases aren't given to boasting, is the national standing of these two modest people. Charles was elected President of the 25,000-member American Rose Society in 1988, having worked up through ARS district and regional offices and a national vice-presidency. He is an ARS Life Judge of Long Standing and a Consulting Rosarian, often called on for advice in rose-growing.

Lee is a North Carolina farm girl by birth, an ARS Life Judge, and so knowledgeable about old roses that she took the first national trophy awarded to old garden roses in 1973.

The Jeremiases operate a small business, Bynum Manor Roses, chiefly as a vehicle for identifying, propagating, and preserving old roses that are adapted to the Southeast. The business was named for the Victorian home on the property, the townhouse of the original owners, the Bynum family. Charles and Lee do no plant breeding, other than watching for mutations that appear to have horticultural value. They sell a few old roses, which are difficult to obtain elsewhere, but the business is strictly secondary to their first love: growing and showing roses competitively. Their huge rose garden unquestionably helps them in exhibiting roses because of the choice it offers in varieties and blooms at various stages of maturity.

No quick answer comes when the Jeremiases are asked why roses mean so much to them. The answers may be rooted in their distinct personalities. Charles is a methodical man, analytical and precise, as one might expect in a chemist who holds important patents from his work in industry. His approach to taking up roses as a hobby in 1959 was typically objective. He cut out color pictures and descriptions of roses he liked, taped them on a board, studied them and rose gardening for a year, and finally bought seventeen plants for his first rose garden.

Lee is a natural gardener, strongly influenced by a dear and knowledgeable grandmother. She loves to recount how, as a wee girl, she grew curious about the progress of a rose cutting. Her grandmother was rooting it under a half gallon Mason jar (which used to be the way most folks started rose bushes). Lee pulled up the plant to see if it was growing roots. Grandmother watched the tableau from the kitchen window, replanted the rose, and delivered a stern but loving lecture that cemented Lee's developing bond with gardening. Years later, when she was established as an authority on old roses, Lee returned to the old home place to help her grandmother identify an old rose that had been growing there for more than a hundred years. It turned out to be 'The Bishop', of the centifolia division.

Following a traditional education at Wake Forest, Lee worked in public relations for several years, then did something she really wanted to do. She took a two-year course in horticulture at Forsyth Tech. Along the way she began specializing in roses and winning top awards as an exhibitor. Judging followed, and she soon became respected for her fairness and helpfulness to exhibitors.

Both Charles and Lee were established rosarians when they married in 1981. They soon settled in at Bynum Manor, a rambling Victorian home surrounded by enormous sweet gum trees. They faced a full acre of neglected lawn, part of which had for years been under horse barns and corrals. Gradually, the side and back yards filled up with roses.

Even veteran rosarians such as Charles and Lee will, after some soul-searching, admit to having a favorite rose . . . or several. Lee likes 'Sombreuil', a fragrant white climbing tea. She calls it a "crowd pleaser." Then, 'Casino', a yellow pillar climber, and 'Dortmund' of the Kordesii class, red with a white eye. From the miniatures, she picks 'Jennie La-Joie', a climbing pink with tiny, exhibition-quality tea rose blooms.

Charles's first choice, "just for its marvelous fragrance," is the old 'American Beauty'. But to show his evenhandedness, he names a newer rose next, the yellow hybrid tea 'Sunbright'. For its historical significance he likes the first-ever polyantha rose, 'Paquerette', with clustered white blossoms brushed with pink. The colors of the tea rose 'Catherine Mermet' endear it to him . . . pink with overtones of lavender and white. From the miniatures he favors 'Rainbow's End', opening pure yellow and turning red.

Fragrance is high on the Jeremiases' reasons for preferring old roses. They recall with satisfaction the reaction of a blind and wheelchair-bound lady brought to the garden with a tour from the Council on Aging. Her attendant was fussing around wheeling her from place to place in the garden, when the blind lady stopped her. With her face wreathed in smiles she cried out, "Just leave me here, honey, I can smell every rose in the garden!" Such memorable experiences more than compensate Charles and Lee for the time they spend with visitors.

Charles has plenty of time for the garden, now that he is retired. Other than the period leading up to and during "Show Time!" at Mother's Day, he spends about sixteen hours weekly with the roses. Lee's job at the radio station leaves her only about half as much time. Visitors are amazed at the amount of work they do, and well, in such a few nours. Both are energetic and organized. Having done every task many times before, they whip through them quickly in order to have more time just to walk among and enjoy their roses.

It is frustrating to have the time and energy but not the space to grow more roses. The few trees on their property cast high afternoon shade, a desirable consideration for roses in the South (but not where summers are cooler). A deep edging each spring, with a sharp spade, cuts tree roots that would compete with the roses. All the incidental space is filled with containerized roses. Generous walkways have been provided to accommodate visitors, so they have no more lawn to convert to rose beds.

Charles and Lee are choosy about the roses they acquire, but they never discard any. A few plants were lost to the bitterly cold Christmas Eve freeze of 1985 when, following unseasonal weather in the 60s, the temperature plummeted to minus 3 degrees Fahrenheit. (Unaccountably, the old teas and hybrid perpetuals withstood the cold better than hybrid teas and floribundas.) A few more were lost to intensely hot and dry summers. The rugosa hybrids suffered most from the heat and dryness.

Chores around the rose garden are shared. "She does the buying, I do the planting," Charles jests. He does the weekly spraying, a necessary but tedious chore. Lee's legs are a bit younger, so she takes care of the miniatures to spare Charles the stooping. These two strong personalities do everything so well in rose-growing that they have found it works better if they labor separately in the garden rather than shoulder to shoulder. Yet, all the planning and preparation for shows is done together.

The Jeremiases have had to adapt traditional rose culture to their southeastern climate, soil, and unusual rose cultivars. Before planting a new acquisition, they research its origin for clues on how to grow and prune it.

New acquisitions usually arrive as small own-rooted or budded plants. Budding on a vigorous rootstock can mean better performance from a weak or disease-susceptible cultivar. However, many old roses are grown "own-rooted," which means not grafted. With the relatively mild winters at Newberry, own-rooted roses survive reliably.

New plants are potted up and grown on for a year, or until a place in the garden opens up. This gives the Jeremiases an opportunity to inspect the new plant for any sign of mosaic virus disease, and promptly pitch it if this transmittable systemic disease shows up.

Some of their roses are grown from cuttings given to them on visits to other growers of old roses, or from branches sent to them for identifica-

*Charles introduces a young visitor, Cory Hamm, to the beauty of old roses.*

tion. The cuttings are treated with Rootone rooting hormone and "stuck" in a propagating bed resembling a cold frame. The bed is filled with a mixture of equal parts of moistened peat moss, perlite, and white quartz sand. Softwood cuttings "take" quickly and form a good root system prior to winter.

The soil at Bynum Manor varies from heavy clay to sandy loam. Only the sandy spots dry out enough to require regular watering. Charles scrapes up basins around plants with a hoe and waters deeply, usually fertilizing at the same time.

The heavier soil has a high water table, and planting holes dug in the spring tend to fill with water. If they do, Charles dumps in a deep layer of gravel with a topping of soil, then positions the plant and backfills around it with native soil. He is careful to settle in the plant by flowing water around it to eliminate air pockets. Tramping down the heavy soil would compact it unnecessarily.

Own-rooted plants are set to a depth where the soil line in the container lines up with the surface of the garden soil. Grafted plants are set in with the bud union an inch or two below the soil line, to discourage sprouting by the understock. By northern standards, their roses, even the miniatures, are set far apart, because of the size to which rose plants develop in the Jeremiases' garden.

Upright rosebushes are grown without support. Climbers and large shrub roses are positioned around perimeter fences or at the back of the yard where wire trellises, resembling grape arbors, help in tying up plants and keeping them under control. The Jeremiases keep roses well away from walls because solid surfaces trap humidity and increase the incidence of foliar diseases.

Over the years, the Jeremiases have brought in so many leaves from neighboring yards that their soil is in excellent tilth. They compost the leaves in a pile so large that it would turn most gardeners green with envy. As the pile builds up, they scatter fertilizer and lime to speed the breakdown and to counteract the natural acidity. After the soil has warmed up in the spring, Charles and Lee dress the decomposing leaves around established rose plants. The mulch discourages weeds, conserves moisture, and prevents soil from splashing on the foliage. The continuing replenishment of organic matter in the soil also partly explains why their roses have never been damaged by nematodes, troublesome in some southern soils.

Charles's training as a chemist helps him select and use rose insecticides and fungicides efficiently. Summers in South Carolina are hot and humid. Without a regular preventative program, red spider mites, mildew, and blackspot would take over. For some time, Charles has alternated weekly sprayings with Orthene and Diazanon for insect and mite control. To prevent fungus diseases he uses Daconil 2787 and Triforene.

*(Left) The old rose 'May Wallace', run up and over an arch of rebar steel, is an attention-getter.*

*(Right) 'Sweet Surrender' is one of the Jeremiases' favorites.*

Sometimes, Actidione PM or Baleton is used, depending on the problem. All these are brand names for proprietary products.

Charles feels that waiting to spray until a problem is evident won't work in the South. "I don't believe in waiting until I see the whites of their eyes," he says. Yet, Charles and Lee are concerned about the amount of spray used, both from the standpoint of environmental responsibility and cost. They put away pump sprayers when they found that an electric Atomist unit did the job with only one-third as much active ingredient. Its only drawback is the long and heavy cord required to maintain the electric current while reaching all corners of the garden.

Recently, Charles began evaluating Safer Insecticidal Soap products for controlling insects, mites, and fungi. He hopes that these will reduce the amount of chemicals required to keep his roses clean, and the preliminary findings look good.

Their rose-feeding program is based on eight- to nine-month Osmocote Controlled Release Fertilizer and a potassium-magnesium source,

*'Dortmund', a shrub rose of the* Kordesii *class, flowers heavily.*

"K-Mag." Four ounces of each are top-dressed around established plants in the spring and covered with mulch. If growth appears to slow or if the foliage color goes off during the summer, Peters Plant Food, Schultz Instant Plant Food, or Ra-Pid-Gro is applied as a foliar spray and drench. Dolomitic limestone is worked into the soil as indicated by the soil tests, which Charles does himself.

The date and severity of pruning depends mostly on the habit of growth of the bush and whether the flower buds are formed on new or second-year growth. The Jeremiases handle the hybrid teas, floribundas, grandifloras, polyanthas, and hybrid perpetuals pretty much alike, pruning to four or five strong canes and shortening these to about two feet in length, somewhat longer than other rose specialists. They wait until January to begin, because such late (for zone 7) pruning causes new growth to come in in February and March, after the coldest weather is past. The new growth usually escapes frost damage because it has had time to harden off before late frosts come. January pruning is, of course, far too early for more northerly gardens.

The rather deep pruning of the exhibition roses concentrates the vigor of the bush into a few strong stems and generates larger blossoms for cutting and show. However, many of the old roses are grown more for landscape value than for exhibition. More often than not they are large, vigorous plants that can't be reduced to the size of modern roses without loss of color and plant vigor. And, some of them, mainly the climbers, bloom chiefly on second-year wood: deep spring pruning would reduce the number of blooms severely. Other old roses grow into shrub forms, some stiffly upright, and others arching and spreading.

*The beautiful hybrid tea, 'Christopher Stone', circa 1935, is still found in some gardens.*

Charles minimizes pruning on shrubby old rose varieties. Pruning of shrubby varieties consists mostly of tipping back unruly canes and removing weak or dead canes at the base. On those which are one-time bloomers, he delays pruning until after blossom drop. At that time he also removes weak canes flush with the crown. The plants bleed little because he paints the cut stems with a black material called "Tree-Cote," to prevent the cane borer fly from laying eggs.

On climbers, Charles first notes the stronger canes formed the previous year. They will be tipped back and saved because most of the blossoms will be formed on them. Then, he uses loppers to remove canes which are two years old, plus the weak year-old canes, by cutting them flush with the crown. Older stems are recognizable by their heavier bark and more knobby appearance.

Lee has found that little pruning is necessary on her miniature roses, other than occasional shaping and training, and removal of weak canes or those which are causing congestion in the center of the plant. Some of her miniatures grow three feet tall by the end of the season but are immediately recognizable from standard cultivars by their smaller blossoms.

For those interested in growing old roses, there are not many sources. Some of the best known have gone out of business, victims of catastrophic weather or of the difficulty of keeping the skilled labor required for propagation. Few people are qualified to operate old rose nurseries because of the encyclopedic knowledge of cultivars required and the extreme accuracy demanded to insure correct identification at every step in propagation and marketing.

Only one class of roses gives the Jeremiases difficulty in growing—the hybrid rugosas. They suffer more than other roses from hot weather and dry soil. Oddly, just one hundred miles north at Winston-Salem, the rugosas do pretty well. It may be that the slightly hotter, longer summers in South Carolina push the rugosas past their stress threshold.

Charles and Lee have some advice for beginners who are considering going into roses as a hobby. First, they advise, don't bite off more than you can chew. Start with no more than a dozen plants. Then, spend a few seasons gaining confidence in growing and in pest control. Before you get serious about showing, attend a few rose shows. Ask for copies of the schedules and read up on the various classes. Buttonhole one of the "helpers," the judges who are at shows to assist exhibitors. Ask them about points to look for or to avoid in showing. Generally, it isn't a good idea to bother exhibitors with questions when they are busy setting up or grooming. Some are so competitive and intent on what they are doing that they don't welcome questions.

Join your local Rose Society, they add, or, if you don't live in a city, sign up as a Member at Large. At Society meetings, rosarians are much more relaxed than at shows. They will cheerfully answer questions about stem length, cleaning foliage, grooming, and potential disqualifications. They can tell you how and when to disbud so that fresh scars won't disqualify your entry.

Most of all, keep a positive mental attitude. Be at shows when the doors open. Take one or two backup stems for each cultivar you intend to enter. Have your entry tags made out in advance. Enter the "Novice" class; some of the advanced exhibitors are so skilled that they could qualify as professionals. And, by all means, bring only as many roses as you have time to groom and set up; be selective in your entries.

On mental attitude, Lee Jeremias advises, "Don't take the decisions of judges personally. You may not win a ribbon your first time out. If you don't, ask a helper what specific shortcoming or disqualification you need to fix in your next rose show. Maybe it was nothing more serious than cutting your stems at the wrong time. We cut our old roses the evening prior to shows, and don't refrigerate them. Many exhibitors of modern roses do refrigerate them overnight. You have to know your cultivars to anticipate how far ahead of prime condition to cut, and how to transport them to shows."

You may not be as fortunate as Charles in his first garden and his first show. He grouped the first seventeen rosebushes he bought into a large raised bed. A lady saw them, stopped and identified herself as a local nursery owner, and complimented Charles's garden as the prettiest rose garden she'd ever seen. And, in his first show, he entered just one rose, a long-stemmed deep red 'Mr. Lincoln'. It took "King of the Show," second best among all entries. ("Queen of the Show" is tops.)

*Lee grooms miniature rose blossoms for a show. She is brushing 'Pierrine'; 'Break O'Dawn' is in the white cup.*

Your experience with roses will be more rewarding, the Jeremiases believe, if you collect a basic library of rose books. There is no single great American reference book on roses. Charles is a tireless researcher and has a large library, including many out-of-print books. Whenever he publishes papers or articles on old roses, he bibliographs to a depth and accuracy seldom encountered outside of universities.

Both Charles and Lee have a strong sense of public service. Their hobby gives them a means of serving others with garden tours while enjoying themselves. Yet it leaves time for Lee to work at a local radio station and for Charles to teach Sunday School and to lecture on roses. They haven't taken a conventional vacation since their marriage. Instead, they travel to ARS district and regional rose shows and to the two yearly meetings of the national.

Lee laughed when asked "What next?" in her career. She quipped, "I want to write a book entitled *Is There Life after Roses?*" Then she admitted she wants to exercise her gift for artistic arrangements—abstract and advanced compositions. Both she and Charles have enrolled as Apprentices in Artistic Arrangements with the ARS but Charles freely acknowledges Lee's advantage. She has an instinctive feel for it but his lifetime of disciplined effort may work against the spontaneity that inspires abstracts.

# More about Roses

The best place to learn about roses is a rose garden, not a book. But it will help if you will take with you on your first visit to a rose garden, a list of the eight major rose divisions generally accepted by the American rose trade:

*Hybrid Teas*   At one time the best known of the divisions, the hybrid teas were created by crossing the old tea rose of China with selections from other species. The original tea roses were marginally winter hardy and lacked the colors deep yellow and dark red. For many decades, rose breeders concentrated on hybridizing to improve this division through greater winter hardiness, broader range of colors and bicolors, repeat blooming, and increased vigor. Unfortunately, the majority of hybrid teas produced in the first hundred years of modern rose breeding lacked strong fragrance; some lacked scent entirely.

Exquisite blossom form is probably the best-known attribute of hybrid teas—high-centered, tightly wrapped, symmetrical in the bud stage, long-stemmed, with few distracting leaves on the upper extension of the stem. Breeders look for other features as well: vigorous plants of medium height, blossoms with strong necks and good holding ability before and after cutting, resistance to major diseases, brilliant color, and a strong, pleasant fragrance, preferably fruity or spicy.

By the year 1940, more than six thousand hybrid tea cultivars had been introduced. Many did not last long in the marketplace and were displaced by superior cultivars. Unfortunately, short-sighted hybridization had introduced or overlooked some undesirable characteristics into hybrid teas: susceptibility to certain major rose diseases, or lack of fragrance. Breeders abandoned the trouble-making lines and have restored the image of hybrid teas to its former glory. However, in the interim, breeding emphasis began to shift to other divisions. If you like to display long-stemmed roses in vases, individually or in arrangements, you should have some hybrid teas in your garden. There are better landscape roses, but none can match the elegance of hybrid teas for cut roses.

*Floribundas*   A floribunda can be recognized at a glance from its medium- to large-sized blossoms borne in clusters. A quick guess can often be validated by a sniff: most floribundas are scentless.

Rose breeders listened to the buying public when they developed floribunda roses. All cultivars are in the short to medium height range preferred for landscaping. The plants are rugged, dark green, and vigorous, except for the yellow colors, which tend to look less robust.

Most floribundas are winter hardy except in the northern Great Plains and upper Great Lakes area, where winter protection is advised. Nearly every color known to the rose world has been incorporated into this division.

Some time ago, rose breeders began infusing more hybrid tea blood into the floribundas to produce larger blossoms with the depth of tea roses. That trend continues and is already blurring the distinction between floribundas and the newer grandifloras. Certain of the newer floribundas have loose clusters of medium-sized blossoms, with tight, high-centered, vase-shaped buds, much like down-scaled hybrid tea blooms.

***Grandifloras*** If you are just starting to buy roses, the place for the grandifloras is in ranks behind lower-growing floribundas and hybrid teas, or in tall flowering hedges.

This greater height, up to six or seven feet in warm climates, is only one of the hallmarks of the grandifloras. Additionally, they have large blossoms of the classic double tea rose conformation, borne in small clusters. Some of the first cultivars in this recently created division were not quite as hardy as contemporary floribundas, but the newer ones are. Some grandifloras lack scent and only a few have strong fragrance.

The distinctions between grandiflora, floribunda, and hybrid tea roses are wavering as breeders strive for repeat blooming, larger and better-formed blossoms, somewhat shorter plants, and intensified winter hardiness. Breeders are also working on strengthening disease resistance and incorporating fragrance in new releases.

***Climbing Roses*** "Climbing" roses are tall bushes with very long canes that can be espaliered, tied to trellises, or run over arbors. Some were developed from tall mutations from bush cultivars and bear names such as 'Climbing Peace'. Others have no bush rose counterparts. You may think of climbers as old-fashioned, more appropriate for the Victorian era when the tall vines could be trained up porch pillars and high walls. But, gardeners are discovering that contemporary landscapes can benefit from the addition of arbors, trellises, and pillars for training climbers. These vertical accents can add considerable interest to otherwise flat landscapes. The Rose Garden at the National Arboretum is an excellent example.

When you buy climbers you may find them divided into three groups:

*Ramblers* Perfect for draping over fences, the late-blooming, nonrepeating ramblers have long, limber stems and numerous clusters of small flowers. Most are winter hardy but, when espaliered against a wall, tend to get mildew disease from the still, moist air.

Some of the famous old ramblers such as 'Dorothy Perkins' have no scent; their appeal was in the tremendous show of color they put on at peak bloom season in early summer. They have largely been superseded by the large-flowered climbers that have heavier, less pliable canes, bloom over a longer span, and which are fragrant. Some of the ramblers can escape in mild climates and infest pastures. Their low, spreading growth and habit of rooting wherever they touch the ground make them extremely difficult to eradicate. (Except for kudzu, 'Dorothy Perkins' is the worst weed on my farm.)

*Large-Flowered Climbers* This group includes not only the popular climbing hybrid teas, but also the half-hardy *Bracteata* and *Gigantea* cultivars known mostly in California. The stems are longer and stiffer than the ramblers and tend to grow more erect.

Most cultivars are fragrant and the newer ones are repeat bloomers. Before you buy, ask about winter hardiness. Severe dieback or pruning can reduce bloom on marginally hardy climbers.

*Some old roses go way back. 'Austrian Copper', an R. Foetida bicolor, left, was introduced in 1590, 'Old Blush', center, in 1752. The Eglantine or Sweetbriar rose, right, was first mentioned in writings dated 1551.*

*Pillar Roses* These plants have shorter, sturdier canes that can be pulled together and tied up to a pillar, or trained up a tall cage. The flowers and foliage are altogether beautiful and the plants are hardier as a group than the large-flowered climbers.

*Modern Shrub Roses* You will be seeing more of these roses as tolerance to extreme cold, disease resistance, and repeat-blooming traits are strengthened. Four distinct types are currently in the forefront of shrub roses: they are hybrids incorporating the species *Rosa rugosa*, *R. rubiginosa*, *R. spinosissima*, and *R. moschata*.

Of these four, much of the recent North American work has centered on *R. rugosa* hybrids. The Canadian Department of Agriculture has recently released new *R. rugosa* hybrids with great cold tolerance, extended bloom, disease resistance, and large, colorful hips. These were developed for low-maintenance landscaping and as a source of winter food for birds.

While shrub roses vary considerably in appearance, you can, with a little practice, recognize them. As compared to the grandifloras, for example, *rugosa* hybrids usually have lower, denser, more solid looking bushes, some with rough-surfaced, ribbed leaves.

*Rosa rubiginosa* hybrids have dense, upright bushes, loads of medium-sized, fragrant, single blossoms, and apple-scented foliage. Traditionally, the *rubiginosa* hybrids have been more important in Europe than in the United States.

*Rosa spinosissima* is a name given to hardy cultivars developed from the wild species *R. pimpinellifolia*. Selections from the species were used as parents in *spinosissima* hybrids. Gardeners use these hybrids as background plants where their tall, open, lanky bushes can arch out to their heart's content. One of the first roses to bloom, the *spinosissima* hybrids are covered with large, fragrant, single or double blossoms.

One of the parents of modern hybrid musk shrub roses is *R. moschata*, the musk rose. It contributed a heavy but pleasant fragrance that characterizes the class, regardless of the modern rose used as the other parent. The vigorous plants grow five feet tall in most areas and up to eight feet high in the South and West. The clustered flowers are short-stemmed, medium in size, semidouble, and numerous, and come in red, pink, or creamy white and yellow shades. The plants bloom over a long period and bear attractive hips in the fall and winter.

*Old Garden Roses*   The name evokes images of quaint, charming rose gardens, but will your dream characters be dressed in medieval or Victorian costumes? Any date before 1867 will do. The American Rose Society chose this cutoff date; any garden rose introduced prior to 1867 will be entered in the Old Garden Rose division. This division is the largest, if not the most popular among all roses.

Most old garden roses are selections from wild species, but some are old natural or manmade hybrids, or mutations. The cultivars you are most likely to see in the gardens of old rose specialists are derived from:

*Rosa alba*, the white rose
*R. burboniana*, the Bourbon rose
*R. centifolia*, the cabbage or Provence rose
*R. chinensis*, the Chinese rose
*R. damascena*, the damask rose
*R. gallica*, the French rose
Hybrid perpetual or remontant rose
Portland rose
Tea rose

*Miniature Roses*   Tiny blossoms, but not necessarily tiny plants, distinguish miniature roses. Miniature roses, however, are not toys; they are sturdy, cold-hardy, reblooming garden and container flowers that are beginning to win high marks in the "Award of Excellence" competition established by the American Rose Society as well as All-America Rose Selections awards.

Some miniature roses grow only fourteen to eighteen inches high and spread out twice as wide; this type makes good container or hanging-basket roses. Others, under long-summer conditions, can reach thirty inches in height. However, if you look at the tiny individual blossoms or blossom clusters, you can immediately tell that they are miniatures, not low-growing, large-flowered standard roses.

It is significant that miniature roses boomed in popularity at about the time that soilless growing media became widely available, when fluorescent lights became the norm for indoor growing, and when controlled-release fertilizers proved their value for rose culture. All these advances made the growing of miniature roses in pots, larger containers, and hanging baskets easier and more reliable.

By the way, "minis" are not just for containers: they do well in outdoor plantings, excelling as edgings, bedding, or low background plants in well-drained soil and full sun. They combine beautifully with perennials, annual flowers, and seasonal bulbs.

Rose breeders have been able to transfer almost all desirable rose traits to miniatures, while retaining a height range of three to eighteen inches (under northern climates)—all colors, winter hardiness, disease resistance, and repeat blooming. Some of the cultivars are scentless. A few climbing miniatures have been introduced but are regarded by most rose enthusiasts as curiosities.

*Polyantha Roses*  You won't find many polyanthas in general nurseries in the U.S.A.; the division has been largely supplanted by the floribundas. This old division is not sufficiently venerable to fall under the Old Garden Rose division. It dates back to the bringing of a pink, semidouble form of *Rosa multiflora* to England. As a parent in crosses, it produced plants with numerous clusters of small flowers. Some polyantha cultivars are single-flowered; others are double.

Note: not to confuse you, but the American Rose Society recognizes many more categories of roses than these few divisions. They do it mostly so judges can compare "apples with apples" and "oranges with oranges" at rose shows. The additional categories include climbing cultivars of standard rose classes, greatly changed selections from species roses, and hybrids between species that don't fall into any of the major divisions. You can find these categories listed in the fine booklet updated annually by the American Rose Society, entitled *Handbook for Selecting Roses*.

*Planting Bare-Root Roses*  You can buy rosebushes as "dormant" or "containerized." Dormant bushes are dug from the growing fields after the leaves have dropped (or have been removed by a defoliant) and are cut back severely, graded, and often waxed to reduce evaporation from the stems. They are usually sold in illustrated bags enclosing shavings around the roots to keep them moist. Containerized roses are grown by potting up dormant roses in containers of 2- to 3-gallon size.

Dormant roses are usually planted in the fall in zone 5 and farther south, and in late spring where winters are extremely severe. In zones 5 and 6, fall-planted roses should be mulched after the surface of the soil freezes, to minimize heaving from freezing and thawing. Spring-planted roses bloom little the first season and should be watered faithfully during the early summer, when they are putting down roots.

Soak the roots of dormant roses in tepid water for a day before planting. Trim off frayed or broken roots and dig planting holes before bringing the plants out in the drying wind. Pour the holes full of water and let it soak in, but don't wet the soil to be used for backfilling. If your plants arrive during very cold weather, pot them up in containers of planter mix and let them develop a root system for a month before tapping them out and setting them in the ground.

Make planting holes for rose bushes 18 to 24 inches across and 12 inches deep. Allow 3 feet space on all sides of the bush, and 4 or 5 feet for climbers or large shrub roses. Mix moistened sphagnum peat moss or pulverized pine bark with the excavated soil, one part to three parts soil, and, if your soil is poor, mix in a cupful of superphosphate to encourage rooting. Shovel a cone-shaped pile of amended soil into the center of the hole, then spread out the roots and fit them over the cone. Lay a shovel handle across the hole and raise or lower the plant until the soil line on the central stem of the plant is about 1 inch below the shovel handle. This places the "bud union," the point where the desirable rose wood was grafted to the rootstock, about 1 inch beneath the surface of the soil.

Depth of planting is extremely important. Too-deep planting can cause roses to refuse to bloom properly or can bring on root rot in heavy soil. Yet, if you expose the bud union fully or partially by shallow planting, the understock may try to shoot up sprouts.

Some authorities recommend filling in 2 or 3 inches of soil around the roots, treading on it to firm it down, shoveling in another layer and treading on it, and so on until the hole is filled level with the surface of the soil around it. This works fine if you amend your soil with organic matter or if it is naturally sandy. However, if you are working with moist, heavy clay, treading on it will squeeze out the air spaces and make it so dense that it won't drain. It would work better if you trickled water in slowly as you shovel in layers, to make the clay flow among and around the roots. The idea is to firm the soil just enough to eliminate big pockets of air, which could dry out the roots.

On poorly drained, heavy clay soils in high rainfall areas, rose beds should be built up 3 or 4 inches above the surrounding soil. That guarantees that the bud union won't be submerged under standing water.

Containerized roses can be transplanted to the garden at almost any time, even when they are in bloom. Northern growers know to get their containerized roses in by late summer so they will have plenty of time to send down roots before the soil grows too cold for root proliferation. Some nurseries rush the sale of containerized roses, before a good root system has formed. You may want to slide a root ball out of a container and check it before purchasing; the root ball should not fall apart and it should not be matted and girdled with roots.

*Planting Containerized Roses*

When setting containerized roses in the garden, be aware that they are usually grown in artificial mixes containing principally organic matter and little or no soil. Roots may find it difficult to grow beyond the confines of the root ball if the texture of the surrounding soil is too different. Therefore, you should amend the backfilling soil with moist peat moss or pulverized pine or fir bark to raise its level of organic matter.

Gently clean the planter mix away from the central stem of the bush and check the depth of the bud union below the surface. It should be about 1 inch deep. If it is deeper, shave off the top of the planter mix until the union is at the right depth. Before setting the root ball in the hole, brush off any roots that are girdling the sides or the bottom. Firm the soil in the bottom of the hole so that it won't settle and position the plant so that the top surface of the root ball is level with the surrounding soil. Settle backfill soil around it layer by layer, by either treading on it or trickling water over the backfill.

Newly planted roses, dormant or containerized, should be watered every three or four days when the weather is dry. A square of the recently introduced spun-bonded synthetic landscape cloth, 2 feet on the side, can be laid over the soil around the plant. Weeds won't come through it. Cover the landscape cloth with hardwood mulch, pulverized pine or fir bark, freshly chipped wood or bark nuggets to keep the soil cool and to conserve moisture.

# *Antique Fruit Trees*

*Elwood Fisher, Virginia Renaissance man, "rescues the perishing" by finding and saving ancient fruit tree varieties for posterity.*

*The apricot cultivar HW 407 escaped spring frosts to fruit heavily at Harrisonburg, Virginia.*

T he "tree fruits" include all the species and cultivars of fruit borne on trees or large shrubs, but not the "small fruits" borne on bushes, canes, vines, or small herbaceous plants. The tree fruits predate most of man's other food plants because man did not have to cultivate them: he simply had to beat the animals to the ripening fruits, and reach or climb up and pick them. Later, man learned how to preserve fruit by drying, and it became one of his principal foods.

By the time the first "permanent" settlers sailed for North America, a huge pool of improved selections from fruit tree species had been developed in Europe. Previously, traders and warriors as far back as Alexander the Great had brought seeds and cuttings to Europe from all over the known world. Significantly, one of the most important items brought to North

America with colonists were fruit tree seeds and cuttings. Parts of the New World proved very favorable to tree fruit culture, but some areas were disappointing. Colonists discovered a number of new fruits in North America, including native plums and beach plums, papaws, persimmons, and the red mulberry, *Morus rubra*. They were also mystified to find peach trees, not realizing that Indian tribes, on their journeys to Florida, had brought back and planted peach pits from old Spanish settlements.

The few colonists who were farmers understood how particular tree fruits can be about site, soil, exposure, and length and dependability of season. It was difficult to transpose European experience to this vast continent, with its wild swings in temperature, extremes of weather, and hungry wildlife. Yet, within a few years, colonists had begun to stake out sloping land near bodies of water or hilly table land shielded by mountains.

Later, as successful home growers expanded and began to sell their fruits and fruit products, locations near navigable waterways became a consideration. Fresh fruit and cider were too fragile or heavy for oxcart transportation over rough roads. Dried fruit and cider became important export items in the colonial economy and, when faster sailing ships were developed, fresh fruit joined the list. Settlements in the West Indies were especially good markets because pome and stone fruits grow poorly in the tropics.

Looking back on the statistics for fruit production in colonial days, it is unbelievable how much fruit and cider were produced by small farmers for home consumption and sale. Fruit was prepared in so many ways: it was dried, made into fruit leathers, boiled down into syrups to use as a sugar substitute, preserved as fruit butters in crocks, but, above all, expressed for fermentation into cider. Colonial cider was strong stuff, running 12 to 15 percent alcohol, yet was the most popular beverage excepting (arguably) water. Northern farmers soon learned how to concentrate cider even further by letting barrels of cider freeze and drawing off the concentrated hard cider liquid.

One reason cider was so important was that European varieties of grapes could not be grown successfully in our climates, despite many attempts. Wine had to be imported. Stills for making liquor from grains were yet to come.

A wide selection of fruits was grown by the home gardeners and farmers for the next three centuries. Apples were the shoo-in favorite, followed by pears, peaches, plums, cherries, apricots, nectarines, quince, figs, and medlars. The old trees planted around settlers' homes languished as towns grew up around them and city people began buying rather than growing fruits and vegetables. A few trees, however, lived to great ages, two hundred years for apple trees in favorable climates.

The concentration of people in cities led to the development of commercial tree fruit orchards in favorable climates, near rail transportation or

*Elwood propagated this ancient pear by grafting a cutting to a seedling pear understock.*

navigable rivers. Apples, pears, and cherries, which are not notably resistant to summer heat or extremely cold winters, were grown in cool, upland areas. Early-blooming peach and cherry orchards were located where bodies of water and sloping land protected them against loss of blossoms or young fruit to late freezes. The mid-Atlantic and southern colonies offered many good peach and fig sites. Among the peach sites were a few especially favored locations where the more demanding apricots and nectarines could be successfully grown. Plums are very adaptable, especially the native species, but have never been as popular as the leading tree fruits.

Until this era, tree fruit cultivars were selected for flavor, juice content for cider making, season of maturity, winter hardiness of the rootstock and scion, season of bloom, self-fertility, and production. Farmers had long since mastered the principles of grafting: in fact, they were as good or better at it than we are now. They had little or no means of insect or disease control, but their tolerance for blemishes on fruit was greater, and they could always consign wormy apples or bruised pears to the cider press or vinegar vats.

Then, as shippers began to control the fruit market, and the equipment and chemicals for pest control became available, specialists in fruit trees emerged. They began to tinker with the dwarfing rootstocks from Europe, to give farmers smaller trees, handier for picking, pruning, and pest control. The thickness of skin, color, size, and holding quality in cold storage became important considerations. Many fine-tasting old fruit cultivars brought from Europe were discarded because of the small or soft fruits of indifferent color, too-dry or too-juicy flesh. Even some of the selections made in North America, early in the life of the Colonies, such as 'Rhode Island Greening', became obsolete.

Tree fruit nurseries geared up to meet the demand for the new cultivars, customized for commercial production. This marketing shift decided the cultivars which would be principally available to home gardeners until a revival of interest in the delicious old varieties occurred. Brief but significant booms in fruit tree growing occurred during the Liberty or War Garden days of World War I and the Victory Garden days of World War II.

All the while, with every passing year, antique tree fruit cultivars were disappearing. Once gone, fruit tree cultivars cannot be retrieved. For a long time, virtually no one seemed to care that this irreplaceable genetic treasure was being allowed to slip away. We are all beneficiaries of the foresight of the few people who did care, and did what they could to save what was still left. Their concern has grown into a worldwide movement with networking and exchanges to lessen the chance of losing rare cultivars, some of which were literally down to only one tree in all the world.

*Elwood shows me that fruit size decreases when the trees are not thinned.*

At his home in Harrisonburg, Virginia, Elwood Fisher maintains one of the finest collections of antique varieties of fruit trees, grapevines, and berry bushes in North America. His orchard and vineyard cover more than half an acre of his back yard and adjacent property leased from a neighbor. And while other fruit tree hobbyists might grow trees for fun or profit, Elwood grows principally because he is concerned about the loss of germ plasm when antique cultivars of fruits and berries die out. His hobby has gained him international notice.

Friends marvel at how much Elwood accomplishes in the time remaining from his teaching position at James Madison University. He leads wildflower tours deep into the mountains of his native West Virginia, teaches courses on identifying and using wild foods, including mushrooms, leads birding expeditions, and is a consulting parasitologist. That's just what he does away from home!

Inside and all around the Fishers' home are signs of his skill as a craftsman. Beginning twenty-one years ago, he and his wife, Madge, took a roughed-in house and gradually converted it into a beautiful home. Outside, hundreds of feet of precisely laid stone walls, more than head-high in places, are his handiwork. Each chunk of broken limestone is fitted with a flat surface out, and the mortar joints are raked and brushed out to a uniform 1-inch depth. The walls break his steeply sloping lot into terraces; they required heavy poured footings and extensive drainage to prevent buckling under hydraulic pressure.

Before we toured their beautiful home and gardens, Madge served us a generous piece of marvelous apple pie. We talked about what led up to Elwood's strong sense of commitment and his well-developed skills as a plantsman, artist, and craftsman.

Fortified with apple pie, Elwood and I meandered around the house and adjacent gardens, with many stops to admire unusual plant material and constructs. The front entrance and heavily used areas inside the home are floored with serpentine, but the construction that really catches your eye is a wall-to-wall fireplace made of strips of serpentine.

Stonework is Elwood's thing; for several years, dynamic Madge busied herself hanging the wall and roof insulation and doing much of the fine finishing inside the house while Elwood was wheelbarrowing seventeen tons of stone through their front door.

More stonework lies outside. All around the house are sculptures made from the stone excavated from the home site and, in the back lawn, you can see the flat tops of huge limestone boulders left in place rather than blasted out. Madge and Elwood chipped out cavities to use as bird feeders and they work beautifully. Inside the home are several of Elwood's whimsical wood or stone sculptures, sleek and functional or slyly amusing.

Alongside the house is an exquisite Japanese garden, actually a deep grotto with walls made of water-worn limestone. Some of the pieces are of awesome size. Elwood described, with understandable pride, how he singlehandedly maneuvered each piece into place using a simple iron pipe tripod to lift, and the power of his International Harvester Scout to skid stones into place. Then, he used hydraulic jacks to tilt and rotate rocks so that they fitted the design in his mind's eye. You can walk across the grotto on thick cylinders of limestone standing on end. (They are actually 16-inch-thick cores from holes drilled on a nearby building site, to accommodate the hydraulic equipment of an elevator.)

Elwood realizes that the time has come to begin winding down some of his more physical projects. Although still in good condition, he is of World War II vintage and has to pace himself on heavy jobs. Reminders of the long hours he works around the house and yard are everywhere but none more telling than the tall poles for streetlights that enable him to work in the yard at night.

Searching out and saving ancient fruit trees, berry and grape varieties, south to Georgia and the Carolinas and north through New York State, has taken much of Elwood's spare time and energy for twenty-odd years. The expense in time and travel has been considerable. He continues his crusade largely because he is uniquely qualified to find and preserve old fruit tree cultivars.

The area of West Virginia where he was raised was settled in the 1700s largely by German immigrants. These good farmers brought cuttings (scions) of fruit trees, berry bushes, and grapevines over with them, often keeping cuttings alive by sticking the cut ends in potatoes. Over the mountains to the east, major landholders of English stock, including Thomas Jefferson, imported starts of apple trees of varieties they or their forebears knew and grew in the old country.

Early on, Elwood was marked for growing fruit trees. His grandfather Shuman, on his farm near Clarksburg, had eighty-four varieties of apples, pears, peaches, plums, gooseberries, and currants. By the time Elwood was seven years of age, his grandfather had him grafting fruit trees. As the two of them traveled around the coves and ridgeland, his grandfather would point out old trees and have Elwood memorize their

*A bird's-eye view of Elwood's orchard shows the density of planting and the size of the trees, all of which have multiple grafts.*

variety names. Elwood told me, with mixed pride and regret, "I have found every apple cultivar that Grandfather Shuman grew except the one named 'Seedless' (without pips). It was developed in Vermont in 1869."

His grandmother Fisher figured equally in teaching mountain skills to Elwood. While Grandfather Fisher ran a country store, Grandmother served as the local folk authority on herbal medicine; she diagnosed by looking at patients . . . the color of their eyes, skin, and nails, condition of their hair, and other signs that old-time general practitioners knew to watch for. Customers got "doctored" while they were shopping for supplies and clothing.

Elwood tagged along behind his grandmother while she collected native plants, and cultivated vegetables and herbs for poultices, potions, antiseptics, emetics, and expectorants. She knew not only where to find the plants she wanted, but when to harvest them and how to store them for maximum potency. Twenty years later, when Elwood went on his first field trip with a botany class, he amazed the professor by identifying every plant and giving its medicinal use.

Elwood remembers his grandmother collecting yellow root, ginseng, black cohosh, golden ragwort, may apple roots, and dozens of other species for medicine, and how his grandfather sold smokeless sumac wood to moonshiners. At night, his grandmother practiced the traditional German "fractur" art of embellishing marriage licenses, certificates, and homilies with traditional German art.

Elwood was only seventeen when, late in World War II, he volunteered for the U.S. Navy. Seeing the world convinced Elwood that he didn't wish to follow the strict Dunkard upbringing of his childhood, but a driving curiosity about other religions and cultures led him into divinity school, and later into studies of art and history and, finally, botany. School followed a hiatus of several years after he came home, during which he worked as a lineman for a power company and as a welder on a pipeline.

Elwood and Madge met when she was teaching home economics in Ohio and he was teaching high-school biology, history, and art. Later, he completed work on his masters in zoology at Miami University. Madge also helped while he went on to get his doctorate in biology at Virginia Polytechnic Institute in Blacksburg. Since he "owed her one," Elwood helped her become certified in library sciences, once he joined the staff at James Madison University. Madge is now a librarian at an elementary school in Rockingham County.

Elwood wasn't thinking about fruit trees during their first years in Harrisonburg; he was busy teaching medical entomology, parasitology, ornithology (Grandma taught him birds, too), zoology, and history of botany. Then, three developments conspired to shape his future for him. First, he watched with concern as southern corn blight disease threatened to decimate the corn crop because geneticists had allowed the gene pool of maize to shrink. Next, the Seed Savers' Exchange asked him to collect seeds of old varieties to assist them in preserving germ plasm. But the turning point came when someone asked him if he knew where to find the old apple variety 'Winter Banana' that had originated in Indiana. Yes, he knew just where to find 'Winter Banana' . . . on Grandfather Shuman's farm, where he had seen it as a lad. But, when he got there, he found that a landslide had hit the orchard, burying two trees. Those two were the only 'Winter Banana' trees on the place and they were dead as a doornail!

That incident started Elwood thinking, and he realized that he was one of the few people in the entire country who knew many old fruit varieties on sight, and where to find them. Coincidentally, he and Madge had moved to their present home and had a large lot for planting trees, berries, and vines.

So began Elwood's quest to find and save old varieties, and he admits that he had no idea, then, how involved and all-consuming it was to become. He used many ingenious methods to find old trees. "I would come into a little town," he recalls, "and ask who around those parts grafts trees for home orchards. Usually, I would start at the town filling station, and would get my answer right there. Professional fruit tree grafters were always local men and were always willing to cooperate when I explained what I was after. Of course, it helped that I grew up in the mountains and could still talk like one of them!

"Circuit-riding ministers are getting hard to find now," he said, "but there were quite a few around when I first began searching for old trees. They rode horseback in the roughest parts of the mountains and, since they were put up and fed by local families, they knew who served the best apple pies. I've had them lead me straight to long-abandoned farmsteads where they had enjoyed apples years before. We found many long-dead trees, but also a few old survivors.

"It took me five years of searching to find 'Winter Banana', and even longer to find the 'Leathercoat' russeted apple mentioned by William Shakespeare. I am still looking for the 'Wasp' apple, also called 'Birdstow Wasp', and Thomas Jefferson's favorite cider apple, 'Talliaferro'. I keep hearing about an apple with the local name of 'Chuke', known in Great Britain as 'Chuket' or 'Teuchat Egg', but have yet to find a tree by that name. It was recorded in Scotland in 1768.

"The luckiest find in all my searching," Elwood said, "was a man who had served for many years as a judge at county fairs. He would ask entrants for cuttings of varieties that placed well in fruit exhibitions. He was ninety-six years of age when I ran across him, and still had twenty-two great old apple varieties, some of which I have found no place else.

"One of my other hobbies, bird watching, ties in beautifully with my searching for old fruit trees. I visit several areas in the mountains during the spring and fall to count or study migrating birds. While driving, I keep one eye peeled for fruit trees, or remnants of old homesteads. Whenever I spot something promising, I will mark it on a map for a visit on the way back home.

"For several reasons, I am having better luck in finding old apple varieties than other fruits," Elwood explained. "First, hundreds of apple varieties were planted in the Colonies; the settlers apparently learned from seamen that stored apples and cabbages could help prevent scurvy during the winter when greens were not available. Also, apple trees can survive longer than most other fruit tree species . . . sometimes more than two hundred years.

"Pear trees usually don't last as long as apples. They need good soil, and tend to be shorter-lived where soils are thin or infertile. Fire blight tends to debilitate and eventually kill trees, especially where bees can bring the bacterium in from other fruits," Elwood continued. "For that reason, the old varieties of pears I have obtained have usually gone through several cycles of renewal by rooted cuttings or grafts. Like apples, pears tend not to come true when grown from seeds. Apparently, their genetic makeup is so complicated from eons of hybridizing, that tremendous variation occurs among seedlings.

"Among the stone fruits, cherries are fairly long-lived," he said. "I've found some trees that must have been sixty to seventy years old. Up in the mountains where it is cool, they can grow the large sweet cherries as well as sour or pie cherries. Growers treasure them so much that they will graft desirable scions onto seedlings to keep the variety going.

"On the other hand," Elwood said, "the relatively short-lived stone fruits such as peaches, plums, apricots, and almonds usually produce pretty good trees when grown from seeds, and they resemble the parent tree fairly closely. The American Indians fell in love with the first peaches introduced by settlers, carried seeds with them all over the mountains, and planted patches which still survive. The red-fleshed 'Blood' or 'Indian' peach was one of their favorites."

Elwood caught my doubting look when he was describing the true-breeding character of peaches and plums grown from seeds. "Oh, yes!" he reassured me. "I've seen some seedlings from old greengage and French prune plums that were superior to the original." He showed me one of his selections, grown from a seed and code-numbered "EF-33-74." It certainly bore out his contention.

"American Indians and settlers alike," he said, "used fruits in a way not generally known today. They fed them to livestock. Lacking any means of preserving the stone fruits other than drying, they fed surplus peaches, plums, and apricots to pigs and cattle. Apples and, to a lesser extent, pears, were stored in caves, cellars, and straw-lined pits."

I asked Elwood about gooseberries and currants, of which he had several attractive varieties. "One of the great gardening disasters, in my opinion," he said, "was the misdirected eradication program against gooseberries and currants during the 1930s. I can recall crews of WPA men combing the hills, valleys, and home gardens to find and burn gooseberry and currant bushes because they were felt to be alternate carriers of white pine blister rust disease, which endangered this valuable timber tree.

"Our old German families were law-abiding, but not inclined to go along with edicts that didn't make sense to them. Consequently, they tended to dig up and store plants of currants and gooseberries and replant them after the eradication crews had moved on. Thanks to them, I have been able to find quite a few of the really old garden favorites. I expect to see more gooseberries and currants planted in gardens as people learn what delicious pies and preserves can be made from them."

1)

2)

3)

4)

5)

## Antique Fruit Varieties

Searching out and saving antique fruit trees, berry and grape varieties have taken much of Elwood's spare time and energy for more than twenty years. He continues his crusade largely because he is uniquely qualified to find and preserve old fruit cultivars such as those shown here: a seedling from an unnamed antique nectarine (1); 'General Hand' plum (2); 'Perfection' red currant (3); 'Medlar of Nottingham' (4); an antique crab apple grown for preserves (5); 'St. Edmund's Pippin' apple (6).

6)

As Elwood's collection of fruit trees expanded, it became apparent that he would soon run out of room. His half-acre lot would hold only seventy-five or so mature fruit trees of standard size. Then, he made a decision that multiplied the capacity of his orchard severalfold. He began grafting several kinds of apples and other species on each of his existing trees, always tagging the grafted scion by cultivar name. He also began cordoning trees by the Belgian system to allow much greater planting density. Some trees were espaliered up walls or trained flat against trellises made by lacing and tying together canes of local bamboo. His trees are crowded, by any standard, and berry canes and bush fruits are chinked in wherever he can find a sunny spot. It isn't the optimum arrangement for growing fruit trees but it has enabled him to save countless cultivars that otherwise might have been lost.

Here and there among Elwood's collection of conventional fruits are oddities such as medlars, figs, almonds, nectarines, quince, and jujube (which grows into a good-sized tree at Victory Garden South). Someday, you might see jujubes on the gourmet produce counters; they are delicious little fruits the size and shape of a large date, apple flavored but rather dry in texture, tan to brown when ripe. Medlars will probably remain obscure; they look a bit like the fruit of quince but smaller. You have to develop a taste for them. Madge made a face when Elwood mentioned medlars. "The nearest next-to-nothing fruit I ever tasted!" she exclaimed. "You have to pick and store them until the pulp ferments before they are worth eating. When they are ready, you have to really work at it to get more than a taste of fruit." (Well, that pretty much explains why more people don't plant medlars.)

Elwood asked me to help him diagnose what was wrong with a medlar tree he had espaliered, for protection, in a corner between a brick wall and a chimney. The margins of the leaves were bleached almost white. I hipshot and guessed at overly high soil pH, which would tie up iron and perhaps other trace elements. This condition frequently occurs where lime from concrete foundations and walls gets into the root zone of nearby plants. Elwood agreed to apply a blend of chelated micronutrients in the fall to see if it restores the desired color to next year's foliage.

What really impressed me about Elwood's orchard was the extraordinary range of flavors in the old apples. Mind you, these were rather small fruits, some no larger than the crab apples you see pickled and colored red. We ate them warm, out of hand, peeling and all. I detected flavors I never knew came with apples: cinnamon, licorice, nutmeg, banana, pineapple (and, once or twice, worm). Elwood explained that certain tart varieties are preferred for cider-making, others for pie-making, still others for drying. You can use antique cultivars for other than their primary uses, but some of the fun in growing them is using them as their

developers intended. Truly, gardeners are missing something good by settling for just the few modern cultivars that are sold for home orchards
today, a sentiment to which Elwood added a heartfelt "Amen!"

"All told, I have nearly eleven hundred varieties of apples here," said
Elwood, "plus three hundred pears, nineteen grapes, some fifty-seven
cherries, twelve apricots, twenty-nine plums, several figs (including the
hardy Siberian and one which is claimed to be seedless), and some thirty
varieties of red, white, or black currants and gooseberries. I have several
kinds of brambles but they tend to get out of hand. I don't know how
much longer I can continue to grow them.

"I feed the whole neighborhood with fruits," he said, "but a lot of it
goes to waste. I have to overpower my instinct to provide food, by re-
minding myself that my most important goal is to preserve the plants
and not to save the fruit crop. But, at the same time, I feel I should learn
how to thin, prune, and spray all the kinds I grow, in order to advise
people on the best regimen for fruit production. I have an obligation to
my neighbors to keep the place clean and not to have my orchard harbor
insects or plant diseases that could spread."

We talked for a long time about ways he might reduce the dreadful
number of hours he has to spend in the orchard spraying, often in the
hot sun. Elwood is a highly conscientious man about protecting the environment but is reluctantly convinced, as am I, that a certain minimum of

*Antique apple
varieties are es-
paliered Belgian
fashion atop a
terrace formed by
one of Elwood's
stone walls.*

*Madge and El-wood Fisher gather apricots in a Welsh trug.*

spraying is required to keep damage from insects and diseases at an acceptable level. Being a scientist, Elwood is extremely careful about spraying, and wears the full recommended regalia of rubber clothing and gloves, goggles, and respirator.

Madge is concerned about the effect on her husband of the heat and hard physical labor of spraying. Elwood uses a gasoline-powered "Solo Port 423" backpack mist blower, which is a great sprayer, but heavy to lug around. He is going to look at the electric-powered Atomist as a lighter, less noisy alternative, which uses less actual chemicals because it micronizes the spray.

Elwood's spraying program begins in the fall, after leaf drop, when he drenches all the trees with a dormant spray of Ferbam and dormant oil. This is his first line of defense against overwintering insects and the bacterial disease peach leaf curl. To control plum curculio and codling moth on plums and apples, he sprays with malathion at blossom drop and again later when the insects begin to emerge.

He sprays at full flower to prevent fire blight, which is destructive in Harrisonburg. He uses Agrimycin or a 4 percent solution of Chlorox. Later in the season, he "target sprays" spot outbreaks of such diseases as quince rust. The fungicide Polyram works well for him against scab, cedar-apple rust, fly speck, and sooty blotch. He also uses benomyl (Benlate) to control powdery mildew on apples, but only when necessary.

He advises using common sense in reducing brown rot damage by concentrating on early varieties of peaches, plums, apricots, and nectarines. Elwood has observed that the disease is much worse on later varieties that mature during hot, humid weather. On the few occasions when warm, humid weather has come at ripening time, he has used Benlate and Funginex to control brown rot on peaches and other stone fruits. "But, I have gone back to using old-fashioned Bordeaux mix on stone fruits and grapes we plan to eat," he said. "I feel it is safer. At times I have used Carbaryl to control Japanese beetles on grapes and roses."

Elwood realizes that thinning fruits, particularly peaches, apricots, and nectarines, would reduce the incidence and severity of brown rot. However, thinning an orchard the size of his is physically impossible for one person, part-time. He has to prop up many overloaded branches to keep them from breaking under the weight of fruit.

"One of my best weapons against the spread of diseases and insects, and the effect of drought," Elwood said, "is mulching between the rows of trees in my orchard. I have all my neighbors save leaves and lawn clippings and I sheet-compost them. I know that the trees are withstanding the drought better. Believe it or not, I didn't water once during our long drought, except when I transplanted new trees. I think that, being healthier, my trees suffer fewer disease and insect problems, perhaps because more predators can live in the mulch than in clean-tilled soil. I frequently bring in 'helpers': toads, salamanders, lizards, and their skink cousins."

Elwood explained "summer pruning" of apple trees to me. It must have seemed to him that I had been living on another planet because, literally, I had never heard of it, nor seen it done. He showed me how, come June 15, he cuts back each shoot with fifteen or more leaves on it. He takes off two-thirds of each shoot, being careful to disinfect his shears between trees or after pruning in an area that appears diseased. Then, in late July, he cuts back to two leaves, the growth put on since the first pruning. Finally, in late August, he repeats the procedure used for the second pruning. The technique, he explained, forces more fruit to form the next year, instead of excessive vegetative growth, and may prevent the tree from getting into the cycle of "biennial cropping," setting a heavy crop every second year.

Elwood is especially skilled at grafting. April is the time for cleft, bark, and whip grafting of scions collected during the winter. Then, from June through August, he does budding, or chip, grafting of both pome and stone fruits.

Cleft grafting is used mostly when topworking existing trees to replace all or part of the smaller limb structure with a more desirable cultivar. He cuts off limbs up to a size of about 1 inch in diameter, splits the ends, and inserts one or two short pieces of scion wood so that cambium meets cambium, and wraps the union and all the exposed cut with a rubber grafting band.

Bark budding is used mostly to start a new branch growing when a tree is lopsided, or to replace a broken branch. You have to wait until new growth is pushing out and make a tee-shaped slice in the bark. Insert a short piece of scion wood with the end trimmed into a "vee," and dab the exposed surface with grafting wax to prevent drying out.

Whip grafting is used to join a piece of scion wood to a slender branch of equal diameter. You can cut both pieces on a slant and join them so that cambium meets cambium or, if you are dexterous, you can match two sawtoothed cuts so that the graft won't slip. Wrap the whip graft with a rubber grafting band and tie snugly.

Budding is used to graft desirable scion wood to young seedlings with strong root systems, and is done by inserting a chip of scion containing a bud, into a cross or tee-shaped cut through the tender bark. Whip a wide rubber band around the graft and tie it snugly. Elwood prefers to do most of his grafting by the chip-bud method because buds done at the right time "take" almost 100 percent. Yet at the many grafting workshops he conducts, he demonstrates every known method because of the special situations which call for specific grafts. He isn't doing much grafting now, because he is concentrating on keeping his present inventory alive and healthy, rather than adding to it.

Although Elwood is an ace at pruning, he balks at trying to describe it, or how to graft, to anyone, other than at workshops where he can also demonstrate the procedures. "I've been pruning so long," he says, "that I do it automatically, like riding a bicycle or laying stone. Every tree of every variety of every kind calls for different pruning. It is an art that has to be explained to a person as you show him or her how to do it, just as my grandfather taught me."

Elwood smiled as he recalled three rigid rules of pruning given to him by Granddad Shuman all those years ago:

1. There are only fifty-two days of the year when you should not prune fruit trees . . . Sundays! (Grandfather Shuman was of the strict Dunkard faith.)
2. Never leave one limb superimposed over another; the bottom limb will be too shaded.
3. Open a tree enough that a bird can fly through it.

Elwood starts his pruning in the winter, right after Christmas, and continues through February. He prunes the older trees first, but waits until February to prune trees that are three years of age or younger. (These require minimal pruning.) Then he moves on to grape pruning and the special pruning required for cordoning and espaliering trees.

I asked Elwood how he felt about disinfecting shears and painting wounds on trees. He grinned and said that professional pomologists, Extension Service personnel, and he agree on disinfecting with Clorox or Lysol spray but disagree on wound paints. They maintain that paint is more cosmetic than effective, but Elwood says he suspects that decay organisms can enter wood at unprotected cuts, especially if the wound is large enough for the wood to crack. He applies a homemade mix of asphaltum diluted with xylene solvent or, in a pinch, a shot of cheap latex paint from a spray can.

Elwood glossed over his feeding program because, in his rich Shenandoah Valley soil, not much is needed. "Oh, I will scatter a little 19-19-19 corn fertilizer under a tree in late summer if it looks a little puny but, truly, I rely on the decaying mulch to supply most of the needs for nutrients. Too much vegetative growth results in poor production . . . the energy goes to shoots, not fruits."

Since Elwood and I are within a year of each other's age, we couldn't avoid the subject of what happens as he loses some of his stamina and when he is finally called to that great orchard in the sky.

"Madge and I have thought about selling this place and moving to a farm after retirement. It would take me about three years and a great deal of work to move all two thousand or so plants I have on this property. I would be willing to do it, if a way could be worked out for a

1)

2)

3)

4)

## Grafting Fruit Trees

Elwood demonstrates his proficiency at grafting fruit trees. Hc prefers the chip-bud method because such grafts done at the right time "take" almost every time. He cuts a chip bud from scion wood (1). Then the chip is fitted to match a chip taken out of the understock branch (2). The bud graft is wrapped with flexible "parafilm" (3) to protect it, then labeled with the date and names of the scion and the understock (4). When slender branches are splice grafted (5), the cut surfaces of scion and understock must match perfectly. Whip the two pieces together with parafilm or a broad rubber band to secure and protect the splice.

5)

foundation to take over my collection for posterity. There isn't any point in moving it if it can't be carried on. I think it is crucial that this country protect the gene pool of its major food crops in the event the standard commercial varieties are attacked by a plague of insects or diseases, or unforeseen events such as destruction of ozone burn or acid rain . . . both of which are already real threats.

"A few others have collections of old fruit trees, grapes, and berries, including individuals such as myself, the restored garden and orchard at Monticello, the Luther Burbank Garden, the Colonial Williamsburg Foundation, and the American Museum of Frontier Culture at Staunton, Virginia. There are a few germ-plasm banks in Europe but they have had to turn to us for new starts on old varieties that have disappeared there.

"Cornell University has over thirteen hundred old apple varieties at their Geneva, New York station. I send them scions of the rediscoveries I have made, and I send scions to several collectors and breeders to reduce the risk of loss. Cornell is undertaking a valuable program of heat-treating and tissue-culturing old apple varieties to rid them of disease-causing viruses carried in their tissue."

I did convince Madge and Elwood to divulge the names of some of their favorite fruit varieties. Elwood winced when Madge chose the modern Japanese apple variety 'Mustu', a cross between 'Golden Delicious' and 'Indo'. Both like 'Tabarza' plum from Iran. Elwood likes the gooseberry 'Kathleen Olenberg' with large, red fruit, and the pearl-like white currant, 'White Imperial'. "My taste buds would soon tire of just one variety of a given fruit," Elwood commented.

After extracting my promise to return someday soon, the Fishers took me over to their regional airport. On the way, Elwood asked a favor. "Have anyone contact me," he said, "if they know anything about the history of the old apple variety named 'Walla Walla'. It has been grown in these parts since 1919 but no one has a record of it anywhere else. What's an apple named 'Walla Walla' doing in the Shenandoah Valley?"

# More about Antique Fruit Varieties

You will seldom find antique varieties at retail stores. When you do, they might be labeled incorrectly, because synonyms are rampant among antique varieties. This is not due to deceptive trade practices but, rather, to the fact that original names of some varieties were lost years ago and local names assigned.

"Some of the supposedly 'lost' varieties have been rediscovered under synonyms," says Elwood Fisher. "For example, I have found very old English varieties, which have been lost over there, under different names in this country." Elwood is a bear on keeping fruit tree names straight and kindly gave me the names of reference books on antique fruit trees.

"These old books, plus some twenty others of the nineteenth century, help me key out unknown varieties. For example, the books describe the shape of the fruit: flat, conical, elongate, round, quadrate, etc. Then, I look up its color: red, yellow, green, blush, striped, spotted, solid, russeted, or smooth. If still in doubt, I can split a fruit and look at the core and the shape and color of the seeds. Even the calyxes, straight, reflexed, or absent due to aborting, can settle difficult identification questions. The season of ripening is also significant, though it varies, of course, from North to South."

Elwood is outspokenly critical of the books written for the general public on the subject of growing fruit trees. When I asked him to name good books on fruit culture he replied, "There aren't any!" Then, he went on to explain that fruits and berries are so regional in their adaptation and demanding in their requirements that no one has written a book which could apply to all climates. "It would take three or four volumes and several years of work to do it thoroughly," he said. "I think that gardeners would be further ahead relying on variety recommendations and pruning and spraying information from their State Cooperative Extension Service.

## Terminology

A relatively modern innovation may complicate your ordering of antique fruit trees. Some nurseries, as a nod to the smaller gardens of today, graft antique scions onto dwarfing rootstocks. For your guidance, here are the terms used to describe the mature height of grafted and own-rooted trees, both antique and modern:

- *Dwarf:* 4 to 8 feet at maturity. (While most trees in this class will grow to 6 feet in height, the M-27 rootstock can produce 4-foot-high trees when grafted to certain scions.)

- *Semidwarf:* 8 to 12 feet.

- *Semistandard:* 12 to 20 feet.

- *Standard:* 20 feet or more at maturity.

The tree size should be listed as a part of the description of a fruit variety in catalogs or on tags. If not, don't buy the tree; you may be getting a full-sized tree when you have room only for a dwarf.

## Dwarf Fruit Trees

A continuing decrease in the size of home gardens and yards has created a new demand for dwarf fruit trees. From the home gardener's viewpoint, the little fully dwarfed apple and pear trees may seem the most attractive, but the semi-dwarfs usually give greater satisfaction and can be controlled to some extent by pruning. In addition to the obvious advantage of being able to pick fruit from the ground or a short stepladder, you can also reach all parts of small trees with an ordinary pump-type sprayer. You are less apt to crowd small trees together, and the incidence of foliage and fruit diseases is lessened by the improved circulation of air. You can easily reach all parts of the tree for pruning, thinning, and summer tipping-back, which can prove especially important in years of heavy bearing. Without thinning and summer pruning, a feast could be followed by a famine. Finally, with a soft landing pad of a mulch under the foliage canopy, you will lose fewer fallen fruits to bruising. As with a child learning to walk, they don't have far to fall.

Peaches grow very fast, and are usually sold as standards, assuming that you will replace them when they overgrow or succumb to borer damage. Yet, certain plum tree stocks, when spliced in between the rootstock and the scion, can restrict top growth.

Cherries are also usually sold as standards although they can be dwarfed on G-9 rootstock. Of all fruit trees, cherries often suffer the worst from bird damage, and dwarfed trees can be reached for covering with bird mesh.

Plums are also susceptible to bird damage, and can be dwarfed with the 'Pixie' rootstock. Neither 'Pixie' nor G-9 are widely available, but are increasing in popularity. They are grown by a nursery called Oregon Rootstocks.

If you can't find dwarfed peaches, cherries, or plums, you can prune these trees relatively severely after two or three years of growth. You may suffer remorse after pruning, asking yourself, "What have I done!," but the tree will form more fruiting spurs and reward you for keeping it within bounds.

## Care and Training

The care and training of young fruit trees soon after planting has changed drastically in recent years, due to new discoveries and new products. No longer do the experts advise gardeners to prune new trees severely at planting time. In fact, they advise minimizing pruning for the first two or three years after planting, except for training to a low head, because pruning very young trees can stunt a tree. By preserving the maximum amount of limbs, twigs, and foliage, you can increase photosynthesis and promote a stronger root system. Once the tree is settled in and growing strongly, you can begin a program of "tipping-back," or shortening limbs, as Elwood Fisher does with his summer pruning.

*"Crop props" support heavily laden apricot branches and prevent breakage.*

You can trick apple and pear trees into producing more fruit by a branch-training technique, discovered years ago. The procedure works better on young trees, especially apples, which tend to head lower. It doesn't take much time and needn't be done precisely. Drive a number of pegs around the dripline and tie stout strings to them. Loop the strings over outer branches and pull them down as far as you can without breaking. Or, you can tie a cinder block to a rope and loop it over a heavier branch to persuade it to bend down. You will see that the outer section of the limb, which is below a horizontal line, will bear more heavily. This works because sugars are partially trapped in a downwardly arched limb, and a high suger level in tissues can cause more fruit buds to form. With each succeeding year, training branches downward will become easier.

Home gardeners in the northern tier of states and at high altitudes have difficulty getting apple trees to survive. But they can copy a technique perfected in Siberia (apples in Siberia?) which results in a bizarre-looking but hardy tree. There, orchardists head the trees quite low and train the branches low to the ground and horizontally, supporting them with pegs and posts. As the tree grows, they train the limbs into a pattern like a four-leaf clover, so they can get into the center without stepping over branches. The trees survive extreme winters and bear good crops because the bulk of their top growth is down near the warming effect of the earth. Snow covers the branches and protects them from drying out and destruction from freezing and thawing.

**Mulching**    Landscape cloth, one of the new weed barriers developed for agriculture and home gardeners, and mulches of various kinds of organic matter combine to save labor and help trees grow and produce to their full potential. Commercial growers have long known that grass and weeds growing under fruit trees can compete for food and water, slowing growth and reducing yields. They are also aware of the damage done by cultivation, either to feeder roots near the surface, or accidentally to tree trunks. One of the saddest sights I know of is a poor little fruit tree with lawn grass growing right up to the trunk, whipped and nearly girdled by a string trimmer.

Commercial growers also know that mulches under the foliage canopy of fruit trees help growth and production in many ways: by keeping down weeds, reducing evaporation, and decomposing into humus while nurturing beneficial soil organisms. There is a downside to mulches such as hay or straw; they offer protection to meadow voles and pine voles as well as to rabbits, all serious pests in the eastern U.S. You need to protect the trunks of trees mulched with hay, straw, chipped wood, pine or fir bark, with a loose wrapping of half-inch-mesh hardware cloth. Commercial growers often protect trunks but don't mulch, mostly because of the cost of labor.

The ultimate mulch combines organic matter with an underlayment of landscape cloth under the entire area beneath the foliage canopy. The fabric looks like a thin blanket. No weeds can penetrate it except nutgrass, which is one of the sedges, and certain aggressive grasses. You could eradicate such ugly customers with a herbicide such as Roundup before planting. Here's the sequence for planting new trees and mulching:

**Planting**    After killing out aggressive perennial grasses and weeds, work lime and fertilizer into the soil according to soil test results.

Plant and water the new tree and wrap the trunk loosely with hardware cloth to protect against mechanical injury and chewing of bark by rodents. Tie the wire on with cotton string so, if you forget to loosen it later, the string will decay and prevent the wire from girdling the tree.

Spray the trunk and inner parts of lower limbs with cheap latex flat white paint. Technically, this isn't necessary except where sunscald or winter burn is a problem. But, why take chances? It won't hurt and, at the least, will keep the trunk from splitting on that warm day in midwinter when the sunny side expands rapidly while the shady side is still frozen.

Cut a square of landscape cloth and make a slit halfway into it. Slip it around the tree as a collar. Overlap strips of the fiber to enlarge the covered area. You can enlarge the mulched area as the tree grows.

Scatter a cup of vegetable garden fertilizer or organic equivalent over the landscape cloth and spread mulch 3 to 4 inches deep. The mulch will protect the fiber from ultraviolet ray deterioration. Don't draw the mulch up close to the trunk. Use pine or fir bark, hardwood mulch, or chipped wood, preferably precomposted. Let me caution citrus belt gardeners not to mulch around their citrus trees with organic mulch; it can encourage serious root and crown diseases.

The fertilizer should prevent nitrogen drawdown. However, if yellowing foliage makes you suspect a nitrogen shortage, drench the mulched area with manure tea or a liquid fertilizer. Don't fertilize late in the growing season; it can tenderize the young tree. Subsequent applications of fertilizer can be made as drenches or broadcast over the mulch and raked in. If you top-dress stable litter or manure over the mulch, you may introduce weed seeds and defeat the major purpose of the mulch.

As the tree increases in size, the layer of mulch can be made deeper to keep aggressive weeds under control by shading or smothering them out.

*Buying*

The selection of modern fruit trees for your home garden is more complicated than simply deciding which sorts you like to eat, and planting trees. You can start by visiting your Cooperative Extension Service office and picking up bulletins on adapted fruit tree varieties and their culture in your climate. Often, the value of Extension Service literature depends on the importance of commercial orchards in your state, and their recommendations will be tilted toward varieties grown commercially. For a balanced perspective, send for catalogs from fruit tree growers in your region, or one of the national suppliers. Here are a few of the things you will learn:

Fruit trees are indexed by the number of "chilling hours" (less than 40 degrees F.) required for blooming. Some with a high number of chilling hours will not bloom or bear fruit in warm climates with mild winters. Most catalogs cover this requirement by listing adaptation to the various climate zones on the U.S. hardiness zone map. The most reputable nurseries will not ship unadapted varieties, even if you ask for them.

While many tree fruit cultivars are moderately self-fertile, production can often be increased by the presence of another tree, of a kind known for good pollination and for flowering at the same time as your chosen cultivar.

Some kinds of fruit trees, notably cherries and Japanese plums, require "two to tango." If a neighbor happens to have a recommended pollinator in his yard, bees will probably carry the pollen to your tree. Or you can graft a piece of the recommended pollinator on the fruit-bearing tree. If fruit set is poor after planting two trees known to pair well for pollination, suspect lack of bees, due to indiscriminate spraying nearby, or rainy or cold weather when blossoms are open to pollen transfer.

Very early blooming cultivars should be avoided in areas prone to late frosts, as this can result in poor or no production.

Certain areas are "frost traps," where frost will occur even though surrounding areas are frost free. These can be basins caused by the topography, or traps caused by obstructions such as buildings, fences, or evergreen trees. Before planting, look all around and try to choose a spot where cold air will drain away rather than be trapped.

Each kind of fruit has distinct soil preferences. While all will grow well on deep, fertile soil, peaches and plums do better on comparatively poor sandy or gravelly soil. Of the tree fruits, pears show the strongest preference for fertile soil. Yet, on fertile soil, especially if forced with fertilizers, pears will produce soft, lush growth that may develop fire blight, if the disease is entrenched in that neighborhood. Few of the tree fruits, except certain plum cultivars, will tolerate poor drainage and, on dense clay soils, will do better if planted on low, wide mounds.

## Care and Feeding

All new trees, and especially those of standard size, need a number of years to set the first significant fruit crop. You have to regard the care they need during those years as you would the feeding and training of a child. If you are faithful in your obligation, both tree and child should reach a healthy, productive maturity. Although early-bearing differs by cultivar, peaches, apricots, nectarines, and plums are generally the most precocious, followed by cherries, pears, and apples. Some apple cultivars don't hit their stride for six to seven years, and a few even longer. Elwood Fisher's experience with 'Northern Spy', for example, is that dwarfed trees should produce in seven to nine years, but standard trees not until fourteen years! I think that the definition of an optimist would be an eighty-year-old gardener planting standard trees of 'Northern Spy'.

All fruit trees need fairly frequent watering the first summer after planting and, later, generous watering when setting fruit. You can taper off for a short time, but resume watering again when trees are forming fruit buds for the next season. Water by flooding around the tree, rather than by a sprinkler.

All fruit trees benefit from yearly feeding at rates per square foot of soil comparable to those of large, greedy vegetables. From 2 to 3 pounds per 100 square feet of soil beneath the foliage canopy should be sufficient. Scatter the fertilizer around the dripline and slightly outside it, where the greatest concentration of feeder roots can be found. Spring feeding is preferred because late summer or fall feeding can tenderize the tree.

## Pests and Diseases

The testimonials from gardeners who grow fruit without chemical sprays or dusts often neglect to mention the amount of fruit spoiled by insects or diseases, or damage to trees by borers. Even the most dedicated organic gardener will search out effective botanical and biological controls and acceptable mineral sprays such as Bordeaux mix and dormant oils. The amount of insect and disease controls you need is dependent on how much damage to trees and how much blemished or spoiled fruit you are willing to accept.

Insects such as borers, codling moths, plum curculios, and the various scales can weaken trees and damage fruit. Diseases such as brown rot, scab, rust, and bacterial leaf curl can have the same effect. If you are dead set against the use of proprietary insecticides or fungicides, ask around for the best organic fruit growers in your area and inquire how they manage it. Start with your local Master Gardeners Association. If you can accept the small amount of environmental impact caused by spraying a home orchard, ask your Cooperative Extension Service for a preventive spray program, scheduled for your area.

A growing trend, particularly at the universities, however, is the inclusion of nontoxic controls in "Integrated Pest Management" programs, which rely on a balance of predatory insects and biological controls. In the South and West, where nematodes are a problem on fruit trees, universities are researching green manure crops which either repel nematodes or will not harbor them.

If you'd like to try antique varieties of fruit trees in your garden, remember that they will grow into standard, full-sized trees. The options are to order antique varieties grafted to dwarfing rootstocks, or to graft scions of antique varieties onto existing trees of the same species. Any way you do it, the result will fully justify the effort.

# *Herbal Arts*

*Her love of growing and drying herbs for seasoning and crafts draws Maureen Ruettgers's family and friends into her hobby.*

*(Left) Drying herbs and everlasting flowers fill Maureen Ruettgers's antique barn.*

**H**erbal arts is a new name for a very old pastime. To sit and weave wreaths from herbs or to dry and toss petals and flower heads into fragrant, colorful mixtures links you with a chain of humankind all over the world, back to the dawn of civilization. We have the leisure time now to practice herbal arts, which relieve stresses and satisfy our creative instincts by busying our hands and stimulating our senses. Ancient Greeks and Romans, Chinese philosophers, and medieval ladies might not have described their motives and gratifications in the same way but they, too, hung herbs and flowers to dry, wove them together with thread, and scented closed spaces with what we now call potpourris, and sprays of lavender, sage, and rosemary.

The herbal arts have advanced on the wave of interest in herbs for culinary, landscaping, and medicinal purposes. As gardeners experimented with herbs for seasoning foods, added silvery or gray-foliaged herbs to landscapes, and soothed upset stomachs with mint teas, they discovered that their attractive and durable flowers or seed heads could be dried for winter arrangements. And, as they grew in gardening, they evaluated garden flowers and wild species for drying and ranged out over the landscape to find natural materials to add variety to their dried creations. The result has been a vigorous revival of the ancient art of decorating with dried plant materials, only more eclectic and considerably faster, thanks to glue guns, monofilament line, desiccants, Styrofoam forms, and floral essences not available to previous generations.

The growing interest in country living and our colonial heritage has spawned research into the part played by herbal arts in the lifestyles of earlier days. Restored settlements such as Colonial Williamsburg, Old Sturbridge, Old Salem, and Plimoth Plantation reproduce the dried arrangements, swags, and fragrant mélanges of dried petals settlers made from the herbs and flowers of their day. All of this has raised our awareness of growing and utilizing herbs as a rewarding hobby, steeped in tradition and lore. Few other hobbies can call forth such strong images of families, on long winter evenings, clustered around lamps or hearths for light, busy with herbal crafts or capturing the images of flowers in needlework or quilts.

Always, there have been lively cottage industries associated with herbal arts. When practitioners reach a certain level of proficiency, and people begin to admire their handiwork, some decide to sell what they make. Today, herbal arts are often displayed at crafts fairs and harvest festivals. Thus it was, too, at medieval fairs and festivals. Lacking tools and the money to buy them, peasants made and marketed what they could from materials they could gather from gardens, fields, and hedgerows. Even the most highborn shopper must have reacted favorably to the cunning combinations of homegrown or found materials.

At herbal arts displays today, many of the hobbyist-exhibitors are well educated; some are trained in fine arts. But many are plain, everyday people with extraordinary talents in growing and utilizing herbs and flowers artfully.

Most of these hobbyists are good gardeners. They grow their own herbs and flowers for drying, and combine them with seed pods, vines, and flowers gathered from the wild. Some buy dried material and floral scents from florists and specialty suppliers at trade fairs or through the mail. They feel their way into the hobby, enticed by the beautiful creations they see at craft fairs and garden club flower shows. They ask questions, attend workshops and seminars, study how-to books, and practice with simple creations. All the while, the people who are good gardeners expand into

*Maureen created this wreath from artemisia decorated with gomphrena and statice.*

growing species and cultivars known to be useful in making wreaths, dried arrangements, bunched mixed herbs for hanging, collages, and potpourris. The more adventurous scout roadsides, stream banks, fencerows, botanical gardens, and vacant lots for weeds and wildflowers, vines, trees, and shrubs with decorative flowers or seed pods.

The typical herbal arts hobbyist does not have the dark, drafty barn so often featured in articles about drying herbs and flowers. Well-ventilated, dark barns are great for hanging hundreds of bunches of garden flowers or herbs for drying. Good ventilation reduces the incidence of molding, and gradual drying in the dark reduces fading and loss of natural fragrance. But, favorable drying conditions can also be created by darkening a room, opening a window from the top, and running an electric fan to keep the air moving.

The majority of herb hobbyists dry their herbs and flowers in darkened rooms, garages, or sheds, often with help from a small heater and a fan. Their gardens produce too much raw material for drying with silica gel, except for particularly fragile blossoms. Hobbyists use cookstove ovens set on the lowest heat, commercial dehydrators, and microwave ovens for drying during rainy weather or to speed up the process to meet show deadlines.

I know many gardeners who are deeply involved in herbal arts. Their hobby involves them year-round, yet accommodates time needed for work, family, or social obligations. Herbs and flowers for drying are easy to grow and don't demand harvesting within a tight time frame. Harvesting and preparing flowers for drying is especially enjoyable, and putting them together artfully can wait until you have spare time and feel creative. I know of no other hobby that has so many dimensions or that involves more sensory stimulation. The fragrances transport you to the garden or fields where you harvested the plants; the bristly textures and muted colors remind you of the fullness and brilliance of the fresh flowers and leaves.

A few miles out from Boston, in the countryside that sent militia for the first battles of the Revolution, and in a home occupied by three generations before the call went out from Lexington and Concord, lives the Ruettgers family. Without a doubt, families who tilled this farm in past years and gardened near the old white frame home grew herbs and flowers for drying, and used them artistically.

Perhaps emanations from generations past guided Maureen Ruettgers into herbal arts, or it could have been a near and dear role model, or an inborn and carefully nurtured artistic talent. Whatever the source, it has produced a good gardener with a gift for landscaping with herbs and flowers useful for drying, and for employing them in highly creative ways.

*Maureen shows me how she selects materials for wreathmaking.*

Maureen Ruettgers is living proof that a young woman can have a satisfying plant hobby while raising a family and doing community work. She and her husband, Michael, have gradually converted the grounds of an historic home into a large, beautiful, and functional garden for herbs and flowers for drying. The old barn that came with the place proved to be a perfect site for drying and storing herbs and dried flowers. Their three children grew up in the garden and at the feet of their mother as she worked away at herb crafts. They took to it naturally, much to the delight of their mother and father.

Michael shares Maureen's love for growing things but he describes himself as "more of an inside man." He loves to cook and preserve the vegetables and grapes he and their son Chris grow. Michael learned gardening from his father at their homes in England and, later, in San Diego.

Maureen is among the many herb growers who are enlarging the scope of the hobby to include herbs for seasoning, for medicinal purposes, and for inexpensive, fragrant decorations for the home. Although she considers herself an herb enthusiast, Maureen grows many annual and perennial flowers, and some wildflowers, for decorative flowers and seed heads. She uses them to enrich her materials for dried herb crafts: wreaths, swags, bunches, sachets, potpourris, and so forth. This infusion of nonherb plants adds color and texture to her garden, which, for much of the growing season, would otherwise show mostly the muted green, gray, and silver colors of her herbs. Maureen grows several of the healing herbs in her garden, not for medicinal use but because they look good in landscapes or can be used in herbal arts.

A tour of the Ruettgerses' garden is a learning experience because of the many uses to which Maureen puts her plants. We began our tour just outside their back door, in view of the kitchen windows:

"The first garden we built here was a 'ladder garden,'" Maureen recalled. "We laid an old ladder on prepared ground and planted in between the rungs with herb plants. We used it to teach visiting schoolchildren how to garden in small spaces: they loved to sample the herbs. The kinds of herbs vary from year to year but are basically the

The "ladder garden" makes a pretty display for French tarragon, center; 'Spicy Globe' basil, foreground; and chives and parsley in the background.

edible herbs that can be bought anywhere as plants . . . sweet basil, parsley, dill, spearmint, thyme, sage, rosemary, and chives. I was trained as an elementary school teacher and it did my heart good to see the difference that old ladder made in getting the story over. We still use the ladder garden with visiting school groups.

"Gradually, we expanded the herb garden to its present size of a quarter of an acre and added beds for perennials, mostly those with interesting flowers for drying, seed pods, or shade-tolerant cultivars. It is hard to find shade-tolerant plants with useful seed pods. I use pods of hosta, one of the best shade plants. Alchemilla, or lady's mantle, one of my favorites, withstands moderate shade and stands up well to wind and rain. It has greenish yellow blossoms that dry well, and the cupped leaves collect large, glistening drops of dew or rain. The drops slide over the leaves like quicksilver. I like to plant lady's mantle in drifts. Out in the sunny areas of the perennial beds, we grow the eryngiums, baptisias, verbascums, horehound, and butterfly weed for decorative seed pods which we combine with dried pods of annuals such as *Nigella damascena, Scabiosa stellata,* and Shirley poppy.

"There really is a fine line of distinction between what nurseries call 'perennials' and the perennial herbs. I suppose that what qualifies a plant as an 'herb' is its usefulness in flavoring, medicines, or scenting. Many herbs have decorative uses as well, and I will confess a fondness for them, but when it comes to choosing flowers for drying or for decorative seed pods I'm not so much of a purist that I discriminate against annual or perennial flowers. I need a wide variety of blossoms, seed pods, and dried foliage for my creations, as well as fragrant herbs.

*Tall artemisia 'Silver King' stands guard for Maureen's drying barn in the background.*

*Masters of the Victory Garden*

*"Here's why I like lady's mantle," explains Maureen during a taping by* The Victory Garden.

"Next to lady's mantle, cinnamon basil is my favorite plant in the garden. It is easy to grow in full sun, and quickly develops a mounded shape. The tip growth of each branch is purple green and the blossom scales are deep purple. The blossom spikes retain their color when dried and, being short, mix neatly in potpourris. The fragrance is intense and clovelike, fresh or dried."

Maureen has found it helpful and pleasing to the eye to divide her garden into two parts: one half, dubbed by the children "The Magic Garden," is planted with pastel colors of flowers for drying, and mostly silvery or gray herbs. The other half, "The Kitchen Garden," is reserved for brighter colored flowers, mostly grown for potpourris, and herbs that are blended in their manufacture. The garden is made up of raised beds separated by mulched walks; the perennial border is elevated two feet and surrounded by a wall of gray fieldstone.

Near the house is a forty-foot-long arbor for grapes, very ornamental and painted white. Maureen's father built it; he is a master woodworker and was restless in retirement. Michael's wine and jelly grape varieties are beginning to climb up and over it. The arbor is a work of art; it looks much like the one at the Victory Garden in Lexington, Massachusetts.

Maureen and her daughters, Polly and Abigail, and I had a great time touring the herb garden. Of all the plant classes, I suppose I know the herbs best, having grown the culinary herbs commercially for several years. Nevertheless, the Ruettgerses were growing several I'd never seen before. Their cooler climate and emphasis on decorative herbs has allowed them to collect and propagate some kinds you won't find outside of the catalogs of herb specialists. Odd species of salvia, thyme, artemisia, and mint kept me guessing, and rarely successfully. Maureen swapped what she knew about unusual herbs for what I knew about container growing, pest control without chemicals, and plant nutrition, in relation to herb growing. The children didn't say much but I could tell they were absorbing the conversation.

In the Ruettgers garden, the plant that impressed me most was the ambrosia, *Chenopodium botrytis*, also called feather geranium or Jerusalem oak. I know it can become a weed in some gardens, but growing it in the hot, dry soil of the South where I live is anything but easy. Maureen's garden was well stocked with ambrosia; she told me she has to thin out and discard surplus volunteer plants every year.

I was particularly interested in her collections of salvias for drying, including *Salvia hordeum* and *S. leucantha*, and numerous artemisias (wormwood). Unusual alliums were blooming all over the place; August is the time for these onion family relatives to shine. I saw yellow, white, pink, and purple varieties from 8 inches to 24 inches in height.

Here and there, around the garden, were herbs growing in containers. I asked Maureen which herbs, in her experience, do best in containers. "The shorter ones," she replied, "especially herbs that trail over the sides of containers; lemon thyme, oregano, and creeping rosemary are good. You need some erect plants of the shorter varieties for vertical accents and foliage or flower color: chives, lavender, or sage, for example. The gross feeders such as basil need larger containers, as does mint."

I was curious to learn if Maureen left any of her containerized perennial herbs out of doors during the winter. "No," she said, "not only because they would die from freezing, but also because the containers would break up from the pressure of expanding ice." Maureen uses terra-cotta containers to blend with her old-fashioned garden. She knocks the plants out of containers in the fall, heels them in for winter protection, and repots in the spring. She takes plants of the tender herbs indoors: bay, lemon verbena, rosemary, and such.

Maureen and I agreed on the difficulty of growing herbs on windowsills during the winter, despite the bland assurances in some books that it is easy. As you travel north, winter days grow progressively shorter and often more cloudy. Herbs have a hard time existing, let alone producing enough new growth for cutting. The overly warm, bone-dry winter atmosphere of many homes also works against plants. You can get around the problems by installing fluorescent lights in a cool room and enclosing the plant growing area with clear plastic sheeting. Under lights is a great place for starting seeds and saving plants and starts of your prized tender perennials.

Maureen's raised beds for herbs enjoy many of the advantages of containers, without the need for frequent watering. She fills them with moderately fast draining soil that holds moisture well, yet never becomes waterlogged. The porous soil is easy to cultivate and to keep free of weeds. Her raised beds reminded me of a similar arrangement for herbs at the Birmingham, Alabama, Botanical Garden. Volunteer herb enthusiasts had converted a steep slope into an outstanding herb garden by using weathered railroad ties to break the slope into level terraces. *The Victory Garden* taped the Birmingham "Herb Army" at work weeding and grooming their wide selection of improved cultivars.

Maureen gets her information on esoteric herbs from a large home library and from her association with the oldest group within The Herb Society, the Massachusetts chapter. "An office I held in the chapter proved invaluable to me," Maureen said. "I was elected librarian. That gave me access to 700 volumes on herbs, some very old and valuable." At one time, The Herb Society's national garden was nearby, at the Arnold Arboretum. It was a valued resource that assisted Maureen in learning the many genera and species that are called "herbs." Now, it has been moved to Holden Arboretum in Mentor, Ohio, near Cleveland.

At chapter meetings, Maureen has met many notables in herb growing: Madeline Hill, Joy Martin of Logee's Greenhouses, and Cyrus Hyde of Well Sweep Farm, to name a few. Some have visited her garden and have shared information and plants. I reminded Maureen of the several *Victory Garden* programs which have featured herbs, among them being visits to Caprilands in Connecticut, to the Denver Botanic Garden, and a wreath-making workshop at Callaway Gardens.

At the time I visited the Ruettgerses, they had just returned from a trip to Europe, and Maureen's daughter Polly was preparing to leave on another trip. Nevertheless, she took the time to show me the flowers and herbs she likes to grow, and how she makes potpourri by mixing dried herbs and flowers from the garden. She and her mother are keeping notes to establish the best stages of maturity for harvesting herbs and flowers for the best color, fragrance, and keeping quality.

I asked Maureen about sources for seeds, plants, and supplies for herb crafts. "You can avoid a lot of trial and error," she said, "by asking a member to recommend you for membership in a local chapter of The Herb Society. If there is no chapter nearby, you can network with other herb enthusiasts in horticultural societies, or within the Master Gardener organization; many of their members grow herbs along with vegetables.

"Some herb enthusiasts bring back seeds from foreign countries, of species not known in this country. Bringing in seeds is permitted, but importation of plants is so complicated that usually only botanical gardens are willing to make the effort. Once in this country, it is a slow process introducing a new species until one of the major herb seed and plant marketers gets behind it. Conversely, greatly improved cultivars can catch on rather quickly, as did 'Dark Opal' and 'Spicy Globe' basils. Also, the seed and plant companies seem to be making an effort to locate and market more flower varieties with potential for drying."

*(Left) Polly gathers roses for potpourri while Abigail holds an armful. (Right) Abigail and Polly mix dried herbs to make potpourri.*

We spent some time in the fragrant drying shed, already filling up with bouquets, swags, wreaths, and the makings of potpourri. "In about two weeks," Maureen said, "every tray in the big dryer will be covered with herbs and flowers, and every hook on the wall will be loaded with wreaths." She emphasized the necessity of darkening all the windows and maintaining good air circulation in the drying room, to retain color and fragrance. Slow microwaving or drying in ovens is being used by

*Herbal Arts* **127**

1)

2)

3)

4)

5)

6)

## Herbs and Flowers for Drying

A basic selection of herbs and ever-lasting flowers for drying includes florist's statice, Limonium statice (1); teasel, which is widely naturalized (2); matricaria or feverfew (3); *Gomphrena* 'Strawberry Fields' (4); *Salvia farinacea* 'Victoria' (5); yarrow, *Achillea filipendulina* 'Moonshine' (in the foreground); and ambrosia (6). All have versatile colors and textures that hold up well in dried arrangements. A variety of techniques, from air-drying to microwaving, are used by hobbyists. Experimentation will show you which method is most effective for you.

other enthusiasts for preserving herbs and flowers, but the Ruettgerses' production would overwhelm home units.

Maureen and Polly use silica gel to dry certain delicate flowers, and most species with blue or purple flowers, which tend to fade in air-drying. The silica gel helps to retain natural colors. Silica gel is a powdery substance. When flowers are imbedded in it, and the powder dusted in among the petals, the silica gel draws the moisture out of the tissues. It has to be shaken off the dried flowers, and can be reclaimed by heating to drive off the absorbed moisture. "We found that we could air-dry the blue flowers of 'Hidcote' lavender so perfectly that they could hardly be distinguished from the fresh. We can't grow and dry enough lavender to meet the demand at our annual sale," said Maureen.

"Members of the Massachusetts chapter come out and help us dig and pot up plants for the sale. We have many other herb enthusiasts in the area; they bring friends to see the dried materials and crafts and to pick up ideas. They especially like our wreaths and necklaces made of spices and can't seem to get enough of Polly's potpourri. We are very choosy about the essential oils we use to reinforce fragrance: some of the commercially available stuff is cloyingly sweet or offensively oily smelling. You can buy essential oils extracted from all the major herbs and fragrant flowers. They add life to potpourris; just stir the contents of the jar gently and the fragrance will come to life again and again.

"In wet years, we have had to cancel the sale. Continuing rains and damp weather can make drying of herbs and flowers difficult for everybody. What a difference a dry summer can make! In just two or three days, herbs can dry sufficiently to keep. Wet seasons have convinced me to install a warm air drying system in the barn similar to the one used here years ago to dry digitalis grown on the farm for pharmaceutical use. Also, the heat would let us work later in the winter here in the barn; without heat, it gets too cold by January.

"One little extra that makes our sales so successful is that we serve an herb lunch, along with herb teas. That alone has persuaded many customers to take up herb growing. It helps that we offer books on growing and using herbs. Books on birds and butterflies also sell well because they naturally go with herbs.

"Above all, I want to do everything I can to lead, but not push, our children into gardening with herbs and flowers. It has meant so much in my life and I hope it will in theirs. We were so proud of Polly for two term papers she did; they were on medieval gardening and heart drugs. She did all the research, including tracing how Mr. James Patch grew digitalis on our land years ago."

That her large garden is both beautiful and functional is a tribute to Maureen's dedication to the aesthetic values and country traditions that the herbal arts represent.

# More about Herbal Arts

Herbal arts, the "craft" side of herbs, is one of many specialties open to the hobby herb grower. It attracts nearly as many herb growers as producing herbs for gourmet cooking. Both of these specialties lead medicinal herbs in popularity, but such has not always been the case. Mankind was using medicinal herbs when diagnoses were by supposition and treatment by trial and error. Scenting herbs were used not only for such civilized purposes as imparting a sweet smell to linens and clothing, but also for masking unpleasant odors and repelling insects. Herb uses are described at length in the writings of early physicians and philosophers, from Europe east through China. Some herbs were gathered from the wild but, as trade and commerce grew, seeds and plants helped gardeners everywhere to grow a broad range of herbs. Improvement by selection began more than two thousand years ago.

Now, gardeners can buy seeds or plants of herb varieties developed especially for drying. These hold their flower colors with little fading, and resist shattering during handling. For instance, the common purple-flowered oregano, *Origanum vulgare*, is no great shakes for flavor, but has superb color, holding power, and stem length for drying. Cinnamon basil, one of the recently rediscovered "rare basils," is perfect for potpourris, where its bronzy purple color and strong, clove-like scent will hold for several months.

The cultural methods for growing herbs for culinary uses are not always compatible with those for herbs to be dried. Herb cookery calls for tender vegetative tips. To produce new vegetative growth, you need to trim off the very flower heads and seed pods that are useful in herbal arts. For this reason, the herb specialist usually grows culinary herbs in the vegetable garden or dooryard plot, and isolates the herbs for drying in a special herb garden. This arrangement also makes best use of the landscaping value of the gray and silver herbs which are so important in herbal arts.

Most gardeners hate to waste the beautiful flowers and seed heads on their herb plants but, every year, many do. They might be pleasantly surprised at how easy and satisfying it is to work with dried materials, and at the extent of their own creativity. Herbal arts is not gender-oriented; many men are quite good at it. Their dried herb and flower creations tend to be large and robust and to include wild materials such as cattails, which can be collected only by slogging through marshes, and teasel weed and rabbit tobacco from the roughest terrain.

**Starting Right**   It is possible to throw yourself wholeheartedly into herbal arts—simultaneously to begin growing special herbs and flowers for drying, all the while scouting for wild seed pods and flower heads. I would counsel moderation. If you are already growing herbs, start evaluating a few new herbs every growing season; learn how to grow and when to harvest them for drying. Experiment with blending them with herbs you already know. Discard the varieties you don't like or which don't hold well when dried and move on to others.

Once you become proficient in herb growing, study the catalogs of seed companies and specialists in flowers for cutting. Select a few varieties which are adapted to your climate and which are specifically recommended for air-drying.

Watch this last point carefully; some suppliers recommend varieties which are so fragile that careful and tedious drying with silica gel is required. Grow a short row of a few new varieties each year, in your food garden, where cutting armloads of flowers won't disrupt the landscape. Anticipate that the colors, even after careful drying, will be subdued when compared to fresh flowers. Of all the colors, blue is the most elusive in drying and the yellows and oranges the least likely to fade. Good clear whites are rare; most dry to cream or dingy shades.

*Drying Herbs*    People who love to tinker can find plenty of room for their talents in techniques for drying herbs and flowers. First place in drying techniques is held by uncomplicated air-drying, using a dark area ventilated by fans. But, air-drying is speeded up considerably by drying for two or three days in a refrigerator, then hanging bunches in the dark to complete drying. Hanging lets stems and leaves assume a more or less natural stance, while laying them to dry on racks or layers of paper towels flattens them like herbarium specimens. Microwaving at low settings can preserve colors at exceptional levels of brilliance, but some flowers tend to collapse and lose their shape. You will have to experiment with settings and duration of microwave drying; it varies from oven to oven. Very slow drying in an electric oven with the door cracked works well; sometimes the oven pilot light alone will do the job in a gas oven. Commercial or home-made dehydrators are good for drying petals for potpourri and seed pods with short stems, but usually lack the capacity to handle long-stemmed flowers.

One of the best rigs for drying is a home greenhouse. Gardeners drape the houses with black plastic to exclude light, hang their harvests of herb and flower stems in bunches, crack the vents to let out moisture-laden air, turn on the fans, and, in less than a week, their plant materials are dried just right, pliable but not

*These wooden drying trays were made by Maureen's father.*

brittle and prone to shatter. Almost as good are large cold frames covered with black plastic, cracked for ventilation, and fitted with a fan in one corner to force out moist air. Such units can dry small wreaths made up from fresh vines, branches, and flowers, but the monofilament thread or thin copper wire used to hold them together should be tightened after drying.

**Making Wreaths**

Wreaths are probably the most popular herbal art. Most are made on Styrofoam or straw forms purchased at florist shops or specialists in flower-arranging supplies. Or, you can weave your own forms from kudzu, honeysuckle, and wild grape vines, or prunings from vineyards. Where I garden in the South, tall silver artemisia, lemon verbena, and anise-scented (licorice) basil grow so large that the limber branches can be half-dried, woven into wreaths, then completely dried before adding decorations.

There is an art to making wreaths perfectly round and symmetrical, or to other special shapes such as ovals and hearts. The professionals use jigs fitted with slots through which the monofilament, thread or wire can be passed for wrapping. But, the real art starts with the decoration; a well-made wreath is solidly covered with a mixture of dried flower and herb heads, frothy dried foliage, tiny conifer cones, seed pods in scale with the size of the wreath, and ribbons to suit your taste. It should be so securely wrapped with monofilament thread in a muted shade of gray, or fine wire, that it will stand up to handling. All decorations should be either firmly threaded into the base or stuck on with a glue gun so that they won't shake loose in handling.

*Wreathmaking*

Maureen demonstrates the art of wreathmaking, using artemisia, sage, and oregano. Using blue-gray thread, she ties the fresh artemisia to a wire ring (1). The real artistry begins with the decoration. Over the artemísia, Maureen arranges sprays of sage leaves with oregano flowers, and ties them securely to the wreath (2). Lamb's ear, gomphrena flowers, sage flowers, and gray santolina add their decorative effects (3). When the wreath is completely assembled, Maureen hangs it to dry.

1)

2)

3)

## Making Potpourris

Potpourris also make excellent gifts when packed in the special decorative large-mouthed jars on sale at pottery outlets. Some gardeners use so many petals that they arrange with local greenhouses and public parks to deadhead their geraniums and roses. Not all dried flowers used in potpourris are fragrant; some are added for color and bulk. Herbal arts specialists are divided on the issue of using floral essences to enhance the fragrance and carrying power of petal and flower blends. Some use none at all. Some load their potpourris with perfume. Others compromise by using only highly refined natural floral fragrances discreetly, along with orris root as a stabilizer and extender.

Bunches of dried herbs are rather plain and simple, but are appropriate for hanging in kitchens. They look at home in kitchens with a colonial or country design but are not out of place with any decor. Sage, rosemary, common oregano, and English thyme cut at first flower stage look good and hold well. There is no denying how attractive mint looks when the stems are cut at the ground and dried when the first flowers are opening, but it tends to shatter, as does basil. Sweet marjoram can be cut when the little seed balls are still green. Common chives and garlic chives should be cut at full flower; garlic chive seed heads are also quite decorative. Ordinary garlic flower heads dry beautifully and don't smell rank. If you consider the many other alliums to be herbs, you add many excellent colors and blossom forms to your flowery workbasket.

## Landscaping with Herbs

Some of the decorative herbs have potential as landscape subjects, as do some of the species grown mostly for medicinal purposes. Landscape architects have begun to appreciate certain of the herb species for their foliage, flowers, and fragrance. Some of the interest is due to the imaginative plantings in the National Herb Garden within the United States National Arboretum at Washington, D.C. Also, designers have seen how Europeans use herbs in conjunction with perennials, groundcovers, and shrubs, often to get special textural effects and silvery colors. Greenhouse growers who produce herb plants for sale often install demonstration gardens to show visitors how herbs will look at maturity in various landscaping situations. As yet, most full-service nurseries market herbs as a class and don't separate the species with special potential for herbal arts or landscaping. That day will come.

Once you get started in herbal arts, you may wish to attend one of the national seminars and trade shows for hobby and commercial herb growers and herb craft specialists. The Cooperative Extension Service at Purdue University and the International Herb Marketers Association sponsor yearly conferences. The lectures are superb and the trade fair attracts all kinds of suppliers and products for herb specialists. Your Cooperative Extension Service office will have dates and locations. Until and if the time comes when you head for the national herb meeting, there is plenty at home to feed your curiosity about herbal arts. Every town of any size has a hobbyist so good at herbal arts that they lecture and give demonstrations. Books on drying flowers and herbs are plentiful and well illustrated. Yet, the best way to learn is by growing and drying your own, and experimenting to make herbal creations that please you. You will seldom go wrong and, when you do, you simply take your less-than-a-masterpiece apart and do it better.

# *Dwarf Conifers*

*Ed Rezek gains international notice for his Long Island collection of dwarf conifers, miniature jewels of the evergreen world.*

*This corner of Ed's back yard displays his exotic-looking collection in an artful landscape.*

**D**warf conifers are not a modern discovery. Interest in these slow-growing, miniature forms of standard plants goes back centuries. They are found in all the forms of standard conifers—ground-hugging, spreading, mounded, ball-like, vase-shaped, columnar, and conical erect plants, and special forms such as weeping and contorted—and in a wide range of colors including blue, variegations of silver, white, or cream-yellow, as well as every shade of green. Such myriad variations make the plants eminently collectible.

The early collectors of dwarf conifers were noblemen or traders with the time and money to devote to scholarly pursuits, including collecting plants from afar and learning how to identify and grow them. The first collectors were probably wealthy Chinese and Japanese hobbyists who, hundreds of years ago, gathered dwarf conifers from the wild to include in their bonsai collections. Though many of their bonsais, then as now, were normal plants artificially dwarfed by severe pruning and root restriction, these collectors sought out and cultivated true miniature conifers as well.

Interest in collecting dwarf and unusual forms peaked during the mid-nineteenth century as wealthy gentry in Great Britain and on the Continent vied with one another for exotic garden specimens. Sheltered courtyards, old walls, granite troughs, rock gardens, and alpine screes accommodated dwarf conifer collections naturally. When wars and hard times took their tolls on the estates, interest in dwarf conifers went into decline, but they were protected at botanical gardens and smaller private collections.

Today, as gardens become smaller in scale and gardeners become more discerning, dwarf conifers are increasingly prized for their beauty and longevity as well as for their compact size and slow growth habit in the landscape. The distinctive forms invite close inspection and contemplation, for many are best appreciated at close range. Landscapers think of them as "designer plants" because, as in designer clothing, their style, uniqueness, and finish are immediately apparent.

The term "dwarf" is a relative one and therefore somewhat misleading. A dwarfed forest tree might grow ten times as large as a dwarfed shrub. However, all dwarfed plants mature at smaller sizes than are normal or typical for the species. At maturity, dwarf plants can range from one-half to only one-twentieth the size of normal plants. Furthermore, dwarf plants grow very slowly, from less than one inch to five inches a year.

Some dwarf and unusual conifers come about as chance seedlings. Others are propagated by cuttings taken from a dwarfed branch of an otherwise normal plant. No one knows all the causes of spontaneous dwarfism in plants, but it may be due to air pollution, radiation, or viruses. Dwarfing anomalies may show up as:

**Juvenile fixation.**   Ordinarily, the foliage of juvenile conifers differs from that of adult plants in form and color. Some plants never "shift gears"; they retain their juvenile characteristics at an advanced age. *Thuja occidentalis* 'Rhineglow' is an example. Others, such as *Chamaecyparis thyoidies* 'Andelyensis', may exhibit fixation, but become unstable later on and revert partially or fully to normal performance.

**Witches' brooms.**   No causal organisms have been found to create these profusely branched and often low-growing malformations on conifers and deciduous plants. As the name suggests, they are congested and resemble brooms. You can reproduce them by cuttings or grafting, and they will often grow into dwarfed or unusual plants. Witches' brooms or grafted

*Their distinctive forms, compact size, and slow growth habit make dwarf conifers the designer plants of the small landscape.*

cuttings made from them rarely set seeds but, when they do, mutations can occur at a higher rate than with normal plants.

Grafting cuttings from witches' brooms to normal rootstock is one way to propagate these curiosities, but the plants sometimes suffer from incompatible grafts, due to different rates of growth of the scion and understock. The rate of growth of grafted specimens (dwarf scions grafted on normal rootstock) can depend on the vigor of the rootstock. Strong rootstocks can sometimes force dwarf conifers to grow too large. Grafts are unavoidable, because certain forms of dwarf conifers don't set good root systems when you try to make cuttings and root them.

***Dwarfed or stunted alpine forms.*** Most of these will start to grow normally when planted in regular garden soil at low elevations. They can, with difficulty, be maintained as dwarfs by growing them as severely pruned bonsai. A good example is *Abies lasiocarpa* 'Sub-alpina' from the timberline in the Northwest.

*An old, over-grown conifer has been opened up by pruning and clipped to train it into a pom-pom form.*

**Fastigiate (narrow, flattened, upright) forms of conventional conifers.** These generally come about as chance seedlings and are identifiable at an early age. The flattening effect is most noticeable in the tips of the twigs, but can also show up as kinked branches.

**Side shoots from erect conifers.**   If you have ever tried to root and grow a cutting from the tip of a side branch of a conifer, you doubtless found it to be stubbornly geotropic. They usually produce prostrate or descending forms that will not turn upright. However, if you injure one of these forms by severe pruning or mechanical damage, or if they are injured by freezing, they can revert to upright growth, resulting in a freakish-looking plant.

Many dwarf conifer specimens are not perfect miniatures of the standard version, but show the effects of the various conditions that dwarfed them. Early attempts at identification left a confusing legacy of mixed-up Latin and variety names. Now, a botanist or knowledgeable amateur can, after a brief inspection, identify each by its genus and species and make an educated guess as to its cultivar name. The shape and arrangement of the leaves, and, if available, cones and seeds provide the botanical "finger-prints."

What is it about these miniature plants that exerts such fascination? Aside from smallness, collectors look for forms that differ from the norm for the species. Whereas a normal tree might be conical in form, a dwarf offspring might grow into a weeping shape, or globose, drum-shaped, creeping, or spreading. Collectors look as well for color variations or variegations: a yellow-foliaged plant from a green parent, a silvery-blue plant from a green parent, a green and white or green and gold variegation from a solid green species. They look for curiously contorted plants resulting from the genetic aberration called "fasciation" or flattening of stems and terminal growth, for thread-leaved foliage where flattened foliage would be normal, and for mimicry of other species in leaves or needles.

Not content with variations from the norm, some advanced dwarf conifer specialists experiment with topiary effects, grafting ball-like or weeping forms onto tall, single trunks to get tree forms, and splicing variegated foliage among solid-colored growth. They prune larger specimens to imaginative designs: spirals, poodle puffs, mushroom shapes, tall columns, Medusa-like branching, and pearls-on-a-string fantasies. They interplant their dwarf conifers with choice small deciduous trees and perennials. They want to do more than simply charm visitors with their collections; they want to overwhelm them with effects not seen since royal gardeners sought to please their lords and ladies.

In the landscape, dwarf conifers are often combined with young specimens of Japanese maples, alpine plants, dwarf perennial flowers, and small-leaved groundcovers. With more commercial nurseries offering a wider selection, home gardeners can choose superior dwarf conifers to replace overgrown or overused shrubs. These plants hold great potential as container-grown specimens for decks, patios, and terraces, where space is valuable and every plant must have year-round impact. Both the visual effects and the maintenance are enhanced by grouping dwarf plants together.

Part of the challenge of growing dwarf conifers is in keeping the surroundings and accessories in scale with the plants, to emphasize their beauty and not purely their oddness. Skillful collectors, like Ed Rezek of Long Island, New York, can work magic in creating miniature landscapes that display their plants to perfection.

*Ed created this spiral topiary form by clipping a* Chamaecyparis pisifera *'Squar-rosa Intermedia'.*

*E*d Rezek of Malverne, Long Island, typifies the new breed of dwarf conifer collectors. Enthusiasts such as Ed can't stop with simply collecting new specimens: their love for their specialty plants compels them to master the art of displaying dwarf conifers. And it is an art, the art of illusion. When the *Victory Garden* crew arrived at Ed Rezek's home, they couldn't resist rubbernecking around the front, side, and back yards. I think it is safe to say that, in the many years of the show's existence, we have never seen such an extraordinary garden!

On a tour of the garden, my eyes told me I was looking at very young evergreens, but Ed told me they were up to forty years old! Tiny ball-like *Chamaecyparis*, wee spruces growing like hand-high Christmas trees, and sculpted miniature topiaries made a bewitching sight.

Ed's yard is the centerpiece of the neighborhood, immaculately kept, rising up in tiers from street level. The back yard is short from front to back but, by designing a peninsula to jut out from the side and past the center of the yard, Ed manages to convey an anticipation of what lies beyond. A tastefully constructed waterfall and pool catch your eye as you round the tip of the peninsula. By stair-stepping deep beds of plants down from slow-growing deciduous trees in the back, to waist-high dwarf conifers in the center and, finally, to very short dwarf conifers in the front, he creates a harmonious and totally artistic effect. The illusion is one of looking at a much larger landscape compressed to miniature scale.

Ed Rezek could sell the plants in his back, front, and side yards for several thousand dollars. But he won't—not the whole collection, not even a single plant. Monetary return never has been a consideration in his hobby of growing dwarf conifers. Ed is not a wealthy man; comfortably situated, yes, but living on retirement income. His wife of more than forty years, Maureen, plans to work a year or two longer before retirement. She is an excellent typist and helps Ed with his many compilations and reports.

"The day I start expecting money or recognition for my dwarf conifers is the day I begin losing the fun of it," Ed says emphatically.

Ed is an agile, energetic man, yet infinitely patient. His is a class of plants that you have to get on your knees to appreciate fully, and that require a full measure of faith from the grower. You'll never hear a dwarf conifer grower boast, "You can almost see my plants grow!" These diminutive plants grow so slowly that, years after the passing of the hobbyist, most will still be wee, little things as compared to the original, standard-sized species. Ed is so advanced in his hobby that the tinier and more difficult the plant, the more he likes it. He showed me a couple of seedling plants that, although several months old, had grown into little knots of foliage no larger than a pea seed.

His production of dwarf conifers, choice variegated conifers, and deciduous trees and shrubs could rival that of a commercial nursery. He grows from seeds and cuttings. Hundreds of plants, started in his ten-by-twenty Everlite greenhouse in pots, fill every spare inch of space in his yard. Prior to joining the International Plant Propagators Society, he learned to root cuttings and germinate seeds of dwarf conifers by trial and error. Now, he has excellent success, using sterile rooting media, mist propagation, and bottom heat in his greenhouse.

Some of his benches hold propagating boxes, filled with perlite and watered with an overhead mist system. At the time of my visit, they were full of recently stuck cuttings, stripped of lower leaves, dipped in rooting hormone, and plunged deep into the rooting medium. Other benches were covered with trays filled with deep pots of potting soil. He uses these to put a compact root system on the cuttings rooted in perlite. His greenhouse space is so valuable that, after a few weeks, he moves the tray of potted plants to a lath-covered holding area wedged in between the garage and the greenhouse.

"You might think I'd want to move to a home with a larger lot to hold all the dwarf conifers and special grafted plants I produce," he said. "But no, my neighbors have helped to keep me here. They have let me help renovate their landscapes with choice evergreens and dwarf conifers that have overgrown my space. I bet I've placed a thousand plants in good homes!"

You can see what Ed means when you drive down his quiet side street. Several of his neighbors have the most distinctive landscapes you ever saw, each bearing Ed's signature—multiple colors or forms of the same species grafted on one plant, elaborately trimmed topiaries, imaginatively trained creeping or prostrate plants, and, more than anything else, dozens of dwarf conifers that would make a retail nurseryman's mouth water.

Ed says, "I got hooked on dwarf conifers shortly after I moved into this house. The guy that built it hauled off the topsoil and sold it: I had to have thirty truckloads hauled in to raise the level of the ground in my side yard and to build up raised beds to hide the high walls of the base-

*Ed's neighbors enjoy a garden landscaped with choice dwarf conifers. Some of these are more than twenty years old, yet are quite small.*

ment. I had the usual 'quick and dirty' landscaping done: I didn't have the money to buy choice plants. So, I ended up tearing it all out about two years later.

"What happened is that I met Joe Reis at the printshop where I worked as an electrotyper. Joe was a true pioneer in dwarf conifers: he ate and slept dwarf conifers. He found out that, while stationed with the Marines in Peking in 1945, I had seen the 'Forbidden City' and had vivid memories of its old and fantastically trained bonsais. Joe showed me how to prune and train dwarf conifers to start bonsais and gave me starter plants for a new landscape." (Ed paused a minute to show me two dwarf Alberta spruces from Joe's original gift: they are now ten feet tall. Then he had to explain to me that some dwarf conifers grow rather large after several years, yet not near as big as the standard species.)

Ed continued his story . . . "Joe Reis was a scrounger. He had to be. The nurseries on the Island didn't handle dwarf conifers, except maybe a few Alberta spruces and other semidwarf cultivars. We'd get the bums' rush when we asked too many questions or wanted the nurseryman to order special stuff for us. One nurseryman said to us, 'This is the stuff

I've got to sell. If you want it, buy it. If you don't, I've got other customers to wait on!'

"So, Joe and I began sniffing out the few collectors on the East Coast and swapping what we had for what they had. We visited the Arnold Arboretum in Boston and Longwood Gardens in Kennett Square, near Philadelphia. Those were exciting days, not only discovering fascinating new plant materials but finding other specialists who were just as crazy about dwarf conifers as we were. When I look back on the dwarf conifers we perceived as outstanding in those days, I have to admit that, today, they'd be rated as rather ordinary 'Old Standards.'

"Other collectors and I had what amounted to a 'dwarf conifer underground' out here on the Island because, with our mild climate, we could grow plant material that would succumb to weather stresses on the mainland. And most variegated conifers won't sunburn or fade here. By word of mouth, we found several other private and commercial growers near enough to us to get together every now and then. All were knowledgeable about dwarf conifers: what one didn't know, another did. We had a ball, exchanging plant material, going plant hunting and bringing back cuttings in Wardian cases like those Darwin took with him."

Ed mused, "Some of the collectors in those days were secretive about their sources. I expect it was because they wanted first crack at anything new their sources might come up with. Other collectors would not sell starts of their plants to a plant propagator, protecting, I assume, their potential for profit. Other collectors, and they were in the majority, shared freely.

"Personally," Ed continued, "I think it is foolish to have a dog-in-the-manger attitude about a plant which you alone have. You could lose it and it could never be duplicated. Whenever I grow or discover a plant that seems to have potential, I propagate it and give a plant or two either to the National Arboretum in Washington, D.C., to the Planting Fields here on Long Island, to the Arnold Arboretum in Boston, or to close friends who are collectors. Should something happen to my original plant, it is not lost, never again to be cultivated. When I share with other collectors or arboreta, I often get something in return that I may prize. It is a two-way street.

"I also send rooted cuttings or scions to friends who operate large wholesale nurseries in Oregon; they specialize in dwarf and unusual conifers. One has a color picture of my garden in their catalog, and another grows many of my developments for retail nurseries." Ed showed me an inventory list from the commercial propagator: an outstanding number of dwarf cultivar names were followed by an I.D. for the source . . . "Rezek."

"It has taken all these years for dwarf conifers to be available in local nurseries on the Island, and I know that only a few old standard dwarfs are available in even the best retail nurseries in other states, except on the West Coast. Dwarf conifers haven't quite 'arrived' in much of this country. But, they'll become well known, just as they have in Europe."

Often, dwarf conifer enthusiasts also grow unusual forms of conifers, not dwarf, but standard-sized shrubs and trees with novel color forms, weeping or creeping habit, unusual leaf or needle formations, attractive bark, or with the potential for shaping into topiary forms. Ed's garden includes multiple-graft trees in various colors or growth habits of the same species and "multigeneric" plants with two or three plants of different kinds twisted and bound together so the trunks would apparently (but not actually) fuse. There are trees with kinks in their trunks, shrubs espaliered up trellises, and hundreds of offspring of dwarf conifers which Ed shared with commercial nurserymen years ago.

Nurserymen in the area regard Ed as some sort of phenomenon because he knows so much about his subject. He knows where and how to look up information on plants and propagation. Early on, he was accepted into the International Plant Propagators Society and attends their meetings in North America and abroad. He was a founding member of the American Conifer Society, and has served on its board since its inception in 1980.

Wherever he travels, Ed watches for aberrations in plants. A trip into a nearby town can turn into a collecting expedition. He is very good at spotting anomalies: color mutations, witches' brooms for dwarfing, growth habit mutations, anything that sets a conifer off from the "type" or standard for the cultivar. He soon discards any plants that lack grace or beauty. However, a sugar maple, *Acer saccharum* 'Monumentale', which grows in his side yard, is more startling than graceful. It is thirty feet tall and twenty inches wide, like a telephone pole with leaves. Ed loves to tell visiting kids that it is "Jack's Beanstalk." They believe it; so do I!

I was curious about how Ed has discovered so many oddities in his small back yard. It has partly to do with the fact that he is working with genetically unstable plants, but more to do with his daily prowling of a relatively small garden: weeding, clipping, and thinning. Nothing escapes his notice and he is out there every day during the growing season.

Right before our eyes, he pointed out a silver-fringed branch on an all-green dwarf conifer, a tightly clustered witches' broom on a tiny juniper, and a ground-hugging seedling grown from seeds harvested from an upright conifer. Later, we discovered that such mutations are more prevalent in urban areas, perhaps due to air quality.

Some of Ed's most productive seed parents are old dwarf hinoki cypress growing around the neighborhood, many from his collection. He gathers and plants the seeds, and watches for variations from the norm. The seeds have grown into many useful and beautiful variations on the

*Two old specimens of* Cedrus Atlantic *'Glauca Pendula', weeping blue Atlantic cedar, are trained on supports around three sides of Ed's house. Posts hold the limber branches clear of the path.*

original . . . the not-so-beautiful-nor-useful were discarded. Apparently, these old hinokis have an involved genetic makeup, which accounts for the wide segregation in offspring from seeds. Ed doesn't do any hybridizing, but relies on genetic anomalies to get new material from seed propagation.

Now that Ed has virtually no room to grow new plants, he is concentrating on making his old plants look better. Out front, he trimmed and trained two old and overgrown bird's nest spruces, *Picea abies* 'Nidiformis', into flat-topped pom-poms. From the street you can see the character of the old and twisted stems with their attractive mature bark.

Ed is changing the top growth of some old but not particularly valuable plants by grafting on new scions from desirable cultivars within the same species. Not content with that, he is tying knots in whippy *Chamaecyparis* suckers, plaiting trunks into incredible forms, and training procumbent plants like Atlantic cedar thirty feet around the sides of his house, where the twigs hang like green icicles.

Now that Ed is so sure of what he can do with plants he seems to be playing with them to amuse himself, his family, and neighbors. But, whatever he conceives has to look graceful, not grotesque, or he will prune it off and start all over. Harkening back to the plants he saw at the Imperial Palace in Peking, Ed grows bonsai and sets the containers wherever there is a little space in his crowded garden. Come winter, he sinks the containers in the ground and the warmth keeps the tiny, artistically trained plants from freezing. He has some bonsai that could grace any collection, including one cork-bark pine with an exquisite line, and a forest of Norway spruce seedlings.

Ed freely admits that three things have helped him to succeed in his specialty of dwarf conifers: an understanding and supportive wife, a job with regular hours (he worked for twenty years as a postman in Valley Stream after leaving the printing industry), and growing up in a family that loved gardening. He credits his automatic watering system for helping preserve domestic harmony: he and Maureen never feel trapped by their garden. They just set the automatic timers on the sprinkling system and the mist emitters and ventilators in the greenhouse and take off!

Ed is a natural teacher, gifted with enthusiasm and quick, sure hands. He taught a neighbor, Regina Scimeca, to graft trees. She showed me her Japanese maple with twelve grafts on it, all taking! Such multigraft trees, after you get over the shock of seeing several foliage and color forms on one tree, can be beautiful. More important, they give gardeners with small yards a way to enjoy several kinds of trees in a small area.

Always teaching, Ed showed me how to wait until axillary buds show on Japanese maples before taking cuttings, and to trim off all the leaves from the scion (the piece to be grafted on the understock, which is the bottom, or rooted, part).

Quick as a wink, Ed stripped the scion, carved the ends into a long "vee" shape, cut a cleft into the bark of the understock, inserted the graft, and whipped it into place with a wide rubber band. "New growth should start in two to three weeks inside this protective baggie," he said; "it maintains high humidity around the graft."

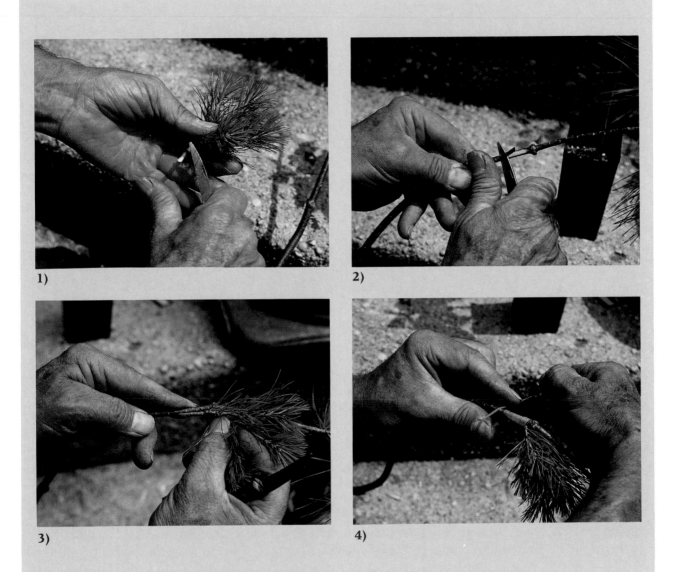

1)

2)

3)

4)

## Grafting Dwarf Conifers

Ed explains the process of grafting dwarf conifers. He begins by trimming the tip of a scion branch into a vee shape (1). He cuts a matching slit through the bark of the understock (2) and slips the scion into the slit so that cambium meets cambium (3). A good bond will start the sap flowing from the understock to the scion right away. Finally he wraps a wide rubber band snugly around the graft and ties it tight (4). To maintain high humidity around the graft, Ed slips a protective plastic bag over it. New growth will begin in two to three weeks.

*Some of the dwarf or compact conifers in front of Ed's home grew too large and dense for their settings. He gave the Chamaecyparis pisifera 'Compressa' a poodle cut and limbed up the golden Taxus cuspidata 'Aurescens' into an umbrella shape to let more light in his windows.*

Ed matches the diameter of the scion to the diameter of the understock when cleft grafting, so that the connective tissue (the cambium) matches up. A good cambium-to-cambium bond will start the sap flowing right away from the understock into the scion, so it won't wilt. He prefers to work with small-diameter branches, less than ¼ inch in diameter. On deciduous trees, he uses new-growth wood from near the tips of branches.

The top growth of a sapling tree can be entirely changed by grafting a desirable scion on the stem of a vigorous but common seedling of the same species. That's the quick way to convert a cheap garden-variety tree into a choice specimen. Ed calls these "high grafts" and often uses them to replace the top growth of common green Japanese maple, *Acer palmatum*, with scion wood from a more valuable crimson or cutleaf cultivar. The branches of choice Japanese maples descend from the main trunk to form a flattened, pagodalike canopy that looks very good in the company of dwarf conifers, and which becomes picturesque with age.

I asked Ed to recommend a starter collection of dwarf conifers and choice, compatible Japanese maples for gardeners just entering the hobby. His list includes many colors, forms, habits of growth that lead to distinctive shapes, and novel foliage characteristics. These cultivars lend themselves to an infinite number of landscape situations:

- *Abies balsamea* 'Nana': Dwarf, globose, dark green, with stomatic lines on undersides of needles.
- *Chamaecyparis obtusa* 'Gracilis Nana' (Japanese hinoki cypress): Pyramidal, medium to dark green, obtuse leaf shapes.

- *Chamaecyparis obtusa* 'Lutea Nana': Dwarf, broadly pyramidal, bright gold, cup-shaped leaves.
- *Chamaecyparis pisifera* 'Golden Mop': Dwarf, mound-forming, with bright gold, threadlike foliage.
- *Chamaecyparis thyoidies* 'Little Jamie': Dwarf, dense, columnar, rock garden plant, purple cast in winter.
- *Juniperus chinensis* 'Procumbens Nana': Low-growing, groundcover-type juniper, ideal for overhanging walls.
- *Juniperus communis* 'Berkshire': Very dwarf, broadly globose, dark green, blue-striated foliage.
- *Juniperus communis* 'Compressa': Very dwarf, spirelike cultivar. Excellent for use in small-space gardens.
- *Juniperus scopulorum* 'Table Top Blue': Silver-blue foliage grows like a table top.
- *Juniperus squamata* 'Blue Star': Dwarf, mounding, with star-shaped, steel blue foliage, a recent introduction from Holland.
- *Picea abies* 'Little Gem': Very dwarf, dense, bun-form plant; diminutive, excellent for the rock garden.
- *Picea pungens* 'Globosa Glauca Nana': Dwarf, globose, dense shrub, with good blue coloration.
- *Picea pungens* 'St. Mary's Broom': Diminutive, mounding blue spruce with conspicuous buds; a real "mini-gem."
- *Picea sitchensis* 'Papoose': Dwarf, compact, broadly conical bush; fine needles with blue striation beneath.
- *Pinus parviflora* ( Japanese black pine) 'Adcock's Dwarf': Diminutive, slow-growing, congested bun; a jewel for a rock garden or small area.
- *Pinus strobus* 'Nana': Dwarf, compact, spreading mound; long, soft, dense bluish-green needles.
- *Pinus sylvestris* 'Repens': Rich green, compact ground-hugger.
- *Tsuga canadensis* (hemlock) 'Cole's Prostrate': Dwarf, slowly creeping, well-branched mound; center wood is exposed; partial shade is best.

As taller companion plants for dwarf conifers, Ed suggests "high grafts" or four Japanese maple cultivars: 'Garnet', 'Crimson Queen', 'Ever-Red', and 'Filigree Lace'.

- *Acer palmatum* 'Garnet': Coarse, dissected, gem-red foliage on a broad, compact mound.
- *Acer palmatum* ( Japanese maple) Dissectum 'Crimson Queen': Mounding, cascading form; deep red, finely dissected foliage and branches.
- *Acer palmatum* Dissectum 'Ever-Red': Leaves emerge with fine silvery hairs; retains good red color in hot weather.
- *Acer palmatum* 'Red Filigree Lace': Fine, threadlike, deep red foliage: the finest cutleaf red in existence.

*A cork bark black pine*, Pinus thunbergiana *'Corticosa Nishiki', has been trained into bonsai form.*

As companion perennials to cover the soil between dwarf conifers, Ed suggests: the compact sedums and sempervivums; *Lamium* 'Beacon Silver', and dwarf *Thymus* (thyme) cultivars. These are smaller than the culinary thyme cultivars. Miniature hostas and dwarf iris such as *Iris verna* and *I. cristata* are quite appropriate for interplanting among dwarf conifers.

As annuals for color spots among the dwarf conifers, he uses (discreetly): tuberous-rooted begonias, New Guinea impatiens, and wax begonias. When they grow so large that they begin to look out of scale, Ed pulls them out and replants with younger plants of annuals.

In his rich topsoil, Ed never feeds his dwarf conifers. His object is neither to starve his plants to retard growth nor to stimulate them into growing rapidly. Rather, he wants them to grow slowly but steadily and retain good foliage color. He has applied a light mulch of pine bark for several years and feels that the nutrients released during its decomposition are sufficient to nourish the slow-growing evergreens. They certainly looked well fed to me!

Red spider mites are a major problem on conifers everywhere; they can be troublesome in hot, dry weather. Ed is planning to use insecticidal soap to increase the effectiveness of his spray program. He is watching with considerable alarm a serious pest on other parts of the Island, the Adelgid hemlock scale. These armor-plated insects are difficult to control, except at the crawling stage. Then, insecticides mixed with spreader-sticker agents will penetrate and kill them.

Slugs are a minor problem, mostly on the hostas Ed uses in shaded areas. Squirrels try, and sometimes succeed, in digging up his precious plants. Ed captures them in a humane trap and carts them off to a large park some distance away.

In Ed Rezek's garden, it is easy to see why dwarf conifers are the designer plants of tomorrow. Experts like Dr. Henry Marc Cathey of the National Arboretum predict that the new American landscape will be composed of smaller, slow-growing, choice plant material, sited with care for maximum impact. Anyone looking for a prototype garden will find it in Malverne, New York.

# More about Dwarf Conifers

Dwarf conifers have been selected from a number of genera. Most of these species are native to temperate climates and prefer rather moist soil conditions. With the growing interest in water conservation and xeriscaping, we may see more interest in selecting dwarfs from warm climates, plants which can tolerate dry soils:

*Abies* (fir)
*Cedrus* (true cedar)
*Cephalotaxus* (plum yew)
*Chamaecyparis* (false cypress)
*Cryptomeria* ( Japanese cedar)
*Juniperus* (southern red cedar)
*Picea* (spruce)

*Pinus* (pine)
*Podocarpus* (southern or Japanese yew)
*Pseudotsuga* (Douglas fir)
*Taxus* (yew)
*Thuja* (arborvitae)
*Tsuga* (hemlock)

Dwarf conifers can be grouped into three divisions by size:

● *Pigmy:* Only one-twentieth the size of normal plants of the species at maturity, the specimens can be quite expensive because they grow so slowly.

● *Dwarf:* One-twentieth to one-quarter the size of normal plants of the species at maturity, these are usually easier to grow than the pygmy types, because of their vigor.

● *Compact:* One-third to one-half the normal size of the species when mature, these should not be confused with young plants of standard-sized shrubs, trees, and groundcovers, which grow considerably faster and up to three times as large.

**Rate of Growth**    The rate of growth of dwarf conifers depends not only on the length and warmth of the growing season but also on precipitation, irrigation, exposure to wind, nutrition programs, and underlying soil. Hobby growers make their soil well drained, and keep it on the poor side, although well fortified with organic matter for water retention and biological activity. Maintaining an organic mulch by adding to it each year or two is standard practice in most dwarf conifer gardens.

Rate of growth can also depend on the interaction of the scion and the understock of dwarfs grafted on normal rootstocks. Grafting is the only practical way to increase certain desirable specimens that may be difficult to root as cuttings, or don't set seeds. Much trial and error has gone into matching scions to understocks that won't force them to grow overly large and that weld into strong unions.

**Buying Dwarf Conifers**    Accumulating a dwarf conifer collection is usually a long-term proposition because of the care needed in acquiring compatible specimens adapted to one's climate. You often see rock garden enthusiasts evolving into dwarf conifer enthusiasts as well, for they already have the site and a feeling for working with small plants.

Use caution when planting balled and burlapped plants. Most sources offer dwarf conifers as balled and burlapped plants or containerized specimens. Generally, the slower-growing the plant, the costlier, because of the time it has to spend in the nursery growing large enough to be sold. Rezek told me that plants can be grown in fields with soils that are too sandy to retain a good, solid root ball, or sold before a new network of roots has proliferated inside the burlap. If the nurseryman knocks these around with careless handling, or if you rush the planting, you can end up with a bare-root plant that may not survive. Ed always leaves the burlap in place, but unties and folds back the top after he has pulled the backfill soil up and around the root ball. He firms the backfill thoroughly to eliminate air pockets that could let roots dry out. I might add that you should avoid plants that are balled in woven plastic; you must completely remove this stuff. Roots won't grow through it.

*Ed uses a lath cover over plants in his holding area for winter protection and for summer shade.*

Prepare the soil for dwarf conifers by thoroughly mixing in a 2-inch layer of moistened peat moss or finely ground composted pine or fir bark to spade depth. If your soil is heavy clay, also mix in 2 inches of sand. This will raise the level of the dwarf conifer bed 3 to 4 inches above the surrounding soil for good drainage. Raised beds give no particular advantage on deep, sandy soils.

## Landscaping

Effective arrangements can be as simple as a small, uncomplicated combination of shape and colors for an intimate corner, a little colony of various shapes and colors among a cluster of large rocks, one or two in a stone trough interplanted with alpines, or on a gritty, gravelly, scree sloping down from a scattering of rocks that appear to have been deposited by a retreating glacier.

Group pygmy plants fairly closely: individual specimens tend to fade into the wallpaper. However, space dwarf and compact types far enough apart so that they do not become crowded with age. Leave generous spaces between groups of dwarf conifers and fill them with choice groundcovers and spring bulbs.

Between groups of dwarf conifers, establish mats of low-growing, nonaggressive groundcovers. You will have to hunt up suppliers of choice groundcovers to get cultivars to set off the color and texture of your dwarf conifers.

## Care

You can keep the interiors of large plants free of accumulations of dead needles by shaking them and, if you can reach the interior, raking and disposing of needles. A few dead needles do no harm, but a deep layer can be unsightly, can shed water, and can actually become a fire hazard around smokers.

Some authorities recommend that you syringe plants with a fine spray of water frequently during warm weather. But Ed Rezek cautions you not to do it on new growth, not until after it has hardened. Water on tender young needles or leaves, followed by hot sun, can cook them. Some of the dwarf hemlocks are particularly susceptible.

Sharp, fine sprays of water can discourage spider mites. One of the best ways to do this is to use a backpack sprayer with plain water or insecticidal soap. Maximum pressure will blast many of the red spiders off, if directed up toward the undersides of leaves. It is difficult to get a sufficiently fine spray with a water hose without so much pressure that needles or leaves are damaged.

## Propagation

Once you have developed the touch for siting and growing these fascinating plants, you may be inspired to try growing them from seeds, collecting them from abnormal growths such as witches' brooms, and propagating them by cuttings or grafting. Growing and propagating dwarf conifers from seeds or cuttings taken from growth anomalies is not really difficult, but it does require more attention and concentration than most other plant specialties.

You really need to see pygmy, dwarf, and compact conifers to appreciate their uniqueness and to get ideas on where and how to use them. Don't be overwhelmed by the complex plantings displayed at public gardens. Start with a small grouping of plants that please your sense of color and balance, and let your collection evolve from there. If you plan to grow your dwarf conifers in containers, select cultivars that are hardy in the next zone to the north to assure their overwintering reliably.

# *Peonies*

*With a good eye, a green thumb, and a little bit of luck, Wisconsin's Roger Anderson makes a breakthrough in peony breeding.*

*(Left) 'First Arrival' was Roger Anderson's first introduction from his efforts to cross tree peonies with herbaceous cultivars.*

**P**eonies are legendary for their opulent, often fragrant flowers in luminous shades, from pastels to deep reds and creamy whites. The vivid hues of the emerging spring growth and flower buds provide color impact long before the blossoms open. After bloom, the foliage is clean and glossy, a handsome foil for later-blooming perennials. Peonies deliver an end-of-season gift; seed pods on long stems can be dried for arrangements. Peonies are long-lived, too; a mature plant can eventually spread to four feet, a commanding spectacle in the perennial border.

The range of peony flower forms include *single*, with the flower's center composed of stamens and pistils, and a single, daisylike layer of ray petals; *semidouble*, with two or more layers of petals in open blossoms, and with the stamens and pistils clearly visible at the center; *double*, or *"fully double,"* nearly ball-like, with many layers of petals concealing the stamens and pistils; and "*Japanese type*," in which the single or semidouble blossoms have a distinctive crested, petaloid or staminoid "boss" in the center.

Most gardeners are familiar with herbaceous peonies, cultivars which freeze to the ground during the winter and regrow each spring from strong, deep rootstocks. All require a long winter dormancy and do not perform well south of zone 7B. Long-stemmed and fragrant, herbaceous peonies are one of the most desirable flowers for cutting. Though the double cultivars that look so spectacular in the garden can overpower arrangements, the single or crested anemone types combine well with other blooms. Early, midseason, or late-blooming cultivars provide an extended flowering season.

The relatively rare early-blooming herbaceous rock garden peonies, *Paeonia tenuifolia*, are very hardy. They average twelve to eighteen inches in height, with fernlike, deeply cut leaves. Some of the cultivars in this class have a blossom form not found in other classes, single with tufted centers.

More unusual are tree peonies, which actually resemble shrubs rather than trees and develop woody, persistent top growth reaching two to four feet or more in height. Their bloom period begins with the late herbaceous types, and extends two or three weeks thereafter. The flowers have distinctive frilled petals with dark "flares" at the base; in some cultivars, the petals are fringed with contrasting colors. In many parts of the United States, tree peonies are more difficult to grow than herbaceous types. The West Coast, Northwest, and protected East Coast sites provide the requisite mild winters and cool summers to produce the classic large, shrubby tree peony forms so coveted as landscape specimens. Where they can be grown, the dramatic size, fragrance, attractive foliage, and characteristic form of the blossoms rank tree peonies with rhododendrons and roses for sheer beauty.

A class recently expanded by breeders in the United States is one that crosses herbaceous peonies with tree peonies. These crosses resemble either true herbaceous or tree peonies, depending on the percentage of traits inherited from a particular parent. Their bloom period corresponds to that of tree peonies.

As a genus, the peonies number about thirty species, some of which are no longer found in the wild. Of these, six or eight have been extensively improved for garden use or incorporated into hybrids. Originally, peonies were brought to Europe from the Caucasus in the sixteenth century, and a different group of species from China and Siberia in the eighteenth century. The first mention of peonies in the United States was a listing of five varieties in M'Mahon's catalog in 1806.

American peony breeding was inspired by the progress made in Europe, notably by Lemoine in France, and by the English nurseryman James Kelway. Lemoine succeeded in crossing the Chinese peony with *P. Witt-*

*manniana*. The Chinese peony, *P. lactiflora*, is the ancestor of most herbaceous peonies and has long been cultivated in the Orient. Lemoine broke with the long-standing infatuation of European breeders with the indigenous *P. officinalis*. Lemoine's crosses became known as "European Hybrids." Kelway focused on selecting from the Chinese peony.

During the prosperous years of westward expansion following the War Between the States, keen American gardeners discovered how well the hardy herbaceous peonies grew in our northern climates. European travel grew, and gadabout gardeners saw and ordered the latest European peony hybrids. Interest peaked in the days of Queen Victoria, when spacious homes and yards provided room to grow large perennials and abundant domestic help freed genteel ladies to exercise their talents in making florid arrangements for their homes and churches.

By 1903, interest in peonies was very high, and the first annual meeting of the American Peony Society commissioned Professor John Craig of Cornell University to plant and observe and standardize the many named varieties of peonies for sale in the United States and Europe. In addition, the Society had Craig rate peonies on a scale of 1 to 10 and recommended that the trade drop all varieties scoring less than 7.5.

During the 1930s, the foremost pioneer American breeder of peonies, Dr. A. P. Saunders of New York State, succeeded in crossing several species and made many desirable selections from the progeny. He also refined certain species imported directly from their native countries. Today, more than half a century later, eight of his herbaceous peonies, twenty-three of his tree peonies, and two of his rock garden cultivars are still being offered.

Between the two world wars peonies suffered a lag in popularity. In part this was due to certain limitations of the plants themselves. The blossoms of some of the older varieties are so large that they fill with water and tip face down during spring rains. The mature plants of some cultivars are simply too large for compact modern gardens, a far cry from Victorian times when tall peonies with blossoms as large as cabbages were in scale with homes. Moreover, the palette of traditional peony colors—shades of rose, magenta, lavender, and dark reds—has been subject to the whims of fashion trends.

Sluggishness among commercial producers contributed to public indifference. For various reasons, many commercial peony growers' offerings failed to keep pace with changing tastes. As their huge inventories of old favorites waned in popularity, these growers were slow to replace them with improved varieties, which tended to circulate within a small group of amateur breeders. Increasing stocks of new peony varieties is slow and expensive; it can be five years or longer between the evaluation of a deserving new hybrid and the production of an inventory sufficient for introduction. Good peony varieties are not cheap. Older varieties average ten to twenty-five dollars apiece, but new introductions, especially those which have received an award from the American Peony Society, can bring two hundred fifty dollars or more.

Even the way in which peonies are sold has held back their progress. Producers ship herbaceous peonies mostly in the late summer and fall, the traditional planting time. Yet, spring is the time when the mass of gardeners wish to buy plants. The peony plants offered for sale in the spring are mostly dormant root divisions, usually boxed in illustrated waxed-paper cartons and kept moist with shavings. If these are not sold within a few weeks, the warmth of the display area will wake them up and sprouting will commence. It is most difficult to transplant a sprouted peony root, with 3 or 4 inches of succulent growth, without its suffering considerable shock.

Several developments have pulled peonies out of their sales slump. Most important, devoted amateur breeders have risen to the challenge to improve the genus; their greatly improved cultivars and hybrids are becoming more widely available. The leading commercial growers of peony plants are now quick to react when an amateur hybridist develops a promising new seedling, by arranging for marketing rights. Some are also funding research and breeding programs of their own. Propagation by tissue culture promises to speed up the initial increase of these new varieties, and nurseries are beginning to grow and sell improved peonies in containers to make planting possible at any time during the growing season.

Yet, hobby peony breeders outnumber the professional plant breeders and, in the foreseeable future, will be having the greatest impact on improving the genus. One successful amateur breeder, Roger Anderson, feels there is plenty of room for more hobby breeders. His story will show you one way to get started in this fulfilling hobby.

*Roger stands before the impressive array of his peony evaluation trials.*

*E*ach spring, the spacious, sloping front lawn of a farm home near Fort Atkinson, Wisconsin, undergoes a transformation. During the winter, little can be seen except long rows of tilled soil crossing the lawn on contour, and the glint of sun reflecting from plant tags. Then, with the melting of snow and warming of soil, strong spears, like bronzy-green asparagus, begin pushing up through the mulch. By late May, cars will be stopping on the farm-to-market road in front of the house to admire the rows and rows of flowers, breathtaking in their color. Roger and Sandra Anderson's peonies are doing their thing again, all twelve hundred plants, tall and short, single and double flowered, ruby-red or green leaved, moving with the slightest breeze, and, later, perfuming the air and exciting the senses.

The star of the peony show is a hybrid produced by Roger, a cross between an herbaceous cultivar and a hybrid with a tree peony as one of its parents. He named his hybrid 'Bartzella'. The plants are semiherbaceous in response to winter, yet the large, citrus-scented blossoms are like tree peonies, a lovely lemon yellow and fully double, with frilly-edged petals. Individual established plants of 'Bartzella' have produced more than sixty blooms each, up to six inches in diameter. The foliage resembles, at first glance, that of an herbaceous peony. A closer look reveals similarities with tree peony foliage. A cross between two species is difficult and unpredictable; that an amateur was able to accomplish it speaks well of Roger's self-taught skills.

The dense, compact plants of 'Bartzella' grow to a height of twenty-four to thirty inches and the sturdy stems won't gooseneck when weighted by rain. The petals have more substance than tree peonies. Plants have survived temperatures of 30 degrees below zero F. They froze back to about three inches above the ground but regrew strongly.

Roger didn't become a peony enthusiast and hybridizer overnight. His was a long and involved hegira, filled with summer romances with other plants, specialties which he explored then set aside to move onward. His journey began at Whitewater, Wisconsin, his boyhood home. All his people farmed, raised purebred Holstein cattle, and grew vegetable and berry crops to feed their families and to sell. His pragmatic father liked to kid

Roger about his fondness for flowers. His favorite line was, "When are they going to be ready to eat?"

It was Roger's grandfather who encouraged his involvement in flowers. Noticing the sturdily built toddler sniffing the gladiolus he raised for cutting, his grandfather nicknamed Roger "Ferdinand" after the famous bull in a children's story. Roger can still remember helping his grandfather harvest long gladiolus stems and seeing, around his yard, plants of old 'Festiva Maxima' peony.

After high school, Roger served a hitch in the military, then returned to truck gardening for several years, to supplement income from an eight-to-five job. They were good but hard years, with Roger and Sandra growing and selling many kinds of vegetables, fruits, and flowers for extra income. His interest in flowers led Roger to Bill Himmler, a local amateur plant breeder, who taught him how to hybridize gladiolus and grow them from seeds. Under Bill's tutelage, Roger learned how to evaluate new breeding lines critically. After taking a long, hard look at the limited market for new and improved gladiolus hybrids and the numerous breeders competing for the business, Roger went into other hobbies. He bred and sold black Labrador dogs, Golden-laced Wyandotte poultry, and Roller pigeons. A dog lover myself, I asked Roger why he moved from dogs to flowers. He answered "Well, I made money breeding Labs, but they tended to wander. I always knew where the flowers were at night!"

Along the way, Roger and Sandra were raising a family of four and making plans for their present hilltop home on ten acres just south of Fort Atkinson. To meet the needs of his growing family, Roger went to work as a purchasing agent for a local meat packing plant and, later, as a machinist . . . his present occupation. He still takes contracts for house painting. "Lets me make money to support my hobby," he says with a smile. (I know what he means.)

About fifteen years ago, Roger was introduced to peonies by his friend Carroll Spangler, who showed him photos of one of the first Itoh hybrid peonies from Japan. It was love at first sight! Roger scraped up forty dollars and sent to Gilbert H. Wild's nursery for plants to use for seed production. Roger told me that at the time, the forty dollars was his life's savings and he really felt guilty about spending the money on flowers. I'm sure that a lot of older gardeners who grew up during the Great Depression can relate to that feeling.

Roger had to wait several years for his small Itoh hybrid plants to produce flowers. They made such an impression that he has purchased more peony cultivars every succeeding year. His collection grew, and provided a large and diverse gene pool among his twelve hundred plants. As he mastered his specialty, Roger refined his objectives in peony breeding, foremost of which was the introduction of the yellow color into hardy herbaceous peonies. The way he got the female parent for the cross that produced his first breakthrough was serendipity itself.

One day, when Roger was visiting Carroll Spangler, he noticed a chance seedling peony in bloom. It was a plant Carroll had found years earlier, growing in an asparagus patch, apparently from a seed dropped there. Carroll took pity on the little plant and moved it to a peony bed where, at first, it produced double blooms. Thereafter, it always produced single blooms.

Roger looked beyond the rather homely single blossoms and saw possibilities for the plant as a parent in hybrids. It was vigorous, produced an abundance of pollen, and set loads of large, fat seed pods. Carroll saw no value in the blossoms for shows and was about to discard the plant when Roger intervened and asked to move it to his garden. He divided the crown of that vigorous seedling into three sections. Strangely, while one grew into a single flowered plant, two produced double pink flowers! Roger used the single-flowered plant not only as a female parent in crosses but also as a pollen donor. Roger has been very thorough about early removal of all anthers on female parents, and is positive that the resulting seeds from crosses with tree peonies have produced true hybrids and not "selfs."

Roger is not the first hybridizer to cross herbaceous and tree peonies. About forty years ago a Japanese (they are mad about tree peonies) named T. Itoh succeeded in crossing the herbaceous peony 'Kakodin' and a hybrid out of *P. lutea*, named 'Alice Harding'. Out of twelve hundred crosses he got nine plants: the offspring of four of these made it to the United States where they became known as the Itoh hybrids. As yet, they are curiosities to most gardeners except peony fanciers.

The Itoh hybrids are proving more valuable to gardeners than either of their parents, and should continue to attract interest for years to come. They are quite winter hardy, and resistant to wind and rain damage. To date, no problems with diseases have been noted. With their ease of growth and low maintenance requirements, they should be a landscaper's dream. Early in the season the bushes take on a symmetrical globe shape, which holds until late in the fall. The plants color up nicely after a light frost.

Actually, Mr. Itoh was only one of a line of peony breeders who sensed the commercial possibilities of transferring the yellow color of *P. lutea* to other peony species. The French breeder Lemoine and, later, A. P. Saunders crossed the Japanese tree peony with *P. lutea* to produce what became known as the Lutea hybrids.

Roger Anderson saw the Itoh hybrids as a means to an end. He felt that he could transfer their yellow, golden, and softer colors to herbaceous peonies, *P. lactiflora*, and retain the best qualities of the three contributing species. It took a few years, but he did it! A few other American

*'Cora Louise',
which Roger
named for his
grandmother,
was his second
tree x herbaceous
peony hybrid.*

hybridizers have succeeded with similar crosses: two named cultivars have come out of their efforts.

Rather than clutter the nomenclature, the American Peony Society has decided to list all Roger Anderson's cultivars and genetically comparable strains from other breeders with the Itoh hybrids. Roger commented, "I should have enough of my hybrids increased to begin selling small quantities on a first-come, first-served basis in 1992. Prices will be rather high, due to the limited number of plants available." Roger and Sandra have named their budding commercial peony plant enterprise "Callie's Beaux Jardin." Says Roger, "Out here in Holstein country that French name

*These two un-named seedling tree x herbaceous peony hybrids are under evaluation. Hybrid 81-08, left, and 81-18 are from crosses Roger made in 1981.*

ought to be an attention-getter!" Visitors are welcome at Callie's Beaux Jardin during bloom season, by advance arrangement.

As we talked peonies, it began to emerge how Roger and Sandra have accomplished so much, with both working full-time jobs. An energetic and physically powerful man, with shoulders an ax handle wide, Roger has worked his way through several hobby plants and up through the ranks to the inner circle of peony breeders. (He would modestly decline the latter distinction, but I feel he deserves it.) Roger is a study in goal-oriented self-discipline.

His wife, Sandra, would like to see the day arrive when Roger will feel comfortable leaning on a hoe handle and admiring the fruits of their labors, rather than working harder every year. Much of her spare time has been spent in the garden with Roger, planting, weeding, labeling, and assisting him in evaluating experimental hybrids. "There are many days," Roger said, "when Sandra spends more time in the yard than I do, patrolling the peony beds, pulling and spraying weeds." But now, with an empty nest, Sandra is going back to school to get her degree in nursing, which has sent Roger scurrying to find herbicides to reduce the weeding problem.

Roger is a likable man but very serious about his work with peonies . . . so serious that he doesn't realize that he can now let up and take the time to extract more joy from every minute of his hobby. I think he realizes that he may be quite close to making his mark in the peony world and doesn't want to risk letting the opportunity slip from his grasp.

Sandra and Roger work together to grow peony seedlings from his precious hybrid seeds. After putting so much work and so many hopes into producing a few hybrid seeds, Roger wants as many as possible to grow and produce plants. Peony seeds germinate slowly, over a period of several months, and should be planted within two months after the pod turns color and before the seed coat dries hard.

Roger and Sandra pick off individual seed pods just before they become fully mature, shell out and label the seeds. He puts the fresh seeds in a plastic bag of moist sphagnum moss, in a warm corner near the furnace. This treatment produces roots on the viable seeds, but no shoots for a while.

As the roots show, Roger places the seeds in a refrigerator for two to three months, or until a growing point emerges. This satisfies their dormancy requirement. Then the seeds are potted in individual pots. When the shoot breaks through the surface of the soil, he sets the pots under fluorescent lights to hasten growth and development.

Their light fixtures can accommodate only about one hundred seedlings, so the Andersons hold back the remainder by sowing the seeds in boxes of growing medium made by mixing sphagnum peat moss with potting soil. In midwinter, they move the boxes to an unheated but sunny garage. Little happens until spring, when the seeds resume growing. By that time, Roger will have moved the indoor-grown plants to the outside to harden off, making room under the lights for additional seedlings. Seeds that germinate even later are potted up and grown outdoors.

The Andersons have almost an ideal situation for growing and evaluating peonies. Their house sits on a high hill, with their two-acre front lawn sloping down to a country highway. The land was once a dairy farm and the only trees are close to the house. The display beds, two to three hundred feet in length, run across the slope to minimize erosion.

The plants are in bloom from mid-May through late June, and attract visitors from all over the Midwest. When I phoned Roger during a dry September to check on how his plants were surviving, he told me, "Hey, don't worry, once peonies are well rooted, they are very drought resistant. And, Jim, I wish you could have been here in late August. My line of Itoh hybrids bloomed again, that late in the season! It was weird seeing peonies repeat!" he said. "I've never seen anything like it before . . . maybe the dry soil set up the situation."

The Andersons have very few problems with their peonies. Their rich, black soil seldom needs fertilizer or lime, and the carpenter bees which tunnel into peony stems elsewhere haven't yet reached Wisconsin. They spray occasionally during damp spring weather to control botrytis and other blights, with either captan or Bordeaux mixture, made by dissolving copper sulphate and hydrated lime in water: about a quarter pound of each in three gallons of water.

1)

2)

3)

4)

5)

6)

## Hybridizing Peonies

Roger demonstrates his procedure for hybridizing peonies. He begins by removing the petals from the bud of the female parent's unopened flower (1). Then he emasculates the female parent by removing the anthers (2). With his finger, he dabs pollen on the receptive stigma (3). Good record-keeping is essential. Colored tape records the details of the cross for posterity (4). Covering with a paper envelope prevents contamination by pollen from other blossoms, carried by bees and other insects (5). Individual blossoms of the female parent peony, 'Martha W.', have been crossed with various pollen parents (6). Roger harvests the individual seed pods just before they are fully mature. The seeds are shelled out and labeled. Peonies germinate slowly, and the Andersons are careful to plant their precious hybrid seeds within two months after the pod turns color, before the seed coat dries hard.

Even though the peony beds are fully open to cold, drying winter winds, the Andersons never lose peonies to freezing. In severe winters, tree peonies freeze back nearly to the ground, but send up new wood from underground buds. These produce large, late blooms.

Roger feels that the good survival is due mostly to good drainage combined with very deep topsoil. He could use Snow Cones to protect flower buds, but doesn't because they would interfere with his getting a true measure of winter hardiness.

We talked for some time about why peonies had not taken off in demand like daylilies and hosta. Considering their beauty, adaptability, longevity, and freedom from problems, they should be ranked with the leaders. "Four things are holding them back," he said: "the slowness of propagation, unpredictable performance from the one-year-old grafted plants sold at retail stores, lack of promotion, and, more than anything else, lack of advanced, committed hobbyist hybridizers. I feel we are on the verge of breakthroughs in peonies that should make them the new frontier in perennial plants!

"We badly need to learn how to increase valuable new hybrids by tissue culture and to accelerate production. To my knowledge no one has succeeded at tissue-culturing peonies in quantities. Vegetative propagation is so slow that desirable new hybrids remain expensive for several years, and are known only to the fanciers who are accustomed to paying fifty to two hundred fifty dollars for a single plant. The cost of patenting a new peony is high; therefore, most new ones go unprotected. The breeder is lucky to recover his development costs.

"This situation produces no funds for promotion of peonies. Consequently, the growth of interest in peonies has been the result of one-on-one missionary work by the enthusiastic members of the American Peony Society, plus the exposure in a few national and regional mail-order catalogs.

"I think the situation is about to change," he continued. "Many other hobbyists such as myself have invested substantially in peonies. To date, it has been a labor of love for me, but my investment in plants is approaching ten thousand dollars. Some of us, myself included, will want to convert our hobby into retirement income and will go commercial.

"One promotion that is attracting attention from other gardeners are the flower shows put on by the American Peony Society. When we get together for annual meetings at various midwestern and Canadian cities, we hold shows in shopping malls, botanical gardens, and the like. We have a number of hobby growers of peonies in southern Wisconsin and hosted the 1989 annual meeting of the American Peony Society at Janesville."

I asked Roger what he had up his sleeve to follow his beautiful 'Bartzella'. "In 1988," he said, "I got my first look at a new batch of hybrids

*Roger's prize tree x **herbaceous peony hybrid, 'Bartzella', testifies to Roger's skill as a breeder. Large, citrus-scented blossoms, as many as sixty on an established plant, adorn the sturdy stems of this semiherbaceous peony.***

between herbaceous and tree peonies. Two of them looked mighty good . . . doubles, with yellow blossoms, tinged coppery gold. They'll be increased, and evaluated elsewhere as well as in Wisconsin.

"Also," he said, "I'm trying to introduce the orange color into herbaceous peonies. I now have seven plants produced by crossing pollen from *P. lactiflora* (herbaceous) onto an orangeish Lutea hybrid tree peony. They are young now but should bloom in two years. I think I have something good, but time will tell. David Reath, over in Vulcan, Michigan, is on a similar breeding track.

"I continue to try crossing the various species to increase my peony gene pool. Sometimes it works, sometimes not. I tried *P. delavayi* but none of my crosses took. However, I did have success with using *P. Potanini* in a cross: it is a tall, shrublike peony with small yellow flowers.

One cross took: the female parent was *P. lactiflora*. The resulting hybrid was a fooler: the first-year plant produced small, dark pink, incomplete flowers. But, on the second year, it grew into a very nice plant, covered with bright red flowers. It could be the start of a new breeding line.

"And, I'm shooting for a true dwarf peony that can be containerized in an eight-inch pot and sold fully grown at four years of age. To get it, I'm using a double-flowered mutation from the fern-leaved rock garden peony *P. tenuifolia* and a dwarf *P. lobata* seedling which grows to a height of only seven to eleven inches. That's a tall order, and I probably won't succeed without several hundred experimental crosses. I won't quit until I get a dwarf with blossoms as large as teacups, even though I may have to wait from four to ten years to see the first flower on a hybrid seedling." (Note, some authorities question the existence of a distinct *P. lobata* species, but Roger and other peony hybridists will use the name to identify a generally recognized breeding line until the taxonomists agree on what it really is.)

"You can find dwarf herbaceous peonies listed now. They grow no higher than eleven to twelve inches and have blossoms about two inches across. But I want to improve on them."

As "starter" varieties for beginners, Roger recommends:

- 'Msr. Jules Elie': A double pink with good plant habit; very fragrant.
- 'Lord Calvin': Double, creamy white, accented with red candy stripes; fragrant.
- 'Wilford Johnson': Large, fragrant, dark pink.
- 'Karl Rosenfield': Double red.
- 'Paul M. Wild': Large, dark pink double; great for shows.
- 'Norma Volz': Large double, blush pink.
- 'Virginia Dare': Arrangers like it for its small white single blossoms.
- 'America': Dark crimson-red single hybrid.
- 'Sparkling Star': Pink single; looks good in flower shows.
- 'Sky Pilot': Pink, tall plants, up to 34 inches when well grown.
- 'Paula Faye': Semidouble, glowing pink; outstanding garden performer.
- 'Cytherea': Coral, cup-shaped.
- 'Eastern Star': White double.
- 'Shawnee Chief': For its red fall foliage color.

In addition, any of the 'Estate' cultivars, developed and introduced by the Klehm family, would be good prospects.

Looking forward to his retirement in a few years, Roger has already started hybridizing other garden plants, such as bearded iris, daylilies, and flowering crab apples. And, he has begun an ambitious program for renewing the landscaping around his house with choice trees and shrubs. Roger has completed putting in a water garden and will landscape it with peonies and amenable perennials.

I aked Roger what makes him so fond of hybridizing. "I guess I can't leave well enough alone," he said. "I love trying to do what no one has done before, or doing it better." You can't beat that for an attitude!

# More about Peonies

I plant peonies partly because I remember the plants in my mother's garden in Memphis and in the cemeteries we visited on Confederate Memorial Day, and on Decoration Day. That's what we called the Memorial Day that everyone celebrates. The connection between peonies and Memorial Day is universal: before the days of plastic containers and plastic flowers, people used to cut armloads of peonies and stick them in half-gallon fruit jars of water to decorate the graves of their war dead.

One of our old family varieties, I believe, was 'Festiva Maxima', a fragrant white peony with crimson flecks. It was introduced in 1851!

People everywhere respond to the powerful nostalgic pull of peonies, to their bountiful beauty, their fragrance and long life as a cut flower. But some gardeners have given up after a brief fling with peonies because they don't understand that how you grow them depends largely on your climate.

Herbaceous peonies require a winter dormancy to rebuild the food reserves necessary to renew plants year after year. Therefore, they will not live for more than a year or two in mild-winter areas. There is no sharp line of demarcation, but the area where herbaceous peonies are difficult to grow corresponds roughly with hardiness zones 8 and 9. It starts at about Virginia Beach, North Carolina, and takes in the low country of the Carolinas and Georgia, including all of Florida, a strip about two hundred miles wide around the Gulf Coast, and all low-elevation areas in Arizona and California. Surprisingly, however, herbaceous peonies can survive for years in certain parts of northern California, perhaps because the summer dryness forces the plants into a pseudo-dormancy.

*Planting*

I asked Roger Anderson what advice he could give to beginners on growing peonies. "If possible," Roger said, "plant herbaceous peonies in the fall. If you have to start in the spring or summer, buy potted plants that can be set in the garden with minimum disturbance to the roots. Good-sized potted plants, when planted in early spring, will probably bloom the first year.

"The more advanced nurseries grow and ship tree peonies in containers from early spring through fall. The plants can be set in place in the garden at any time during the growing season but spring or fall planting, when it is cool and rainy, creates less stress on the plants.

"Peonies like loose, airy soil, with plenty of organic matter such as peat moss, rotted leaves, or pasteurized manure worked into the soil before planting, because the peonies are going to be there a long time," Roger said. "I don't like to use sawdust as a soil conditioner or mulch because it continues to cause nitrogen deficiencies in the soil.

"Planting depth is critical to the success of peonies. When planting herbaceous peonies in the northern states, locate the 'eyes,' which are the buds that produce the shoots for the coming year. Look for the tallest ones. These should not be positioned more than two inches below the surface of the surrounding soil, and preferably a bit less. If you plant the crowns deeper, chances are the plants will not bloom. Conversely, if you position the eyes level with the surface of the soil, they could freeze or dry out during a severe winter.

"However, in the South and West where winter temperatures don't drop much below 20 degrees F., plant herbaceous peony crowns so that the eyes are about level with the surface of the soil or slightly above. The shallower planting exposes the eyes to colder temperatures and helps to satisfy the requirement for winter dormancy. "Fall is the best planting time for herbaceous peonies because strong plants may bloom the following spring. However, many herbaceous peonies are sold bare-root in early spring for planting as soon as the soil can be worked. They may produce only vegetative growth the first season.

"I plant tree peonies deeper than herbaceous hybrids, and position the 'union' (where the rootstock joins the scion) 5 to 6 inches below the ground level. Where rainfall is heavy and soils are tight clay, be sure to raise the beds for tree peonies and modify the soil with organic matter.

"Plant bare-root tree peonies in the fall, between September and the end of November, or until the soil freezes. You can plant containerized tree peonies from early spring through fall. Here in Wisconsin the dates are April through November. I mulch fall-planted peonies to keep them from heaving out of the ground due to freezing and thawing.

"With herbaceous or tree peonies, the depth of planting is the same for both bare-root and containerized plants. You can't always go by the depth of the soil in the container. The sure way is to gently feel your way in from the side and brush away enough soil to see the eyes. Once you know where they are, you can position the new plant at just the right level.

"When planting any new peony, don't let the roots dry out while digging the hole, and settle it in with plenty of water. If there is no rain, give it water two or three times weekly. Spring-planted crowns will need watering several times during the first season, but fall-planted peonies develop a strong root system during early spring months to support the plants from then on.

## Mulching and Fertilizing

"I use little or no fertilizer when planting because, for two or three weeks after planting, the roots can't take up fertilizer," Roger said. "The fleshy roots are busy sending out a new network of fibrous feeder roots to absorb water. At this stage they are very sensitive to excesses of fertilizer. In my rich soil, I work in a handful or two of bonemeal around each plant, about two weeks after blooming, or in the fall. On less fertile soil, I would recommend a standard commercial fertilizer of a low-nitrogen analysis, drilled in a circle around the dripline of the plant in the early spring, per manufacturer's directions. It has been my experience that feeding late in the spring, when plants are making new growth, can disturb flowering, and should be avoided.

"Wisconsin winters are severe, so I mulch new plants to prevent the soil around them from heaving due to freezing and thawing. Heaving can uproot plants and expose the roots to drying. Composted chipped wood from tree trimmings is good for mulching: it won't blow away like straw or settle into a dense layer like leaves. Piling the fresh-chipped tree trimmings with a little nitrogen and occasional sprinkling will start the decomposition process and prevent nitrogen drawdown. The pile should be started in the spring or summer and turned once or twice to prevent fermentation due to lack of oxygen.

"If you live where winters are severe, pull two or three inches of mulch right over the crowns after the ground starts to freeze and mice have found a home elsewhere. Remove the mulch in the spring when the worst of the cold weather is past but before sprouts show. If you forget and fail to pull the mulch away from the tops of crowns, the plants could suffer from excessive moisture and perhaps contract diseases. I like to use pine boughs for mulching; they stay put and are easy to remove. But, I don't always have them available.

## Pests and Diseases

Roger told me: "In the North, the major pests of tree peonies are carpenter bees, deer, and rodents. I protect against deer, rabbits, and mice by surrounding plants with fine mesh wire. Carpenter bees are not as easy to control. They enter peony plants through the scar left from cutting stems, and the young burrow down to the roots, killing the plant. You can prevent their entry by sealing cut places with soft wax or tape.

"Ants are often perceived as pests of peonies, when actually they do no harm. I can recall telling this to an older lady who, while an excellent gardener, was convinced that ants had to be on peony flower buds before they would open. Perhaps I was a bit less than tactful in telling her that it was 'nonsense and an old wives' tale,' because she took it personally and gave me a severe tongue-lashing.

"Maybe someone can suggest how to convince people that the ants aren't eating the peonies. If they'd just take a good look, they would see that the ants are merely tending aphids like we tend milk cows. They want the sticky honeydew the aphids excrete, or the droplets of sweet sap on the flower buds.

## Care

"Peonies prefer full sun, except in the middle South and the West. My peony-growing friends there tell me that afternoon shade on peonies lessens the stress from intense heat and dryness. Also, tree peony blossoms hold up longer when they are protected from hot afternoon sun.

"There is little need to 'deadhead' spent blossoms except for cosmetic purposes," Roger continued. "I've seen plants grow to a great age with no one removing spent blooms. Flower arrangers would be happy to take all your long-stemmed seed pods. The pods split open when dry and are great for winter arrangements. However, you do need to remove the top growth from herbaceous peonies when it freezes back in the fall, to lessen problems with foliage diseases. The frost-killed tops twist off easily. Leave the tops on tree peonies or Itoh hybrids. After the new growth has started, you can trim the tops to about three-quarters of an inch above the topmost bud on each shoot, to tidy up the plants.

"Notice that I haven't talked about dividing peonies? You shouldn't do it unless a clump needs to be moved. New divisions can take two or three years to hit their stride. I've seen fifty-year-old clumps that have never been divided, still blooming vigorously."

**Regional Differences**

Let me add that peony culture in the South differs slightly from northern practices. Growing up in climatic zones 6 and 7, I saw my parents apply rotted manure two to three inches deep as a mulch on herbaceous peony beds after the tops had frozen. They were careful not to cover the crowns with it. The mulch seemed to slow the emergence of spring shoots by a week or so, just enough to keep the buds from being frozen during late cold snaps. Every two or three years they would apply a top-dressing of lime before mulching with manure, to keep the soil from becoming too acid.

Like Roger Anderson, we had few insect and disease problems with peonies. However, this was before Japanese beetles began invading the upper South. Unfortunately, the late-blooming peonies can still be in flower when the first of the Japanese beetles arrive. Now, we hang beetle traps 100 yards upwind from our peony and rose plants to trap as many as possible on the wing. We also patrol the garden mornings and evenings during the worst of the beetle season to handpick the critters. We drop them into a can of kerosene. Thankfully, the beetle season lasts only a month or so where we live.

Unlike Roger Anderson's rich, deep, black soil, southern soils are generally poor. To grow good peonies, you need to fortify the soil with organic matter to improve nutrient holding capacity and drainage. We feed peonies with a balanced garden fertilizer once, in late summer. Our soils are so low in nitrogen that a low-nitrogen fertilizer can't supply enough nitrogen to meet the needs of peonies. Deep, fast-draining, sandy soils have little capacity for nutrient storage and call for an additional feeding right after blooming is completed. We mulch peonies as Roger does, using compost or hardwood bark mulch.

If you like the idea of growing peonies and want to start out right, the catalogs of peony specialists would be a good place to get a feel for the cultivars, their classes, sizes, colors, advantages, and limitations. In surveying the catalogs, you may be attracted to the old standbys because of their modest price. Let me recommend that you consider buying fewer, but better, cultivars. The newer introductions are so dramatically improved, and peony plants last so long, that the additional cost for modern cultivars is an investment which will repay you many times over.

# *Wildflowers*

*It took thirty years of study and work, but now Weesie Smith's woods teem with choice southeastern native plants.*

*(Left) A trail mulched with wood chips leads from the forest and up stone steps to the Smith home.*

Great expanses of wildflowers in full bloom can knock your socks off with their vivid colors, movement in the wind, and the extra added attractions of butterflies, skippers, moths, and other colorful insects. These native or domestic stands of plantings are what "hook" many gardeners on wildflowers. But what keeps them involved has to do with the need to live closer to nature: if you can't go out into the woods and fields as often as you like, bring small reminders of the great outdoors into your garden.

Unlike garden flowers, wildflower plantings in full sun depend on a succession of bloom, one species overgrowing and following another, all season long, rather than a few kinds of highly selected flowers remaining in color for extended periods. Dominant species come and go, with pinks and blues much in evidence in the spring, followed by earthy yellows, reds, and mahoganies; and white, purple, and gold in the fall. Almost always, the annual grasses are very much a part of the scene; you learn to view them not as weeds but as a foil for the flowers.

The past two decades have seen an enormous growth of interest in native stands of wildflowers and in bringing wildflowers into home gardens. The crossing over of many gardeners into conservation and restoration of wildflower sites has swelled the ranks of wildflower enthusiasts. Any meeting of native plant hobbyists will be a happy jumble of home gardeners with no training in horticulture, nurserymen with a special interest in wildflowers, and botanists and naturalists, either professional or self-taught.

Planting wildflowers in gardens and tended woodlands is not a new idea. After all, the first garden flowers were transplanted from the wild or grown from seeds or bulbs found in the wild. It is safe to say that the first flowers were domesticated because they were the prettiest plants around, at the least prettier than weeds, and perhaps fragrant. Some would have been "bee plants" grown to supply foraging bees with a nearby source of nectar and pollen.

Home gardeners have an easier time than botanists when it comes to distinguishing between wildflowers and weeds. To nonprofessionals, if a native North American plant is showy in bloom or graceful in foliage, even for a short period of time, it is a wildflower. Most nonprofessionals would expand the usual definition of a weed as a "plant out of place" to include all plants with tiny, nondescript flowers and awkward growth habits, even when they are part of the native plant population. Botanists prefer not to use the pejorative term "weed": they tend to group all wild, nonintroduced flora as "native plants." They refer to all introduced plants as "exotics."

All garden flowers were at one time wildflowers but have been so extensively hybridized and improved that they would have a hard time surviving if transplanted to the wild. Many have been so dwarfed and loaded with flowers that they are dependent on gardeners for supplementary plant food and water.

*(Right) One of Weesie's "affinity groups" incorporates blue Phlox divaricata; white foam flower, Tiarella wherryi, the Japanese Solomon's seal, Polygonatum odoratum 'Variegatum'; the groundcover Epimedium x warleyense and, foreground, hardy cyclamen.*

By definition, wildflowers are unimproved species. Plants within species are not as alike as peas in a pod. Individual plants or isolated populations often show quite a bit of variation from the plant designated as "typical," or "the norm," which has caused great confusion in nomenclature. This gene pool diversity is one of nature's devices for insuring survival of the tens of thousands of species in the wild. It also provides sharp-eyed plant breeders candidates for improvement and introduction as garden flowers or landscape specimens.

Always, there have been nature-oriented gardeners who prefer wildflowers "as is" . . . who appreciate their often spartan simplicity and informality. Almost as soon as the first colonists arrived here, these early naturalist-gardeners began moving wildflowers into their gardens by seeds, bulbs, cuttings, and transplants. Those with talents in botany began active seed, bulb, and plant exchanges with the Old World and with other parts of the Colonies. Some North American species were instant "hits." Others

became the stuff of legends, such as the beautiful flowering shrub *Franklinia alatamaha*, sent to Europe and no longer found in the wild.

Native North American wildflower history and lore is really more about people than plants because it concerns the early plant explorers such as John Bartram, who gathered and sent seeds, plants, and bulbs to foreign collectors. In some instances, plants and seeds were collected on research, military, or strategic explorations of middle America and the West, by Audubon, Lewis and Clark, Fremont, and others. European plant explorers came over, either out of scientific curiosity or on commissions from wealthy collectors. Catesby, Michaux, and others are remembered by species they discovered. Thomas Jefferson broke with the reliance on exotic flowers for gardens and tried our native wildflowers at Monticello.

The incredibly rich and varied flora of the New World has enchanted European gardeners since the first boat returned with glowing descriptions of our plants and animals. To this day, interest in propagating North American wildflowers for garden plantings is stronger in Europe than in the United States. Our wildflowers are capable of getting started, surviving, and multiplying despite wide fluctuations in temperature and rainfall. Except for dryland species, ours are easier to grow in Europe than some of their more temperamental species are here.

The early involvement of Europeans with our wildflowers explains why, in colonial days, seeds of some North American species were shipped back to us for planting in gardens. The Europeans were growing species from all over North America, including Mexico, at their botanical gardens when our own garden seed industry was limited to a few industrious Shakers in the East. Some of the varieties had been selected for uniformity, larger flowers, and a better range of colors, but many looked essentially as they did growing in the wild. Thereafter, for many years, the emphasis among European and American seedsmen was on converting American wildflowers into improved garden flowers rather than on propagating wildflowers as Nature put them on this earth.

Wildflowers deserve all the attention they are now receiving, and more. Some rival garden flowers in beauty, durability, and ease of growth. They can add character and interest to otherwise bland seasonal grasslands, forests, and rocky slopes. With all of this going for them, why do so many gardeners slight them in favor of named cultivars of garden flowers?

Some of the resistance is the result of the "regionality" of wildflowers. Each species or subspecies gradually evolved to fit a certain rather narrow ecological niche, and some are not happy unless the grower can provide a similar environment in his garden or woodlands. You have to devote more thought to planting wildflowers and native trees and shrubs than to establishing garden flowers. You have to think of wildflower plantings as "restoring an original picture" rather than "creating a new picture," as you do with garden flowers.

Four developments during the last two decades have conspired to simplify the growing of wildflowers. First, several regional greenhouse-nurseries have begun to produce plants of a wide range of species of native wildflowers, trees, and shrubs for sale. They have worked the kinks out of propagation and can offer sound advice on landscaping with native plants. Second, certain wildflower groups have worked hard to popularize native plants, such as prairie wildflower associations in the Midwest, mountain wildflower groups in the Appalachians, and horticultural societies everywhere. Third, seed companies are promoting mixtures of wildflower seeds as an alternative to large expanses of high-maintenance turf grass. Last but not least, easy-to-follow books on propagating native wildflowers from seeds, cuttings, and division are becoming available.

More and more Americans are becoming concerned about preservation of the environment and the conservation of resources, including native plants. Some are concentrating on protecting or enhancing wildflower sites; others on establishing sanctuaries for wildflowers in their private or public gardens and woodlands. Others are pushing officials to establish wildflowers on roadsides and large open sites such as the land around airfields.

Before the term "conservationist" became stylish, Weesie Smith of Alabama combined her love for wildflowers and gardening with an intense and active concern for preserving irreplaceable sites. Her knowledge of southeastern wildflowers is so vast, her motives so simple and straightforward, and her personality so warm and sharing that it rubs off on everyone she meets.

*Weesie's steep land features rock outcroppings that she has planted with native ferns and flowering plants.*

*I*t is hard to envision Weesie slogging through the swamps of Alabama, or picking her way through deep, brush-clogged ravines to find and identify wildflowers. A tall, slim, gracious lady of great beauty, she charmed the *Victory Garden* audience when we featured her garden. With her education, energy, and natural talents, Weesie would have had little trouble running a sizable business. But she chose family life, gardening, and wildflowering.

In 1957, Weesie and Lindsay Smith built their present home on a deeply wooded, steeply sloping lot of more than four acres on the outskirts of Birmingham, Alabama. She laughed when she recalled how they had to convince their contractor that they really wanted to build on such rough terrain, and that they had to insist he remove only the trees that were in the way of the lane and the house. (In those days, contractors preferred to clear and flatten building lots.)

For a while, Weesie gardened conventionally, landscaping mostly the sunny areas around the house. She had already been bitten by the wildflower bug, but now she had the space to bring them into her garden. Over the years, she and Lindsay constructed winding paths throughout the heavy woods on her property, and removed dead trees to open up the dense canopy of foliage. Then began a continuing wildflower planting program that includes native plants from all over the Southeast and some related wild species from afar.

The *Victory Garden* TV crew taped Weesie Smith's wildflower garden at peak bloom time. I saw species that were new to me, including the forest understory tree, *Stewartia malacodendron*, also called the silky camellia, and *Luecothoe populifolia.* She had great swatches of the common herbaceous wildflowers such as deciduous ginger, and little clumps of rare plants such as terrestrial orchids. Down in a deep ravine, she had sunk plastic bags in the ground to create a boggy environment for southern rain orchids, *Habenaria clavellata.*

Weesie's gardening interests include more than native wildflowers. "Years ago," she said, "Lindsay and I built a 'pit greenhouse,' sunken into a hillside, with the south side open to the sun. We installed drainage tiles and insulating glass slanting toward the winter sun. Down in the concrete block pit, it is cool and dry, and almost never requires heat. I start seeds of wild species and cultivated plants under banks of fluorescent lights over benches, then move the seedlings to a bench beneath the slanted window to grow to transplanting size.

"That ten-by-thirty-foot greenhouse," he continued, "has the propagation capacity to quickly overload our property with wildflowers. So, I use much of the space to force cool-loving, winter-blooming pot plants such as freesias into bloom to use as holiday gifts."

Downslope from the Smiths' house are several terraces, supported by boulders removed during construction. On these contoured banks, Weesie has planted exotic rock garden plants and perennials such as tree peonies and the "roof iris," *Iris tectorum*. Odd little bulbous plants spring up through the rock walls, but she often has to replace them because of the depredations of chipmunks, mice, and voles.

Weesie refers to these areas as her "cutting gardens" because she relies on them to produce sprays for arrangements throughout the growing season. She calls a similar garden nearer the house her "cottage garden"; it receives more sunlight than any other site on the property.

"These tightly managed gardens look okay where I have them," she said, "but I choose carefully the wildflower species I plant close to the house. To me, most wildflowers look best in a natural setting, away from manicured lawns and flower beds . . . out where they appear to have been 'born free.' Conversely, I am very careful not to turn aggressive cultivated ornamentals loose in my wildflower area. The shade-loving woody and herbaceous exotics can become real pests, competing with native wildflowers. Two of the worst in our area are the ivies and vine myrtle."

Weesie was drawn into wildflowers in the late 1950s when her children were still small. She and Lindsay were, and still are, avid hikers and canoers and felt at home in the outdoors. Identifying wildflowers came naturally to Weesie, and during the first years of their marriage, she grew a few without knowing much about them. But she felt the urge to learn more about the environment, and especially Alabama soils, how they were formed, and how they influence plant populations. So, she completed several courses in natural and physical sciences, beginning with geology.

That was the scene when a wildflower enthusiast entered Weesie Smith's life—the late Eleanor Brakefield, a pioneer in the "dig and save" movement for conserving wildflowers threatened by construction projects. Eleanor persuaded Weesie to come along on a wildflower rescue expedition. In those days, dams were going up all over Alabama, often flooding priceless ecological niches; suburbs were expanding; freeways were being pushed through. Irreplaceable wildflower sites were being drowned, bulldozed, or asphalted over.

"I soon found myself caught up in the race to save whole populations of wildflowers from being wiped out," said Weesie. "From the beginning, I centered on saving shade-loving species of herbaceous wildflowers, shrubs, and small trees and transplanting them to our lot. Our property is heavily wooded and bringing in more sun-loving species than we could accommodate in our few patches of sunlight would have been pointless. I was already an experienced gardener, but I soon found that I had to learn a lot about each wildflower to succeed with it."

So began the gradual conversion of the Smiths' wooded lot into a wildflower garden. Weesie's studies in geology helped her to analyze native plant sites and to approximate them in her home garden. Cleaning out the invasive Japanese honeysuckle, muscadine grapevines, and catbriers from four acres by hand-pulling familiarized her with every square inch of the property. She probed here and there and located dry, rocky outcroppings, moist seeps, and areas of deep, fertile loam.

"There were virtually no understory plants worth saving," she said. "So it simplified the removal of about four hundred dead pine trees, killed by pine bark beetles. Later, I contacted the city and commercial tree companies and found them only too happy to dump chipped wood and leaves on our property. I wheelbarrowed it into areas I had marked for planting wildflowers. It wasn't long before I had a deep layer of decaying organic matter over much of the forest floor, and was building paths of chipped wood.

"Our five children were busy being kids," said Weesie: "they helped a little, but I couldn't expect them to share my commitment to wildflowers. I tried taking them on wildflower digs, but found the two incompatible. Instead, Lindsay and I diverted their energy into exploring northern Alabama.

"Lindsay helped by clearing honeysuckle and fallen tree limbs, but he was working long hours building his practice and couldn't go along on dig-and-save missions. After a while, I realized that wildflowering is basically a solitary pursuit, except when you are on field trips with like-minded enthusiasts. You can enjoy wildflowers without knowing much about them, but there are so many species that really knowing them can become a lifelong learning experience. Many gardeners have never ventured deep into woods and wetlands, and are more familiar with the bright annuals and perennials that grow in full sun. The rugged roadside flowers pretty well take care of themselves, but not the forest understory species. You can't just plant them and let them grow wild: they require varying degrees of management.

"When I advise gardeners on starting wildflower gardens," said Weesie, "I take them through a short checklist. I suggest that they first consider the duration and density of sunlight that falls on the site. Any site that receives a half day or more of full sunlight should be planted with

*Weesie gathers fragrant freesias in her pit greenhouse.*

sun-loving meadow flowers. The shade-tolerant species will do better beneath deciduous trees, but some have a tolerance for sun that doesn't appear in catalog descriptions. Densely shaded areas can be improved by limbing up trees or dropping and chipping unthrifty specimens."

Weesie has formed a conclusion about "shade-loving" wildflowers that has a lot of merit. She feels that many species are found only in the woods in the wild because of heavy competition from other plants out in the sun. She has found that many forest species will adapt to situations where they receive morning sun, and afternoon and evening shade. "But," she says, "they won't survive in the sun unless the soil is rich in organic matter and is kept moist." I think that Weesie's discovery opens up many possibilities for gardens that have little shade.

"Beginners need to locate different soil types on their property. Dig into the soil at various places on the site. If the soil is uniformly heavy, you may have to modify some spots with sand to suit the preference of some species for fast-draining soil. Southeastern soils are almost always acid and relatively poor, which suits most wildflower species just fine.

"There isn't much you can do to prepare soil beneath trees for planting wildflowers, other than raking the leaf litter to the side, spreading a two-inch layer of composted wood chips or pulverized pine bark as a mulch, planting through it, and pulling the dry leaves around the plants.

"Competition from tree roots is fierce; wildflower plants need help to get started on the forest floor. Fall is a good time to transplant wildflowers to wooded sites because the trees are going dormant, and rains will lessen the watering chore while getting plants established and well rooted. Spring is a poor time to transplant because the trees are leafing out and roots are competing for soil moisture.

"The forest landscape will become more natural looking as the stands of wildflowers thicken and spread from the few plants you plug in beneath trees. Contented wildflowers set seeds and reproduce abundantly.

*A pea gravel walk leading to the pit greenhouse is bordered with the azalea R. 'George Taber' and Phlox divaricata.*

Some species have backup systems for reproduction, rhizomes or bulbs as well as seeds.

"The big difference in just growing wildflowers and gardening with wildflowers," said Weesie, "is using landscaping skills to enhance their natural beauty. For example, whenever I acquire a new species, my first priority is to choose for it the best possible site, one with the proper amount of shade and moisture, and the most appropriate soil. We have both heavy clay and sandy soil on the place, which gives me some flexibility. Then, I look up at the forest canopy and down at the soil, and try to sense the effect of wind and winter exposure on the site. My aim is to do everything I can to start that new plant off right, because, once it is planted, I can't change its surroundings.

"I don't wish to make wildflower gardening seem difficult," she said, "because it is as simple as growing zinnias and tomatoes. It is just that the needs of most wildflowers are different from those of garden flowers. If beginners will take a little time to try to understand wildflowers, they won't be disappointed in their attempts to grow them. In the wild, each species adapts to certain soil, climate, and exposure situations; the trick in growing them is to try to duplicate those conditions in your own garden or woodlands.

"Let me back up," Weesie said, "and remind beginners in wildflowering never to remove plants or seeds from national or state parks or nature preserves. Actually, it is best to defer collecting until one knows for sure whether a species is abundant or rare. Generally, the summer-flowering meadow and roadside wildflowers are fairly abundant: collecting a few seeds shouldn't hurt. Just leave a few heads to drop seeds for next year's plants.

"I have to caution beginners about the 'localness' of many wildflowers. Only a few, and they are meadow flowers such as gaillardia, coreopsis, liatris, and phlox, will grow in varied locations around the country. For example, in Birmingham, we are on the southern edge of adaptability for species that are more at home in northern Alabama, Georgia, and Tennessee. We know from experience not to go into southern Alabama and bring back wild plants. They are accustomed to mild winters and more rainfall. Rarely will they survive our cold winters, tremendous variations in winter temperatures, and periodic droughts.

"This is why the first wildflower books you buy should be publications of your state wildflower or horticulture society or, at the most, books published for a discrete climatic region such as our Southeast. As you get deeper into the subject, you may wish to buy one of the college-level books published for each state or region, bearing the title of *Flora of* a particular state. These are heavy books, but you will need them when you begin delving deeply into wildflowers. They list and describe many species not found in general garden encyclopedias."

*Two treasures from Weesie's woodland garden:* Cypredium kentuckiense, *a recently named species of lady's slipper orchid (left); and the adaptable forest floor native bloodroot,* Sanguinaria canadensis.

I asked Weesie which "surefire" wildflowers she would recommend as starter plants for woodlands. She reminded me that her recommendations would stand only for the Southeast and told me that the first plants she moved to her woods were:

- Bloodroot, *Sanguinaria canadensis*
- Blue phlox, *Phlox divaricata*
- Liverleaf, *Hepatica spp.*
- *Trillium spp.* (she now has fifteen species)
- Jack-in-the-pulpit, *Arisaema triphyllum*
- False Solomon seal, *Smilaceae racemosa*
- Solomon seal, *Polygonatum biflora*

I certainly concur with her choices, because the woods around my farm are rich in these species. One more I would add is a sun-tolerant plant with yellow and green daisylike flowers, *Chrysogonum virginianum*, usually found where a fallen tree has opened the forest canopy to let sunlight through. And the wild deciduous azaleas: they especially like moist soils along creeks and around seeps.

Weesie has mixed feelings about the current rage for "wildflower meadows." These are areas planted with mixtures of flower seeds made up of sun-loving native American species and exotics from other parts of the world, often laced heavily with grass seeds. "I would feel better about them," she said, "if they were made up totally of North American wildflowers, because I am wary of introducing species which could become invasive weeds, such as cornflowers. They are probably okay for yards where they are not likely to escape, but I'd rather see only natives planted along highways, where roadside plants might escape into agricultural land."

Weesie offered this advice to gardeners trying to propagate wildflowers or to increase stands on their property. "With my greenhouse and banks of fluorescent lights, I have an ideal setup for starting seeds and growing plants of wildflowers. However, a beginner could get by with one fluorescent light fixture in a cool corner of a basement or unheated room. Get fresh seeds if possible. Fresh seeds of many wild species will germinate within a week or two, but let them dry out and turn dark, and they may not come up for six to twelve months! If your supplier ships plants or bulbs, query them on the source; buy from only the specialists who propagate their plants and not from those who take them from the wild."

Weesie doesn't shy away from being called a "conservationist" as well as a wildflower gardener. "It took only a trip or two with experienced wildflower specialists," she said, "to convince me of the scope of ecological loss we were facing in Alabama. It was abundantly clear that very few people seemed to understand that it was irrevocable. And even fewer were doing anything about it. In all of northern Alabama, not more than a dozen of us were fighting for conservation. But we pulled others into a loose-knit coalition and began to press for the protection of significant sites. We began to log the locations of scarce species of wildflowers and, in the process, discovered some that were previously unknown.

"One of our most significant accomplishments was protecting unique ecological niches along the ravines in the northern sector of the Sipsey River wilderness. Lindsay and I had hiked through them and were convinced of their value. With help from all over the state, indeed from the entire United States, our coalition of concerned citizens was able to have some deep ravines set aside as wilderness area. These were all in the northern sector of the Bankhead National Forest; we were too late to save similar ravines in the southern sector; they were flooded by a dam impoundment.

"We hadn't been as successful in getting the ear of highway officials," she said. "Until recently, they seemed more interested in subduing the environment with herbicides than in putting wildflowers to work in beautifying roadsides." Fortunately, this is beginning to change.

Weesie told me that her wildflowering trips were fewer nowadays because of the demands her home gardens place on her time and energy. When we taped the *Victory Garden* show there, we were amazed that one person, with occasional help for heavy jobs, could manage such a large area of wildflowers. Weesie admitted ruefully that she is no longer expanding the garden but is concentrating on maintaining it. "There are days," she said, "when I think about removing trees to let in more sunlight for my wildflowers, then I remember that we need the shade to keep the house cool and to discourage sun-loving weeds from coming in. It's a trade-off.

"Nowadays, rather than rushing out on dig-and-save missions, I find myself spending more time at home, protecting my weak wildflowers from the more aggressive species, replacing plants or stands that have been damaged or wiped out by voles. Much of my time is spent pulling out and composting ferns. I think that, if I left our woods unattended, ferns would take over and run out most other species.

"Every now and then I get a pleasant surprise like a little patch of three birds orchids, *Triphora trianthophora*, which apparently came up from seeds. They grew in chipped wood I had spread on a path. The seeds may have been picked up in the bark of a tree dragged across the land during harvesting. The little orchids seem willing (or able) to grow only in the path, perhaps because no other plants are growing there. They come up, bloom, set seeds, and die back in five or six weeks, so I don't try to move them. I just block off a four-foot section of the path in late July."

Weesie shared with me some of the challenges and triumphs of collecting and moving wildflowers. "When the children were small," she said, "we had one of those huge station wagons. We'd load it with newspapers and canvas carrying bags and head for a dig-and-save site. We always asked permission to enter such rescue sites, unless the bulldozers were already going. Then, we'd try to get ahead of them.

"One of the conservationists active then, Eleanor Brakefield, taught me how to move wildflowers at any time of the year. She would worry a plant out of the ground to save as much as possible of the root system, lay it on a newspaper, fold the paper over the root ball, roll it up, soak the wrapped roots in water from a creek or seep, label the plant by species and location, and stand it up in a canvas bag. Sometimes we lugged plants for miles, sweating and swatting at mosquitoes, gnats, and ticks. It was thrilling when we crept down steep inclines on rough, rocky roads that were more like trails, but there were times when, with tires spinning and throwing gravel, I doubted if we would make it back up those hills!

"I had a good eye for spotting wildflowers . . . still do," said Weesie. "But another conservationist, Josephine Henry, beat us all. It would be fair to call her a plant explorer because she traveled all over the country identifying plants, recording their locations, and profiling their sites. On the few occasions I was lucky enough to travel with her, she would use binoculars to locate spots of color at great distances. When you are in such rough terrain that each step is work, being able to go straight to a patch of plants is a lifesaver."

1)
2)
3)
4)
5)
6)

## Southeastern Wildflowers

A gallery of typical southeastern wildflowers from Weesie's collection: the Atamsco lily, *Zephyranthes atamasco* (1), grows from bulbs and likes light shade and moist soil. The Florida flame azalea, *R. Austrinum* (2), brightens open woods in midspring. *Phaecelia bipinnatifida*; the celandine or woods poppy, *Stylophorum diphyllum*; and the cinnamon fern, *Osmunda cinnamomea* (3). *Trillium luteum*, one of Weesie's fifteen trillium species (4). Green and gold *Chrysogonum virginianum* tolerates sun (5). *Hepatica americana* (6), liverleaf, a widely known early spring flower. Weesie reminds beginners that success with wildflowers depends on respecting their often limited adaptability. Most species are suited only to the particular conditions of soil, climate, and exposure of their region.

I asked Weesie about memorable "digs." She recalled the day she and Lindsay whizzed past a clump of wild red lilies on a bank alongside the interstate freeway they were traveling. She fixed the spot in her mind and determined to come back and see the lilies. So, the next morning, she told Lindsay she'd be right back and took off for the remembered spot. When she sighted the lily, she realized that it was just past an exit. She kept on going to the next exit, which proved to be eighteen miles down the road! Thirty-six miles later, she found the lilies, dug up just one, wrapped it in sphagnum moss, and sent it to a botanist friend, Joab Thomas, at the University of Alabama. He pronounced it to be a previously unknown species, more like *Lilium michiganense* than *L. canadense* or *L. superbum*, yet resembling all three. After more study, it will be classified. Perhaps it was fateful that Weesie dug that one bulb. The clump on the highway has disappeared, but their salvaged specimen is reproducing through stolons and can be perpetuated.

Weesie also recalled collecting on a 100-degree day near Peterson, Alabama. The site had long been used for field trips by university students in botany but was slated for obliteration, due to the construction of a new lock and dam. "We carried heavy canvas bags of plants for what seemed like miles through that heat and humidity. But it was worth it! We were saving plants of Alabama croton, a relic from the Silurian geologic era, and snow wreath, *Neviusia Alabamensis*, a beautiful little deciduous shrub.

"Later, I had to travel into central Alabama to rescue from a scheduled spraying with herbicide a plant I consider the star of my garden, a rare yellow ladies slipper orchid, *Cyprepedium kentuckiensis*. It has larger, slightly later flowers than the more abundant yellow ladies slipper, *C. pubescens*, and is lighter yellow in color. In my garden this precious plant has thrived and is multiplying nicely."

Weesie paused and, with a concerned look, told me, "I hope I'm not giving you the idea that I'm rushing around Alabama ripping off rare wildflowers. For many years, I got my plants solely on dig-and-save missions, where the plants would have been destroyed, along with their site. In those days, thirty years or so ago, virtually no nurserymen propagated wildflowers. Every now and then, I'd see advertisements in our *Alabama Farmer's Bulletin* for wild plants being sold by farmers. Usually, I would drive out to see the plants to assure myself that they were not an endangered species and, if not, that they were dug in a way which would insure survival.

"We in Alabama owe a debt of gratitude to two nurserymen for promoting nursery-grown wildflowers. Years ago, commercial 'collectors' would raid wild plant populations and sell them by mail or to pharmaceutical companies or mail-order nurseries. Some still do, and I deplore it. That's why I feel so grateful to my nurseryman friend, Tom Dodd, for

*Accustomed to such feats on her collecting missions, Weesie adroitly walks a fungus-fringed log over a deep ravine.*

popularizing all sorts of woody native Alabama plants, especially the azaleas and rhododendrons. And Dan Coleman, even though he never seemed to have enough plants in his nursery to meet the demand, brought several choice species into public notice. At first, they propagated the traditional ways, by cuttings and layering. It was so slow. Now, they use mist propagation and container culture to reduce the time from cuttings to sales size. Tom Dodd grows most of his native shrubs from seeds to maintain a wide gene pool and has evolved into a wholesaler."

I asked Weesie what advice she had to offer people who are just becoming interested in wildflowers. "The single most important step is to find a local wildflower society or a wildflower group in a local horticultural society. Then, begin going on field trips with them. At first, you may feel totally out of place, listening to the botanists and old-time wildflower specialists reeling off latin binomials and reminiscing about great field trips they have taken. They will be patient and sharing with you, and will show you how to use the picture book guides to identify species.

"Books and seminars are just fine, but they aren't sufficient unto themselves. I've never met an armchair wildflower specialist who knew what he or she was talking about. There is simply no substitute for time in the field, in the company of knowledgeable specialists. Most of these specialists are not botanists or biologists but come from all walks of life. Anyone who loves nature can fit into these groups.

"I wouldn't even dream of trying to plant wildflowers in my garden before seeing or studying how they, or a closely related species, actually grow in the wild. From that, I can make educated guesses on the type of soil, level of acidity, soil moisture preference, and sun or shade requirements of the plant."

Weesie Smith is grateful that getting to know wildflowers led her into the preservation movement. She feels that the two are inseparable; no one can know and love wildflowers without being concerned about their shrinking habitat. She feels blessed that her hospitable land provided a safe harbor for many wildflowers that would otherwise have been lost. But most of all, she values the person/plant interdependence that grows out of wildflower gardening—the pleasure they bring to her, year after year, in return for the time she took to learn their likes and dislikes.

## *More about Wildflowers*

Most wildflower beginners aren't ready to become activists in wildflower conservation, and they aren't up to the more challenging aspects of propagation. They want to start with something simple, sure-fire, and inexpensive. Growing wildflowers from seed mixtures is the answer.

*Planting Wildflower Seeds*

One of the best ways to get to know the common varieties of sun-loving wildflowers is to plant a row or two in your food or flower garden, using a wildflower seed mixture. Start with at least an ounce or two of seeds to be sure to get a good stand and a representative number of plants of each species in the mixture. Sow the seeds in a row or band so you can tell where the flower seedlings leave off and the weeds begin. The mixtures contain both cool-weather and warm-weather annuals. Plant them in the fall or spring; summer planting won't give the cool-weather annuals a chance to show off before hot weather burns out the plants.

A gardening encyclopedia or a wildflower reference book will help you learn the names of the flowers in the mixtures: the references with color pictures will give you a better batting average. Some are common American wildflowers but many are rather obscure European species. Let the plants dry up at the end of the season; then pull them and scatter the seeds over the row. You should get a good stand of the stronger species the following year and another opportunity to identify those which baffled you at the first try.

Establishing large meadows of wildflowers from seed mixtures is a bit more complicated because you have to eliminate heavy stands of grass and weeds to get a good stand. Flower seedlings are small and comparatively weak, and strong grass and weeds can swamp them before they develop plants large enough to compete.

The success of wildflower seedings depends partly on the soil being rather poor, and not heavily loaded with seeds of grass that spread from stolons to make dense mats. Wherever the soil is naturally fertile, moist throughout the year, and seeded with grass, the grass will soon push out all the wildflowers, except the rugged species with large-enough plants to overgrow or thrive between tufts of annual grasses. Casual observers can get the impression that wildflowers prefer poor, dry soil. Not true. They grow there because Nature has adapted many species to grow on soils too poor, dry, or infertile to support a thick stand of stoloniferous grass. Some western wildflowers survive by growing in the open areas between clumps of bunch grasses.

Start a year ahead, during the summer. Plow and rototill the soil. Fumigate the soil to kill weeds, grasses, seeds, and root-rot organisms. Use a chemical such as Vapam or methyl bromide when the soil is warmer than 60 degrees F. If you are an organic gardener, cover the moist, tilled soil with clear plastic, batten it down tightly, and let the accumulated solar heat of summer kill most of the weed seeds. Allow six to eight weeks to "solarize" the soil. Alternatively, soak the area a few times and rototill when the soil is dry enough to work. Several tillings will kill many sprouting seedlings and greatly reduce the weed seed count. Planting thickly and tilling under a summer green manure crop such as soybeans will also help reduce the weed population. During soil preparation, incorporate limestone as indicated by soil tests, and a phosphate source. Incorporate a balanced fertilizer only if the soil is exceedingly poor or if it is raw subsoil. Supplementary nitrogen has a way of encouraging the bad guys to take over.

During the past few years, *The Victory Garden* has taped programs at several botanical gardens where wildflower meadows have been established. Consistently, the thickest stand of wildflowers, the greatest range of species, and the fewest weeds and aggressive grasses were seen where the soil had been fumigated. Furthermore, fumigated plots repeated better and longer; one still looked good after three years, requiring only the pulling of a few aggressive weeds before they set seeds.

After fumigating or "solarizing" large areas, work the soil into a seedbed and use a disc, spring-tooth harrow or rake to make furrows about 2 inches deep across the area. If you garden in zone 7 or south, scatter seeds at the recommended rate in late summer or fall, then drag the soil with a square of cyclone fence to cover seeds lightly with soil. You can either "water up" the seeds with a sprinkler or let them emerge with the fall rains. Either way, they will go through the winter as small seedlings and bloom the following year.

In zones 6 and north, get the soil ready and delay seeding until late fall, just before the soil freezes or early spring. Broadcast the seeds and cover them lightly with straw, not weed-infested hay. The mulch will prevent seeds from washing away and will reduce the loss to foraging birds. Few seeds will come up until late spring; the freezing and thawing will hasten and improve germination. The meadow will bloom the following season. However, some of the slow-growing perennials may form rosettes and not bloom for yet another year.

*Starting and Transplanting Seedlings*

An even better way is open to gardeners who are prepared to start wildflower seeds in flats. At the time you begin preparing the soil, fill shallow plastic or fiber "seed flats" with planter mix and plant them with seeds of wildflower mixes or individual adapted wild species. You don't need a greenhouse: start them under the shade of a tree, up on a table out of reach of pets and mice. Once the plants have grown enough to fill the flats with a mat of roots, and before they bloom, plant entire flats by scraping shallow holes into the prepared soil. Soak the holes before setting-in the flats. Consider the flats as "islands" of flowers scattered randomly across the prepared soil.

As the islands of flowers grow, water occasionally and cultivate in between them to kill emerging weeds and grasses. By late summer, many species will have completed flowering and will have set seeds. Discontinue cultivating and let the seeds drop or blow onto the bare soil surrounding the islands. Scatter a few wildflower seeds on the loose, bare soil to hasten the process of filling in. Wildflower islands can be transplanted in early spring, but this means you have to start seeds in a greenhouse or under lights in late winter.

A few enlightened nurseries have begun to grow what they call "plugs" of wildflowers, which are similar to the flats previously described, and are planted in the same way. They know how to start the species that are difficult or slow to germinate. Some offer plugs of individual wild species as well as mixtures of adapted species.

Some of the widely available North American species are easy to start and dependable in wildflower meadows: coreopsis, *Gaillardia, Rudbeckia, Ratibida, Bidens, Echinacea* or coneflower, *Liatris* or gayfeather, *Helianthus* or sunflower, *Phlox drummondi* and *P. subulata,* various lupins and fall-blooming asters are good examples. You can buy seeds of them from wildflower specialists, grow plants, and set them in colonies in meadows, the way they would grow naturally. This is the best way to establish a meadow of purely American wildflowers.

**Planting in Shady Areas**

A wooded landscape presents a different set of challenges and calls for a different group of wildflower species than sunny meadows. In nature, some forest floors seem hostile to wildflowers; others teem with them. In my climate zone 7, the richest concentrations of hardwood forest-floor flowers are on steep hillsides away from the afternoon sun, and they always seem to be thicker toward the base of the hill. Scientific research indicates that the degree of shade is not nearly as important as root competition for water. Slopes away from the afternoon sun don't dry out badly, and flowers on the lower end of the slope benefit from water seeping from in-soak higher up the hill.

This information suggests how you could grow wildflowers under trees with aggressive surface roots which suck the water out of soil. Rake the area free of leaves and loose duff and lay down a layer of spun-bonded synthetic "landscape cloth." Buy the cloth as wide as you can, because you will need to overlap joints 6 inches. Shred the leaves with a rotary mower and mix them with finely pulverized pine bark and moistened peat moss, mixed on a 3:1 ratio. Include a few shovels of topsoil from beneath the trees. Add a phosphate source but no limestone, and no nitrogen or potash fertilizer. Spread the organic mulch 3 to 5 inches deep over the landscape cloth, and you are ready to plant.

Planting seeds under trees is futile. Start with adapted plants purchased at a native-plant nursery. Spring or early fall transplanting should give you the best results. The landscape cloth should prevent tree roots from competing with the wildflowers until they get a good start. After three or four years, tree roots will find a way to grow into the moist mulch and you may have to fish around, find the heaviest of them, and snip them off with pruning shears.

Generally, the best competitors for forest-floor plantings are the hardy perennial species that come on with a rush in early spring, bloom, and restore their stored carbohydrates before the forest canopy shuts out the sunlight they need for growth and reproduction. In my climate, wild ginger, hepatica, blue-eyed grass, anemone, bloodroot, several species of wild violets, and two species of dwarf iris like hardwood forest situations. Several species in these genera will grow as far north as zone 4.

Some of the most hospitable forest situations are moist glens between trees where the light or dappled shade excludes most grass but allows summer-blooming wildflowers to thrive. The steep banks of healed ravines are ideal for plants such as *Trillium*, *Dodecatheon*, or shooting stars, which need more moisture than most wild species.

**Landscaping with Wildflowers**

An increasingly popular use of native plants is for surrounding intimate garden rooms, retreats, or sanctuaries in landscapes. You can go all the way and transform a thoroughly domestic garden by landscaping it entirely with native plants. Use shrubs for screening, medium-height to tall wildflowers for color, and low-growing wildflowers for groundcovers. Look for slow-growing plants that mature at small sizes. In the trees and shrubs you may have to settle for improved cultivars of native species. Your Cooperative Extension Service can supply you with a list of adapted native trees and shrubs. If the list seems uninspired, check your library for books on native plants of your region. Most of them will be about herbaceous wildflowers. Only a few will instruct you in landscaping with larger native plants. These definitive books will tell you how large a tree or shrub will grow at maturity, its rate of growth, and its soil preference.

When searching for native plants, write down a few facts about each contender: mature height and spread, season and duration of bloom, fragrance, attractiveness to butterflies or their larvae, fruit or berries for wild birds, fall color, winter bark and form of branches, special soil requirements, and water needs. If you live in an acid-soil area, stick with the species that like acid soil. Concentrate those which like moist soils around ponds or streambanks or near a water faucet. Make raised beds for the species such as azaleas that need perfect drainage. Leave generous spaces between trees and shrubs: give them room to grow. You will enjoy watching plants develop their natural form, and they will be healthier.

One of the easiest ways to use wildflowers is to set plants into mixed borders of perennials, shrubs, and roses. Many of the native wildflowers are just as beautiful as exotic cultivars; their inherent vigor enables them to survive where exotics could succumb to insects, plant diseases, and weather stresses. Collectively, more herbaceous wildflowers are planted in this fashion than in any other way. Gardeners usually start out with rugged species that will adapt to almost any garden situation, then gradually work their way into more demanding flowers. The lists given previously for meadow and forest floor plantings are good starting points. Native orchids and plants which require hosts to thrive are not for beginners.

Most nurseries display wildflower plants among other perennials and sort them out by sun- or shade-loving species. When you do find a native American species, it may very well qualify as a wildflower by definition, but won't naturalize well over much of the United States.

With this in mind, if you like the looks of flowering meadows planted with exotics, by all means plant them. But, not if your garden is near agricultural land; exotics can escape and become pests. Personally, I'd rather be selective and use only North American wildflowers, especially those native to my region.

I am optimistic that gardeners in the United States and Canada will come to appreciate the incredible variety and beauty of our native North American wildflower species and will demand plants or seed mixtures only of species native to their regions. When that day comes, the seed companies will be forced to mass-produce seeds of native North American wildflowers instead of garden flowers originally from other parts of the world.

If you want to know and grow wildflowers, it has to be more than a summertime romance. You can learn a bit by growing and observing a few species each year and you can benefit from seasonal wildflower walks sponsored by your state parks system. But you will become proficient by attending meetings of your local wildflower society or horticultural society. Go along on their walks in the woods and meadows. They know what is blooming, and where to find it. Hardly a bush, tree, vine, or groundcover escapes their notice. They exclaim just as jubilantly over common Jack-in-the-pulpit as they do over showy orchids. A plant doesn't have to be in flower for them to know it. They are naturalists as much as gardeners and will help you through the most difficult part of wildflower gardening . . . getting to know the plants. In their company it will be a pleasant voyage of discovery.

# Lilies

*Ruth and Hugh Cocker find southern Minnesota just right for their hobby of breeding and showing hybrid lilies.*

*P*erhaps it is fragrance that makes lilies seen years ago linger in your mind like the memory of a lost love. Or their compelling presence: they draw attention away from lesser flowers by grace and perfection, by colors that make catalog pages pale by comparison. There is no blue lily, nor black, and I would hope never to see one. Give me, instead, the sunny yellows, strawberry and candy-apple reds, delicious pinks, and waxy whites. Throw in a few stripes, penciled or picoteed petals, spots and aureoles . . . and you have enough variety to fill a lifetime of gardening with joyful discoveries.

Combined with other flowers, groundcovers, or dwarf shrubs, or displayed against a hedge of conifers or hollies, lilies display their charms to best advantage. Their graceful flowering stems, elaborate as chandeliers, move in the slightest breeze and animate gardens. Some lilies have been refined so much that you can barely see the foliage between the flowers, but some blend into surroundings like a fawn in a sun-dappled glen.

*(Left) The Cockers' lily evaluation plot dazzles the beholder on a summer day.*

Were you to gather and plant bulbs from each of the ninety-odd lily species, then label each with its flag of national origin, your garden would look like a gathering of the United Nations. Then, you would discover that Northern Hemisphere nations from around the globe would be represented, but there would be not one flag from south of the equator!

About half of the species are native to the Asian landmass, about one-quarter from Europe, several to North America, and a few to Japan. One, the southernmost in origin, is native to the mountains of the Philippine Islands and was not discovered until the late 1940s. Doubtless, a few species remain to be discovered.

This enormously varied gene pool has given us some of the most beautiful plants in the world, so spectacular that the flowers were offered to propitiate the gods of ancient civilizations. But, secular needs were fulfilled as well as sacred: the bulbs were used for food and, later, for their medicinal properties. As human cultures mingled through trade and conquest, lilies began to cross boundaries. The Romans introduced Asian and Middle Eastern lily species to Europe as they fanned out to establish forts and footholds for the Christian religion. During the Dark Ages, monastery gardens sequestered the bulbs, which might otherwise have been eaten. Literature of the 1500s mentions *Lilium martagon*, a Turk's cap lily, and *L. chalcedonicum*.

In the 1700s, the eastern American natives, *L. canadense*, *L. superbum*, and *L. philadelphicum*, made their way to Europe. Importation to Europe of Japanese species such as *L. japonicum* did not begin until the 1800s. The lilies native to the western United States were little known until after the Gold Rush, but created a sensation when they arrived in Europe. Unfortunately, because of their demanding cultural requirements, they proved difficult to grow in Great Britain.

Plant explorers found and introduced *L. Henryi* and *L. leucanthum* in the early 1900s: the dauntless E. H. Wilson brought back *L. regale*, *L. Sargentiae*, and *L. Davidii* from Asia between 1905 and 1908. Shortly thereafter, *L. amabile* was introduced from Korea. Many bulbs perished in transit, forcing plant explorers to retrace their steps hundreds of miles back into mountainous terrain, to dig and ship replacements.

Early lily breeders made some significant crosses but lost them to diseases transmitted through vegetative reproduction. Had they known that disease-free lilies can be grown from seeds, more long-term hybridizing successes might have been reported during the 1800s and early 1900s, when other specialty plant species were rapidly being improved.

*(Right) These un-named Asiatic hybrid lily seedlings bred by the Cockers are still under evaluation.*

The Japanese had been improving their indigenous species all along, but mostly by selection, until they crossed. *L. martagon* from Europe with their own *L. hansonii*, to create the first of the Martagon hybrids. The hybrids had larger individual flowers, more of them, a wider range of colors, and extended life due to thicker petals.

*Lilies*

The Boston nurseryman Charles Hovey reported making crosses in 1843, and the renowned plant breeder Francis Parkman made a three-way cross in the 1860s, using *L. speciosum*, *L. auratum*, and *L. candidum*. The Bellingham hybrids, incorporating mostly western North American species, were made in 1899 by Robert Kessler of Los Angeles, but languished until 1932 when they were introduced by the USDA.

Perhaps the most severe obstacle to the improvement of lilies was the lack of a strong, skillful, committed, and well-financed breeder/grower/marketer. But such a man, Jan de Graaf, came along in the late 1920s. He began working for, and later bought, Oregon Bulb Farms in the fertile Willamette Valley.

With so much untapped potential to exploit, Jan de Graaf set about directing the work of a crew of skilled plant breeders in making up to thirty thousand crosses every year. Prior to that time, no other lily breeder had made crosses on such a large and organized scale and embracing so many species. In the process, Jan de Graaf's hybridizers helped to establish the chromosome counts of the various species and to perfect ways to save pollen from early bloomers for use on late-flowering species, and vice versa.

The various lily species are relatively easy to cross. For some reason, they have not developed the elaborate defenses against cross-pollination that complicate the cross-breeding of other genera. In fact, the only defense of lily flowers is against self-pollination, undoubtedly Nature's scheme to prevent the gene pool from shrinking. Lily flowers display their reproductive organs with the innocence of little children and readily accept bee- and wind-delivered pollen from other flowers.

With Jan de Graaf, as with other breeders, success came as much from the courage to discard good, but not great, hybrids as from the ability to recognize and propagate the pivotal selections. He employed European know-how in freeing his foundation bulbs of viruses by production from seeds and popularized the term "strains" of lilies, meaning sibling bulbs grown from seeds. Strains produce lilies that are reasonably similar to each other, but not as alike as peas in a pod. De Graaf also produced cultivars of lilies by what we now call "cloning," vegetative reproduction from scales, bulblets, or stem cuttings. Cloning is mandatory in new award-winning cultivars, where each bulb has to produce a plant and flower almost exactly like every other one bearing the name.

De Graaf seemed to have a sixth sense for the colors, flower and plant sizes, and plant habits that were desired by both home gardeners and commercial growers of pot plants. Beginning with 'Enchantment' in 1942, De Graaf's "Jagra" line of hybrids became world famous. More than any other cultivar, 'Enchantment' marked the turning point in lily breeding. It remains the most popular lily hybrid worldwide. Among other famous Jagra cultivars and strains are the trumpet type Aurelian hybrids and the late-blooming Oriental hybrids. His 'Pink Perfection' strain, 'Red Band' hybrid, and 'Golden Splendor' are popular around the world.

In 1968 Jan de Graaf sold his business and, in succeeding years, the company lost momentum. Numerous smaller companies in the northwest United States, the Great Lakes area, and southern Canada moved in to capitalize on the swelling demand. Dutch bulb producers began growing the cultivars needed for the American market. At the same time, some private lily hybridizers began licensing bulb producers to increase their backyard businesses. Other lily enthusiasts, with promising seedlings from their own hybridizing, elected not to expand, but to keep their hobby secondary to growing and showing lilies.

The decision to begin breeding a specialty plant marks a turning point in the lives of hobby growers. Successful plant breeders have a special status at plant society meetings because other advanced hobbyists know how much forethought, work, and determination is required in crossing, evaluation, and follow-through. For Ruth and Hugh Cocker, lily breeding sets the pace of their days, the rhythm of their seasons, and most of the goals for their gardening.

*Hugh and Ruth collect pollen from choice male parents to be saved for hybridizing.*

On a breezy June day, I visited Ruth and Hugh Cocker at their five-acre farmstead on the outskirts of Rochester. Their comfortable home is shaded by trees they planted shortly after buying the place in 1950. Black walnut and butternut trees line the approach drive. The most obvious feature is an impeccable half-acre patch of closely spaced lily beds in the side yard and another smaller field of lilies and perennials in the back. Hugh told me that, if all the rows in the beds were lined up end to end, they would measure amost two and a half miles!

Anchoring the farmstead is a neat red haybarn built by Hugh . . . an artifact from the days when he raised and showed Shetland ponies. More than two dozen grazed their pasture at one time. Now, the barn comes in handy for storing lily bulbs in sand over winter.

The Cockers have always been hard workers. At his boyhood home in Canton, Minnesota, Hugh helped his parents with general farming as well as with their spring business of growing and selling bedding plants, perennials, and gladiolus bulbs. Moving to Rochester after finishing high school, he went to work part-time for Ruth's parents in their business, Whiting's Flowers. Ruth and Hugh married while he was serving the air force as a gunnery instructor in B-17s in Florida. The noise battered his hearing. Hugh jokes, "The phone keeps ringing in my right ear, but I've learned not to answer it."

Home again, Hugh worked full-time at Whiting's and after-hours did carpentry. In 1973 he was employed by the city of Rochester as head gardener for the Plummer House estate garden. He and his crew brought the neglected grounds back to their original beauty. He retired in 1986 to devote full time to growing and hybridizing lilies.

Ruth is a small, wiry, brisk woman who chuckles a lot as she recalls her lifelong involvement with plants. "There were few child labor laws in the late twenties and early thirties," she said. "My parents were good to me but, as soon as I was big enough to help, they put me to work with an older brother delivering vegetables to rooming houses in Rochester. Even back then, Rochester was a national medical center, and families would stay in the rooming houses to be near loved ones. We would wash and trim radishes, carrots, onions, and rhubarb, and load them into a coaster wagon. Dad would give us a ride in the morning on his way to work. We would make the deliveries door to door, and there were lots of rooming houses in Rochester. When we were down to odds and ends, we'd pull the wagon home.

"At age eight, I was assigned one street corner adjacent to a Rochester hospital, my older sister another. Every weekday during the summer, I would make up bouquets from buckets of flowers my parents grew, and sell them for twenty-five cents to people visiting patients. Early on, I learned not to put fragrant flowers in hospital bouquets, because the scent can bother sick people. To this day, I have to force myself to recognize fragrance in lilies as a trait desired by most people."

Ruth never lost her interest in growing flowers for florists. Today, sales of stems of lilies, coral bells, balloon flowers, baby's breath, and statice help to pay for their lily hobby.

In the early 1960s, Ruth had become interested in hybridizing daylilies and had worked up to twelve hundred experimental hybrids in her trials. Then, their orbit intersected that of lilies.

"Mentally," she said, "we had been preparing to explore lilies for some time. Back in 1967 we had joined the North American Lily Society. A friend, Louise Koehler, cemented the decision when she gave us eleven of her unnamed hybrids. We loved them and still do. But, it was Earl Tesca, a crusty, opinionated hybridist, who showed us how to recognize potential in lilies and to settle for nothing but the best."

Ruth and Hugh loved working with the lilies. Eventually they offered to move Earl Tesca's collection to their farm. Until his death, Earl continued to work in the lily trials, teaching the Cockers what he knew about hybridizing and lily culture. His breeding emphasis had been on the early "Asiatics" which he felt had the greatest potential for northern home gardens and for cutting. Ruth and Hugh offered to register any of Earl's hybrids in his name, and have honored their promise.

The sudden acquisition of several thousand lily bulbs, representing more than four hundred species and crosses, forced Ruth to make a wrenching decision. "I knew I couldn't work with both: one had to go," she said. "When I made up my mind to get out of daylily hybridizing, I sat down in the middle of my 'babies' and had a long cry. Then, I got up, and dug and bagged all my plants of 'Hems', fifty plants per bag. I hauled those bags all over town and gave plants to schools, county and city parks, and 4-H clubs, hoping to create an interest among youngsters in growing daylilies. And, do you know that, to this day, I can still recognize my hybrids growing around Rochester public gardens and homes!"

Ruth and Hugh gradually transformed what they had learned from Louise Koehler and Earl Tesca into their own set of criteria for breeding lilies. Each breeder has his own vision of "the perfect lily" and, realizing that it is not likely to be achieved with one masterful stroke of the pollen brush, settles for a long-range program of gradual improvement.

The secret of successful lily breeding is to recognize good parents and to know the traits they pass on to progeny. It isn't as simple as it may appear. Some characteristics are linked to others; some are recessive, others are dominant. You can even get entirely different results when you make a "reciprocal cross" by changing roles between the male and female parents.

The time-honored route to gradual improvement is to start with a desirable parent that has a particular shortcoming. The breeder tries to replace that trait with a more desirable characteristic from another species or hybrid by crossing. If the result is promising, but not sufficiently attractive, the breeder may "backcross" to intensify the desirable trait. All of this takes time, careful and critical note-taking, and a great deal of luck. Yet, it is infinitely superior to random crossing.

I asked Ruth if there is a shortcut to recognizing good parents for hybridizing. "If there is, I wish someone would tell me," she said. "I know that certain lines set seeds well and I tend to use these as female parents. And I know that certain lines produce lots of variation when used as male or pollen parents. I don't mind sharing that kind of information with other lily hybridizers because, even if they duplicated my crosses, they would probably get different results. Any new lily hybridizer is going to plow old ground for a while until he or she discovers parent lines that 'notch' and produce interesting offspring."

Ruth took me through the steps of hybridizing lilies, a simple operation because the reproductive parts are so large and easily accessible. She forced apart the petals of a nearly open flower, reached in with her fingers, and pulled off the anthers with their load of unripe pollen, to emasculate the flower. Then, she covered the female stigma with a little square of aluminum foil and squeezed down the corners to form a cup. "Easier and faster than bagging to keep out foreign pollen," she explained, "and hardly visible except from close up.

"In two or three days the stigma will be covered with stigmatic fluid and sticky—receptive to pollen," Ruth explained. "I harvest pollen from desirable male parents just before it is mature enough to shake loose. I catch it in little rectangular snap-top plastic boxes like those used for faucet washers. After the pollen has dried for a day or so, I outfit each box with its own short-handled cotton swab. The pollen will keep all season in the refrigerator; I understand you can freeze it, but I've never needed to do that."

Ruth showed me how to hybridize by transferring dried pollen from one of the storage boxes to a receptive stigma. She removed the protective aluminum foil, pollinated the stigma, and replaced the foil to exclude windblown or insect-vectored pollen from a different source. I

1)

2)

3)

4)

5)

6)

## Hybridizing Lilies

The Cockers demonstrate the steps of hybridizing lilies. Pollen from desirable male parents is collected, labeled, and boxed, then stored in the refrigerator (1), where it will keep all season. The female parent's receptive stigma is swabbed with pollen on a Q-tip (2); afterward Ruth covers the stigma with a square of aluminum foil to keep out foreign pollen. The cross is labeled with the code numbers of the parents (3), then Ruth records the cross in the "Stud Book" (4). When the pods are nearly ripe, the seeds are shelled out (5). The seeds from one hybridized pod are planted in a single pot (6). These seedlings are ready to be separated and transplanted into garden rows for growing to evaluation stage.

thanked her and started to move on, but Ruth stopped me and said, "Hold on, Jim; we're not through yet." She wrote on the tag the date of the cross and the code numbers of the female plant and the pollen donor, then looped the tag over the completed cross.

She told me that she goes back later and looks for crosses that have "taken," those that show swollen ovaries, indicating successful cross-pollination. Only about one-third of Ruth's crosses take; these are entered into her "stud book," a permanent record of pedigrees. For ease of retrieval, crosses are entered alphabetically and numerically. Regrettably, some of the seeds from crosses don't germinate: these failures are also noted in the stud book for future guidance.

I asked if they have tried any hybrids between species. "No, we leave that to the scientists who understand how to manipulate genes and germ plasm. Interspecific crosses are difficult. We find plenty of potential for improvement just in crossing within the same species," said Ruth.

When I asked the Cockers for their checklist for evaluating new hybrids, they told me that "everything was in their heads," and commenced pouring out information as fast as I could take notes:

"We look first for color and flower form. You might describe it as 'overall impact.' This first screening can be done on the first or second year of bloom and will eliminate 90 percent of the hybrid seedlings. An entirely new color is highly unlikely, so we look for clarity of straight colors and new combinations of markings and background colors. Earl Tesca preferred only a few strong colors, and 'spotless' at that, with no markings or spots on petals. We don't have a bias against any color, and our taste runs toward the modern bicolor or tricolor patterns and spots.

"We look for symmetry, width of petals, lively texture, and number and conformation of flowers that is new for that particular class. There are places in every garden for upright, outfacing, and nodding blossoms; open-faced, flaring, or reflexed. Size isn't everything; the maximum overall impact can also be attained by greater numbers of rather small individual blossoms. Bright colors aren't everything; we've found some lovely pastels.

"Plant height has to be in scale with the 'inflorescence,' or the total frame of flowers. Short plants tend to be more wind-resistant but, if they are dwarfed too much, you can't cut the inflorescence without weakening the bulb. So, our preference is for vigorous, medium-height plants.

"Our experience in flower shows and selling cut flowers conditions us to look for flower substance and holding power. We want flowers that look crisp week after week in the garden and that will hold well when cut for arrangements. The thickness of petals has a lot to do with this.

"Flower colors should not fade with age or sunlight; we call this trait 'color-fastness.' We grow all our lilies in full sun so we can judge this factor critically.

*Hugh and Ruth show me their early-flowering Martagon hybrid lilies. Note the pendant blossoms.*

"Of late, we have been breeding for more flowers per stem, that open sequentially. Some of our lines have as many as five buds per stem branch, as opposed to the usual two or three. This means that lilies will continue to bloom longer and, with deadheading of spent blossoms, will last longer in arrangements.

"We watch for endurance of bulbs; they should come back year after year, increase strongly, and not tend to die out. With this screening, we also cull out the hybrid seedlings that tend to be severely hurt by late spring frosts.

"Out in the open, and not staked, out lilies are exposed to high winds and thunderstorms. We look for strong stems that don't break or topple, and that recover quickly after being bowed down by rains. We don't have many lily diseases in Minnesota and, with our preventative spray program, we don't let virus-carrying aphids get a start. Consequently, most of our selection for disease resistance is done by eliminating the lines that show susceptibility to leaf spots and bulb rotting.

"As for earliness . . . at first, we were taken with the extra-early Asiatics but found that they emerge too early in the spring. The growing point can be frozen so badly that the bulb will not bloom or even may die. Consequently, we are gravitating toward second-early and later types to lessen the damage from late spring frosts.

"Most of our breeding is with the Asiatics and the Martagons, neither of which has much fragrance, if any. To introduce fragrance to these lines, we would have to cross them with the later-blooming Trumpets or

Orientals and backcross to restore earliness. We don't have the time for such an ambitious project."

Actually, Earl Tesca's passion for perfection has, in a way, delayed the introduction of a line of lily hybrids under the Cocker name. "We respected Earl so much," Hugh said, "that we felt obligated to continue evaluating his hybrids and to register the outstanding lilies after his death. That took several years.

"We have registered only one of our own hybrids, 'Carolyn Marie', named after one of our daughters. We have six or so more ready to register with the Royal Horticultural Society in England but have been vacillating. Now we are sure enough of our own judgment in lilies to say, 'Okay, this is the best we can do in improving this class . . . perhaps the best anyone in the world can do. The time has come to register our own hybrids, increase and introduce them.' Meanwhile, we will continue hybridizing in other classes."

I asked Ruth and Hugh how many lily awards they had won. Ruth gave one of her chuckles and asked, "Do you really want to know?" Then, she proceeded to drag out enough silver to start a mint, plus a cut-glass award from Czechoslovakia, a bronze medal from Poland, and fancy porcelain plates in presentation cradles. Ribbons were laced together like fish on a stringer; they weighed so much that Ruth grunted when she hoisted them up to show me.

"It has gotten to the point that people expect Cocker seedlings to win in the classes where we specialize," said Ruth. "We never take lily shows for granted, however. We are fortunate to have thousands of lilies from which to choose, and we cut and condition stems carefully. For local or regional shows, we cut stems early in the morning, tag them with cultivar names or code numbers, stand them in glass milk bottles filled with water, bag each head, and load them into our van for transport. National conventions of the North American Lily Society are another matter. When we have to fly, we reduce the number of stems over what we usually show, pack the stems carefully, and check them as baggage.

"As for stem length, it doesn't hurt the bulb to cut stems. Just leave about a third of the stem and leaves for photosynthesis. We have cut stems from the same bulb year after year and have noticed only a slight decrease in the size of the plant and spray of blossoms. However, you can kill bulbs by taking the entire stem when cutting. We had a severe hailstorm one summer, which stripped some plants of leaves. We lost a number of these, and the damage would be comparable if you cut off stems at ground level.

"When we are setting up for shows we cut off a bit of each stem to balance the stem length to the size and optical weight of the blossom truss. We advise home gardeners to nip off the anthers of lilies they bring in the house because the pollen can stain clothing and tablecloths. We

*Ruth loads up for a show. The carrying trays hold lily stems in bottles of water.*

*The Cockers have amassed an impressive collection of trophies from their participation in lily shows.*

don't do that for shows, of course, because blossoms must be complete for judging. We find that sun-warmed water is taken up by cut stems faster than cold water right out of a tap.

"Our satisfaction really doesn't come from winning lily shows. Sure, we'd like to win "Best in Show" at the NALS someday, but aren't going to fret if we don't. We get our kicks out of renewing old friendships at local, regional, and national shows, including many lily people from Canada and other foreign countries. We love shoptalk and sharing lily know-how with people just getting into lilies as a hobby plant."

We talked about the place of lilies in landscaping. The Cockers' home landscape reminded me of "the shoemaker's children." It is neat and attractive, but includes no lilies. "We forget about taking care of the lilies we plant around the house," explained Hugh, "so we concentrate our lilies in the test plot." But, they have a good feel for how to use them massed in exhibition beds, or mixed with perennials and annuals for flowering borders. Their lectures on lilies explore the many ways lilies can be used in home gardens.

"In lectures," said Ruth, "I always tell home gardeners that they shouldn't believe everything they read in garden books. For example,

*Surrounded by lilies, Ruth and Hugh point out 'Rochester'. The white is 'Mont Blanc'; the yellow in the foreground is 'Earl of Rochester'.*

*Masters of the Victory Garden*

books will tell you to group three to five bulbs of the same lily cultivar to make 'drifts' of the same height and color. That's good if you can afford it. But, good lily bulbs are not cheap. If you are on a tight budget, you can buy one each of several kinds, space them widely, and let each bulb increase to make a drift. Sure, the recommendations for planting tall kinds in the back and shorter kinds toward the front always apply, and you shouldn't mix colors indiscriminately. But, it's no problem if you make bad combinations; just wait until late fall and move the bulbs."

Ruth added, "I prefer to see lily bulbs interplanted with low-growing annual flowers or nonspreading perennials. Lilies don't really hit their stride until the second or third year after planting. The filler flowers help to cover the bare dirt while the lily clumps are thickening, then the lilies begin to shade the ground around them. This serves to keep down weeds and reduce evaporation of water."

The Cockers are blessed with deep, fertile, sandy loam soil. Much of their nutrient supply comes from decaying organic matter. Ruth and Hugh gather and work in leaves saved by friends in Rochester; consequently, their soil is in beautiful condition. However, to maintain a good level of mineral nutrients, they top-dress a light application of balanced fertilizer around April 1, before the lilies begin to emerge.

The high level of organic matter may explain why they have been able to replant the same area in lilies for several years with no outbreaks of bulb diseases. It also increases the speed and depth of in-soak of rain-water and encourages root proliferation by bulbs. On the flip side, it also encourages all sorts of rodents: moles, voles, gophers, mice, and shrews. But their talented cat, Dixie, kept them under control until her demise. Even the abundant rabbits gave their yard a wide berth. Deer are all around but have bothered them only once, when they browsed a few seed pods. Then, Ruth got some human hair from the beauty shop and tied balls of it around the lily plots; it did the job.

Hugh offered this advice to gardeners who are just beginning to grow lilies: "In the North, the weather in late fall may be so wet and cold that planting becomes impossible, and you will have to store bulbs until spring planting time. When it happens to us, we store our common bulbs in boxes of sand in the barn. They freeze solid but it does no harm. However, we pack our most valuable bulbs in plastic bags without holes, fill them with moistened peat moss, and seal them tight. We store the bags in a refrigerator in the basement, set at about 40 degrees F. to keep the bulbs from freezing. In tight bags, the bulbs hold without sprouting until we can prepare the soil in April.

"Spring planting works fine for us," said Hugh, "but there is a solid reason for planting in the fall when possible. Lilies have contractile roots that anchor them like holdfasts. Being accordion-pleated, contractile roots can increase or decrease in length. They can pull shallow-planted bulbs down to a depth where the bulb feels comfortable. I think that adjustment goes better in the fall, when the soil is loose and moist."

The Cockers use Treflan pre-emergence herbicide to maintain clean beds, and mulch with pine needles. In our walk through their plantings I saw Ruth remove only three weeds, all so small that I didn't notice them until she stooped to pull them out.

"You have to keep an eye on the clumps," Ruth cautioned. "After a few years, five on the average in Minnesota, the clumps will thicken up so much that they will begin to run down in vigor. The stems will be shorter than is normal for the cultivar, and look puny. The plants are doing everything but waving and shouting at you to signal that it is time to lift, divide, and replant them. We wait until the frost has killed the tops in the fall before digging and replanting."

Hugh grinned at that thought and said, "Some of those big old clumps of lilies will give you a struggle, especially if the soil is wet. A big clump can weigh twenty pounds, dirt and all. You have to lay it on the grass and blast the soil off with a spray of water before you can see and get at the individual bulbs. I can usually pull the bulbs apart but sometimes have to use a sharp knife. We don't have bulb disease or nematode problems in southern Minnesota, so there is no need to dip or dust our bulbs with fungicides or insecticides."

As we walked through their lily trials, the Cockers pointed out plants with brown lower leaves, evidence of late frost damage. Some plants were oddly stubbed-off, their flower buds apparently blasted. "It's the very early ones that get hurt badly by late frosts. They look unhappy, but will survive and develop new flower buds for next year," said Hugh. "That's one reason why we like the mid-season Asiatics; they emerge a little later and usually escape frost damage."

Ruth and Hugh pondered and waffled for a long time before answering my request for a short list of starter varieties for beginners. (When you know and love so many cultivars, it is genuinely difficult to boil down the list to a few.) At last they agreed on these selections:

- 'Connecticut King': Yellow with orange center, midseason.
- 'Black Beauty': Dark crimson with white edge, late.
- *Tsingtauense:* A species lily, orange, early; it prefers partial shade.
- 'Henryi White': Blooms just after midseason.
- 'Carolyn Marie': Wine-colored, midseason.
- 'Claude Shride': A dark red, early Martagon hybrid.

"Where winters are severe, stay away from the class of lilies called Oriental; they are not hardy. Avoid the unusual species lilies until you get a feel for lilies; with certain species you have to practically duplicate the conditions under which they grow in the wild."

*Ruth gathers lily trusses to be sold to local florists.*

With their tremendous and varied experience, the Cockers have long held memberships in local, regional, and national organizations, and have served them well. Hugh was President of the Northstar region of NALS for two years and served two three-year terms as a Director. Ruth was Secretary of the Northstar region for two terms. Over the years, their lily patch has given the Cockers rest from their busy schedules and restored their psyches.

Thomas Jefferson said, "The greatest service which can be rendered any country is to add a useful plant to its culture." Perhaps the Cockers' deep enjoyment of their hobby springs from the value their work will have for future gardeners.

# *More about Lilies*

**Buying Bulbs**
The first order of business, if you are interested in growing lilies as a hobby plant, is to send off for catalogs from specialty suppliers of lily bulbs. Freshness of bulbs is very important to success in growing, and the best place to get fresh, carefully harvested bulbs is from mail-order suppliers.

Specialty bulb growers will ship you new crop bulbs as soon as possible in the fall or early winter, after digging. They can't do it any earlier, because bulbs shouldn't be lifted until the foliage has turned color. The major United States producers of lily bulbs are in the Northwest, where digging of the Asiatics doesn't begin until late October and, for the later Orientals, not until well into November.

Gardeners in northern states are then faced with shipments that come in after the ground is frozen. Experienced lily growers anticipate the late delivery. They prepare lily beds in advance, dig the holes, cover the soil with mulch to keep it from freezing, and slip the bulbs in the holes when they arrive.

Growers in Holland, where lily bulbs mature even later than in the United States and Canada, have to wait until spring to ship and sell over here. This causes no great problems with home gardeners because, when spring-planted, good-quality bulbs will bloom the same growing season. However, the plants won't be quite as vigorous the first year as those grown from fall-planted bulbs. Gardeners should be wary of bargain-priced lilies, for while mail-order lily specialists price their bulbs according to size, small bulbs can be sold at retail to novices without their knowing that they will take longer to measure up to their bred-in capacity.

Lily bulbs are a difficult product for mass marketers to sell in the spring, because the bulbs begin to sprout shortly after they are displayed in a warm area. They are sometimes packed in plastic bags, which force the sprouts to turn and twist. Such distorted growth will usually produce a stunted plant that will rarely bloom the first year.

Experienced local nurseries know to pot up lily bulbs when they show signs of sprouting in the package. Some will offer plants in full bloom for transplanting to the garden, but these are not a good buy. All that top growth will stress the root system when the plant is set in the garden, and the plant may not survive. Young, green containerized lilies will adjust much faster and better when transplanted.

*Lily Classifications*

Lily enthusiasts have organized lily hybrids and species into ten "divisions," which are internationally accepted. Ideally, all catalogs and labels should carry the name of the division, because the excellent European books on lilies refer to them frequently and they are used in lily shows. Of the ten lily divisions, five are important in North America. If you have only the cultivar or strain name, here are some hints on finding its proper division:

*Asiatic Hybrids.* Most of this germ plasm is from species originally from Asia. The goal of hybridizers has been to create early-blooming, adaptable, short-to-medium-height, disease-resistant plants. The colors range from pastels to bright and include a few dark shades. The only shortcomings of this division are lack of fragrance and a decided preference for the cooler weather of the northern and midwestern states. The NALS describes these as "the early-blooming and easy hybrids."

*Martagon Hybrids.* Taller than most of the Asiatics, the Martagon hybrids have pendant Turk's cap blossoms and whorled leaves. In favored locations, the Martagons will spread into large colonies and naturalize. Colonies have been known to live for more than a century. Slower to get started than the Asiatics, the Martagons prefer about the same climatic conditions.

*Trumpet and Aurelian Hybrids.* These generally tall, magnificent lilies bloom after most of the Asiatics are spent, and are second only to them in popularity.

The powerfully fragrant Trumpets are recognizable more by their petals than by blossom form. The petals have a waxy sheen and dark-colored outer surfaces: purple, brown, or green. The newer Trumpets, especially, are easier to grow than the Orientals. Within this division are cultivars with blossoms that look not at all like trumpets, that are, instead, bowl-shaped and outfacing, pendant, or nodding. Some have open-faced flowers, with petals flaring back from the center attachment.

The early Trumpet hybrids utilized *L. regale* × *L. sulphureum* crosses to get golden and sulfur-yellow colors. Jan de Graaf made hundreds of selections from *L. leucanthum* (centifolium), then crossed the best of these with *L. Sargentiae, L. sulphureum,* and *L. Brownii.* The most significant results were the cultivar 'Pink Perfection' and the large, varied class called the "Aurelian hybrids." This division of lilies is intermediate in hardiness between the Asiatic and Oriental hybrids. Most cultivars are fragrant; the flowers are borne in large trusses.

*Oriental Hybrids.*   Easily recognizable, these have enormous individual blossoms. The first crosses were between *L. speciosum* and *L. auratum,* and many hybrids have since been developed from this approach. Later, *L. auratum* was crossed with *L. japonicum* and *L. rubellum* to get plants with less massive frames. Out of these crosses came the "Imperial Strain," which added gold center bands to petals, expanding the color range of the basically deep red, pink, or white flowers. The most recent hybrids within the division include genes from disease-resistant species or from the short, large-flowered, upfacing *L. nobilissimum.*

In North America, the Oriental hybrids perform best on the West Coast and in favored locations in the East and Upper South. They grow well in warmer parts of Great Britain but even better in New Zealand and cool zones of Australia. They are not nearly as cold hardy as the Asiatics, but will tolerate hot weather better, if given afternoon shade. Their elegant presence brings entirely different reactions from viewers than do the saucy, bright-faced Asiatic hybrids. They have an innate dignity. Thus, they have to be sited with greater care in the landscape than do the Asiatics.

*Species Lilies.*   If you could see the species lilies growing wild in native populations, you could understand why you cannot satisfy the requirements of all species with one garden soil, one site, one feeding and watering regimen, and one schedule and method of propagation. Most grow in rather cool areas, at specific latitudes, altitudes, and sun exposures. The North American Lily Society recommends that, despite the fact that some of the true species lilies are easy to grow, novices should start with the hybrids, which are less demanding. The species lilies range in size from miniature to head-high and require research to appreciate the great range of choices. A good place to look up species of native American lilies is in wildflower books for your region.

**Planting**

Have your soil tested before preparing soil for lilies. Most lilies prefer a soil pH range of 6.0 to 6.5, but the Oriental hybrids prefer somewhat more acid soil in the range of pH 5.0 to 6.0. The pH of soil can be lowered (made more acid) by working in 1 pound of agricultural sulfur per 100 square feet of sandy soil, or twice as much for heavy clay soil. Apply yearly until the desired pH level has been reached. Except on vegetable garden soil, which contains residual nutrients from fertilizers, mix in 3 pounds of 5-10-10 fertilizer per 100 square feet.

Lily bulbs can be sunk into the soil in open spaces between low-growing conifers, dwarf rhododendrons, or groundcovers, where they will benefit from the organic litter and from their roots being in the shade. Incorporate a little fertilizer and, if needed, lime, before planting.

When your bulbs arrive, you can dust them lightly with captan fungicide or dip them in a Benlate solution. If they look dry and a bit shrunken, put them in a sack of moistened peat moss for a few days until they plump up. If your bulbs arrive with the roots trimmed off or rotted, send them back. Well-rooted bulbs will start off much faster and give better first-year performance.

Follow the directions received with the bulbs for spacing and planting depth. The rule of thumb is to cover the bulb with soil to a depth twice that of the *diameter* of the bulb. (Lily bulbs are usually rather flattened from top to bottom.) When you see recommendations to cover bulbs with 6 to 8 inches of soil, they are the type that forms a root system on the stem above the bulb, as well as contractile roots below the bulb. Conversely, when you see directions to cover bulbs with 2 to 4 inches of soil, they are the type that forms roots only at the bottom of the bulb, or are of a species that will rot if planted deep.

If you decide to plant "on the flat," you will discover that the bottom of your planting holes will be below the level of the surrounding soil, not the best situation for drainage. Instead of digging holes, work up the soil in the bed and buy some bags of planter mix. Set the bulbs on the top of the prepared soil and pour the planter mix over them to cover the bulbs to the recommended depth. This is a fancy way of building a raised bed, but it elevates the bulb to warmer, drier soil levels where the drainage is better.

As you plant each bulb, mark it with a more or less permanent label. Drive in a stake 3 to 5 inches away from each bulb of taller varieties.

## Fertilizing

A preplant application of fertilizer won't be enough to feed lilies through the growing season unless your soil is quite fertile. Typically, lily enthusiasts side-dress a low-nitrogen fertilizer on the soil around lily plants as soon as new growth begins to show: 2 to 4 tablespoons per plant should suffice. Be sure not to get any fertilizer on the foliage. One or two foliar feedings with water-soluble fertilizer before flower buds form may work better on sandy soils.

## Pests and Diseases

Several minor leaf spots may attack lilies in zones 7 and 8, and elsewhere during wet summers. They are not critical but can disfigure foliage. In northern and midwestern areas the only major fungus disease is botrytis or gray mold, a muggy weather problem, which starts as spots on the leaves and gradually involves flower buds. Micronized copper sprays are effective. Wide spacing between plants and siting lily beds out in the open helps lily foliage to dry faster and to minimize foliage disease.

Even more important, spray at the first sign of aphids. Keep weeds pulled too; some weed species can harbor cucumber mosaic virus and transmit it to your lilies through aphid vectors. If any foliage looks mottled, light green against dark, dig out and discard the bulb without delay. Mosaic virus symptoms are nothing like nutrient-deficiency signs, light or off-color foliage. Try supplemental feeding if you are in doubt: foliar feed or drench around plants with fish emulsion or one of the water-soluble fertilizers high in potash; they are labeled for feeding ornamentals.

## Dividing and Transplanting

Don't move or divide lilies unless there is a good reason for it. However, taking up lilies to speed up increase is a different matter. As plants mature, young plants will begin to come up, growing from new bulbs that form around the mother bulb. In the fall, you can dig these young bulbs and spread them out in drifts or use them to start new lily beds. Tiny new bulbs may get lost if you transplant them into the landscape, unless you label them carefully.

The stems of some lilies run for some distance underground before turning up one to two feet away from the old bulb. This is an especially good habit among low, rather open shrubs, which act as an understory, even giving stems some support. These are called "stoloniferous" lilies after their underground stems. The American lilies with stolons form new bulbs on the ends.

Some species, such as *L. tigrinum*, set numerous bulbils—little dark, shiny beads—in leaf axils. These can be taken when they begin to loosen prior to dropping off, and rooted to make new bulbs. Or when the foliage turns brown, you can bend the stem over at the base, cover it lightly with soil, and new lily plants will grow along the stem the following year. You may see small bulbs forming right at the surface around stem-rooting hybrids; if so, heap up a few inches of soil to cover them until they are large and well-rooted enough to take up for division.

Certain lilies can be increased from bulb scales. Plunge the scales with the scar down, in trays of moist vermiculite to root, or alternate layers of scales with layers of moist vermiculite in a plastic bag. Bottom heat will speed the process but, since you will be doing it in late summer, you probably won't need extra heat. Tiny bulblets will form around the scale and, when these begin to show green shoots, detach and pot them up in a seed flat mix to grow to the size of a quarter before setting them out in a nursery row.

## Hybridization

Watching lilies develop and bloom from bulbs you planted and nurtured is thrilling, no doubt about it. But, the ultimate thrill is to become the proud hybridizer of a seedling lily that is more beautiful than either of its parents. Don't bother with haphazard crossing; instead, start with one of the newly introduced polyploids. They have extremely complex genetic backgrounds, which enhance your chances of developing a fine new hybrid. Just make sure that the catalog listing says that they are fertile.

To succeed in crossing polyploid lilies, you need to play a little "numbers game." The chromosome number of the gametes of most lily species is 12. Normal or standard lilies are diploid; that is, they have a chromosome number of 24. Triploid lilies have a chromosome number of 36, and the chromosome number of tetraploids is 48. Your best results will come from crossing diploids with diploids, triploids with triploids, and tetraploids with tetraploids.

Lily catalogs lump all cultivars with more than the normal chromosome number under the catchall term "polyploid." This classification developed only recently and includes some of the most exciting new lilies seen in many years.

# *Peppers*

*Fun, fellowship, community service, and creative satisfaction are harvested along with Ann and John Swan's Pennsylvania pepper crop.*

*(Left) The colorful sampler shown here displays some of the sweet, mild, pungent, and hot peppers grown by the Swans.*

**P**eppers are one of the most important food crops in the world, but you'd never know it from looking at typical produce counters. One small bin of green stuffing peppers and a few jalapeños in the gourmet section would be representative. However, as you travel south through Mexico and into the Caribbean and Central America, you enter the home-land of peppers. Peppers everywhere! Fresh, dried, pickled, roasted, fried . . . mostly hot, but many with subtle flavors that are wasted on us Norte Americanos.

Whoever first referred to the genus *Capsicum* as "peppers" started a confusing situation that seems insoluble. The name "pepper" was already being applied to *Piper nigrum*, the tropical spice pepper, before explorers brought back garden peppers from the New World. Most Europeans refer to garden peppers correctly as "*Capsicums*," but it seems doubtful whether the Latin name will ever catch on here.

Collectively, sweet and hot peppers may rank second only to tomatoes among garden vegetables worldwide. In many nations, hot peppers are the single most important condiment. Use of garden peppers in the United States, mostly fresh in salads, is "small potatoes" compared to other parts of the world. The use here is increasing, thanks to the promotion of golden and mature red sweet peppers and the increasing interest in Mexican, Southeast Asian, and Pakistani cuisines, which call for hot and mildly hot peppers.

Peppers spread all over the tropical and semitropical parts of the world with the early explorers. The seeds are easy to keep and transport, and will remain viable for several years. Curiously, the "hottest" cuisines in the world are not found in the New World, where garden peppers are native, but in Africa, Pakistan, Thailand, and China. Many countries offer side dishes of fiery pepper sauces and vinegars, so that diners can season foods to individual tastes. It is possible that the bland taste of the basic foods of these countries led them to welcome the addition of hot peppers for seasoning.

Early explorers reported that Amerindians grew peppers for more than flavoring. They appreciated hot peppers as an appetite enhancer, an aid to digestion, an expectorant, and an aphrodisiac. When the Europeans arrived, peppers had long been domesticated. However, a few wild stands survive, and are harvested annually for vine-dried hot peppers. Old-timers in the South maintain that homemade sausage made with hot peppers keeps better and that peppers tame the taste of wild game. No self-respecting truckstop in the deep South is without bottles of red "Louisiana hot sauce" and pickled hot peppers on every table. The hot, vinegary juice from pickled peppers is used mostly to flavor boiled mustard and turnip greens.

Peppers were first reported in North America in the Florida and New Mexico gardens of Spanish garrisons. Soon thereafter, numerous varieties of both sweet and hot peppers arrived with planters from the Caribbean settling in the South. Yet, seeds of sweet peppers had arrived early with colonists from Great Britain, France, and Holland, and spread south and east with frontier expansion. This may account for the overwhelming national preference for sweet peppers.

Thomas Jefferson planted peppers at Monticello, perhaps ordering seeds from Bernard M'Mahon's catalog. In his 1806 offering, M'Mahon states: "The capsicums are in much estimation for culinary purposes . . . the 'Large Heart-shaped' is the best." He named other varieties: 'Cherry', 'Bell', and 'Long-podded'.

Taxonomists have squabbled over the botanical arrangement of the genus *Capsicum* for centuries. One of the major drawbacks to classifying the various varieties by species was that most of the United States taxonomists and agricultural botanists were at northern universities. In short-season

*A harvest of "hots." Clockwise from the top: 'Anaheim TMR 23', 'Tabasco', 'Frogmore', an unidentified wild species, 'Habañero', 'Hungarian Yellow Wax'; center, 'Jalapeño M.'*

areas, culture of the late-maturing sweets and hots was difficult, and growing of the true tropicals was impossible. However, in recent years, with the aid of laboratory techniques such as electrophoresis, taxonomists have been able to distinguish the subtle differences among species.

Classifying peppers is difficult partly because pepper plants cross so readily. Fortunately, wild specimens of certain pepper species can still be found, which gives scientists a starting point. They have been able, working with ethnobotanists, historians, and archaeologists, to project the centers from which the various *Capsicum* species spread throughout the world.

*Hortus III* lists only two *Capsicum* species as important in North America, *C. annuum* and *C. frutescens*. Five "groups" are listed under *C. annuum*; these include virtually all the sweet and nontropical varieties of hot peppers. Within *C. frutescens* is the Tabasco pepper, the source of the heat for the best-known brand of Louisiana hot sauce, which is fermented for a year before bottling. Vinegar-pickled hot peppers are often of the 'Serrano' variety or of 'Tabasco'. Certain of the tropical species or forms won't grow well in this country because they developed under specific conditions of night length, duration of season, and day and night temperatures that we can't duplicate in continental United States gardens.

Everyone, it seems, is more aware of peppers these days. The press coverage generated by the many chili cookoffs, which have now spread coast to coast from the original in Terlingua, Texas, has helped. People everywhere are recognizing and using sweet peppers as well, to add color and flavor to salads, and for their high vitamin content. Still, we have only just begun to appreciate the great variety and potential of the many easily grown pepper varieties and hybrids. Elizabeth Snyder, in her book *Uncommon Fruits and Vegetables*, puts it this way: "With the Mexican and Southeast Asia food explosions in this country of late, we had best begin to make an effort to understand which [pepper] is which and how to use them."

A good place to start would be the produce stand of a grocery serving Mexican-Americans or Southeast Asians. You'll see fresh fruits of the bluntly conical, black-green 'Jalapeño'; the slender, twisty 'Red Chili'; the considerably longer and milder 'Anaheim' or 'New Mexico Chili', or the variably hot, horn-shaped 'Hungarian Yellow Wax'. Dried pods of 'Ancho' and 'Poblado' will be for sale for making powders, and the small, pungent, fruits of 'Serrano' and 'Bird Pepper'. Few of the varieties popular in Southeast Asia and Pakistan are seen here; emigrants from those countries have adapted pretty well to the Mexican varieties.

There is, as well, a big difference in flavor of the various kinds of sweet peppers. Connoisseurs agree that the best flavors are not to be found in the big, blocky bell peppers sold on produce counters, but rather in the medium-sized tapered or horn-shaped peppers such as 'Gypsy' hybrid or the sweet strains of 'Hungarian Yellow Wax'.

Each sweet, mild, or hot pepper variety has its own distinctive flavor; these flavors change with maturity, and in cooking, drying, or pickling. Pepper enthusiasts have learned to tune their tastebuds to the nuances. For John and Ann Swan, a flirtation with peppers more than thirty years ago has blossomed into an infatuation that adds zest to their lives.

*John and Ann prefer to allow their sweet peppers to ripen red before picking.*

John and Ann Swan of West Chester, Pennsylvania, are the kind of people who have fun growing any kind of plant, be it a flower, vegetable, tree, or shrub. They are good-natured, sharing people who have developed into crackerjack home gardeners and are enjoying every minute of it. Peppers are one of the plants that add spice to their lives and those of everyone around them. Red, yellow, green, purple . . . sweet, mild, hot, and fiery peppers; name a variety and chances are they will have grown it. In their big garden, their pepper patch dominates.

Plunked down in the middle of a large raised-bed food garden, their pepper patch gives the Swans room to try a few new varieties each year, while supplying pecks of peppers of their favorite varieties. The food garden is only the beginning of a beautifully integrated landscape. Flanked by huge, curving beds of perennials and decorative herbs, their side-yard area melds into spacious peninsulas planted with shade-loving species, mostly native plants. In the background are great trees. Atop a rise above the food garden are a culinary herb garden and a sizable wildflower meadow garden. All around the house are choice shrubs, groundcovers, and bulbous plants. The Swans are serious gardeners, no doubt about it!

English born and brought to the United States in infancy, John credits some of his love for flowers to his mother, "who loved to gather and arrange great armloads of flowers, like a proper Englishwoman." Not so with Ann Tucker Swan. Born in Bermuda of an English mother and a Bermudian father, she came to the United States with John as a war bride after World War II. (John was stationed in Bermuda with the U.S. Army Air Corps.) Ann, who describes with relish her growing up as "the only girl on an island with a school for boys," came by gardening from both sides.

Ann's father founded and headed up the Nonsuch Island Training School for wayward boys. They were taught numerous skills, and gardening was, perforce, high on the list. Imported food would have been too costly to satisfy the appetites of growing boys. Her parents taught Ann how to prepare the eclectic foods of Bermuda, reflecting cuisines that merged on the island: British, African, Portuguese, and Caribbean.

In particular, Ann learned how to use peppers to make food more interesting.

"Our friends in Bermuda included people from many parts of the world," recalled Ann. "Each grew his or her own kind of heirloom peppers, sometimes several kinds per family. They pickled the small, red, very hot 'bird peppers' in sherry or rum and used them as condiments for fish chowders and stews. A dash of either of these hot sauces made a memorable Bermuda version of the Bloody Mary. Bermudians grew and used lots of cucumbers, as do I, and put them up as spicy pickles, sometimes with hot peppers. In Bermuda, all surplus vegetables were preserved; the cost of imported food provided incentive."

Gardening had to wait while John finished his degree in English at the University of Pennsylvania and Ann began a career at Smith Kline Laboratories in Philadelphia. "I wasn't good at waiting," said Ann; "I soon had an office full of plants!" John went to work in marketing communications at the DuPont Company. Thirty years ago, they bought a lot near West Chester, Pennsylvania, and later expanded it to three acres. They named their mini-estate "Frogmore" after a famous manor house in England.

"It was not until we began building our house that we took a close look at the land," said John. "We had wondered why the property was strewn with rocks and was rougher than the surrounding farmland. Then, an old farmer in the neighborhood told us that our land was the site of an abandoned dump for rock rubble blasted from a serpentine stone quarry. Ever since before the American Revolution, and up until the early twentieth century, chunks of rock had been hauled from the quarry to our lot. In some areas of the lot, rock was thirty feet deep! We had been unable to recognize the extent of it because of a tangle of underbrush, vines, shrubs, briars, and trees. The saving grace was a cart trail that wound through the piles at ground level, and a more or less rock-free area where we built our home. The old trail, which led down to a creek in the back, became our woodland garden.

"My back still aches," said John, "at the memory of the rocks Ann and I removed and piled aside to make room for our first food garden. That experience taught me why the settlers in this area built homes of stone . . . they needed a place to put them when clearing their fields!" Ann added: "We hauled in soil and dumped it over the rocks; we grew beans and corn at first, stuff we could direct-seed. Neither of us had done large-scale gardening, so we began with simple crops. Our first failure was asparagus; it just didn't produce well for us. Early on we began composting, as my father had taught the boys to do on Bermuda. John and I could get lots of manure locally, loads of leaves from our trees, and field hay from our open pastureland. Years ago, we began saving and recycling all garden refuse and kitchen scraps."

In their then-new garden, Ann could hardly wait to get started growing her fondly remembered peppers, especially the tiny, very hot bird peppers. She sent to Bermuda for seeds and began what has proven to be an absorbing hobby of evaluating hot, mild, and sweet peppers in the garden, and preparing or preserving them in many ways.

"Our friends considered me slightly balmy," Ann said, "until they tasted my bird peppers pickled in sherry. Just a few drops turns bland dishes into party foods!" Her days of sailing a ketch from Nonsuch Island to mainland Bermuda for shopping showed in her description of refilling empty pepper-sauce bottles. "As the tide goes out, pour in more sherry. The flavor will hold through one complete refilling."

*A plant of 'Cubanelle' pampered by the Swans with a plastic pot reservoir, a wire cage, and salt-marsh hay mulch.*

"I can't get the same kind of sherry we used years ago on Bermuda, but from all the kinds I've tested, one seems to approximate the taste I remember . . . Taylor's Golden Sherry. It is neither too dry nor too sweet.

"John helped me so much with my pepper hobby and, later, as I branched out into herbs," Ann said, "he built a thousand-square-foot vegetable garden on a slope so steep that he had to terrace it with railroad ties, three high at each step. I wheelbarrowed and dumped in soil mixed with spent composted manure from a nearby mushroom grower.

"After we completed that job, he and I tackled the piles of stones around the place." As Ann spoke, I tried to imagine the number of man and woman hours needed to load, move, offload, and set the thousands of stones in evidence. They were neatly laid without mortar, in back-sloping walls. I estimated the walls at about five hundred feet total, ranging in height from two to four feet. The stones have begun to collect a patina of moss, lichen, and ferns. Here and there, choice perennials are chinked in. Carefully chosen prostrate shrubs and creeping groundcovers break the stark gray-green lines.

"If only we had been able to afford a tractor and a scoop loader," John added, "we could have finished the job in a year or two. But, we were young and strong. The hard work, year after year, may have been a blessing. We still have the energy and endurance to do whatever we wish, be it gardening, volunteer work, or travel."

Their shared excitement crackled as they told how they discovered a wild pepper on an island in the Galapagos Archipelago. "On the side of a still-active volcano, at some distance, partly hidden by tall grass, we caught a glimpse of pepper red. We picked our way through the underbrush and, sure enough, found a tall, shrubby, pepper plant with small pods. It was the first wild pepper we had seen in our travels and we had to have it for our pepper trials.

"We brought seeds home and grew plants, only to find our Galapagos pepper was a promiscuous little devil. After only one generation, we lost the original line due to natural crosses with other varieties. One of those accidental crosses, it turned out, was a 'keeper,' a small-fruited pepper we named 'Frogmore' after an estate in England. We are still growing it.

"Many of the exotic pepper varieties are available from seeds ordered from specialty catalogs. We've picked up seeds of local varieties in Ecuador, and have found a few more wild kinds," says John. "Friends give us some; that's how we got started with 'Rocotillo'; it came from Puerto Rico. We order seeds of Mexican and southwestern specialties from Seeds and Plants of the Southwest, in Santa Fe, New Mexico, and from Horticultural Enterprises in Dallas. Stokes Seeds in Buffalo is another good source with a wide selection of sweet and mild peppers. The Pepper Gal in Largo, Florida, has an interesting list as does Park Seeds in Greenwood, South Carolina."

*The Swans' pepper patch, which is planted on terraces, ascends a steep slope.*

Ann is delighted with an heirloom pepper they were given by a friend who found it in South Carolina. It is one of the distinctive small-fruited hot peppers native to the tropics and has adapted to temperate climates. It is a different species from standard hot peppers: the foliage is smaller and the plants bushier. No one knew its name, so they dubbed it 'Ethel Jane' in honor of the person on whose property it was found.

"Space is limited in our garden," John said. "Before we order seeds, we decide how many fruits of each variety we will need to grow for our own kitchen and for the Pennsylvania Horticultural Society's 'Harvest Show.' Then, we project how many plants we'll need to produce them. Finally, we add a few varieties that we've never grown before. After dropping the varieties that were unsatisfactory or indifferent the previous year, that brings us up to twelve to fifteen varieties, three to ten plants per variety. That's all we have room for in the food garden. Ann plugs a few plants of the more ornamental hots into sunny perennial beds, and that relieves a bit of the pressure for space.

"I always draw a plot plan of the vegetable garden so we can rotate crops," John continued. "We don't like to plant peppers in the same location two years in a row. We don't rely on memory; a plot plan reminds us of what we planted, when and where, from year to year."

John does most of the propagation for the Swans' garden. "I start pepper seeds in the basement beginning the second week in March," he said. "I plant three seeds per cube in Jiffy 7s, which I buy a thousand to the case to save money. When the seedlings have their first set of true leaves, I scissor out the surplus and leave one strong seedling per cube. Pepper seeds germinate best at 70 to 75 degrees F. I get good results by setting trays of moistened and seeded Jiffy 7s in the furnace room for germination. I cover the trays with sheet plastic to keep moisture in and marauding mice out.

"As soon as the seeds show green sprouts, I remove the plastic and move the trays of Jiffy 7s to fluorescent-lit shelves and grow the plants to the six-leaf stage at about 65 degrees, 60 at night. Then, I do something that I feel makes a real difference in pepper growing. I pot up the Jiffy 7 plants in four-inch plastic pots filled with a half-and-half mixture of screened soil from the vegetable garden and a potting medium named 'Pro-Mix.' I don't sterilize the soil used in the mix; so far, we've been lucky not to have any root rot in our plants.

"After three or four weeks, the seedlings will have filled the pots with roots but, in an average spring, won't be pot-bound. At that season of the year, we begin listening to the weather-band radio. We really need to get our pepper plants in the ground around May 15, after hardening off for two weeks, in order to maximize production. So, around May 1, weather permitting, we begin setting trays of plants outside, along a sunny, sheltering wall. Wind is the real villain; if it kicks up during the day, we cover the plants to keep the stems from being damaged. If the temperature drops, we bring them indoors. Every cold night we bring them in. We have learned that you must not allow pepper plants to become shocked by cold temperatures or whipped and weakened by drying winds.

"We can actually see the plants changing as they harden off. The stems and leaves thicken and become stiffer. The leaves turn dark green. New internodes are short. We know that, when we set a hardened-off pepper plant in the garden around May 15, it won't be shocked by transplanting.

"We've developed a system of transplanting that works for us. Our soil is fluffy and weed-free from tilling in late fall and adding composted manure from a mushroom grower. We line out rows three feet apart and set pepper plants thirty inches apart, to get the maximum number on each terrace. How we set them in makes a big difference, we feel.

"We mix a handful of 5-10-5 granular fertilizer into the quart or so of soil excavated to make a planting hole. We set the plant in just deep enough to match its soil line with the surface of the garden soil, perhaps half an inch higher. If the plants are overgrown due to weather delays, we straighten out girdling roots before planting and backfilling.

"Next, and we may be the only gardeners doing this, we cut the bottoms out of six-inch nursery pots and set them around the pepper plants, small end down. We twist them this way and that to sink the bottom rim one and a half to two inches deep into the soil. These pots shelter young seedlings not only from cutworms but also from stem-whipping winds. They reflect and concentrate heat, and give us a reservoir for watering. We pour water into them slowly, to avoid washing soil around. Those bottomless pots are one of our 'secret weapons.'

"Another secret weapon is a stack of large, rigid, empty three-gallon plastic nursery pots we stow in the garden house. If night temperatures threaten to fall below 50 degrees, we cover pepper plants with inverted pots. We're not so much concerned with frost after May 15 as we are with the chilling effect of cold wind and cold rain. We didn't have to buy the containers; they came with perennials and shrubs we purchased.

"As anyone knows who has grown peppers," John said, "they sit still for two or three weeks after planting, regardless of the weather. Nothing

1)

2)

3)

4)

## Protecting Peppers

The Swans employ an arsenal of techniques to protect their peppers until harvest. Bottomless plastic one-gallon pots shelter new transplants from wind and cutworms, as well as reflecting and concentrating heat (1). Baskets and nursery containers cover pepper plants against late spring frosts (2). Old shutters supported above plants reduce the stress from extremely hot weather (3). Old madras bedspreads pulled over cages protect plants against fall frost (4).

*Masters of the Victory Garden*

you do will make them add size. I think that the plants are developing roots like crazy. When the soil warms in June, the plants take off and grow with a rush. Some of our hot varieties don't put on much growth until late July.

"When fast growth starts, we set a cage around each pepper plant. The cages serve three purposes: they keep plants from toppling in windstorms, they minimize breakage of brittle limbs, and they keep our feet from compacting soil near the plants. We have tried growing peppers without cages but lose production to toppling and breakage. We like red-ripe peppers and let so many fruit hang on the plants that they are especially vulnerable to breakage.

"We make pepper cages of the reinforcing wire mesh used to strengthen concrete; it works much better and lasts longer than the thinner, less substantial fencing such as dog wire. All our cages are eighteen inches in diameter. We make some of them thirty inches high for short varieties and some forty-eight inches for taller peppers. The net height is six inches less because we snip out the cross wires on the bottom ring. That leaves spears that stick into the ground to prevent the cage from tipping over in a storm. The cylinders last for nearly ten years; we're on our second set. In late June we dress two to three inches of salt marsh hay over the entire vegetable garden, for moisture retention, weed control, and reduction of soil temperature. Salt hay is particularly good because it holds up for a long time, contains no weed seeds, and does not support fungus diseases."

It's important not to cultivate around pepper plants. Instead, hand-pull weeds growing around the plants and rake soil out of the walkways to pull up around the plants and to bury weed seedlings.

John continued: "The mulch really helps our plants to withstand extreme heat and dryness. During a heat wave, some of our sweet varieties, especially 'Gypsy' and 'Cubanelle', looked as if they were about to die. Watering kept them barely alive but didn't seem to help the problem. We laid old louvered shutters across the tops of the cages and the shade saved the plants. Hot weather always reduces fruit set, except on the hot varieties, even though we water deeply every two or three days. Peppers can stand only so much heat and dryness."

The Swans rarely find it necessary to give their peppers supplementary fertilizer. "The 5-10-10 we mix in at planting time is enough to produce a good crop on our soil," said John. "The mushroom compost, being composed mostly of straw and horse manure, probably contributes most of the other nutrients needed by vegetables. If I see an occasional plant growing slowly, I will give it a shot of liquid plant food, but never of a high-nitrogen analysis."

I asked Ann how many peppers they harvested from the seventy plants in their garden, and which was the most prolific variety. "I have no doubt we lose some production," she replied, "by minimizing picking until the 'Harvest Show' in late September. Even so, we get up to five pounds of fruit per plant, especially from 'Cubanelle' and 'Gypsy'. Some of the hots such as 'Bird' pepper, 'Thai Hot', and 'Tabasco' have hundreds of fruits but they are so tiny and hard to pick that we are lucky to get half a pound per plant.

"Personally," Ann said, "I much prefer red-ripe sweet or mildly hot peppers over the immature green fruit. The flesh is sweeter and thicker. And, since I roast, sear, or sauté most fruits rather than eating them raw, the thick mature skin slips right off. I am willing to sacrifice yield for such quality. As it stands, the day before the 'Harvest Show,' every inch of space on the basement floor and the family room is covered with baskets of ripe peppers, labeled by variety. By the way, I clip off large-fruited peppers with a pair of sharp Felco shears. Snapping or twisting them off can break limbs.

"After the show, we concentrate on preserving all the peppers we can before hard frost," Ann said. "Light frosts don't worry us because we lay old cotton bedspreads over the crops. The Madras spreads are rather light, but rarely blow off, and they dry out quickly after a rain. We've tried the new spun-bonded floating row covers, but they tear on the cages and are hard to anchor. I hate the way they feel when they are wet! I'd rather dry the bedspreads on the vegetable garden fence, fold and store them between frosts."

The plants' heavy foliage canopy in the fall tends to shield the lower half of the plant and, often, the fruits that are borne down low. Even though a light frost can blacken the outer shell of foliage, you can continue to pick peppers for a while. But frost makes a warm-weather vegetable act like a wounded deer; it may run for a while but is doomed to a short life. You'd be better off either picking all the fruits before a frost and freezing them, or pulling the entire plant and hanging it in a cool basement to supply you with fresh peppers for up to a month.

"A killing frost doesn't ordinarily come before mid-October, so we have about three weeks to harvest and preserve our pepper crop. We freeze 'Gypsy' or 'Canape' diced, or halved and seeded, along with whole fruits of the pungent 'Rocotillo'. The 'Jalapeño M' fruits, we pickle. We lay fruits of the thin-fleshed hots on old window screens and dry them in the furnace room. Fortuitously, we turn on the house heat at the same time we need heat for drying.

"I hate the dry hot pepper flakes served in Italian restaurants and pizza parlors!" said Ann. "I prefer a powder I make by grinding and mixing selected hot and mild peppers to taste. I try to make my mixtures hot, but not so hot as to kill the flavor."

She showed me how she prepares hot pepper powder for the Philadelphia unit of The Herb Society, which sells it as a fund-raiser. She combines flavorful mild peppers such as 'Fushimi' and 'Zippy' and removes the calyxes (caps) from the dried fruit. Then she adds about 10 percent by volume of a very hot dried pepper such as 'Thai Hot', 'Bird', or 'Tabasco'. She runs these through her food processor, tastes the mixture to be sure it has the right degree of heat, then runs it through her blender to make a fine powder. She seals the powder tight in small bottles to preserve the flavor, labels and dates them, and they are ready for use. I tasted some of Ann's blends and, to this old hot-pepper lover, they seemed just right!

I asked Ann if she wore rubber gloves when working with hot peppers. "No," she replied, "the flush of heat I get from the active ingredient makes my arthritic hands feel better. But I always take out my contact lenses because the flying powder will bring tears, despite my laying a damp towel over the food processor and blender."

For her pepper jelly, another fast-selling item for their fund-raisers, Ann prefers to use mature red fruits of 'Gypsy' and 'Canape' hybrids, or 'Hungarian Yellow Wax'. They tried the paprika variety 'Szegedi', but it lacked production. They shy away from the large-fruited bells because

## Pepper Preparations

An assortment of Ann's "pepperations" tempt the palate: hot and pungent dried peppers for mixing into powders (1); bottled hot "Sherry Peppers," "Hot Pepper Vodka," and "Spiced Sherry Peppers" (2); frozen peppers: 'Rocotillo', in the foreground, and 'Cubanelle' (3).

1)

2)

3)

the flat-topped fruits tend to catch water and rot. She finds other uses for mature red peppers; for her, 'Gypsy' makes fine pimiento peppers for canning. Others, such as the mildly pungent 'Anaheim TMR 23', she chars, removes the skin and seeds, stuffs into pint plastic containers, adds a pinch of salt, applies lids, and freezes. Thawed, they are in a handy increment for adding to cooked dishes.

One of Ann's newest but most popular productions are pickled cocktail peppers of the 'Rocotillo' variety, flavored with dill. These are funny little pungent, but not fiercely hot, peppers, flat like flying saucers. Green when immature, they turn yellow, then red when ripe. She mixes the three colors for pickles.

Also new are experimental hot mustards made with powdered dry 'Habañero' and 'Thai Hot' peppers. Ann is perhaps best known for the Bermuda specialties, sherry pepper and rum pepper. To make them, she stuffs tall, slender jars one-third full of red-ripe fruit of small, thin-skinned hots such as 'Bird', 'Tabasco', 'Thai', and 'Ethel Jane', fills them with sherry or rum, caps them, and lets them sit in the dark for at least a month before use.

Ann gave me two more pepper recipes before I left their pleasant company. "For breakfast, try 'Cubanelle' peppers sautéed in light olive oil. Serve them with grilled tomatoes. And for a pepper jelly that will take the blue ribbon, use red-ripe bell peppers and add either horseradish or freshly ground ginger."

The Swans' hobby has given a new focus to their travels and has attracted a new and expanding circle of friends who swap pepper seeds and stories with them. They have been at it so long and have researched peppers so thoroughly that they just might be the best-informed amateur pepper growers in the country. I think they are, and I hope they keep on growing and sharing for many years.

# More about Peppers

**What's in a Name?**

The names of the *Capsicum* species and groups are complicated, but there is a reason for it. Long ago, seeds were transported from centers of origin in the New World to distant points where distinct "varieties" evolved or emerged from selection by man. If you could grow plants of a taxonomic variety side-by-side with representatives of its original species, you would see few differences except for those achieved by primitive methods of selection. Plant scientists can make the connections, however, despite the differences, by comparing similarities that only taxonomists can appreciate.

Eventually, when a taxonomic "variety" becomes sufficiently uniform and true to type, it may be given a "cultivar" name, which is botanical argot for "cultivated variety." Were you to compare cultivars with their original species side-by-side, you might see great differences in the size, shape, and number of fruit, plant habit, season of production, and disease resistance. Yet, taxonomists can look closely at antecedents and descendants and see their relationship.

So, there may be types of peppers for which three entities exist: the original species, the crudely improved and variable variety, and the greatly improved modern cultivar.

For maximum clarity, cultivar names should always appear in single quotation marks such as 'Yolo Wonder' or 'Anaheim Chili'. Few seed catalogs follow this modern nomenclature and prefer merely to capitalize the first letter of the cultivar name or to print it in boldface. Further confusing the issue, seedsmen also prefer to refer to their open pollinated strains of vegetables as "varieties" rather than cultivars.

Dr. Jean Andrews's book, *The Domesticated Capsicums*, contains a chart of domesticated pepper varieties which could be considered a *Capsicum* family tree. The apparent redundancies in naming are unavoidable. Explanatory notes have been added.

● *Capsicum annuum* var. (variety) *annuum:* Representative cultivars would be 'Jalapeno', 'Gypsy', or 'Park's Whopper'. Most of the sweet and hot peppers popular in temperate climates are in this group.

● *Capsicum annuum* var. *aviculare:* A representative cultivar would be 'Chiltecpin'. The bird peppers are in this variety. The plants are generally tall, open, and rather small-leaved, and the fruits are tiny, variable in shape, and very hot.

● *Capsicum baccatum* var. *pendulum:* 'Kellu-uchu' and 'Pucauchu' would be representative. These varieties do not perform well at our latitudes.

● *Capsicum chinense* var. *chinchi-uchu, habañero,* and *rocotillo:* Habañero and rocotillo are late maturing, but can be grown at our latitudes. The plants are rangier but otherwise superficially similar to popular varieties of *C. annuum.*

● *Capsicum frutescens:* Representative varieties would be *tabasco* and *uvilla grande.* Both have erect, quite hot fruit on large, late plants.

● *Capsicum pubescens* var. *rocoto:* No mistaking these plants: the leaves have a faintly furry look and appear thinner than those of our garden peppers. Not well adapted to temperate climates.

The *Capsicum* family trees don't show 'Habañero' and 'Rocotillo' as cultivars, even though seeds are available under these names. I believe it is because these are primitive and highly variable varieties from which other named cultivars were later selected. Any Jamaican, for example, can tell you that their version of *habañero* — some call it 'Scotch Bonnet' — can differ in hotness and flavor from village to village.

You won't find many hybrids among the hot peppers, but you may encounter the term "strains." A given variety may have several different strains, depending on who grows the seeds. Each producer has his own specifications for the variety, and selects toward it, when choosing seed parents. After a few generations of selection, his strain may differ from the original, yet will still look enough like it to pass. For example, certain strains of 'Hungarian Yellow Wax' are distinctly nippy while others are perfectly sweet. You can't tell the difference without tasting them. Sometimes, strains become accidentally mixed by field-crossing with another variety. That can result in mild-flavored peppers in a supposedly hot variety or—surprise!—hot peppers in a supposedly sweet variety.

## Adaptability

I can remember when peppers were the prima donnas of food gardens. Those old varieties sulked in hot weather and cold: if the temperature didn't suit them, they would blossom, but wouldn't set fruit. The new hybrid peppers perform well in all the contiguous states, but the bearing season in the northern tier of states, even with the aid of heat-trapping mulch, is rather short.

When you order pepper seeds or plants, remember that peppers originated in or near tropic latitudes. If you garden in an area with short or cool summers, choose the early varieties or hybrids, those that will mature in sixty to sixty-five days. This means you can't grow the great big stuffing peppers because they mature rather late. Take heart: the smaller-fruited hybrids are more productive anyway, and often are better flavored.

## Mulching

Peppers respond well to mulches but what you use depends on the average soil temperature in your garden during the summer. Peppers like warm soil, but not hot. The hot varieties of peppers can tolerate hot soil, but would yield better if mulched to hold down maximum soil temperatures. This is why John and Ann Swan's salt marsh hay mulch produces good results for them. Such organic mulches are recommended across Middle America and farther south and west, rather than plastic.

Plastic mulches, however, work better in northern zones such as 4 and 5 and the upper edge of 6. They trap solar heat and keep the soil warmer than in surrounding areas. Experiments in Duluth, Minnesota, confirm that clear plastic mulch is most effective in their cool climate, applied after the soil warms up, and covered with organic mulch later for shading. Weeds will grow beneath clear plastic due to the warmth, humidity, and transmitted light, but the organic mulch will shade them out.

Black plastic mulch is not recommended for zones 7 and south, unless you run drip irrigation tubes under it and spray-paint the areas over root zones with flat white. In warm climates soil temperatures can rise alarmingly beneath black plastic, particularly on dry, sandy soil, and can stress plants by killing the roots in the surface layer beneath the plastic. The white paint reflects sunlight and reduces soil temperatures. White plastic mulch is available but is expensive.

## Buying Seeds and Plants

Pepper enthusiasts soon learn to order pepper seeds from companies that conduct field performance trials in a climate similar to theirs. Their "average plant height" figures can be relied on. Field trials also reveal the varieties or hybrids that are more tolerant of heat, cold, drought, or wet soil than others, and resistance to locally serious plant diseases.

Pepper breeders believe there is a genetic linkage between the ability of peppers to set fruit at low temperatures and at high. One appears to go with the other, to a point. There is a threshold of heat, about 86 degrees F., beyond which the bell or sweet peppers won't set fruit. You can expect peppers not to set fruit, when temperatures remain cooler than the low 60s for extended periods.

**Pests and Diseases**

Certain pepper hybrids have been bred for resistance to locally prevalent plant diseases. Your State Cooperative Extension Service will list these in their "Recommended Varieties" publications. They name resistances to specific diseases rather than, as some seed catalogs do, merely using the general and not particularly enlightening term "disease resistant."

One of the features we at *The Victory Garden* advise new gardeners to look for in pepper varieties is resistance to tobacco mosaic virus disease, TMV. This virus can cripple pepper plants, shut down their production, and make the plants look distorted and mottled. Many old bell pepper varieties have no resistance whatsoever, but most hot peppers have high levels of resistance. There are degrees of resistance: steer clear of any variety or hybrid labeled as "Tolerant of TMV"; you need maximum resistance in peppers, not merely tolerance.

Peppers have few problems with insects, but leafhoppers and thrips can rasp foliage and cause fruiting buds to drop. These can be controlled by spraying with insecticidal soap. A few species of larvae such as tomato fruit worms can bore into peppers; these are more difficult to control; your County Agent can suggest spray programs.

**Planting**

Peppers benefit from 2 to 3 percent organic matter in the soil, just enough to make it accept and store water, and to keep it biologically active. Too much organic matter can result in runaway release of nitrogen in warm weather, with resultant lush growth and inhibited fruit set. Peppers also like raised bed culture and drip irrigation; during dry seasons, drip irrigation can produce significant yield increases over watering by sprinkler.

Don't overplant peppers. Two or three plants will keep the average family in salad and stuffing peppers all summer long, and one plant of hot peppers will suffice. That leaves room to try new varieties and hybrids, and I hope you will. The incredibly beautiful ornamental peppers make fine heat-resistant plants to set among your garden flowers. Not all catalogs will tell you whether their ornamental varieties are hot or sweet; most are hot.

**Boosting Yields**

You can increase pepper production in many ways: by wrapping pepper cages with clear plastic for a few weeks after planting (leave a chimney for warm air to escape), by picking fruits weekly to reduce the drain on plant vigor, by installing drip irrigation, and by growing them with the aid of plastic mulch in cool climates. Some gardeners save plastic milk jugs, cut out the bottoms and remove the caps, and set them over young plants. The idea is to shield the plants from cold wind and rain and to accumulate a little heat to make them grow faster than unprotected plants. It works, and it also keeps out cutworms.

Most people miss out on one of the major advantages of peppers. They are so productive that only a plant or two of each variety can give you all the fruits of one kind that you can eat or put away for winter. Why plant several bushes of one variety of pepper when you can mix them up and have many different fruit sizes, shapes, colors, and flavors? Just one season of growing peppers will convince you that they really are easy to grow, and will inspire you to experiment with a wide variety. You'll have the makings for international cuisines and good old American cooking right at your fingertips!

PHOTOGRAPHS BY
**GARY MOTTAU**

DRAWINGS BY
**DANA GAINES**

# THE NEW VICTORY GARDEN

### BY
## BOB THOMSON

### WITH
## JAMES TABOR

# THE NEW
# VICTORY GARDEN

# ACKNOWLEDGMENTS

This book owes a great deal to many whose names do not appear on the cover but without whom it would not have come into being. First, thanks must go to Russell Morash, creator of the "Victory Garden" series on Public Television. He's an acknowledged leader in how-to television, and viewers everywhere must count themselves fortunate for his talents in bringing good gardening to American television. William D. Phillips, my editor at Little, Brown, is the stuff of every author's fondest dreams. Through a seemingly endless project, he never lost his sense of direction — or humor. James Tabor, the book's writer, patiently transformed manuscripts and tapes into finished form. John Pelrine, the "Victory Garden" series producer, contributed endless hours of his time and an inestimable reservoir of gardening knowledge. Former gardener Rudy Perkins added to that vast pool of gardening wisdom, as did Kip Anderson, current overseer of the Victory Garden itself. Gary Mottau, whose photos make this book a true feast for the eye, displayed an uncanny ability to catch the garden over and over at just the right time. Dianne Schaefer's artistry blended all the elements together into a beautiful union, and Dana Gaines's illustrations have added clarity to difficult-to-describe processes. Michael Mattil's tireless scrutiny (and well-timed comic relief) as copy editor assured that the book would come to you without flaw or inconsistency.

Special thanks must go to those who helped with the features that complement the book's gardening chapters. The National Wildlife Federation's Craig Tufts supplied invaluable information about birds and their habitats. Gladys Phillips helped create a lovely section on wreathmaking. The Goodell family of Westminster West, Vermont, whose extraordinary cider has been famous in New England for a good many years now, gave professional depth to my amateur's love for cidermaking.

My literary agent, Donald Cutler, deserves special mention along with Colleen Mohyde, Bill Phillip's able assistant, who kept all the many pieces together.

All of us at the Victory Garden are grateful to those who have made our regional gardens a reality: Lexington Gardens in Lexington, Massachusetts, Callaway Gardens in Pine Mountain, Georgia, and Rogers Garden Center in Newport Beach, California.

A final word of thanks to those who have supported "The Victory Garden" over its very fortunate long life. First, WGBH-TV in Boston, our producing station, and all public television stations across the country for bringing "The Victory Garden" to their viewers. And our corporate underwriters — those businesses who believe gardening is so worthwhile and want to be a part of bringing it to American viewers: Peter's Professional Plant Food, Monrovia Nursery Company, and the Mantis Manufacturing Company.

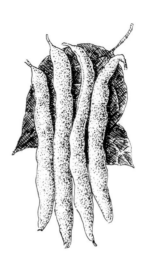

All photos by Gary Mottau with the exception of the following:

Max E. Badgley — pages 189 (left), 190 left column (bottom 3 photos), right column (top photo), 191 middle column (both photos), 192 middle column

Lee Jenkins — pages 190 right column (bottom), 191 left column, right column, 192 right column

Robert L. Wick — pages 193 (all), 194 left column, 195 center column

Russell Morash — pages 5, 17, 36 (bottom), 100, 232, 272–3

Rudy Perkins — pages 234, 235

*This book is dedicated to my wife, Betty,*
*my daughter, Kathy,*
*and to my sons, Scott and David*

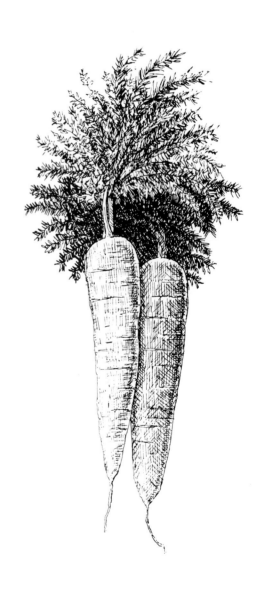

# THE NEW
# VICTORY GARDEN

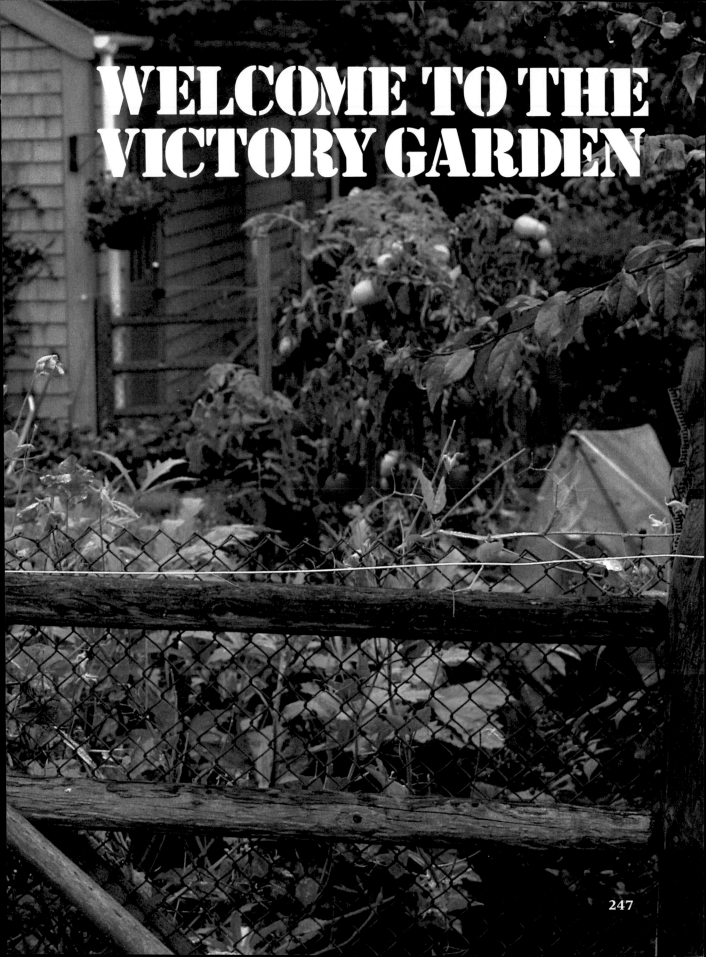

# WELCOME TO THE VICTORY GARDEN

# WELCOME TO
# THE VICTORY GARDEN

In the spring of 1979, I was beginning my twenty-fifth year in the gardening business. My predecessor, Jim Crockett, was getting ready for his fourth season as host of "Crockett's Victory Garden," the acclaimed PBS series. As a fellow "media gardener" (I'd been doing a Boston-based radio show for almost twenty years), I was keenly aware of Jim Crockett's work. I admired it very much and never missed an opportunity to watch Jim as he puttered around the little patch behind the WGBH-TV studios in the shadow of Harvard Stadium.

One day that spring, quite unexpectedly, I received a call from Russell Morash, the show's producer. We chatted a bit, and then Russ came to the point. Jim Crockett was ailing. If the current season was to be completed, the Victory Garden would need a little help. Russ asked if I could lend a hand. I agreed at once, feeling that it would be a privilege to work with Jim, who had helped create a truly unique television series.

We began working together about the middle of May 1979. I quickly discovered that Jim was as straightforward and friendly in real life as he was on camera. We worked well together, and I admired not only his considerable gardening expertise but his sheer courage, as well. Jim Crockett was suffering from cancer then, but he never once complained. His gaze and handshake remained firm throughout those months, and his spirit was bright, though I knew he was hurting. One afternoon, when we had finished taping a segment of the show, Jim drew me aside. "I need to talk to you," he said, and went on to explain that his latest prognosis had not been encouraging. "I'm flying out to a special clinic," he told me. "I want you to keep on doing the program while I'm gone, Bob. Will you do that?"

I assured him that I would, and promised to do my best until he returned. He said that he expected to be gone a month, maybe two. Tragically, four weeks later we received word that he had passed away. I was terribly saddened, as were millions of viewers who had fallen in love with this exceptional man.

"The Victory Garden" needed a new host, and Russ Morash asked me to step in. I thought that carrying on the "Victory Garden" heritage would be a fine way to honor Jim's memory, so I agreed to give television a try. That was seven years ago.

They've been a momentous seven years for vegetable gardening. In that time, I've seen more exciting changes and advances than in my previous three decades in the business. The plant breeders have created wondrous new vegetable varieties, for one thing. Ten years ago, there was no such thing as Sugar Snap peas or supersweet corn. These well-known varieties are

only two of a whole host of newcomers that are changing the face — and flavor — of gardening. We've also been blessed with many new hybrid varieties, giving us increased disease resistance, vigor, and plants bred specifically for small-space culture. And it's not only the vegetables themselves that have changed. Cultural practices have kept pace, too, and I've stayed abreast of them in the Victory Garden with raised beds, intercropping and succession planting, and high-yield techniques. There have also been dramatic changes in pest-control methods. Not so long ago, gardeners drenched their soil with strong chemicals. Few do so any longer, and my practice in the Victory Garden reflects this changing consciousness. I use physical barriers, manual removal, and organic pesticides. Nor have I ignored the generation of new gardening aids — black plastic mulch, Wall O' Water, spun polyester row covers, and more.

So much has happened, in fact, that a whole new book for vegetable gardeners really is necessary. I wrote this one both to bring you up to date on the remarkable advances in varieties, tools, techniques, and cultural practices, and to supply as well all the timeless basic information you need to grow vegetables successfully. This book is organized very much like its distinguished companions in the Victory Garden book series, in a month-by-month format, because that's how gardeners garden. When you're thinking about peas in May, you should be able to look them up in the May chapter and find what you need to know about their care and culture at that time of year. Thus the bulk of the book is devoted to eight chapters representing the gardening months of March through October. Each chapter begins with an alphabetized list of crops and the things we do with them in that month. If you want to know when to harvest tomatoes, simply check the front page of each month under the "Harvest" heading, then locate the "Tomatoes" section in the appropriate month. (Believe it or not, it's June!) If you need to know how to start summer squash seeds indoors in March or April, turn to those months, find the "Summer Squash" entries, and start reading. And if you want to learn about the entire cultural cycle of a crop — corn, let's say — simply start reading in the first month that crop appears (April, in this case, when I plant the seeds in peat pots) and follow the entries all the way through the subsequent months.

In addition to these comprehensive monthly chapters, there are two more chapters, "Beginnings" and "Endings," which detail early- and late-season activities. "Beginnings," which precedes the March chapter, describes the things I do to prepare for a long, intensive growing season in the Victory Garden. And in "Endings," which follows the October chapter, I tell you how to put the garden to bed for the winter, and suggest some worthwhile activities for the long, cold hiatus.

For gardeners just getting started, or for those who'd like to update their know-how, I've put all the information on the latest cultural practices up front in the very next chapter, "Steps to Victorious Gardening." This is the chapter to begin with for a thorough immersion in the skills I've been teaching on the "Victory Garden" television series for so long. And even serious veteran gardeners will find this chapter to be "must reading," because it distills the years of Victory Garden experience into essential knowledge and techniques they just won't find anywhere else.

Finally, I've included special features as companions to the gardening months themselves. In some cases, these features provide additional information on certain topics that most gardeners will find especially useful — container gardening, say, or the selection and care of tools. In others, I've focused on topics that have given me great pleasure over the years in the Victory Garden, such as wreathmaking and gardening to attract birds. I've even included a feature profiling several Victory Garden contest winners, drawing valuable cultural lessons from each victorious garden.

Conspicuously absent from this book are the complicated frost maps found in many other gardening tomes. After having squinted over such maps and charts for many years, I've finally

**I'm getting ready to share my enthusiasm for oak leaf lettuce as the television camera focuses in.**

concluded that they're worse than useless. Because they cannot indicate the frost characteristics for any local microclimate, they invite gardeners to risk their crops on dangerously general information. I think that's a disservice. A valley garden and a mountainside garden in the same-color area on one of those maps have very different frost dates and microclimatic conditions. Instead of including one of those colorful but misleading little maps, I'm going to offer this advice: To learn about the growing conditions in your particular microclimate, consult your local county extension service agent. He or she will know about the frost dates and growing conditions for *your* backyard, and that's what you need to grow the best vegetables.

I've also avoided giving a general planting timetable other than the one I use for my crops in the Victory Garden. It's just not possible for me, a New England gardener, to tell you, a gardener in Spokane or Tallahassee, when to plant, with utter precision. What I *can* do is describe the principles I use to arrive at my gardening schedule for planting, fertilizing, harvesting, and so on. Those principles, applied to your garden, will be as useful there as they are in the Victory Garden itself. My last expected spring frost date, April 20 (determined after consultation with my county extension agent and years of practice), is the pivotal day upon which all the rest of my gardening year is based. Once you've established that date for your own garden, the rest of the schedule and planning falls into place rather easily. I'll tell you exactly how to make the plan and create the schedule — for *your* garden — in the chapter titled "Beginnings."

And there you have it. That's enough introducing. Let's get right to the heart of things. As I've said so many times on the air, welcome to the Victory Garden!

My Victory Garden techniques assure a bountiful harvest, including a well-grown spring cauliflower that I'm especially happy about. I replant open areas as soon as a harvest is taken. The black-plastic-covered raised beds provide added warmth for cucumbers on the A-frame trellis and some newly set out squash seedlings.

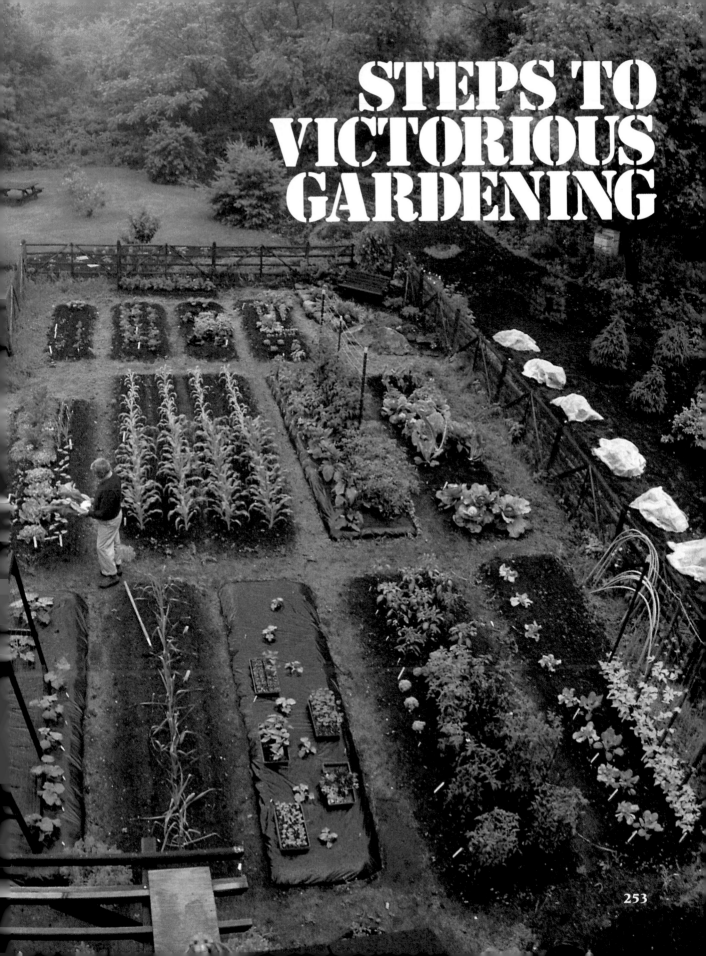

# STEPS TO VICTORIOUS GARDENING

# STEPS TO VICTORIOUS GARDENING

Tending a garden is a never-ending learning experience. I experiment constantly with new varieties, schedules, and techniques, carrying on my semiscientific campaigns in the least exact but most exciting laboratory of all: the great outdoors. There, no two springs are ever alike, no single harvest is ever exactly the same as any other, no frost is absolutely predictable. Thus, I set down my steps to victorious gardening with confidence tempered by an awareness that my own education is ongoing. When I say "victorious" gardening, I mean that these steps are lessons that the garden has taught me, and that have worked well. I never feel as though I have made the garden submit to my whims, any more than the adventurous climbers who reach the summits of big mountains feel that they "conquer" peaks. Like them, I view my adventure as a partnership with nature. I consider myself a good steward on this bit of land I call the Victory Garden, but never its master.

In this chapter, you'll find all the lessons I've learned from the years of intensive culture in the Victory Garden and that I've been sharing on the television program. Included are site selection, soil preparation, varietal selection, starting seeds indoors, buying seedlings, planting out, mulching, using season extenders, watering, thinning, weeding, managing pests and diseases, harvesting, making and using compost, and more. All the skills and techniques are laid out in the order in which you'll use them in the garden itself, beginning at the beginning with site selection and ending with harvesting.

## Site Selection
A good vegetable garden demands sun — the more the better. Six hours is really minimum. Those hours should be full, not filtered, for sturdy growth. Step one, then, is to give the garden all the sun a piece of property allows. Everything else will be severely compromised if the garden does not receive those essential hours of sunlight.

Ideally, the garden should be located away from the shade cast by buildings and trees. That should also keep the garden well away from the root systems of trees, which will steal essential nutrients and water. Tree roots will reach out at least as far as the trees' outermost branches — the so-called drip line. Keep the garden's borders beyond that line, and the vegetables will be safe from thirsty tree roots.

Slope is important, too. If the garden is located on too steep a slope, soil will erode and nutrients will be washed away. Terracing is advisable on hillsides much steeper than 15 degrees. A

gentle slope to the south is actually ideal, as it promotes drainage and exposes the garden to more sunlight.

Size is another consideration. The Victory Garden has expanded over the years, from the small Boston garden to several other locations. Each of the new gardens is larger than the original. From that experience comes one of my cardinal rules: Start small and build on success, rather than retreating from large failure. I've found that I can always push back fence lines when time, confidence, and energy allow. For beginning gardens and gardeners, I think that a 15x15-foot plot is perfectly adequate.

## Soil Preparation
Along with lots of sunlight, a successful vegetable garden requires well-prepared soil. Bad soil is a handicap, but *any* soil (as so many Victory Garden contest winners have demonstrated)

can be improved tremendously. The Victory Garden itself is a case in point. When the first Victory Garden was born in the parking lot behind the WGBH-TV studios in Boston, the land was rubble, and what little soil there was served only to separate the debris. That first season, Jim Crockett added dozens of bales of peat moss to improve the structure of that junkyard soil. In my years, I've continued to add peat moss, homemade compost for tilth and fertility, and coarse builder's sand for drainage. There's premium soil in that garden now, soil that holds moisture, retains nutrients, provides good aeration, and crumbles like chocolate cake in my hand. It took a lot of work, year after year, to create that superb soil, and from that genesis comes another cardinal gardening rule: Great soil is not built overnight, but it *can* be built. Never be discouraged by bad soil. With patience and work, virtually any soil can be improved enough to produce excellent vegetables.

Soil quality is determined by three characteristics: composition, pH, and fertility. These three are like the legs of a stool. All must be present; if any one is missing or impaired, vegetables will grow poorly or not at all. If soil is too loose and sandy, or too heavy and clayish, aeration, drainage, and nutrient retention will suffer. Similarly, because vegetables require a pH range of 6.0–7.0 for optimum growth, soil that is too acid or alkaline will impair their development. And soil that is deficient in nutrients (especially in any of the "big three" — nitrogen, phosphorus, or potassium) cannot support healthy crops.

**Composition**  The first step in preparing soil for vegetable gardening is understanding soil composition. Basically, there are three types of soil: clay, sand, and loam. Clay soils are composed of densely packed clay particles. They do not drain well, nor do they provide good aeration. Clay soil is hard to work, and, because of its density, is slow to warm and dry in the spring. Sandy soil is made up of large, irregular granules that neither adhere to each other nor retain moisture well. Water flows through unimpeded, washing out nutrients. Loam, the third basic soil type, is a combination of sand, silt (particles that are between clay and sand on the soil spectrum), and clay, with varying amounts of organic matter.

Each soil type has a different feel. Clay soil, when squeezed, will form a dense, sticky ball. When wet, clay soil feels slick and greasy. Sandy soil feels gritty, and is so loosely structured that it may not hold its shape even when squeezed hard into a ball. Loam molds readily into a ball when squeezed, but crumbles easily, too.

All gardeners long for loam. The ideal gardening soil would be a deep loam, a bit on the sandy side, with a crumbly, chocolate-cake feel. This dream soil would have a high *humus* content — at least 5 percent and preferably more. (Humus is decayed plant and animal material, a dark, crumbly substance that is essential

Spring soil preparation and
pea seedlings in peat
strips, ready to be set out.

for good vegetable gardening.) As much as 50 percent of its total volume would be given over to pore space, which in turn might contain water or air. This loose, crumbly structure is open enough to allow penetration by roots, and firm enough to support the plants above those root systems. Equally important, the high proportion of organic matter allows the soil to retain enough moisture, nutrients, and air.

My summer-sown buckwheat cover crop is turned under just at flowering. Green manure crops like this add invaluable organic material at a very low cost.

Not many of us are lucky enough to find that kind of soil ready and waiting for our vegetables, so improving the soil structure is a basic part of any vegetable gardener's activity. The foundation of soil improvement is organic matter. *Any* soil — heavy clay or dusty sand — benefits from the addition of organic matter. Fortunately, there are lots of sources for this prime ingredient of good soil. Peat moss, which I mentioned above, is one. It's available in bales from garden supply houses and, while relatively expensive, is an excellent way to improve soil structure quickly. Sawdust is fine, too, if you have access to a sawmill or woodworker's shop. Animal manure is another amendment that improves soil structure. Manure contains some nutrients, and contributes to soil fertility as well. Green manures are grassy or leguminous crops that can be planted any time and later dug into the soil. Winter rye and buckwheat are two green manure crops that have become Victory Garden standards. And of course there is compost, perhaps the best all-around soil improver. Compost is a potpourri of organic materials (plant residues, grass clippings, kitchen wastes, and so forth), soil, lime, and fertilizer that decomposition has blended into a dark, crumbly, humus-rich mass. Later in this chapter, I'll give detailed instructions for creating large amounts of rich compost with a minimum of effort. For now, it's enough to know that compost is an unbeatable addition to any garden.

There are good reasons for all this stress on organic matter. It's full of large, spongy particles that "open up" the soil, making it easier for water to percolate in and then helping retain that water once it has entered. Organic matter is also a repository for soil nutrients. It holds minerals absorbed from the soil, provides a medium in which beneficial bacteria thrive, and fuels soil microorganisms that help produce nutrient-rich humus. Finally, organic matter increases soil's porosity, and it is in the porous spaces between particles that air — which the plants need for growth — resides.

I like to add most soil amendments to the Victory Garden in the fall. The beds are ready for replenishment after producing successive crops all season long, and the winter months provide time for manure and partially decomposed organic matter to break down fully. When the beds have produced their last, I add 2 inches of well-rotted manure or compost. (If I can find only fresh manure, I'll use that now, because it will have a chance to break down over the months.) I also add ground limestone to adjust the pH, and fertilizer to boost nutrient content. Fertilizer goes down at the rate of 2 pounds of 10-10-10 for every 100 square feet of bed area. I'll explain how much limestone to add in the next part of this chapter. I turn all this — manure or compost, limestone, fertilizer — into the soil. Then I rake the beds into shape and sow a cover crop of winter rye, using 1 pound of rye seed for every 100 square feet of area sowed. I rake the seed in lightly, water it well, and keep the beds moist until germination occurs. Come spring, that rye will be turned under 4 to 6 weeks before planting time, adding still more organic matter to the soil.

Fall is not the only time I can add organic matter to the soil, of course. Finished compost and well-rotted manure can be turned into the soil at any time, as can peat moss and other organic materials. Similarly, coarse builder's sand (the remedy of choice for gluey clay soils) can be worked in any time.

Gardeners just getting started will have to strip sod from the ground before they can add any amendments to the soil. For this bit of work there is nothing more valuable than a *very* sharp spade. First, I cut down through the grass, making parallel cuts 12 inches apart to form strips of sod. Then I lever up the foot-wide strip as I go, working the spade along underneath, cutting off the top inch or so, and rolling the sod back on itself until the mass becomes too heavy to move easily. When that happens, I

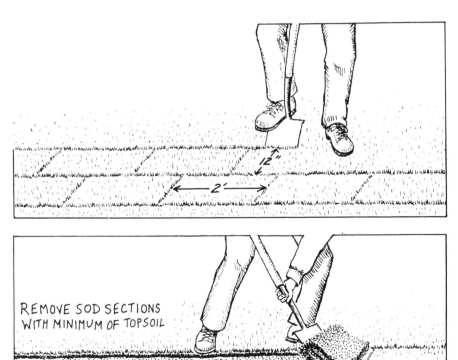

REMOVE SOD SECTIONS
WITH MINIMUM OF TOPSOIL

cut the roll loose and lay it to one side. After the whole garden area is cleared, I use my spading fork to turn up the topsoil to a depth of 12 inches, forking in organic material (compost or manure) as I go, and adding enough lime to bring the pH into the 6.5 range. The stripped sod goes into the compost pile, where it will decompose into more rich, organic matter.

**pH Level**   The second important indicator of soil quality is pH, which is nothing more than the degree of soil acidity or alkalinity as described by a number from 0 to 14. Zero is completely acid, 14 completely alkaline. The midpoint, 7, indicates neutrality. The pH level is important in vegetable gardening because soil for most vegetables must be between 6.0 and 7.0 on the pH scale for best plant growth. In acid soils with a pH below 5, phosphorus is not released readily, and other nutrients (notably magnesium, potassium, and calcium) tend to wash out. High acidity deters the breakdown of humus, invites diseases like clubroot, and discourages earthworms. Very alkaline soils (with pH above 7.5) have their own problems. High alkalinity keeps trace elements locked up in the soil, deters the production of humus, and can contribute to a toxic buildup of chemical salts.

I've heard stories about gardeners who assess their garden's pH by tasting the soil, but I've never actually *met* anyone who does it that way. I've experimented with some of the do-it-yourself testing kits available at hardware stores and garden supply centers, but I don't much like them. The color-coded reagent has always seemed difficult for me to match with the little charts they provide. I much prefer the more accurate and dependable alternative of having my sample tested by the county extension service. For a very reasonable fee, the service gives me a computerized printout on my soil, including the current pH, levels of nitrogen, phosphorus, and potash, and levels of important trace elements like iron and boron. The test report also includes helpful recommendations for amending the garden soil, tailored to my particular needs. When I take a soil sample, I make sure to take soil from at least four different locations throughout the garden, to give the chemists a true cross-section. I also make sure to use a clean trowel to dig the soil, and clean double plastic bags to hold it. I avoid touching the soil with my hands, because body oils can contaminate the sample. Finally, I avoid any area that's recently been enriched by fertilizer, compost, or manure, because all of those will affect the test results.

I like to test for pH in the fall and again in the spring. The fall test, performed after the long, intensive growing season, tells me how much lime I must add to bring the pH back to the 6.5 level that's optimum for most vegetables. Lime works slowly in the soil, which is why I add it in the fall — by spring, it will have done its job. The tests usually reveal that our season-end pH has dropped to around 6.0, and I add lime accordingly. My rule of thumb is that 70 pounds of ground limestone will raise

When collecting soil samples for testing, be sure the trowel is clean and use double plastic bags. To provide a good cross-section for analysis, I take samples from at least four different locations in the garden.

the pH of 1000 square feet of garden soil one full point — that is, from 5.5 to 6.5. There's nothing esoteric about liming. When I add organic matter in the fall, I work limestone in at the same time, incorporating enough to bring the pH back into that desirable 6.5 range.

I test the soil pH again in the spring, before planting time, so that I can make any last-minute adjustments that may be needed — usually only a light dusting of ground limestone before I turn under the cover crop of winter rye, adding well-rotted manure or finished compost if I have any available.

The methods described above will work for most gardeners east of the Mississippi River, where centuries of heavy rainfall have leached away alkaline elements and left the soil generally acidic. Western gardeners may find themselves with the opposite problem. On the other side of the Mississippi, where rainfall is somewhat lighter, alkalinity has remained higher. Soil tests there may indicate the need for agricultural sulfur, which will lower the pH. Twenty pounds of sulfur will lower the pH of 1000 square feet of garden soil one full point, from 7.5 to 6.5. Sulfur can be incorporated just like limestone, by broadcasting or mechanically spreading over the soil and then forking or rototilling in.

*Fertility* Fertility is the third component of healthy soil. For successful vegetable gardening, soil must contain adequate amounts of the "big three" macronutrients — nitrogen, phosphorus, and potash. Nitrogen is important to plant protein formation and to the creation of chlorophyll, the pigment that fuels photosynthesis. Nitrogen is also essential for strong foliar growth. Yellowing leaves are one sure sign of nitrogen deficiency. Phosphorus is required for strong root development, disease resistance, and fruit formation. Phosphorus-poor plants will look stunted, and may have reddened stems or leaves. Potash is necessary for vigorous growth, and plays a key role in disease resistance. Browning leaves and retarded growth are telltale signs of potash deficiency.

Plants also need substantial amounts of three secondary nutrients — calcium, magnesium, and sulfur. These are usually found in adequate supply in most soils. Also generally present in sufficient amounts are the important micronutrients, also called trace elements: iron, manganese, boron, chlorine, zinc, copper, and molybdenum.

As I've already mentioned, I use a lot of organic matter in the Victory Garden, and this has some nutritive value. Manure is relatively high in nitrogen, for instance, and compost will introduce adequate amounts of micronutrients. I also use chemical fertilizers, though, and I think it's silly to avoid one or the other as a matter of rigid principle. Both organic matter and chemical fertilizers have their place in any soil management program. It's my feeling that a balance of organic matter and chemical fertilizers is best for the garden and the gardener. I advocate the use of chemical fertilizers mostly because they're efficient. Organic materials, whatever their virtues, are not as efficient suppliers of plant nutrients, for example. It takes twenty pounds of cow manure to provide the same amounts of nitrogen, phosphorus, and potash found in *one* pound of 5-10-5 fertilizer. It's also true that organic materials do not contain balanced proportions of essential plant nutrients. They must be combined in various ratios to give growing vegetables an adequate diet, and it can become downright confusing juggling recipes of bonemeal, blood meal, greensand, wood ashes, tankage, and the like.

My preference, then, is to rely heavily on organic matter (animal manure, compost, green manure crops) to improve soil *structure*, and more on chemical fertilizers to produce balanced fertility. I've found that this combination is both good for the soil and very efficient in terms of time and labor. As I'll say over and over again in this book (and on the air!), I believe strongly in achieving maximum yield from every hour I spend in the garden.

All chemical fertilizers carry a three-number designation. Among the most common are 5-10-5, 10-10-10, and 5-10-10. These numbers refer to the percentages of nitrogen, phosphorus, and potash (in that order) contained in the bag of fertilizer. The remaining material in any bag is simply inert matter used for binding and forming. Different formulations of the "big three" are useful for different crops. A 5-10-5 fertilizer is best for fruiting crops like squash and tomatoes, which benefit from

**Side-dressing corn: Here I've opened up a narrow, shallow trench to apply the fertilizer, which I'll cover up with soil.**

extra phosphorus; 10-10-10 is better for leafy vegetables like lettuce, spinach, and cabbage, as the extra nitrogen promotes vegetative growth. And certain crops, most notably peppers, benefit from 5-10-10 because they need extra potash.

Fertilizers like those described above release their constituents into the soil quickly. Their breakdown begins as soon as they're dug into the soil and come into contact with water contained in it. They continue to release their nutrients for a period of time that varies depending on rainfall, temperature, and soil disturbance. No standard chemical fertilizer will provide nutrients steadily over an entire Victory Garden growing season of five to six months, though. To provide certain crops with additional nutrition during the season — especially long-term crops like winter squash or melons, which can take from 100 to 120 days to mature — I rely on slow-release fertilizer. Chemically the same as other commercial fertilizers, the granules of slow-release types are coated with a water-permeable material that releases the nutrients more gradually than do standard fertilizers.

I also use a balanced liquid fertilizer for foliar feeding, initial watering-in of seedling transplants, and as a quick-fix boost for any plants that show a nutrient deficiency during the season. Water-soluble fertilizers, as their name implies, are meant to be mixed with water. They come in crystalline and liquid forms, and my favorite is a balanced 20-20-20 formula.

Fertilizing in the Victory Garden is really an ongoing process. In the spring, when I turn under our cover crops of winter rye, I like to add 5 pounds of 5-10-5 fertilizer for every 100 square feet of bed area for most of the crops. I'll use the same amount of 10-10-10 for leafy vegetables (lettuce and Swiss chard, for example), and 5-10-10 for the peppers, with their big appetite for potash. During the season, when I'm preparing the raised beds of long-term crops like squash and melons, I add 5 pounds of slow-release 14-14-14 per 100 square feet of bed area before laying down the beds' black plastic mulch.

Side-dressing is another way to make sure that each crop receives all the nutrients it needs throughout the growing season. Peppers, for instance, benefit from additional fertilizer after their first fruits set. It's good to side-dress broccoli, after harvesting the primary head, with half a handful of 10-10-10 per plant. In the calendar-month chapters that follow, I give specific, month-by-month instructions for side-dressing, but the thing to understand here is that there's nothing at all complicated about the process. It's nothing more than using my cultivator to scratch half a handful of fertilizer per plant into the soil around the plant's base.

I use balanced water-soluble fertilizer liberally. When seedlings are transplanted from 4-inch pots to individual cell-packs after having been started indoors, I water them in with a starter solution of 20-20-20 liquid fertilizer diluted to half strength. Later, when these transplants are set out into the garden, they receive another watering-in with half-strength solution. I keep my eye on all the crops during the growing season, too, and whenever I spot yellowing leaves, unusually slow growth, or other signs of nutrient deficiency, I give the needy plants a drink of 20-20-20 at full strength.

Finally, when fall arrives and the Victory Garden beds are coming empty, I fertilize the soil with 2 pounds of 10-10-10 for each 100 square feet of area before sowing the cover crop of winter rye.

There are a few fertilizer cautions worth mentioning. One is to keep chemical fertilizer 3 or 4 inches away from plant roots and stems. Direct contact with either will cause burning, resulting in checked growth or a dead plant. Be careful, also, to avoid overfertilizing, which can be more harmful than underfertilizing. Finally, don't use fertilizer during very dry weather, unless you can water adequately. Roots can't take up the nutrients unless there is enough moisture in the soil. In the Victory Garden it's not a problem, because I can water the crops pretty much at will, and I make sure they receive at least 1 inch of water per week during the growing season. Gardeners who live in very dry areas, or who are subject to water-use restrictions during the summer, will need to be more careful with the chemical applications.

## Compost

As I indicated in the previous section on soil preparation, compost is probably the best all-around soil improver available to the vegetable gardener. I've used compost in the Victory Garden from the beginning, but my method for producing compost has improved a bit. At first, I used a conventional three-bin compost system. One bin was for ready-to-use, fully reduced compost. Another contained partly decayed, intermediate material. The third was for new matter. This three-bin system, in optimal conditions and with lots of turning, could produce finished compost in three months. Note well that phrase, "lots of turning," and then understand when I say that all the turning was the rock upon which my three-bin system finally came to grief. As I got busier in the Victory Garden, the turning just wasn't getting done. More pressing activities always seemed to demand my attention and, though I am as devout a lover of compost as any gardener on earth, my compost production dwindled.

Now I've hit upon a different and better way to make compost. The new system eliminates one bin altogether. Instead, I fill two larger bins with the same ingredients that went into the three-bin system. But here's the big difference: no turning. The larger bins generate enough heat to speed decomposition without requiring all that turning, and I like that. Physicists talk about elegant formulas, by which they mean formulas that work with utmost efficiency. I like to garden by that same principle: maximum output from minimum input. It's not that I don't en-

**Adding ground limestone will hasten the breakdown in our compost.**

FERTILIZER

LIME

2" SOIL

6" ORGANIC
MATERIAL

joy spending time in the garden — I've been at it for more than thirty years and loved every minute. But as I've said on the air, gardeners in this day and age just can't afford to waste time or energy.

In the next chapter's feature, "Victory Garden Structures," I give detailed instructions for building a sturdy two-bin composter like the one I use. Here, I'll explain how I make the rich compost that goes into the Victory Garden beds. To start my first pile, I lay down a 6-inch layer of organic material or manure, or a mixture of both. The organic material might include leaves, garden refuse, tomato vines, and lawn clippings. The latter should not be used alone, because they will mat together and prevent air circulation. It's also important to use clippings from lawns that have not been treated with weed killers or insecticides, because these can remain active and damage crops later on. Similarly, diseased garden refuse of any kind is denied entry into the Victory Garden composter. I also stay away from bones or meat, which decay too slowly, cause bad smells, and attract digging animals. I do include household waste whenever possible: vegetables, fruits, eggshells, and coffee grounds. On top of this first 6-inch layer I add 1 to 2 inches of soil, then 2 handfuls of lime, and 2 more of any garden fertilizer. The lime ensures a correct pH, and the fertilizer maintains a proper balance of essential nutrients. After the first layer's sequence is complete, I repeat it several times until the bin is filled. Then I go to work on bin number two.

As I build the layers, I'm careful to leave a depression in each pile's center. This collects water and channels it down into the pile, where it's needed — along with oxygen — for decomposition to occur. Moisture control is important, too. Each layer should be about as wet as a damp sponge, but not soaking. Too much water drives out air, which causes anaerobic decomposition to occur. From anaerobic piles come bad smells that will not endear you to your neighbors, so avoid overwatering.

If I complete a pile in early summer, that will give me ready compost for fall. My second bin, completed at season's end, will be ready during the following spring. Decomposition takes place more quickly during the heat of summer, so the March-started compost is often finished faster than my fall batch. I know that the compost is finished when there is no longer any heat in the pile, and — more important — when the compost is dark brown and crumbly.

## Raised Beds

The practice of raised-bed culture was probably originated by the Chinese thousands of years ago. French market gardeners near Paris improved some of the techniques in the late 1800s, and in the last ten years, raised-bed culture has undergone a real renaissance.

In the Victory Garden, I now grow almost everything (corn and a few vining crops are about the only exceptions) in raised beds. The advantages are many. Raised beds provide a greater depth of rich topsoil, which is the primary growing medium for all vegetables. This extra helping of premium soil allows for a greater concentration of nutrients, and a more economical use of fertilizer and amendments. In traditional flat-plane culture, all the garden areas — walkways as well as growing areas — receive fertilizer and organic matter, though they do no good in noncultivated areas. With raised beds, the amendments go only to those areas where crops will grow, cutting down on wasted material — and time. It's also true that because feet and machines travel on the footpaths and not over the beds, soil compaction is kept to an absolute minimum. This means that the soil remains loose and friable, providing excellent drainage and aeration and allowing growing roots to penetrate without difficulty. The high fertility of the beds allows for very intensive gardening practices: intercropping, succession planting, and extended seasons. The soil warms up earlier in spring, and stays 6 to 10 degrees warmer throughout the growing season. Raised beds also lend themselves nicely to the most efficient way to keep the garden watered — drip or trickle watering. And when heavy rains drench other gardens, washing away seeds or seedlings and submerging young plants in early spring, the raised beds float snugly above the deluge. The only extra attention raised beds require is a bit more watering during the hottest days of summer, when their greater exposed surface area causes them to lose more moisture than flat beds.

I've heard people say that the big drawback to raised beds is the work required to create them, but I think that's a myth.

**Opening up a trench to bury the corners of the black plastic.** ▲ **I've stretched the plastic taut before burying the edges all around.** ▶

*Any* garden requires a certain amount of working-up in the spring: tilling, forking, raking, and so on. Raised-bed gardens require about the same work. When I make my raised beds, instead of raking the soil smooth and flat, I rake it into the raised formations that will be our beds. It's not really any more work than that required for flat culture.

Here's how I go about making raised beds in the Victory Garden. The best time to do this is in the spring, following a thorough fall program of soil amendment like that described earlier. As soon as the soil can be worked, I add any last-minute amendments (compost or manure, lime, fertilizer) and till or fork them under, along with the green manure cover crop that's been growing all winter. Next, I excavate the pathways that will separate the beds. I like to have fairly wide pathways, about 24 inches, and I string two lines to help me keep my digging straight. I take about 3 or 4 inches of soil from the pathway and deposit it on top of the adjacent soil, working the length of the bed. All my Victory Garden raised beds are 48 inches wide, and most are 8 feet long. I string lines 48 inches apart to help me form the beds, too, so that they're just as neat and eye-pleasing as the pathways. To make the beds themselves, I use my rake to form the soil between the paths into a flat-topped mound about 8 inches high, with a base width of 48 inches and sides that taper up at about a 45-degree angle to a top that's 36 inches wide. (See accompanying illustrations.) I have to work a bit with the flat side of my rake to shape the top and sides of the bed and to smooth the pathways in between beds, but when I'm finished I have raised beds that will last the whole growing season. Once created, these raised beds need only minor reshaping with the rake at the beginning of each season.

Planting in raised beds is easier than flat-plane planting because the beds are higher, requiring less bending and stooping. The 48-inch width is not only convenient for the gardener — the bed can be worked from both sides — but good for the vegetables, too, since I never have to stand on the growing surface. My actual planting practice is the same as it would be for conventional gardens, whether I'm setting in seedlings or seeds. I can sow in single rows, wide rows, or simply broadcast the seed, depending on the crop I'm growing.

## Varietal Selection

In my thirty-plus years of gardening, I've stayed with a few varieties for a long time. I still grow Butter and Sugar corn, for instance, and I've grown Buttercrunch lettuce for over a decade. Most of the Victory Garden crops, though, are of more recent vintage. I spend a lot of time reviewing seed catalogs and trying out the new varieties. I'm always on the lookout for varieties that combine disease and insect resistance and good eating quality. I'll hazard an observation here, too, that a good many growers still use the same varieties they were seeding twenty years ago. I think that's a shame. Though I'm pretty conservative in most matters, I'll try any new, promising varieties as soon as I can get my hands on them. Many problems that plague the garden can be overcome only when breeders discover a wild strain of disease-resistant plants and work that desirable quality into a new variety for home gardening. Other kinds of advances, as well, make new varieties attractive. Dr. Clint Peterson's new A+ carrot is one example. The A+ is sweet and delicious, and packs *twice* the vitamin A content of previous varieties. I want vegetables like that in my garden — and on my table.

The best way to stay abreast of such developments is to read as many seed catalogs as possible. I'm on the mailing lists of dozens of companies, and I spend many enjoyable winter hours poring over the catalogs. Though the catalog descriptions occasionally run to extremes, many have excellent cultural information. I also read as many articles as I can in the leading garden magazines, and I talk to lots of other gardeners, all of whom have something to tell me. They're just like me: Whenever I produce a masterful new crop, bragging rights come with it.

Another excellent source of information on new varieties is an organization called the All-America Selections Committee. This

A recent All-America favorite of mine — Jersey Golden Acorn — yields a good harvest of superb-tasting squash on compact vines. Good yield with great taste in less space is a real improvement.

group of seed industry professionals conducts annual field trials of promising vegetables and flowers in regional gardens across the country. Qualified judges give awards to varieties that display superior performance when grown alongside the best existing varieties. Before long, these varieties show up in the catalogs and on seeds racks. While All-America Selections may not show spectacular results in all gardens, using them increases the chances of producing healthy, vigorous crops. For more information on garden planning and crop choice, see the chapter entitled "Beginnings," which immediately follows this one.

## Starting Seeds Indoors
I start the vast majority of crops grown in the Victory Garden indoors, rather than planting out directly in the soil, even when warm summer weather would allow me to direct-seed if I wished. I emphasize indoor starts for my crops because of the

greater control this gives me over growing conditions during the critical early stages of the plants' lives. Indoors, the plants are assured freedom from wind, cold, and drought. They are started from seed in a sterile growing medium, so diseases can't attack them, nor are they subject to assaults from insects or other pests. I can control the amount of light they receive, and keep them free from competition with larger, more established garden crops. All in all, starting seeds indoors lets me produce the hardiest, healthiest seedlings possible.

I start a few tomatoes (my super-early crop) and some onions and leeks indoors in February, but the bulk of my indoor seeding takes place in March and April. I use a soilless growing medium called "Redi-Earth," which is a commercial variety developed at Cornell University. The mix is a blend of peat moss, vermiculite, and nutrients, and is available at garden centers and from some seed catalogs. The mixture is free of weeds and disease organisms. In addition, it's porous enough to keep the seeds moist without inviting rot, while providing good aeration and drainage. I add this mix to plastic 4-inch pots that have been sterilized by washing in a solution of 1 part chlorine bleach and 7 parts hot water. New pots need not be sterilized.

Before I fill the pots, I moisten the growing medium in its bag, which not only prevents my being smothered by billowing clouds of fine peat moss but saves time, as well. Next, I fill my 4-inch pots to the brim, and firm the surface by pressing down with the bottom of another 4-inch pot, leaving a ½-inch space to allow for watering. To compensate for the various kinds of attrition that can keep new seed from coming up or attack it once it does, I sow twice as many seeds as I plan to transplant into the garden. Thus the eventual growth of 10 cabbages, say, requires my sowing 20 seeds at this early stage.

To sow, I crimp the seed packet into a V and then tap the seed out with my index finger. After they are sown, I cover the seeds with this same soilless mix to a depth equal to about three times their diameter. Planting too deeply retards emergence, while shallower planting increases the risk of drying out.

I set the pots in a tray of warm water and let them remain there until capillary action has drawn water up and moistened the surface of the growing medium. When I can see the moisture from this bottom-watering, I remove the pots from their tray. Thereafter, I keep a close eye on them. The medium must never be allowed to dry out, or to become soggy. Either will spell the demise of germinating seeds. This bottom-watering is the technique I use for all my indoor-started seeds. It's much neater than top-watering, but — more important — it prevents seeds from being washed out of the growing medium.

To germinate, seeds need constant moisture and bottom heat, but not fertilizer. Like camels, seeds carry a long-distance supply of nutrients with them, and at first the sprouting seeds will

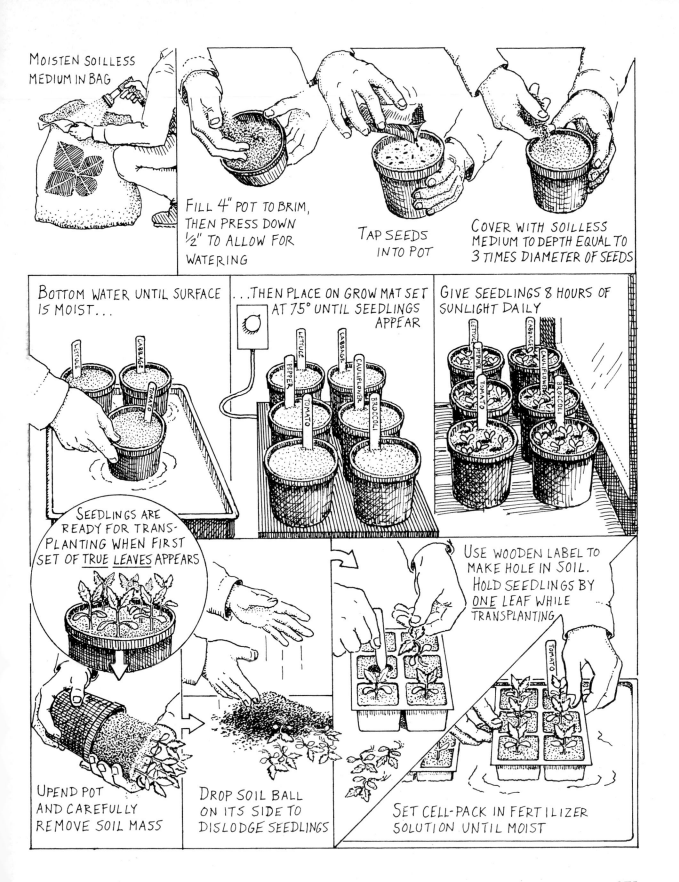

MOISTEN SOILLESS MEDIUM IN BAG

FILL 4" POT TO BRIM, THEN PRESS DOWN 1/2" TO ALLOW FOR WATERING

TAP SEEDS INTO POT

COVER WITH SOILLESS MEDIUM TO DEPTH EQUAL TO 3 TIMES DIAMETER OF SEEDS

BOTTOM WATER UNTIL SURFACE IS MOIST...

...THEN PLACE ON GROW MAT SET AT 75° UNTIL SEEDLINGS APPEAR

GIVE SEEDLINGS 8 HOURS OF SUNLIGHT DAILY

SEEDLINGS ARE READY FOR TRANS-PLANTING WHEN FIRST SET OF TRUE LEAVES APPEARS

USE WOODEN LABEL TO MAKE HOLE IN SOIL. HOLD SEEDLINGS BY ONE LEAF WHILE TRANSPLANTING

UPEND POT AND CAREFULLY REMOVE SOIL MASS

DROP SOIL BALL ON ITS SIDE TO DISLODGE SEEDLINGS

SET CELL-PACK IN FERTILIZER SOLUTION UNTIL MOIST

**Steps to Victorious Gardening** 271

feed on these quite satisfactorily. While the professional growers adjust temperatures precisely to the needs of different crops, the home gardener need only provide a soil temperature of about 75 degrees to insure optimum germination of vegetable seeds. At the Victory Garden, I set the pots directly on a grow mat to give them this steady bottom heat. Made especially for propagating, a grow mat is a 2-foot square of rubber in which electrical cables are embedded. Setting the mat's thermostat at 75 degrees provides ideal soil temperature and foolproof germination.

As soon as the seedlings poke through the surface, I move the pots off the heat and into bright light, then water them conscientiously, for they must not be allowed to dry out. Full, strong sun, coupled with nighttime temperatures of 55 to 60 degrees, will produce the sturdiest seedlings that will survive later transplanting outdoors. At this stage, at least half a day of full sunlight is important. Without that much, I would be reluctant to grow seeds indoors unless I supplemented natural light with fluorescent grow-lights.

Standard blue-white fluorescent tube lights are adequate for growing seedlings indoors. These can be used to supply all the light seedlings receive, as in a basement, or they can be used to augment sunlight from windows. It's possible to buy special

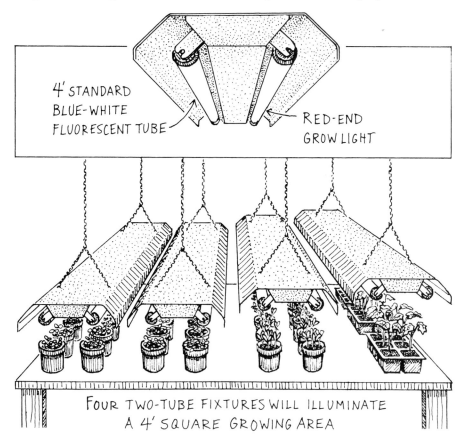

4' STANDARD BLUE-WHITE FLUORESCENT TUBE

RED-END GROW LIGHT

FOUR TWO-TUBE FIXTURES WILL ILLUMINATE A 4' SQUARE GROWING AREA grow-lights, at hardware stores and garden centers, that emit more light from the red end of the spectrum and that have been designed especially for indoor plant growing. Probably the best arrangement is to combine a standard blue-white tube with one of these special red-end grow-lights, thus providing the plants with a wide range of red and blue light wavelengths. Two 4-foot fluorescent tubes provide enough light for a growing area 4 feet long and 1 foot wide. By aligning 4 two-tube fluorescent fixtures, a 4-foot-square growing area can be lit. Fluorescent lights do not heat up, so plants can be placed very close to them — 3 inches or so. Most growers don't know this, but more light comes from the center of the tubes than from the ends, so it's a good idea to move the seedlings around every few days to make sure they all receive equal amounts of light. And don't make the mistake of leaving the lights on twenty-four hours a day. Plants need some darkness to develop properly. Eight hours of darkness is enough, and an automatic timer never forgets.

Germinating seeds will stay in their 4-inch pots for 2 to 4 weeks, until they produce their first set of true leaves. These aren't the first leaves that appear. Those are seed leaves (also called cotyledons), and they will dry up and shrivel as the seedling grows. The true leaves are the *next* to appear, and they look like smaller versions of the plant's real leaves. When the true leaves are evident, it's time to move the seedlings on to cell-packs. These are light plastic containers that vaguely resemble egg cartons and may have 4, 6, 8, or more individual cells for growing seedlings.

To separate the seedlings, I gently upend the 4-inch pot, so that the soil mass drops into my hand, and here I am very careful not to damage any of the delicate seedlings. Then I drop the soil ball, from a height of about 6 inches, onto its side on the potting bench. This breaks up the soil, loosens the seedlings, and makes it much easier for me to isolate individuals without undue damage to roots and stems. My cell-packs are filled with the same soilless growing medium, pre-moistened, and each cell is firmed. A 4-inch wooden label is the perfect tool for making a hole in the growing medium. Into this I insert my seedlings, holding them by the leaves, never by the stem, and burying them up to their seed leaves, one seedling per cell. Setting them in too deeply could check growth or kill weak ones; not deeply enough gives spindly, weak seedlings. I firm the medium gently. Once transplanted, the seedlings are given a watering-in with a solution of balanced water-soluble fertilizer (I like 20-20-20) diluted to half strength. I use the same bottom-watering technique with the cell-packs that I used earlier when the seeds were first planted in the 4-inch pots. The planting medium takes up the liquid until fully saturated, and the delicate seedlings are not disturbed by a heavy shower of water. This bottom-watering settles the medium, and also eliminates the inadvertent washing away of soilless mix.

The object of all these steps — planting seed indoors, watching for true leaves, transplanting to cell-packs — is to provide unchecked growth for the plants. Any number of mishaps (temperature fluctuations, insufficient or excessive watering, inadequate light, overly aggressive fertilization, to name a few) can check plant growth, but one of the surest ways to accomplish it is to leave a plant growing too long in one container. Progress halts when root mass exceeds soil volume, and while the plant may survive thereafter, it will never be as healthy or productive as it would have been without overcrowded roots. To prevent this, I periodically pop my plants from their containers to check the roots. If I see that the roots have filled up the soil mass, I move them to larger containers. But if I have my planting times figured correctly, I should not have to do this, and, in fact, I prefer not to. All this potting-up takes time from a busy gardener's spring schedule.

I transplant most of my seedlings only this one time, from 4-inch pots to cell-packs. Then, after they've hardened off (spent 5 days in the cold frame adjusting to outdoor temperature and moisture conditions), I set the individual seedlings into the garden soil as soon as temperature and soil conditions allow. This produces plants more vigorous than those that have been pampered and nursed along under limiting indoor conditions for too long. On the rare occasions when I want a few larger seedlings (broccoli, perhaps, or tomatoes), I'll move them from their cell-packs into individual 4-inch pots. This will give me very sturdy seedlings that could be set out in the cold frame or (in the case of tomatoes) in plastic-wrapped cages that will give me a 3- to 4-week jump on the season.

The only variation in the procedures described above occurs when I'm seeding crops that are extremely sensitive to transplant shock: melons, for instance, or cucumbers. To minimize this shock, I sow seeds for crops like these in peat pots or peat strips filled with soilless growing medium. Peat pots can be set directly into the garden soil, where they disintegrate, allowing young roots to expand unimpeded. The one drawback to peat pots is that they tend to dry out. I pay them special attention after the seeds have germinated, keeping them moist at all times. When they're set into the garden, I peel the tops from the peat pots, because those tops, if left exposed to air, would wick away moisture and dry out the root mass below.

**These peat strips for starting peas, beans, and sweet corn have meant weeks-earlier harvest for all three.**

## Buying Seedlings

Though I like to start my own crops from seed whenever possible, I realize that I'm fortunate to have a greenhouse and the good conditions necessary to grow strong seedlings. Without the light and temperature needed for strong seedling development, it makes sense to buy them at a good nursery or garden center. I like to shop early for best selection and to get the seedlings before they've grown too long in their containers. I look for healthy foliage and I check the undersides of leaves to make sure they're free of insects. I like young, stocky seedlings, and avoid, weak, leggy, long-stemmed plants. And I'm never afraid to slip the plant out of its cell-pack to check its root system. If all I see is a mass of roots and no soil, it goes back on the shelf. Plants like that have sat too long in the container and won't perform well in the garden. Finally, I shop at garden centers that enjoy good reputations. They're never the cheapest, but customer satisfaction and repeat business are important to them. They'll have the best plants, and the really good ones will replace any seedlings that die off quickly — an indication that something was amiss in the greenhouse — or show signs of disease that could have been incurred early in their development.

## Planting

There are two primary ways to plant vegetables in the garden: sowing seeds directly in the soil, and transplanting seedlings that have been started indoors. Sowing seeds directly involves no magic. It does require knowledge of the soil temperature each crop needs to germinate and of the crop's sensitivity to frost (if I'm planting in the spring). In the monthly chapters that follow, I give specific, crop-by-crop requirements for direct seeding, so that's the place to look for individual instructions for beans, say, or pumpkins. There's a good bit of variation between crops' germination temperature requirements and frost sensitivity, so it's hard to generalize. Once the timing is established, though, the planting procedures are similar for all the crops. I head for the garden with my seed packets, rake, trowel, and planting board. When I plant single or wide rows, I cover the seeds with soilless growing medium three times as deep as their diameter. I use the growing medium rather than soil because it's free of weed seeds, disease organisms, and insects, and because it offers less resistance to the germinating seedlings than more solid soil does. I gently firm the growing medium with my hand, then water the seeds in well with a very fine spray from the watering can or hose. As is the case when starting seeds indoors, seeds sown in the garden must be kept moist to germinate.

The other way to get plants into the garden is to transplant established seedlings. Before *that* happens, though, they must be "hardened off" in the cold frame for 5 days. The Victory Garden cold frame is nothing more than a portable wooden box, about 4 feet square, with a hinged top covered with clear plastic. Full instructions for building a cold frame just like the one I use appear in next chapter's feature. Seedlings rushed directly from the indoors to the open garden can suffer shock from the sudden temperature fluctuations, wind, and reduced water supply, and this shock can impair their growth forever after. In the cold frame, they become accustomed more gradually to wider temperature variations, reduced water, blowing wind, and longer hours of direct sunlight.

A straight line and careful seeding make for a neat look to the garden and less thinning later on. The watering can at the end of the row won't let me forget to water in.

I like to set the cell-packs of seedlings or individual pots into the cold frame on an overcast day to ease them into the harsher outdoor conditions. I try to keep the frame cover closed that first day, and here I'll admit that managing a cold frame takes some getting used to. It must be vented on warm, sunny days so that the seedlings don't overheat, but it must be closed early enough on cool days to build up heat for the evening. Though I don't use one, it's possible to buy cold frames with automatic venting devices, which can be set to open and close the cover at a certain time each day, or when the internal temperature reaches a certain point. There's nothing wrong with automatic venters like this, but I've come to prefer the intimacy with my crops that I gain from making the adjustments myself.

When the seedlings have been hardened off, they go into the garden. I dig their planting holes one by one, pop a plant from its cell-pack, and set it into the hole. Planting depth varies from

A warm spring day means my cold frame is opened wide to keep cool seedlings of lettuce, broccoli, leeks, and Chinese cabbage.

**These broccoli seedlings are set in deeper than they grew in their cell-packs because they will root along their stems. To fill in the space until the broccoli needs it, I've interplanted quick-growing leaf lettuce.**

crop to crop. Those that root all along their stems, like tomatoes, go in deeper than they were growing in the cell-packs or pots, so that strong root systems will develop. Others (like lettuce) that will not root along the stem are planted the same depth they were growing in their seedling containers. I add soil to fill the hole around the seed ball, then firm the soil on top, leaving a slight depression around the stem to collect water. When all the seedlings have been planted this way, I give them a thorough watering with a solution of balanced water-soluble fertilizer diluted to half strength.

## Mulches

Mulches are one of the gardener's best friends. Where they're used, they reduce or eliminate weed growth and, therefore, weeding. Mulches help the soil retain moisture by slowing evaporation. They stabilize soil temperature, and lessen the likelihood of rot for crops like squash and melons. One type of mulch, black plastic, even discourages a few types of insects from attacking plants. A welcome by-product of all this is that mulches reduce the gardener's work load. You'll never hear me complain about that.

Mulches may be organic or inorganic. Organic types include salt marsh hay, grass clippings, compost, sawdust, newspapers, and more. Inorganic mulches include aluminum foil and clear and black polyethylene plastic. Organic mulches must be at least several inches thick to quell weeds effectively and conserve moisture, and they must be replenished throughout the growing season as they become compacted and decompose. Not so the inorganic plastic mulches, which is one main reason why I favor them, in the Victory Garden, over the organic types. Black plastic mulch — the kind I use most widely — can be forgotten, once it's in place.

I use black plastic mulch throughout the Victory Garden, and will confess right here to an unabashed fondness for the homely stuff. It makes weeding a thing of the past, greatly reduces the need for watering, and helps warm spring soil for those early crops. Plentiful moisture, the absence of weed competition, and warm soil produce great crops. Every one I've grown under black plastic has outperformed those left unmulched.

Plastic mulch is available at garden centers in rolls of varying length, width, and thickness. For the Victory Garden's raised 48-inch-wide beds, I use black plastic that is 6 feet wide and 3 mils (or .003 inch) thick. It's possible to buy mulch plastic in thinner, .002-inch versions, but I like the thicker type, which resists ripping and is sure to last a whole season.

Which crops do I single out for black plastic treatment? Heat-lovers like peppers, eggplants, and cucumbers benefit especially from the soil-warming effect of the plastic. Weed control with rambling, long-vining crops like melons and winter squash is much easier with black plastic, so they're covered, as well. I don't use it for crops that come quickly — radishes, spinach, beets — because all the laying down and taking up would be too much work. Nor do I use it for crops that are spaced very closely in the rows, like carrots or lettuce. Finally, it's not helpful to crops that like to grow cool: the brassicas, spinach, and kale, to name three. (I'll give specific mulching instructions for each crop later, in the monthly chapters.)

Here's how I use the plastic mulch. Bed preparation comes first. I make sure that all soil prep — adding manure or compost, lime, turning under cover crops — is complete. Then, before the plastic goes down, I add 5 pounds of slow-release 14-14-14 fertilizer per 100 square feet of bed space. Next, while the crop in question is hardening-off, I lay the black plastic over the bed and bury its edges all the way around the bed's borders. The extra foot on each side of my 6-foot-wide strips gives me plenty of plastic to work with. In addition to giving the garden a nicely tailored appearance, this anchors the plastic securely, even in the wildest New England gales. Come planting time,

The soil under the black plastic mulch will be many degrees warmer than ground uncovered, which means quick, unchecked growth for these tomato seedlings.

whether for seeds or seedlings, I cut 4-inch squares in the plastic and plant my seeds or seedlings through the openings. At one time I just cut crosses in the plastic, but stopped that practice after discovering that wind whipped the little flaps back and forth, administering quite a beating to delicate seedlings.

Now that I've expressed this fondness for black plastic, let me admit that I also use organic mulches for certain crops. Asparagus, for instance, is mulched with salt marsh hay or grass clippings when newly planted shoots appear above the soil. Leeks, late in the season, will receive a thick mulch of salt marsh hay or grass clippings to keep them from freezing in the rapidly chilling soil. (Neither of these trench-grown crops lends itself to black plastic mulching.) Organic mulches, when used in the spring, are not laid down until the soil has had a chance to warm up because, unlike the heat-absorbing black plastic, they'll keep the heat *out*. That makes them valuable during the hot summer months, though, and they're laid down at that time to protect certain crops from too much heat, and to help conserve moisture as well. Let me give this general warning for grass clippings, one of my favorite organic mulches: They must not be laid down too thickly (about 2 inches deep is maximum) in hot weather, or they will mat and generate too much heat for the safety of the plants beneath.

**Broccoli appreciates an organic mulch like salt marsh hay to keep its root zone cool. It will cut down on weeds, also. ▲**

**The Wall O' Water tower fits over young plants to protect them from the cool nights and gusty winds of spring. ▼**

## Season Extenders

People mark their garden victories in different ways, but one of my goals is to harvest something from the garden every day from mid-April through Thanksgiving. In our New England climate, that takes some doing. I've come to rely heavily on my season extenders for that 8-month harvest season. I use the cold frame, Wall O' Water towers, and a spun polyester fabric. I'm especially enthusiastic about this fabric, which helps the crops in many ways. It offers several degrees of frost protection, for one thing. For another, it keeps insects at bay. I don't have to disturb it for watering, because water passes right through. Finally, it affords excellent light penetration. It's possible to lay the spun polyester right on top of the emerging seedlings of some crops, and it's so light that the growing plants will lift it right up. I prefer to support it with hoops of PVC tubing or #12 wire, though, so that the plants are spared even the minimal resistance that the very light fabric offers.

The Victory Garden cold frame is used primarily for hardening off, but it does extend the growing season of a few crops — especially lettuce — several weeks in the spring and fall. As I've said elsewhere, the cold frame is essentially a 4-foot-square box with a hinged lid that is covered with plastic. Heat is trapped inside the covered box, and the inside temperature can be adjusted by opening the lid to vent off excess warmth.

To protect tomatoes, peppers, and eggplants against frost, I use Wall O' Water towers. These are flexible plastic tubes, large

This beautiful crop of spring brassicas was protected from early cold and troublesome insects by spun polyester fabric, which is supported by hoops of bent PVC tubing.

enough to fit over the young plants. Once in place, channels in the Wall O' Water are filled with water, which retains warmth from the sun through cool nights. They also protect seedlings from wind and, to some extent, from insects.

## Basic Care Techniques

*Watering*   Plants obviously need water for good growth. They need it consistently, and I make sure the garden gets 1 inch of water per week throughout the growing season. That amount is easily measured by putting a can in the path of my sprinkler with a mark 1 inch from the bottom. I water in late afternoon, so that little is lost to evaporation from a hot midday sun, but early enough so that the plants dry off before evening. Early in the season, when the plants are delicate, I prefer hand-watering with a hose-end sprayer that has a fine rose attachment to break the force of the spray. After the seedlings have developed, my watering device of choice is an oscillating sprinkler that provides a fine spray and even distribution.

The most economical way to water a garden where water is precious is a drip or trickle system. Either of these delivers water very slowly, and the water is absorbed completely and deeply, avoiding runoff, because the rate of flow is so gradual. The Israelis have used this principle to make the desert bloom — literally — and drip and trickle systems can also be used to deliver fertilizer and insecticides in liquid form. A drip or trickle system, which uses a tube or hose with many small holes in it, may be above ground or dug in permanently below the surface. These systems can be quite complex, with different zones, timers, and programs for different crops. Such systems are quite expensive, though, and these days you can spend a

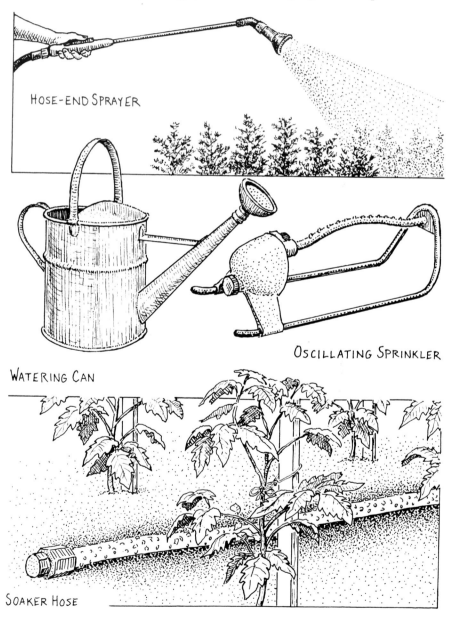

HOSE-END SPRAYER

OSCILLATING SPRINKLER

WATERING CAN

SOAKER HOSE

fortune on watering technology — as on many areas of gardening equipment — if you choose. I've had excellent luck with my tried-and-true oscillating sprinkler and rose-equipped watering can, however, and recommend those for all but the biggest, most elaborate gardens.

*Thinning*  Plants must be thinned to their appropriate spacing, or they will never develop fully. I thin early, always after a rain or watering, when the plants can be pulled most easily from the moist soil. This first thinning is done when the seedlings are 1 to 2 inches tall. I cull out weaker seedlings and leave the sturdiest

The bag of Victory Garden tricks for beating the season and the bugs includes raised beds, black-plastic-covered beds, plastic-wrapped tomato cages, cold frame, spun polyester over PVC hoops, and cheesecloth to protect delicate carrot seeds.

My three favorite weeding tools: the Cape Cod weeder, a red-handled three-prong cultivator, and an action or scuffle hoe for stand-up work.

behind — or at least that's the rule by which I *try* to do my thinning. In many cases, *all* the seedlings will look equally strong, but I still have to thin to the correct spacing, hard-hearted though it may seem. Not all thinnings are discarded, by the way. Some are transplanted to fill gaps left by poor germination, and others (spinach, say) are eaten in salads. When I'm thinning in the garden beds, I use one hand to protect the strong seedlings in place while I pull the culls with my other hand. Individual spacings vary from crop to crop, and I describe each detail in the monthly entries.

*Weeding*    In any good growing environment, weeds thrive, too. They compete with vegetables for moisture and nutrients, and they can harbor insect pests. Where I've used thick organic or black plastic mulch, my weeding is eliminated or reduced. Where weeding is necessary, I do it every week, after a rain or thorough watering, but not while the foliage is still soaking wet, because disease can be spread through the wet leaves. When possible, I work the soil over with my scuffle hoe (see the "Victory Garden Tools" feature in March for a detailed description of this largely undiscovered marvel), which is the easiest way I've found to accomplish this task. The three-pronged cultivator is handy for in-close weeding like that required for onions, beets, and some brassicas.

## Pests

One of the biggest differences between the way things used to be done in the Victory Garden and the way they are done now is my handling of insect pests. Over the years, I've developed a philosophical attitude toward them. Yes, it's possible to wage all-out chemical warfare and produce a relatively insect-free garden. But I, for one, am exceedingly wary of chemical pesticides. As I will say throughout this book, I don't think it makes sense to treat crops with exotic compounds that may do worse things to me than to the bugs. As a result, I've developed a pest management program in the Victory Garden that relies heavily on nonchemical deterrents. Experience has proven that I can produce beautiful, healthy crops without toxic chemicals.

My first line of defense is varietal selection. Whenever possible, I choose varieties that I know are resistant to attack from insects, or that have demonstrated an ability to take a few licks and keep on producing. Timing is my next weapon. My overwintered spinach will be ready to eat before the leaf miners become troublesome. A second sowing of summer squash, in midsummer, is usually spared from vine borer infestation. Whenever possible, I time plantings to minimize contact with insects. This requires an intimate knowledge of their rhythms and cycles in my garden, of course, but taking the time to keep records and plan my plantings is, to my mind, a better way than soaking the soil with insecticides. We're really talking about vigilance here, and I *am* vigilant when it comes to insects. I visit the garden often, so that I spot problems early on. It's often easy to deal with insects when they've just begun their invasion. Aphids, for instance, can be hosed off. Colorado potato beetles can be picked off by hand. Vine borers can be surgically removed from plant stems. It doesn't really take all that much more time or effort than spraying or soil drenching, and the end result leaves me feeling more secure. In the feature titled "Pests and Plagues" in June, I give descriptions, accompanied by color photographs, of insects most troublesome to the home gardener. Refer to that section for a thorough grounding in insect identification.

I'm very enthusiastic about the spun, bonded polyester fabric (one brand name is Reemay) that I now use in the Victory Garden. As I mentioned in the "Season Extenders" section of this chapter, this fabric provides some frost protection, and is also effective against insects that chew, lay eggs, bore, or otherwise attack the plants. The fabric can be laid directly onto the soil, after which it is lifted by the growing seedlings, but I prefer to support it with hoops of PVC tubing or #12 wire. Mosquito netting, which I've used in the past on beet crops, also works well, but the spun, bonded polyester seems to be more effective.

My use of crop selection, timing, black plastic, and polyester fabric has greatly reduced insect problems in the Victory Garden. Usually, the few bugs that do manage to infiltrate my barriers can be removed manually or sprayed off. Once in a great while, however, I'll still need to apply an organic pesticide. Three of these form my Victory Garden organic arsenal. *Bacillus thuringiensis*, sold under the trade names Attack, Dipel, and Thuricide, is effective against caterpillars like cabbage

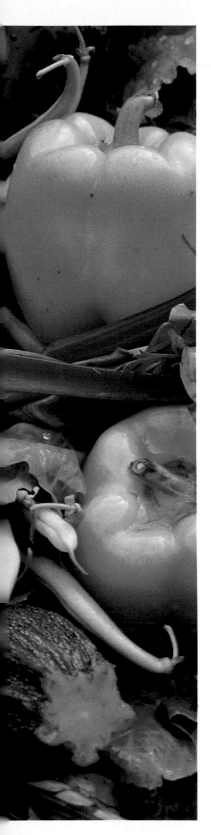

loopers, cabbage worms, corn earworms, European corn borers, and gypsy moths. Despite its scary name, *Bt* is a bacteria that is harmless to humans. It can be dusted or sprayed on the plants, but I prefer to spray a solution because it gives more complete coverage, especially on the undersides of leaves. Rotenone is another organic insecticide, which means in this case that it is derived from plants. It is effective against asparagus beetles, cucumber beetles, flea beetles, aphids, and caterpillars. Though potent, its toxicity is short-lived. I apply it as a 1-percent-solution spray. Pyrethrum, derived from the flower heads of some chrysanthemum varieties, is a good choice for white fly control. Red Devil is a particularly handy commercial mixture of rotenone and pyrethrum.

Even with organic pesticides, I practice careful handling techniques. I wear gloves when mixing the solutions, and gloves and a mask when spraying or dusting. I never store unused solution, but dispose of it when I'm finished.

My last line of defense against insects is really no defense at all, but tolerance. I know that no matter how religiously I observe the garden, and no matter how carefully I erect my barriers and apply organic insecticides, I'm going to lose a few plants here and there to bugs. That's okay. Bugs, bothersome as they may be, are a part of nature's scheme, too. I figure they're entitled to a leaf or two, as long as they don't get out of control.

## Harvesting

In the Victory Garden, I plan to stagger my harvests, so that I don't suddenly find myself with 50 crookneck squash in their prime, or 100 lettuce plants ready for pulling. Lettuce is a good example of how I do this, because I harvest lettuce from May through October. I've always got a cell-pack or two of lettuce seedlings coming along. I use the cold frame to get lettuce seedlings off to an early start, and then use it again later to keep them going into the fall. Staggering techniques also apply to cabbage, tomatoes, corn, and many of my other crops. By planting successive generations, I receive successive, smaller harvests that just keep on coming. This requires a sense of timing, but that's where my garden plan (see the chapter titled "Beginnings") comes in handy.

I believe in harvesting early and often. I give specific harvesting instructions for each crop in the monthly chapters that follow, but that early-and-often principle is my guiding light throughout the season. Vegetables that are harvested young are the tenderest and most flavorful. There's no sense in leaving vegetables on the vine or in the ground beyond their prime. And after harvesting, I use them as soon as possible. If there's a surplus, it goes to friends and neighbors. I never made an enemy by handing over a bagful of fresh-picked ears of corn.

**The payoff!**

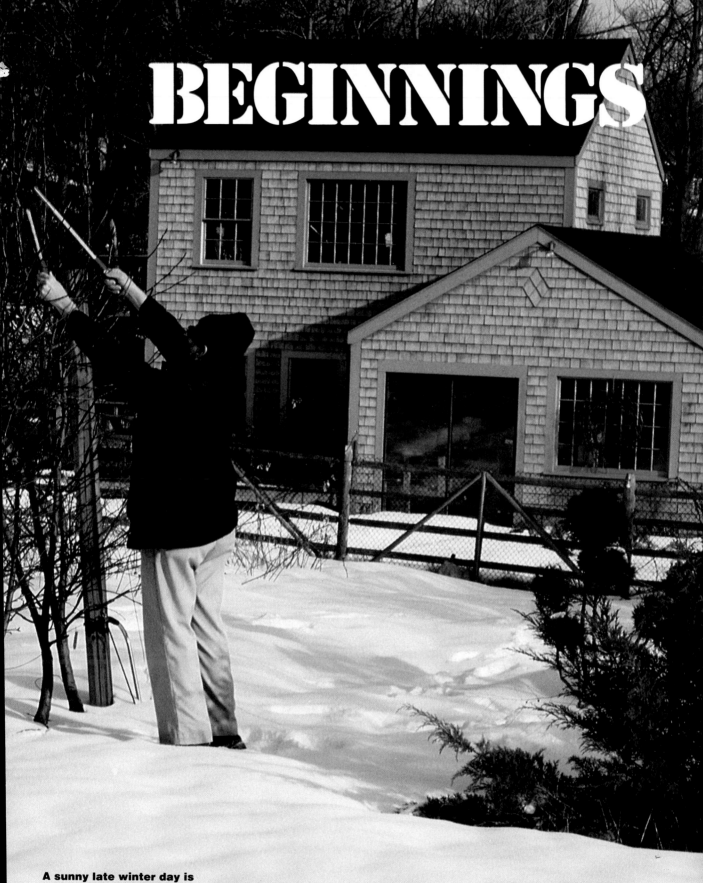

# BEGINNINGS

A sunny late winter day is a great time to prune fruit trees and berry bushes.

# BEGINNINGS

My gardening year begins quietly in January, pleasantly anticipated as I shovel snow or cut firewood, taking shape by the fireplace as I mull over the many seed catalogs that have arrived in the mail, and culminating in a day of serious planning, when I sit down with graph paper, pencil, and seed packets to plot out my garden beds. It's certainly possible to throw a garden together in May on a wing and a prayer, but I much prefer not to. I do think of gardening more as an artistic creation than a scientific project, but I also like to create my garden in an organized, systematic way. Planning minimizes labor and mistakes and maximizes output. Planning is also an instrumental part of the Victory Garden philosophy of constant, three-season productivity. With all the intercropping and succession planting and crop rotating I do, I'd be lost without a coherent plan to make sure everything's in the proper place at the proper time.

The first step, really, in planning the garden is varietal selection, making a list of all the vegetables I'll be growing in the coming season. The majority of these will be modern varieties that have performed well, but I always have my eye out for new vegetables that promise improved taste, better disease resistance, greater insect tolerance — or a combination thereof. I'm especially amenable to All-America Selections. These vegetables have been test-grown by specialists at twenty-eight sites across the country. Each year, new candidates are grown next to the best similar varieties. Thus the newest grows next to the best, and must show clear improvement under widely varying growing conditions to be judged a winner. I've rarely been disappointed by All-America Selections, which include such triumphs as Sugar Snap peas, Gypsy peppers, and Savoy Ace cabbage.

Next, I use pencil and graph paper to draw a diagram of the garden, showing every bed. I use a ½ inch to 1 foot scale, but that's less important than making the diagram accurate enough to show each raised bed and vegetable-planting area. That may sound overly meticulous, but it's not. It's the only way to judge accurately how much seed I need to buy, and to provide an adequate supply of vegetables for the number of people I want to feed.

When I assign crops to beds, I consider several things. Long-term crops like parsnips go on the perimeter of the garden, where they won't be disturbed by the comings and goings related to other beds. Corn I locate on the north or west side of the garden, so that the tall mature plants won't shade lower crops. I plant brassicas (broccoli, cabbage, Chinese cabbage, cauliflower, and Brussels sprouts) in beds where they have *not*

**Start indoors**
Celery
Leeks
Onions
Tomatoes (super-early)

A sure sign of the season to come — seed catalogs and seed orders. ▶

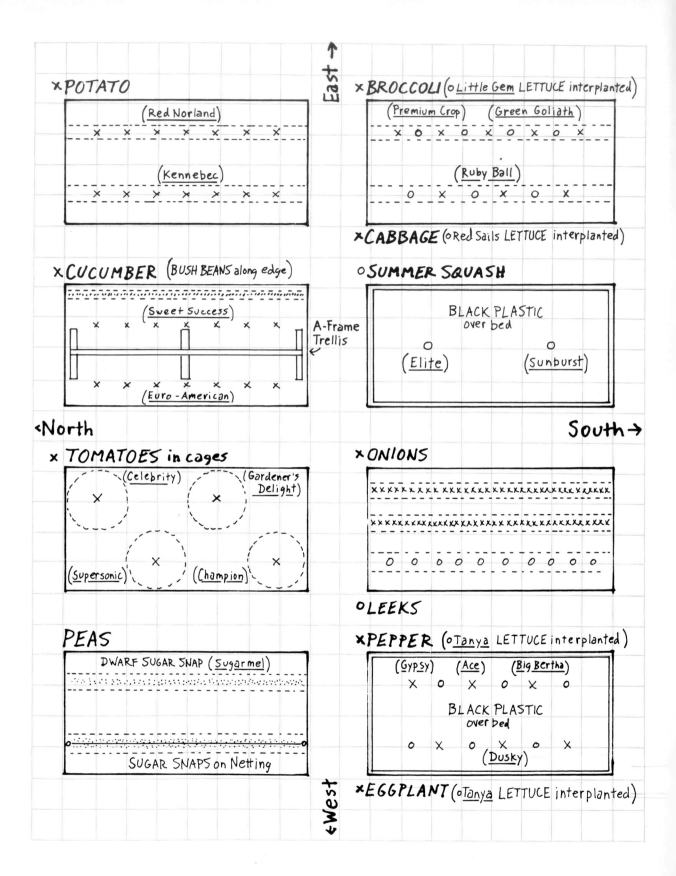

×POTATO

(Red Norland)

(Kennebec)

East →

×BROCCOLI (○Little Gem LETTUCE interplanted)

(Premium Crop)   (Green Goliath)
× ○ × ○ × ○ × ○ ×

(Ruby Ball)
○ × ○ × ○ × ○ ×

×CABBAGE (○Red Sails LETTUCE interplanted)

×CUCUMBER (BUSH BEANS along edge)

(Sweet Success)
×   ×   ×   ×   ×   ×   ×

(Euro-American)
×   ×   ×   ×   ×   ×   ×

A-Frame
Trellis ←

○SUMMER SQUASH

BLACK PLASTIC
over bed

○             ○
(Elite)       (Sunburst)

‹North

South →

× TOMATOES in cages

(Celebrity)        (Gardener's Delight)
×                  ×

(Supersonic)   ×   (Champion)   ×

×ONIONS

××××××××× ×××××××× ×××××××× ×××××

×××××××× ××××××× ××××××× ×××××××

○ ○ ○ ○ ○ ○ ○ ○ ○ ○

○LEEKS

PEAS

DWARF SUGAR SNAP (Sugarmel)

SUGAR SNAPS on Netting

×PEPPER (○Tanya LETTUCE interplanted)

(Gypsy)   (Ace)   (Big Bertha)
×    ○    ×    ○    ×    ○

BLACK PLASTIC
over bed

○    ×    ○    ×    ○    ×
(Dusky)

‹West

×EGGPLANT (○Tanya LETTUCE interplanted)

grown for a year or more, to stave off clubroot. And where legumes have grown, fertilizing the soil with their nitrogen-fixing roots, I plan to plant heavy feeding crops like squash.

With seed lists and diagrams in hand, it's time for scheduling. I write down *lots* of projected dates. For each crop, I record the date it will be started indoors, the date it will be moved to the cold frame for hardening-off, the date of planting in the soil, and the projected date of harvest. Planting dates for direct-seeded crops are also faithfully recorded. April 20 — my last expected spring frost date — is the linchpin for all this scheduling, and I give specific dates for all the above steps, for each crop, in the monthly calendar entries. Here, though, I'll say that experience has taught me to be flexible, and to consider my carefully recorded schedules as educated guesstimates. I'm never offended by having to juggle the schedule a bit to accommodate late blizzards or early warm periods. That's all part of the game, and it's great fun later to compare actual harvest dates with those I projected back in January. Whenever a bed will be used for succession planting, I record the pertinent dates for the crop and bed, too. Finally, I double-check estimates of indoor growing time, amount of seed required, and harvest dates.

My growing season is really divided into three periods: spring, summer, and fall. Each subseason has a plan of its own, and a schedule. And all my plans go into the Victory Garden journal, where they're kept year after year. I make notes on them during the season, recording thoughts on timing, weather, soil conditions, and each variety's performance. A final word about plans and schedules: I'm not rigid about either of them. No gardener can afford to be, if he values his sanity. I make adjustments to the garden plan every year, and each season rearranges some of my best-laid schedules. Even with these necessary and inevitable changes, though, the Victory Garden is vastly more efficient — and enjoyable — for having been created according to plan.

As January draws to a close, I set aside my completed garden plan and schedule and make sure that I have everything I'll need for the next growing season. I prepared my tools back in November and December, so I don't have to worry about them. I make sure that I have a good supply of pots, cell-packs, peat pots, and peat strips for seed starting and transplanting. I check my supply of sterile potting medium and 4-inch wooden labels. (A label in each pot gives a quick chart of seed-starting and transplanting times, as well as the correct variety that's growing there.) I check the heating pad, and make sure that I have enough lime, fertilizer, black plastic, and spun, bonded fabric to get through the spring. As seeds come in, I sort them and file them alphabetically in a shoe box or plastic file cabinet.

And then, at last, February arrives, bringing with it the very first planting of the new Victory Garden year. It all starts with celery . . .

**Celery**   While the television crew was traveling through Utah one year, I met an ingenious "Victory Garden" contest finalist named Delbert Thompson. A lanky, booted Westerner, Delbert was also a bishop in the Mormon Church. Since growing food was one way Delbert had found to practice the Mormon philosophy of self-sufficiency, he took his gardening very seriously. All of Delbert's crops were impressive, but his long, creamy stalks of celery really caught my eye. I asked him how he grew such beautiful celery, and he showed me his secret weapon: 10-inch sections of PVC pipe that he collected, free, from the discard piles of nearby construction projects. Delbert simply slipped these over the growing celery plants when they were young.

In order to produce the most nutritious celery possible, I've given up blanching in the Victory Garden, but that story about Delbert and his PVC pipe does point up the fact that celery is a crop which needs a bit of extra attention. It's a *very* long-term crop, which can take the whole growing season to mature, and that means some extra care. My variety of choice has been Improved Utah-52-70R.

I'll be transplanting celery seedlings to individual cell-packs in mid-March, so I start them from seed indoors in mid-February. I plant the seeds ½ inch deep in 4-inch pots filled with soilless medium, bottom-water thoroughly, and set them on the heat pad at 75 degrees. I'll have seedlings up in 5 to 7 days, and as soon as they're evident I move the pots to full sunlight — a windowsill or shelf in the greenhouse. There they will remain until mid-March, when they've moved into individual cell-packs.

**Leeks**   Leeks are relatively disease resistant and insect free, and few things are more rewarding than pulling a trophy leek from the ground in September. Garden-grown leeks will make grocery-store specimens (if you can find them) seem puny and bland by comparison. I'm quite a fan of leeks now, but must confess that it was not always so. I guess I thought that the gourmets just made too much fuss over this crop, which does require a lot of care and a very long growing season. A cold day in late November changed all that, however. I was working in the garden, covering strawberries with a deep mulch of hay. The ground was frozen iron-hard, and it looked as if snow would begin to fall at any moment. I came inside frozen to the bone, and discovered my television colleague, Marian Morash (chef-in-residence for the "Victory Garden" TV series), rehearsing a segment we'd be shooting soon. "Hey Bob, want some soup?" she asked, and I quickly agreed. *Anything* hot would have been welcome at that point! After a few spoonfuls from the bowl she handed me, though, I realized that her creation was not only hot — it was the best soup I'd ever tasted. "What *is* this stuff?" I asked her. "Why, leek and potato soup," she exclaimed. "What *else* would you eat on a day like this?" Thus occurred my conversion to leek-lover. Leeks take a *long* time to grow, so I start

A good variety of leek seedlings ready for Victory Garden evaluation. Modest beginnings for our fall-harvested giant leeks.

my leek crop indoors in late February. In 4-inch pots filled with soilless medium I sow the seeds and cover them with ¼ inch of the medium, then bottom-water until the pots are moist all the way from top to bottom. The pots are set onto my heat pad at 75 degrees, which will produce seedlings in about 7 days.

Giant Musselburgh and Titan are my favorite varieties. As their names imply, they produce *big* vegetables — 1½ inches in diameter and up to 18 inches long. Giant Musselburgh has been around for more than seventy-five years, so I know that it's stood the test of time and emerged as one very dependable performer.

**Onions** I want to be able to plant onion seedlings in the garden in late April, and that means starting them indoors in mid-February. I've started onions in plastic trays and Speedling flats, but I've returned to my standard 4-inch pot. It's plenty deep, easy to handle, and easy to buy in quantity. I fill the pots with soilless medium, sow the onion seeds ¼ inch deep, bottom-water well, and set the pots on my 75-degree heat pad. I'll have seedlings up in a week, and I move them into full sun. After a couple of weeks, I thin the seedlings so that there's about ½ inch of space between them in the 4-inch pots. I don't bother transplanting these onions to cell-packs (there are too many of them), but let them grow along in the 4-inch pots until it's time to transplant them into the garden in April.

**Tomatoes**   One of my goals with tomatoes is to be the first kid on my block with red, ripe fruit. By breaking all the rules, I'm now able to do that. I actually grow two crops of tomatoes in the Victory Garden these days — my steady, dependable main crop, which I begin to harvest in July, and my super-early, labor-intensive crop, which I begin to harvest — are you ready? — by June 1. To do that, I have to alter my planting schedule radically. Tomatoes cannot produce ripe fruit until they have matured. A variety that must grow 65 days to maturity, in other words, can't produce fruit in 55 days, no matter how ideal the growing conditions. To allow for this rather elementary fact, I seed my super-early tomatoes, indoors, in February.

For this crop, I like Jet Star and Early Girl. Both are prolific producers with relatively compact vines. In mid-February, while the winter winds are still howling outside, I start one 6-cell-pack of each variety, sowing 2 seeds per cell ½ inch deep in the soilless medium. I bottom-water the packs until the growing medium is thoroughly moist, then set them on my 75-degree heat pad to germinate. The seedlings will be up in a week. I move them to full sun in a warm location (70 degrees or more is good) and, after another week, thin to the strongest seedling in each cell.

In mid-March, I transplant each seedling to an individual 4-inch pot filled with soilless medium, setting the seedlings deeper now than they were growing in their cells — right up to their true leaves, in fact, because tomatoes will root all along the stems. I bottom-water them at this transplanting with a solution of balanced, water-soluble fertilizer diluted to half strength, give them a day out of full sun to recover from the trauma of transplanting, and then set them back in the sunniest, warmest location I have.

In mid-April, each seedling is transplanted once more, this time to individual 1-gallon plastic containers filled with soilless medium. Again they're set in deeper than they were growing in their previous pots, to allow for more root formation. By now the seedlings will be 6 to 8 inches tall and growing very vigorously. I feed them again with a drink of water-soluble fertilizer (again diluted to half strength), give them another day's respite from full sun, and then put them back on my sunny windowsill or in the greenhouse. During the next 3 weeks, I keep a close eye on the weather. Whenever there is a warm, sunny day without high wind, I carry the tomatoes outside to take advantage of those prime conditions. (I'm also ready to hurry them back

Tomatoes are worth that
special effort.

inside at the first hint of dropping temperatures, rising winds, or heavy precipitation.) These outdoor visits serve to harden the seedlings off, and to give them as much of a head start as possible before I set them out — permanently — on May 5. A week before, I work in 5 pounds of 5–10–5 for every 100 square feet of bed. Then I plant them in the open garden, setting them in deeper than they were growing in their gallon pots, spacing them 36 inches apart in the raised beds. The plants will be up to 3 feet tall by this time, which makes them too big for Wall O' Water protection. Instead, I surround them with cages made

**Turning in soil-improving winter rye *in small batches* makes this task much easier.**

from concrete reinforcing wire. For detailed instructions on building these cages see this chapter's feature, titled "Victory Garden Structures."

When the tomatoes have been transplanted, I water them in with full-strength water-soluble fertilizer and then cross my fingers. Actually, the mini-greenhouses, coupled with the very early start in February and successive transplantings, have just about eliminated tomato fatalities. I can almost always count on harvesting red, ripe tomatoes now by June 1. And when I bite into that first sweet, juicy Early Girl, I know all the work was worth it.

**Winter Rye**  My cover crop of winter rye has been green all through the cold, blustery months of New England winter, keeping the raised beds in shape, protecting against wind deformation and runoff damage. The cover crop has also been storing nutrients that will be released when it's turned into the soil. Winter rye's contribution to soil structure is even more important. When it's turned in, and decomposes, the organic material helps produce a loose, friable soil that is ideal for vegetable growing.

I've found that winter rye in the Victory Garden takes from 2 to 4 weeks to break down completely, so during our inevitable January thaw I turn under the beds that I'll be using for early spring plantings — crops like the brassicas, for example. (I give specific planting schedules for each crop in the monthly chapters that follow.) Then I follow along with a turning-under schedule that anticipates sowing times by 3 or 4 weeks. I turn the rye under with my spading fork, working from one end of a raised bed backward, taking 4-inch sections with each lift. I turn the mass over to bury as much green matter as possible, then break up the turned soil by smacking it sharply with my fork.

# VICTORY GARDEN STRUCTURES

During the long winter months, I ease the burden of indoor captivity by spending time in the workshop, repairing some of the Victory Garden's structures or making new ones. Over the years, through trial and error, I've come up with designs for five important gardening aids that I think are worth passing on.

**Composter** You'll hear me say over and over that good gardens are built on a solid soil improvement program, and the heart of soil improvement is composting. A compost bin is simply essential. My new, two-bin composter is a real improvement over former designs.

Here, step-by-step, is how I built the new composter. See the accompanying illustration for construction details.

## Materials

*11 8-foot pieces of pressure-treated 2x4*

*6 ⅜x3-inch lag bolts (bottom)*

*6 ⅜x6-inch carriage bolts (sides to back)*

*4 ⅜x4-inch carriage bolts (top rails)*

*20x4-foot piece of galvanized dog wire (2x4-inch mesh)*

*¾-inch galvanized staples*

**The durable, indispensable Victory Garden cold frame.** ◄

**1.** Make three 4x4-foot panels, using 2x4 lumber cut into 48-inch lengths and then nailed together.

**2.** Make one 4x8-foot panel, also using 2x4 lumber.

**3.** Attach galvanized "dog wire," using galvanized staples, to all four frames.

**4.** Attach the panels to each other, as shown, using 5-inch carriage bolts inserted through drilled holes.

**5.** Nail 2x4x8-foot bars of 2x4 onto the bottom and top of the bin's front. These make the bins more rigid and keep them from deforming under the pressure of all that compost they'll eventually contain. (You'll find my detailed instructions for making compost in the chapter entitled "Steps to Victorious Gardening.")

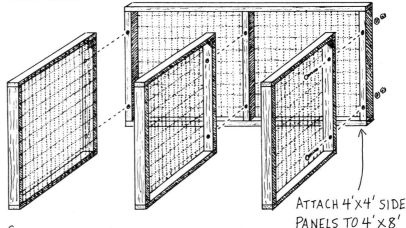

CONSTRUCT PANELS OF PRESSURE-TREATED 2x4 LUMBER. STAPLE GALVANIZED DOGWIRE TO ALL PANELS

ATTACH 4'x4' SIDE PANELS TO 4'x8' BACK PANEL WITH 5" CARRIAGE BOLTS

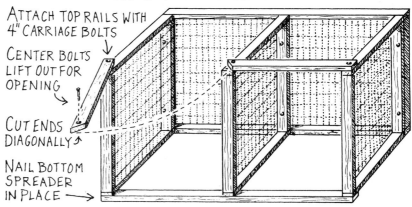

ATTACH TOP RAILS WITH 4" CARRIAGE BOLTS

CENTER BOLTS LIFT OUT FOR OPENING

CUT ENDS DIAGONALLY

NAIL BOTTOM SPREADER IN PLACE

**Cold Frame** A second essential piece of garden hardware is the cold frame, which gives me at least 2 months of extra growing time. It also provides a place to harden-off seedlings and hold over plants that might need help through the winter. I've designed a Victory Garden cold frame that's built to last. Here's the step-by-step construction method. Refer to the accompanying illustration for details.

**1.** Cut a 48½-inch 2x8 diagonally, as shown. This cut can be made with a table saw, or by using a circular saw with a cutting guide tacked in place. These diagonals will eventually become the slanting top pieces of the cold frame.

**2.** Next, cut the cold frame sides, front, and back from 2x8 lumber. For the sides, cut two pieces 45½ inches long. For the front, cut one piece 48½ inches long. For the back, cut two pieces 48½ inches long.

**3.** Now assemble the sides by nailing 1x3 cleats in place, as shown. Assemble the two back pieces the same way.

**4.** Insert eye screws near the ends of the sides, front, and back. Connect the four sections together by threading ½-inch wooden dowels through the aligned eye screws.

**5.** Cut 2x4 lumber for the cold frame top. The two side pieces should be 45½ inches long. The front and back pieces should be 48½ inches long.

## Materials

*32 feet of pressure-treated 1x1*

*3 8-foot pieces of pressure-treated 2x8*

*2 8-foot pieces of pressure-treated 2x4*

*1 8-foot piece of pressure-treated 1x4*

*4 3-inch galvanized corner brackets*

*2 galvanized or brass loose-pin hinges (heavy duty)*

*1 4-foot piece of ½-inch dowel*

*2 8-foot wooden battens, ¼x1½ inches*

*4x4-foot piece of plastic sheeting (4 mil)*

*4x4-foot piece of galvanized dog wire (2x4-inch mesh)*

*36 1½-inch galvanized screws (#8)*

*1¼-inch galvanized box nails*

*¾-inch galvanized staples (#14)*

*1 4x⅜-inch carriage bolt*

*10 galvanized screw eyes*

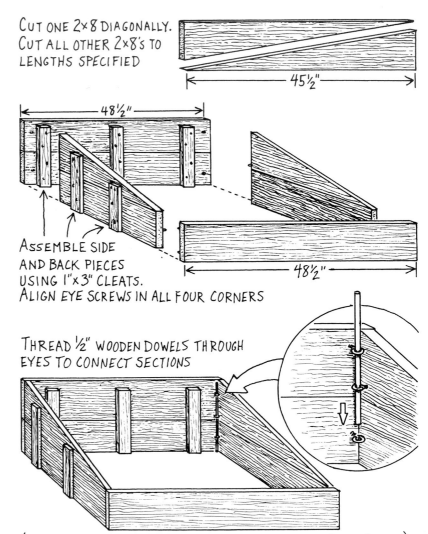

CUT ONE 2x8 DIAGONALLY. CUT ALL OTHER 2x8's TO LENGTHS SPECIFIED

45½"

48½"

48½"

ASSEMBLE SIDE AND BACK PIECES USING 1"x3" CLEATS. ALIGN EYE SCREWS IN ALL FOUR CORNERS

THREAD ½" WOODEN DOWELS THROUGH EYES TO CONNECT SECTIONS

(REMOVE DOWELS TO DISASSEMBLE AND TRANSPORT COLD FRAME)

**6.** Nail or screw the four top pieces together.

**7.** Now cover the top of the frame with galvanized wire fencing (with 4-inch holes) and staple the fencing to the 2x4s with galvanized staples.

**8.** Lay clear plastic (polyethylene sheeting) over the fencing, cut so that there is a 3-inch overlap of plastic all around.

**9.** Fix the plastic in place by nailing furring strips along the outside of the 2x4 frame.

**10.** Attach the top to the cold frame box with loose-pin hinges.

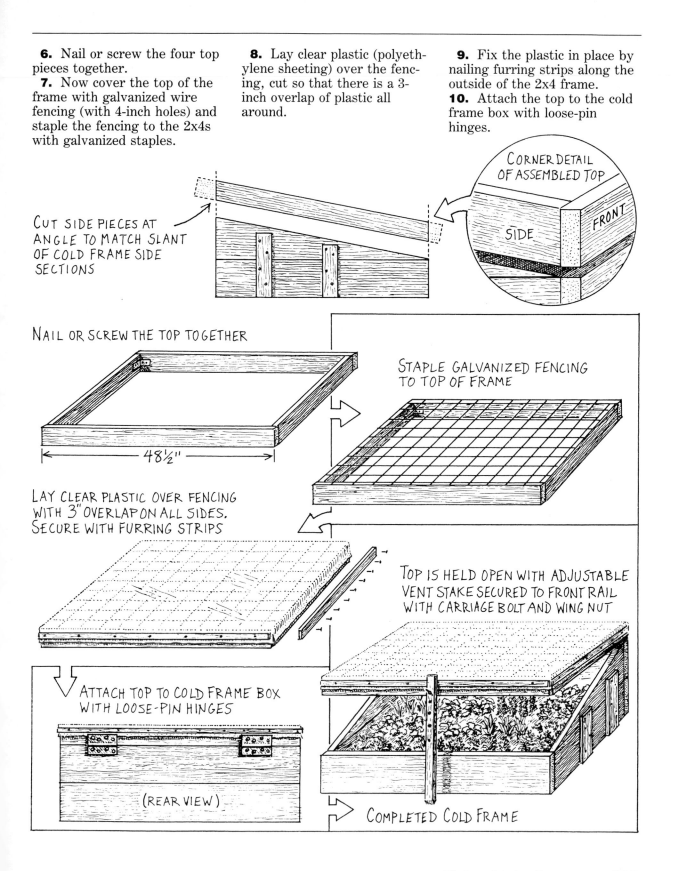

CUT SIDE PIECES AT ANGLE TO MATCH SLANT OF COLD FRAME SIDE SECTIONS

CORNER DETAIL OF ASSEMBLED TOP

SIDE

FRONT

NAIL OR SCREW THE TOP TOGETHER

48½"

STAPLE GALVANIZED FENCING TO TOP OF FRAME

LAY CLEAR PLASTIC OVER FENCING WITH 3" OVERLAP ON ALL SIDES. SECURE WITH FURRING STRIPS

TOP IS HELD OPEN WITH ADJUSTABLE VENT STAKE SECURED TO FRONT RAIL WITH CARRIAGE BOLT AND WING NUT

ATTACH TOP TO COLD FRAME BOX WITH LOOSE-PIN HINGES

(REAR VIEW)

COMPLETED COLD FRAME

**Planting Board**  In addition to the composter and cold frame, I've had fun making planting boards in the Victory Garden workshop. Planting boards are unbeatable for creating furrows and easily spacing transplants. I use redwood, spruce, or pine. Redwood is more expensive, but it stands up to weather better than pine, which requires a coat or two of preservative stain. Here's how to make the Victory Garden planting board:

**1.**  Start with a 48-inch piece of 1x6 redwood, spruce, or pine.

**2.**  Bevel both sides of one of the plank's long edges to 45 degrees. A table saw or a circular saw can be used to do this cutting.

**3.**  Cut notches at 6-inch intervals in the other edge. Large notches are 3 inches deep. Small notches are 1½ inches deep. The planting board, as the illustration shows, will have four small notches and three large notches when finished.

**4.**  Drill a ⅜-inch hole near one end for convenient hanging.

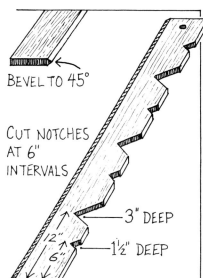

BEVEL TO 45°

CUT NOTCHES AT 6" INTERVALS

3" DEEP

1½" DEEP

12"

6"

**Tomato Cages**  Another project I like to tackle over the winter is making tomato cages. These are the lazy man's choice for controlling the growth of tomato plants, and I recommend them. I buy raw materials from a masonry supply house: one roll of the reinforcing wire used to strengthen poured concrete. The wire has 4-inch openings, and is quite stiff. I buy wire that's 5 feet high, to make sure that my vigorous tomato plants don't cascade over the top, which

happens often with 48-inch cages. Making these cages is easy. I use stout wire cutters to cut through the wire, allowing 80 inches per section, which, when rolled into a cylinder, will make a cage 24 inches in diameter. I secure the cages into their cylindrical shape with several twists of tie-wire, then trim the bottom cross pieces off, leaving a ring of sharp little probes that will stick into the ground and hold the cages upright.

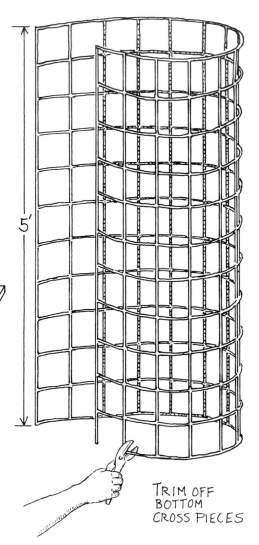

5'

TRIM OFF BOTTOM CROSS PIECES

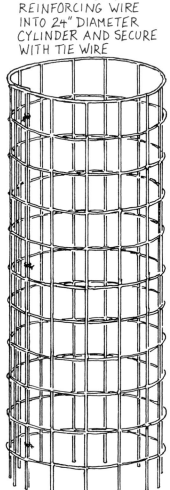

ROLL 80" SECTION REINFORCING WIRE INTO 24" DIAMETER CYLINDER AND SECURE WITH TIE WIRE

**Trellis**  Last but not least, I take time to make the Victory Garden A-frame trellises that I use for cucumbers and some other sprawling crops.

## Materials

*10 8-foot pieces of 2x3 redwood or weather-treated lumber*

*16x6-foot piece of galvanized dog wire (4x6-inch mesh)*

*2 3-inch brass-plated hinges*

*4 18-inch reinforcing rods*

*1¼-inch galvanized screws*

**1.** Cut three 6-foot pieces of 2x3 redwood or stained pine.
**2.** Cut four 4-foot pieces of the same wood.
**3.** Trim the ends of all the pieces, as shown, to make half-lap joints.
**4.** Secure the pieces together, as shown, with 3-inch round-head wood screws.
**5.** Nail or screw braces in place at all four corners.
**6.** Attach reinforcing wire to the frame with galvanized staples. It's possible to substitute string, or wide-mesh nylon netting, for the metal wire, if you prefer.

**7.** Repeat steps 1 through 6 to make the second half of the frame, and attach the two sections with brass loose-pin hinges.

The completed A-frame is 6x8 feet, a two-sided trellis that will support 96 square feet of growing space while occupying less than 20 square feet of ground. That's almost a five-to-one return!

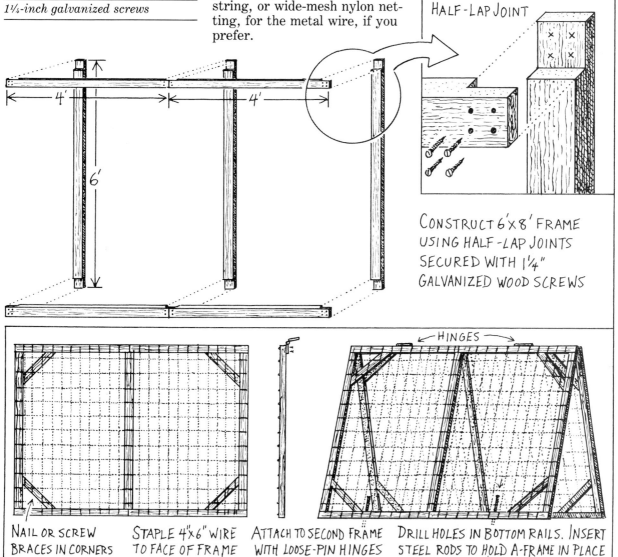

HALF-LAP JOINT

CONSTRUCT 6'X 8' FRAME USING HALF-LAP JOINTS SECURED WITH 1¼" GALVANIZED WOOD SCREWS

4'     4'     6'

HINGES

NAIL OR SCREW BRACES IN CORNERS

STAPLE 4"X6" WIRE TO FACE OF FRAME

ATTACH TO SECOND FRAME WITH LOOSE-PIN HINGES

DRILL HOLES IN BOTTOM RAILS. INSERT STEEL RODS TO HOLD A-FRAME IN PLACE

MARCH

309

# MARCH

March is mostly a winter month, and carries the threat of a late-season blizzard, at least in my region, despite those tantalizing, lengthening hours of daylight and occasional balmy days. Thus I have learned the hard way that disappointment awaits if I move too quickly; this is a month of promise, but also one of caution.

Since March provides plenty of sunlight for indoor seed sowing, I do quite a bit of that. I'll also be caring for the celery, leeks, onions, and tomatoes that I started indoors back in February. It's important to keep the seedlings well fed and watered without overdoing it. Plants can use fertilizer only if they are growing vigorously, with all the light and warmth they might require. Reduce the light or turn down the heat, and one must let up on the fertilizer. Otherwise the seedlings will develop as poor, spindly plants. The same advice follows for water. Seedlings kept too wet will suffocate. They must dry out between waterings or precious oxygen will not get to the roots.

Seed sorting occupies some time, as well. I sort all my packets alphabetically. At the same time, I like to double-check all the seed packet instructions to make sure the producers haven't sprung any new techniques on me.

Not all my March activities take place indoors. There's quite a bit to do outside, and planting is the part I always look foward to most. I'll be planting peas and onion sets outside, and spinach, too. Beyond that, I'll be turning under some of the winter rye, pruning raspberries and blueberries, and moving mulch off the strawberry plants. I'll dust off my cold frames and set them up in the garden's sunniest spot. And March is a good time, too, for me to catch up on those little odds and ends that never quite seem to get done when I'm too busy planting and harvesting. Fencing and trellises, for instance, can always use a sharp eye. It's a lot easier to mend the fence now before weeds disguise the weaknesses and before the woodchuck gets hungry. I'll check my hoses, too, repairing the broken sections because I know I won't have the time later. I'll give the compost bins a once-over, replacing any staples that have loosened and making sure the corners are still secure.

Finally, I'll be taking some of my seed from storage, and since I've protected the seed, it should germinate well enough. To reduce identification problems, I store seeds right in their packets, but I put the packets into tightly capped coffee tins or jars sealed with tape. It's important to keep the seeds cool and dry during storage. Humidity should remain below 65 percent, temperature between 32 and 40 degrees. A refrigerator is a good place to store the seeds. Adding rice, silica gel, or cornstarch to the jars will absorb moisture and reduce the chance of unwanted germination.

**Start Indoors**
Broccoli
Cabbage
Cauliflower
Chinese cabbage
Lettuce
Peas

**Transplant**
Broccoli
Cabbage
Cauliflower
Celery
Lettuce

**Plant in Garden**
Onion sets
Peas
Shallot sets
Spinach

**Victory Garden broccoli, ready for harvest: heads tightly budded, no yellow ing or flowering.**

**Broccoli**   I am joined by many these days in my fondness for broccoli, which is gaining popularity faster than any other home garden vegetable and giving the traditional front-runners — tomatoes and lettuce — a serious run for their money. Of course I relish the taste of fresh-from-the-garden broccoli, but I like it equally because it is not dauntingly difficult to grow. Nor is broccoli a stingy crop. If I harvest the central heads from my plants when they are tightly budded, before any yellowing or flowering has occurred, the plants will continue to grow tasty side shoots for several more weeks.

I have grown some very fine broccoli in the Victory Garden, but the best stand I ever saw grew happily in a community garden complex in Plymouth, New Hampshire. I'd traveled there to visit one of our contest finalists — a young couple attending a nearby college — and while their whole garden was outstanding, the broccoli was really special. I had never seen bigger, healthier plants, even in the carefully tended show gardens of professionals, and I asked the young people to tell me their secret. Smiling, they pointed to a stream flowing over nearby rocks. They explained that every spring, the stream, swollen with snow melt, overflowed its banks and flooded the surrounding land. When those waters receded, they left a superrich soil in which the broccoli, in particular, thrived.

Though I have no overflowing stream, I do grow very good broccoli each year, thanks in large part to the Victory Garden program of soil improvement and fertilization. I start the broccoli plants indoors in mid-March, following my usual indoor seed-sowing practices, sowing twice as many seeds ¼ inch deep in the 4-inch pots (which are filled with soilless medium) as I will eventually want plants in the garden. The pots are bottom-watered until the medium is thoroughly moist, then set onto the 75-degree heat pad. Seedlings are up in 5 to 7 days. When the first true leaves show, the seedlings are transplanted into cell-packs and then given a one-day respite from full sunlight. Bright, indirect light is fine while they adjust to their new quarters. They are then bottom-watered again, this time with a solution of a balanced liquid fertilizer (20-20-20 is the formula I use, but there are other variations that will work as well) diluted to half strength, then returned to full sun. Three or four weeks later the cold frame receives them for hardening-off. A word here about transplanting depth for broccoli seedlings: Like certain other vegetables (tomatoes, for instance), broccoli will grow roots all along its stem. Thus the plant is set into the cell-pack more deeply than it grew in the 4-inch pot, right up to its seed leaves. This will allow the development of a strong, vigorous root system, and it's a process that I'll repeat with every crop that has this growth pattern.

I have several favorite broccoli varieties. Goliath has consistently performed well in the spring garden, as has Grand Duke. Premium Crop is a recent development, an All-America Selection that has also grown nicely in the Victory Garden. And Green Valiant produced absolutely huge heads in my fall garden.

**Cabbage** While most members of the brassica family (which includes broccoli, cauliflower, Brussels sprouts, Chinese cabbage, kale, kohlrabi, and rutabagas) prefer cool weather and do not grow well in hot, cabbage is the exception. *This* brassica will grow well throughout the season, unaffected by warm weather. Despite this advantage, though, I have to admit that I grow less cabbage now than I used to. Time has tempered my tendency to fill up the early spring garden with cabbage plants. Why so? Simply, I don't really need more than half a dozen heads, even though I do love cole slaw.

There are many varieties of cabbage, but only two general types, and I grow them both: the smooth, ball-headed cabbages and the crinkly-leaved Savoys. I'm very fond of Ruby Ball, an early red cabbage, for its good harvest and manageable,

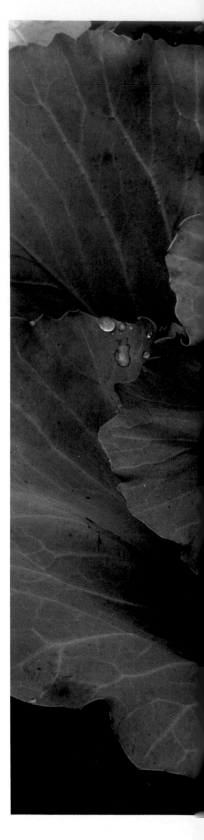

Ruby Ball, one of my favorite early cabbage varieties, produces an abundant harvest of cantaloupe-sized heads that leave room for intercropping lettuce seedlings.

cantaloupe-sized heads. These are somewhat small as cabbages go, but they leave room for the intercropping of lettuce, which maximizes yield from available space. Stonehead is another fine early variety that produces handy, 4-pound heads a week or so earlier than Ruby Ball. And of the Savoys, Savoy Ace is my favorite, an outstanding recent All-America Selections gold medal winner.

In early March, I seed cabbage the same way I seed broccoli, planting twice as many seeds as I will eventually want plants in the garden, in 4-inch pots filled with soilless growing medium. I cover the seeds with ¼ inch of the medium, then bottom-water until it is thoroughly moist. They go onto the heat pad at 75 degrees, which will produce seedlings in about a week. As soon as they're up, they're moved to a sunny windowsill and there they'll remain until they produce their true leaves, at which time I transplant them to individual cell-packs and bottom-water with half-strength water-soluble fertilizer.

**Cauliflower**  Cauliflower has given me (and I imagine I am not alone) more than a fair share of trouble. Clubroot, a disease caused by soil-borne organisms, is one problem. More serious is cauliflower's sensitivity to temperature. Cauliflower cannot stand heavy frost and bolts in hot weather. It grows best in average temperatures of 60 to 65 degrees. If the plants are subjected to 5 days of temperatures in the 40- to 45-degree range, they will be overstressed and that will initiate premature flowering, a survival mechanism that is wonderful for continuance of the species but that severely limits the harvest.

It is essential, then, to wait until all danger of frost has passed before moving cauliflower seedlings into the garden. It is just as essential for the crop to mature before the hot summer weather begins. In the Victory Garden, April 20 is my last expected spring frost date. Working backward to allow 8 weeks for germination and indoor growth, I start seed indoors in the first week of March. The seeds are planted in 4-inch pots filled with soilless medium, covered with ¼ inch of the medium, and bottom-watered thoroughly. I keep the pots at 75 degrees on the heat pad, and will have seedlings in 5 to 7 days. When they're up, I move them to a sunny windowsill until the first true leaves show. Then I prick out individuals and plant them up to their seed leaves in cell-packs filled with soilless medium. They're bottom-watered with water-soluble fertilizer diluted to half strength, given a day out of full sun, and then set onto the sunniest spot I can find. They will remain there until late April, when I will move them to the cold frame.

Early Snowball and Snow Crown are two early varieties that produce firm 8-inch heads, reaching maturity in about 50 days from setting out into the garden. White Sails has produced gigantic heads for me in the spring garden, and Burgundy Queen has proved to be a good, reliable purple-headed hybrid.

Celery's long growing season — 150 to 180 days — means that I start the seedlings indoors in February, then transplant them to cell-packs in March.

**Celery** It's time to transplant the celery seedlings from their 4-inch pots to individual cell-packs filled with soilless medium. When the true leaves are visible, I move them to the cell-packs, planting them the same depth they were growing in their 4-inch pots, then feed them with a solution of half-strength water-soluble fertilizer by bottom-watering. A one-day break from full sunlight eases the shock of transplanting, and then they're ready for full sunlight once again.

**Chinese Cabbage** Chinese cabbage is a very broad category, with many different types that vary in their heading quality. In general, it's a more tender (some would say more refined!) form of the cabbage we Occidentals know as great round heads in the garden. Chinese cabbage is very temperature sensitive, though more recent breeding efforts have produced some relatively weather-tolerant varieties. That aside, timing is still the most important factor in growing this delicious vegetable. Chinese cabbage grows best in cool weather, but can't tolerate more than a light touch of frost. I'll want to move young seedlings into the cold frame in mid-April, so I plant the seeds indoors in mid-March. Chinese cabbage does not tolerate transplant shock well, so I plant 2 seeds in each 3-inch peat pot filled with soilless medium. The seeds are covered with ¼ inch of soilless medium, and the pots are bottom-watered until uniformly moist. Then they go onto the heat pad at 75 degrees, which will produce seedlings in a week or less. When they're up, I move them into full sunlight.

**Leeks** The leeks I started in 4-inch pots in February will grow along happily in those same pots through the month of March. I feed with liquid fertilizer at half strength every other week until May set-out. I keep them in full sun, water regularly, and just watch them grow. I used to rush the leeks into the spring garden as soon as possible, but I no longer do that. One year, in a scheduling mix-up, I let the leeks remain indoors until early May, about 3 weeks after the last frost date in this area. When I finally got them into the garden, I didn't have much hope for a good crop. Surprise: They turned out to be the best leeks I'd produced in the Victory Garden. Now my practice is to keep those seedlings growing indoors well into May, to give them the longest head start possible. My new rule is that bigger transplants grow the best leeks. The February start indoors, coupled with 3 months of indoor growing time, gives me those big, healthy transplants.

**Lettuce** One of the greatest dividends of my work in the Victory Garden has been the opportunity to share the wisdom of gardeners around the world. That kind of communication is invaluable, and keeps opening my eyes to new wonders. I never really gave lettuce its due, for instance, until I visited Wisley, the Royal Horticultural Society's 250-acre garden not far from London. There I met head gardener Bertie Doe, a small man in his sixties. Bertie managed with absolutely no difficulty whatever to infect me with his passion for lettuce, and my own attitude toward the crop has never been the same.

Bertie showed me more than a dozen different varieties of lettuce developed by English breeders, extolling the virtues of each with unbridled zeal. I followed him dutifully, discovering how much there really was to learn about lettuce, but after more than an hour of crouching and touching and tasting and listening I had to call a halt.

"Bertie," I said, "these are all terrific, but I have to pin you down. Tell me two favorites that will be perfect for the home gardens back in the States."

"Tell them to grow Tania and Little Gem," Bertie said without hesitation. "And don't sell your own Buttercrunch short." He walked me to the end of the garden, and, as we were shaking hands, said, "By the way, the French have a great heading lettuce. It's crisp, tipped with red, and slow to bolt. Called Marvel of the Four Seasons." He hesitated, as though about to say more, and then laughed. "And now you'd better move right

Leeks always look frail in March, but 2½ months of controlled indoor growing conditions will produce super-sturdy seedlings for May transplanting. ▲

My first lettuce harvest, compliments of the cold frame. I keep several generations of lettuce growing at all times; as soon as mature plants are harvested, new seedlings take their place. ▶

along before I think of six more really good ones!" I have no doubt that he could easily have done so.

I came home and tried Little Gem, perhaps Bertie's true favorite, and found that its soft, buttery leaves really did justify that overused "melt in your mouth" superlative. Marvel of the Four Seasons was just as good. Since then, I've discovered Red Sails and Webb's Wonderful, and both have also become favorites. These days, thanks largely to Bertie Doe, one of my great joys is an early April cold frame filled with six different kinds of lettuce, all resplendent in various shades of red and bronze and green, as rich in textures as they are in colors. These varieties are not only eye-catchers, of course. Their taste makes grocery-store stuff seem like nothing but roughage — which is not far from the truth. Iceberg lettuce, though the least nutritious and blandest tasting, dominates shelves because it is tough enough to store well and to endure the rigors of long-distance travel. That's fine for the merchants, but not so good for us salad lovers.

All three main types of lettuce — headed, looseleaf, and butterheaded — are best grown fast and cool, so I start seeds indoors in the first week of March. I sow the seeds in 4-inch pots filled with soilless medium, cover them with ¼ inch of the medium, and bottom-water. A heat pad temperature of 75 degrees gives me seedlings in 3 days. Then they go to my sunny windowsill. When the true leaves are evident, I transplant the seedlings to individual cell-packs filled with soilless medium, setting them in at the same depth as they were growing in their original pots. They're bottom-watered with half-strength water-soluble fertilizer and given a day out of full sun, then moved to a location where they'll get full sun but cool temperatures in the 60- to 65-degree range. They'll remain there until early April, when I move them to the cold frame for hardening-off.

Starting two dozen lettuce plants in March will produce 24 beautiful, mature heads all ready for harvesting over a 2-week period in May. After that, the lettuce will pass its prime. To avoid overload and to ensure the longest possible harvest, I stagger plantings of lettuce in the Victory Garden. There are always several generations of lettuce seedlings growing, and whenever a space opens up, these youngsters are ready to fill it. My goal is to have 12 to 24 lettuce seedlings every 2 weeks. This guarantees a continued harvest throughout the season, giving fresh greens from April to Thanksgiving.

**Onions**   While onions can be grown throughout the world in soils ranging from muck to loam, certain regions produce superb onions, thanks to a fortuitous coincidence of climate and soil composition. One year, for instance, I visited Ron Andring, a Victory Garden contest finalist living in Walla Walla, Washington. Ron's home sat on a small, in-town corner lot, and in his unusual garden much space was devoted to protein crops like soybeans and peanuts. But his Walla Walla onions, creamy white and big as softballs, were the garden's crown jewels. I admit to a serious case of envy, because I knew that those onions, even with the most meticulous care, would not produce for me back in Boston as they had for Ron there in Walla Walla, where soil and weather were absolutely perfect.

Similar "miracle" onions also grow around Vidalia, Georgia, and on Maui, in the Hawaiian Islands. Naturally, each region claims that its onions are the sweetest on earth. The "Victory Garden" TV show's director, Russ Morash, is relentless in his search for the truths of gardening, and each time we visited one of these famous onion regions, he would ask me to verify the sweetness factor of that region's star performer.

"Come on, Bob, they say they're sweet enough to eat like apples," he would urge. "Tell us if that's true."

Well, I came, I saw, and I tasted. And I can affirm that these are all wonderful onions, excellent cooked, super when sautéed. But I would *not* recommend eating them like apples, and I have dripped a trail of tears from Vidalia, Georgia, to beautiful Maui to bring you that bit of invaluable advice.

In the Victory Garden, I plant onions from seed and from sets. Sets are young onion plants whose growth was interrupted just as they were forming bulbs. In this area, a bag of 100 costs about $1.29, and I mention the price because I know that some gardeners feel that sets are much more expensive than seeds. I disagree. By the time I add up costs for pots, soilless medium, and my own time (the most valuable commodity in any garden), all of which seeds require and sets do not, sets turn out to be cost-efficient indeed. For any garden where time and labor are supershort, they're unbeatable. Sets are also a terrific way to introduce kids to gardening. Little fingers have great fun pushing those onion bulbs down into the soft, cool soil. In fact, the only drawback to sets that I can think of is the fact that fewer varieties are available than is the case with seeds.

Onions I'm growing from seed were started indoors in February, but in March I plant onion sets outside, when the soil is dry enough to work. I buy sets that are no bigger than a dime (½ inch in diameter, maximum, is a good rule) because larger bulbs are more likely to go to seed, and anything smaller may not grow with the vigor I'd prefer. Onions are voracious feeders, so I fortify their raised beds with 5 pounds of 5-10-5 fertilizer for every 100 square feet of bed space. Then I rake the bed smooth and string lines to keep my planting straight.

Planting the bulbs is simple. I push them in with my fingers until their tops are just barely exposed, making sure to leave their stem ends pointing up. The bulbs are spaced 3 inches apart in the rows, with 12 inches between the rows themselves. I water them in well and forget about them for a while. My favorite onion variety from sets has been Stuttgarter Riesen, which has performed well here.

I plant onion sets in March as soon as the soil is dry enough to work. Stringing a line keeps my garden orderly, and that's important. I believe it should please the eye as well as the palate.

**Peas** Though winter confinement leaves me itching to get a spade in my hands again, most crops just aren't ready for the great outdoors in March, at least in the Victory Garden area. Peas, happily, are an exception. Not only can they be sown directly in March, the *best* peas are sown and grown in cool, 60- to 65-degree daytime air temperatures. In anticipation of this early planting, I prepare the soil well back in the fall ("Steps to Victorious Gardening" discusses my fall soil amendments), so that when spring arrives and the soil has warmed to the 40- to 50-degree range, all systems are go.

Planting peas, by the way, almost ended my gardening career before it got started. My father was a professional engineer, a precise man who insisted on planting his peas by March 17 — Saint Patrick's Day. This was an admirable enough goal, but in Massachusetts the ground was cold and wet, and the sharp east wind would chill a little guy like me right to the bone. Nothing daunted, Dad and I would bundle up and head for the garden. We'd string a line and make the furrow 2 inches deep and wide as a hoe. Dad wanted a double row of seeds, and he insisted that each seed in each row be 2 inches apart. Not 1½ inches or 2½ inches, but 2 inches — exactly. There *was* a purpose to his precision. He had seen me sow with a heavy hand on occasion, and I think he wanted to add discipline to my gardening skills. Those were Depression times, after all, and there was nothing to waste. His message was clear: Use what you need, but waste not a bit in the process — even if winter winds *are* turning your fingers blue.

My sowing these days is more carefree, but before I head outside with my seeds, I do two things to make the job easier. First, I soak the seeds overnight in room-temperature water to soften the skin and hasten germination. Then I treat the seeds with powdered legume inoculant. Peas belong to that marvelous family of plants called legumes, which feed themselves as well as the garden by pulling nitrogen from the air and storing it on their roots. They can do so probably because they evolved in Spartan growing conditions, which forced them to seek from the atmosphere nourishment they could not derive from poor soils. A bacteria called *Rhizobia* clusters in thick nodules on their roots, and these nodules are the nitrogen factories. *Rhizobia* is contained in the legume inoculant (a black powder, perfectly safe to use) that is available from garden centers and through seed catalogs. One dollar's worth will inoculate 10 pounds of seed. I dust my pre-soaked seeds with the powder immediately before planting, because prolonged exposure to air will reduce the bacteria's potency.

While I'm enthusiastic about legume inoculants, I'm much less so about the fungicide that some growers use to stave off the rot that can attack seeds in cool, damp soils. Commercial growers, who can ill afford to lose crops, counter the problem with a potent fungicide, but it has been under suspicion for some time as

**By starting pea seeds indoors in March, I produce a very early June harvest, and eliminate the need to treat seeds with chemical fungicides.**

a carcinogen. I stay away from it altogether. Instead, I have taken to starting some pea plants indoors in March. The benefits of this indoor start are several. Most obvious, I don't have to treat the seeds with fungicide. But I also enjoy a much earlier pea harvest — as early as June 1, in fact. That's a record in my area, and means I can expect a *doubling* of the pea harvest before the truly hot weather arrives. Indoor starting seems to work well with English peas, sugar types, and snow peas. I plant 2 seeds per cell in 2-inch peat cells, which come 12 to a strip. The cells are filled with soilless growing medium, and the seeds are covered with ¼ inch of that mix. I bottom-water the peat strips in a flat plastic tray, and set them on the 75-degree heat pad to germinate. At that temperature, I have seedlings up in about 7 days. I move them off the heat pad, let them grow for another week, and then thin to the stronger seedling in each

cell. They go into the greenhouse to grow on until mid-April, when they'll move to the cold frame for 5 days of hardening-off.

While I'm heartily in favor of started pea plants these days, I also still direct-seed peas, though I start a little later than I used to. At one time, I'd be out digging the pea trench as soon as the soil was dry enough to work in March — old habits die hard, especially those forged by a pea-loving father. Now, though, I wait for the soil temperature to pass 45 degrees, which minimizes loss. To sow my peas, I first excavate a trench 2 inches deep and as wide as the bottom of my square-edged spade: about 8 inches. Then I add 2 pounds of 5-10-5 fertilizer, scratching it in to the bottom of the trench. I just broadcast the seeds into the trench, looking for a casual spacing of about 1 inch between seeds. This thick sowing is closer than many seed catalogs recommend, but I like it because it increases yield and because the closely spaced plants help support each other in bad weather. As soon as the peas are covered with an inch of soil, I erect the trellis that will support them when they grow to their full 6- to 8-foot height. (This is not true of the shorter varieties like Sugar Rae and Sugar Anne, which grow 24 to 26 inches tall.) I make my trellises from snow-fence poles and nylon net-

**Four steps to superb peas. When the soil has warmed to 45 degrees, I dig the pea trench 2 inches deep and 8 inches wide, and broadcast the seeds casually. Then I sprinkle the seeds with legume inoculant and cover them with a full inch of soil.**

ting with 4-inch-square openings. The metal poles are pushed about 18 inches into the ground at either end of the rows, and the netting is strung between them.

There are many varieties of peas out there — shelling peas, English peas, snow peas — but I will say here and now that I'm devoted to peas of the Sugar Snap family. These remarkable peas were developed first by Dr. Calvin Lamborn of the Gallatin Valley Seed Company in Twin Falls, Idaho. Lamborn was seeking to increase yields and to breed out the distorted pod found on edible-podded peas in the 1960s and before. Ten years of crossing thick-fleshed shell peas with edible-podded varieties finally produced a true breakthrough. This standout had large, sweet peas and a crisp, sweet pod, both of which actually became tastier as the pea grew to full maturity. Lamborn called his creation Sugar Snap, and introduced it in 1979. It was immediately voted an All-America Selection, won a gold medal shortly thereafter, and not long ago was voted the top all-time All-America winner by gardeners across the country.

The Sugar Snap pea is so desirable because it makes for one-stop shopping for the gardener. In their early stage, Sugar

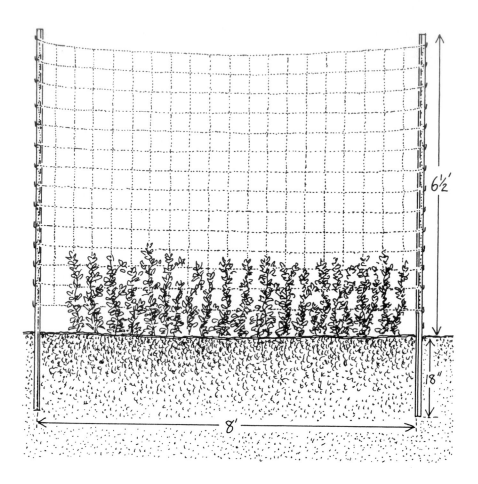

Snaps can be eaten like snow peas. Later, when the pods are developed, they can still be eaten in the pod — no shelling required. And they are exquisite simply munched raw, right off the vine. Because they are so tasty, and because they require no work beyond the growing, I myself see no need now to grow peas that do require shelling. Not everyone will agree with me, of course, but I admit my prejudice right here so·that my frequent references to Sugar Snap varieties later on will be less of a surprise.

**Shallots** Just as I will never rival Vidalia's onion, I will never grow exhibition shallots in the Victory Garden. New England is not prime shallot territory. Still, they are delicious enough that they are worth growing.

Shallots are planted from sets — small bulbs — as are some of the other onion members in Victory Garden beds, but my eyebrows raise every time I see the shallot-set prices in seed catalogs. A half-pound of these little delicacies will cost five dollars or more. They're not really as expensive an investment as that price would make them seem, though, because each little bulb will later produce 6 to 10 shallots.

**Shallots, planted as sets in March, grow rapidly in the Victory Garden's super-fertile soil. Shallot sets are good investments — each bulb produces 6 to 10 shallots.**

To make sure that they receive all the nutrients they need, I work in 1 cup of 5-10-5 fertilizer for every 10 feet of row before planting. Then I space the shallot sets 6 inches apart in the rows, and push each set about two-thirds of its length into the soil, leaving the pointed end up. When green shoots appear, I give the sets a drink of water-soluble fertilizer. I'll also put back into place any sets that have popped up out of the soil or have been disturbed by birds.

**Spinach** Growing spinach in the Victory Garden has taught me about microclimates. Despite virtually identical cultural practices and soil amendment programs in both the Boston and suburban Victory Gardens, I have never been able to coax a truly fine spinach crop from the Boston garden. In the suburbs, though, the spinach flourishes, and I'd match it against spinach grown anywhere. For a long time I wondered why these two gardens, separated by only ten miles and blessed with the best soils modern care could provide, produced such different spinach crops. After years of observation, I think the reason may be heat. It's possible that the urban garden's March and April weather may be just a few degrees too warm on just a few too many days — enough to make the difference. Despite being one of the most cold-tolerant crops, spinach is very sensitive to warm weather.

Because of that touchiness about heat, I sow the spring crop outdoors in late March. My cultural practice here is unusual, but it's worked very well for me in the Victory Garden, so I can recommend it wholeheartedly. The first step is to work the soil well and add 5 pounds of 10-10-10 fertilizer for every 100 square feet of bed.

Most garden instructions call for planting spinach in single rows, giving adequate spacing between plants in the row. Instead, I make a shallow trench with the back of an iron rake, about 12 inches wide and 1 inch deep. Then I sow seed directly into the depression, leaving about 1 inch between seeds. Happily, spinach seeds are white and not tiny, so they are easy to plant this way. Once covered with ½ inch of soil in this wide row, they will germinate even in cold, wet soils in about 10 days. As the plants become large enough to touch one another, I harvest every other seedling for a fine-tasting spinach salad. Soon the leaves will be big enough for cooking. By then the spacing is 6 inches, just what those seedsmen recommend.

This March planting of spinach helps prevent confrontations with hot weather, and as extra insurance against trouble I choose quick-growing early varieties like Melody and America, which will mature in 40 to 50 days. America is an especially good choice if I'm late sowing seeds, because it's more heat tolerant than some other early varieties and will resist bolting for up to 2 weeks in hot weather.

# VICTORY GARDEN TOOLS

In the garden, a few good tools can make an amazing difference between hard times and good times. Visit the shed of any experienced gardener and you will find a set of well-made tools, freshly oiled, their keen edges gleaming. I learned long ago that there are no bargains in tool buying. The only sensible purchase is a tool that is well designed, expertly crafted, and sturdy enough to last season after season. There may be more frustrating things than seeing the spading fork's head part company with its handle right in the middle of spring soil preparation, but I can't think of any just now. Good tools promote both peace of mind and pleasant gardening, and that, after all, is what we're after. Good tools are not cheap, but then neither is it cheap to replace shoddy junk season after season. When you've just laid out money for the third "inexpensive" spade, the wisdom of a strong initial purchase becomes clearer.

This doesn't mean, however, that I spend as much for a garden shovel as for my firstborn's college education. Any number of wily businessmen, capitalizing on gardening's ever-increasing popularity, would have you believe that you simply *must* have aerospace-quality stainless-steel tools, with handles of exotic woods from the dark

**Five well-made tools are the mainstay of my Victory Garden arsenal: rake, spade, spading fork, scuffle hoe, and trowel.** ◄

forests of distant lands. Nonsense. My philosophy is to buy well, but not to overbuy. Leave zirconium/titanium alloys in the nose cones, where they belong.

When I said earlier that a *few* good tools make gardening easier, I wasn't kidding. Most gardeners — myself included — do perfectly well with the Big Five: *spading fork*, *rake*, *hoe*, *spade*, and *trowel*. There are certainly other tools that I use in the Victory Garden. Some save time, some save labor. But one can do without them and still produce beautiful crops. One can't do without the Big Five, and I'll say honestly here that I think most gardeners would do well to spend more time selecting the basic tools they do use. Consider how much care goes into the choice of a set of golf clubs, for instance, or into the purchase of skis or a tennis racquet. Garden tools, like this other equipment, will be used often in their season, year after year, and a great deal of energy will be directed through them.

**Spading fork** This is arguably the most-used tool in the garden. For many years I have had a four-tined steel model. Steel gives, rather than snaps, when it hits large rocks and roots. If the tines are bent, I can re-form them. I have a couple of cast-iron forks, but they are heavier and more brittle, and I'm always afraid they will break when the going gets tough. My favorite spading fork has square tines with a

6-inch spread. You can find models with a much wider bite, but I like a spread of 6 to 8 inches. This lets me get into tight places, but also turns up a respectable swath of earth when I'm digging in earnest. My fork measures 40 inches from tine tips to handle, which is just about right for my six-foot height. Good forks come in shorter and longer lengths, however, so be sure to shop around for the one that fits your body best.

**Rake** My preference is a 16-inch model with a straight top. Bow-top rakes may be stronger, but they're heavier, too, and I don't try to move any boulders with my rake. It's a light-duty tool, used for smoothing tilled ground, clearing out small stones, breaking soil clods, and covering seeds. I like the flat top, too, because I can simply flip it over and give my beds a final smoothing. I prefer a long handle — 60 inches or more — to give me a long reach, but I have long arms and a back conditioned by thirty years in the trenches. As with forks, you'll have to choose a weight and length suited to your own comfort.

**Cultivating hoe** The number three tool in my arsenal is a cultivating hoe. I use an "action" hoe (called, by some, a "scuffle" hoe), and in my travels I'm continually amazed at how many people *don't* use this marvelous little device. An action hoe allows me to cultivate

**The scuffle hoe in action. Though twice as efficient as a conventional hoe, this handy tool is overlooked by most gardeners.**

while walking backward *or* forward. The two-edged blade is also twice as efficient as the single-bladed conventional hoe. Whenever I use my action hoe, I think of those animated TV commercials in which safety razors slide along, lopping giant whiskers off below the skin line. That's just how the action hoe decapitates weeds, loosening the soil at the same time. Whenever I hear people complain about how much work it takes to keep their gardens well groomed, I know they haven't discovered the action hoe yet. As with my other tools, I make sure the handle is of good, close-grained wood, and that the head is of sturdy steel — carbon, not stainless. Carbon steel can be sharpened easily, and that's why I choose it for all my edged garden tools.

**Spade** I use my flat-bladed spade to excavate trenches, cut pathways, and plant large, container-grown stock. That's heavy construction by garden standards, and my spade will take more punishment and stress than any other garden tool. For that reason, I pay special attention to its selection. The wooden handle must be smooth, tight-grained, and completely free of knots, flaws, or interruptions in the grain. I like a handle that's all one piece of wood, right up to the forked end, and reinforced with a wedge where the handle opens into its Y shape. The union between handle and metal spade gets extra attention. Cheap models have a short neck of light-gauge metal with a seam running the neck's length. The wooden handle is inserted into this flimsy tube and then secured, usually with a single rivet. This arrangement can be counted on to split like a scallion the first time any real leverage is applied. I look instead for a one-piece steel throat 10 to 12 inches high — long enough, in other words, to continue a full third of the way up the wooden shaft. The spade's blade is equally important. Stainless-steel spades can be had at considerable cost, but again I prefer a blade of high-quality carbon steel for the same reason that professional chefs use carbon-steel knives: They are easier to sharpen. A sharp spade is one of the greatest labor-savers in the garden, and I sharpen my own with a file frequently. The spade rewards me by slicing easily through turf, roots, and compacted soil.

**Trowel** The humble trowel completes my list of must-have garden tools. I use a one-piece cast-aluminum trowel, with a thick, curved handle. The handle fits me so comfortably that I feel as if I'm shaking hands with a friend each time I pick it up. The scoop is 6 inches long, and the handle is encased in red plastic. I've learned the hard way that my trowel is the easiest garden tool to lose, and that red handle makes it the easiest to find, as well.

**Additional tools** I can hear gardeners everywhere exclaiming, "What about the rototiller!" To tell the truth, with my raised beds I don't use a heavy one anymore. When the Victory Garden was in its early days, and flat-plane culture was being used, the big rototiller was an important part of the arsenal. I've moved on to 4-foot raised beds, though, keeping pace with gardening advances, and I put a lot of work into preparing and shaping those superfertile raised beds. Once I've done so, I don't want to ruin them by running a heavy tiller down their length. However, the new hand-held lightweight tillers are ideally suited for raised-bed maintenance.

Other hardware does come in very handy. A *pocketknife* is one such item. I use mine so often that I'm almost inclined to make the Big Five a Big Six. Opening a ripe melon, for instance, demands instant access to a keen blade. Squash and eggplants should have their stems trimmed cleanly from their vines, as should pumpkins. I also need to snip lengths of twine to tie up cauliflower leaves. I carry a "Swiss army"–type knife with several blades and tools.

I also find handy a *metal watering can*, big enough to hold 2 or 3 gallons. Mine produces agentle, rainlike flow from its "rose" end, which can be removed for cleaning. Plastic cans are lighter and cheaper than the galvanized steel variety I use, but they won't last as long. Either the handles will give way after a season or two, or the flimsy, screw-on rose will strip its threads.

I use a *garden cart* and a wheelbarrow in the Victory Garden. The cart is the largest I could find, with a 14-cubic-foot capacity and big, bicycle-style wheels. I've used it to haul everything from cordwood to sand, and I'm always amazed at how easily the thing rolls along, no matter how badly I've overstuffed it. A good wheelbarrow with an inflatable tire is useful, too, in the Victory Garden's raised beds and narrow aisles. Here, the maneuverability of the wheelbarrow is hard to beat.

A *gas-powered string trimmer*, for a garden the size of the Victory Garden, is something of an indulgence — but a justifiable one. The trimmer saves me a lot of time cleaning up around the beds, and time is my most valuable commodity. By keeping down tall grass, I minimize insect hideaways and keep the garden looking picture-perfect. With a string trimmer, I'm spared the toil of scuttling along on hands and knees, snapping away at grass with clippers. There are very powerful models available, but for my garden purposes, a light, 2-horsepower trimmer, weighing about 12 pounds, is adequate. I use a shoulder strap to support the trimmer's

**My planting board, with cutouts at 6- and 12-inch intervals, eliminates time-consuming measuring.**

weight, which makes the going considerably easier.

My homemade *planting board* is very convenient in spring, when I'm laying out the garden. Easy-to-read markers take the guesswork out of spacing plants and save time by eliminating repeated measurements. The board's beveled edge creates a precise seed furrow, too. (See the feature in the chapter titled "Beginnings" for my detailed instructions on how to make the Victory Garden planting board.)

*Garden lines on bailers* help me mark out straight edges for my beds, and keep planting rows straight, too. I use cast-aluminum bailers wrapped with 50 feet of mason's line, which is sturdier and less likely to tangle than standard twine.

There are several other tools I'm glad to have in the shed, too. A short-handled, *three-prong cultivator* is dandy for weeding close to plants and for scratching in side-dressings of

fertilizer. A standard *garden hoe* is the tool of choice for hilling-up leeks and potatoes. I use a *soil thermometer* to tell me when some very frost-sensitive crops can be planted in spring. (I like thermometers with sturdy metal probes that can be plunged into the soil, and with easy-to-read circular dial scales in sturdy steel casings.) Finally, I've found that a *compression sprayer* with a plastic body is very helpful. The hose-end sprayers work well, but there are times when the portability and superfine spray of the pressure sprayer is unbeatable. A 2- or 3-gallon capacity is adequate without being too heavy for comfortable carrying with a shoulder strap. I make sure that the sprayers I buy have brass components at the spraying end, because steel is sure to rust or corrode after a season or two.

That's about it. My tool philosophy, in a nutshell, is to buy the best without falling for advertisers' gimmicks. And when it comes to tools that I use infrequently — post-hole diggers, say — I rent rather than buy. It just doesn't pay to spend the money and then have the tool sit idle for years and years.

Finally, I take good care of the tools I do buy. After every use I wipe them clean with a brush or coarse cloth like burlap, and then anoint them with a rustproofing coat of oil. I sharpen the edged tools often with a file, and I hang *every* tool in the same place in the shed after each use so that I'll find it, gleaming and ready, the next time I need it. The only thing more frustrating than a broken tool is one that's disappeared entirely.

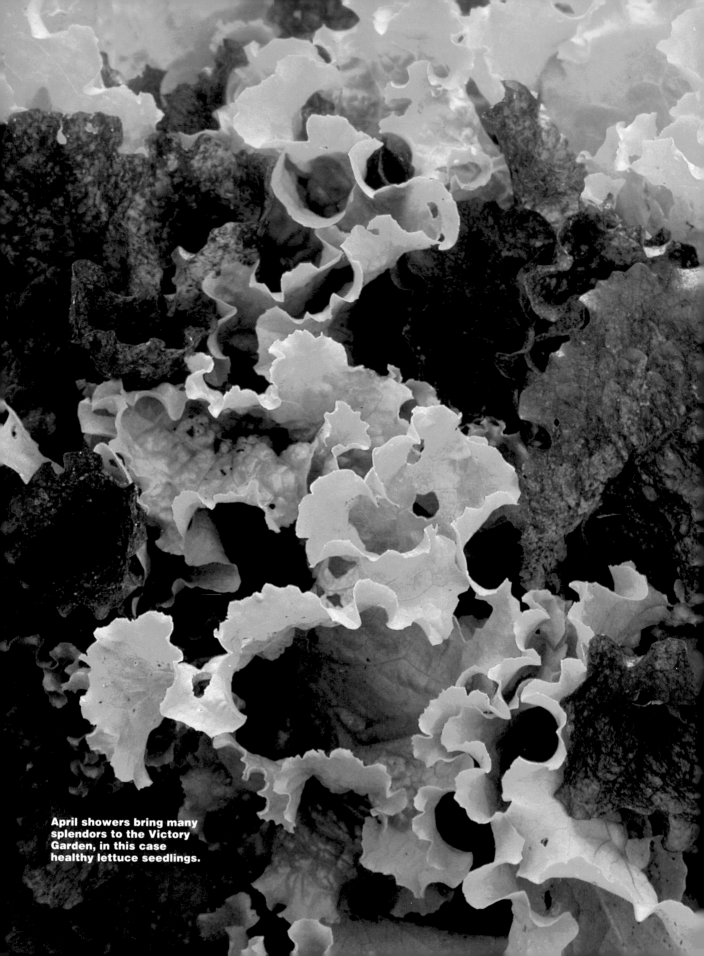

April showers bring many splendors to the Victory Garden, in this case healthy lettuce seedlings.

APRIL

# APRIL

If March is the month of promise, it is in April that the dreams that have sustained me throughout the long winter begin to come true. Plenty of rain will fall early in the month, and days will be, on average, 10 degrees warmer by month's end. April weather is more uniform than was the case with March, and I see the passing of my last expected frost date in the Victory Garden region: April 20. It's still too early for most bugs, a blessing for garden and gardener alike, and all of these fortuitous developments can breed a heady excitement.

These days, I temper that excitement with reserve. It's tempting to rush out every single transplantable item from the greenhouse or windowsill, of course. In fact, at one time I did just that. But over the years, I found that setting plants out too early brought later problems. Even crops that like the cool 40- to 60-degree April temperatures — cabbage, broccoli, and beets, for instance — will suffer quality and bolting problems if jolted by *too* great a fluctuation between day and night temperatures. So with these and other sensitive crops I have learned to be patient rather than pressing. The reward for my April patience is trouble-free crops through the rest of the season.

April may still be, however, the busiest month in the Victory Garden. More than a dozen crops are planted outdoors, and almost that many are started from seed inside. In addition to those important tasks, I'll be turning under more beds of winter rye, laying down black plastic over some of the raised beds to warm them up, and tending to the compost bin. This is the month to start a new asparagus bed, a major project in and of itself. And I'll be getting the trellises and netting ready for use with crops that need them — beans, peas, melons, and cucumbers.

**Start Indoors**
Beans
Corn
Cucumbers
Eggplant
Melons
Okra
Peppers
Summer squash
Swiss chard
Tomatoes

**Transplant**
Broccoli
Cabbage
Eggplant
Lettuce
Peppers
Tomatoes

**Plant in Garden**
Asparagus
Beets
Carrots
Chinese cabbage
Kohlrabi
Lettuce
Onions
Parsnips
Peas
Potatoes
Radishes
Turnips

**Screen**
Broccoli
Cabbage
Chinese cabbage
Radishes
Spinach

**Asparagus**  April is the month to create an asparagus bed, and asparagus crowns are the prime ingredient. Crowns are young asparagus plants, one to two years old. It's possible to grow asparagus from seed, but doing so means a minimum three-year wait before first harvest. That's why most gardeners start new beds with crowns, which will shorten the waiting period by a full year.

When I was a youngster, Dad and I would travel to a nearby farmer's spread to buy our asparagus crowns. We paid two cents apiece for them, and they looked like small octopuses or squid. Nowadays I don't have to track down willing farmers for my crowns because they're widely available at garden centers. I pay a bit more for them now, but the varieties on today's market, like Jersey Centennial, are hardier and much more disease resistant.

The secret to producing award-winning asparagus is soil preparation and more soil preparation. Asparagus will come from these beds for decades (some well-preserved beds have produced for more than one hundred years), so it makes sense to prep the soil with extraordinary care. There's only one chance to do so! Step one is to lay out the beds as soon as the soil is workable and dry in the spring. In the Victory Garden, I laid out two beds in an area 30 feet long and 8 feet wide, which gives room for 30 crowns. (Ten plants per person will produce enough stalks to satisfy most asparagus-lovers.) In each 30-foot bed, I dug out

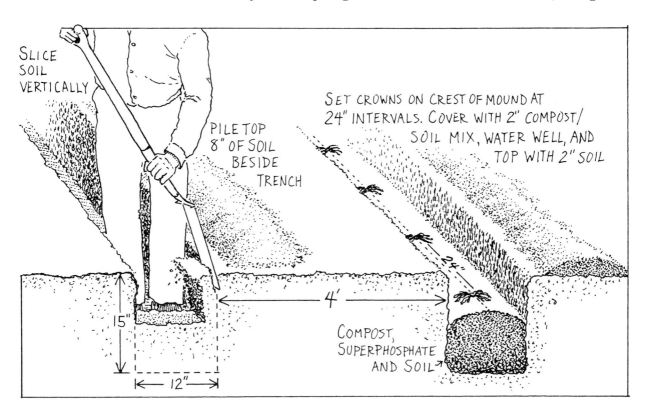

SLICE SOIL VERTICALLY

PILE TOP 8" OF SOIL BESIDE TRENCH

SET CROWNS ON CREST OF MOUND AT 24" INTERVALS. COVER WITH 2" COMPOST/ SOIL MIX, WATER WELL, AND TOP WITH 2" SOIL

15"

12"

4'

24"

COMPOST, SUPERPHOSPHATE AND SOIL

two trenches 12 inches wide and 15 inches deep. The trenches were 4 feet apart. I strung lines to keep my digging straight, and cut the sides of the trench dead vertical. An excavating trick I learned from my father made the earth moving considerably easier. I dug right down to the 15-inch depth, then cleared a space large enough to stand in — about 3 feet long and 1 foot wide. I stood in that hole and just sliced away soil with my spade. The loose slices fell toward me like slices of cake. It was easy to scoop them up and lay them to one side. Here's something else I've learned: I put the top 8 inches of soil (the very best stuff) to one side, and deposited the remaining subsoil in my compost bin.

After digging the trench, I shoveled in about 4 inches of well-rotted manure or compost. Next came a secret weapon: superphosphate, a fast-acting, commercial fertilizer especially effective for root development because of its potent phosphorus content (the analysis is 0-20-0; it's made by treating raw rock phosphate with sulfuric acid, which makes the phosphorus much faster-acting). I scattered 5 pounds per 100 square feet of bed into the trench.

**Before planting asparagus crowns, I trim off any broken or torn roots. After soaking the crowns for 10 minutes, I set them atop the mound at 24-inch intervals.**

When the compost or manure and superphosphate had been added to the trench, I blended in half of the soil I'd set aside earlier, using a hoe to draw the whole mix together into a mound that ran the length of the trench.

Then, at last, it was time to plant the crowns. I bought mine at a garden center where they were kept refrigerated prior to sale, and I made sure that they didn't dry out before I had a chance to plant them. (Damp peat moss works well to hold them in the interim.) I checked each one carefully for root damage, because the crowns are often pulled roughly from their home beds. Broken or torn roots were trimmed back to healthy tissue, and then I gave the crowns a bath in tepid water for 10 minutes. Properly moistened, they were set out at 24-inch intervals atop the long mound I'd created earlier. The crowns should be centered right over the mound's crest, with their roots flowing downward over the mound's flanks. When all were in place, I gently spaded in a mixture of compost or manure and some of the remaining topsoil I'd laid to one side, covering first one side of each crown and then the other with 2 inches of this mixture. I gently firmed the loose soil, and watered it well to firm and settle it further. Finally, I covered the crowns with 2 more inches of soil. By this time the trench was about half-full, and I was almost finished. As a last step, I blended the remaining loose soil with compost or well-rotted manure, using 1 part compost or manure to 3 parts soil, and piled this mix on the ground back from the edges of my trench. As the new shoots emerged over the next weeks, I added this enriched soil a little at a time, spreading it carefully around them until the trench was filled and level with the surrounding soil. I also side-dressed the rows with 10-10-10 fertilizer in June and October . . . but now I'm getting ahead of myself. I'll remind you about that when the time comes in later monthly chapters.

Cultivation is important to young asparagus plants. Until I saw shoots appear from the planted crowns, I weeded the beds by hand. Once they're up, I use the three-pronged cultivator. It was time well spent, because weeds or grass would have competed for nutrients, moisture, and light.

**Beans** Beans, like peas, are a most rewarding crop to grow because they feed the garden as well as the gardener. I needn't go into the contribution they make to our own nourishment; the fact that over 500 varieties are cultivated attests to our love affair with the bean. And beans, like all legumes, do their part for garden fertility. A benign bacteria called *Rhizobia* colonizes on the roots of beans and other legumes. *Rhizobia* takes nitrogen from the air and converts it into forms usable by plants — the process we call nitrogen fixation.

In the Victory Garden I grow both bush and pole beans. Bush beans are prolific producers, mature quickly (50 to 60 days), make good use of available space, and require no support sys-

tems. The only real drawback to bush beans is their relatively short bearing time. Two weeks is usually the extent of my bush bean harvest from any one sowing, though succession plantings every 2 to 3 weeks let me beat that problem. One sowing of pole beans, on the other hand, produces an extended harvest of 6 to 8 weeks. Pole beans do take longer to mature (60 to 75 days) and, though their yield at any one time is smaller, the overall harvest is about the same. Toward the end of their life cycle, they are more susceptible to disease than bush beans. Finally, pole beans, as their name implies, require support of some kind — poles, trellises, or screens.

Several years ago I laughed when I discovered young bean plants offered for sale at my local garden center. Ridiculous, I thought, to buy beans the way one might buy petunias. I'd never thought of seeding beans indoors and then setting them out as started plants. Somebody else obviously had, though, and, as I thought more about it, I could see why. Gardeners want early crops, with no skips in the row, and started bean plants give them those advantages. With just a little extra effort, it's possible to have beans 2 weeks earlier than direct-seeded crops — without those gaping empty spots in the rows. I start my bean plants indoors about the first of April, using peat strips filled with soilless medium. The seeds are planted 2 to a pot about ½ inch deep, bottom-watered until all the medium is moist, and then set onto the heat pad at 75 degrees. The sprouts will be up in a week or so, thinned to the stronger seedling, and moved to a sunny windowsill, where they'll grow until it's time to harden them off in the cold frame. When they're planted out, the peat strips will go right into the ground, so the beans will suffer no transplant shock. Just as important, they'll start life outdoors undaunted by still-cold soil. In the past, I might have endured a 30-percent loss of the earliest direct sowing of bush and pole beans. The seeds of some varieties just would not germinate fully in soils below that 60-degree mark. With this new approach, there are far fewer casualties.

My favorite bush bean varieties are Contender, Provider, Bush Blue Lake, and a French variety called Triomphe de Farcy. The best wax variety I've grown is called Beurre de Rocquencourt. The pole beans I keep coming back to are Kentucky Wonder, Scarlet Runner, and Blue Lake. And a friend recently sent seeds of a variety called French Crystal, which I tried and which indeed turned out to be exceptionally tasty.

**Beets** I don't know how many times I've opened a gardening book to the beet section and read the following: "Beets are one of the easiest vegetables to grow." Perhaps they are in the utterly controlled environment of the laboratory or experimental garden, but I have found beets to be a much tougher real-world customer than those nice book entries would indicate, especially in cool April soils. Just getting the seeds to germinate is often difficult when they've been sown directly in the garden, for instance. And that's not the only problem. For several years when I first came to the Victory Garden I was rewarded by good luck with just about every crop — except beets. Though the tops were lush and lovely, the beets themselves were puny. Thinking that soil nutrients might have been lacking, I doubled the amount of fertilizer I'd been using, then sat back and waited for my crop of superbeets. Imagine my surprise when I found, beneath still more magnificent tops, pencil-thin and sadly anemic beet globes. Exasperated, I sought a beet-expert friend, who finally revealed the error of my ways. I'd been *too* kind to those beets, which rebel at overzealous feeding. Improving soil *composition*, the beet aficionado suggested, would produce better beets than pumping up their diet. My expert friend was correct. These days, I make sure that the beets' soil is stone-free and heavily laced with copious amounts of rotted manure or compost and any other organic matter I can work in — but *not* extra fertilizer.

Before I plant beet seeds outside in mid-April, I speed their sometimes reticent germination by soaking the seeds in tepid water overnight. Then, outside, I string a line the length of the beets' raised bed and use my planting board to make furrows ½ inch deep the length of the bed. I plant the seeds in the furrows with a foot between each row and 1 inch between seeds, then cover them with ¼ inch of soilless medium and give them a good watering-in.

My favorite beet varieties are Pacemaker II and Warrior, hybrids that have performed well. Burpee's Golden is a yellow-orange globe variety that produces excellent greens, which I en-

After soaking them overnight to speed germination, I plant beet seeds in soil that's enriched with compost or well-rotted manure and lightly fertilized.

joy just as much as the beets themselves. Since most beet seeds produce several seedlings per seed, I've recently tried a variety, Mobile, which seedsmen have developed to produce only a single sprout. This promises to eliminate the annoying chore of thinning the beets when they first emerge. It's an interesting new direction and, though Mobile won't replace my tried-and-true favorites like Pacemaker II, it adds variety while saving a bit of labor at the same time.

**Broccoli** The broccoli seedlings I started indoors in March will be ready, in mid-April, for their trip to the cold frame. I give them 5 days there, and then make ready for planting them in the garden. First step is to select a raised bed in which brassicas have *not* grown the previous season. This rotation is a defense against clubroot, which can linger in the soil all winter after plants have been pulled in the fall. Next, I work in 1 cup of 10-10-10 fertilizer for every 10 feet of row, as a last-minute amendment to provide adequate nitrogen and phosphorus, both of which are typically unavailable in cool soils. When I dig the planting holes for the broccoli plants, I add and blend with the

Broccoli and lettuce seedlings make good interplanting neighbors. The lettuce will be harvested before the broccoli grows large enough to need the extra room.

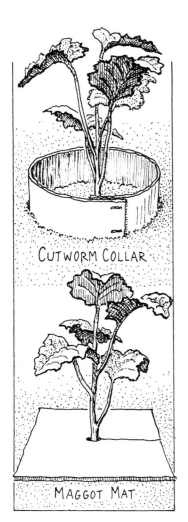

CUTWORM COLLAR

MAGGOT MAT

soil half a handful of lime per hole. This will elevate the pH to about 7.5, which is yet another safeguard against clubroot. Then, at last, it's time to set the broccoli plants into the soil. They'll be 4 to 6 inches tall by now, and I set them into the ground an inch deeper than they were growing in their cell-packs. Broccoli, like tomatoes and certain other crops, will root all along their stems, and setting them in a bit deeper each time they're transplanted lets them develop the strongest possible root systems. Spacing for broccoli is 18 inches between plants and 24 inches between rows, which leaves plenty of room for big, healthy plants to grow and room, as well, for the interplanting of lettuce. Finally, I water the seedlings in with water-soluble fertilizer diluted to half strength and then turn my attention to protecting them from insect invaders. At one time, I fiddled with all kinds of antibug alternatives: cutworm collars, maggot mats, organic insecticides. Now I've found a one-stop bug stopper: spun, bonded polyester fabric. I cover the broccoli beds with this fabric these days, supporting the fabric with hoops of #12 wire, the ends of which are pushed into the soil about 6 inches. Some sources advise laying the spun, bonded fiber right down on the soil, and letting the growing seedlings push the fabric up as they enlarge. I prefer to support the fabric with hoops, so that the seedlings are spared even that little bit of extra effort at this early stage in their development. The fabric protects against all the insects that pester broccoli — cabbage moths, flea beetles, aphids, and root maggots. In addition, it traps heat, which is an advantage with this early planting. Watering is no problem, because moisture passes right through the porous polyester fabric. Any way you look at it, this fabric is a big breakthrough for the home gardener. The stuff is even reusable from season to season.

**Cabbage**   One week before my last expected frost date — April 20 — I move the cabbage seedlings into the cold frame for 5 days of hardening-off. While they're making the transition, I put the finishing touches on their beds. Cabbage, like the other brassicas, is a heavy feeder. To accommodate that appetite, I work in 1 cup of 10-10-10 fertilizer per 10 feet of row. My fall soil amendment program has provided for a different pH in the cabbage bed than the rest of the Victory Garden enjoys. My standard throughout the garden is 6.5, in which most vegetables thrive. A higher pH seems to inactivate the clubroot organism, however, which has been troublesome in my cabbage beds. Thus I lime the beds in fall to produce a pH of 7.5 for the cabbage plants, and work in another half-handful to each planting hole.

When I set the plants into the garden soil, I allow 18 inches between the small-headed varieties and 24 inches between the larger. The plants will need all this room eventually, but now it lets me interplant lettuce. I set the cabbage seedlings into the ground so that their seed leaves are just above the surface (they'll root all along the stem, producing sturdier seedlings),

Cabbage seedlings look like this when they're ready for 5 days of hardening-off in the cold frame.

and then I give them a watering-in with soluble fertilizer diluted to half strength. Finally, I cover the seedlings with polyester fabric supported on hoops of #12 wire. The fabric will protect against cabbage moths and cabbage loopers.

A final word of warning: Cabbage, like broccoli, is susceptible to clubroot infestation. To minimize this, I plant my cabbage in beds where other brassicas have not grown for several seasons.

**Carrots**   I learned a lot about carrots when I was a youngster working on a farm, and one of the first things I learned was weeding. That was my task, and I crawled along the endless sandy rows doing the job by hand. As I grew taller and stronger, I was allowed to push a wheel hoe between the rows. That was better than toiling on hands and knees, but it required sharper concentration — the price for failure was greater. Those rows were close together, and a moment's inattention could easily wipe out a whole swath of young carrot plants.

I'm even less fond of weeding and thinning today than I was then, so it's fortunate that I've learned a much easier carrot routine: pelleted seed. I've also learned to avoid a few "accepted" practices. Take planting out, for instance. Many sources will tell you to sow carrots outside as soon as the soil can be worked. Don't. Carrots are very sensitive to cold, and there's no better shortcut to carrot catastrophe than too-early sowing. They're slow germinators anyway, and that recalcitrance is aggravated by cool conditions.

The real key to superb carrots, though, is superb soil. Carrots most appreciate loose, deep, sandy soil that will present no obstructions to the tiny, developing taproot. To achieve that fine soil, my initial bed preparation for the carrots included the addition of 2 inches of coarse builder's sand, and a very careful culling to remove stones, clumps, or anything else that might get in the way of those taproots.

Carrot germination rates increase rapidly when soil temperature rises above 55 degrees, so I wait until the ground is at least that warm before planting seeds outside. Usually, the soil will be that warm as soon as the last expected frost date in my region — April 20 — is past. When that times comes, I rake the prepared bed smooth and make ¼-inch-deep furrows with my planting board, spacing the rows 1 foot apart. I usually plant 3 to 4 rows, about one bed's worth. I used to fuss with the terribly fine carrot seed in an effort to achieve very regular spacing, knowing that much later work could be avoided if I could sow one seed every ½ inch. Memories of those long days on hands and knees made me wary of the thicker sowings recommended in some catalogs. No matter how careful I was, though, sooner or later I found myself down on hands and knees for extended sessions of thinning. Now I've taken to pelleted seeds, and thinning is almost a thing of the past. Several of the major catalogs carry pelleted carrot seeds, and the cost is quite reasonable — about $1.25 for 1000 seeds. The increased ease of handling (each pellet contains one seed and is about the size of a buckshot) makes the slightly higher cost more than worthwhile. Seed tapes are yet another alternative to sowing straight from the packet. The tapes are 15 feet long, with seeds spaced every ½ inch, and cost about $2. The tape itself dissolves after planting, leaving behind a furrow filled with well-spaced seedlings that need little, if any, thinning.

Whether I'm using loose seed, pellets, or tapes, I cover the seed with ¼ inch of soilless medium, which reduces weed growth in the new bed and means still less work after the seedlings sprout. I gently water the seeds in well, and keep that covering of soilless medium moist. It's a thin layer, and thus can dry out quickly in full sun. Carrots can take up to 3 weeks to germinate, and those seeds need constant moisture the whole time.

Because overzealous watering can actually wash away freshly planted loose seed, I've occasionally resorted to covering the seed rows with cheesecloth in very dry weather. This permits frequent watering without disturbing the seeds. It also breaks the force of heavy rains.

Although superbly groomed soil really is necessary to grow foot-long carrots like Imperator, breeders have recognized that not every gardener will be able to create such favorable growing conditions. To help gardeners, they have produced varieties like Danvers Half-Long and Short-and-Sweet expressly for heavy,

A cheesecloth covering keeps newly sown carrot seed from washing away in heavy spring rains.

stony soils. In those bygone days when I was trudging along on hands and knees, there really were only a few varieties for carrot growers to choose from. They had to take the time and do the work necessary to produce perfect soil. Now, with the new varieties, gardeners have the option of suiting the carrot to the soil, rather than vice versa.

Carrots can be bothered by wireworms, which tend to inhabit freshly opened ground and then disappear after several years. Wireworms will bore little tunnels through the carrots. The brownish worms are about ¾ inch long and are much less active in established garden beds. A friend recommends burying half a potato in the garden if wireworms become troublesome. The worms, so he claims, will be attracted to the potato, which can be pulled out in several days. I've not tried the technique, but it was so intriguing that I decided to include it here anyway.

In addition to Danvers Half-Long and Short-and-Sweet, which I mentioned above, I like Pioneer and Trophy. And I'm especially fond of the new variety, A+, which has a very high vitamin A content and a wonderfully sweet taste.

**Cauliflower**   I can't think of cauliflower without remembering one trip I took with the "Victory Garden" television crew to an international gardening exposition, the I.G.A. show, in Munich, West Germany. The Germans had provided an immense hall for exhibitors to display their prize vegetables, and we spent hours shooting exhibit after exhibit. Toward day's end I thought I'd seen just about everything — giant vegetables and ingenious displays — until I turned a corner and confronted the Germans' ultimate cauliflower extravaganza. There before me was a full-sized lifeboat, filled to the gunwales with broccoli and adrift on a foaming sea of cauliflower. There's nothing like an international gardening exposition to help one see vegetables in new ways.

In late April, after the last expected frost date (April 20) has passed, I move my cauliflower seedlings out into the cold frame for 5 days of hardening-off. I am cautious about that date, because cauliflower is the most weather-sensitive brassica. Too much cold too early in life will cause an undersized curd or premature flowering. Too much heat later on may simply prevent any curd at all from forming. It's a narrow "window of opportunity" to slip through, but the reward is one of the garden's tastiest vegetables.

**Chinese Cabbage**   The Chinese cabbage seedlings started back in March will be 3 to 5 inches tall by mid-April, and it's time to move them out to the cold frame for 5 days of hardening-off. While the seedlings are doing that, I prepare their beds by working into the soil 1 cup of 10-10-10 fertilizer for every 10 feet of row. With the bed raked smooth, after the seedlings have had their 5 days in the cold frame, I peel back the tops of the peat pots (to keep them from wicking away moisture and drying out roots) and set them into the soil at the same depth they were growing. Plants are spaced 12 inches in the rows, with 24 inches between rows. When the peat pots are all in, I water the seedlings with a solution of complete liquid fertilizer diluted to half strength. Finally, I cover them with hoop-supported fabric to protect against root maggots and any other insects that might develop a hankering for this tasty crop. And as with broccoli, cabbage, and cauliflower, I try to maintain a crop-rotation schedule that avoids placing Chinese cabbage where other clubroot-prone crops have grown in the past several seasons.

**Corn**   Corn used to be a problem in the Victory Garden — and lots of other places. In the first small garden behind the WGBH-TV studios, I was always short of room. Also, the early varieties that I tried were disappointing. When I finally did produce a decent crop (and here's the problem that corn growers everywhere shared), I had to rush the ears from plant to pot with great urgency because corn's sugar converted to starch so quickly after picking. Moving out to the suburban garden solved

my space problem, but corn's tendency to lose its sweetness so quickly continued to frustrate me. Even more frustrated, I knew, were the millions of people who had to buy their corn in supermarkets. I loved the taste of corn, but was dismayed by the amount of work required to produce so fragile and unstable a crop.

Then, several years ago, corn breeders responded to the bad reputation of supermarket corn. They delivered from their laboratories a genetic advance designed to vastly improve commercial corn's eating quality. In short, they produced varieties of corn that would hold their sweetness for a long time — up to 2 weeks. This, of course, delighted supermarket shoppers, who can now avail themselves of corn that tastes almost as though it came from the plants moments ago. And even those of us who grow corn in our own gardens appreciate the new "supersweet" varieties, as they're called. I do like to eat my vegetables fresh, as I've often said on the air and in this book, but I resent having to behave like the Marx Brothers in a Chinese fire drill in order to eat a vegetable before it degrades. Now I'm spared that indignity by the supersweets.

There are two supersweet genotypes available to home gardeners these days. "Sugary enhanced" varieties include Burgundy Delight and Platinum Lady, as well as all varieties that carry the designation "SE" or "EH." These are somewhat more tender and a bit sweeter than standard varieties, and their sugars do not convert to starch as quickly after picking. They do not need to be isolated from standard sweet corn varieties when planting.

"Shrunken gene" types (also called $sh_2$ varieties), on the other hand, should be isolated from both standard and sugary enhanced corns. Cross-pollination will produce disappointing ears with woody, starchy kernels in both crops if shrunken gene corn and standard or sugary enhanced types are planted closer than about 25 feet in home gardens. That's a minimum spacing, and 40 feet is better, if the room is available. The reward for this extra care, in the $sh_2$ corn, is *much* higher sugar content and slower conversion to starch after picking. Varieties of this type include Starstruck, How Sweet It Is (a 1986 All-America Selection), and Florida Staysweet.

Corn, once it's up, does very well in cool weather, but the seeds will just not germinate in soil that is too cool — below about 45 degrees. Growers used to get around corn seeds' tendency to sit in the soil and rot by applying a fungicide to the seeds. That fungicide has now fallen into disfavor, and may soon be banned in a number of states. I much prefer the natural alternative anyway, by which I mean sowing the corn seeds indoors and letting them develop while waiting for the soil to warm to about 60 degrees.

In early April, therefore, I soak corn seeds overnight to help speed their germination. This is particularly important with the true supersweet, or $sh_2$ varieties, which must absorb twice as much water as normal corn to germinate. I sow the seeds 2 to the cell in peat strips filled with soilless medium, bottom-water to moisten the medium all the way through, and then set the pots on my 75-degree heat pad. The seedlings will appear in about 5 days, and then they go to a sunny spot to grow until their move to the cold frame in early May.

A word about my Victory Garden experience with early corn varieties: I've never had much success with any of them. They gave me poor ears that turned out woody and tasteless, and I've decided that — in my growing area, anyway — there's a pretty strict relationship between taste and days to maturity: The more days, the better the taste. Now I use a midseason variety like

**Corn-growing has been revolutionized by the introduction of supersweet varieties, which lose their sugar content much more slowly than standard types.**

Burgundy Delight for my early spring corn planting. Given an indoor start and warm soil, this and other midseason varieties have worked very well for me.

I do grow a mixture of standard varieties and supersweets these days. Silver Queen and Butter and Sugar are among my standard favorites. In addition to the supersweets mentioned above, I like Early Sunglow, Kandy Korn EH, Pearls 'n Gold EH, and Snow Queen EH.

**Cucumbers**   I love fresh cucumbers, and for some time I had heard stories about the Dutch, whose tables sport fresh cukes all year round. Those stories made me very curious, and several seasons ago I had a chance to investigate. I arrived in Holland a day or two ahead of the "Victory Garden" television crew, and struck out on my own to the Floriade, a vast international horticultural exhibition on the outskirts of Amsterdam. Ostensibly, my mission was to scout the exhibits and single out those that would be suitable for inclusion in the show. Secretly, though, I was on the trail of the year-round cucumber I had heard so much about.

**Trellised cukes form up perfectly, have added protection from insects and rot, and are a snap to harvest.**

After hours of fruitless hunting, I sought refuge from a driving rain in one of the exhibition's greenhouses. I expected to find flowers inside. When I stepped through the door, though, I was confronted by rows of vegetables: eggplant, pole beans — and cucumbers! The wily Dutch were growing their cukes in large tubs something like sawed-off whiskey barrels. A simple drip irrigation system watered the plants. Two parallel rows of tubs, spaced 4 feet apart, ran the length of the greenhouse. The tubs were separated by only a few inches in the rows. From a horizontal rod 8 feet above the tubs hung nylon netting with 4-inch-square openings. The netting stretched downward in two sheets and was fastened to a frame on either side of the tubs, forming a large A-frame.

Cucumber vines grew up both sheets of netting, completely covering them with leaves and blossoms. Some cucumbers formed on the netting itself, but most hung through, dropping down vertically between the two angled netting sheets. Harvesting was a snap, and productivity was far above average, as it should have been in such ideal greenhouse conditions of temperature, humidity, spacing, and circulation. Perhaps most impressive of all, though, was the cucumbers' perfect shape. Cucumbers grown on the ground — even on black plastic — would rarely achieve such perfection.

Having discovered the Dutch secret for supercukes, I rushed home and tried the netting A-frame idea in the Victory Garden. With some modifications, which I'll get to in May, the trellising system has produced supercukes on this side of the Atlantic, too. (Though not, alas, year-round cukes!)

I can't set cucumbers out until mid-May, and to have 6-inch plants ready by then I start my cucumber seedlings indoors in mid-April. I fill 3-inch peat pots with soilless growing medium and plant the cucumber seeds 2 to a pot, ½ inch deep. (I use the peat pots because cucumbers are very sensitive to transplant shock, and peat pots, which go right into the ground themselves, minimize that trauma.) The pots are bottom-watered until the medium is completely moist, then set on the heat pad at 75 degrees. I'll have sprouts in about 3 days. After they've been up a week, I pinch out the weaker seedling in each pot, give them a day out of full sun, and then move them to the greenhouse or a sunny, south-facing windowsill.

I've come to like Sweet Success, a 1983 All-America Selection, as well as Dasher, Green Knight, and Euro-American. Pickling varieties that have done well in the Victory Garden include Peppi, Liberty (another AAS), and Country Fair.

**Eggplant**  The English use a French word — *aubergine* — for eggplant, which is an Asian crop. That kind of diversity is reflected in eggplant's various forms, too. Out at the Peto Seed Company in California, for instance, horticultural expert John Waterson showed me literally dozens of varieties of eggplants they were "trialing." When I asked him why so many kinds were being cultivated, he explained that disease resistance was one of the company's goals. Just as important, though, was the desire to develop varieties that would satisfy differing cultural expectations of what an eggplant should be. National preferences, apparently, place more emphasis on size and shape than on taste, which explained the golf balls, tennis balls, softballs, eggs, and other odd configurations he showed me. Given the chance to taste-test half a dozen very different shapes, however, I had to confess that I couldn't tell them apart!

All of which does not mean that I am not a lover of eggplant. I am, and to ensure a good supply later in the summer, I start my eggplant seed indoors on April 1 — 3 weeks before my last expected spring frost. Eggplant is susceptible to fruit rot and wilts, with verticillium wilt being especially troublesome in my cool growing area. Once it gets into the soil, it is there forever. Thus I've selected dependable Dusky, which is resistant to this wilt, as the Victory Garden eggplant variety. I sow 12 to 15 seeds in a 4-inch pot filled with soilless medium. I keep the heat pad set at 75 degrees, and in 5 to 7 days my sprouts are up. They reside on a sunny windowsill until I see true leaves — about the middle of April — when I transplant them to individual cell-packs.

Dusky, which resists verticillium wilt, is my eggplant variety of choice. In April I start seedlings indoors, planning for a May move to cell-packs.

**Kohlrabi** One warm summer day a few years ago I was sitting in the Victory Garden, jotting down notes for an upcoming TV show. It was a drowsy afternoon and I was deep in thought until a small voice broke the silence — and my concentration. I'd thought I was alone, but a little girl stood not five feet away. Right behind her stood a big brother and a set of parents.

"Excuse me, sir, but aren't you Bob?" she asked me again, and I admitted that I was, and we had a talk. It turned out that they were from Iowa, visiting New England for the first time. Back home, they had a large kitchen garden in which they grew most of the vegetables I grow, but in much larger quantities. We talked gardening for a while, and then they told me how excited they'd been by things they had never seen before: the ocean, Bunker Hill, *Old Ironsides*. As we strolled through the garden, their eyes went wide when we encountered something else they'd not seen before: kohlrabi. "Looks like a space station," the brother said. The little girl just shook her head: "It's *funny!* I bet I wouldn't like it!" Dad, however, said he'd like to try it back home, so I told him what I'd learned about growing and harvesting this unusual member of the cabbage family. He went on his way determined to grow a crop or two, but I imagine he had a tough time convincing his daughter that such an oddity could be worth eating.

Perhaps because of that odd appearance (it *does* look like Sputnik), kohlrabi has never achieved wide popularity in the U.S. My travels have shown me that it is quite popular in Ger-

Kohlrabi is a short-term crop (45 to 60 days) that adapts to a variety of climates and soils. Though the English feed kohlrabi to cattle, I eat it as a gourmet snack.

many and India, though in England gardeners are more likely to feed kohlrabies to their cattle than to their families. While it may never be the darling of chic eateries, I certainly think kohlrabi deserves better treatment than that. One of my favorite tricks, for instance, is to cut the raw globes into slices like potato chips and then scoop up hearty dollops of dip — a tastier and less fattening way to snack when the urge hits.

Kohlrabi is rugged enough to grow in a variety of climatic conditions and soils, so I direct-seed my crop in the Victory Garden soil in mid-April. Because kohlrabi, like other members of the brassica family (which includes broccoli, cabbage, cauli-flower, and Chinese cabbage, among others), is prone to clubroot infestation, I try to plant it where members of this family of plants have not grown in the last few years. It's a heavy feeder, so before planting I work in 5 pounds of 5-10-5 fertilizer for every 100 square feet of bed. Then, a week before our last expected spring frost date — April 20 — I sow the seeds, placing them ¼ inch deep and 2 inches apart in the rows, which are 12 inches apart. I cover the seeds with ¼ inch of soilless medium, water thoroughly, and wait for the seedlings to appear in a week or two. When they're up and growing, I thin them to the final spacing of 6 inches.

Kohlrabi, which matures in 45 to 60 days, is a short-term crop. Like all fast growers, it needs consistent watering for unchecked growth. My Victory Garden regimen of 1 inch per week ensures that regular supply of moisture.

Grand Duke is the variety I've come to favor. It's an improved hybrid and, unlike its predecessors, will not turn woody if left too long in the ground.

**Lettuce**  I've been growing lettuce indoors since early March, and by early April there are seedlings all over the place. I have them growing in many stages. One generation is emerging — just — in the 4-inch pots. Another is farther along in cell-packs, and a third has just been planted. My oldest seedlings will be ready in early April for 5 days of hardening-off in the cold frame.

With one exception (the lettuce I grow in a cold frame, which we'll discuss in a moment) most Victory Garden lettuce is interplanted, meaning that it is set in between already established plants of crops like broccoli, cauliflower, and cabbage. Interplanting is one of the best ways to increase my yield from limited garden space and, while some gardeners may claim to have "invented" the practice, it's really nothing more than copying nature. In the wild, many different types of plants with different growth patterns and nutrient needs commonly share the same space quite amicably. The trick is to keep in mind that plants that don't compete with each other for light and soil nutrients can be most successfully interplanted. Lettuce, for instance, will be ready earlier, and will be out of the ground before the brassicas mature, thus offering them no competition for moisture and nutrients.

Wherever I have 18 inches between plants, as is the case with broccoli, I set one lettuce plant equidistant between the two broccoli plants. If I have 24 inches between plants — in the Savoy cabbage rows, for instance — I tuck two lettuce plants in. The lettuce seedlings are planted exactly to the same depth they were growing in their cell-packs, as planting them too deeply will slow their growth and can kill the growing points of the plants. I give them all a welcome watering-in with my balanced

It's my standard Victory Garden practice to give newly transplanted seedlings (broccoli and lettuce, here) a drink of water-soluble fertilizer diluted to half strength.

water-soluble fertilizer diluted to half strength, and that's all they need for now.

That's half the drill for April lettuce. At the same time I interplant my lettuce seedlings in the garden proper, I prepare a cold frame bed. This cold frame crop will back up my other lettuce plants in two ways. One, it will give me the earliest possible fresh lettuce. Two, the cold frame crop is insurance. Come what may — hurricanes, Easter blizzards, rabbit attacks — my cold frame lettuce is safe and sound.

To make the cold frame bed, I mark off a 4x4-foot plot in the garden's sunniest spot. Then I enrich the soil by forking in 1 pound of 10-10-10 fertilizer for the bed. I rake the soil smooth, then cover it with the cold frame, allowing several days for the soil to warm. Leaving the cold frame in place, I plant lettuce seedlings 9 inches apart, spacing the rows 12 inches apart. In each row I transplant 5 seedlings of the same variety. The seedlings are watered-in with balanced water-soluble fertilizer diluted to half strength and the cold frame lid is lowered. When the April sun is very bright, bringing the temperature in the cold frame to 75 degrees or higher, I vent it to prevent the seedlings from being cooked.

**Melons** The comprehensive Thomson taste test is applied to virtually every Victory Garden contest selection, and no part of this examination pleases me more than the melon assessment. I've sampled some truly super fruit, but the very best melons in memory grew in Jeanette Hanson's Grand Island, Nebraska, garden. We traveled there to record footage for the "Victory Garden" television series, and after we'd taped from one end of Jeanette's garden to the other, she said, "Bob, I've saved the best for last. Follow me!"

I did, and I could tell by the rich scent that Jeanette's melons were perfectly ripe. Awaiting us there were 15 or 20 cantaloupes, a cutting board, and a sturdy knife. "Try a slice," Jeanette invited me, and for a moment all thoughts of taping were forgotten as the whole crew moved in for their share of the harvest. Those melons were the sweetest I've ever tasted, with tender orange flesh and a melt-in-your-mouth quality. Two factors enabled Jeanette to grow such superb melons. One was the rich Nebraska soil, and the other was the strong Nebraska sun, shining down hour after hour on the flat, treeless countryside.

In the Victory Garden region I don't have that strong Nebraska sun, nor do many gardeners in the United States. I've found, though, that I can give melons the growing season they require by covering the soil they grow in with black plastic, which heats it up sooner and keeps it warm longer than bare soil. Rich, sandy soil is just as important for successful melons, so my initial soil preparation for the melon bed included 2 inches of coarse builder's sand. Every season thereafter, the standard Victory Garden soil amendment program adds 2 inches of compost or manure to the melon bed, as well as the green manure cover crop of winter rye, which is turned under in the spring. Finally, I know that melons are especially heavy feeders, and I keep them happy with slow-release 14-14-14 fertilizer and periodic applications of water-soluble fertilizer. I'll give specific instructions for all these melon tasks as they come due, month by month. In April, I start melons from seed indoors.

During the last week of the month, I sow 2 melon seeds per 3-inch peat pot filled with soilless medium. I cover the seeds

with ½ inch of the medium and then bottom-water the peat pots to moisten them from bottom to top. They're set onto a plastic tray with all the pots touching, which keeps them from drying out too quickly, and the plastic tray goes atop my heat pad, which I set at 75 degrees. I'll have seedlings up in about a week. Then they're moved to full sun. After another week, I thin to the stronger seedling in each pot by snipping or pinching off the weaker seedling at soil level. Then I set the survivors in a sunny spot, still in their tray, where daytime temperatures will be consistently 75 degrees or higher. They'll grow there 4 to 5 weeks, after which I'll move them to the cold frame for 5 days of hardening-off.

I've experimented with a lot of cantaloupe varieties in the Victory Garden, and have come to favor both Ambrosia and Marble White. Ambrosia has produced exceptionally sweet fruit that average 4 to 5 pounds and are mildew resistant as well. While I favor cantaloupes, it's possible to grow other kinds of melon — Crenshaw, honeydew, and watermelon — using the same procedures I've described above.

**Okra**   Whenever I mention okra to friends, I think of the spicy crab gumbo I was once served down in New Orleans (or "Nawlins," as my Southern friends call their hometown). That gumbo was magic, bubbling in a huge pot from which wafted the aromas of bayou, open sea, and exotic spices — and that Cajun stew tasted every bit as good as it smelled.

In the minds of most gardeners, okra is exclusively a Southern crop. It's true that okra thrives under the conditions of heat and humidity characteristic of Southern gardens. Probably the finest okra I've ever seen, in fact, flourished in the North Carolina garden of Chuck and Marian Brackett, contest finalists. Their okra stood a good 6 feet tall, with stems at least 2 inches thick, and the plants were festooned with bright red and yellow flowers. It was an impressive display made possible by the long days of bright, hot sunlight, high humidity, and by Chuck's copious applications of a rich manure tea that he brewed using an oak whiskey barrel and a minnow can.

I can't claim to have grown okra that spectacular in the Victory Garden, but we have turned out some perfectly respectable crops. In early April, I start the okra indoors by planting 2 seeds in each 3-inch peat pot filled with soilless medium. The seeds are covered with ¼-inch of medium, bottom-watered, and then put onto the heat pad. Okra seeds will germinate within a 2-week period at 75 degrees. After the seedlings have grown a week in full sun, I thin out the weaker in each pot by snipping it off at soil level. Then the plants go to the sunniest, warmest windowsill or greenhouse shelf I have for the remainder of April and all of May. They'll be set out into the garden in June, but only after the soil has warmed to a consistent 60 degrees.

Blondie, a 1986 All-America Selection winner, is more compact than other varieties and does well in limited space like the Victory Garden's. Clemson Spineless is another of my favorites, and both have done well — though not spectacularly, as I said — in our cooler Northern climate.

**Onions**   In early April, the onions that have been growing indoors since February are set into the cold frame for 5 days of hardening-off. I prepare the beds in the same way I did for the onion sets in March: 5 pounds of 5-10-5 fertilizer for every 100 square feet, forked into the soil.

I plant the started seedlings outdoors after our last frost date, April 20. They're set in at the same depth they were growing in their container, with a spacing of 2 inches in the rows and 1 foot between rows. Here's a planting tip I learned the hard way. Despite the fact that I use raised beds for onions in the Victory Garden, and despite very conscientious soil amendment every year, I noticed for several seasons that the outermost row of onions was never as vigorous as other rows. It took me a while to understand that I was planting the outside rows too close to the edge of the raised beds. Onions have shallow root systems that

**Heat-retaining black plastic mulch helps me grow respectable crops of okra, a hot-weather-lover, in my cool New England climate.** ▶

**April's onion seedlings. I've learned to set the shallow-rooted onions at least 6 inches from the bed's edge to prevent damage by foot traffic.** ▼

branch out laterally, rather than penetrating deeply. Those outside rows were suffering foot damage from traffic along the adjacent walkways. Now I plant my first row at least 6 inches from the edge of the bed. I also give the onions a watering-in with complete water-soluble fertilizer diluted to half strength.

I used to recommend using some of these seedlings as scallions, but have come to realize that green onions (bunching onions from seed) are much better to eat in salads. The flavor is milder, the outer skin is thinner, and the edible white sections longer than is true with bulbing varieties. Given all this, my strategy in the Victory Garden has been to create a separate scallion row, where I plant scallion seeds every ¾ inch, allowing 16 inches between rows. The scallions will never grow large enough to need the extra room that bulb-onion spacing provides, but the extra 4 inches between the rows allows me to hill around the scallions for pale, blanched bases. Soil preparation and other planting methods are the same for my scallion seedlings as for the bulb-onion seedlings.

**Parsnips**   I am always surprised when I hear people say that parsnips are not a very popular crop. They are hardy enough to survive the coldest regions, and frost actually improves their flavor by converting starches to sugar. That sugar content, in

**Eighteen-inch-deep planting holes for parsnips are easy to dig with a pointed crowbar. Each hole is filled with a blend of soil and compost.**

fact, is the sweetest of any root crop. Sliced like potato chips, then sautéed in butter, they are really superb eating. They're nutritious, as well — full of B vitamins, vitamin C, and potassium. They do require a long growing season, though. The parsnips I plant in April will not achieve maximum size and sugar content until October, a full 7 months later. And parsnips, like all the long-rooted crops, must have deep, loose, rich, well-drained soil.

In early April, I go out to the parsnip beds, located at the edge of the garden so that they won't be disturbed by the care of short-term crops. I take with me my seeds and a tool that is called, in the building trades, a crowbar. This is a steel bar, 6 feet long, with a chisel-like point on its business end. I use the crowbar to make planting holes for my parsnip seeds. I thrust the bar 18 inches deep, then rotate it several times to create a cone-shaped hole 6 inches in diameter. I space these holes 9 inches apart, and fill each hole completely with a mixture of soil and an equal amount of sifted compost. Three *fresh* parsnip seeds are pushed ½ inch deep into each hole. I stress "fresh" here because parsnip seeds are notorious for losing vitality if stored over time. I cover the planting hole with soilless growing medium, which helps keep weed growth down. And because the parsnip seeds will take a minimum of 2 weeks to emerge, I interplant radish seedlings to mark the row. In several weeks, long before the parsnips will need the space, I will harvest the radishes and thin the parsnips to one healthy plant per hole.

**Peas**   In April I will have pea seedlings several inches tall in my peat strips, and they go into the cold frame for 5 days of hardening-off on April 15. Then I plant them in the garden, pre-spaced in the peat strips, peeling off the tops of the peat cells to prevent undue moisture loss from wicking action. The plants are set in to the same depth they were growing in their cells, and watered in with water-soluble fertilizer at half strength. I watch them carefully after this to make sure that the quick-growing plants are not wanting moisture. Usually my 1-inch-per-week ration in the Victory Garden is sufficient, but these peas really are fast movers and may outstrip even that generous water supply. I'm also prepared to rush in with a drink of balanced water-soluble fertilizer at full strength if the leaves begin to look a bit yellow. That can happen in early spring, when cold soil retards nutrient uptake.

The peas that were direct-seeded will be grabbing the trellis by now, and they also receive careful watering and a boost of water-soluble fertilizer if the need arises.

**Peppers**   In the April 1981 issue of *Horticulture* magazine, a gardening expert wrote, "Nothing presents the gardener with a greater challenge than green peppers. Every season this member of the nightshade family frustrates thousands of North

American gardeners." In the April 1982 issue of *American Horticulturist*, another expert wrote, "Sweet peppers are one of the most popular home garden vegetables because of their easy culture." Who's a gardener to believe?

My own experience has shown that peppers are not really that much more difficult to grow than tomatoes or potatoes. It's important not to set them out too early, because the best growing temperatures are from 70 to 75 degrees (air temperature) during the day. I don't set out peppers into the garden until June, but I start them indoors in early April. I sow 12 to 15 seeds per 4-inch pot filled with soilless medium and cover the seeds with ¼ inch of the same material. The seeds are bottom-watered, and the ideal germination temperature of 75 degrees provided by my heat pad produces seedlings in about one week. As soon as they're up, I move the seedlings to full sunlight in a location where daytime temperatures will remain at 70 degrees or higher. By April 30 the seedlings show their first true leaves, and I transplant them to individual cell-packs filled with soilless medium.

Big Bertha, an old standby, is still my favorite variety for a large, thick-skinned stuffing pepper. Ace is another excellent stuffer, but Gypsy, a thinner-skinned, white and yellow pepper, was a 1981 All-America Selection that has grown very well in the Victory Garden. It produces heavily and tastes like the champion it is.

**Potatoes**  Like most people, I never thought of the potato as a colorful crop, but when I visited the Chelsea Flower Show in England, I saw something that changed my mind. Peter Seabrook, the English television gardener, introduced me to a kilted Scotsman who was a potato specialist. The fellow's exhibit of more than 300 potato varieties included specimens that were not only white but blue, purple, yellow, and other shades as well. His potatoes were as colorful as his kilt.

I think I am not the only gardener who has made the mistake of considering potatoes too prosaic for home cultivation. In fact, potatoes are excellent candidates for the backyard garden. The taste of fresh, homegrown potatoes far surpasses anything that the supermarkets can offer. In addition, potatoes are prolific, yielding half a bushel from a 20-foot row.

Traditional wisdom holds that to start potatoes, one should bring home a bag of seed potatoes from the garden center, cut them into pieces, treat the pieces with a fungicide, dry them on a windowsill for 3 days, and then, finally, plant them in prepared trenches. All of which illustrates that traditional wisdom is sometimes more traditional than wise.

My own approach is different and much easier, and derives from my Victory Garden philosophy of achieving maximum yield with minimum effort. It's not that I object to putting in my time in the garden. I do that virtually every day, and have done so

for over thirty years, and have loved every minute of it. But every ounce of energy I can save by being more efficient with potatoes, to take one example, can go to the good of other crops or to the garden as a whole. Anyway, here's how I grow potatoes.

First, I buy only those seed potatoes that are "certified," meaning that they have been grown specifically for use as a seed crop in soil guaranteed to be free of the fungi and other diseases that plague potatoes. I buy early in the season to get a good selection of varieties and sizes. That's important because the U.S., unlike Europe, has not yet standardized the grading of seed potatoes. Egg-sized potatoes are perfect — easy to handle and economical, since they are sold by the pound. If I'm forced to buy larger potatoes, I'll plant them whole rather than go through that time-consuming cut-dust-dry-wait routine. Planting a 40-foot row with cut and treated potatoes may save $2, but it costs a lot more than that in my time. Even more important, planting whole, certified seed potatoes greatly reduces the risk of disease.

In mid-April, I open a trench 6 inches wide and 6 inches deep. Potatoes don't like a richly organic soil, so I do not add manure or compost at this point. Recent studies have shown that pota-

**I save time and effort by planting whole certified seed potatoes in the Victory Garden. Egg-sized potatoes are perfect for handling and 9-inch spacing.**

toes are quite sensitive to variations in pH, and actually prefer an acid soil, around 5.7 on the scale. Much below that, and yields will be reduced. Much above, and the crop is more likely to succumb to scab. Since 5.7 is more acid than the 6.5 that prevails throughout other areas of the Victory Garden, I set aside a patch of ground early on, and make sure *not* to treat that patch with limestone. This seems to work well, because I always get great potatoes, but it would be possible to lower that pH with agricultural sulfur (see "Steps to Victorious Gardening" for amounts to use) if I had to.

In the bottom of the trench, I loosen the soil and scratch in 1 cup of 5-10-5 fertilizer for every 10 feet of row. I then toss the seed potatoes into the trench, leaving about 9 inches between potatoes. Rows are 24 inches apart. Finally, I return about 3 inches of soil to the trench, so that the potatoes will be covered by a full inch of dirt.

Because potatoes are susceptible to many diseases (wilts, mosaics, blights, blackleg — to name a few), disease resistance is important when selecting varieties. Red Norland is excellent, a very early variety that produces high yields and resists scab. Kennebec, a late-season white variety, produces big tubers that are among the finest tasting I've grown. This variety is also resistant to mosaic and blight, which makes it a favorite of mine. Irish Cobbler and Red Pontiac are other varieties I've tried and liked.

**Radishes**   Easy to sow, murder to grow. That *used* to be my line on radishes. Flea beetles and other bugs attacked their tops. Root maggots assaulted the bottoms. If grown too slowly into hot weather, they turned into four-alarm fires. They could also suffer from clubroot, a disease that is very hard to eradicate once it gets a foothold. Nowadays, though, my line on radishes is softer. I've discovered spun, bonded fiber, which holds the bugs at bay — a major victory in the Victory Garden. And I grow very-fast-maturing varieties to ward off the bad case of hots that plagues radishes which grow on into summer weather. I'm now able to focus on radishes' undeniable assets. They grow quickly to maturity (anywhere from 21 to 45 days), making them a great crop for those of us who love instant gratification. They're amenable to less than superior soil, too. And they happily take up residence among other garden crops, making them perfect for my Victory Garden regime of interplanting.

Probably my favorite variety is Easter Egg, a blend of seeds that produces a colorful harvest of red, white, pink, and purple radishes that are as much fun to hunt as they are to eat. Champion is a fine traditional radish, bright red and round, about 1 inch in diameter when ripe. And Cherry Belle, an All-America Selection, can mature in *3 weeks* under the right conditions!

Radishes are a shallow-rooted crop that grow well in the standard Victory Garden pH of 6.5. They like loose soil, and to give

**Colorful Easter Egg radishes.**

them that I fork up the radish bed to a depth of 6 inches in early April, working in at the same time 5 pounds of 5-10-5 fertilizer for every 100 square feet of bed. I rake the soil smooth, then string lines to make my rows in the raised bed. With the planting board I make furrows ¼ inch deep, then sow the radish seeds 1 inch apart in the rows, with 6 inches between rows. I cover the seeds first with ¼ inch of soilless medium, water in, and then set in place the fabric row covers supported by #12 wire hoops. With soil temperatures between 50 and 60 degrees, I'll have seedlings in 7 to 10 days. When they're 1 inch tall, I

**My fast-maturing spring radish varieties are planted in April and harvested in May. Bug problems are largely a thing of the past, thanks to protective spun polyester fabrics.**

thin every other seedling, leaving a final spacing of 2 inches for these early varieties. This sowing may well be ready for harvest early in May, and I'm careful to take the radishes as soon as they're ready. They remain in top eating condition for only a few days.

**Spinach**  The spinach I planted in March is ready for thinning in April. My rule for thinning is simple: When the leaves touch, I thin. The thinned seedlings will be about 2 inches tall, and are perfect in salads. Spinach this tender one just can't buy.

After thinning, I erect hoop-supported covers of fabric over the spinach rows. This barrier will prevent flies from laying eggs that would eventually turn into the dreaded leaf miners. At one time, this insect was the bane of my spinach crop, but no more.

**Summer Squash**  Summer squash is the darling of gourmets these days. They like the blossoms as well as the tiny, immature fruit. The blossoms are prepared tempura-style or sautéed, and they are delicious indeed. At the Mayfair Hotel in Miami recently, the "Victory Garden" television crew was treated to tiny crookneck squash, lightly sautéed. I won't soon forget their delicate flavor.

The only problem I've had with squash in the Victory Garden is overabundance. I seem to end up, always, with more zucchini than I can use for the combined demands of television taping, cooking, and demonstrations. That means the neighbors are assured, each year, of fresh Victory Garden squash. Then again, I guess that's not such a horrible fate.

I want to plant my squash seedlings outdoors in May, so I start them indoors in late April. I sow 2 seeds per 3-inch peat pot filled with soilless medium, cover the seeds with ½ inch of soilless medium, and bottom-water. They receive a germination temperature of 75 degrees over my heat pad, and give me seedlings in about 5 days. After another week, I thin to the stronger seedling in each pot, and leave them growing in full sunlight where the daytime temperatures will remain between 65 and 70 degrees. On May 1 they'll go to the cold frame for 5 days of hardening-off.

My favorite varieties include Elite, a green zucchini; Sunburst, a yellow scalloped 1985 All-America Selection; and Peter Pan, a green scalloped summer squash that took an All-America award of its own in 1982. Finally, Sundance is a fine crookneck variety that I like.

**Swiss Chard**  There are mentions of chard by Greek writers as early as A.D. 400, but most of the references include warnings that the growth is indigestible and fit only for the common people. Thankfully, that attitude no longer holds sway and Swiss chard now takes its place in the Victory Garden with no apologies whatever.

I have seen lots of good chard crops, but none finer than that grown by Peter Abbot, our first Victory Garden contest winner. I remember that we arrived at Peter's house very late, after a hectic day of travel and taping elsewhere. Surveying his garden by the glare of our car headlights, we picked it as a regional winner at once. When I asked him about the secret of his success the next day, he pointed toward a couple of big concrete towers, which had served as shore fortifications that protected Boston during World War II. When the military abandoned those towers, pigeons and gulls moved in. Peter used their nitrogen-rich guano to fertilize his garden, and no crop responded as handsomely as his Swiss chard, which also received doses of rinsed, ground seaweed. His plants grew 18 inches tall, and were brilliantly colored ruby and green.

I don't plan to move my seedlings outdoors until the first week of May now, which means that I start them indoors in the first week of April. I sow the seeds in 3-inch peat pots — 2 seeds per pot — cover them with ¼ inch of soilless medium, and bottom-water. The seeds germinate in 5 or 6 days over the heat pad at 75 degrees and as soon as they're up I move them into full sunlight where the daytime temperatures will stay at 65 to 70 degrees. After a week or so in full sunlight, I'll give them a drink of complete water-soluble fertilizer diluted to half strength.

I have grown Fordhook Giant, an old standby, with consistent success. Ruby Red has done well in the Victory Garden, too. Both varieties will mature in 50 to 60 days and will provide a continuous supply of leaves all the way through to fall frost.

**Tomatoes**  Tomatoes are the most popular home garden crop, bar none. *Everybody* loves tomatoes nowadays. That wasn't always the case, though. The tomato's botanical name, *Lycopersicum*, is Greek for "wolf peach," a reflection of the belief, once held by many, that tomatoes were poisonous and to be avoided.

Not so today, of course, and gardeners know that there is no tomato like that grown and ripened in the home garden. Supermarket varieties, grown for commercial use, must be picked when green and then gassed into ripening. Mechanical harvesting and shipping require a tough skin, not the most desirable eating characteristic. Seed catalogs these days overflow with tomato varieties. There are standards, hybrids, cherries, orange tomatoes, yellow tomatoes, giant tomatoes . . . on and on. To make sense of all this diversity, it helps to know that all tomatoes fall into one of two categories: determinant or indeterminant. These terms describe the plants' growth habits. Determinant varieties set a certain number of flowers, grow to a certain height, and produce a certain, predetermined number of fruit. This is a plus in some growing conditions — container culture, for instance. Indeterminant varieties, on the other hand,

Swiss chard is a long-bearing crop that supplies leaves from June until frost. I start the crop indoors in peat pots in early April. ▶

will keep on growing, flowering, and fruiting until frost kills them. In frost-free climes, indeterminant varieties actually become perennial plants.

Tomatoes are also imbued with varying degrees of resistance to diseases and insects. Four of the most common and dangerous tomato afflictions are verticillium wilt, fusarium wilt, tobacco mosaic, and nematodes (not a disease, but a destructive worm that lives in the soil). Better Boy VNF, for instance, is resistant to verticillium and fusarium wilts, and to nematode infestation. Some varieties are bred to resist all four: Celebrity VNFT is such a tomato, and it's a favorite of mine. Not only disease resistance figures into my varietal selection with tomatoes, though. I also like Sweet 100 and Gardener's Delight, both cherry types. Though not particularly disease resistant, Sweet 100 will beat any other variety for sheer production — the cherry tomatoes hang like bunches of grapes from those fragrant, green vines. And Gardener's Delight is my personal flavor favorite, blending just the right combination of sweet and acid elements. My full-sized main crop picks are Celebrity, Superfantastic, Jet Star, and Better Bush. The latter is a strong determinant variety (something of an exception that really gives the best of both types: good continuous production on a compact plant with indeterminant flowering habit), sturdy and potatoleaved, that produces a very healthy crop of 6-ounce tomatoes. It's an excellent choice for small spaces. Big Boy is the one to pick for dependable production of large tomatoes. It will give a steady supply of 1-pound fruit. For what it's worth, though, the largest tomato ever grown (look it up in *The Guinness Book of Records*) was a 6-pound, 7-ounce monster of the Delicious variety.

On April 1, I sow the seeds, indoors, for my main crop of tomatoes. The seeds are planted in 4-inch pots filled with soilless medium, covered with ¼ inch of the mix, and bottom-watered thoroughly. I sow early, midseason, and late varieties — all at the same time. The pots go onto my 75-degree heat pad, producing seedlings in a week. They're moved to a sunny, warm spot and left to grow until true leaves show, later in the month. Then the seedlings are transplanted to individual cell-packs filled with soilless medium, bottom-watered with water-soluble fertilizer at half strength, and given a day out of full sun to recover from transplant shock. Then, I set them back into full sun, water consistently, and wait for warmer weather.

**Turnips**  I'm afraid that turnips have received something of a bum rap. I've heard them called tasteless, and peasant food, and a few other unpleasant things. Not true. Spring turnips steamed with butter are an elegant dish indeed. To have those ready for harvest by late May or early June, I sow turnip seeds directly into the garden when the soil has warmed to at least 50 degrees — usually by mid-April. I prepare the bed by turning it

Sweet 100 is the champion producer among my tomato varieties, giving up fruit clusters like bunches of grapes.

A month from now I'll be harvesting small, tender turnips from this bed. For now, shallow cultivating lets the tender seedlings develop free from competing weeds.

over with my spading fork and then raking the soil smooth. I use the planting board to make furrows, and then plant the seeds ¼ inch deep, ½ inch apart, with 12 inches between the rows. When the seedlings are 3 to 4 inches high, I thin them out to their final spacing of 3 to 4 inches in the rows. In a month or 6 weeks, I can expect to have small turnips ready for harvest. The pungent greens are good in salads.

# CONTAINER GARDENING

Growing vegetables in containers is both satisfying and a lot of fun. Container gardening is the perfect solution for apartment and condominium dwellers, or for any gardeners who are short on growing space. Even gardeners who do have ample space are not always blessed with perfect growing conditions. In some yards, for instance, the sun may not shine on plantable areas, but blazes down, instead, on driveways, decks, and other service areas. With container gardening culture, it's possible to take the plants to the sun. Container gardening is as versatile as it is helpful, too. Just about any vegetable — even sweet corn — can be grown in containers.

Some of the gardening guidelines for growing good vegetables also hold true for those grown in containers. First of all, they must be in a location that receives at least 6 hours of sunlight each day — *direct* sunlight. In addition, the soil must be good, one that holds water but drains well, supplies plenty of nutrients, and breathes. And like plants in the garden, plants in containers must be fed.

There *are* some differences between conventional culture and container gardening. The

**Container culture makes vegetable gardening possible for urban apartment-dwellers and anyone else who's short of space. As you can see at left, there's no shortage of varieties suited to container growing.** ◄

**Container-grown plants need more frequent watering than those grown in garden soil. A hose-end attachment that creates a superfine spray is ideal.**

biggest, I think, is that container-grown plants need more water. Because their pots are exposed to sun and air, plants in containers dry out more quickly than those in the soil. They need more frequent watering, and I often water my container crops daily during peak growing. This frequent watering washes away fertilizer and other nutrients in the soil, so feeding must also be more frequent. I feed plants in containers with slow-release fertilizer at the time of planting, and continue feeding weekly through the growing season with a complete (20-20-20) water-soluble fertilizer.

Soil, of course, is as important to plants in containers as it is to those in the ground. Filling many containers with soil can be both troublesome and expensive if you have to buy every pound from a garden center or nursery. I've learned to make my own mix for container culture, both because I plant a lot of container crops and because I like the satisfaction of creating my own "special blend." To make the mix, I blend in a wheelbarrow equal parts of sifted garden soil (run through a ½-inch mesh), sphagnum peat moss, and coarse builder's sand. The peat moss holds moisture. The sand assures good drainage. The soil brings a host of nutritious organic matter to the mix. This is a good, heavy mix that will support heavily fruited crops like tomatoes, peppers, and squash. For vegetables like lettuce, chard, and any others in containers that might be moved around often, I substitute perlite for the builder's sand. The perlite is much lighter, and serves the same function as the sand, promoting good drainage. A tip here that I've learned the hard way: Fill large containers where they will ultimately be positioned. If you have to move them after they're full, they'll be pretty heavy. Finally, with certain crops that are prone to diseases — eggplant, say — I use a commercial soilless growing medium.

When choosing containers, I let my creative urges run free. Some are utilitarian, some are beautiful, some economical. All have a place. Terra-cotta is the classic choice, for good reasons. It's elegant, with a natural look that blends with any environment. Terra-cotta is practical, too. It's heavy enough that it won't blow over in a strong wind with a heavy load of fruit. It also breathes well, and that is good for the plants. Terra-cotta does have a few drawbacks, though. Its breathability means that the rate of water loss is increased, and *that* means more frequent watering. Terra-cotta is brittle, too, and can break easily if dropped, whacked with a hoe, or subjected to a cracking frost.

I also like whiskey barrel halves for container culture. Their rustic good looks appeal to me, and they hold a lot of soil. They're readily available from garden supply houses, nurseries, and hardware stores, and they'll last almost as long as terra-cotta. I've discovered, by the way, that they're considerably less expensive when bought whole, rather than cut in half. It's no chore at all to snap a line around their middle with a chalked string and then saw them in half, using either a power saw or a handsaw. I especially like whiskey barrels placed in the garden at the ends of rows, with vegetables and flowers planted in them.

Recently, I discovered fiberglass containers. The best of these are richly adorned with nice detailing and, even better,

**Whiskey barrels make excellent vegetable-gardening containers. Place large containers like these where you want them *before* filling with soil!**

**Zucchini grown in a container can be just as vigorous and healthy as that grown in the garden itself, as this Burpee's Hybrid shows.**

are *very* light. Fiberglass being what it is, they'll last for years. They're a bit expensive, but their longevity should offset that initial expense. They're just the thing to dress up formal areas like decks and porches.

I've also collected, over the years, a number of nursery cans of both metal and plastic. These make fine pots for vegetables, too, when I recycle them after they've held a shrub or tree. No matter what kind of container I choose, I make sure that there are several holes at least ½ inch in diameter in the bottom, to assure good drainage so that the plants won't drown. And I'll admit that I don't really have a favorite type of container. Each has its place in the yard or garden, and I make use of them all, as the location requires.

Size is as important as type when choosing containers. I think that most gardeners err by not giving their plants enough soil volume in which to grow and mature. It's hard even for the veteran gardener to remember just how large a 6-inch tomato seedling will become. When I select containers, I'm perfectly content to err on the side of excess. I like containers that will hold at least 5 gallons of soil, and, because I like to mix flowers with the vegetables, most of my containers are even larger than this. It's true, too, that a large container means less frequent watering and fertilizing.

After I've drilled the holes in any new pots that don't have them, I fill them with my soil mix or soilless medium to within 1 inch of the top. When the plants are in place and watered, the soil level will drop another inch, and that will leave plenty of room for future watering.

Breeders have devoted a lot of attention in recent years to developing varieties that are suited to small-space and container culture. Thus we now have cucumbers and squash that grow on short vines. Those are only two examples, and I study the catalogs every year to keep up with the latest advances in container varieties. One new tomato variety that's pleased me in containers is Park's Better Bush. It's well named because it does have a very compact bush habit but fruits heavily. One plant, alone, will fill a half whiskey barrel.

**Container cauliflower, thriving in half a whiskey tub. A key to successful container culture is giving plant roots sufficient room. Too big a container is better than too small.**

Champion is another good tomato variety for container growing. I stay away from the cherry types and the beefsteak tomatoes because the plants just grow too large. Peppers are great in containers, too. I've been happy with Gypsy and Ace, and I ring the pepper plants in their containers with annual flowers that will cascade over the rims: alyssum, nierembergia, browallia, petunias, and dwarf small-flowered zinnias. A single stake for the pepper plant in each container keeps it standing tall under a heavy fruit set. Eggplant also shines in pots, especially with soilless growing medium, which assures they'll be spared the ravages of verticillium wilt. Eggplants are beautiful dressed with purple alyssum. I'm never afraid to show my vegetables off, displaying them as proudly around the yard as if they were ornamentals. Their colors and textures enhance any piece of land.

Most of the brassicas, especially broccoli, cauliflower, and cabbage, will do well in containers. I've grown combinations of Premium Crop broccoli and Little Gem lettuce in the spring garden with excellent results. White Sails cauliflower, grown with a decorative fringe of Red Sails lettuce, is another striking combination. And a bold planting of Brussels sprouts with hardy kale at their base will last right through the cool of fall.

Cucumbers also do well in containers, and we benefit now from the breeders who have shortened cukes' vines and given us bushlike behavior. Because they trail out over the pot (you could stake them upright, but why bother?), I like to grow an upright, strong an-

**Strawberries have long been a favorite of container gardeners. The berries are easily protected from birds, and, kept off the ground, are less prone to rot.**

nual like large-flowered zinnias to add a strong vertical contrast. The same arrangement works beautifully with summer squash.

Have you ever thought of okra in a container? A recent All-America winner called Blondy is a dwarf variety well suited to container culture. It's beautiful, too, with its hibiscus-like flowers. Lettuce and Swiss chard do well in pots, and carrots will, too, if you give them a tailored, stone-free soil.

Here are two last tips for growing vegetables in containers. If plants are positioned against a wall, make sure to rotate the pots so that the growing stems don't start leaning toward the sun. And consider putting *very* large containers on dollies, which makes turning and moving much easier on the human back.

The gardener's bench for overseeing the vegetable garden is highlighted by brilliant red azaleas. A bit too much time sitting has given the weeds a chance to grow, but they'll soon be looked after.

MAY

# MAY

If forced to choose my most satisfying gardening month, I would probably pick May. Everything growing is still young, vigorous, and unblemished, at least in the beginning of the month — living proof of that old saw about hope springing eternal. The weather has stabilized nicely by now, and shirtsleeves are the uniform more often than not. And in May, *everything* needs attention. I have plenty of crops up and growing in the garden. The greenhouse and windowsills are filled with seedlings. Cold frame lettuce needs watering and venting. Most important, perhaps, is the warming soil, which by midmonth will support my most delicate crops.

May is also the month in which I take the first spring harvests of asparagus, lettuce, radishes, and spinach. With planting and harvesting going on at the same time there is a symmetry, a bringing together of beginning and end, that appeals to me very much. I don't lose sight, though, of my goal of season-long productivity. Thus I'll be keeping tabs on my succession plantings of lettuce, and making sure that long-season crops like leeks and winter squash receive careful attention.

Rewarding though it is, May is not totally carefree, being the month when pests come on strong. Leaf miners and Colorado potato beetles can gain a foothold in May, as can aphids and flea beetles. I pay very careful attention to all the crops when I'm in the garden at this time of year. My use of physical barriers, varietal selection, and black plastic mulch has greatly reduced insect problems. A few bugs always manage to sneak in, though, and I deal with these by removing them manually or with organic pesticides. Four-legged pests will also visit in May. During the 1985 season, in fact, I had fine early crops of peas, cabbage, and broccoli nibbled to nubbins in *one night* by woodchucks. A whole family of the toothy creatures burrowed under my chain-link fence and devastated the garden. Now I make sure that the fencing extends down at least 12 inches into the ground.

**Start Indoors**
Brussels sprouts
Pumpkins
Winter squash

**Transplant**
Brussels sprouts
Eggplant
Lettuce

**Plant in Garden**
Beans
Cauliflower
Corn
Cucumbers
Leeks
Lettuce
Melons
Summer squash
Tomatoes
Winter squash

**Fertilize**
Carrots
Chinese cabbage
Kohlrabi
Peas
Potatoes

**Screen**
Beets
Cauliflower
Cucumbers
Potatoes

**Harvest**
Asparagus
Lettuce
Radishes
Spinach

**Mulch**
Asparagus

By early May, this asparagus is almost table ready.

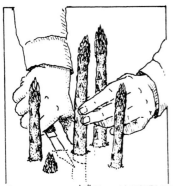

SLICE SHOOTS ½" BELOW SURFACE

**Asparagus** The whole "Victory Garden" crew was dining at a fine Liverpool restaurant one evening after a long day's shooting at a nearby gardening exposition called the Garden Festival. Our host this night was a representative from that exposition, and, while the staff served our meal, he explained to us how very important asparagus growing was to this particular part of England. He launched into a detailed description of how meticulous asparagus farmers lovingly blanch the already-tender stalks by hilling up soil early on in the spring as shoots appear, causing the stems to stretch and stretch, creating unique, pale stalks at least 12 inches long. So involved did he become in extolling the virtues of English asparagus that he failed to notice, on the plate at his elbow, half a dozen superb examples of that very crop. It was hard to keep from smiling, because we had all been munching contentedly on our own asparagus throughout his explanation.

May is the month when I begin harvesting spears from my own established bed in the Victory Garden. I look for shoots that are as thick as a piece of chalk (about ½ inch in diameter), 6 to 12 inches tall, and in tight bud. I use a sharp penknife to slice the shoots off about ½ inch below the soil surface — a trick I learned from my English asparagus-growing friends. Leaving the exposed cut protected by the soil lessens the likelihood of later disease or insect damage.

Asparagus loses its sweetness quickly after harvesting, but it is possible to slow that loss somewhat by setting the freshly harvested shoots stem-down in a dish of water in the refrigerator. I almost hesitate to pass on that advice, however, because one of my reasons for gardening is to enjoy the taste of vegetables when they are *fresh*. I much prefer to hustle the shoots from plant to pot, steam them lightly, and dine like a king.

The new asparagus bed planted in April will need hand-weeding in May. It must be done with caution, so that the delicate crowns and shoots are left undisturbed. When the weeding is complete, I mulch the sprouts with salt marsh hay, shredded wood bark, or 2 inches of grass clippings to suppress weeds and conserve moisture. Two inches of grass is the maximum, by the way. A thicker layer invites matting, which can allow too much heat to build up underneath, damaging or killing the tender young plants. If I do any further weeding or cultivation, I'm very careful in this bed, because the crowns' delicate rootlets can radiate as much as 2 feet from the central plant and they're only 4 to 6 inches down. Easy does it!

**Beans** I direct-seed varieties of both bush and pole beans in late May, only after I'm absolutely sure that the soil has warmed to at least 60 degrees. This is important enough for me to use and refer to my soil thermometer before sowing the beans. If the soil is too cool, the bean seeds will lie there and rot. Before planting, I treat seeds of both types with legume

inoculant, using the same method described for peas in March. I prepare their raised beds a little differently than most other crops', forking in 5-10-5 fertilizer at the rate of 2, rather than 5, pounds for every 100 square feet of bed. This reduction is made possible by the beans' nitrogen-fixing ability.

For pole beans, I plant a single row, spacing the seeds 2 inches apart and 1 inch deep. For bush beans, I use wide-row planting, scattering the seeds 1 to 2 inches apart, 1 inch deep, in a row 6 inches wide. I cover all the freshly planted seeds with 1 inch of soilless medium and water them in well. If the early growth of either variety appears slow, it's probably because the cool soil is retarding intake of nutrients. This problem is easily remedied with a dose of balanced (20-20-20) water-soluble fertilizer at full strength.

I've tried all kinds of support systems for pole beans in the Victory Garden: single poles and stakes, A-frames, and so on. After all is said and done, I've come to like wide-mesh nylon netting with 4x4-inch or 4x6-inch openings strung between 8-foot metal snow-fence stakes driven 18 inches into the ground. The stakes and netting go up quickly and are easy to remove

**With a well-used hoe, I'm opening a wide row for seeding bush beans. A casual 1- to 2-inch spacing is fine.**

and clean come fall. The netting's large openings make harvesting simple. I erect this netting above my row of pole beans at planting time. No thinning of these seedlings is necessary, and in 2 weeks I'll have small plants getting their first grip on the bottom of my netting.

**Beets** The beets I sowed in April will have produced healthy seedlings by May. I like to thin the seedlings now, before they get too large, leaving 2 to 3 inches between plants. If I have gaps elsewhere in the garden that I'd like to fill, I can use these seedlings. They'll transplant just fine if I moisten the soil and then lift them out carefully with a plant label. After thinning, I water the beets with liquid fertilizer, and then I erect protective screening.

Don't think May is too soon for screening. May is the month when leaf miners make their first appearance, and they like nothing better than to feast on the young, tender beet leaves. The first sign of miners is white egg case clusters on the backs of the foliage. Later on, the symptoms show up as fine tunneling that soon turns to limp, gray, mushy leaves; the miners are there chewing their way through the inner tissue of the leaves. I've found it best to screen early, before any signs of the miners

**These young, well-spaced beet seedlings are almost weed free thanks to salt marsh hay mulch.**

appear. Having experimented with various systems, I've settled on supporting hoops of #12 wire with polyester fabric draped over them. I make the hoops long enough to give 12 inches of clearance over the plants at their highest point, and I bury the borders of the netting all the way around the edge of the bed. This barrier system has several advantages over chemical applications. For one thing, once the barrier is in place, my plants are protected — period. No repeated application required. Perhaps more important, the barrier is hazardous to no one's health.

**Brussels Sprouts** There is nothing I love more than a plate of freshly steamed Brussels sprouts anointed with golden, dripping butter. They're a superb vegetable for the Thanksgiving feast, and my affinity for them was frustrated somewhat by my early experience in the Victory Garden. For several seasons I started the Brussels sprouts as early as possible. When this produced less than satisfactory harvests, I began starting them much later. That approach worked no better. It took a visit to northern California, where I saw Brussels sprouts thriving in cold, coastal regions, to put me on the right track. I know now that the key is to have healthy plants with established sprouts by the time cool fall weather arrives. That means (in my region) starting the plants indoors in mid-May. I plant the seeds in 4-inch pots filled with soilless medium. The seeds are covered with ¼ inch of the medium and bottom-watered until thoroughly moist. Seven days over the heat pad at 75 degrees produces seedlings, which I keep on a sunny windowsill until their true leaves appear. This is usually in early June, and that's when I transplant them to individual cell-packs and bottom-water again with half-strength water-soluble fertilizer.

I have grown Jade Cross E, Prince Marvel, and Achilles with success in the Victory Garden, but Jade Cross E has been the most consistent performer of all the varieties.

**Carrots** The seeds I sowed in April will have produced, by now, wispy, grasslike carrot seedlings. I thin those seedlings before they are 2 inches tall. If they're allowed to grow any larger, removing them will disturb the threadlike taproots that are left behind. My strategy is to water or wait for a good rain and then thin when the soil is still wet and loose. Because I use pelleted seed most of the time now, my thinning chores are greatly simplified. If I've sown a variety that is not available in pelleted seed or in seed tapes, though, it's back to the tried-and-true methods from the old days. This work must be done with two hands, and, if the seedlings are very close together, it's a matter of holding one delicately with the fingers of my left hand while I pluck out a neighbor with my right, leaving a final spacing of 1 inch between seedlings. I'm careful not to compress the soil around the stems of the remaining seedlings.

**A well-grown Brussels sprout plant in late summer. ▶**

**Carrots at just the right stage for thinning. ▼**

After thinning, I side-dress the beds with 5-10-5 fertilizer at the rate of 5 pounds per 100 square feet of bed. I spread a band of fertilizer by hand on either side of the carrot rows, then scratch it into the soil with a three-pronged cultivator, taking care to keep the fertilizer from coming into contact with any of the seedlings.

**Cauliflower**   After 5 days of hardening-off in the Victory Garden cold frame, my cauliflower seedlings are ready for planting in the garden during the first week of May. Because cauliflower (like broccoli, Brussels sprouts, cabbage, kohlrabi, and certain other brassica family members) is susceptible to clubroot, I try to rotate this crop so that it's planted in a bed where other likely clubroot victims haven't grown for three or four seasons. In the Victory Garden, clubroot has been a major problem, and this rotation is one of my primary defenses (along with liming the planting holes) against the disease. I recognize that it's not as critical a problem in all parts of the country as in mine, but for those who are victimized as I've been, rotation and liming have proven effective safeguards.

The seedlings are planted an inch deeper than they were growing in their cell-packs, and before setting them into their holes I work in half a handful of ground limestone per hole to keep the pH up around 7.5 and stave off the dreaded clubroot. Spacing for the cauliflower seedlings is 18 inches between plants and 24 inches between the rows. When they're in place, I give all the seedlings a watering-in with balanced water-soluble fertilizer diluted to half strength. To protect them from the variety of insect pests that can attack cauliflower seedlings, I set up hoop-supported netting now. This one-time task takes the place of maggot mats and chemical insecticides.

**Chinese Cabbage**   In May, the Chinese cabbage crop needs fertilizing, weeding, and watering. The idea is to keep the plants growing fast to provide a June harvest before sizzling weather sets in. I fertilize the plants twice this month with complete liquid fertilizer at full strength. I make sure that they receive at least 1 inch of water per week, too. But the water or rain brings its own problems: hungry slugs. The first symptom is a number of dime-sized holes in the outermost leaves. Checking the plants and hand-picking these slimy vegetarians is the safest way to protect the crop. This means a night patrol or two, because that's when the slugs are most active. Weeding is another effective defense, because a neat, well-weeded bed leaves them fewer places to hide.

**Corn**   The corn I started indoors in April will be ready for planting in the garden after 5 days in the cold frame for hardening-off. Corn is planted in blocks, by variety, and I make each block 8

The labels in the photo read:

CHINESE CABBAGE
Nagoda 50

CHINESE CABBAGE
2 Seasons Hybrid

**Getting to the weeds among the Chinese cabbage is a necessary chore to ensure a good harvest — I also keep my fingers crossed for cool weather.**

feet square. The blocks are located on the north or west side of the garden so that the plants, which eventually grow to 6 or 8 feet, will not shade other crops. Block planting also allows for wind pollination (corn is a wind-pollinated crop), which would occur less efficiently or not at all if the corn plants were set out in single rows. With the advent of the new supersweet $sh_2$ varieties, I have had to adopt new spacing techniques. Various catalogs recommend different spacing requirements between supersweet and standard varieties, but I've found that 25 feet is really a minimum to keep the two types from cross-pollinating. If cross-pollination between supersweet and standard varieties does occur, *both* are spoiled, so it's worth working hard to avoid contact.

Corn is one of the few crops, by the way, for which I revert to flat-bed culture. Before laying out the beds, I work in 5 pounds of 10-10-10 fertilizer for every 100 square feet of bed — corn is a very heavy feeder. Then I string an 8-foot line every 2 feet for the 4 rows that will make up each bed. I mark each row by sprinkling limestone over the smooth-raked soil. When I have

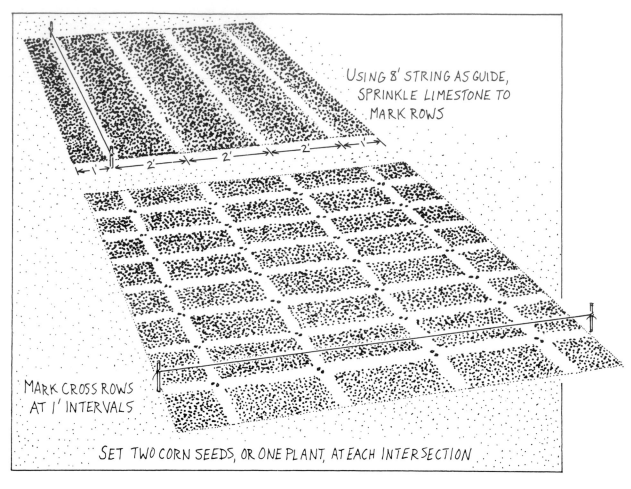

USING 8' STRING AS GUIDE, SPRINKLE LIMESTONE TO MARK ROWS

1' | 2' | 2' | 2' | 1'

MARK CROSS ROWS AT 1' INTERVALS

SET TWO CORN SEEDS, OR ONE PLANT, AT EACH INTERSECTION

the rows marked out, I go back and string my 8-foot lines across the row markings at 1-foot intervals. (This is easier drawn than written, so see the accompanying illustration.) I mark this second set of lines with limestone, too, thus ending up with a design like a tic-tac-toe diagram. Wherever two lines intersect, I set in a corn plant. This gives me a spacing of 1 foot in rows and 2 feet between rows, which is more real estate between rows than you'll find recommended in some sources. But I have discovered over the seasons that corn — as well as a good many other crops in the Victory Garden — does much better if the plants are given ample elbow room. For a time I did experiment with extremely close spacing (1x1 foot) but ended up with stunted plants and frayed nerves — hilling-up and other work was inconvenient. The crowded plants seemed to be fighting for light, water, and nutrients, and I found it hard to do the necessary cultivation with them jammed in too tightly. I've come to favor the more spacious 1x2-foot spacing, which has produced happier plants and, in this case at least, a happier gardener.

In early May, after the corn seedlings have spent 5 days hardening off in the cold frame, I set them into the ground. Because

**The corn seedlings I started in peat strips are hardening off in the cold frame before their move to the garden. ▶**

the peat pots will dry out if their tops are left exposed to air, I peel the tops off.

In mid-May, I sow a second generation of corn outdoors, using varieties like Butter and Sugar, Butterfruit, Silver Queen, Kandy Korn, and Symphony. I sow 2 seeds 2 inches deep every 1 foot along the row, and thin to the stronger seedling in a couple of weeks.

**Cucumbers** The cucumber seedlings I started in April will be moved into the cold frame for 5 days of hardening-off in mid-May. While they're doing that, I prepare the cucumber beds. Cucumbers are heavy feeders, and they like richly organic soil, so I work in 2 inches of compost and augment that with 5 pounds of slow-release 14-14-14 fertilizer for every 100 square feet of bed. After those amendments have been turned in and the soil raked smooth, I cover the raised bed with black plastic, burying the borders under the soil all around. The plastic warms the soil, saves moisture, and cuts weeding.

After their stay in the cold frame, I plant cucumber seedlings through 4-inch squares cut in the plastic every 12 inches. I peel the tops off the cucumbers' peat pots (to keep the porous peat pots from wicking away moisture from the soil), and set them into the soil at the same depth they were growing.

People with large gardens can grow cucumbers on the ground without difficulty, but the same crop can be grown in about one-fifth the space with some kind of vertical support. After a good bit of experimenting, I've settled on an A-frame support made of redwood, secured with staples and weatherproof glue, and covered with galvanized dog wire stapled to the frame. The wire has 4x6-inch openings. The frame is 8 feet long and 6 feet high, and is anchored into the raised bed with long steel reinforcing rods that extend 16 inches into the ground. There's another advantage to growing cukes vertically, by the way: They grow nice and straight. Whenever I grow cukes on the ground, many will curl. That has no effect on flavor, but who really wants bent cukes? More important, perhaps, keeping the fruit off the soil reduces the likelihood of rot.

Though I don't do so, it's possible to sow cucumber seeds directly in the soil. Timing is very important. The seeds won't germinate at all in soil cooler than 50 degrees, and will germinate very slowly in soil that's 68 degrees. Seventy degrees or warmer is best, and that's not usually found until early summer. If I were to direct-seed cukes, I'd fortify the beds and lay the black plastic down 2 weeks before I wanted to plant, then monitor the soil temperature with a thermometer to be safe. When the soil was at least 70 degrees, I would sow the seeds through 4-inch squares cut out of the plastic. The seeds would be sowed in pairs, 2 inches apart and 1 inch deep, spaced every 12 inches. I'd cover them with ¼ inch of soilless medium, water well, and keep moist until germination.

**Space-hungry cucumber seedlings are kept in bounds on the Victory Garden A-frame trellis — one very good way to get the most out of the garden.** ◄

Early tomatoes are warmed with plastic-wrapped cages and spun polyester fabric temporarily pulled off PVC tubing. Letting tomatoes sprawl like this is not my preferred method, but was suggested for early determinate types, which crop early and then die off.

Cucumber beetles have been somewhat troublesome in the Victory Garden, and I've found an effective defense. It is a weekly dusting with the organic pesticide rotenone.

**Eggplant**  My seedlings will be at least 2 inches high by now, and showing their first true leaves — the sign that it's time to transplant them into individual cell-packs filled with soilless medium. I bottom-water with water-soluble fertilizer diluted to half strength, protect them from full sun for a day, and then move them to my sunniest windowsill. In June I'll set them into the cold frame for 5 days of hardening-off before moving them into the open ground or into containers.

**Kohlrabi**  My kohlrabi seedlings will be up by now, and it's time to thin them down to a final spacing of 6 inches in the rows. They are heavy feeders, and to make doubly sure that they receive all that they require, I give them a generous drink of complete water-soluble fertilizer around the middle of the month.

**Leeks**  In early May, I move my leek seedlings into the cold frame for 5 days of hardening-off. While they're doing so, I excavate the leek trench. The key to good leeks is blanching, and the key to good blanching is trenching. I *have* seen it done other ways. At the Royal Horticultural Society's Harvest Show in London, gardeners produced 4-foot leeks with 18 inches of beautifully blanched stalk by growing them in flue tiles — the kind used to line chimneys. Superrich soil filled the tubular tiles, and the resulting leeks were indeed spectacular. They also required a great deal of TLC, as do most of the eye-popping specialty crops grown for such international shows. Trenching is a more traditional method of blanching leeks, and I've been perfectly satisfied with it.

I dig my trench 9 inches deep and as wide as my spade, about 8 inches. I put half the soil I remove on one side of the trench, and half on the other. Into the bottom of the trench goes 2 inches of compost, which I blend with an equal amount of soil. When I set the leek seedlings into the trench, I use a trick I learned from master gardener Peter Chan, certainly one of the most knowledgeable small-space gardeners on earth and a keen observer of how plants perform. Peter showed me that leeks send leaves out from their stalks in only two directions. Thus it is possible to align the seedlings so that all the leaves extend the same way. This keeps them from interfering with the growth of neighboring plants, provides maximum exposure to sun and air, and allows for a close spacing. Over the seasons, I've found that orienting the leaves about 15 degrees off the parallel line of the row makes maximum use of space and still keeps the leeks from touching. I space them 9 inches apart in the rows, and plant them to the depth of the union between the roots and leaves.

**Excavating my leek trench against a string line helps keep the bed neat. ▶**

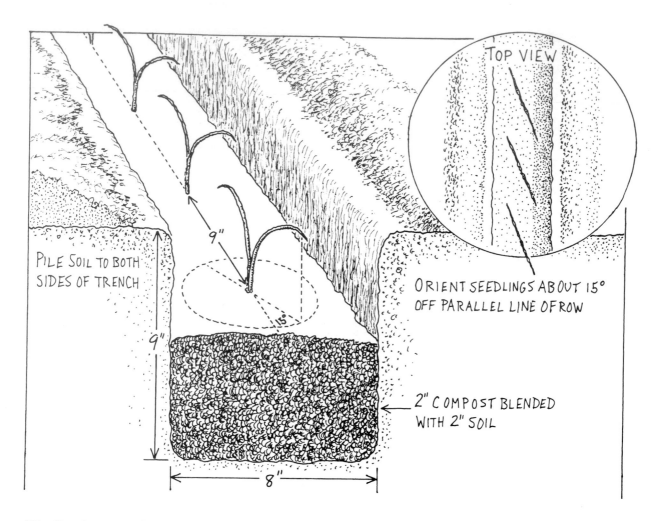

TOP VIEW

PILE SOIL TO BOTH SIDES OF TRENCH

9"

9"

15°

ORIENT SEEDLINGS ABOUT 15° OFF PARALLEL LINE OF ROW

2" COMPOST BLENDED WITH 2" SOIL

8"

Finally, I water the seedlings in with complete water-soluble fertilizer (20-20-20) diluted to half strength. The remaining soil standing beside the trench will be used to hill-up around the leeks as they grow in subsequent months.

**Lettuce**   In May I'll be harvesting the lettuce from my cold frame, and, a little later, from the garden itself. I pop in lettuce seedlings whenever a space appears between tomatoes, peppers, and eggplants, thereby assuring a steady supply of succulent, delicious greens all month long. All the lettuce that I plant now will be cell-pack seedlings 3 to 4 weeks old that I have been growing indoors, using hot-weather-tolerant varieties like Slowbolt, Summer Bibb, and Webb's Wonderful.

**Melons**   No description of melon planting would be complete without reference to "Victory Garden" contest finalist Reverend Ralph Miller and his "zoodoo" melons. Reverend Miller lives up north in New Hampshire, not generally considered prime melon country. From his garden, though, come some of the sweetest,

**Dinner for two grows happily between cabbage and broccoli. ▶**

juiciest melons I've ever tasted. This clergyman, you see, lives not far from a petting zoo that houses zebras, antelopes, and many other species of exotic fauna, all of which produce a steady supply of high-octane manure. The Miller melon patch receives hearty doses of this "zoodoo," and that, according to the reverend, is responsible for the super melons he grows in a decidedly less-than-super climate. The story points up an important fact about melon culture, namely that this crop requires a very rich soil to thrive.

In early May, I move my Victory Garden melon seedlings out to the cold frame for 5 days of hardening-off. While they're toughening up, I prepare their raised bed. I amended the soil the previous fall to bring the pH in line, and added 2 inches of manure or compost for a rich, organic composition. Now, before planting the seedlings, I fork in 2 inches of compost and 5 pounds of slow-release 14-14-14 fertilizer for every 100 square feet of bed space. I rake the bed into shape, then cover it with black plastic, burying the borders all around. When I'm ready to plant the melon seedlings, I cut 4-inch squares out of the plastic, spacing the squares every 2 feet. After peeling back the tops of the peat pots (to keep them from wicking away moisture), I set them in at the same depth they were growing. Then they're watered in well with half-strength water-soluble fertilizer.

That's how I do it in the Victory Garden, but it is possible to sow melon seeds directly in the soil. With that method, I would wait until the soil was 70 degrees or higher. Two seeds would be spaced 24 inches apart, and sowed ½ inch deep through 4-inch squares in the black plastic mulch. I would water them in and, when the seedlings were 2 to 3 inches tall, thin to the stronger seedlings, leaving a final spacing of 2 feet.

**Peas**  About this time in their growth cycle, my peas' nitrogen-fixing ability may be impaired by cool soil. If I see yellowing leaves, I give them a drink of complete water-soluble fertilizer.

I also watch the tall Sugar Snaps to make sure they're getting enough support. If they seem to be wandering around, I'll tie extra string at 12-inch intervals parallel to the ground. This will help to tuck the vines into the netting and keep weak clingers securely attached to my supports.

**Potatoes**  My potatoes are ready, in May, for their first hilling-up. The foliage will be at least 6 inches tall by now, and the very young potatoes forming on the roots need protection from the sun. If they're exposed to light, they will turn green, and a poisonous substance called solanine will be produced in their skins.

Hilling-up is easy. I begin by side-dressing each plant with half a handful of 5-10-5 fertilizer. Then I fill their trench with 4 inches of soil, mixing in the fertilizer at the same time and being

In May the Sugar Snap peas are well up on their 6-foot nylon trellis against an old, sweetly fragrant lilac backdrop. ◄

The row of potatoes on the left has been filled in and hilling-up will begin shortly. The row on the right will be filled to level when the plants get a few inches taller.

careful not to cover the growing points. The soil cover keeps roots deep and cool, and the tubers forming up are completely protected from harmful sunlight.

I'm also keeping an eye out for the Colorado potato beetle. If I see just a few of the beetle's bright orange eggs under my leaves, I'll pick them off by hand or remove the affected leaves. This ravenous insect is the bane of all potato growers. A friend of mine on Nantucket Island grows potatoes for the restaurant market. He simply has given up trying to control the Colorado bugs. "So what if they get the foliage?" he reasons, "I only want small potatoes anyway."

I suppose giving in to these nasty little creatures is one way of dealing with the problem, but I don't lose gracefully here in the Victory Garden. An idea that shows promise is covering potatoes with the spun polyester fabric that I use to protect other crops from insects. Although a few bugs emerge from the soil under the covering, the fabric protects against flying invaders. One interesting side effect of this tactic, however, is that the beetles move on to their second-favorite meal in the garden — eggplant. Thus I have to be very vigilant after I put the fabric in place, to make sure that one crop's gain is not another's loss.

**Pumpkins**   When I was a child, I would go out into our family's pumpkin patch and walk among the pumpkins, which seemed huge. They weren't real giants — probably in the 10- to 20-pound range — but my vantage point was a lot lower then. Giant pumpkins did not disappear when I outgrew the family patch, though. Not long ago I saw a pumpkin grown by Howard

**With luck, May's seeding of pumpkin will produce the perfect candidate for the Halloween jack o' lantern.**

Dill of Nova Scotia that weighed nearly 500 pounds! Giant-pumpkin-growing has become quite a craze, in fact, and 400-pound monsters are common sights at contest weigh-ins. The gardeners who produce these giants work up superfertile soil, and allow each plant to produce only one pumpkin by plucking all other flowers from the vines. Variety selection is also crucial: Atlantic Giant is the one that produces the real monsters.

I haven't room in the Victory Garden for giant pumpkins. In fact, I barely have room for the normal varieties. This long-season crop takes up a lot of space, and is really better suited to very large gardens than to compact operations like mine. I get by, though, with varieties like Spirit Hybrid, New England Pie, and Jackpot, all of which produce shorter vines and 7- to 10-pound fruit.

In May, I start the pumpkin seeds in 3-inch peat pots, sowing 2 seeds per pot early in the month. It's possible to direct-seed pumpkins in the garden in May but, as with many Victory Garden crops, I prefer to start the seedlings indoors. This gives me better control over temperature, moisture, and light early on. The seedlings are protected from pests and diseases, and critical garden space is left free for spring crops like lettuce and radishes. I use my heating pad to give the seeds their ideal germination temperature of 75 degrees, making sure that I don't let their growing medium dry out. Consistent watering right from the start is very important to pumpkin development.

If I were to sow pumpkin seed directly into the soil, I would warm it up by laying black plastic down several weeks before my June 1 planting date. Then, come June, I'd cut 4-inch squares 24 inches apart in the plastic, and plant 2 seeds 1 inch deep in each square. They'd be watered in and then left alone for 2 weeks, when I'd thin to the stronger seedling.

**Radishes**  In May I enjoy an excellent radish harvest, taking the radishes from the soil as soon as they're large enough to eat. I like to pluck them out by their greens, rinse with the hose, and munch them right there. I know that spring radishes won't hold their peak quality very long, so I harvest the whole crop when they're ready, even if the result is more than I can use right then. Stored in plastic bags, they'll keep nicely in the refrigerator for days.

In August, I'll plant my fall radish crop. Until then, the weather will just be too hot for successful radish growing.

**Spinach**  I'm harvesting beautiful, mature spinach from the Victory Garden by now, and I use a technique that leaves the grit in the garden, where it belongs. Instead of yanking out the spinach plant root and all, I cut the plants off at ground level. This gives me the leaves, which I want for salads and cooking, but does not shower sand and soil over the remaining plants.

**This month the spinach is ready for harvest — just waiting to be snipped off.** ▶

**White Icicle radishes.** ▼

**Summer Squash**   During the middle of May, I move my summer squash seedlings into the cold frame for 5 days of hardening-off. While they're doing so, I add 5 pounds of slow-release 14-14-14 fertilizer to their bed. Squash are heavy feeders and will need every bit of nutrient material I can work into that soil. Next, I stretch black plastic over the bed and bury the edges of the plastic sheet. Then I cut 4-inch squares in the plastic, giving a single row of plants spaced 4 feet in the bed.

Summer squash and zucchini seeds can be planted directly in the soil, though my practice is to start the seedlings indoors. For direct sowing, I'd plan on waiting at least a week after the last spring frost date, and on making sure that soil temperature is at least 60 degrees. Black plastic, laid down 2 weeks before planting day, will warm the soil much more rapidly. For planting, I'd cut 4-inch squares in the plastic and sow 2 seeds per hole, 4 feet apart. When the seedlings were up, I'd thin to the stronger plant.

**Tomatoes**   I aim for a late-May planting of my main-crop tomato seedlings. That timing puts a month between them and the last expected spring frost, and gives them 60- to 65-degree soil temperatures as well. Air temperatures will be relatively stable in the 70- to 75-degree range — ideal for tomato seedlings.

On May 20, I set my seedlings into the cold frame for 5 days of hardening-off. While they're adjusting, I work 5 pounds of 5-10-5 fertilizer for every 100 square feet of area into their raised beds. For planting in the raised beds, I make 2 staggered rows with 2 feet between rows and 3 feet between the plants themselves. I set the plants in the soil right up to their true leaves, to encourage root formation all along the buried stem. They get a drink of balanced water-soluble fertilizer diluted to half strength, too.

If May or June weather turns inclement, I protect the seedlings with Wall O' Water towers. These are flexible polyethylene multichambered constructions that provide the last word in outdoor microclimate control. The Wall O' Water's tubes are filled with water, which gains heat during the day, creating a warmer miniclimate for the tomatoes. That heat is retained at night, moderating the cooler evening temperatures as well.

Now is also the time to consider support systems, and I will tell you that in my years of gardening, I've tried them all. I've let tomatoes sprawl on the ground, over hay, and on black plastic. I've trained them up single stakes. I've trained them up elaborate string trellis affairs, and along both single and multiple string runners to overhead wires. And I've used cages. Before I say which I like best, let me pass on a few lessons learned the hard way.

One thing I can confirm is that pruned, vertical tomato plants (using, say, two leaders on string to wire overhead) do ripen faster than those left to sprawl. They also suffer a reduced

**At lilac and tulip time when most folks are just thinking about putting their tomatoes in, the pampered Victory Garden early crop is 3 to 4 feet tall and in flower.**

yield. Even in the Victory Garden, I don't get something for nothing. In general, it's true that pruning hastens ripening at the expense of yield, and tomatoes are no exception to this rule. In very short season areas, it might make sense to use this method to avoid loss of late ripeners, but I don't use it in the Victory Garden.

I've also found that sprawling tomatoes on black plastic produce unequaled yield, but commandeer more real estate than I can afford to surrender. This method will cause some increase in fruit rot, too.

Another conclusion based on years of trial: Single stakes with single leaders are undesirable. This system reduces foliage cover too drastically, with poor production from each plant resulting.

After all is said and done, I have come to favor tomato cages. They make the very best use of available space by promoting vertical growth. The fruit, when it appears, is held aloft and thereby protected from feet, slugs, pests, and rot. Harvest from a cage is easier, requiring less bending and stooping. And cages create a neat garden that is visually pleasing. I think this is not

unimportant. A garden that creates a sense of order and beauty will be doubly rewarding, certainly more so than one that is only half a step removed from the weed patch.

I've tried the cages available from garden supply centers and seed catalogs, but they're too short. Most are only 4 feet tall, and my indeterminant varieties would routinely cascade up and over the tops of these cages. Now I make my own cages, 5 feet tall, from steel reinforcing wire with 4-inch openings. I buy the wire from masonry supply houses. For detailed tomato cage directions, see the feature titled "Victory Garden Structures." I put these cages in place as soon as the weather allows me to remove the Wall O' Water towers once and for all.

**Winter Squash** Winter squash take twice as long, on average, to mature as summer squash, but in other ways they're quite similar. Both gobble up garden space with their long vines, and both are very heavy feeders. I tried solving the space problem by training vines up trellises, but supporting the very heavy fruit was just too difficult. More recently, I've been experimenting with bush varieties of winter squash that require

**Concrete-reinforcing-wire cages will last a good many years and are my favorite way for training tomatoes.** ◄

**In this system, I've trained each tomato plant to a double leader and woven them in and out between sturdy twine strung on 8-foot-high snow fencing.** ▲

about half the 10 or 20 square feet occupied by each plant of standard-vining varieties.

I want to set my winter squash seedlings into the garden on June 1, so I start them indoors on May 1, sowing 2 seeds per 3-inch peat pot filled with soilless medium, covering the seeds with ½ inch of medium, and then bottom-watering. (I use the peat pots because winter squash are very sensitive to transplant shock.) On the 75-degree heat pad the seeds will germinate in about 7 days. Once they're up, I move them to the sunniest, warmest spot I have, keeping the peat pots moist but not soaking. After 2 weeks, I'll thin to the stronger seedling in each pot, then let them grow in peace until the last week of the month, when they're moved to the cold frame for hardening-off.

It's also possible to direct-seed winter squash now. When the soil has warmed to at least 60 degrees, I prepare the squash beds by adding 2 inches of compost and 5 pounds of slow-release 14-14-14 fertilizer per 100 square feet of bed. Black plastic goes down next, and I bury the borders all around. I cut 4-inch squares out of the plastic, spacing every 5 feet for larger varieties and 3 feet for the smaller, bush varieties. Into each square cutout I plant 3 seeds ½ inch deep, allowing about 2 inches between seeds. They're covered with soilless medium and watered in well. The seeds in each cluster will germinate in about 7 days, and a week later I'll thin to the strongest seedling in each spot.

**Waltham Butternut — a real winner!**

As far as varieties go, I'm very fond of Waltham Butternut, and not only because it was developed by Bob Young at our nearby suburban experiment station in Waltham, Massachusetts. This winter squash comes ready in 90 days, producing manageable 12-inch fruits with wonderfully sweet flesh. Waltham Butternut also peels easily, and is even somewhat resistant to vine borers. That's a lot to recommend it! Sweet Mama hybrid and Jersey Golden Acorn are more modest in their demand for space, and Jersey Golden Acorn has a fine, sweet flesh. Blue Hubbard, the classic New England squash, is — to me, at least —. the tastiest of them all, and I grow a crop every year. Turk's Turban is a dramatic decorative addition to any garden, with flying-saucer-shaped fruits that mature into bright shades of red, yellow, white, and green.

# VICTORY GARDEN HERBS

Not surprisingly, herbs are some of the more enduring plants cultivated by man over the ages. They improve the subtlety of food, sweeten the air with beautiful fragrances, and for centuries have been used as healing agents. Their presence is long-lasting when dried and used in sachets and potpourris. They can decorate wreaths, and add graceful touches to table arrangements. My particular fondness is for those which supplement vegetables from the garden, so in the Victory Garden I grow herbs chosen for their usefulness in cooking. Sweet basil is an indispensable complement to tomatoes. Dill goes perfectly with cucumbers. Tarragon is a must for roast chicken. And chives brighten the taste of eggs.

I've reserved a small area for my culinary herbs, just off the back door of the house and literally steps away from the kitchen. I fear that if the herbs were 150 feet away in the main garden, their impromptu use would decrease dramatically. Herbs love sunshine, and this location gives them at least 6 hours of full sun. The best and most fragrant herbs are grown in full sun, under somewhat drier conditions than in the

**The culinary herb garden just outside the kitchen door.** ◄

**A selection of sweet basil ready to be set in the garden.**

vegetable garden. That's another reason why I think it's a good idea to give them their own spot, where water can be meted out more sparingly. The herbs in my kitchen garden do well with a pH of 6.5, and in fact will be content with a pH anywhere from 6.0 to 7.5. Good drainage is essential, so I ensured that with 2 inches of sand and peat moss when I prepared their bed. I also worked in compost (a couple of inches), because there will be both perennial and annual herbs in the bed and I want to get it in good shape at the time of creation. Any deficiencies will be harder to correct later on.

My herb garden is divided in half, and each bed measures 6

feet by 5 feet. I wanted a formal look to this garden, in part because it's traditional but also because it's next to the house. Herbs, by the way, enjoy a reputation for being a bit rank, and some do grow vigorously. But an untidy look is more the result of poor maintenance than any innate unruliness. There's no reason for an unattractive herb garden. Frequent "pinch-pruning" (the reason we grow these little wonders in the first place!) is usually enough to keep them in line.

To give the herb garden a sense of history, I planted a hedge of boxwood on the front border. The boxwood can't be used in the kitchen, but it is lovely to behold. I keep the hedge neatly trimmed at 1 foot high, and it is a very attractive first layer in my planting. The two beds are separated by a 2-foot-wide gravel pathway that provides easy access to all the herbs.

**Sweet basil** is an annual grown from seeds sown indoors in April. I follow the same indoor-seed-starting procedures for herbs that I use for vegetables (see the chapter titled "Steps to Victorious Gardening" for details). Basil will not tolerate any frost and even resents a chill, so I don't set it out into the garden until the middle of May. This 6-week jump indoors produces sturdy transplants for the garden. The thing to bear in mind with basil is that it will try very hard to go to flower and seed. While this is attractive, it shortens the herb's productive life, so I cut basil frequently, or use my forefinger and thumb to pinch off its topmost, succulent growth. Dark Opal is a handsome, deep-colored variety that is ornamental as well as useful. It will get stiff competition now from a 1987 All-America winner named Purple Ruffles. Another excellent, new variety that makes a wonderful edger to the herb garden and produces heavily for the table is Spicy Globe. This variety has a dwarf habit and most of the plants will hold to a tight ball shape that looks finely clipped but is, in fact, the herb's natural habit. As is the case with all the herbs I'll mention, basil can be purchased as started plants at garden centers or, as mentioned above, started from seed.

**Chervil,** an annual, is parsley's exuberant first cousin. It grows quickly and comes easily from seed. I sow seed directly in the ground at the end of April, and have harvest-ready plants in June. Chervil has a delicate, anise-licorice flavor that is best appreciated right after harvest. I make another sowing in a month because the plants tend to be short-lived. It's lovely and graceful in flower, and chervil will reseed if left to itself. I prefer to choose its location myself (the middle of the bed), so I keep the plants under control. Chervil does well in cool weather and, unlike most of the herbs, will do well in a bit of shade.

Chives' colorful bloom adds a pleasing touch to this perennial member of the onion family.

**Chives** are a hardy perennial, whose flowers add a rich purple color to an otherwise basically gray and green herb garden. Chives produce that mild onion flavor so indispensable for omelettes and chowders. The plants are started from seed indoors in March, for set-out in late April. About 15 to 20 seeds are sown in a 4-inch pot filled with soilless medium. I use one pot for each clump of chives I want. They're transplanted to their spot, where they grow together afterward. I sow 6 pots of garlic chives and 6 of regular chives as well. They're all harvested by cutting the tops with a knife or, better still, with scissors. If the plants go too long without harvesting, they'll form flower heads which are quite beautiful and do not affect the flavor in any way. They're a fine ornamental addition to the herb garden and, with their 12- to

14-inch height, are good edging plants. Harvest will last well into fall. Old clumps may need to be divided and set into newly enriched ground if they begin to decline or crowd out their neighbors.

**Dill** (or dill weed, as it is sometimes called) is a wonderful annual in the kitchen but short-lived in the garden, requiring successive sowings. I start a first generation in the greenhouse in mid-March for a late April set-out, then plant a few seeds in the open ground at the same time and also at monthly intervals through the season. Dill is a must when cucumbers come in, and beyond succession plantings, it's of easy culture, requiring only a single stake per tall plant to hold the seed head up.

**Marjoram** is a mild, sweet-flavored herb related closely to oregano. Though people don't

As delicate as it is desirable — dill coming into flower.

always distinguish between the two, the flavors are different. Marjoram is an annual easily raised by seed that I sow in mid-March for set-out in the garden in early May. Six plants provide well for the whole season.

**Mint** relieves the heat of summer and cools many a dish and drink. There are many flavored mints — spearmint, peppermint, pineapple, and apple. They make fine iced teas, and their strong flavors carry through well, but they can be terribly invasive in the garden. Thus I like to contain these rock-hardy perennials, especially in a small space. I grow several flavors, and each is set in the ground in a 5-gallon container with the top rim of the pot 1 inch above the soil. This keeps these spreaders from taking over the garden, and a 5-gallon container will give them all the root they need and me all the

mint I can use. Seeds can be started indoors in March for garden set-out in April. The garden center can also supply one or two different flavors, which prevents having to buy whole packets of seeds that will never be fully used.

**Oregano** is stronger and more pungent than its close relative, marjoram, and is the herb people think of when they think of pizza pie. I start oregano plants from seed in mid-March for set-out in early May. Unlike marjoram, oregano is a hardy perennial, and 6 plants will suffice. Both of these herbs can spread 1 foot, and get to be about as tall. Frequent pinching of both for table use will keep a fresh supply of leaves coming and produce a bushier plant.

**Parsley,** though tough once started, is not easy to get going. The trick to sowing parsley is to get the seeds to germinate. I often soak the very hard seeds overnight in warm water before sowing a dozen or so in a 4-inch pot. An alternative is to nick, or "scarify," the seeds with a file to hasten sprouting. I sow indoors in mid-March to have young plants ready for the garden in May. Parsley has different leaf textures, one being more savoyed, or crinkled, than the other. The smoother varieties clean more easily, but are not as rich-looking. Besides putting half a dozen plants in the garden, I always grow a few in pots that will come indoors after the growing season to provide a garnish into winter. They do have large root systems, so I use 8-inch pots and give regular liquid fertilizing through the season.

As useful as it is beautiful, parsley benefits from frequent snippings.

**Rosemary** is a tender perennial. In mild areas of the country it will become a handsome, long-lived, woody shrub, but for most of us it needs indoor wintering-over, and thus lives in a large terra-cotta container that travels in and out with the seasons. One choice plant of rosemary suits me, because this marvelously pungent herb requires a chef's gentle touch. I buy rosemary plants as I need them in the spring from a good garden center. I use a soilless mix for planting in the pot, because it's light and makes transporting in and out easier. Rosemary needs watering only once a week, except in midsummer, when I double that. Feeding every other week with water-soluble fertilizer will keep this herb in good health. Generally pest-free (as

Oregano backed up by sage — find room for it too if you can.

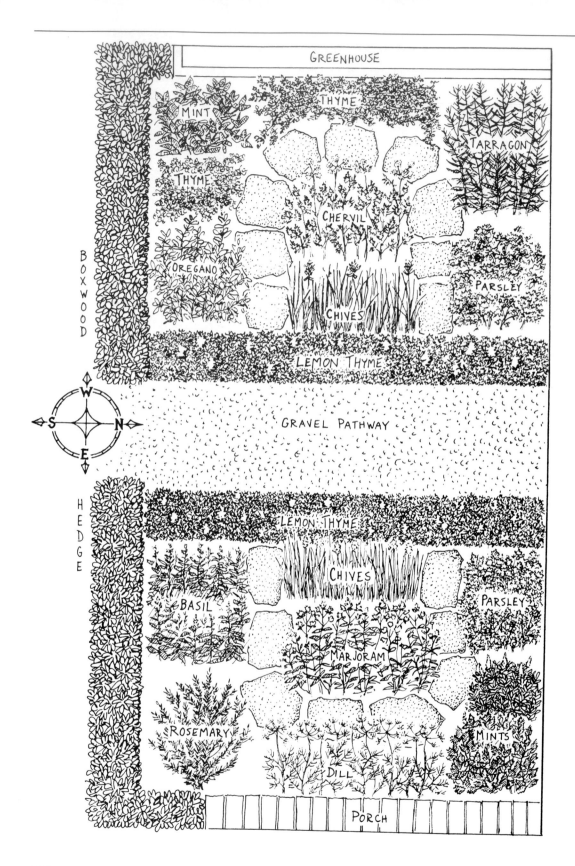

GREENHOUSE

MINT
THYME
TARRAGON
THYME
CHERVIL
OREGANO
PARSLEY
CHIVES
LEMON THYME

B O X W O O D

W
S
N
E

GRAVEL PATHWAY

H E D G E

LEMON THYME
CHIVES
BASIL
PARSLEY
MARJORAM
ROSEMARY
MINTS
DILL
PORCH

This rosemary is a veteran of many moves into the garden and back indoors for winter protection.

are all the other herbs), it can be troubled by spittle bugs, which conceal themselves under a white, frothy bubble on the stems of the plant. I simply wash them off. If the demand on leaves is not heavy for the kitchen, rosemary will often flower with small, blue-violet blooms that sparkle among the green, needle-like leaves.

**Tarragon** *must* be French. Any other is banished from the kitchen. This is a slow-growing but hardy perennial, and I need several plants to supply the table. The best tarragon for table use is propagated from cuttings, and will not come true from seed. Thus I avoid seeds altogether, and buy plants from good garden centers. I was reminded of one way to distinguish French from Russian (the unwanted) tarragon by a delightful passage from the writing of herb matri-

arch Adelma Grenier Simmons: "The best way to tell with Tarragon (meaning French) is to pick a piece and bite it and it will bite you back. It stings your tongue. It must taste of anise." I give tarragon plenty of room to grow, as it will come 2 feet high or more, and spread to that dimension. It's a good choice for the back of my basically low-growing culinary garden. It's also one of the few herbs that I dry for winter use. In the fall, I gather several 12-inch braids of this pungent herb and keep the stems together with an elastic band. As the stems wither, the elastic retains a tight hold. I hang the bunches away from the sun in a warm location with good air circulation, and use them as needed.

**Thyme** is a moody perennial that will last many years if treated kindly and watered carefully. It needs very good

A favored spot in the herb garden is reserved for French tarragon.

drainage to prevent winterkill, and I can't guarantee that it will come back year after year. I look on thyme as a short-lived perennial. It's welcome and useful, despite this tendency to come and go, for it begs to be touched to release its memorable scent. It softens garden edges nicely, adding a bit of free form to otherwise formal areas, so I let thyme spill freely out into the walkways, where passing feet will bruise the leaves and release that delicious scent. There are many varieties of thyme, and it pays to sniff them all at a good garden center or herb farm. Lemon thyme smells remarkably like real lemons, and makes a fine edger. I use it on both sides of my kitchen herb garden. Woolly thyme is almost a pet, and golden thyme adds rich color to the bed. Common thyme serves the table best. I plant all these wonderful, ground-hugging varieties from started plants, because thyme is hard to start from seed.

As I mentioned earlier, all the herbs in my garden do well with minimal care, my standard pH of 6.5, and about half the water I give to the vegetables. Herbs do need to be weeded, and my three-pronged cultivator does this nicely. Actually, I minimize this task by applying a 2-inch mulch of cocoa bean hulls. This is an attractive, brown mulch of small hulls that blends nicely with the reserved textures of the herb garden. Once it's settled down, the mulch — despite being very light — doesn't blow around. The hulls are slow to decompose, and serve several years before requiring replacement.

In June, I keep an eye on more than a dozen crops, waiting for the moment of perfection to harvest. Peas, one of my favorites, will be ready by midmonth.

# JUNE

# JUNE

With its long, warm days and frequent, torrential showers, June is an exciting month in the Victory Garden. Lush foliage is flowing over the garden's raised beds as the effort expended over earlier months pays dividends. I've already completed the spinach harvest, and will be making quite a few more this month: broccoli, cabbage, turnips, cauliflower, radishes, peas, beets, and chard. Early tomatoes will be ready, and so will scallions. I'll take lettuce, too, and the leeks, planted in open trenches 6 inches deep back in April, will now be backfilled to the level of surrounding soil. The wispy green shoots, with their leaves all perfectly aligned, stand guard over their territory as neatly as a platoon of soldiers with shouldered arms.

Of all the June events in the Victory Garden, none pleases me more than the harvest of peas. Later in the month I will be strolling through the beds, plucking those tender beauties from the vines — and eating quite a few of them right there. I'm not distracted, though, from succession plantings of lettuce, nor from the careful attention to watering that June crops often need.

Weeding and cultivating actually help offset some of those watering demands, by reducing the competition for moisture in the beds. I don't look upon either of these as hard labor, because the little time I spend weeding and cultivating produces so much reward for the crops. My black plastic mulch, of course, drastically reduces the amount of weeding and cultivating I have to do. I use that mulch wherever possible, and it's one of the greatest time- and labor-savers in the garden. Where it can't be applied, I use salt marsh hay or do the weeding and cultivating by hand, always aware as I'm grooming the soil that this activity is really my first line of defense against insects. In addition, the dust mulch that cultivating creates actually slows evaporation from the soil. Even as I'm performing this summery care, though, I have one eye on the fall crops of pumpkins, winter squash, broccoli, cabbage, and Brussels sprouts.

**Start Indoors**
Broccoli
Cabbage
Kale
Lettuce

**Transplant**
Broccoli
Brussels sprouts
Cabbage
Kale
Lettuce

**Plant in Garden**
Beets
Cabbage
Lettuce
Rutabagas

**Fertilize**
Asparagus
Kohlrabi
Leeks
Melons
Onions
Swiss chard

**Screen**
Cauliflower

**Mulch**
Asparagus

**Harvest**
Asparagus
Beets
Broccoli
Cabbage
Cauliflower
Chinese cabbage
Kohlrabi
Lettuce
Onions
Peas
Shallots
Summer squash
Swiss chard
Tomatoes
Turnips

**Asparagus**  Since planting the asparagus crowns in their trench, I have been adding the rich mixture of topsoil and compost or manure around the shoots as they grow taller. By late June, the trench will be filled in and level with the surrounding soil. When that happens, it's time for me to scratch in a side-dressing of 1 cup of 10-10-10 fertilizer per 10 feet of row all along both sides of the trench, and then to refresh the mulch of salt marsh hay or grass clippings that I laid down in May.

After I've finished harvesting asparagus from the established beds, I side-dress them, too, scratching in 1 cup of 10-10-10 fertilizer per 10 feet of row and then mulching with 2 inches of grass clippings or salt marsh hay to suppress weeds and conserve moisture.

**Beans**  The bush beans and pole beans that I started indoors can be set out with safety during the first week of June. After hardening them off for 5 days, I separate the peat strip seedlings into individual cells, and space them 3 to 4 inches apart in a 10-inch-wide row. I set them in as deeply as they were growing in their peat cells, and peel off the tops of those cells so that they won't wick away soil moisture. I water the seedlings in with balanced, water-soluble fertilizer diluted to half strength, and then tend to the bush limas. I've been growing varieties like Fordhook #242 and Henderson Bush Lima since April, and they can go out, too, using the same hardening-off and planting procedures described above. Even more than standard bean varieties, limas were very chancy in cold soil. The new setting-out of started seedlings greatly reduces my lima mortality rate.

From now on, I can plant a new row of bush beans every couple of weeks to ensure a steady harvest throughout the season. I seed them directly in the soil now, and continue this successive planting of 10- to 15-foot rows through the season.

**Beets**  My April planting of beets will have produced 2-inch globular roots that are ready for harvest in June. I like to get them out of the ground before they are any larger because the increased size and age can bring a tough woodiness to the beets. Some of my recommended hybrid varieties do stand a bit longer in the garden, but even these I prefer to harvest young. Harvesting is a breeze. With the Victory Garden's loose, friable soil, I'm able to grasp the beets by their tops and gently pull them right out. If I notice any leaf miner damage at this point (sometimes a few manage to circumvent even my careful screening — don't ask me how!), I cut the leaves and discard them. They do *not*, of course, go into the compost pile. I've found it easier to clean beets outside by just washing them down with the garden hose. After I've done that, I trim the tops off, leaving about 1 inch of stem attached to the globe to minimize bleeding.

It's also time to sow another crop of beets, using the same steps described in April. Because the weather is so much

The key to my easy-growing, easy-harvesting Victory Garden beets: loose, friable soil, sifted to remove stones and amended with compost or well-rotted manure.

warmer, this June crop will need more careful attention to watering, and the seed bed must be kept moist until germination occurs.

**Broccoli**   In June I harvest the first of my spring broccoli planting. Broccoli heads are made up of hundreds of individual flowers, and with this vegetable we're actually eating the flowering part of the plant. Thus it's important to take it when the flowers are tightly wrapped and just at or before the individual flowers show any yellowing. Flowering can be triggered by several factors: a warm or cold spell, or aging. This means I keep a vigilant eye on the plants as their time approaches.

When I harvest from side-shooting varieties, I do so in a way that lets the plants keep producing for several weeks. I remove the main head with a cut across the stem a couple of inches below the point where the head and stem meet. This will allow the plant to develop many more smaller heads on side shoots, which are just as tasty as the big head. After the primary harvest from any of my broccoli plants, I side-dress by scratching in half a handful of 10-10-10 per plant.

Even though there is no danger of frost, I'll start my fall crop of broccoli indoors to give the plants every possible benefit from the controlled conditions of watering, temperature, and an insect- and disease-free environment. I sow the seeds in 4-inch pots filled with soilless medium, then bottom-water. With a germination temperature of 75 degrees on my heat pad, I will have seedlings up in about 7 days. Then I move them to full sun and wait for the true leaves. When those show, I transplant the seedlings to individual cell-packs filled with soilless medium and bottom-water with a balanced water-soluble fertilizer diluted to half strength. They receive a day out of full sun to ease transplant shock, and then they go back to a sunny spot to grow for a week or so. Finally, I give them 5 days in the cold frame for hardening-off before setting them into the garden soil.

I'm an advocate of indoor starting, but it's possible to sow broccoli seeds outdoors, too. If I were to do so, I'd sow 4 seeds in a cluster at 18-inch intervals, cover them with ¼ inch of soilless medium, and water in well. Later I'd thin to the strongest seedling in each cluster.

**Brussels Sprouts**   Brussels sprouts fit very nicely into the Victory Garden scheme of things because, despite being a long-season crop that requires 3 months or more to mature, they grow vertically and make excellent use of available space. I'm so fond of their taste, though, that I'd probably grow them regardless. In early June, I transplant my seedlings from their 4-inch pots into individual cell-packs. Given a drink of half-strength water-soluble fertilizer, they'll grow happily on a sun-bathed windowsill or in the uncovered cold frame while I prepare the raised bed for their arrival. (To ward off clubroot, I plant them

Slicing off only the main broccoli head stimulates the development of side shoots, which will continue to produce for weeks.

in a bed where other brassicas haven't grown for the last several seasons.) Like the other brassicas, Brussels sprouts prefer a slightly sweet soil, and I add enough lime to their beds to raise the pH to around 7.5. Because of my problem with clubroot, I like a pH of 7.5 for Brussels sprouts. I'll also add 2 inches of compost to the soil of their bed, working the compost in well with my spading fork. Toward the end of June the seedlings will be about 6 inches tall, and ready to be set out into the garden. I space them 24 inches apart, and I plant only one row of Brussels sprouts, because each plant of Jade Cross E. will produce 75 to 100 sprouts. The seedlings are set in the ground a little deeper than they were growing in their cell-packs, and I water them in with water-soluble fertilizer diluted to half strength.

Aphids seem to have a particular fondness for Brussels sprouts, and have given me fits in the Victory Garden. Once the tiny insects find their way onto the undersides of leaves and into the sprouts themselves, they're just about impossible to

dislodge. My best defense against this kind of invasion has been careful vigilance. At the first sign of aphid presence, I spray the leaves with a strong blast from the garden hose, hoping the force of water will flush most of them off. If that doesn't dislodge them, I'll dust with rotenone or spray with pyrethrum.

**Cabbage**   Cabbage heads are ready for harvest when they're well formed and solid, and it's important to take them when they're ready. Cabbage that stays in the ground too long is likely to split. Splitting heads can also be caused by overly generous or irregular watering, or from excessive water uptake after heavy June rains. To minimize this problem, I use my spade to trim the roots of any cabbages that will stay in the ground longer. I cut down through one side, just outside the lower leaves.

To take the heads, I cut just above the soil level and then, as with all the brassicas, pull and discard the roots. This helps prevent the spread of clubroot.

In early June, I start the seedlings for my fall crop of Victory Garden cabbage, following the same indoor-planting techniques I used in April. Come July, I'll transplant the seedlings to cell-packs, harden them off, and set them into the garden. Savoy Ace and Ice Prince are my favorite fall varieties.

Though I prefer starting the seedlings indoors to give them the best possible growth, it's acceptable to sow the seeds of a fall crop directly into the soil. Were I to do it this way, I'd cluster 3 seeds at 24-inch intervals, cover with ¼ inch of soil-less medium, and water in well. I'd keep the seed bed moist until germination, then thin to a single strong seedling in each cluster.

**Cauliflower**   In the late 1940s I was a fledgling in the nursery business — a budding entrepreneur — and on purchasing trips I traveled the length and breadth of Long Island, home not only of beautiful nurseries but of thriving truck farms as well. Those truck farms devoted much of their acreage to cabbage, broccoli, Brussels sprouts, and especially cauliflower. Stopping one day for lunch at a roadside diner, I got into a conversation with a grizzled old fellow who'd obviously been farming for a long, long time. Why, I asked him, was so much cauliflower grown on Long Island? Perhaps thinking that I was some kind of spy, he ignored my question and spoke, instead, about trucks and tractors and the weather. As I was leaving, I told him that I was in the nursery business, and left him a card to prove it. Then I headed for my truck. After looking at the card he called me back. I came eagerly, thinking that he'd treat me to the secrets of this region's spectacular brassica crops. I was all ears as he glanced at my card once more and said, "Well, we grow cauliflower 'cause we're near a damned good market!" And that was it. Well, not quite. After I'd thanked him again and was about to go, he said, "Stay in the nursery business. It's interestin' work. Growin' cauliflower is too damn monotonous."

In the ideal climate of Long Island, with its rich soil and moisture-laden air, growing cauliflower may have been so easy that it *was* monotonous. In the Victory Garden, unfortunately, the culture of this finicky crop has been more of an adventure. The most common problem has been the root maggot, which attacks the plants' water delivery system, making them droop and wilt on warm days. The repeated wilting triggers early maturing of the plant, and usually results in very small heads. The maggot is the offspring of an egg-laying fly, however, and I reasoned that tenting the crop with polyester row covering would discourage the insects. It worked, and now I routinely protect the cauliflower rows with fabric supported on hoops of #12 wire.

Yellowing heads is another cauliflower problem. To prevent the plants from discoloring, it's necessary to blanch the heads — shield them from sunlight. This is done by tying leaves up over the emerging heads, by breaking the leaves over the heads, or

Cauliflower heads must be protected from direct sunlight, which causes yellowing. I tie the leaves into a cover, using garden twine, as soon as white heads begin to form.

by growing varieties that are self-blanching. I like the tying technique best, because the self-blanchers produce somewhat smaller heads and the broken-leaf method seems to weaken the plants a bit.

Once the blanched cauliflower is 8 to 10 inches in diameter, snow white, and tightly grained, it's ready for harvest. I pull the whole plant out, cut the head free, and discard the roots. No composting for these or any brassica roots — too much risk of spreading clubroot.

**Celery**   Now that our weather has stabilized and I'm sure that the celery seedlings will not be subjected to temperatures below 50 degrees (which would cause them to bolt), I'll plant the seedlings in the garden. First they'll go into the cold frame for 5 days of hardening-off. While they're getting used to the weather, I'll prepare the celery bed by working in 2 inches of compost or well-rotted manure with my spading fork, taking care to loosen the soil very deeply — a full 12 inches. I'll also work in 10-10-10 fertilizer, allowing 5 pounds per 100 square feet of bed. When the seedlings are ready for planting, I set them into the soil with a spacing of 6 inches in the rows and 12 inches between rows, then water in with water-soluble fertilizer.

At one time, most celery was blanched by hilling-up, but blanching, which does rob the stalks of some nutritional value, has become less popular. Blanching also means more work, even if you use an ingenious method like that of Delbert Thompson, described in March. My own preference now is not to blanch celery, but to let it grow green and crunchy, full of all the vitamin

It used to be common practice to blanch celery, but unblanched celery is actually more nutritious. For the few plants I do blanch, 12-inch planks laid against the celery do the job neatly.  ▶

A and nutrients that exposure to sun will create. If I *were* to opt for blanching, though, I doubt if I'd use the hilling-up method. It's a lot of extra work, for one thing, but I've also found that hilling-up allows soil to fall down between the plant's stalks, making them not only gritty when harvested but more susceptible to rot. Instead of hilling, I'd probably plant the celery in 9- or 12-inch blocks, creating a "self-blanching" bed. It's also possible to lay 12-inch-wide planks up against the plants, with stakes on the outside to keep the planks from tipping backward away from the plants.

**Chinese Cabbage**   In June, my crop of Chinese cabbage will be ready for harvest. I keep an eye on the thermometer throughout this month, watching for several days of temperatures above 80 degrees. If 3 such days come back-to-back, I go ahead and harvest the Chinese cabbage plants — even though they may not be completely mature — to get them before they bolt.

This panorama of the June garden shows off several of my favorite Victory Garden techniques: raised beds with spacious walkways, black plastic mulch, A-frame trellises, and protective spun polyester fabric supported on PVC hoops.

In June I plant the egg-plant seedlings through 4-inch squares cut out of the black plastic mulch covering their bed. I'm careful to handle the seedling by its root ball rather than by the fragile stem and leaves.

To harvest, I remove the whole plant from the soil, then cut the top growth off with a sharp knife. I discard the roots and, as with all the brassica roots, avoid putting them into the compost bin because of the danger of spreading clubroot.

As soon as possible after harvesting the Chinese cabbage, I plant a crop of beans in the same bed. The beans, with their nitrogen-fixing talent, will help replenish the soil that the heavy-feeding Chinese cabbage has depleted.

**Eggplant**  During the first week of June, I begin final soil preparation for my eggplant seedlings. While they're hardening-off, I work in 2 inches of compost and 5 pounds of slow-release 14-14-14 fertilizer for every 100 square feet of bed. I rake the bed into shape, then place the black plastic, burying its borders all the way around. I cut 4-inch squares in the plastic 24 inches apart and plant the seedlings through these when they're ready, setting them in to the same depth they grew in their cell-packs.

Verticillium wilt has become a problem with my Victory Garden eggplant crop. Commercial farmers fumigate their soil to defend against wilt, but I prefer to outrun the problem with a disease-tolerant variety like Dusky and a fertile soil that helps keep healthy plants growing fast, one step ahead of the disease.

**Kale**  Kale is the toughest customer in the Victory Garden. Extremely cold tolerant and resistant to most bugs and diseases, kale is rich in both vitamins A and C and in iron as well. Six ounces of kale, in fact, deliver twice the vitamin C contained in 6 ounces of orange juice. As if that were not enough, kale supplies as much calcium as an equal volume of milk! And

The greenhouse is still busy in June. Kale, for one, gets an indoor start early in the month.

when all else has been harvested out of the Victory Garden, kale remains. It's become a must in my winter garden.

I start my kale seeds indoors in early June, sowing them in 4-inch pots filled with soilless growing medium and covering the seeds with ¼ inch of that medium. Over the 75-degree heat pad, I will have seedlings in 5 to 7 days. When they're up, I move them to full sunlight, and at the first appearance of true leaves I transplant the seedlings to individual cell-packs. After that, they're given a day's break from full sun while they recover from transplanting shock and are then set back onto a very sunny windowsill or into my versatile cold frame. Kale is a fast grower, so I'm careful not to let that medium dry out while the seedlings are growing in containers. In July I'll set seedlings into the open ground, being sure first to harden them off for 5 days in the cold frame.

**Kohlrabi**   Short-term crops like kohlrabi enjoy rapid growth, so I side-dress the plants with 1 cup of 5-10-5 fertilizer per 10 feet of row in the first week of June.

Good kohlrabi is *young* kohlrabi, so I harvest them at the end of this month, when they're about golf-ball-sized (and definitely before they're as big as tennis balls). If allowed to grow beyond 2 inches in diameter, they quickly lose dinnertime appeal. Grand Duke, my variety of choice, won't go woody, but it will toughen a bit. I harvest by breaking off the leaves, then cutting the stem about 1 inch below the ball.

When the bed is vacant, I work in 5 pounds of 10-10-10 fertilizer for every 100 square feet of bed space and then plant lettuce seedlings or beans in that space. Legumes are a particularly good follow-up crop for the heavy-feeding kohlrabi, as their nitrogen-fixing roots will help replenish the soil.

**Leeks**   Leeks are very heavy feeders, so I side-dress them in June with 1 cup of 10-10-10 fertilizer for every 10 feet of row, keeping the fertilizer at least 2 inches from the leek stems. I also weed now, carefully, with my short-handled three-pronged cultivator. And I'm not disheartened by the wispy, grass-blade appearance of the June seedlings. They *will* develop.

**Lettuce**   The lettuce just keeps on coming. By this time of the season, I'm planting only varieties that are heat tolerant: Red Sails, Mission, Great Lakes. Whenever a space opens up — in the kohlrabi bed, for instance — I pop in lettuce seedlings. They appreciate some shade now, and the taller crops — peas, beans, trellised cucumbers — give them just that. Careful attention to watering is important, too, now that the hot days are here to stay.

As far as harvest techniques are concerned, I've read about, listened to, and tried a good many. Some gardeners like to pick only the outer leaves at first. Some take only the tender inner leaves. Some actually "crew-cut" the loose-leaf types down to within 2 inches of the soil, hoping that the plant will produce more leaves. I'll tell you what I've concluded: It doesn't make much difference *how* I harvest lettuce. One way's as good as another. The important thing is to use the lettuce I've harvested as soon as possible. The fresher the better, and *that* is the crux of lettuce harvesting! Equally important, in June's heat, is to watch for evidence of pre-bolt. At the slightest tinge of bitterness in the outer leaves, or hardening or knobby formations in

It's time to side-dress the leek seedlings with 1 cup of 10-10-10 fertilizer for every 10 feet of row. My plant labels, clearly marked with waterproof pens, are withstanding summer showers to keep me informed.

**Use number 1,421 for the trusty Victory Garden knife. I've had good success growing small icebox-type watermelon in the cool Northeast.**

the center, I rip the plant out and replant with new lettuce. The old has gone by when those signs appear.

**Melons**   In June I water the melons regularly, making sure that they receive at least 1 inch of moisture per week. I don't have to worry about weeding or cultivating because the black plastic mulch eliminates those chores, but I do make sure that the vines are kept on the beds and out of the aisles. In June and July, I will give the melon plants a nutrient boost of complete water-soluble fertilizer, and then bide my time until August harvest arrives. There is simply no comparison between store-bought and homegrown melons. The store-bought variety are generally picked green to allow for shipping and storage time. Contrary to popular belief, though, melons don't ripen to full flavor once they're off the vine, so if you've never taken a crop all the way in the home garden, chances are you've never tasted what a melon can *really* accomplish.

**Okra**   Down in the Victory Garden South, Jim Wilson is able to produce a veritable forest of okra. Thriving in the heat and humidity, the plants grow at least 6 feet tall, and I just can't grow beauties that size up north. Okra needs 100 days of very warm soil and air temperatures, and can be stunted badly by cool temperatures in June. But if the weather is benign, I can depend on a decent, if not spectacular, okra harvest in August.

The plants that I started indoors in April will be ready for 5 days of hardening-off in early June. Before planting the seedlings, I'll work in 5 pounds of 14-14-14 slow-release fertilizer for every 100 square feet of bed, and then cover the soil with black plastic, burying the edges just as I did for the cucumber and melon beds. I plant the seedlings through 4-inch squares cut into the plastic, 24 inches apart, setting the plants in the same depth they were growing. And I peel off the tops of those peat pots, to keep them from wicking away moisture.

**Onions**   The very nice thing about onions is that they can be harvested throughout the growing season, as they are needed. My scallion patch will be ready for harvesting throughout June. In my main bed, the onions planted from sets will be ready first. I can take onions at this point if I wish, and I usually harvest a few now. I'll keep on harvesting throughout July and August, and the foliage tops of the main-bed onions will turn brown and wither during these months, indicating storage-ready onions underneath.

This is a good time to watch for root maggot damage, which will be revealed on top by discoloring at the onions' tips. There's not much to be done except watch carefully and pull the afflicted at once. I tried spreading wood ashes to discourage these egg-laying insects by creating a gritty barrier around the plants, but any appreciable rainfall washed them right away (the ashes, not

the insects, alas). Now I just follow my watch-and-pull strategy if the maggots appear, but they've never really been a serious problem.

The onion beds will need cultivating this month, and I do it — carefully — with my three-pronged cultivator. Onions have shallow roots and are easily checked if those roots are disturbed. This is also the time to side-dress with 1 cup of 5-10-5 fertilizer for every 10 feet of row.

**Peas**   The pea harvest has never been earlier, now that I plant seeds in peat strips and set out seedlings in the open garden in mid-April. The first year I tried this technique, I was astonished by the results, and continue to be just as pleased. That year, I got first peas (the variety was low-growing Sugar Anne) on June 1, or *3 weeks* earlier than ever before. Other, later-maturing varieties followed closely.

Harvesting various types of peas is not without its subtlety. Snow peas can be harvested any time before the pods swell. So can sugar-podded types, though their flavor is vastly improved if one waits until the pods are about to burst from their skins. With standard garden peas (which I rarely grow any longer), the key is not so much in harvest as it is in use thereafter. These, like corn, lose their sugar content very quickly after being picked. That means being ready to shell and cook these old-fashioned types within minutes of the harvest. The pea harvest will last 3 to 4 weeks, and when the plants have finally produced their last I pull them up by hand, taking as many roots as possible, and add them to the compost bin. With these legumes there's no danger of spreading disease (the case with brassicas and clubroot, for example), and the peas are a rich source of nitrogen in the compost.

**Peppers**  Rather than use a specific date for planting peppers, I keep my eye on the weather forecast. When I'm satisfied that the nighttime temperatures won't fall below 55 degrees, I feel safe in setting the peppers out. Sometimes that's as early as the middle of May in my region, and sometimes I have to wait until early June. Each year has its own personality, and I try to be sensitive to that. The real key, though, is to err on the side of caution, because peppers love warm weather and loathe cold. At one time, when it was standard practice to rush all crops out into the garden as early as possible, I had quite a few pepper crop failures. One year the peppers produced their usual two flushes of blossoms, but no fruit. They'd been set into the garden too early, and a spate of cool, rainy weather forced the blossoms before the plants were ready to bear fruit. Later, another unexpected blast of cool weather did the same thing, after it was too *late* for the plants to fruit. The key, I think, is waiting until the soil is at least 60 degrees and nighttime temperatures won't go below 55 degrees. If, despite my thermometer-watching and cautious scheduling, an untimely set of cool days threatens the peppers, I'll protect them with Wall O' Water towers.

Peppers *love* growing under black plastic, which conserves heat and retains moisture. *I* love the plastic because it eliminates weeding and greatly reduces watering chores.

Peppers are heavy feeders that produce a long harvest, so I give them a thorough job of soil preparation. In addition to the standard Victory Garden fall soil improving, I work up the peppers' soil while they're hardening-off in the cold frame for 5 days (after those temperatures have stabilized). I add both 2 inches of compost and 14-14-14 slow-release fertilizer (5 pounds per 100 square feet of bed) to their soil. Then I lay down the black plastic mulch and bury its borders. The 4- to 6-inch seedlings are planted through 4-inch squares cut out of the plastic every 18 inches, with 24 inches between the rows. After the seedlings are in, I water them with half-strength liquid fertilizer.

I've found that in the Victory Garden I have few problems with insects or diseases with the pepper crop. For a while I used cutworm collars, but neglected to do so one season with no damage at all. Nor have I ever staked my pepper plants, though I know some gardeners who do. Adequate, consistent watering is much more important, and I am careful about that all season long.

**Pumpkins**  June is pumpkin-planting month in the Victory Garden. It's always hard to believe that the 6-inch seedlings I set out now will eventually grow into plants with 8-foot vines and 10-pound fruit — but they always do!

The planting procedure for pumpkins is similar to that for squash and cucumbers. I move the seedlings to the cold frame on June 1 for 5 days of hardening-off, and while they're doing that I prepare the pumpkin-bed soil. The standard Victory Garden pH of 6.5 is ideal. Pumpkins like a rich, highly organic soil, so I work in 2 inches of well-rotted manure or compost to give them that, and at the same time add 5 pounds of 14-14-14 slow-release fertilizer for every 100 square feet of bed space. Then I cover the beds with black plastic, burying the edges all the way around and cutting out 4-inch squares every 24 inches. When the seedlings have completed their 5 days in the cold frame, I set them into the ground at the same depth they were growing in their peat pots, first tearing the tops off those pots so that they will not be exposed to air and dry the seedlings out. Last of all, they receive a drink of complete water-soluble fertilizer diluted to half strength.

Woodchuck neighbors have demonstrated a real affinity for my Victory Garden pumpkins, and I tried several defenses before finally resorting to chicken-wire fencing, 4 feet high and buried a full 12 inches beneath the surface. That buried border is important. Woodchucks aren't great climbers, but they can burrow like mad.

A gourmet's delight, my shallots are ready for harvest when their tops wither and fall over. After harvesting, they should be cured in a dry, cool area.

**Rutabagas**  Rutabagas, also called Swede turnips, or just plain "Swedes," have an image problem. Too many gardeners make the mistake of thinking of them as food fit only for starving armies. I once believed that, remembering my grandmother's Thanksgiving table and the inevitable yellow lump of overcooked mush she said was good for me. But rutabagas allowed to grow into fall weather and harvested the day before Thanksgiving are a different — and very rewarding —experience. Started this month in the open garden, the seeds will quickly germinate. Once they're up, I can almost forget about them until harvest time. They're not particularly finicky about soil, so I don't even bother working extra compost or manure into their raised bed. They do like my standard pH of 6.5. I plant the seeds in mid to late June in ¼-inch-deep furrows, with 6 inches between the seeds and rows 12 inches apart. I group 3 seeds in each spot, cover them with soilless medium, and water them in well. Seedlings will be up in 5 to 7 days, and I'll thin to the strongest seedling in each group a week later. This is a long-term crop that won't be ready for harvest until early October, and the rutabagas need two more things for proper growth: cool weather and plenty of moisture. The Victory Garden climate provides the former, and I take care of the latter, giving them at least 1 inch of water per week.

**Shallots** My March-planted shallots can be harvested any time now. I watch the tops, and I know that the bulbs are ready for use when the tops wither and fall over, which usually occurs in early June in the Victory Garden. There's nothing easier than digging or pulling out these gourmet bulbs, and they'll store very well for a long time in any area that's reasonably dry and no warmer than 40 degrees.

**Summer Squash** Summer squash develops quickly from its bold yellow flowerings. My squash rule is to harvest young and frequently. For me, gardening is a way to get vegetables at the peak of perfection, the way they *aren't* in all too many grocery stores. Summer squash that is allowed to sit too long on the vine overgrows its maturity, loses flavor, and develops tough skin. I like to get these delicacies when they're small enough to hold in my hand, 6 to 8 inches long. And I keep picking them throughout the season, because this stimulates the plants to keep producing more fruit. As soon as the blossoms have turned

**Summer squash the way I like to harvest it: young and tender. The blossoms are eminently edible.**

brown and dried, the little squash have reached prime picking condition. Don't be surprised if some of them are thumb-sized when this happens — that's when they're at the peak of flavor.

Occasionally I'll see some blossom-end rot (caused by incomplete pollination) at the first flowering of my summer squash crop, and this is usually the result of unsettled weather. I'm never overly alarmed by the rot, because I know that when the weather settles down the plant will be just fine. I just discard any mushy-ended fruit that results.

**Swiss Chard**   In June I harvest Swiss chard, when the outer leaves are 6 to 12 inches long. It's the outer leaves I take, snapping a few from each plant all the way down the bed. Cutting for once, is not recommended, as the plants seem to recover better from having the leaves snapped off cleanly. By taking the mature, outer leaves only, I stimulate the plant's inner-leaf growth. This continual regeneration will provide a steady harvest of foliage throughout the summer and into the early fall.

After harvest, I give the plants a side-dressing of 10-10-10 (a half-handful per plant), scratched in well with my cultivator. That and conscientious watering will be all this sturdy crop needs.

**I harvest only a few outer leaves from each Swiss chard plant in June, snapping the leaves cleanly at the plant's base. ◄**

**A super-healthy winter squash seedling, ready for transplanting. My use of sterile soilless growing medium eliminates disease and provides plenty of nutrients during the plants' critical early growth phase. ▼**

**Turnips**   If June stays cool and moist, the turnip harvest can be spread over the season. If the forecaster predicts an early hot spell — a week of weather over 80 degrees, say — I'll go ahead and harvest the whole crop. They'll taste just fine after a week or two in the refrigerator, but that hot weather can put their fine flavor off if they're left in the ground. As with most Victory Garden vegetables, I like to harvest the turnips when they're small and tender, no more than 2 inches in diameter. And the tops will add a body punch to a fresh garden soup.

**Winter Squash**   The seedlings I started back in May are ready for planting out now, in early June. While they're hardening off in the cold frame for 5 days, I prepare their raised beds. I add 2 inches of compost and 5 pounds of 14-14-14 slow-release fertilizer for every 100 square feet of garden space. When these have been forked in well, I rake the soil smooth and then spread black plastic over the raised bed, burying the borders all the way around. I cut 4-inch squares in the plastic, spacing them every 36 inches for bush varieties and 5 feet for the larger, long-vining types. After peeling the tops of the peat pots back (to keep them from wicking away soil moisture), I set them into the soil and water in with a welcoming drink of balanced, water-soluble fertilizer at half strength.

# PESTS AND PLAGUES

Insect pests and diseases are both inevitable parts of gardening. Their impact can be minimized by following the sound cultural practices outlined in "Steps to Victorious Gardening," but there comes a time when every gardener must deal with insects and diseases. In this chapter, you'll find descriptions and pictures of the most common pests and plagues, along with my specific solutions for each.

**Aphids** are troublesome everywhere. What they lack in size (¹⁄₁₀ inch) they make up for in quantity, reproducing with a fervor that would make rabbits blush. Aphids suck juices from leaves and transmit diseases in the process. The many species of aphids come in a variety of colors. They can reproduce with or without a mate, and give birth to eggs as well as living young. Ants frequently live with aphids, because the latter secrete honeydew, which is a food source for the ants. It's a nice symbiosis: Ants do their part by protecting the aphids, and even moving them to lusher pastures. Aphids are present throughout the growing season, and my first line of defense is to keep a clean garden and to buy plants that are insect-free. I keep the perimeter of the garden weeded, thereby reducing areas where they can hide. And I compost all refuse immediately. Early, small infestations of aphids can be sprayed off with a strong stream of water. If they begin to accumulate, I dust the plants with fast-acting rotenone.

**Leaf miners** destroy leaves by tunneling between leaf surfaces. There are many species, and adults will lay eggs on leaf surfaces of a variety of vegetables. These eggs are usually yellow, making them easy to spot, and they appear to be lying at right angles to the undersides of the leaves. The eggs hatch and the larvae then tunnel in between the leaf surfaces, eventually creating leaves that resemble topographic maps and that are

*Leaf miners*

also rendered inedible. Miners are particularly troublesome on spinach, Swiss chard, and beets. They do tend to come in cycles, being most troublesome in spring because that's the season of lush, green, leafy growth. In days past, this was a very difficult pest, because the best control was a systemic insecticide that would be absorbed by the plant and then ingested by the miner. Contact insecticides were ineffective because the larvae were protected by the leaves. In those days, I watched carefully for the eggs, and crushed them whenever I found any. That reduced, but never really controlled, a leaf miner invasion. Now I cover miner-susceptible crops with spun polyester fabric at planting time. This barrier prevents adults from laying eggs. It's nontoxic and very effective.

*Aphids*

**I no longer use chemical insecticides in the Victory Garden. Spun, bonded polyester fiber offers chemical-free protection while admitting both sunlight and moisture. This late-June potato foliage, which would have been riddled by the Colorado potato beetle, is untouched and growing beautifully.** ◄

*Imported cabbage worm*

*Adult form*

*Cabbage looper*

*Adult form*

**Cabbage moths** produce two harmful pests: the imported cabbageworm and the cabbage looper. The former is a green caterpillar produced by a moth with white and black spots. The green looper crawls with a distinctive looping motion, and is produced by a brownish moth with a silvery spot in the middle of each wing. Both caterpillars eat the leaves of all brassicas. Control these days is easy and safe: agricultural fabric, which keeps the moths at bay. *Bacillus thuringiensis* kills any that manage to slip in. *Bt* is an effective control alone — without the fabric. *Bt* must be ingested by the caterpillars to kill them, so some leaf damage results while the sprayed leaves are eaten. The change is insignificant, especially if *Bt* is sprayed while the caterpillars are small. Both types of caterpillars produce several generations through the season, so I watch for them all summer long.

**The Colorado potato beetle** was once a restricted and little-known bug. Now that potatoes are widely cultivated, this insect is troublesome everywhere. It's become a national nuisance, and has been dosed with more than a fair share of DDT. The adult is yellow with black stripes on the wings and black dots on its orange head. It will lay yellow-orange eggs on the undersides of leaves. The eggs hatch into fat red grubs, which chew ravenously through potato foliage. They can completely destroy the leaves, preventing tuber formation or causing poorly developed spuds. They *must* be controlled. My favorite method is to cover the crop (having ro-

*Colorado potato beetle*

tated the bed, because adult beetles winter-over in the soil) with polyester fabric draped over tall hoops of #12 wire. Dusting with rotenone is another approach, but it's difficult to get complete coverage. Hand-picking is practical on small patches of potatoes.

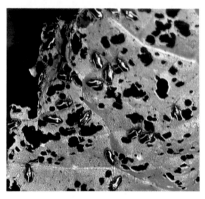

*Flea beetles*

**Flea beetles** are spring pests, often feeding on newly set-out and young plants. They are small, about 1/10 inch, and hop like fleas when disturbed. Their chewing riddles leaves. There are a number of species, all of which feed on brassicas, eggplant, and potatoes. Their damage is unsightly (it looks like dozens of tiny buckshot holes in the leaves) but not usually fatal. Agricultural fabric will keep many out, and a rotenone dusting should control the rest.

**Squash vine borers** are worrisome pests east of the Rockies. The borer is the caterpillar of an orange and black, clear-winged moth that also has coppery forewings. It will lay eggs at the base of summer and winter squash, pumpkins, cucumbers, and melons. The eggs hatch a white grub that enters the soft, succulent stems of these plants. Left unchecked, the grubs will kill plants. Breeders have produced some borer-resistant varieties with toughened stems, but the borers continue to be a problem. My solution is to drape agricultural fabric over the vines, with the ends of the fabric secured with stones or pieces of wood, leaving plenty of slack. As the plants grow, they'll push up the feather-light fabric, which keeps moths away from the plants. An alternative is to dust the base of the plants weekly with rotenone. Once infestation occurs, surgery is the only remedy, and I describe the procedure in detail in the July summer squash entry.

*Squash vine borer*

*Spotted cucumber beetle*

*Striped cucumber beetle*

**Cucumber beetles** feed not only on cucumbers but also on squash, melons, beans, and peas. There are two varieties of beetles, striped and spotted. Both are about ¼ inch long. The striped beetle has a pale yellow or orange body, with three black stripes running the length of its body. The spotted cucumber beetle is greenish yellow, with a small black head and 11 (count 'em) black spots on the back. Beetle larvae live in the soil, feeding on roots and stems. Of greater concern is the fact that they spread bacterial wilt and cucumber mosaic, which can lead to total vine collapse. Netting is very effective, as is a weekly dusting with rotenone, if the plants are grown in the open.

**Cutworms** are the larvae of night-flying moths, and can wreak havoc in the garden. The larvae emerge from below the soil surface, girdle the young stems of plants, and chew them off at ground level. There are few more dispiriting sights than a cutworm-devastated garden after an evening foray. Frequent cultivation will unsettle the bugs, and bring them to the surface, where birds will rejoice over the easy pickings. There are many species and, among them all, the cutworms can remain active through the season. Individual plants can be protected easily with cardboard collars 3 inches in diameter. I cut 9-inch strips, fold them into circles, and staple the ends together. Then I slip the collars over individual tomato, pepper, and eggplants — if it looks like a bad cutworm year. The Victory Garden, fortunately, hasn't suffered greatly from cutworms, so I haven't

*Cutworm*

included this collar defense in any of the monthly vegetable entries, but it *is* effective. Cutworms will not climb over the collars and, if they're pushed 1 inch deep into the soil, the worms can't burrow under, either.

**Root maggots** have bedeviled me in the Victory Garden. They can attack all members of the brassica family, as well as onions. The adult fly lays eggs at the bases of the cabbage, broccoli, cauliflower, Brussels sprout, radish, and turnip plants. These eggs hatch into maggots that chew and suck on the roots. They can easily kill plants or, in the case of broccoli and cauliflower, stress the plants into premature heading or flowering. They are more damaging in the Victory Garden in spring, but they are also present with fall crops. Control is by barrier — agricultural fabric. A rotenone dust applied weekly to the base of the plants will offer protection, too. Individual plants can be protected by placing 4-inch tarpaper squares at the base of each plant. A slit from one side

*Corn earworm*

of the square to its center allows it to fit around the plant's stem. Because it requires less work and no chemicals, I favor the use of fabric.

**Corn earworms** are the worst corn pests in the U.S. and can visit any patch. The adult is a night-flying moth that lays eggs on corn leaves. The larvae chew leaves and thereby stunt plant growth. As the corn ears develop, they enter through the silk and work their way from top to bottom, eating kernels as they go. Breeders are working on very tightly wrapped cobs that make it difficult for the larvae to enter, but that development seems a few generations away just yet. That said, it's also true that damage in the Victory Garden has never been severe. My solution is to cut

out the small affected areas with my pocketknife. I've also sealed the silks with several drops of mineral oil from a medicine dropper, which prevents the worms from crawling down into the ears. The time to do this is just when the corn ears are beginning to fill out.

**Tomato horn worms** are among the most frightening garden pests. If they were bigger, they'd fit perfectly into a grade-B Japanese monster film. They can grow up to 5 inches long, and they blend in frustratingly well with tomato foliage. They have orange antennae, which they extend when disturbed. With these "horns" showing, the creatures can be rather daunting. Fortunately, there are several effective controls. Hungry birds love them. They're easily hand-picked. *Bacillus thuringiensis* kills them. Certain parasitic wasps will also destroy them. Without control, however, they have an insatiable appetite for tomato foliage and fruits. Their name is a bit misleading, because they'll also go after the leaves and fruits of peppers, eggplants, and potatoes.

*Tomato horn worm*

*Root maggot mat*

Most vegetable diseases are caused by fungi, bacteria, or viruses. Most viruses and some bacteria are transmitted by insects, and can be minimized by controlling insect populations. Of the three types of disease, fungal problems are perhaps the most common. Disease damage from all three types can range from minor cosmetic damage to total plant collapse.

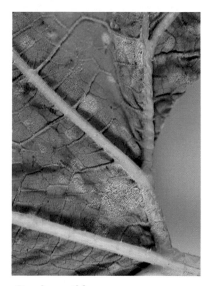

*Powdery mildew*

**Powdery mildew** manifests as a white powder on leaf surfaces. The infestation can be limited to the surface only, in which case it's not severe enough to weaken or kill the plant. The disease commonly afflicts squash, melons, cucumbers, and beans. If infection is severe, plants can be killed.

My defense is to space plants adequately for good air circulation, and to avoid late-afternoon waterings that send plants into evening with wet foliage. In areas where powdery mildew is very troublesome, a fungicide may be in order.

**Damping off** affects seeds and newly emerged seedlings, and is caused by soil-borne fungi. Under ideal conditions — excess moisture, primarily — a whole crop can be lost. Seedlings may fail to emerge, or after growing 2 inches, may simple topple over and die. I have solved this problem by starting seeds in sterile, soilless growing medium. Good cultural practices like adequate spacing in the seed flats or pots and careful — not excessive — watering are also important.

*Damping off*

*Anthracnose*

**Anthracnose** is quite common, unfortunately, though it occurs primarily in the eastern U.S. It commonly affects beans, peas, cucumbers, and melons. Black, sunken spots appear on fruits, and the veins on the undersides of leaves turn black. The disease spreads easily in wet weather, and can be distributed throughout the garden by an unwitting gardener walking about when foliage is wet. Control involves watering early in the day, so that foliage can dry before nightfall. It's also wise to avoid working with anthracnose-susceptible crops when their foliage is wet.

*Leaf spots*

**Leaf spots,** though sometimes caused by bacteria, are most commonly caused by fungi. Leaves develop spots, sometimes turn yellow and die. Humid weather in summer encourages the development of this disease. Tomatoes are sometimes affected, but virtually any plant can develop leaf spots. I try to control this by avoiding excessive watering, and by working in the garden when plants are dry. Good garden sanitation is also important.

**Clubroot** has been devilish in the Victory Garden, and it's troublesome on brassicas throughout the U.S. The causative organisms live in the soil, and have been variously classified as slime molds and fungus. They're very long-lived, and extremely hard to control. They can cause severe wilting during the day. Mature leaves turn yellow and drop, and roots become swollen and distorted. The plants are usually stunted, and may often die. The disease attacks all members of the brassica family throughout the country. It's impossible to dig out clubroot once it's established, as the organisms can survive in the soil for years. Rotation in new gardens is one important control. Beds, once planted to brassicas, should not be replanted with them for at least 5 years. In all but the very largest gardens,

*Clubroot*

this is hard to put in practice, however. In the Victory Garden, I've managed to grow decent brassica crops despite widespread clubroot infestation by heavily liming the planting holes of the most susceptible brassicas (I include this measure in the appropriate monthly vegetable entries for specific crops). A pH of 7.5 in brassica beds seems to check the growth of clubroot. It's also important to keep plants growing vigorously, with ample nutrients and consistent watering.

Fusarium and verticillium wilts are both caused by soil-borne fungi. They are difficult to tell apart.

**Fusarium wilt** plagues cucumbers, tomatoes, asparagus, peas, peppers, and potatoes. The plants' lower leaves will yellow and curl up during the hottest part of the day, and then will recover — for a while — during the night. After a bit, the whole plant withers and dies. There is no chemical control for this wilt. Instead, I plant disease-resistant varieties, and pull and destroy infected plants at once.

*Wilt on eggplants*

**Verticillium wilt** can afflict many plants, including tomatoes, eggplants, peppers, and potatoes. Symptoms include yellowing of lower leaves, poor fruit production, and curling leaves at the tip of the plant. It's possible to fumigate or drench the soil with certain chemicals to control this disease, but I prefer to keep the Victory Garden as chemical-free as possible. To that end, I plant disease-resistant varieties of vegetables and destroy any infected plants as soon as I find them.

**Bacterial wilt** of cucurbits is, as its name implies, caused by bacteria rather than fungi. It can occur anywhere in the U.S., and most commonly affects melons, cucumbers, pumpkins, squash, beans, potatoes, and onions. Leaves will wilt during the day and, at first, recover overnight. Eventually the vine dies. There's an easy way to test for this disease. If you cut through a wilted stem and squeeze out white, sticky sap that forms a thread when you touch a plant label to it and draw the label away, you've got bacterial wilt. Since the disease is spread by cucumber beetles, the best way to control it is by keeping the beetles at bay, as described in their entry in the "Insects" section.

*Bacterial wilt*

**Viruses** are numerous, and affect many plants all over the United States, including tomatoes, peas, peppers, corn, beans, cucumbers, and celery. Symptoms may vary widely, but the most common include mottling, streaking, puckering, and curled leaves. To minimize the incidence of virus infection, I always select disease-resistant varieties. Good garden sanitation — prompt clearing of trimmings and refuse — is also important. And since many viruses are spread from plant to plant by insects that suck — aphids, for instance — insect control is another primary defense.

The disease list above is not exhaustive, but it does include the most common and damaging maladies that may strike the home vegetable garden. An invaluable source of information and advice is the oft-mentioned county extension service agent, both for insect and disease problems. Don't hesitate to call up these helpful men and women whenever you encounter a bug or illness that baffles you. A list of county extension offices, with addresses and phone numbers, is included in the appendix at the end of this book.

Mulched pathways keep the garden accessible in all weather and let me pick the day's harvest without tracking mud back into the house.

JULY

# JULY

July is payday. Hot summer weather and warm soil are urging all the crops into high-gear growth. The corn harvest, certainly one of the gardening season's high points, will begin in mid to late July. My first main-crop tomatoes will be ready in July, too, and their appearance causes just as much excitement as the corn. Bush and pole beans will be at their tender best and need frequent picking during this busy month. In fact, I'll be harvesting over a dozen crops, and planting quite a few more, with an eye on the fall season just ahead.

As July's heat settles in, I prefer to move my gardening time to the cool of early morning. Watering, weeding, and thinning are quite pleasant in the freshness of the new day. If I've provided well for feathered friends, I'm often rewarded this time of year with their early-bird feeding on garden pests. Speaking of which, my routine of checking for pest presence continues (see "Pests and Plagues"). Vigilance is the first line of attack. I'm ever ready to wash some off, and to use organic sprays to deal with the few that penetrate the fabric barriers.

Because the soil in the Victory Garden has been producing so intensively for several months now, it's time to pay particular attention to side-dressing and, as each bed is harvested, to replenish it with compost or well-rotted cow manure, and fertilizer. This midseason rejuvenation allows me to keep every square yard of real estate producing intensively all season long.

Here's how I accomplish it. First I broadcast fertilizer (5-10-5 or 10-10-10, depending on the crop that's coming next) at the rate of 5 pounds per 100 square feet of bed, then add 2 inches of compost or well-rotted manure to the cleared bed. I go to work with my spading fork or small tiller, turning over the soil and mixing the ingredients into the top 6 inches. With my raised bed system and emphasis on shorter rows, this task is never overwhelming — a comfort in the midsummer heat.

**Start Indoors**
Cauliflower

**Transplant**
Cauliflower
Cabbage

**Plant in Garden**
Beans
Beets
Broccoli
Carrots
Cucumbers
Kale
Peas
Summer squash

**Fertilize**
Celery
Leeks
Parsnips
Peppers
Tomatoes

**Screen**
Broccoli
Cabbage
Cucumbers

**Harvest**
Beans
Beets
Carrots
Celery
Corn
Cucumbers
Peppers
Potatoes
Summer squash
Tomatoes

**Mulch**
Beans
Beets

**Beans**  I came across a wonderful assortment of beans at a community garden near Pearl Harbor in Hawaii. Among the gardeners were recent Asian immigrants who took particular pleasure in beans. Glenn Tanaguchi, a county extension agent, was especially enthusiastic about winged beans, a legume with long flaps extending out along their length. Every part of the plant was edible — leaves, stems, even roots. There were also yard-long beans, thin as a pencil but actually stretching up to 3 feet long. As I mentioned in an earlier entry, the diversity of beans is truly amazing. And in pointing out this great variety, I'm getting around to a picking point. With all these, including those I grow in the Victory Garden, it's a good idea to pick young and often. In July my May bean planting will begin to

Tender snap beans complement summer squash and sweet basil.

come ready, and I look for quality, not size, when harvesting. Keeping the harvest picked actually extends the bearing time, too, as the plants are urged on to continued production by the removal of mature beans.

It's also time to plant another generation of bush beans, and to keep planting new short rows every 10 to 14 days for continuous harvest. Planting directions are similar to those of the earlier spring bush beans. I do tend to be more vigilant in my watering during these warm summer months, because I don't want the germinating seeds to dry out. I've found that a light mulch — just enough to cover the ground — of salt marsh hay or grass clippings spread right on the seed bed is an excellent way to keep the beds from drying out under that July sun.

One caution that I've learned the hard way: I do not travel through the bean plants when they are wet. To do so is an excellent way to spread leaf diseases like anthracnose, so when there's water on the foliage, I tend to other projects.

**Beets**   I'll finish harvesting my first planting of beets this month. My second generation is coming along, and now it's time to think of September with a July seeding. I always look forward to this sowing because I know that, in the Victory Garden region at least, the dreaded leaf miner will be much less troublesome from now on. Why that is I'm not sure, but I've observed that insect invasions seem to come in cycles with predictable rhythms.

Planting procedure for the beets this month is no different from the methods used in April. I soak the seeds overnight in tepid water to hasten their sometimes reluctant germination, then plant them outside in the loose, stone-free soil of the Victory Garden's raised beds. That carefully prepared soil is the key to good beets. In hard or stony soil, the beets just won't grow into the moist-fleshed, globular beauties that are so prominently featured in all the seed catalogs. Spacing is 1 inch between seeds and 12 inches between rows. After I've covered the seeds with ½ inch of soilless growing medium, I'm careful to keep the rows well watered in this warmer summer weather. Any seeds that dry out simply won't germinate. The best beets are those that have grown quickly, so my end-of-the-month thinning to 3 inches is followed by a good watering with a balanced water-soluble fertilizer. The beets will produce harvestable tops in early August. The globes themselves should be ready by Labor Day.

**Broccoli**   The seedlings that I started indoors in June are ready for planting in the garden now. I plant this fall crop in the bed that grew a spring crop of peas. I lime the planting area and scatter 10-10-10 fertilizer at the rate of 1 cup for every 10 feet of row. This is turned in and raked smooth. I also blend in half a handful of lime to each planting hole. A slightly alkaline soil (at pH 7.5) seems to inhibit the spread of clubroot. The seedlings are set in so that the seed leaves, their lowest set of leaves, are just above the surface of the soil. Broccoli will root along the stem and this will help produce a sturdier seedling. Plants are spaced 18 inches apart in the row, with rows 2 feet apart. With a double-row planting, if I set the first plant in the second row between the first and second plants in row one (i.e., stagger the planting), I will get the most out of the space. After planting, I water the seedlings in with a complete, water-soluble fertilizer, diluted to half strength. Because cabbage moths are still active, I protect the seedlings with fabric.

**Cabbage**  Cabbage is one of the real stalwarts of the fall Victory Garden. My June-sown seedlings will supply the table well into October, and they're ready, in early July, for transplanting to individual cell-packs filled with soilless medium. They're hardened off for 5 days, then planted outside in the soil. Procedures are the same as those used in the spring, except that spacing is

**The July harvest includes cabbage, sweet peppers, and mild onions. This month I'll set out my cabbage destined for fall harvesting.**

Picture-perfect reds: beets and onions.

more generous (24 to 30 inches) because fall varieties produce larger plants. Row covers, supported by wire hoops, will keep cabbageworms and root maggots at bay. If any caterpillars manage to sneak in, I spray with *Bacillus thuringiensis.*

**Carrots** New England is known for its "bony" soil, of course, and in the old days settlers had to work hard before they could plant. The stones they took from the fields were plentiful enough to build walls all around those fields, and anyone with 8 inches of topsoil was considered very lucky indeed. I think of those rugged farmers often when I harvest carrots in the Victory Garden, not because the soil in my beds is that bad, but because it's so very different. I've worked hard on the Victory Garden's raised beds, adding sand, peat moss, and compost, amending with fertilizers, and testing for pH and nutrient content. Nowhere has the effort paid off more handsomely than with my carrots. And at no time is this more apparent to me than when I harvest the carrots: All I have to do is grasp a handful of lush green tops and pull gently. The soil is so deep and friable that the carrots pop right out.

In July, I plant the fall crop. I don't really do anything different from what I did in April except covering the newly seeded rows with salt marsh hay to keep them from drying out and watering the rows twice daily, rather than once.

**Cauliflower** Although I start the seedlings of most other fall brassicas — broccoli, cabbage, Brussels sprouts — in May and June, I delay starting cauliflower until July. Earlier sowings have often yielded disappointing results if the cauliflower headed in August heat. Cauliflower likes to mature in the cool of fall. Breeders have made considerable progress in tempering cauliflower's intemperance for heat, but fall is still the best season.

I sow the seeds in 4-inch pots filled with soilless medium, covering them with ¼ inch of the medium and then bottom-watering. The moistened pots go onto my heat pad at 75 degrees, and I'll have seedlings in about 7 days. They're moved to a sunny spot, and when true leaves unfold I transplant seedlings to individual cell-packs. They're bottom-watered with water-soluble fertilizer at half strength, and given a day out of full sunlight before going back into full sun. For this fall sowing I always try two or three new varieties, to see how they hold up against my recent favorite, White Sails.

**Celery**   Near the end of this month, I side-dress the slow-growing celery plants with 1 cup of 10-10-10 fertilizer per 10 feet of row. The plants are big enough now that I feel safe in twisting off a few of the larger outer stalks for summer munching. The main harvest will begin in September.

**Adult candy. . .on the cob!**

**Corn**   The corn that went into the garden in May will come ready for harvest in mid-July, having survived attacks by crows, raccoons, and insect pests like the corn borer — if I'm lucky and clever. I've read about, and tried, lots of different methods for holding this hungry army of animal invaders at bay. Some gardeners I know recommend putting a paper bag over every ear of corn to protect them from birds. This sounds fine, and the pictures of stalks with two or three bagged ears look convincing. But it's a huge amount of work to bag *every* ear on a corn crop. And there are few more frustrating things than walking out into the garden on the morning after a windy night to find all those carefully placed bags blown throughout the neighborhood. Birds just haven't been that much of a problem in the Victory Garden. If they were, I'd be inclined to defend against them with scarecrows or a prowling platoon of hungry housecats. Raccoons are another matter. They are determined and ingenious. I'm winning the raccoon war, but just barely. The protection begins with a good stout fence about 4 feet high. Then to the top of the fence, running around the entire perimeter of the garden, I mount a single strand of uninsulated aluminum wire. The wire is connected to a device that generates an electrical pulse every second, shocking animals that touch it. Another raccoon deterrent seems to be rock music. A "Victory Garden" contest winner in Knob Hill, Pennsylvania, put a radio under a plastic pail right in the corn patch, tuned it to the local rock station — and never suffered a loss. I've also experimented with humane traps, and have caught quite a few raccoons. But, having caught them, I'm left with the disposal problem: either take them for a long ride in the country, or put them in a weighted bag and toss them in a nearby pond. I'm never mean enough for the pond toss, so it's always a matter of chauffeuring two or three bewildered raccoons to new homes.

Of all the pests that can ravage corn, though, the European corn borer is among the most troublesome. In days past, gardeners sprayed with strong chemicals, but I'd rather lose the crop than eat it after it's been treated with chemicals that could do worse things to my insides than to the bugs themselves. I'm also willing to accept less than perfect ears. I usually go out with a pocketknife, expecting some damage from corn borers and corn earworms. Spraying with *Bacillus thuringiensis* will take care of corn earworms, the 1½-inch-long moth larvae that attack not only corn but beans, peppers, and tomatoes as well.

There are probably as many suggestions for telling when the corn crop is ripe as there are pests that attack it. I still like to watch the silk on the ears. When the silk is all light brown, and the ear feels full from one end to the other, the corn is probably ready. The silk should still be silky, and not at all shriveled. I will also peel back the corn leaves wrapping the ear and puncture a kernel. If the fluid in the kernel is milky rather than clear, I know the corn is ready. I try not to use the peel-and-puncture method too much, though, because if the corn is not ready, it's left hanging on the stalk partly exposed, making a sweet-smelling target for birds and bugs.

**Cucumbers**   There's always a bountiful July harvest of cucumbers in the Victory Garden, and it's a good thing — I'm especially fond of cucumbers. I rub the soft spines off the long European types and munch them right in the garden, in fact. Even though I harvest young and often, the cucumber vines invariably peter out before the end of summer, so a second generation of cukes goes in this month. The soil's warm enough now that I can direct-seed without any problem, and I prepare the beds just as I did for my earlier sowing (see May), working in compost and slow-release fertilizer before applying black plastic, then sowing the seeds, and finally setting up the A-frame support.

Cucumbers are seldom ravaged by insects, but can be destroyed in short order by an unstoppable bacterial wilt spread by the cucumber beetle. The agricultural fabric that protected a number of spring crops will keep these insects at bay, too, when draped over the cucumber vines. Dusting with rotenone will also help. Some varieties, like Sweet Slice and Sweet Success, have varying degrees of disease tolerance (though not total resistance) bred in.

**Kale**   One of the inspirations for planting kale is the vision of it standing tall well into December, the heavy green leaves holding firm even under several inches of snow. That said, finding real estate for 6 plants in the busy midsummer garden is never easy. And since kale is a brassica, it should not be planted

**Hilling-up corn and weeding are both accomplished in this one step.** ▶

**A mild, burpless cucumber grows straight and long on the Victory Garden A-frame trellis.** ▼

where relatives have recently grown. To do so invites clubroot and that, like bad debts and psoriasis, is very hard to get rid of once it's established. I prepare the kale bed by adding 1 cup of 10-10-10 fertilizer for every 10 feet of row, then raking the bed smooth. The transplants, now deep green and 4 inches tall, are set in the same depth they grew in the cell-packs. Spacing is 18 inches in the row, with 24 inches between rows. I water them in with half-strength water-soluble fertilizer and then pretty much forget this hardy crop. Kale can look after itself right through the season. A later side-dressing (5 pounds of 10-10-10 for every

Kale and cabbage are set in in July for fresh eating from September into November.

**This one last feeding and hilling will stretch these leeks to trophy proportions.**

100 square feet of bed) and a lookout for aphids (they can be washed off with a hard hose spray) when the weather cools should be all the attention kale needs.

**Leeks**  The leeks that were planted in May, looking for all the world like anemic grass blades, have grown into robust sentinels in the July garden. Now's the time to give them a final feeding and hilling. The trench has been filled and brought level with grade, and I side-dress with 1 cup of 10-10-10 fertilizer for every 10 feet of row. When that's done, I draw soil from the bed 2 inches up along the leeks' stems. The object is to get the leek to stretch up and out from the thick stem that develops below.

**Parsnips**  My spring-sown parsnips sometimes suffer from the out-of-sight, out-of-mind syndrome. They are tucked off in a remote corner of the garden, fretted over until they finally come up, and thinned to a single plant per hole. But then they're forgotten. Really, though, after the care that went into preparing each specially designed planting pocket, there is little to be done. A side-dressing boost in July will encourage them to reach to the bottom of the cone I made for them and to thicken up nicely for cool-season eating. Each parsnip gets a half-handful of

5-10-5 fertilizer in a ring around the plant. I scratch the feed in and give the bed a thorough weeding, and yes, forget the parsnips . . . for now.

**Peas**   I look forward to July for sowing many of the crops that do best maturing into cool fall weather. Peas, however, are an exception. I can't tell you how many fall pea harvests have been disappointing in the Victory Garden. The problem is that if fall comes too cool too fast, the peas' growth is checked before they have time to flower and fruit well. I wish I had a pat answer for this dilemma, but I haven't met anyone yet who can successfully command the weather gods. At least *starting* the peas this time of year is easy. Germination is so reliable now that I seed the peas directly in the soil without a worry. I dig their trench 2 inches deep and 8 inches wide, after having worked in 5 pounds of 5-10-5 fertilizer for every 100 square feet of bed to replenish the nutrients depleted by the very active spring and summer growth. I treat the seeds with legume inoculant and then plant them as I did earlier, broadcasting casually for a spacing of about 1 inch. I draw an inch of soil over them, then keep the bed moist until the seeds sprout. This is also the time to erect the trellises for tall-growing varieties like Sugar Snap. Bush types receive a more natural trellis: branches left over from spring prunings. I just push these into the ground beside the emerging pea plants, which grab the branches and climb right on up.

**My row of parsnips, safely off in one corner of the garden, are doing beautifully in their individually tailored planting pockets.**

**Peppers**   Though Americans are accustomed to eating their peppers green, Europeans think that this borders on the uncivilized. They like their peppers red. In fact, almost all peppers will turn red if left on the vine long enough, though from the astronomical cost of sweet red peppers in the grocery stores you'd think they were rare and exotic varieties. They aren't. Growers charge more for them because consumers want the bright colors. When we grow our own peppers, we can take them any way we choose, of course, and in July my first peppers will be large enough to pick. While I leave a good many more on the vine to sweeten and turn red, it is a good idea to pick peppers as they become table-sized, encouraging the plants to produce many more.

When harvesting, I cut the fruit from their vines, leaving ½ inch of stem on the pepper, and I take care not to loosen the main plants themselves in the soil. I also side-dress each plant with half a handful of 5-10-5 fertilizer per plant, scratched in around the base, to encourage a second set of fruit.

**Potatoes**   My Red Norlands that always come first will already have had a few tubers lifted from under them, and this month will see the vines dying off. When the plants show decline, I'll lift one hill at a time for the table, using my spading

One of my garden favorites — and a special taste treat!

fork gently to turn up the tubers. My mid- and late-season varieties should continue to grow through the month, if I keep the Colorado potato beetle at bay. The fabric covering the potatoes is not quite wide enough to afford total protection, because the vines are so robust that they lift it right off the ground, allowing beetles to slip beneath. However, it does reduce their damage considerably, and gives the plants a few more weeks of unchecked growth. It also means less time spent waging hand-to-hand combat against adult beetles and orange egg cases alike.

July's zucchini is bold, beautiful, and the perfect size for harvesting.

**Summer Squash**   The bright yellow blossoms of summer squash, so soon followed by young fruit, really hold center stage in the July garden, but a single-minded pest can quickly lay waste to the whole patch if I'm not careful. The squash vine borer is active in July, at least in these parts. Females lay eggs at the base of my squash plants. These hatch larvae that feed on the interior flesh of the vines. A deposit resembling sawdust, collecting at the base of the vine or at the point of entry, is the first sign of infestation. Dusting the base of the plant with rotenone can help, if done early in the worms' life cycle. Once the leaves begin to go limp, though, more drastic measures are called for, because this is a sign that the insect has nearly killed the plant. I use my pocketknife to slit open the stem and cut out any borers that are feeding on the squash. This is major surgery, and to help with recovery, I hill up over any area that has been opened, then water well. Squash will root along the stem, and if I've acted early enough, this should save the plant.

Here's another measure, passed on to me by a viewer, that works well and that requires no chemicals. I cut foot-square pieces of aluminum foil, make slits from one border to the center, and slip these mats, shiny side up, around the base of the squash vines. Glare and reflection may disorient egg-laying adults, or the eggs may simply get cooked by solar radiation. Whatever, I suffer no borer damage with these metallic mats in place.

In mid-July I sow another crop of summer squash, using the same techniques described earlier, and after the middle of this month the vine borer is, in my region anyway, much less of a problem.

**Tomatoes**   July has barely begun when Early Girl, Sweet 100, and, a bit later, Gardener's Delight are basket ready. Celebrity, Champion, Better Bush, Jet Star, and Superfantastic come midmonth, and the Beefsteaks (those one-slice-makes-a-sandwich tomatoes) close out July.

Tomatoes in cages are easy to look after, and now that they're supporting plants that look me squarely in the eye (I'm 6 feet tall), my cages really come into their own. This month, I'll side-dress the plants after the first harvest, scratching in half a handful of 5-10-5 fertilizer around the base of each plant, taking care not to let the granules touch the stem itself. The disease-resistant hybrids I grow are flourishing this time of year, undeterred by wilts or mosaics that were once so troublesome to tomato growers. And my Victory Garden regimen of regular watering (1 full inch per week) and carefully maintained pH (6.5 throughout the garden, save the acid-loving potatoes) prevents blossom-end rot and some of the other physical blemishing (catfacing, for example) that can plague this crop.

**You'll need a napkin ready for these juicy tomatoes.**

# VICTORY GARDEN BERRIES

Some of gardening's sweetest rewards come from the berry patches. Fresh-picked strawberries, raspberries, and blueberries slipped from the bushes at peak perfection are tasty delights, indeed. The berry patch is really the garden's dessert shoppe, and all three — blueberries, raspberries, and strawberries —are of easy culture.

**Blueberries**  I plant blueberries in the spring where they will receive at least 6 hours of direct sunlight. They are perennial shrubs, so siting is important because they will occupy their spot for years. Six bushes will provide well for a family once they've come fully into their own, which takes several years. I plant three different varieties that come ripe at different times during the season. Blueberries are listed as early, midseason, and late in catalog descriptions. Choosing these three varieties will extend the berry harvest a full month. Each group should be represented in the garden. Blueberries are available from garden centers and through the mail, with the latter likely to provide the best choice, especially if you deal with a berry specialist. Blueray (early), Bluecrop (midseason), and Herbert (for late season) are

**High bush blueberries ready for the Thomson taste test. ◄**

good choices. Having more than one variety also improves pollination and increases yield.

Blueberries prefer an acid soil with a pH of 5.0, rich in organics and well drained. I add several inches of peat moss mixed in thoroughly to each planting hole; 5 inches of sawdust mulch covers the patch, and both help lower the soil pH. The plants are set 6 feet apart in 2-foot squares cut out of lawn, at the same depth they were growing in the nursery. I water them in with water-soluble fertilizer for a strong start. Pruning at this early stage is limited to cutting back any broken or crossing branches and damaged roots.

It will take a couple of years for these bushes to bear a significant amount of fruit. I fertilize every year in June with

half a handful of 10-10-10 fertilizer for every 12 inches of height, and keep the sawdust mulch 5 inches thick around each plant.

The only pruning necessary for the first 2 or 3 years is to remove crossing branches, spindly, twiggy growth, and head back exuberant shoots. I maintain a couple of inches between branches and encourage the thicker, stronger branches to develop. The best berries are on 2- to 3-year-old wood. These will continue producing for several years, then peter out.

When the plants are fully established, I remove about 20 percent of the oldest wood every year, and old, declining branches are removed at ground level.

**A row of blueberries mulched with sawdust. I prune back thin, spindly top growth (above), and remove any crossing branches (below).**

**As soon as the berries start to color up, I cover the bushes with tobacco netting.**

Mind the birds when berries become ripe. I protect my patch with tobacco netting strung over lengths of bent plastic tubing, but I always leave a bush or two exposed, in line with my philosophy of sharing a bit of the garden's gifts with the birds (see the feature on "Gardening to Attract Birds"). One last tip: Color is not the best indication of truly ripe blueberries. I wait 2 to 3 weeks after they've turned a ripe, rich blue, and then let the occasional tasting tell me when they're just right. Tough job, but someone has to do it. And an especially nice fall treat is the bright color of the blueberry leaves, which makes them a good choice as a landscape plant.

**It doesn't get much better!**

**Raspberries** Raspberries are true homegrown treasures. They're so fragile that they want to be vine-ripened, and really should be enjoyed immediately. There are red, black, and gold raspberries, and they can fruit from early through late summer. Those that fruit in late summer are called, illogically, fall bearers. They're *all* delicious!

They're also eager bearers that can be invasive, so they inhabit a separate corner of the Victory Garden. Like blueberries, they need full sun for at least 6 hours and a rich, free-draining soil. The pH level should be around 6.0. I have two rows of raspberries, each of which is 2 feet wide and 15 feet long, with 4 feet between rows.

Raspberry plants can be bought in the spring from garden centers or from mail-order houses, and I make sure to buy stock that's certified to be disease free. The best time to plant any of the three varieties is early spring. I prepare the soil by working in 3 inches of well-rotted manure or compost before setting the canes out.

The canes are planted 2 feet apart in the row, at the same depth that they grew in the nursery. I make sure to water the canes in well and then set up their training system.

I've adopted my training system from a cane fruit specialist I met at the Royal Horticultural Society's Trial Gardens in Wisley, England. For both June- and fall-bearing varieties, I use this system, which keeps the bushes looking neat and provides easy access to pickers. First, I sink 8-foot cedar posts 30 inches deep into the ground at each corner of the raspberry patch. Then, at 30-, 45-, and 60-inch intervals above ground level I string guy wires of vinyl-wrapped, multistrand cable around the 4 posts, securing the wires with galvanized staples. These wires contain and guide the canes as they grow.

Now, about pruning. Raspberries bear in different ways, and this bears on how they're pruned. Summer-fruiting raspberries fruit on wood that grew the previous season. Fall bearers (really late-summer bearers, as I mentioned earlier)

bear on the current season's growth. In the first year for fall bearers, no pruning is necessary. After the first year, though, fall bearers are cut right back to the ground, leaving just an inch of stubble. They'll put on vigorous vegetative growth the next season, flower, and fruit — after which they'll be cut right back down to stubble again — and every season thereafter. Summer-fruiting raspberries produce canes one year that flower and fruit the following year. In that same fruiting year, they make new vegetative growth for the following season's crop. All the canes that have fruited are removed from summer bearers each fall. These spent canes will be brown and woody-looking. For either type of pruning, stout shears and sturdy gloves are a must.

In June I apply a side-dressing of 10-10-10 fertilizer to the area around each raspberry plant, using 1 pound for every 10 feet of row, then lay down a

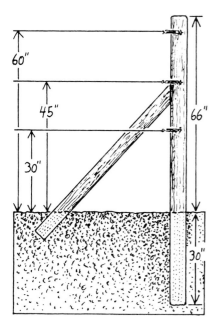

**Prune back old canes of summer-fruiting raspberries.**

4-inch mulch of sawdust. I water the patch consistently throughout the season, delivering the Victory Garden standard of 1 inch of water per week.

June-bearing raspberries will be ready for the taking in — what else? — June. The fall-bearing varieties will come ready in late July, August, and September. It's important to pick raspberries as soon as they ripen. When they're ready to go, you'll find that they slide easily from the little white core that remains on the stem. I use small containers to pick these little jewels, so that those on the bottom are not crushed as I go along. I don't wash the delicate berries, either — that seems to dull their fine flavor and can hasten rot, even when they are refrigerated.

A fall application of well-rotted manure or compost will improve next season's crop.

**Strawberries** The glossy photographs and glowing catalog descriptions of strawberries never prepare me for the plants that the mail brings in early spring. A tangle of roots, some still clotted with dead leaves, maybe a hint of green here and there — sorry-looking specimens indeed. The plants come in bundles of 25 or 50, all held together with a single rubber band. Remember, I tell myself, all great strawberry beds started this way.

There are two kinds of strawberries. Everbearing varieties yield lightly through the summer, then produce their main harvest in mid to late summer. June-bearing varieties yield primarily in late spring and June. Though their bearing time is shorter, the overall yield from June bearers is greater. Different varieties are suited to different climatic conditions throughout the country (as well as being imbued with degrees of resistance to different diseases). Your local county extension agent or garden cen-

be at soil level. If it's too high, the plant will dry out; if too deep, the growing point will suffocate and stop growing. After the original plant is in place, it will produce runners, and these will root and create daughter plants. Three of these daughter plants are allowed to develop, each about 10 inches from the mother, arranged so that the 4 form a square, with the plants at each corner. In the first year of planting, the mother plant will produce lightly or not at all. Next season, the mother plant will produce heavily, with the new daughter plants also producing well. After this second season, the original plant and 2 daughters are taken out, leaving one new mother to produce 3 new daughters. This system balances the plants' constant spawning of new plants with berry production. The goal is to maintain both, and this system does that. You obviously have to pay some attention to

ter fruit specialist is the best source of advice on which varieties will do best in your particular area.

It's true that strawberries are perennial plants, but one set of plants can't be counted on to produce forever. After a couple of seasons, production from original plants (also called "mother" plants) will decrease, while susceptibility to various diseases will increase. For this reason, strawberries are grown in a way that ensures continual production of new plants. I've tried lots of systems, and have settled on two as being highly desirable. I'll get to them in a moment. First, soil preparation. Spring is the best time to plant strawberries, and a traditional bit of wisdom holds that it's permissible to do so when deciduous trees are beginning to leaf out. When planting time

**Sweet strawberry success.**

arrives, I soak the straggly plants in a bucket of water to awaken their root systems. While they're doing that, I prepare the soil. My standard Victory Garden pH of 6.5 is fine for strawberries. I work into their beds several inches of compost or well-rotted manure and then go about planting. With either of the systems I'll describe in a moment, spacing between rows is 24 inches.

The first system is the more economical of the two, with slightly lower yields and smaller individual berries. It's called the *spaced matted row* system. In this growing scheme, mother plants are spaced 24 inches apart. They're set in just at the point where roots and stem meet. This is called the crown, and it must

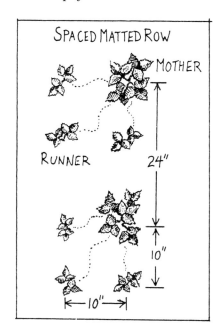

the plants, pruning and directing them after the initial planting, but the reward is a berry patch that will keep on producing for years.

My other system is more extravagant and less work, and uses the black plastic of which I've grown so fond. Before planting, I soak the new plants in water and prepare the raised bed just as I did for the previous type of planting. Before setting the strawberry plants in, though, I work 5 pounds of 14-14-14 slow-release fertilizer into the soil for every 100 square feet of bed, along with several inches of rotted manure or compost. Then, after raking the bed into shape, I stretch the black plastic over it and bury the edges all around. I cut 4-inch squares from the plastic every 12 inches and set the plants in just to the point where roots meet stems, as described above. And that's it. The shoots sent out will quickly wither on the plastic. That means only the main plants grow, and they do *grow*. This system truly produces superplants. The black plastic eliminates competing weeds, conserves moisture, provides more heat for early fruiting. Berries stay clean on the plastic, and, because each plant puts all its energy into producing berries, the latter are huge and supersweet. Depending on the variety I plant, I may have a light harvest the first season and then a super harvest the next year, or just one grand harvest during the second growing season. This system requires that I plant new strawberry plants each season, but the reward in size and quality of berries — as well as the reduced work with the

**My preferred strawberry system: plants spaced 1 foot apart on black plastic. This gives me premium berries with almost no weeding and no runners to space out.**

black plastic — has led me to favor it, and it's the system I use most in the Victory Garden.

With either system, the Victory Garden regimen of 1 inch of water per week is fine. After harvest, with the first system, I fertilize the plants with 5 pounds of 10-10-10 fertilizer for every 100 square feet of bed space. And I mulch the plants in the matted row system with about 3 inches of salt marsh hay, to keep the berries clean and off the ground once they begin to form. Finally, with either system I pinch off the blossoms that form during the first year. This produces the strongest plants possible.

The berries in both systems will be delectable to birds, so I protect the beds with fine-mesh black plastic netting supported on #12 wire hoops or bent PVC tubing.

Strawberries are ready for harvest about a month after

the plants have bloomed. I harvest only berries that are completely red, and I never pull the berries themselves. Instead, I pinch off the stem behind it with my fingernails and thumb.

Varieties I like are Fairfax, an old standby, Earliglow, Sparkle, and Ozark Beauty. As I mentioned earlier, the varieties best suited for your area may well vary, so consult your local county extension agent or garden center fruit specialist.

**So that I get more berries than the birds, I cover the bed with nylon netting.**

The August garden shows broccoli getting ready to head, onions drying off, corn needing to be picked for dinner, and Inca marigolds adding a bit of color on a gray day.

# AUGUST

# AUGUST

August's harvest is rich, with all the heat-loving crops coming into full productivity. Melon and pumpkin vines seem about to consume the garden. Eggplants glisten after the morning watering. The Gypsy peppers continue to amaze me with the number of fruit set. Later on, the lima beans are ready to pick, and I'll probably not be able to survive all the zucchini. It's a heady time indeed, but experience has taught me to keep my wits about me now. The days will be getting cooler and shorter, and these mainstay crops from the tropics won't be around, at least in New England, much longer. Thus, despite the bounty, I need to be ready for next month's much cooler weather. That means finding space to set out cauliflower, Chinese cabbage, radishes, lettuce, and spinach. With an early August start, all these lovers of cool weather should produce beautifully through September.

August is also the month when I'm saddled with a particularly enjoyable chore: visiting many of the exceptional gardens entered in my annual "Victory Garden" contest. Every year I'm gratified — and educated — by excellent backyard gardeners all over the country. These vegetable-gardening enthusiasts have developed many ingenious techniques of their own to deal with vagaries of terrain and climate. I'm always impressed by the length to which serious gardeners will go to harvest superb vegetables, and I've noted that two things are common to virtually every one: maximum use of garden space, and careful, regular attention to soil preparation. Those are the keys to successful, productive vegetable gardening, and where they're practiced, the crops flourish.

August, despite the overflowing harvest baskets, is not without problems. Hot weather brings with it the need for vigilant watering. If the weather is really scorching, I pay particular attention to the weeds, which can compete with vegetables for soil moisture, and to my mulches, which I'll deepen just a bit to lessen evaporative loss.

**Start Indoors**
Chinese cabbage
Lettuce

**Transplant**
Lettuce

**Plant in Garden**
Beans
Cauliflower
Chinese cabbage
Lettuce
Radishes
Spinach
Turnips

**Fertilize**
Chinese cabbage
Eggplant
Okra

**Harvest**
Beans
Eggplant
Melons
Okra

**Mulch**
Spinach
Turnips

An unusually warm summer rewards me with a good crop of pole lima beans, but New England's unpredictable weather has taught me that the best bet is with bush varieties.

**Beans**   My crop of bush lima beans will be ready for picking late in August, while the pole beans planted in June have been producing steadily all month. I like to harvest both types of beans when young, because I've found that older beans are too tough for my taste. I keep an eye on the pods and pick them daily if necessary. I want to send the plants the right message: "Keep producing." Pole beans I harvest while they still snap cleanly and before the bean seeds fully develop. With the limas, I let the pods fill out completely, but harvest well before the pods turn yellow.

During the first week of August, I plant a last crop of beans, using quick-maturing bush beans like Provider and Contender. I seed in a wide trench as I did in May, working in 5-10-5 fertilizer at the same rate to get them growing vigorously. I cover the seeds with ½ inch of soilless medium and keep the bed moist until the seeds sprout. This crop must grow quickly through August so it has time to set a good crop for a late September harvest.

**Cauliflower**   July's seedlings will be ready, in August, for their move to the open garden. I try to pick a cloudy day for this, to help ease the shock of transplanting. The beds will have been limed to raise the pH to 7.5 to help protect against clubroot, and I'll work in 5 pounds of 5-10-5 fertilizer per 100 square feet of bed. I've taken 2 crops off the bed where cauliflower is being planted, and it's very important to fertilize now so growth is vigorous.

After 5 days in the cold frame, I set the seedlings, which are now 4 to 6 inches tall, into the soil a little deeper than they've been growing in their cell-packs, spaced 18 inches apart. I give them a welcome watering of water-soluble fertilizer, too. Keeping the plants well watered is not easy to do on those sweltering days, and as I deliver early-morning and late-afternoon waterings I often envy my father, who, at eighty-five, is still an avid cauliflower grower. He spends 4 or 5 months each year in Maine, where cauliflower thrives. He's not far from the seacoast town of Camden, and there he can grow cauliflower right through the summer. The days often begin wrapped in a blanket of thick coastal fog, which burns off during the late morning and then rolls back in during late afternoon. Cooled and moistened by this ocean air, the cauliflower flourishes.

**Chinese Cabbage**   Come the first of August, I'm ready to plant out the fall crop of Chinese cabbage. About 6 choice heads is what I'm after for the late September and early October harvest. This season change from warm August to cool fall suits their growing needs just fine. If I have enough open ground, I'll seed out directly into a bed enriched with 5 pounds of 10-10-10 fertilizer per 100 square feet. Three seeds are planted ½ inch deep at 12-inch intervals, and I'll thin to the strongest seedling in a couple of weeks. If space is tight, I'll sow indoors in 3-inch peat pots and move into the mid-August garden when there's room. He who forgets that Chinese cabbage resents being transplanted will suffer plants that prematurely flower, so setting out young plants in peat pots is the perfect solution to that problem. I peel back the tops of the peat pots when I set them in, so the August sun doesn't wick moisture out. I also water them in with a water-soluble fertilizer — this heavy feeder appreciates all the nutrients it can get.

**Cucumbers**   The cucumber vines that have given their all are pulled and composted now. In the space left by their departure, I can plant a quick crop like lettuce. But if I have enough of that growing elsewhere, I'll replenish the cucumber beds with 2 inches of compost or manure, lime as needed to adjust pH, and add 2 pounds of 10-10-10 fertilizer for every 100 square feet of bed. Then I'll sow the cover crop. If the harvest has been completed in early August, I'll sow 1 pound of quick-growing buckwheat for every 100 square feet of area. Buckwheat is frost tender, and I'll turn it under before it's killed by frost in September or October. If my cucumber harvest has lasted until late in August, I'll go ahead and sow winter rye seed, which will take the beds through the winter.

**Eggplant**   I like eggplant when they're a bit immature — 2 to 3 inches long — but most I leave to size up fully. These get the time-tested ripeness evaluation. I gently press my thumb into the fruit. If the shiny black eggplant dulls and stays a bit dented, it's ready. (If the flesh springs back and shines, then I'm

The taste, of course . . . but also the beauty of eggplant and Ruby Swiss chard.

too early.) I snip off the fruit and 1 inch of stem. I expect my eggplants to produce right through September, and to keep them growing strongly I side-dress with half a handful of 5-10-5 fertilizer around each plant after first harvest.

Another word about verticillium wilt: It may have claimed a few fruit by this time, though Dusky, my favorite variety, has some tolerance to this disease and usually holds up nicely. I've also found that less-tolerant varieties can survive if they're side-dressed and given weekly feedings with water-soluble fertilizer. It may be that the extra nutrients keep them growing just fast enough to stay one step ahead of the disease.

**Lettuce**   This month I'll be starting, indoors, my fall crop of lettuce. I sow the seeds in 4-inch pots filled with soilless medium, just as I did back in the spring, and bottom-water the pots to moisten the medium thoroughly. I put them on a heat pad at 75 degrees to produce seedlings in 3 days, and then move them to a sunny spot. When the seedlings' true leaves show, I transplant them to cell-packs filled with soilless medium, bottom-water again, and give them a day out of full sun to recover from the trauma of transplanting.

**Melons**   I doubt if there's a crop I look forward to harvesting more than melons. For Northern gardeners they might be called the ultimate challenge; up here it's difficult to achieve the same sweet flavor and tender flesh that come so much more easily to hot-clime growers. Varietal selection has a lot to do with my Victory Garden success, and I'd still nominate Burpee's Ambrosia as my favorite — the one melon I'd take to a desert island with me. But I also know that too much moisture at the time of ripening affects taste adversely. While there's not much to be done about rainfall, I can be careful with watering. The trick is to give enough, but not too much. My approach, which seems to work well, is to hold watering, once fruit has set and reached full size, until the plants just begin to show signs of wilting.

Soon after that, the long-awaited harvest will arrive. There are two reliable indicators of ripeness in a melon. The first is a heady fragrance that grows stronger as the thermometer climbs. The second is a slipping disk. At the base of the stem that attaches the vine to the fruit, there is a ½-inch disk that will recede and start to pull away from the melon when it is ripe. If the disk slides off the fruit with gentle thumb pressure, I know the melon's ready to go.

When the last melon's been harvested, I pull the black plastic off the bed and, if it's in good shape, roll it up for use next year. I work in 10-10-10 fertilizer (2 pounds for every 100 square feet of bed), add 2 inches of manure or compost, and rake the bed smooth. Finally, I sow my soil-replenishing cover crop of winter rye, using 1 pound of seed for every 100 square feet of ground sowed.

**My favorite cantaloupe, Burpee's Ambrosia Hybrid, is nearing full ripeness. When the disc that joins stem to fruit begins to shrivel, get the knife ready.**

**Okra**   The key with okra (even more than with most vegetables) is to harvest early. I cut them at 3 to 5 inches, leaving a bit of stem behind. After taking the first harvest, I side-dress with 5-10-5 fertilizer (1 cup per 10 feet of row) to coax continued fruiting.

**Radishes**   It's time to sow my fall radishes in the Victory Garden, a crop I always anticipate with more pleasure than that of spring. Fall radishes are consistently superior to those grown in spring — large, juicy, cool-tasting — because they so much prefer maturing in cool weather.

Before planting, I replenish the hardworking soil by scratching in 1 cup of 5-10-5 fertilizer for every 10 feet of row, and turning in 2 inches of compost as well. With the bed raked

The mid- to late-August-sown radishes are well spaced and soon will be free of weeds for unchecked growth. The Victory Garden cold frame is back out to extend the growing season well into fall.

smooth, I use my planting board to make ¼-inch furrows, and sow the radish seeds 1 inch apart, with 6 inches between rows. I cover them with ¼ inch of soilless medium, water well, and wait for the seedlings to appear in about a week. When they're up, I thin out every other plant, leaving a final spacing of 2 inches.

Since these radishes will be growing into cool weather, I can choose from lots of varieties: whites, multicolored, cylindrical (Icicle or Breakfast), and even the white, rose, or black-skinned long-storage radishes. The point is that I needn't stick with the red globe types only.

**Spinach**   It's been too long between fresh spinach harvests, but now that the weather is cooling, it's time to plant a midmonth sowing for September eating. I first work in 1 cup of 10-10-10 fertilizer for every 10 feet of row, then rake the bed smooth. Then I open the spinach trench, 12 inches wide and 1 inch deep. I scatter the seed the length and width of the trench, spacing the seeds about 1 inch apart. An inch of soil covers the seeds. At this time of year, I like to mulch lightly right over the seed bed with salt marsh hay before watering. This will help keep the bed evenly moist while the seeds germinate. They'll be up and growing before long, and — once again — here's my fail-safe harvest rule: When the leaves touch, pick. There will be several harvests before individual plants stand 6 inches apart, the first one being small but *very* tender greens that make superb salads.

**Turnips**   I said before that turnips are tasty, and that's true. They're also a rich source of nutrients with most of the vitamins C, A, B, E, and minerals concentrated not in the roots but in the greens. An ounce of turnip greens, for instance, has 5 times the amount of vitamin C that's contained in an equal amount of root. That might explain why turnip greens are so popular in the South.

I'm looking for roots with my August sowing of turnips, though, and have chosen two varieties with good flavor, Purple Top and Golden Perfection. I plant seed ½ inch deep in prepared furrows, allowing 1 inch between seeds. One foot separates the rows. I cover the seeds with ¼ inch of soilless medium, water them in, and then thin to a final spacing of 4 inches in the rows when the seedlings are 3 to 4 inches high. In late August, if the weather is still hot, I'll mulch the bed with 2 inches of salt marsh hay to keep moisture in and to keep the plants cool.

An August sowing of Purple Top turnips will produce beauties like these to be enjoyed this fall.

# SECRETS OF THE SILVER TROWEL GARDENERS

Since 1979, the "Victory Garden" television show has sponsored an annual vegetable gardening contest. Each year, viewers send in crop lists, diagrams, and photos of their gardens. A preliminary screening reduces the entries to a manageable number. Then our judges make on-site evaluations. From this select group, the finalists are chosen. I visit these with our television crew to record segments for national broadcast on the PBS television series. And from this *crème de la crème*, viewers vote for their favorite. We've showcased the finest gardens throughout this country, and I've learned many useful lessons from these masterful gardeners.

The one common element linking *all* the great vegetable gardeners I've visited is meticulous attention to soil preparation. My own program, pretty conscientious in its own right, is outlined in "Steps to Victorious Gardening." I've been impressed, over the years, with the great lengths to which other gardeners go to enhance

This beautiful and very productive garden is tended by 1986 contest finalist Nan Norseen. Intensive cropping on raised beds with mulched paths, surrounded by lawn, caught our judges' eye. ◄

soil in some pretty unlikely locations. For instance, I'll never forget Andrew Biggerstaff of Portland, Oregon. He was in his late eighties when I met him, and had been gardening all his life. Now retired, he'd *really* become involved in gardening. He lived on one of the hills overlooking Portland, and as we snaked up the steep, winding roads I wondered where on earth he'd find a flat square foot to cultivate. He lived right on top of the hill, and, with the exception of a small level area to one side of his house, the land was very steep. He built 75 steps on either side of the garden, which measured about 80 by 80 feet. And he had tamed the ferocious slope singlehandedly by creating a number of stone wall–contained terraces. Looking after the garden was no easy task, but Andrew solved it with compost and lots of manure. The latter was dropped off at the top of his driveway, where he loaded it into wheelbarrows and then sent it down a chute to whatever level he happened to be working on. He'd set a barricade across at that level, then go down and shovel the manure onto his beds. He grew superb vegetables in this unlikely setting and, with his raised terraces, could garden comfortably at waist level. From Andrew I learned that nothing will keep a determined gardener from his creative endeavors.

I've often sung the praises of leaves as a great source of organic material, and Bob Hardison of Chapel Hill, North Carolina, used them as well as any gardener I've seen. Every year he collected all the leaves on his property, then prevailed on the city to drop a truckload or two as well. He kept them in a cinderblock pen and added them to his compost piles as they emptied. His vegetables thrived on the leaf-enriched soil in his beds.

North Carolina produced another ingenious finalist, Chuck Brackett. His specialty was manure tea. He'd created wood-enclosed raised beds, carefully engineered and featuring elaborate trellising to support his 8-foot tomato vines and equally rambunctious pole beans. Chuck composted and used rotted manure, but also gave his plants frequent boosts with manure tea, adapting the principles of moonshine stills to brew his rich solutions. His basic ingredients were 55-gallon barrels, water, manure, and something to suspend the manure in the barrel. Rather than tying the manure in a burlap bag (traditional but short-lived, as the burlap soon rots), Chuck took a 5-gallon plastic pail and cut several slits in the sides, 1 inch wide and 5 inches high.

He lined the pail with aluminum wire screen, and filled it with manure. A lid held everything in place. This "secret weapon" was suspended in the barrel and steeped for at least 24 hours. The result was a rich liquid fertilizer that plants took up readily. His was such a realistic-looking operation that revenue agents flying over the countryside looking for stills occasionally landed and came by for a closer inspection. Seemed that it wasn't hard to convince them that *his* brand of mash wasn't for human consumption.

Chuck also constructed custom beds that impressed me. They were raised beds walled with brick, with aluminum wire screening covering the soil. To each bed he'd add organic material, adjust the pH, and then custom-fit the season's insect barriers. Some were short, for lettuce and other greens, while others were as much as 3 feet high to allow for growth of taller plants. The overall system was as effective as it was attractive.

One of the most eye-pleasing gardens I saw anywhere belonged to Ewing Walker in Maine. He lived right on the rugged coast in a beautifully restored old home. His vegetable gardening had to be aesthetically pleasing as well as satisfying for the table, to complement that lovely old house of his. His solution was to make raised beds 3 feet above grade, with grass strips lying between. He framed the beds with 6x6 timbers, painted to match the house. The beds were beautiful to look at, and produced vegetables that the bony, unenhanced coastal soil alone could never have managed. Raising the beds so high helped warm the growing area after the long Maine winter, and made for stoopless gardening as well.

Ewing was doing with grass strips what I'd seen done at a number of other contest gardens: incorporating the vegetable garden into a small backyard landscaping plan. Rather than cut an entire patch from the lawn, contest winner Helen Rood, outside Minneapolis, placed individual wide-row beds between grass strips. This gave her access to the garden even during the soggiest weather, and lent an especially refined look (not unlike the maze gardens of stately English mansions) to her yard.

Contest finalists have overcome lots of challenges in their zeal. During the contest's first year, I visited a doctor in rural New York state. His practice was at home, and he left time in his busy schedule, every day, to spend an hour or so relaxing in the garden. His area harbored quite a deer population, which he eventually frustrated with an 8-foot fence all around the garden. That kept them on the right side of the fence, an important achievement to someone who put up as much produce as Dr. Pike, who had an elaborate system of climatically controlled root cellars with rooms at different temperature and humidity levels that allowed him to keep the harvest well into the new year.

Good gardeners tend to be a resourceful lot. Our winners the first year lived right along

A few years ago this now lovely Camden, New Jersey, garden sported only trash, debris, and weeds. Then two dedicated gardeners transformed it into a Silver Trowel Award winner.

the Massachusetts coast, in a particularly windy location. They buffered that by locating the garden in among trees. They also had a sandy patch of ground to contend with, and for help they turned to the sea, hauling up loads of seaweed. It's a fine organic amendment with ample trace elements. They'd rinse the salt off and let it dry in the sun before using it in compost and for mulching. This partly explained the incredible richness of their greens, spinach, chard, and so forth — but not entirely. Credit also had to go to their special fertilizer — sea bird guano collected from a derelict military facility built during World War II to guard Boston Harbor. Gulls and other shore birds found this concrete tower a

useful sanctuary, and this "livestock" took no looking after.

Finally, there was the couple in Camden, New Jersey, who did more than their part to reclaim a former dump site. Michael Devlin and Valerie Frick turned an eyesore into a garden where food, flowers, and herbs thrived. They were even able to use a discarded engine block, turning it into a planter! This intrepid couple personified one of the characteristics I've encountered again and again in my garden visits — the feeling of immense satisfaction that derives from reclaiming badly used land.

That's one of the pleasures of gardening, but certainly not the only. The list is inexhaustible, in fact, and each time I've looked on as a new gardener has regaled me with tales of his super tomatoes or sugar-sweet corn, I've realized this anew. There's no end to it!

The Victory Garden journal is one of my most important aids. Memory dims as the months pass, but the journal never fades. Here, I'm noting how this season's new varieties of kale and summer squash performed: vigor, yield, insect and disease resistance, maturing time, and so on.

# SEPTEMBER

# SEPTEMBER

Weather can be my undoing in September. Tropical storms with damaging winds often work their way up the coast. And if a harvest moon comes near the end of the month, especially on clear and windless nights, it could bring a killing frost with it. I'm prepared to go out and cover frost-tender crops like tomatoes, peppers, and eggplant for a night or two because I know that this brief cold spell will generally be followed by a period of good growing weather.

In September, the coming on of cool-season crops offers some welcome additions to the table. Planting does slow considerably except in the dusted-off cold frames, which I keep filled with lettuce seedlings. Beds that open up are quickly seeded with soil-improving winter rye, and compost that's been breaking down in summer's heat is ready to be spread over the raised beds.

There are lots of notes logged in my Victory Garden journal this month. My memory from year to year is not nearly as reliable as notes recorded through the season. I find them particularly helpful with new varieties and techniques. I note yield under favorable and not-so-favorable growing conditions; disease resistance; eating quality; vigor and productivity; timing — was I too early or too late? Here's a sample remark:

*Experiment with mail-order potato eyes disappointing — yield low — vines looked stunted. Stick to whole, small tubers.*

I planted a short row of potato eyes, which have recently been appearing in mail-order catalogs. They weigh almost nothing to ship and are easy to handle, so I tried a row. In this particular season, they were disappointing, taking up as much space as seed potatoes but producing only a fraction of the crop. No improvement there, so I'll go back to whole, small tubers until something new comes along.

Here's another:

*Parsnips — mistake to plant a crop before parsnip — delayed parsnip seeding not doing as well.*

I tried to get an early spring crop on the bed where parsnip was to go. That worked all right but held the bed too long. By the time I seeded parsnip, it was late and resulted in acceptable but not trophy-sized parsnips.

The grammar may not be flawless, but the information I record on the spot, when everything is fresh before me, will prove invaluable next season and beyond. What's the old saying about those who don't understand history being doomed to repeat it? Not so in the Victory Garden.

**Plant in Garden**
Lettuce
Spinach

**Fertilize**
Broccoli
Spinach

**Harvest**
Beans
Broccoli
Cabbage
Carrots
Cauliflower
Celery
Chinese cabbage
Leeks
Lettuce
Peas
Radishes
Summer squash
Turnips
Winter squash

| PLANT | VARIETY | SOURCE | DATE SEEDED | CONTAINER | DATE GERM. | GERM. | 1st TRANS. | 2nd TRANS. | COLDFRAME/OUTSIDE | GARDEN | 1st FLOWER OR HARVEST | COMMENTS |
|---|---|---|---|---|---|---|---|---|---|---|---|---|
| Tomato | Patio | Stokes | 3/17 | 4" | 3/23 | Good | 3/30 | 4/29 | into 3 | 5/9 in wall o water |  | Still no ripe fruit by 7/19 |
| " | Better Boy VFN | Stokes | 3/17 | 4" | 3/22 | Good | 3/30 | 4/29 |  |  | 7/16 | Cracking of first fruit. Good fruit set. |
| " | Celebrity | Harris | 3/17 | 4" | 3/22 | Good | 3/30 | 4/29 |  | 5/9 wall water | 7/12 | First fruit at orange-pink stage 7/19 Vine small |
| " | Supersonic | Harris | 3/17 | 4" | 3/24 | Good | 4/3 | 4/29 |  | 5/9 " |  | Good fruit set |
| " | Whopper VFNT | Park | 3/17 | 4" | 3/22 | Good | 3/30 | 4/29 |  | 5/9 " |  | Weaker set than Campbell 1327, Revolution |
| " | Better Bush | Park | 3/17 | 4" | 3/23 | Good | 3/30 | 4/29 |  | 5/9 " |  | Very heavy set, but many fruit malformed |
| " | Revolution | Twilley | 3/17 | 4" | 3/23 | Good | 3/30 | 4/29 |  | 5/9 " | 7/16 |  |
| " | President | Park | 3/17 | 4" | 3/23 | Good | 3/30 | 4/29 |  |  |  |  |
| " | Floramerica | Burpee | 3/17 | 4" | 3/22 | Good | 3/30 | 4/29 |  | 5/9 " | 7/16 | Earliest of regular size tomatoes again. Fruit smaller this year |
| " | Quick Pick | Park | 3/17 | 4" | 3/22 | Good | 3/30 | 4/29 |  | 5/9 " | 7/7 |  |

A sample journal page. Four months from now, when I'm ready to plan next year's garden, the information will prove invaluable.

These Kentucky Wonder pole beans are only one of a dozen or more varieties I grow every year. I'll be harvesting beans all through the month.

**Beans** My midsummer-sown beans are producing abundantly in September. In fact, with the repeated sowings of short rows, I've had fresh beans for the table continuously since mid-June.

When I was a kid, we grew two types of beans in our garden — bush beans and pole beans, one variety of each. Now I might grow 15 varieties a year, still modest compared to a gardener close by who grows over 200 varieties annually. He's determined to help preserve the rich gene pool among this most valuable crop, so his collection contains varieties long since out of the commercial trade. His efforts are important because some of these varieties are exceptionally flavorful, some are highly disease resistant, some very productive. In fact, one of my favorite beans is an heirloom type, White French Crystal. They are not easy to come by, so I save a crop for seeding next year by allowing a few vines to ripen their bean pods fully. They are shelled when the pod has shriveled but before they split and spill the beans. I store them in a cool dry spot (a covered jar makes a good container) over the winter and then have good bean seeds ready for next year's planting.

When the bean beds finally are finished, I cut the vines off just above ground level, leaving their nitrogen-fixing roots in the soil. I scratch the soil lightly with my cultivator, adding 2 pounds of 10-10-10 for every 100 square feet of bed, then seed winter rye right over the wide bean row, and water in.

**Broccoli** I harvest broccoli right through September and into October. It will tolerate a bit of frost, so I water with water-soluble fertilizer this month to encourage continued side-shooting. I also keep an eye out for aphids, which tend to be troublesome on fall brassicas. A strong spray of water keeps infestations in check by washing the bugs right off the plants.

When the broccoli harvest plays out, I pull the roots and discard them, to avoid leaving clubroot organisms in the soil. Then

I give the beds my standard fall soil improvement. I work in 2 inches of compost or manure, lime as needed, and 2 pounds of 10-10-10 fertilizer per 100 square feet of bed. This is raked smooth, and then I sow 1 pound of winter rye seed for every 100 square feet of bed. Finally, I water in well and keep the beds moist until full germination occurs.

**Cabbage**  I think we have to thank the English for expanding our horizons with cabbage, especially the fall types. My winter reading has included some wonderful books by British estate gardeners, and their notes and preferences on cabbage varieties really point out the care they take with varietal selection for almost every month. This doesn't translate so well over here with our harsher climate, but it has made me more attentive to the fine art of selecting cabbage varieties.

My Victory Garden intensive culture is shown at its best here: Growing beautifully in the single 4-foot bed are Savoy cabbage, kale, Swiss chard, oak leaf lettuce, and Brussels sprouts.

I find my September bed filled with ball-head green and red types and the beautiful Savoy Ace, a Japanese breeding success, with its commendable size, nicely savoyed leaves, and creamy yellow heart. These cool fall months are really perfect for cabbage because growth is good but not so exuberant that everything comes at once. The cabbage holds well in the ground and can be harvested as convenient.

It's usually late September or early October before all my fall cabbage is out of the ground. When it's finally finished, I prepare the beds for next year by adding 2 inches of compost or manure, lime as needed, and 2 pounds of 10-10-10 fertilizer for every 100 square feet of bed. I sow 1 pound of winter rye seed for each 100 square feet of area, water in well, and keep the seed bed moist until germination occurs.

**Carrots**   I'll be harvesting carrots throughout the fall, taking them as I need them from the Victory Garden's beds, rather than making a once-over harvest. This is really my favorite carrot season, too. The carrots that I pull and munch now are even sweeter than those grown from spring into summer, because carrots prefer maturing into cool weather.

The carrots catch your eye here, but my Victory Garden soil is the real star. Stone free and enriched with compost and manure, it provides the loose, friable composition carrots must have to develop without splitting and forking.

The September garden in full swing. Many gardeners quit when summer ends, but there's plenty of fall action in the Victory Garden. Beans, squash, lettuce, and leeks are ready for harvesting; the fall crop of radishes has just been planted.

**Cauliflower**   By late September my fall crop of cauliflower is ready for harvest. The caulis get individual scrutiny as they size up this month. Under cool, early fall conditions, the heads should stay in good shape in the ground until the table calls, but I don't assume anything, and check regularly for curd separation or yellowing. If I see either of those, I harvest quickly.

When the harvest is finished, it's time to give the cauliflower beds their fall soil preparation. I work in 2 inches of compost or manure, lime to raise the pH to the 6.5 level (no brassicas will be growing here next year, as I follow my brassica crop rotation plan, so I don't want the higher pH of 7.5 that I use in brassica beds), and 2 pounds of 10-10-10 fertilizer for every 100 square feet of bed. With the beds raked smooth, I sow 1 pound of winter rye seed for every 100 square feet of area, water well, and keep moist until germination occurs.

**Celery**   In September — at last — I can expect to harvest the celery plants that I started from seed way back in February. I'll harvest whole plants, cutting them off just at ground level. The

**I harvest cauliflower when the head is tight and white, before any yellowing or separation occurs. Blanching produces that beautiful creamy color.**

After seven months (I started them indoors in February), my celery is finally ready for harvest. With garlic and red onion, they make a lovely picture.

green, crunchy stalks are a welcome taste treat now that fall is arriving.

Celery has been in the ground for a long time, and has taken a lot out of the soil, which will welcome my fall rejuvenating. I work in 2 inches of compost or manure, lime as needed to adjust the pH, and 2 pounds of 10-10-10 fertilizer for every 100 square feet of bed. That's all turned in well and raked smooth, and then I sow 1 pound of winter rye seed for every 100 square feet of area. I water the seed in well and keep the beds moist until germination is complete.

**Chinese Cabbage**   It's time to harvest my fall planting of Chinese cabbage, but first a word about slugs. The moist ground beneath the succulent Chinese cabbage heads is prime slug habitat, and slugs like the taste of this delicious brassica as much as the rest of us. The generous spacing that I give each plant will cut down on the slug population a bit, and careful cultivation also helps send them on their slimy way. But slugs can be even more troublesome in fall than spring. There are a whole host of home remedies. Some folks put beer in saucers to attract the slugs, which then expire from drowning or wretched excess or both. Long-frustrated gardeners also take fiendish delight in sprinkling salt on slugs' tender bodies. Ingenious devices called slug hotels, available at garden supply houses, allow the creatures to check in but not out. I've also tried spreading wood ashes or gritty substances like diatomaceous earth around the bases of plants, but rain seems to wash these abrasives away all too easily.

As long as the weather stays cool, I'll continue harvesting 5-pound heads of Chinese cabbage into October. When the last has been pulled, I'll begin my fall soil-enrichment program. See "Steps to Victorious Gardening" for my soil-enriching instructions.

**Leeks**   Leeks can be harvested at any time during their growth, but I like to leave them alone until early September, when they'll be fully mature. By then, there should be 10 to 12 inches of blanched, glistening white, mild-flavored stalk under the soil, with the leek leaves spread out like beautiful fans on top. I use a spading fork to harvest them, pushing it into the ground several inches from the plants and making sure to bury the tines deeper than the plants are growing. Then I nudge them up and out with a back-and-forth motion.

My row of leeks will provide for the table right through till Christmas if I lay down a thick mulch of salt marsh hay in November to prevent freezing. If my appetite can't keep up with the supply, I'll try to winter-over a few, taking them in the spring before they go back into active growth.

**Lettuce**   In September I plant my lettuce seedlings in the cold frame, first forking into the soil 1 pound of 10-10-10 fertilizer for the 4x4-foot bed. I set the lettuce into the soil the same depth they were growing in their cell-packs, water in well with half-strength water-soluble fertilizer, and close the cold frame lid. Once in a while September will bring an unusually warm, sunny day, and I keep an eye on the cold frame temperature. If it starts to climb over 75 degrees, I vent the heat to keep the seedlings safe.

**Peas**   If September's weather has been kind to my fall peas (warm for good growth without a checking frost), I'll have a good year. But even in a bad year, a crop failure is the beginning of next season's soil-improvement program. If I don't get a crop, I turn the vines right into the soil. Then I work in 2 pounds of 10-10-10 fertilizer for every 100 square feet of bed, 2 inches of compost or manure, lime as needed, and rake the bed smooth. I sow 1 pound of winter rye seed for every 100 square feet of bed space, and that's that until next spring.

I've used my spading fork to lever up this beautiful leek. They can be taken any time during their growth, but won't be fully mature until September. That gorgeous root system is made possible by the Victory Garden's specially conditioned soil: carefully adjusted pH of 6.5, annual addition of compost or manure, and systematic fertilization throughout the season. ▶

My cold frame provides early lettuce in spring and late lettuce in the fall. These Little Gem seedlings, planted as my summer squash harvest winds down, will come ready in October. That gives me fresh salad greens nine months out of twelve!

If there's a good year, and therefore a harvest, I take peas as long as possible to encourage the plants to keep producing. When they've finally given up, I cut the spent vines off at ground level and compost them. They're a bit tough by now and will break down better in the compost bin. The roots I leave in the soil, loosening it with my three-pronged cultivator before working in 10-10-10 fertilizer and manure or compost. The winter rye goes down last of all, to provide a good, thick stand that will hold the soil in place over winter and add a substantial amount of organic matter come spring, when it's turned under.

**Radishes**   I'm in no great hurry to harvest my fall radishes. They're actually improved by cool weather, growing slow and sweet this time of year. I don't leave them *too* long in the ground, though, because they tend to turn woody and tough when old.

Root maggots have not been a problem with the fall radishes, so I don't even bother with protective fabric. And once the harvest is complete, I make the bed ready for winter by working in 2 inches of manure or compost, lime as needed, and 2 pounds of

10-10-10 fertilizer for every 100 square feet of bed. Last, I sow 1 pound of winter rye seed for every 100 square feet of area and water well.

**Spinach**  The fall crop will be maturing now, and to keep it growing vigorously, I give the bed a drink of water-soluble fertilizer early in the month. I *am* fond of this fall crop, which has no leaf miner worries, never bolts (the hot weather is past), and even tastes better, thanks to the right temperature cycle of warm-to-cool weather.

At the end of the month, I'll find an open bed and open another trench, 12 inches wide, 1 inch deep, and about 15 feet long. Here I'll direct-seed a crop of spinach that will grow a little before going dormant for the winter. This crop will come ready for harvest in March and April, and may be the best of all, having grown completely untroubled by pests of any kind. One thing is certain: It's a most welcome sight — and taste — come early spring!

**Summer Squash**  This crop is very frost sensitive, so I keep my ear on the weather reports in September. If the squash are hit with a frost, they will rot on the vine. When frost is predicted, then, I harvest all the fruit, or, failing that, at least try to cover the vines with a sheet of clear plastic, which will give a couple degrees of frost protection and a longer harvest.

Fall spinach, well fed with water-soluble fertilizer in early September. This crop will provide greens for the Thanksgiving feast. I'll seed another, at month's end, for wintering-over.

When that harvest is finally finished, I pull up the plants, take them to the compost bin, and put away the black plastic for use next season. Then I give the squash beds my standard fall soil improvement. I spread enough lime to bring the pH into the 6.5 range (after getting back results from my soil test), then add 2 inches of compost or manure. I also work in 2 pounds of 10-10-10 fertilizer for every 100 square feet of bed area. With the soil raked smooth again, I sow 1 pound of winter rye seed for every 100 square feet of area and water in well.

**Turnips**  With turnips coming on this month, I'll have all the fixings for a traditional New England boiled dinner, one of my favorites. These quick-growing, tasty turnips that come in September are much better for having matured into cool weather. I'll harvest them at 1½ to 2 inches across, when they're at their tender best. They will keep the table well supplied while their big, even tastier cousins — rutabagas — size up to provide great eating in October and on to Thanksgiving.

**Winter Squash**  If you've been looking for squash entries between here and the June planting, you've been frustrated — there aren't any. That's because so many of the traditional garden "chores" — extra fertilizing, weeding, cultivating, chemical warfare — are eliminated by my streamlined Victory Garden cultural practices. Starting the squash indoors virtually eliminates seedling failure, so replanting is a thing of the past. The slow-release fertilizer feeds the hungry plants all through their growing cycle. (If any deficiencies occur, I nip in with quick-fix feeds of water-soluble fertilizer — but they rarely occur.) Insects are held at bay by the plastic, which also conserves water and completely eliminates the need for weeding and cultivating. Thus here it is September — harvest time — almost before I know it.

Frost now becomes a factor in the lives of my winter squash. I think everyone knows that summer squash vines are highly sensitive to frost, but not everyone knows that winter squash vines are also sensitive. Both can be done in by a hard, early frost, although winter squash are somewhat tougher, and will stand a few degrees of frost without harm.

The September garden is literally a treasure trove of colorful winter squash. Tasty Blue Hubbards are coming ready now. So is Waltham Butternut, and the Jersey Golden Acorn. Color is the best indicator of readiness for all of these. Waltham Butternut turns a uniform tan, and loses its green cast. Hubbard becomes gray-blue all over, and Jersey Golden Acorn turns shiny yellow. I cut all with 2 inches of stem attached, then cure them off the vines in the sun for a few days before putting them in cool storage (50 to 60 degrees) for the winter. I handle them gently, because bruises invite rot, and I don't crowd them or stack them on top of each other. It's important to leave space among the fruits.

The winter squash beds have performed long and hard for months now, and it's time to treat them to my regular Victory Garden season-end rejuvenation. I work in 2 inches of compost or manure, lime as needed to adjust the pH to 6.5, and add 2 pounds of 10-10-10 fertilizer for every 100 square feet of garden area. With all that blended in, I rake the beds smooth, sow 1 pound of winter rye seed for every 100 square feet of space, and water well.

**A Blue Hubbard winter squash, still green. When it's gray and uniformly smooth, I'll harvest by cutting it off with 2 inches of stem. Though they look tough and gnarly, *all* winter squash should be handled gently, as even small bruises promote rot. ◄**

**Resembling tiny pumpkins, these Gold Nugget squash are firm, deep orange, and ready for harvest. The mulch of salt marsh hay keeps fruit off the damp ground, retarding rot. ▶**

# MAKING CIDER

The countryside close to where I grew up was dotted with farms, and several of our neighbors pressed their own cider every fall. I well remember autumn trips to one of those farms. My father and I would drive down when the orchards were groaning with Macs and Cortlands. We could smell the tang of the cider press half a mile down the road when the wind was right. At the farm, we'd find mounds of scoured, gleaming apples waiting for the press inside the small mill. Dad always brought along a load of gallon jugs, and the farmer filled them with golden cider fresh from the press. When all the jugs were full, he'd hold a wooden dipper under the stream and give me a taste. I've never forgotten it. The cider was dark and thick, a perfect blend of tang and sweetness, cool enough to quench thirst and rich enough to fill me right up.

There aren't as many cider mills around as there used to be, nor are there as many presses in American homes. That's a shame, because cider is as American as apple pie, and maybe more so. Though the apple was unknown in North America, seeds were brought over by colonists from England in the 1600s. Our most famous apple planter was John

**Key cidermaking ingredients: clean, sound apples, a sturdy cider press, spotless containers, and a thirsty gardener.** ◀

**To make pomace (the pulp from which juice is expressed), I first feed apples into the hand-cranked grinder. You can also make the pomace with a blender or food processor.**

Chapman, immortalized in legend as Johnny Appleseed for his planting beyond the Alleghenies in the early 1800s. But apple planting got off to a much earlier start. Historical records show that the first true New Englander, Peregrine White (who was born on the *Mayflower* as she lay at anchor on May 20, 1620), sowed apple seeds in Massachusetts when he grew up. Apple raising and cidermaking reached a peak in this country in the mid-nineteenth century, when almost 80 percent of the population made farming their daily work. We've changed a lot since then, of course, and many of us have lost our ties with the old farming ways. But just

as many are anxious to regain some of that connection with the land, which is one reason for gardening's dramatic increase in popularity.

You don't have to grow an orchard, or live next door to a cider mill, to enjoy the matchless taste of fresh, sweet cider. A very reasonable investment of time and money will produce excellent home-pressed cider. I've made cider at home often, and I enjoy not only the superb taste but also the feeling of self-sufficiency I get from making my own cider. There are few home creations that taste better, and I don't know of many that are easier, either.

I buy cider apples from a local orchard. It is *very* important to use only ripe, sound apples. A "sound" apple has no bruises, worm damage, disease, or rot. The skin is smooth and intact. I buy apples by the bushel, knowing from experience that I'll get about 2 gallons of cider from each bushel. I've also picked my own in the fall, which is a nice way to save a few dollars and have a fun family outing at the same time.

At home, I wash each apple very thoroughly, making sure to clean out the area around the stem, where chemical sprays tend to accumulate and form a residue. Cleanliness, by the way, should be raised almost to the level of fanaticism in cidermaking. Cider is very nearly as volatile as milk, rich with organisms and bacteria, and I sterilize every single cidermaking implement. That means all the scoops and ladles, the cider press itself, our pomace cloth, cheesecloth, containers, lids — *everything*. I use boiling water for the cleaning; soaps and detergents don't do the job. They won't disinfect adequately, for one thing, and they can leave a residue that taints the cider.

Cidermakers agree that it's best not to use one variety of apple, but to blend two or three kinds for the finest flavor. Just *which* varieties to blend has been debated since pre-Christian times, when cider was already a popular drink in Europe. I've found that a reasonable compromise is to blend three varieties, two sweet and one tart — Delicious, Cortland, and MacIntosh. Some friends of mine in Vermont have been pressing cider as a family business for a hundred years, and they're *still* experimenting with different blends, so I never feel bad about trying a new combination. And I never hesitate to ask the advice of local orchardists, who are sure to have their own favorite combinations.

There's no magic to pressing cider at home. It requires only a bit of patience and elbow grease. It's changed little, in fact, in hundreds of years. I use a small manual press, bought from a mail-order

I'm adding washed apples to the press's attached grinder. Pomace collects in the wooden vat, which I've sterilized with boiling water.

The three stages of cidermaking, all in one view. At the top, a half-ground apple. In the middle, pomace collecting in the hardwood vat. And down below, pure cider already flowing into the sterile container. Cider is clear when first expressed, but contact with air quickly turns it a characteristic tawny brown.

house, several of which advertise in magazines like *Yankee*, *Country Journal*, *Organic Gardening*, and *Harrowsmith*. Cidermaking supplies can also be found in the Yellow Pages, but look under the "Winemaking Equipment and Supplies" heading.

The use of a food processor to make pomace (the pulp that's squeezed for juice) saves a tremendous amount of time and labor, but it's not the only way — particularly for traditionalists. I have friends who make pomace by slicing the apples very finely with a wooden slaw cutter. And I've read about a hardy homesteading couple who pound their apples into pomace in a big tub with one end of a 5-foot log!

My home press holds about 2 gallons of pomace when it's full. I use a wooden scoop to ladle in pomace and to press it down from time to time as I go. Juice will begin to flow at this point, so I keep a sterilized container under the press's spout to catch this early runoff.

When the press is full of pomace, I set the round wooden platen in place. The only thing left is to engage the metal screw and start turning. *Slowly.* Here's where patience comes in. Cider starts to flow as soon as the handle is turned, and it's tempting to keep right on going. Be warned that cider

And that's it. The cider I've pressed is ready to drink as soon as it starts to flow into the jug. In fact, I doubt if there's a better time to drink it, when it's so fresh that it tingles all the way down. There are ways, though, to keep the cider, and I've used each of them at one time or another. Unless cider is refrigerated, fermentation will begin at once. The expressed liquid is rich with microscopic yeast organisms present in the apples' skin, and, given only the right temperatures, these industrious little microbes will immediately begin turning the sugar into alcohol — and eventually into very fine vinegar. I keep cider as long as 2 weeks in the refrigerator. I've also tried freezing cider to keep it longer, and this works perfectly well — for months, in fact. The only caution is to leave space in the plastic jugs (I don't use glass for freezing — too much danger of cracking) for expansion.

**The final product, ready for the taste test.**

should not be hurried. Pressing out 2 gallons of pomace should be an all-day affair. That doesn't mean I stand around staring at the press. I give the platen a few more turns to start, and then repeat the process every half hour, giving one or two full revolutions each turning. I'll make ten visits to the press during the day. And if I'm really anxious to engage in the ultimate Yankee frugality to get the last drops of es-

**Pressing the pomace is an all-day process. I tighten the press's platen one or two turns at a time, then leave it alone for an hour. The reward for my patience is fresh, pure cider that can be enjoyed fresh or kept in the freezer for months.**

sence from my pomace, I'll let the press sit overnight, making the final turns the next morning.

A frost-spared early October garden, still fully productive. One of my garden aims is to extend the growing season as late as possible into the fall, which means being ready to cover frost-tender crops like beans when cold is forecast.

# OCTOBER

# OCTOBER

In October, the Victory Garden philosophy of intensive culture really comes into its own. I'm still harvesting brassicas, leeks, rutabagas, and lettuce out of the cold frame. The threat of a killing frost sends me out with baskets and boxes to capture the last of the peppers and the remaining tomatoes. The vegetables, in other words, are still coming on strong. Broccoli, Brussels sprouts, cabbage, and kale will give a great harvest right through the month. I learned years ago from my father that Brussels sprouts are helped to mature at this time of year by pinching off the top 6 inches of stem and by pulling off the lower leaves. This stops any additional top growth and sends all the energy into the rapidly developing sprouts. Leeks, Swiss chard, and spinach don't even need this minimal attention. They're all thriving in the cool weather.

Still to come this month is the harvest of pumpkins, and many herbs will be bunched for drying. Braided onions hang in the potting shed. Potatoes and squash are stored for winter.

The Victory Garden will soon have more vacant room, as the last of the crops are taken. I'll continue to amend the soil with compost, manure, lime, and fertilizer. In October, I take soil samples to test for pH and nutrient content. Fall is the best time to correct the pH, as both lime and sulfur take time to act. That pH, as I've said elsewhere, is the key to unlocking nutrients in the soil. If the pH is not close to neutral (between 6.0 and 7.0), many soil nutrients just aren't available to the plants. I never guess at pH, but rely on my county extension service test results. I'm not usually given to unequivocal statements about gardening, but here's one: This attention to pH is one of the most important things I can do for the garden.

Another October certainty is that deciduous trees will lose their leaves. I take my own leaves, and all those that neighbors will bestow, and put them in one of the compost bins, where they'll break down over the winter, turning into next season's most friable soil amendment.

Finally, I take a few special minutes to lean on my spading fork or rake and savor this very special time, the last days of the last month of my growing season. The garden and I have been working together since February, and in a way it's a bit sad, like saying good-bye to an old friend. That sadness never lasts long, though, because I'm so proud of all that we've produced together over the months — the taste of those early tomatoes is still strong on my tongue — and because I know that the gardening year never truly ends. Cycles complete themselves, rhythms change, pace alters, but the garden is always alive and thriving, appreciating my contribution to its growth and awaiting the approach of spring's flourish.

**Plant in Garden**
Winter rye

**Mulch**
Asparagus
Kale

**Harvest**
Brussels sprouts
Kale
Lettuce
Parsnips
Pumpkins
Rutabagas
Tomatoes

**Asparagus**   It's time to give the asparagus beds their wintering-over top dressing of manure. I spread 2 to 3 inches of well-rotted manure over the entire bed this month. Nutrients from the manure will work their way into the soil all winter long, steadily and gradually. And the manure, as always, enhances the soil composition wherever it goes.

**Brussels Sprouts**   In early October, I pinch off the growing tips of the Brussels sprouts plants to drive energy into the developing sprouts. I also prune out the yellowing lower leaves. When the sprouts reach golf-ball size and are tight leaved, like mini-cabbages, I start harvesting from the bottom up. I take the

Pinching off the top and snapping off the lower leaves hastens the maturing of Brussels sprouts from the bottom up.

sprouts by breaking them off with a twist of the fingers. It's trendy now in some of the more fashionable food boutiques to uproot a whole stalk of Brussels sprouts and present them to the table just that way. It's an impressive offering, and I save one such stalk for the Thanksgiving feast at home.

**Kale**  Kale is one tough plant, able to survive inclement weather, drought, and rough treatment. It even improves with cold weather and frost, so I'm in no hurry to harvest all the kale too soon. I'll leave a few plants, in fact, to overwinter completely, bedding them down under 6 inches of salt marsh hay in late November for use next February. When I do harvest kale, I snip individual leaves from the plants, taking them from the outside without disturbing the central growing point. Leaving that point alone prolongs the harvest considerably.

**Lettuce**  This may be the most satisfying lettuce harvest of all. I have gone to the October cold frame and found the plastic cover entirely frosted over, only to lift it up and discover, inside, perfectly healthy lettuce plants waiting to be picked. There's little to equal the taste of fresh Red Sails, Buttercrunch, and other savory types at this time of year.

When the harvest is completely finished, I go through the same fall soil preparation for the lettuce bed that all my other Victory Garden soil receives. A soil test tells me how much lime I need to add to adjust the pH back to the desired 6.5 range. In addition, I work in 2 inches of well-rotted manure or compost for soil structure. The bed receives a pound of 10-10-10 fertilizer, and then I broadcast the fall cover crop of winter rye, sowing the seeds thickly. They're watered in, and that puts the bed to bed for the winter.

**Parsnips**   I sample the first parsnips after a good hard October freeze. This crop not only survives cold weather, it is much improved for being left in the ground over winter. The cold helps convert starch to sugar, producing much sweeter parsnips. Most of the crop will be harvested by late fall before hard frost

A few fall-dug parsnips, well shaped and long thanks to the customized planting holes I prepared in April.

locks them in the ground, but I like to sample an early parsnip or two this month. There's no special trick to the harvest. I dig the roots with a spading fork, working both sides of the parsnip row, plunging the fork in well back of the plants and gently levering the soil up by pushing the handle down. At this time I think back to those oversized ice-cream-cone holes that I made with the steel bar. If the parsnips are as big as the holes, I'll be a happy gardener.

**Pumpkins**   It's easy to know when pumpkins are ready for harvest. They turn that bright, uniform orange we all associate with Halloween jack-o'-lanterns. The vine will die off, and that's also a sure sign that the pumpkins are ready. I harvest them by cutting through the vine with my pocketknife, leaving 2 inches of vine on the pumpkin. I also handle the pumpkins carefully, making sure I don't pull the stem away from the pumpkin while I'm harvesting, because the open wound that results will be more likely to rot.

When the harvest is finished (and I do try to get all the pumpkins before the first hard frost hits, because they'll turn black and rot if punished by a deep freeze), I roll up the black plastic for use next year. Then I put the pumpkin beds through my usual Victory Garden fall soil amendment program. After testing for pH requirements, I add the necessary amount of lime, and work in 2 inches of well-rotted manure or compost and 2 pounds of 10-10-10 fertilizer for every 100 square feet of bed space. After raking the soil smooth, I sow 1 pound of winter rye seed for every 100 square feet of bed, water in, and wait for spring.

**Rutabagas**   Like parsnips, rutabagas' flavor is much improved by a good, hard frost. I wait until we've received one of those and then harvest a rutabaga or two. The globular rutabagas sit there, half in and half out of the soil, just waiting to be lifted free by their tops. Nothing to it. The harvest will actually last over several weeks as the seedlings tend to grow at different rates, giving plants that come to maturity at different times, rather than all at once.

By the end of October, I still have plenty of rutabagas waiting to be harvested. Since very hard freezing of the ground will not occur until December, it is perfectly suitable to leave them in the ground right up to Thanksgiving.

**Tomatoes**   There are still tomatoes in the early October garden. Many are green, and it's tempting to let them fully ripen on the vine. I can get them through the light frosts of September by wrapping their cages in polyethylene, but an October frost is usually much harder. If one is forecast, I go ahead and harvest all the remaining tomatoes: green, semigreen, and red. Those with blemishes go to the discard pile. The rest are stored.

These Jersey Golden Acorn squash will fill the day's harvest basket of season's end tomatoes and peppers, broccoli, and a lovely Chinese cabbage.

A classic New England assortment of winter squash and pumpkins.

Any tomato with the slightest blush of pink will eventually ripen off the vine, but conditions must be just right. They must be cool and dry, and it helps to put a piece of apple in the storage container (I use a Styrofoam cooler). The ethylene gas given off by the decaying apple aids the tomatoes' ripening. Each one is wrapped in newspaper before going into the cooler. While these — even when fully ripened — will never match the beauties I pulled fresh from the vine in August, they'll certainly do next month. And green tomatoes have *their* uses, too, as any lover of green tomato relish can attest.

My last bit of tomato housekeeping is to pull the tomato cages, clear them of any leftover foliage or vines, and store them for next season. Empty vines go to the compost bin. Then I prepare the beds for winter by working in 2 inches of compost or manure, 2 pounds of 10-10-10 fertilizer for every 100 square feet of bed, and enough lime to bring the pH to 6.5. I work all this into the soil, rake it smooth, sow 1 pound of winter rye seed for every 100 square feet of area, and water well.

**Winter Rye**   I'm sowing my winter cover crop of rye on the Victory Garden raised beds this month as they come open. The practice is the same for all the beds. When the harvest is complete, I work 2 inches of manure or compost into the soil, add 2 pounds of 10-10-10 fertilizer for every 100 square feet of bed area, and lime as needed to adjust the pH to 6.5. That's all worked in well, raked smooth, and then I broadcast 1 pound of winter rye seed for every 100 square feet of area being sown. It's watered in and the beds are kept moist until germination occurs. The rye will grow over the winter, holding the beds' shape and, come spring, contributing its organic matter to soil structure when I turn it under before planting.

A good thick stand of winter rye with mums, Mission lettuce, and Inca marigolds. Next year's successful garden begins with fall soil improvement.

# WREATHMAKING

When I talk about preserving the harvest, many people think I'm talking about canning or freezing food. Here's another way to preserve the yield of garden and fields. I'm talking about wreathmaking, a craft that was practiced among American colonists and that can still beautify our homes as it did theirs.

To make wreaths, you'll need a few things from the hardware store. Of primary importance is wire for attaching materials to the frame. A bunch of 2 dozen floral wires costs about 59 cents; a whole spool is only about $3. Number 24 wire is a good all-purpose choice. Wire cutters make the job of snipping off pieces much easier, though an old pair of sturdy scissors will do. Needlenosed pliers save my fingers when twisting wire, and serve as tweezers when positioning the materials. Wreath frames are essential. Wire frames are either flat or box-wire types. There are also Styrofoam or floral foam frames. A 12-inch wire frame costs about 79 cents and a 12-inch foam frame about $2.50. You will need something to fix materials to the frame, and I think the very best way is with a light hot-glue gun. Fifteen dollars buys a good gun, which will glue almost

**The American native bittersweet winds easily around and makes a simple, rustic addition to the Victory Garden tool shed. ◄**

**Gathering American bittersweet.**

anything. I've added an on/off switch 5 inches down the cord from the glue gun's handle, to extend the life of the tool. Glue sticks sometimes come with the gun, and extras cost about 20 cents each. Finally, you will need a special corner where mess can be ignored until you get around to recycling all your materials.

The list of wreath ingredients is almost endless, and starts, of course, in the garden. From the flower garden, everything from peonies to hydrangea, from roses to dusty miller, and clematis, delphinium, and foxglove seed pods. From the vegetable garden, rhubarb flowers, celery leaves, ornamental kale, carrot tops, okra pods, leek and chive seed heads, and whole, tiny red peppers. The herb garden is another gold mine, providing

flowers from marjoram, mint, tarragon, chives, and lavender as well as the seed heads and seed pods from lovage, dill, coriander, chervil, and sage. Sage, bay, parsley, and savory leaves work fine, too. In fact, just about any herb you grow can be an eager candidate for a wreath.

I have seen tendrils of wisteria, branches of birch, bittersweet, weeping willow, forsythia, and pussy willows all used. They are so flexible that they can be coiled or woven into natural wreath frames, to be used as they are, or decorated further. It's even possible to use many roots as frames, securing the ends with a quick twist of wire or weaving them into each other for a purely natural connection. Look also for berries, seed pods of locust and tulip trees, clematis, delphinium, larkspur, and foxglove seed pods, cones from pine, hemlock, spruce, and evergreens like juniper.

It is also possible to range farther afield, collecting goldenrod, clover, red sumac, tansy, heather, teasel, Queen Anne's lace, and an endless number of weed flowers and wonderful grasses and pods. It's not necessary to know all their names to appreciate their lovely forms and textures. Finally, don't forget to bring bayberry back from the shore, and remember that cemeteries and arboretums are wonderful collecting grounds for the polite guest.

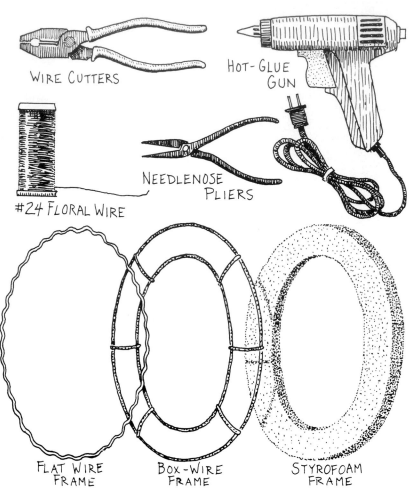

WIRE CUTTERS

HOT-GLUE GUN

#24 FLORAL WIRE

NEEDLENOSE PLIERS

FLAT WIRE FRAME

BOX-WIRE FRAME

STYROFOAM FRAME

Gathering can go on from early spring to late autumn. Try to pick on dry days, in early morning, just after dew has evaporated. Most flowers are best harvested at the peak of bloom, and trial and error is the only way to develop a sense of timing here. It's better to harvest earlier than later, in some cases cutting just as the buds begin to unfurl their color. Those just showing and others at peak bloom are the real eye-catchers in a well-done wreath. But it's nice to work in variety and interest by including flowers at all stages.

After picking, I strip all the leaves from the stem except one or two near the flower itself. Leaves retain moisture and retard the drying process. Stripping outdoors, right after picking, allows me to leave the mess outside.

There are lots of ways to preserve this harvest, but I stick with two simple methods. One is highly traditional, the other ultramodern. The traditional method, practiced by our forebears, is air-drying. It's easy, cheap, and produces materials in good quantity. It also works on almost anything that grows. To begin, loosely bunch together about 6 of the same type stems and wrap them with a rubber band 2 inches from their ends. Tie again with string and leave a loop for hanging. Choose a drying spot that is dry, dark, and has good air circulation. I hang bunches from the edge of a top pantry shelf. Be sure that the bunches hang freely, and aren't crowded. Drying this way will take 10 days to 2 weeks, after which you can leave the bunches hanging until you want to use them, or store them in cartons away from dust. If you'd like to see them on display, set them upright in baskets throughout the house, avoiding the moist bathroom and direct sun.

The ultramodern drying method is to use a microwave oven. Although it limits the size of materials, it does a perfect job of drying, locking in the exact natural colors. Leaves that yellow in air-drying remain a brilliant green. Experiment by placing a leaf or two on half a paper napkin and covering with the other half. Top this with an inverted ovenproof custard cup to keep the leaves from curling. Set the oven on high and leave it on for 2 minutes. As with foods, let the materials relax out of the oven for 5 minutes while the internal heat continues to dry them. If they're stiff and dry to the touch, they're finished. If almost dry, let them sit out overnight. If still damp, return for another minute in the oven. Experiment with ferns, English ivy, and forsythia. Since

I'm using twine to hold my wreath of American bittersweet in good form.

the microwave perfectly captures the colors of a fall leaf and a pansy, why not a rose?

With a wealth of dried materials on hand, you're ready to start making wreaths. A word of advice: If you're not adept with a glue gun, practice first. Plug it in, load with glue according to the instructions, and wait 2 or 3 minutes, so that when you press the trigger, melted glue (it's really plastic) dribbles out. Practice on an old basket or mushroom box. Frame around the rim of either with a sampling from your collection, starting with larger pieces, like pine cones. Hold the gun point right above a spot on the cone, pull the trigger, and hope. You should play around until you can regularly produce a neat, single spot of glue the size of a pea. When the little spot is in place, release the trigger and make a

clean getaway by twisting the nozzle up and away. Quickly connect your cone or other material to the naked rim. Stick with this trial-and-error practice, and you'll be surprised at how quickly you become expert. The trick is to produce the right size drop for the material, just large enough to hold it in place, but no larger.

Now let's go step-by-step through the building of an herb wreath, one of my favorite kinds. First, assemble the materials: a 12-inch saw-toothed wire frame, enough artemesia (or other material) to cover the frame's surface, herbs of your choice, and the basic tools and supplies listed earlier.

Cover the entire surface of the frame with artemesia, or a substitute, anchoring it with a piece of the wire looped over and around the boughs. Don't worry too much about neatness and visible wire. This is your base, and will be covered.

For the next layer, wire on bunches of tarragon, lemon balm, savory, mint — whatever herbs you have harvested. Use the needlenosed pliers to twist the wire tightly around these bunches. Vary the textures, colors, and shades. If a bit of wire shows, tuck in a sprig of lavender or thyme or rosemary. If you are using a glue gun, camouflage any bothersome spots by gluing on a chive or marjoram flower, or dill or fennel heads.

As with any recipe, don't hesitate to substitute, and, above all, don't avoid making because you lack the suggested ingredients. If you don't have artemesia, try lamb's ears, oregano, catnip, or basil. Try it freshly picked, and let it dry on the frame. Vary appearance by using a box-wire frame, which will allow you to attach a much larger selection of materials.

If you want to break off your herbs for cooking, attach them mostly with wire. If the wreath will be purely decorative, you can rely more on a glue gun. Add to the design by wiring or gluing on nutmeg, nuts, or cinnamon sticks. Glue on rich green microwave-dried bay or sage leaves. Stretch the theme and trim with tansy, yarrow, goldenrod, berries, or tiny hemlock cones.

Finally, cut off any wire ends. Decide where you want the top of your wreath to be, and wrap a wire hook around the back of the ring for hanging. There you have it! Your own creation, beautiful, aromatic, and useful. Yet another way to use the things that grow all around us.

I gather all the leaves I can in fall because they are such good soil-improvers. I mulch them, compost them, and sometimes spread them right on the garden and till them in before sowing over with winter rye.

# ENDINGS

# ENDINGS

The gardener's year is circular; November and December are the months that close the circle. Though I'm already looking forward to the next season's activities, I appreciate this quiet period. It's a time to relax, reflect — and take special delight in the harvest that the Victory Garden provides right through Thanksgiving. It's one of my gardening goals to grace the table with fresh vegetables come the end of November. I want this special meal to include freshly dug leeks, kale, parsnips, Brussels sprouts, as well as stored potatoes, onions, rutabagas, and winter squash. Careful mulching is essential if I'm to enjoy this late-season bounty. I mulch around the leeks, parsnips, and Brussels sprouts after they've had several frosts, but before the ground freezes. When that happens, I use leaves or salt marsh hay, laying the mulch quite thick — 6 to 12 inches. Both mulches work well. Leaves are almost always readily available, and they're a fine soil conditioner. Come spring, I'll dig them right into the soil. Any extra leaves will fill one of the compost bins over winter. I also lay down a 6-inch mulch of leaves or hay on the strawberries now. And both raspberries and asparagus are mulched with 2 to 3 inches of manure.

A few more projects close up the garden for winter. To leave it tidy, ready for next year, I bring in all the equipment I've used over the season. I gather tomato cages and stack them together in the garage. Trellises come down and receive any necessary repairs before they go into storage. After the last lettuce harvest, I take the cold frames apart and store them. I bring watering cans and hoses inside, and blow out underground hose lines with a compressor. (A bike pump with a special fitting will work just as well.) After I fill the compost bins almost to the top, I add a final 2 inches of soil, water well, and then cover with black plastic. This will keep the pile active into early winter. Pots are sorted and cleaned, and any broken ones are discarded.

I'm orderly with my tools. Anything that can be hung *is* hung on pegboard. Before they go to their assigned spots, all tools are cleaned. I wire-brush working ends and metal surfaces, then file all the edged tools. All metal surfaces are wiped down with motor oil, to prevent rusting. I clean wooden handles and give them a fresh coat of linseed oil. The occasional painted handle receives a fresh, bright coat. Pruners, hose-end attachments, string lines, and other small items are "filed" together in an old bureau. Finally, I make a list of items that will need to be replaced come next growing season.

One tradition of long standing at my house is having a live Christmas tree. Several of the landscaping evergreens around my home spent time indoors as living Christmas trees, and

**I like to give all my hand tools a good cleaning before putting them away for winter. This includes scraping off soil, oiling metal ends, sharpening edges, and rubbing over wooden handles with linseed oil. ▶**

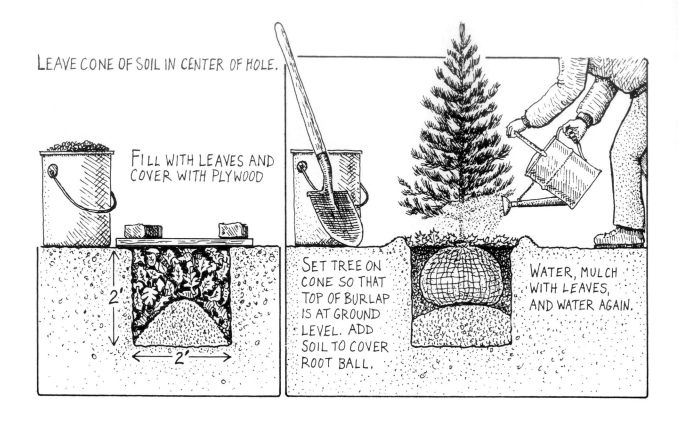

LEAVE CONE OF SOIL IN CENTER OF HOLE.

FILL WITH LEAVES AND COVER WITH PLYWOOD

2'

2'

SET TREE ON CONE SO THAT TOP OF BURLAP IS AT GROUND LEVEL. ADD SOIL TO COVER ROOT BALL.

WATER, MULCH WITH LEAVES, AND WATER AGAIN.

there are few things more satisfying than watching a 3-foot spruce mature over the years.

Before I go shopping for our tree, I prepare the hole in which it will eventually be planted. Because the tree will one day grow into a fully mature forest tree as much as 30 feet tall, it needs ample separation from house, outbuildings, and other trees. I'm also careful not to set it too close to the garden, where shade would rob sun and spreading roots would steal moisture and nutrients from my vegetables. The tree's planting hole is dug 2 feet deep and 2 feet in diameter. I keep the soil from this hole in a large bucket, and store it in the garage or cellar, where it won't freeze. Then I fill the hole with leaves and cover it with a piece of plywood.

Next comes shopping for the tree. Spruce and pine are the most popular Christmas choices. When shopping for a live one, I look for good, dark green color and secure needles. A vigorous shake should not dislodge needles from a healthy tree. Another test is to bend a single needle between thumb and forefinger. If the needle is supple and bends easily, springing back to its original shape, the tree's healthy. If the needle is brittle and snaps, I look for another tree.

During the Christmas season, the tree stays indoors only 3 to 5 days. Exposing it to a longer period of dry warmth is a main cause of winterkill. I keep the root ball moist in a waterproof container (the very large plastic tubs available from nurseries and garden centers work well for this) with about 2 inches of water. I also moisten the burlap-covered root ball daily, and provide humidity for the tree by spritzing it thoroughly every day. After its brief stint indoors, the tree goes outside for planting. I remove all the leaves from the protected hole, and place some of the stored soil in the hole, creating a cone. The root ball goes on top of that cone, and the burlap is left on the root ball. It will rot away and the roots will grow right through it. It's important to plant the tree at the same depth that it was growing in the field, and this means that the top of the burlap should just be covered with soil. After the root ball is in place, I fill the hole with my remaining soil. Then — and this is very important — I water the tree in well. Next I spread leaves all around the base of the tree to help retain warmth and moisture, and then I give the tree another good soaking. Many live Christmas trees die during the winter from drying out, because rain is infrequent and snow is not a usable water source. Whenever there's a thaw in January or February, I go outside to water the tree. And I spray the needles with an antidesiccant, which lets them breathe but slows the rate of water loss.

In December the seed catalogs begin to arrive, and I spend many an hour by the well-stoked fire, turning pages and fantasizing about next year's harvests. I like catalogs that are easy to read, illustrated in color, and full of helpful cultural information. Some companies, for reasons I've never understood, insist on printing their information in microscopic type. My eyes glance off such user-unfriendly catalogs, and they don't get much of my business. I do pay attention, though, to the catalogs from various specialty houses, which offer Oriental vegetables, heirloom varieties, and the like. These complement nicely my assortment of catalogs from the major houses and provide a look at varieties that mainstream houses can't afford to stock.

Finally, December is gift-giving month, and I enjoy this chance to share the garden's glory with friends and relatives. I give relishes, braided twists of onions, potpourri, gardeners' aids (like the planting boards I make in the Victory Garden workshop; see the feature titled "Victory Garden Structures" for instructions), and wreaths (which I've described in a separate feature, "Wreathmaking"). Subscriptions to gardening magazines also go into the stockings of friends, as do copies of the "Victory Garden" video.

# GARDENING TO ATTRACT BIRDS

I've mentioned elsewhere my early morning visits to the Victory Garden, when I watch birds helping themselves to a hearty breakfast of insects from the various crops. The birds are beautiful, of course, but their visits serve a very real purpose, reducing plant damage from insect pests and lessening my own de-bugging work. Birds are a welcome addition to the Victory Garden and its environs, and I know that I am not alone in my fondness for them. Something like 70 million people now attract birds with feeders, spending an estimated $500 million annually on birdseed. There's good reason for such enthusiasm. Birds are faithful, and will pay regular visits to any backyard that offers them food — from feeders or more natural sources. Their color and flash add beauty to any home environment. And of all wildlife, birds are the least likely to cause problems for the gardener and homeowner.

Many people start out creating a backyard wildlife habitat with bird feeders, and there's not a thing wrong with that. When I was a boy, we had several feeders around our house,

**I like the natural look of this house feeder, hung at a convenient height for re-filling. ◀**

**Chickadees being offered a two-course meal — suet in the cage and seed in the cylindrical feeder.**

and a large nesting box as well. I remember the pleasure of seeing bright flocks of evening grosbeaks come to the feeding tray in winter, and of watching new chickadee families learn the ropes during the summertime. I liked especially the little red hummingbird feeder, and found the tiny, brilliantly colored ruby-throated hummingbirds endlessly fascinating.

One of the nicest things about bird feeders and bird-baths (birds need water, too!) is that they provide almost immediate results. While other aspects of creating a backyard

wildlife habitat may take months or even years to pay dividends, feeders and baths will collect birds in a few days. There are really six basic kinds of feeders, each with certain things to recommend it. The best all-around type, and the one to have if you're having only one, is the cylindrical plastic feeder. Available from hardware stores and garden supply houses, these are best supported on a pole away from large trees and the eaves of your house, from both of which squirrels may leap. Fill the tubular feeder with sunflower seeds of the black oil or striped kind, and nothing else. Sunflower seeds are more popular with more kinds of birds than any other seed, and they provide more fat and energy than do other varieties, an important consideration during cold winter months. Tubular feeders will attract not only seed-eaters, but birds that normally eat insects as well, when the insect population dwindles in winter: nuthatches, chickadees, titmice, and woodpeckers.

The feeding table is really nothing more than a flat plywood tray with a roof, supported 1 to 3 feet from the ground. Bigger birds that like to walk around in their food will come to the tray, as will

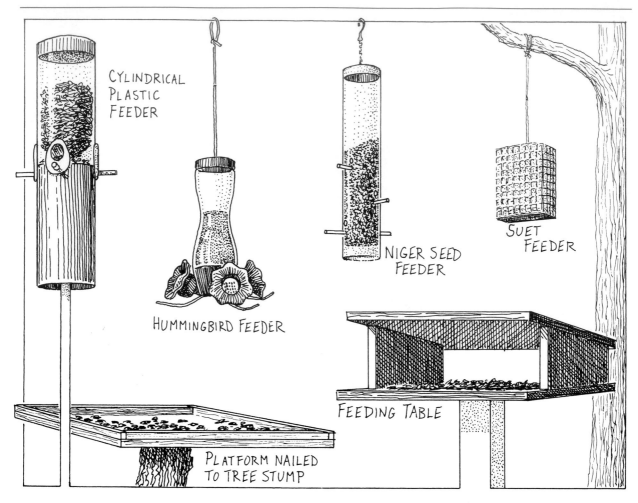

CYLINDRICAL PLASTIC FEEDER

HUMMINGBIRD FEEDER

NIGER SEED FEEDER

SUET FEEDER

FEEDING TABLE

PLATFORM NAILED TO TREE STUMP

gregarious types that like to dine with four or five buddies. You'll see cardinals, mourning doves, blackbirds, finches, and evening grosbeaks pecking happily in your feeding table.

Suet feeders are a third type, and are especially important in winter. Suet is a certain kind of fat (the hard fat around the kidneys and loins of cattle and sheep), which you can find at butcher shops or meat counters. A winter suet feeder invites birds you might not see otherwise — a variety of woodpeckers and nuthatches, Carolina wrens, yellow-rumped warblers, and, in the coldest winters, red-shouldered hawks or

American kestrels. A suet feeder is nothing more than a wire mesh cage hung from the trunk or branch of a tree 6 to 8 feet off the ground.

Hummingbird feeders are usually red plastic or glass containers that hold sugar solutions. They're red because hummingbirds have been found to associate that color with high concentrations of nectar in flowers. A hummingbird feeder should be easy to clean, and cleaned often — every other day — with hot water or a mild

detergent. Use a sugar solution that is 1 part table sugar to 4 parts water.

Niger seed feeders, sometimes called thistle seed feeders, are tubular plastic feeders with very small holes for the very small seed. Niger seed will attract some species, like pine siskins and red polls, that might not gather around other feeders.

Finally, a small platform nailed to a tree stump makes an ideal fruit feeding table for birds. Mockingbirds, bluebirds, catbirds, thrashers, thrushes, and robins all eat a lot of fruit in the winter. Raisins and currants are best, but orange halves will bring orioles, too.

Birds need water as well as food, and many homeowners make the mistake of thinking that wildlife naturally finds ponds and streams to drink from and bathe in. In urban and suburban areas, such natural sources may be few and far between, so providing a backyard water source is a sure way to attract wild birds. A birdbath need not be complicated at all. Any shallow container will do: from a ½-inch deep, 6-inch wide saucer to more traditional pedestal-mounted birdbaths standing 3 feet high. The birdbath should be light enough to tilt easily for cleaning, and not too deep. Birds don't like water deeper than ½ inch. They bathe and drink from the same water, so the bath should be cleaned daily and refilled with clean tap water — no additives!

Bird feeders and baths are an easy, inexpensive way to begin attracting wild birds to your yard, but they do not provide the natural habitat wildlife needs. To really make the best environment for wildlife, you need to think in terms of living plants. Landscaping and gardening with wildlife in mind will create an environment that provides four essential elements: food, water, cover, and a place to raise young. Consider this fact: With the very best feeders, you may attract up to fifteen kinds of birds. With landscaping and gardening, you can expect visits from more than *eighty*.

The first step in creating a habitat for birds and other wildlife is to develop a land

**A downy woodpecker enjoying a winter's meal at the suet feeder.**

scape plan. Make rough sketches, identifying what's on your property already. Don't just put down the trees and shrubs. Show everything, as illustrated in the accompanying sample plan. Include large deciduous trees, all shrubs and flowering plants, and fruits, as well as heat pumps, swing sets, driveways, outbuildings, and other structures. Early fall is a good time to begin making your inventory. Walk around out there and see what's been growing well and what's been struggling. Look at areas of bright sun and shade, at areas where your land borders that of neighbors, and — of course — at your garden. Through all the surveying, try to be thinking like an animal. Ask yourself which plants provide good food, protective cover, and shelter for raising young. If you're not too sure which varieties *are* best, you

may want to talk to an expert. When we created the new Lexington Victory Garden outside Boston, we worked with some of the best experts in the business, people like Craig Tufts of the National Wildlife Federation. You may not have access to such expertise, but don't disregard your county extension service agent, who's likely to be a wealth of free information. If you'd like to do some reading on your own, I'll pass on three sources that I've found very helpful. A fine starting point is the National Wildlife Federation's "Gardening With Wildlife" kit, available from the National Wildlife Federation, Dept. BN, 1412 16th Street NW, Washington, D.C. 20036. *The Bird Feeder Book* by Donald and Lillian Stokes, published by Little, Brown, provides information on common birds. Ortho Publishing's *How to Attract Birds* is a reasonably priced guide to a very wide range of birds and their preferences. And for the really serious enthusiast, there is *The Audubon Society Guide to Attracting Birds*, by Stephen W. Kress, published by Scribners.

Once you've familiarized yourself with the kinds of birds that frequent your area, and with the general lay of your own land, it's time to make a detailed landscape plan, to scale, on graph paper. As you do this, bear in mind that you're working to create a backyard environment that will provide the four essentials for wildlife survival mentioned earlier. The ideal plant for attracting and maintaining wildlife will be evergreen, with extremely dense growth, thorny and heavily branched, and will provide fruit or berries all year round. Unfortunately, that ideal plant doesn't exist. What we try to do in the Victory Garden, and what you can do at home, is to use our tactic of succession planting to provide a group of plants that all work together to meet the needs of birds.

Food is our first consideration. No one plant will provide fruit or berries all year, so in spring we depend on grape holly and shadbush (also known as amelanchier), which bloom and bear fruit by May and produce through July. I also like to share a little of my berry crops with the birds. Any berries grown for human consumption will delight the feathered friends: blueberries, strawberries, blackberries, gooseberries, currants, or raspberries, for example. I protect most of my berry crops with netting, but I always leave a few plants open for the birds. Dwarf fruit trees — plums, cherries, or peaches — are another source of food for the birds in spring and summer.

Much more critical than those two seasons, though, are fall and winter. The best solution is to provide the birds with massed bunches of plants that make good cover *and* food sources. Berry-bearing shrubs are an especially good bet. Berry bushes will attract birds likely to be different from the seed-eating birds at your feeder, and the bushes that produce berries in fall will hold

*Pyracantha* **is a choice ornamental, offering berries that birds love.**

*Viburnum dentatum.*

fruit into late winter, when birds may be finding wild food in short supply. Firethorns, or *Pyracantha*, and flowering dogwood are excellent berry bushes, as are the mountain ashes, winterberry hollies and junipers such as the Eastern red cedar.

I also like the native viburnums, which are especially heavy fruit-setters. Arrowwood viburnum, American cranberrybush, and black haw viburnum will all form a dense shrub mass, and will bear fruit from September through January or February.

Privets are exellent choices for hedging, because they provide fine bird cover with their thickly intertwined branches, *and* if you've left some unpruned to flower they'll hold fruit — blue or blue-black berries — late in winter. Likewise, tree holly holds fruit until April or May. For a wide variety of shapes and forms, I favor the cotoneaster group, which gives a range of food-bearing plants from growth that crawls on the ground to plants 8 to 10 feet tall. A few are evergreen, with berries from early fall through late winter, and very adaptable to many different soil conditions. Junipers are also excellent, providing thick cover and, in the female varieties, an ample food supply. The junipers do need strong sun, but they can be downright spiny, making some of the best cover planting around. I'd hate to be a housecat trying to chase chickadees into a big Hetzi juniper!

As you can see, by planning and planting with the birds in mind, I can offer them food sources throughout the year. The grape holly and Amelanchier start things off in early spring, after which the birds feast on their ample supply of natural foods, augmented tastily by a few of our Victory Garden berries. Come fall, the viburnums, berry-bearing species, and cotoneasters sustain the birds, and berries and fruit produced by those plants keep them going through the winter, as well.

For hummingbirds, I plant as many red, tubular-shaped flowers as I can. Scarlet salvia, (an excellent bedding plant), cypress vine, scarlet petunias, and scarlet gladioli are excellent hummingbird-attracting annuals. Good hummingbird perennials include bee balm, Texas sage (an annual in the North), wild columbine, and trumpet honeysuckle.

Birds like seeds as much as they like berries and insects, of course, and your supermarket is far from the only source of seed. I've discovered over the years that growing my own birdseed is more fun than hauling home bags of supermarket stuff. Sunflowers are perhaps the best of all, but marigolds, cosmos, and zinnias add color to the garden, are heavy seed-producers, and, in the case of the marigolds, help protect the garden from certain pests. These flowers produce seeds that the birds love. Four-

**Annual salvia is a real hummingbird pleaser.**

**Pokeweed (*Phytolacca*).**

o'clocks and petunias attract birds in droves, as do the bright yellow flowers of the St.-John's-worts. The best way to insure a hearty seed supply is to resist the gardener's habit of pinching off fading flowers to keep the plants in full bloom. Let the flowers wither, and the seeds will swell in their pods. This will produce lots of birdseed, plus seed for next year's planting of flowers.

Though shrubs and bushes, along with flowering plants, are the most important sources of food and cover for birds, trees can also be helpful. Many people think only of large deciduous trees when landscaping their yards, but in fact a greater number of smaller trees may be a better option for the average-sized yard to which the homeowner wants to attract birds. Semidwarf or dwarf fruit trees, crab apples, hawthorns, flowering dogwoods, and Cornellian cherry are all good choices. They produce fruit and lots of spring color, along with pleasing fall foliage. I also think the sassafras is a superb choice. Though not widely available, it produces perhaps the most spectacular fall foliage of any tree. The female trees produce fruit, and the leaves are quite aromatic, producing the pungent, surprising scent of gumbo filé, an essential ingredient in Cajun cuisine.

# APPENDIX: AGRICULTURAL EXTENSION SERVICES

## Alabama

Agricultural Extension Service
Bulletin Room
Alabama Cooperative Extension Service
Auburn University
Auburn, AL 36849
(205) 826-5323

## Alaska

Agricultural Extension Service
University of Alaska
2651 Providence Avenue
Anchorage, AK 99504
(907) 277-1488

## Arizona

Agricultural Extension Service
University of Arizona
Tucson, AZ 85721
(602) 626-2438

## Arkansas

Agricultural Extension Service
Cooperative Extension Service
University of Arkansas, USDA
1201 McAlmont, Box 391
Little Rock, AR 72203
(501) 376-6301

## California

Agricultural Extension Service
University of California
Davis, CA 95616
(916) 752-0412

Agricultural Extension Service
San Joaquin Valley Agricultural Research Extension Center
9240 South Riverbend Avenue
Palier, CA 93648
(209) 646-2794

Agricultural Extension Service
Department of Botany and Plant Sciences
University of California
Riverside, CA 92521
(714) 787-3432

## Colorado

Agricultural Extension Service
Department of Horticulture
Colorado State University
Fort Collins, CO 80523
(303) 491-7018

## Connecticut

Agricultural Extension Service
University of Connecticut
Storrs, CT 06268
(203) 486-3435

## Delaware

Agricultural Extension Service
University of Delaware
Newark, DE 19711
(302) 738-2531

Agricultural Extension Service
University Substation Division
R.D. 2, Box 48
Georgetown, DE 19947
(302) 856-5250

## District of Columbia

Agricultural Extension Service
1351 Nicholson Street, N.W.
Washington, DC 20011
(202) 282-7403

## Florida

Agricultural Extension Service
Agricultural Research Center
3205 S.W. 70th Avenue
Fort Lauderdale, FL 33314
(305) 475-8990

Agricultural Extension Service
University of Florida
Gainesville, FL 32611
(904) 392-2134

## Georgia

Agricultural Extension Service
University of Georgia
Athens, GA 30602
(404) 542-8861

## Hawaii

Agricultural Extension Service
University of Hawaii
3190 Maile Way
Honolulu, HI 96822
(808) 948-7256

## Idaho

Agricultural Extension Service
University of Idaho
Box 300
Boise, ID 83701
(208) 334-3209

## Illinois

Agricultural Extension Service
Extension Specialist, Floriculture
205 Ornamental Horticulture
Building
University of Illinois
Urbana, IL 61801
(217) 333-2123

Agricultural Extension Service
Extension Vegetable Specialist
208 Vegetable Crops Building
University of Illinois
Urbana, IL 61801
(217) 333-1969

Agricultural Extension Service
Extension Specialist, Pomology
104 Horticulture Field Lab
University of Illinois
Urbana, IL 61801
(217) 333-1522

## Indiana

Agricultural Extension Service
Department of Horticulture
Purdue University
West Lafayette, IN 47907
(317) 749-2261

## Iowa

Agricultural Extension Service
2 Northcrest Drive
Council Bluffs, IA 51507
(712) 328-0077

## Kansas

Agricultural Extension Service
Department of Horticulture
Kansas State University
Manhattan, KS 66506
(913) 532-6170

## Kentucky

Agricultural Extension Service
Agricultural Science Center
North, Room N-318
University of Kentucky
Lexington, KY 40546
(606) 257-2874

## Louisiana

Agricultural Extension Service
Louisiana State University
Baton Rouge, LA 70803
(504) 388-4141

## Maine

Agricultural Extension Service
University of Maine
Orono, ME 04473
(207) 581-2771

Agricultural Extension Service
Highmoor Experimental Farm
Monmouth, ME 04259
(207) 933-2100

## Maryland

Agricultural Extension Service
University of Maryland
College Park, MD 20742
(301) 454-3143

Agricultural Extension Service
Vegetable Research Farm,
Route 5
Salisbury, MD 21801
(301) 742-8788

## Massachusetts

Agricultural Extension Service
Bowditch Hall
University of Massachusetts
Amherst, MA 01003
(413) 545-2250

Agricultural Extension Service
33 King Street
Northampton, MA 01060
(413) 584-2556

## Michigan

Agricultural Extension Service
Department of Horticulture
Michigan State University
East Lansing, MI 48824
(517) 355-5178

## Minnesota

Agricultural Extension Service
University of Minnesota
St. Paul, MN 55108
(612) 376-7574

## Mississippi

Agricultural Extension Service
Box 5426
Mississippi State, MS 39762
(601) 325-3935

## Missouri

Agricultural Extension Service
University of Missouri
Columbia, MO 65201
(314) 882-7511

## Montana

Agricultural Extension Service
Plant and Soil Sciences Department
Montana State University
Bozeman, MT 59715
(406) 994-4601

## Nebraska

Agricultural Extension Service
377 Plant Science Building
University of Nebraska
Lincoln, NE 68503
(402) 472-2454

## Nevada

Agricultural Extension Service
University of Nevada
Reno, NV 89507
(702) 784-6981

## New Hampshire

Agricultural Extension Service
Plant Science Department
University of New Hampshire
Durham, NH 03824
(603) 862-1200

## New Jersey

Agricultural Extension Service
Blake Hall
Box 231
Rutgers, The State University
New Brunswick, NJ 08903
(201) 932-9393

## New Mexico

Agricultural Extension Service
New Mexico State University
Las Cruces, NM 88003
(505) 646-1521

## New York

Agricultural Extension Service
Cornell University
Ithaca, NY 14853

## North Carolina

Agricultural Extension Service
Department of Horticultural
Science
North Carolina State University
Raleigh, NC 27607
(919) 737-3131

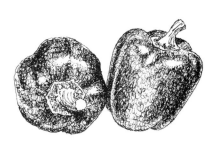

## North Dakota

Agricultural Extension Service
North Dakota State University
Fargo, ND 58102
(701) 237-8163

## Ohio

Agricultural Extension Service
Ohio Agricultural Research
Development Center
Wooster, OH 44691
(216) 264-1021

## Oklahoma

Agricultural Extension Service
Oklahoma State University
Stillwater, OK 74078

## Oregon

Agricultural Extension Service
Oregon State University
Corvallis, OR 97331
(503) 754-3464

## Pennsylvania

Agricultural Extension Service
102 Tyson Building
University Park, PA 16802
(814) 863-2194

## Puerto Rico

Agricultural Extension Service
Departmento de Horticultura
Recinto Universitario de
Mayaguez
Mayaguez, PR 00708
(809) 832-4040, ext. 3004

## Rhode Island

Agricultural Extension Service
University of Rhode Island
Kingston, RI 02881
(401) 792-2791

## South Carolina

Agricultural Extension Service
Department of Horticulture
161 P&AS Building
Clemson University
Clemson, SC 29631
(803) 656-3011

## South Dakota

Agricultural Extension Service
Horticulture and Forestry
Department
South Dakota State University
Brookings, SD 57007
(605) 688-5136

## Tennessee

Agricultural Extension Service
University of Tennessee
Box 1071
Knoxville, TN 37901
(615) 974-7324

## Texas

Agricultural Extension Service
Texas A&M University
College Station, TX 77843
(713) 845-7341

## Utah

Agricultural Extension Service
Utah State University
Logan, UT 84322
(801) 750-2258

## Vermont

Agricultural Extension Service
Hills Building
University of Vermont
Burlington, VT 05401
(802) 656-2630

## Virgin Islands

Agricultural Extension Service
Box L
Kingshill, St. Croix, VI 00850
(809) 778-0246

## Virginia

Agricultural Extension Service
Virginia Polytechnic Institute
Blacksburg, VA 24061
(703) 961-6723

### Washington

Agricultural Extension Service
Washington State University
Pullman, WA 99164
(509) 335-2511

### West Virginia

Agricultural Extension Service
West Virginia University
Morgantown, WV 26506
(304) 293-4801, 4802

### Wisconsin

Agricultural Extension Service
University of Wisconsin
Madison, WI 53706
(608) 262-0768

### Wyoming

Agricultural Extension Service
Plant Science Division
University of Wyoming
Box 3354, University Station
Laramie, WY 82071
(307) 766-2243

# THE
# VICTORY GARDEN
# LANDSCAPE GUIDE

PRINCIPAL PHOTOGRAPHY
DAVID M. STONE

# THE VICTORY GARDEN LANDSCAPE GUIDE

## BY
## THOMAS WIRTH

### WITH THE ASSISTANCE OF
### JAY HOWLAND

*To the memory of my maternal grand-
mother, Louise Schwab Schaller, who
nurtured my roots at a very early age*

# ACKNOWLEDGMENTS

I am greatly indebted to Russell Morash — originator, producer, and director of the PBS "Victory Garden" series. Russ provides the stimuli and atmosphere needed to bring out the best in those around him, and by example sets the highest standards of artistry and do-it-yourselfism. Jay Howland put forth a tremendous effort as writer in the preparation of this book, and I am certain it would never have been completed without her. Jay transformed my nearly illegible scribbles and sketches into logical order and readable English, always capturing the essence of what I was trying to say. William D. Phillips, senior editor at Little, Brown, was an uncompromising and enthusiastic supporter during the growth of the book. His acute sense of purpose kept everyone in focus and made us all feel good about hard work. Bill passed the baton to Laura Fillmore during the concluding phase, and it was she who gave the content a much-needed final pruning and reordering. Jack Foley of the WGBH design department is responsible for the design of the book. He masterminded the format to incorporate artfully a voluminous mass of information, photographs, and drawings. David Stone took most of the wonderful photographs — and became less terrified of knocking on strange doors as time progressed. And Marianne Orlando added her fine hand to produce the expert illustrations.

Many of my professional friends at Sasaki Associates provided receptive ears and responsive suggestions. Joe Hibbard was particularly helpful during the early stages, and Paul Gardescu urged simplicity and the concept of landscape as space — ideas I hope I have succeeded in communicating. Mas Kinoshita, my mentor for nearly a decade, whose holistic approach to design is contagious, is present in many places in this book. My friends at universities, arboretums, and nurseries across the country, too many to mention, have been most generous teachers over the years. I did call on Wayne Mezitt of Weston Nurseries in Hopkinton, Massachusetts, and William Flemmer III of Princeton Nurseries in Princeton, New Jersey, to review preliminary plant lists, and I am grateful for their many suggestions.

I cannot omit all the people at Little, Brown, from Mike Mattil, the tireless copy editor, to Peter Carr, who was in charge of manufacturing the book. Or Don Cutler of the Sterling Lord Agency, literary agent for WGBH, with whom I had long discussions early on about the original outline for *The Victory Garden Landscape Guide*. This book has also benefited indirectly from the generosity of George J. Ball, Incorporated, and of Public Television stations, who together sponsor the "Victory Garden" television series.

And finally, a tribute to my family: Helene, my wife, who has labored to keep the larder full while I was writing, and our five children. Each has good reason to feel that this book is partly theirs, too.

# INTRODUCTION

The "Victory Garden" series first aired on public television back in 1975. Originally titled "Crockett's Victory Garden," it began as a show dedicated to growing vegetables. Its setting was a garden in Boston, Massachusetts, right outside the studios of WGBH-TV. Its heart and soul was Jim Crockett, an inspiring gardener and a man much loved by all who were lucky enough to know him — whether in person or through the television series. His knowledgeable successor as host is Bob Thompson, and with Bob at the helm "The Victory Garden" is going strong, watched by millions of viewers every growing season.

Over the years the show has broadened its scope to embrace everything from houseplants to flowers to greenhouse culture to landscaping, in addition to the garden vegetables that were the foundation for the whole thing. And four books have grown out of the series: *Crockett's Victory Garden*, *Crockett's Indoor Garden*, *Crockett's Flower Garden*, and *Crockett's Tool Shed*.

In many ways this book follows the lead of the volumes that preceded it. Like both the books and the show, *The Victory Garden Landscape Guide* responds to Americans' enthusiasm for gardening and their fascination with the natural environment. And as Jim Crockett's and Bob Thompson's involvement grew out of their respective personal backgrounds, I have come to the "Victory Garden" show and to this book from a lifetime of working in the landscape both as a professional and for my own pleasure.

Growing up in rural Pennsylvania, I started gardening with my grandmother in a patch all my own at the age of six. At an early age I also started observing and enjoying the structure of the landscape. There was an old stone tower on a hill in a nearby state park, and I often climbed up and looked out over rolling fields of different crops, contoured ribbons of green and gold, dotted with stone farmhouses and barns. I loved the sight. I was an active 4-H club member, too, and each summer we would travel to the state university for vegetable-judging contests. One of these was held, coincidentally, at the landscape architecture department; and I'll never forget that day. I was totally distracted from the vegetables by the terrific drawings and photographs on display. Then and there I decided that a landscape architect was what I wanted to be, that the built environment fascinated me as much as the natural one.

I spent four and a half years studying horticulture and landscape design at Rutgers University, and two studying landscape architecture at the University of Michigan. Meanwhile I worked at jobs ranging from sod farming to landscape contracting to maintaining landscapes at New York World's Fair pavilions, along with several stints in professional offices. All this hands-on experience led to a long-term position as a member of the firm of Sasaki Associates in Watertown, Massachusetts, where I was part of many teams that designed and oversaw the construction of landscaping projects all over the country.

I still do a great deal of building. It was while I was in the midst of turning a huge old 1800 barn into a family home (which now houses five kids, a very busy wife, four cats, and a dog) that WGBH-TV asked me to appear on another television series, called "This Old House." I've designed and supervised several on-camera landscape transformations for that series, and whenever a special landscaping opportunity comes up on "The Victory Garden" I happily step in. On the show we have tackled many of the challenges facing homeowners: small spaces, steep banks, shady areas . . . in fact, this book grew from all the possible situations we felt our audience might encounter in their own landscapes.

This book is for everyone, from the city apartment-dweller to the suburbanite to the owner of wide-open rural spaces. One of my central themes here is that *any* place can benefit from thoughtful planning, well-informed choices of plants and construction materials, and the application of a few imaginative ideas. And you may be surprised — even if all you have is a stoop or a small backyard — at how many good ideas you have once you start learning how to think about landscaping.

As with the other Victory Garden books, the major part of *The Victory Garden Landscape Guide* (Part II, The Landscaping Year) has a calendar format that follows the twelve months of the year. Each month's entries look at aspects of landscape design, plantings, construction, and maintenance that are in keeping with that season. The twelve-month structure, first adopted in *Crockett's Victory Garden*, has proved tremendously helpful in all the Victory Garden books, but especially in the *Landscape Guide*: it breaks a large and complex subject into manageable, accessible areas of interest.

Yet in many ways *The Victory Garden Landscape Guide* departs from the pattern set by its predecessors both in subject matter and in treatment. A landscape is an entire environment for living, very different from a vegetable patch, a flower bed, or a greenhouse. And a landscape matures not over a summer but over a lifetime. Trees, shrubs, vines, and ground covers can be a big job to plant. Some trees and shrubs grow to a huge size, and they can live for dozens or hundreds of years; deciding what to plant becomes a long-term design decision, not a springtime experiment. Besides, most of these plants are fully as important in the landscape in the dead of winter as they are in spring and summer. The same is true of landscape construction: it's large scale, permanent, and a year-round fixture of the place where you live.

The complexity of the subject has called for yet another departure from Victory Garden tradition — Part I of this book. I have not plunged straight into the first month of the landscaping year, as the earlier books did, but have begun instead with an introductory section, Landscaping Essentials, which provides a brief primer on landscape design. Its goals are to open your eyes, stir your imagination, help you answer some important questions, alert you to some pitfalls, and assist you in setting priorities and making workable plans.

Part I is designed to help you see the possibilities of your situation by perceiving the world in landscaping terms and approaching your project (or problem) with an informed attitude. Basic principles and broad guidelines are the subject in Part I. Part II, on the other hand, invites you to roam from month to month, finding the particular items that pertain to your situation. There are assorted "Landscaping Opportunities" to consider: city gardens, the look of your garden in winter, and easy-maintenance landscaping are among them. There are suggestions and plant lists for all purposes and circumstances as well as monthly maintenance tasks and horticultural projects suited to different seasons. I'll introduce you to all kinds of landscape construction challenges — drainage, stairs, walks, and decks — and to the materials you'll use in building.

Being a successor to *Crockett's Victory Garden* and *Crockett's Flower Garden*, this book tries to build on, not duplicate, much of the specific gardening advice those books contained. For instance, while I heartily endorse the making of compost heaps and the use of compost as soil enrichment and/or mulch, I won't repeat here the excellent composting instructions given in *Crockett's Victory Garden*. Rather than reiterating planting and cultivation information that has already been well covered, I'll focus on ways to use plants in the larger setting; and I'll deal primarily with plants that have not appeared in the previous volumes.

As for prescribing solutions to landscape design problems, this book steers clear of ready-made formulas. Throughout the book I'll look at varied settings, present data about construction materials and their uses, and suggest a wide range of plants to meet given needs. I'll introduce you to the landscape's components and offer you the tools and procedural guidelines for forming them into an environment you can enjoy. Perhaps you're interested in putting some container plants on your patio or grouping shrubs to soften the edge of a lawn. Or maybe you want to redesign and rebuild your backyard from the ground up, put in a terrace, establish a hedge, even install an ornamental pool or fountain. You can find ideas for all these situations here. Browse and investigate. The search for solutions is always exciting, and the final achievement yet more so.

**Drafting a chapter at my outdoor table in the shade of young red oaks transplanted from nearby woods.**

# PART I LANDSCAPING ESSENTIALS

Since the beginnings of time, people have yearned to organize and beautify their surroundings. And probably since the beginnings of time (certainly throughout my experience), people have felt some degree of insecurity or anxiety about their ability to do it. Yet in a very fundamental way, it is precisely the people who inhabit a landscape who are best qualified to decide how it could best function, look, and feel.

One of my chief aims is to convince you that you *can* design an improvement to your property — or a whole new landscape — if you go slowly and learn to look around you. The slowness, the process, is as important as the final product. There's no great mystery about shaping your environment, once you grasp the basic principles of design and composition and come to terms with your raw materials: the soil, the climate, the plants and other material you have at hand.

Landscape design is at once fine art, applied art, and natural science. It combines the disciplines and the fascination of all three. A well-conceived and well-made landscape will be beautiful to all the senses (that's fine art); comfortable and functional in its plantings, structures, and spatial arrangements (that's applied art); and energy-efficient, not too demanding of maintenance, and healthily self-sustaining (that's science). Partly because landscaping is a combination of arts and sciences, and partly because it's a large and long-term assignment, it is natural to feel a little timid about it. But every one of us has the instincts required. A landscaping project is eye-opening to do, rewarding when completed. And it is great fun.

**Opposite: early-flowering Korean azalea brightens the border planting at the lawn edge, while shadblow blooms in the background.**

# 1  THE ELEMENTS OF DESIGN

**Opposite: Landscape masses: (A) Space is well defined by enclosing elements. (B) Space leaks out with removal of background mass. (C) Removing canopy destroys space. (D) Cluttering or overfilling dilutes space.**

The terminology of design is really nothing more than a specialized shorthand, a series of code words used to label qualities of objects or spaces. Happily, in landscape design, the objects and the spaces — and their qualities — are all part of everyone's daily experience. So learning the language is no problem.

This chapter is partly an extended glossary, to let you know what I mean when I use any given term, and partly a preview of the applications of these elements of design. I'll often mention issues to bear in mind and questions to ask as you go about designing, redesigning, or modifying your landscape.

The five elements of design are *mass*, *form*, *line*, *texture*, and *color*. A glance out your window will afford you with examples of all five. It will probably also suggest to you why mass, form, and line are the essence of landscape design — and how texture and color reinforce and enrich the effects created by the first three. In a landscape, mass, form, and line are the cake; texture and color are the frosting.

**Mass**  Mass is volume of space, whether occupied or empty. Every object in the landscape has mass: your house, the trees and shrubs and structures around it, everything that rests on or emerges from the ground plane. Empty space has mass too, for the purposes of landscape design, because the volumes of spaces have to be related to the volumes of objects in and around them.

Visualize for a moment a three-story Victorian house set in front of a wooded area, with a huge evergreen hedge to one side, a shrub border on the other, a stone wall across the front of the lot — and a single

**The dominant mass is "negative space" defined by the hollow in the ground, the backdrop of greenery, and the overarching tree limbs.**

A.

B.

C.

D.

*Orlando*

magnificent sugar maple in the front lawn. The masses of the house and the sugar maple live happily in the mass of space defined by the encircling hedge, shrubbery, woods, and wall. But alter any one of these components and you will significantly alter the spatial relationships of the whole picture. For instance, removing the woods or the evergreen hedge will allow the space around the house to leak out, so to speak, in all directions. Removing the sugar maple will make the house seem overpowering. Filling the space between the house and the tree with other plantings or structures will dilute the power of the composition by breaking up one mass: the mass of space.

Artists speak of positive space (meaning space occupied by tangible objects) and negative space (meaning space occupied by air); and negative space is at least as important as positive. So think of mass as space, and you're on your way to understanding a pivotal element of design.

Masses are obvious and easy to take for granted. The bigger they are, the easier it is to forget all about them; and a common mistake when you're starting out is to get involved prematurely in minor things like selecting shrubs, shopping for furniture, planning details of a fence or a flight of steps. But none of those details will look quite right in the end, if you don't think through the arrangement and balance of your major masses — including spaces — first.

**Form**   Form means shape. We are surrounded by a host of natural and man-made rectangles, squares, circles, ovals, triangles. Consider the natural geometry of the pyramidal growth of a Norway spruce, not to mention the gables of houses or garages. Circles and ovals? Look at the natural egg shapes of cedar trees, the plump forms of rhododendrons, the soft rounded line of a hilltop or knoll, the rough shoulder of a rock out-cropping. Rectangles and squares are a little trickier to find in nature, but they abound in the structures people build, from walls to terraces to houses.

The forms I've been mentioning are all geometric and more or less regular; you could plot their outlines mathematically. What about free forms, those flowing irregular shapes that are far more common in nature than the geometric ones? Free forms are a tantalizing subject, because while there has been a great vogue for their use in gardens and land-scapes over the last century or two, they're the hardest of all forms to use successfully in landscape design. Done with sophistication and skill, free-form designs can convey a feeling that is marvellously casual, natur-alistic, and, well, free. Done without sophistication or skill, they can con-vey a feeling that is merely confused.

And it's not only free forms that convey feelings. Every kind of form carries with it a collection of associations based on everyday human experience, and those associations arouse age-old emotional responses. (The table here lists a few.) Forms actually affect the way you feel as you live, work, and play in your landscape.

## Forms

| Form | Association | Emotional connotation |
| --- | --- | --- |
| Circle | Egg, breast, ball, wheel | Soft, quiet, perfect, unbroken |
| Square | Block, cube | Stable, rigid, fixed, equal |
| Rectangle | Box, table, house | Narrow, directed, stable |
| Triangle | Pyramid, spire, knife | Sharp, strong, tense |
| Free | Amoeba, blob, squiggle | Loose, casual, undefined, imperfect |

So plan your landscape forms carefully. Should they be angular? Four-square? Fat and rounded? Lofty and attenuated? A landscape design consisting of a series of rectangles, for instance, will evoke an altogether different complex of emotions from one that employs ovoid or irregular shapes.

When choosing plants for form, take into account the size and the location of the plant. The soft shapes of dwarf white pine or mugho pine or the rounded cushion of a Sargent weeping hemlock are appealing on an intimate scale; the tall spheres and ovals of maples, beeches, or oaks are grander and must be seen from a distance to be appreciated. (Bear in

**Below, left: This man-made curvilin-ear form has a gen-tle, flowing shape.**

**Below, right: The naturally rounded form of cutleaf red Japanese maple also conveys a sense of softness and repose.**

mind, too, that many roundish trees branch near the ground, their lowest branches even sweeping the earth if allowed to do so. The effect is pleasant but does take up a lot of space.)

Other tree forms include picturesque types like weeping birches or gnarled, contorted pines; the vase or fan shapes of trees whose branches spread up and out, creating arched spaces beneath; and columnar or fastigiate forms that punctuate the landscape with strong verticals like exclamation points.

With each kind of form, think about its effect not only in itself but in relation to surrounding plantings and structures. There will be some forms you can't change, like the shapes of your house or the neighbors' garage or the wooded lot across the street. Plan the forms on your property to complement and harmonize with what exists; to screen it if necessary; and to suit your own personality and taste.

**Line**  Lines not only define edges and direct the eye; they are an important source of excitement and interest in themselves. Some landscape objects are mainly linear, like fences, driveways, walks, tree trunks and branches, boundaries of plantings or lawns, or the horizon. In winter, in the North, the landscape seems to consist mostly of lines — bare twigs, dry grasses, crisp edges of things. In summer the world leafs out; mass and form and color and texture come into their own; and line ceases to dominate.

As with forms, different kinds of line elicit different emotional responses. Straight lines give a feeling of formality, firmness, repose. Jagged lines and sharp angles suggest tension, excitement, stress. Curved lines are more relaxed and picturesque; irregular curves look "natural." A straight driveway is austere and efficient, whereas a slightly curved one is inviting, even mysterious or romantic.

Haphazard or controlled, rigid or swooping, stark or ornate, lines can distract, entertain, calm, or irritate the eye. Before you choose a picket fence, decide whether that zigzag edge is right for you. If you're

**Of all landscape elements, the tracery of tree branches against sky most completely exemplifies line and its effect.**

Line applied to man-made structures: strong, crisp lines of wall and pavement echo the architecture and draw the eye to the focal point at the corner of the house.

contemplating adding an S-curve to your drive, visualize how it will go with the lines of the house or the plantings on either side. In a tight site where rectilinear structures prevail, you will generally find it easier to work with square angles and straight lines, or with well-disciplined curves, than with random lines. With more space or in a natural setting, you have more latitude to cultivate free-flowing naturalistic effects.

**Texture** Visible texture is produced by the play of light and shadow on surfaces. Tangible texture is what you can feel with your hands, your feet, any part of your skin. Texture is perhaps the most sensual element of design, since it appeals to both sight and touch; and yet, like its sister element, color, texture plays only a supporting role in landscaping. It is, for the most part, something to decide on after the large questions of mass, form, and line have been dealt with. Practical considerations (such as slipperiness or tactile comfort) aside for a moment, textures are chiefly of interest for their ability to enhance the major effects you have been working on.

Still, there is much that you can do with texture. A landscape that was completely uniform in texture would be monotonous indeed. Textural variety affords visual relief, drama, even excitement. And since everything in nature, organic and inorganic, has its own texture, achieving this variety is a pleasure. There are countless kinds of grasses in a meadow and ground covers in the woods, and infinite degrees of roughness or smoothness in stone or wood. An herb garden is a perfect example of textural variety. Among the myriad shades of green and the different leaf and stem sizes and shapes, there are dozens of textures, from glossy to velvety to hairy. The textures enrich form, line, and color and create a tapestry of green on green.

Coarse visual textures result from strong contrasts of light and shadow — light washing the topmost surfaces, shadow filling the spaces between — as in a rubblestone wall or the foliage of a large-leaved tree

like a maple. Coarse textures impart an informal, bold, or rustic feeling. But because they can be uncomfortable to the touch, some coarse landscape textures can also be uneasy to the eye. To many people, rough-textured walks, drives, or seating areas are annoying or even threatening.

Coarse-textured plantings make such a strong statement that they need to be used with discretion. I'd generally recommend using no more than one-third coarse-foliaged trees or shrubs in a residential planting composition. Yet within that limitation, they definitely have a part to play. If you have decided on a shady, wooded corner at the far end of your yard, big-leaved maples or rhododendrons or viburnums (for instance) will add to the bucolic air. You can also use coarse-textured plantings to heighten an impression of perspective, by placing the coarser textures in the foreground and progressively finer ones farther away. Or you can use a single coarse-textured specimen as a focal point.

**Texture at work in the landscape: in the Japanese bonsai garden of the National Arboretum, fine foreground textures contrast with the coarser-textured foliage of background plantings.**

Fine landscape textures range from uniformly smooth and shiny surfaces to surfaces where there are only minute contrasts between light and shade: a smooth concrete walk, a smoothly finished wooden surface, a fine-leafed shrub like boxwood, a new-mown lawn. They express restraint, refinement, quietude; a neat or even formal feeling. If you want to give an elegant tone to a yard or patio, smooth finishes and fine-textured shrubbery will do the job: plants like small-leaved azaleas, cotoneasters, or spireas.

Finer-textured trees and shrubs often look best planted en masse for maximum impact. This is true, for instance, with birches, willows, spireas, or junipers. Many of these plants naturally tend to grow in clumps, so this is a very logical way to arrange them.

As you think about plant textures for your landscape, don't forget the winter. Evergreens remain the same throughout the year; but the textures of the bare twigs, branches, and trunks of deciduous plants come into their own once the leaves fall. For the most part, you'll find that the texture of the naked plant is closely related to its foliage texture. A Japanese maple's branches and twigs are as fine as its foliage; a red oak, sugar maple, or shagbark hickory has branches as coarse-textured as its leaves.

**Color** This last of the elements of design is another "secondary" or supporting element, but extremely important both for what it can do and for what it should not do. Used properly, whether as background or

**Color, rather than
texture, brings this
rock garden alive.**

as accent, color will enrich the beauty of a landscape. Used improperly,
color can be so distracting or abrasive as to ruin an otherwise good design.

If this seems paradoxical, think of photography. A black-and-
white photo reveals mass, form, and line, the three linchpins of landscape
design. A color photo of the same subject can actually camouflage them.
Or think of classical Greek statuary: to people nowadays it is almost dis-

tressing to imagine those elegant forms and serene lines decked out in garish pigments, as scholars say they originally were.

The primary colors of landscaping are nature's basic palette: green, brown, and blue. There are the greens and browns of vegetation and soil, and the blue of the sky present everywhere as reflected light. In nature, bright hues are reserved for accent — like the crimson of red-stemmed shrub dogwood or the white of birch bark — and for seasonal fireworks like spring and summer flowers and fall foliage.

Similarly, in a planned landscape the basic colors will be nature's triad of green, brown, and blue; but there's plenty of scope for artistic use of color in year-round accents (whether structures or plantings) and in seasonal displays.

Colors, like forms, lines, and textures, have their own set of emotional associations. Cheerful yellow. Frivolous pink. Businesslike beige. Restful green. Romantic mauve. They also have "temperatures." In an interior, you can warm a room up by painting it peach, or cool it down with blue-gray. Landscape color works the same. You can use pale flowers and bluish foliage to "cool" a hot sunny area, or you can plan for brilliant fall foliage if the autumn is cold where you live. In shady corners, you can plant flowering shrubs or perennials in clear, bright colors. And since cool colors seem to recede and pale colors to enlarge, you can use color to create illusory depth of perspective. A small and crowded garden, for instance, will feel more spacious if pale, cool colors predominate. A feeling of intimacy will result from the use of warmer, more intense colors.

There are a few dos and don'ts to keep in mind when you plan colors for your landscape design. Where flowers are concerned, avoid juxtaposing clashing colors like pink blossoms against red brick masonry, or orange side by side with magenta. And with all landscape plantings — whether leaves, bark, or flowers are the colored element — avoid crowding too many different hues in the same area. Confusion and conflict detract from the beauty of any one color.

**White paper birches really sing against a dark-painted house and the dark greens of evergreen shrubs and ground cover.**

Compose with autumn foliage color as well as blossom color in mind. Here, white birches, red and yellow maples, and dark green conifers make a beautiful fall triad.

Do consider using large masses of color. For winter effects, think about the soft green of the twigs of a Thurlow willow or the reddish glow of Virginia rose, whose twigs make a dense ground cover. In summer you have the whole palette of flowers and flowering trees and shrubs to work with. Massed blooms of a single color can be magnificent — a bed of pink azaleas, a bank of yellow forsythia. So can a mass of one color next to its complementary color(s), such as blue complemented by oranges and yellows. Or cluster purples, red-violets, and pinks together; or reds, yellow-oranges, and yellows.

To make the most of colored plantings (as with everything else in landscape design), take into account the setting. A contrasting backdrop such as a dark-colored wall or a stand of hemlocks will set off white birches or white flowering dogwoods. For the vivid bark and blooms of an Oriental cherry a light-colored backdrop is better — a white building or an open grassy area. And sunlight has an important impact, whether picking up a haze of golden twigs in wintertime or backlighting the shimmering foliage of beech trees in summer. You can make the light work for you to intensify every chromatic effect.

Mass, form, line, texture, and color. Each element plays a vital part. None can work alone. How effectively you assemble these elements determines how well the overall picture will succeed.

# 2 PRINCIPLES OF COMPOSITION

To compose means "to put together." Landscape composition puts together plants and all the other elements of a particular scene to make pleasing combinations of masses, forms, lines, textures, and colors. From a visual standpoint, a successful composition is one that brings its different components into harmony and unity. The effect of a well-arranged composition is more than the sum of the effects of the masses, forms, lines, colors, and textures that make it up.

In this chapter I'll try to give you a sense of the underlying principles or rules that make every composition work. I keep these five principles in mind throughout the process of design, and they serve as guidelines or controls for every choice I make. They are *scale*, *balance*, *rhythm*, *emphasis*, and *simplicity*.

**Scale**   Scale means relative size. If something is "out of scale" it's too big or too small for its location and surroundings; if it's "in scale" it is, like the baby bear's chair, just right. Proper scale is absolutely central to landscape design. It is interesting that a concept as easily grasped as scale can also be quite elusive to pin down in practice. It takes a certain amount of experience or training before you feel sure about scale in landscape design: you have to develop an eye for it.

The key to scaling things in the landscape is the human body. This is true because everything that is planted or built in a landscape has to fit the people who will live with it. Human height establishes sight lines — and they in turn decree how high or low a screening hedge or wall should be. Human breadth is the yardstick for the comfortable width of a pathway. Seats, benches, low walls for sitting on, all have to be tailored to the length of human legs. Human paces measure out the proper depth for steps and terraces. The human form determines the dimensions of houses, sheds, and gazebos; and these structures set the scale for the plantings around them.

**Foreground elements establish the scale of the vista to Mount Vernon. Without the gate and wall, relative sizes are uncertain.**

Bad examples of scale are a lot easier to come up with than good ones. If a picnic table dwarfs a small patio, a giant evergreen overshadows the facade of a house, or a rock garden is lost in the vastness of a formal lawn, an uncomfortable tension results. Very often, when I find myself in a generally pleasant landscape that feels wrong in some undefined way, and I analyze the feeling, I find that what is bothering me is a problem of scale.

**Any landscape structure or planting too large or too small for its surroundings is "out of scale" and detracts from the harmony of the composition.**

SCALE

**Balance**   Balance is partly, but not wholly, a matter of scale — because balance has to do not only with the relative sizes of things but with all the other attributes that go to make up their visual "weights" in the landscape. Such attributes include dark versus light colors; massiveness versus delicacy; brightness versus shade; rough textures versus smooth ones; curves versus angles; even noise versus quiet.

What constitutes a well-balanced landscape is partly subjective. For instance, some people are happiest in a very stark, sunny, wide-open environment, while others seek out sheltered grottos of shade and a feeling of great privacy. On the other hand, even an objective outside observer can sense whether the overall composition of a landscape, within its general type, is balanced or unbalanced.

The urge to bring order out of chaos is a deep-seated human instinct, and that's one reason why balance is so important. Also, equilibrium implies a kind of security. It might seem that symmetry would be the easiest route to a balanced landscape composition. After all, if you put two identical weights on a pair of scales, you bring them into balance. Why not just put identical evergreen shrubs on either side of the front door, identical flowering trees at either corner of the lot, and a round pool in the exact middle of the backyard? No, it won't work — at least not with the informal layouts and facades of most American homes. Symmetry is rarely found in the wild landscape, and perhaps for that reason a perfectly symmetrical garden or landscape design has a very strained and

**The driveway was moved to this location, where the horizontal mass of the handsome natural rock outcropping will be balanced by the upright mass of spruces planted on the opposite side.**

The diagram above and the photo at right show well-balanced composition. The arrangement of flower pot, lamp fixture, and wall sculpture is informal yet carefully planned.

Symmetrical planting at each side of the door is very awkward for this entry approached from one direction. In the second photo, asymmetry in planting and an added step in the landscape make a balanced composition.

stiff feeling, unless it is part of a totally symmetrical larger space. (Symmetry was, of course, the rule in formal gardens from Rome to the Renaissance; but that kind of formality is mostly inappropriate in America today, besides being very demanding and expensive to maintain.) Achieving balance is a more subtle matter, a matter of instinct, experience, and — even for practiced eyes — careful experimentation.

**Rhythm**   Rhythm means the predictably repeated elements in a landscape. A degree of regularity or repetition of masses, forms, lines, textures, and/or colors is necessary to a satisfactory composition. To realize how necessary, think what a hedge would look like if every plant in it were of a separate species. Or imagine a paved walk that combined bricks, paving stones, cobbles, rubblestone, and tiles. Or picture a massed

The key to the effect of this Japanese garden, above, is rhythmic repetition in depth. Gravel mounds and close-clipped yews echo the triangular shapes of the hilltops beyond.

Repetition of form and line: pyramidal branching of weeping hemlock (at left) accompanies the peaked cap of the fence and roof over the gateway. Fence boards and lattice are rhythmic vertical elements.

planting consisting of seventeen different sizes and shapes of trees. Even nature's "massed plantings," otherwise known as woods, are made up of grouped colonies of trees of the same species and similar size.

Excessive repetition can be boring. But there are some things, like pavements, walls, fences, and shrub orders, that really demand a regular, consistent treatment. In a way, rhythm in the landscape has a reassuring effect. The predictable elements in a visual composition, like the predictable patterns in a musical composition, make an expression of unity and completeness.

**Emphasis** It may be that the single most important factor in a successful composition is the choice and handling of emphasis. Just as a person tries to highlight his or her own best assets, just as a painting must have a central subject or focal point, a landscape should be given a focus or concentration of significance. Emphasis is a way to bring out the latent personality or unique character of a place. Without emphasis, a design can't help but be somewhat bland and characterless.

This is not to say that every family should go overboard and rush out to divert a river into their backyard or construct a monument on their front lawn. Often, giving emphasis to a landscape design is a matter of tact — of gently guiding the eye to the chosen focal point; of allowing an existing feature or quality to assume its natural dominance. The center of emphasis could be an attractively framed doorway, a view of a hill or a pond in the distance, a grand old tree, a charming or interesting piece of sculpture. Emphasis can be developed through bold impact or through subtle enrichment. In a very small garden where the whole thing is treated as a jewel, the garden is its own emphasis. The more sprawling or featureless a landscape, on the other hand, the greater its need for shaping and framing and direction.

**Simplicity** There are two good reasons why, in landscape design as perhaps nowhere else, "less is more." The first reason is practical:

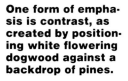
One form of emphasis is contrast, as created by positioning white flowering dogwood against a backdrop of pines.

simplicity saves money, time, and irritating (but hard to undo) mistakes. The second is aesthetic: a simple design is far more likely to work out well than an overly ambitious one.

Even simplicity, of course, can be carried too far. A perfectly flat expanse of green grass is simple, all right, but not much else. Sensitive restraint is the keynote here. A landscape design can achieve an effect of pleasing simplicity by staying away from artificiality or fussy detail; by limiting the variety of different colors, textures, or forms that are used; and by rationing the number of kinds of plants and construction materials. Even within all those constraints, a landscape can be as functional, comfortable, inviting, and richly green or flowery as anyone could wish.

In fact if you think of a landscape you know and enjoy — a landscape you always feel peaceful in — you'll probably discover that it is basically uncomplicated. Maybe there is a nicely settled feeling to the house; maybe the house is framed by one or two big old trees and some reasonably disciplined shrubbery; maybe a sunny side yard is sheltered by a screen of more of the same kind of shrubbery; maybe there is a flower garden behind the house, giving way to woods or an open field with a glimpse of blue distance; maybe a rambling stone wall ties the whole place together. A place like that can be beautifully simple, and simply beautiful.

As you look at the space around your house and consider ways to refurbish or redesign it, concepts like "balance" and "scale" — basic though they are — may seem rather abstract in relation to the questions you're asking yourself: Where can I clear a level place to sit or play? How do I create a visual boundary for the front lawn, yet still allow sunlight and a sense of openness around the house?

**Simplicity of materials, forms, and lines gives this Bucks County farmhouse landscape great strength and serenity. Note the absence of foundation "landscaping."**

These are really spatial questions. In answering them, you'll move from concepts and principles to more practical structural matters. You'll probably want to spend a lot of time outdoors pacing off distances and envisioning possibilities. Chapter 3 helps you see how to open, enclose, or frame volumes of space in your landscape.

# 3 THE STRUCTURE OF THE LANDSCAPE

One of the first things many people do to clarify their thoughts when they are planning a space — whether a living room, a vegetable plot, a patio with grouped furniture or container plants, or a roomy front lawn — is to make a rough thumbnail sketch or map of what might go where. This can be a helpful preliminary exercise, but it has one notable limitation for landscape planning: it is two-dimensional. In this chapter I'd like to encourage you to keep thinking about your situation in three-dimensional terms.

A landscape architect tries to form enclosures and openings that relate to each other and to the whole, in much the same way as an architect works out the design of a building. The only real differences (apart from differences of scale and function) have to do with media, since landscape architecture incorporates not only structures but earth and sky, changing climate, and living vegetation.

I'll distill these primary three-dimensional or structural concerns into four terms that are favorites of mine, and that are certainly familiar to everyone: *spaces*, *edges*, *views*, and *entries*.

**Spaces** Spaces are the "rooms" of the landscape, and it is natural and useful to approach them in ways closely analogous to the ways you'd handle rooms in a house. In a typical residential landscape, whose space is limited, different units are best treated intimately so as to give a sense of charm and fascination. In a more expansive situation you can use space in a grander manner, developing vistas and panoramas (as well as sheltered nooks) much as the great houses of the past used galleries, halls, and ballrooms (as well as cozier spaces). In the smallest situations, such as city gardens or closely circumscribed suburban lots, I'm always looking for ways to enlarge the apparent size of the landscape — perhaps through the placement of plantings or structures; through color or texture; or by exploiting a view of space beyond the legal property line, what I call "borrowed landscape." Your eye takes in all the space it sees, whether that space technically belongs to you or not. Which is another of the delightful facts peculiar to landscape design.

In any landscape there has to be a hierarchy of spaces: the large and the small, the visual and the utilitarian, all fitting together and supporting one another to make up an attractive and livable whole. Take, for example, a house with a front yard. Consider that yard first as an element of the neighborhood around it. Then look at the yard as the entire space bounded by the house, the street, and the side property lines. Within that, look at the subordinate spaces. There might be the space into which you drive your car; then a walk through a natural pocket of trees and shrubs to the front door; then the area around the front door,

The canopy of pine boughs and walls of surrounding shrubbery form an outdoor living space or "room" whose appeal is enhanced by the placement of furniture.

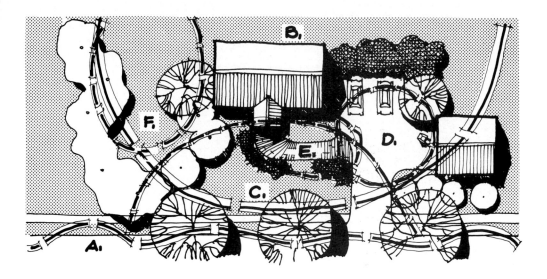

**LARGE SPACES**
A. STREET SPACE
B. HOUSE
C. FRONT YARD

**SMALL SPACES** ·
D. ARRIVAL SPACE
E. ENTRY
F. SIDE YARD

**Consider the relationships of spaces with each other and with the setting.**

with a recessed entry which is another space in itself. The largest space of all might be primarily of visual "use" — the plantings, ground covers, and lawn between house and street.

The challenge and the excitement of dealing with spaces lie in how you enclose or define them. And they do have to be enclosed or defined. That is a fundamental job of landscape design, just as a job of architecture is to establish the sizes and shapes of rooms within a building.

**Edges** I use the word "edges" to mean two different things. One group of landscape "edges" are the planes that enclose spaces — the floors, walls, and ceilings of outdoor rooms. The second group are junctions or meeting points where different planes or materials coincide.

Look first at the horizontal plane: the ground. It's tempting to think of the ground plane as flat and more or less neutral. Certainly that's the easiest way to picture it. But by manipulating the topography and texture of the "floor" of the landscape you can achieve some of the most delightful and unexpected effects of all — and often with the least effort or expense. Think of the way you will set apart a small wooded area if you drop the level of the lawn a bit below it. Or imagine the instant effect of seclusion if you recess a sitting area below the grade of the shrubbery that surrounds it.

Vertical edges, the "walls" of the landscape, affect the definition of spaces the most. The sides of the house and other permanent structures are major vertical elements, and there is little you can do to change them. You can, however, soften or screen them if you want. And you should pay attention to their materials and overall style so as to harmonize with them whatever additions you have in mind. Other landscape walls can range from the solid but symbolic (like the low stone wall that stops neither the eye nor anything else) to the transparent but impassable

(like the thorny barberry hedge). Walls can be as picturesque as a grove of birches or as plain as a board fence. Some walls block both view and wind, so as to provide winter shelter; others block the view but let wind breathe through for summer ventilation. Your choice depends on your particular landscape needs.

The topmost ceiling of all landscape spaces is the sky. Yet there are subceilings that can be equally important, either because they contribute to a feeling of privacy and coziness; or because they afford shelter from sun, rain, or snow; or because they are in proportion to a smaller-scaled landscape space. These subceilings include foliage, trellises, or roofs of decks or porches. Some ceilings are dense enough to block out sunlight and the sky altogether. Others let light dapple through all year round. Others cast dense shade in summer but admit sun in winter.

Under my second definition, landscape edges are the boundaries or junctions where two planes or surfaces meet. Where lawn meets shrubbery, where patio pavement meets lawn, where a wall meets the flowers at its foot: all are edges. So are the visual "meetings" of things, like the irregular profile of a tree against the sky or of a group of shrubs against the side of a garage. Walks and pathways are always a big edging challenge, being such strong linear interruptions to the ground plane. The Japanese have always been past masters at careful transitions between structures and the landscape.

When you think about edges and edgings, take into account your general attitude and the character of your place. Some personalities — and some landscapes — go best with soft, undefined edges. Some people prefer things crisp and hard-edged. Some like a lot of ornament and interest in their edges. Here you have to make your own decisions; but as a general rule you will have the best luck if you work for simplicity.

Consistency of materials and style is another important goal. An informal rubblestone wall will look funny abutting a conservative brick house; a tightly sheared boxwood hedge will be out of place bordering an open meadow-style lawn. As always, coordinate edging elements with their surroundings for the most pleasing result.

**Views**   There has long been a dictum among landscaping professionals that views should be pictorial: they should be ideal for photographing or painting. I don't necessarily agree. In fact some of the most satisfying and exciting landscapes I know are almost impossible to photograph — or paint, for that matter. There's an old cartoon that shows two artists looking out their studio window at a stupendously gorgeous sunset over distant rolling hills, one artist saying to the other, "Corny, isn't it?" Like sunsets, many views are more than the sum of their parts. They involve transitory angles of light combined with sound, atmosphere, even smell.

It is true, however, that fine views, particularly when enframed, can be pictorial. When you consider views purely as seen images, you realize how important it is that each view have the elements of a well-

**This deck was designed to take advantage of the pleasing outlook and existing vegetation. Surrounding trees make a frame, and a simple low railing allows an uninterrupted view.**

composed picture. There should be a background, a middle ground, and a foreground, and well-planned transitions among them. And there should be something — whether planting, structure, or just a certain slant of light — to give a focal point to the composition.

The eye will never tire of looking at beautifully arranged images. For that reason I do recommend that important windows of the house have a considered view, windows being natural frames. Some windows' views will be more important than others, of course. And you should be cautious about getting into heroic measures to frame some far-off vista at the expense of valuable landscape details nearer by. Sometimes the distant view is not worth the compromises you may have to make. In such cases you may actually enjoy the view more if you're obliged to take a short walk to see it.

Speaking of walking, you should also think about the different ways you see views depending on whether you are moving or standing still. You've probably experienced the most extreme example of these differences: your perception of a certain spot when you pass by it in a car, and your changed perception of the same place when you are on foot. If you stop walking and sit down, still other qualities of the view will capture your attention. Duration makes the difference. Japanese gardens recognize and play upon these different ways of seeing through "positions of pause": a pathway may be deliberately made to turn or a pavement to change to a more rubbly texture, which forces you to slow down and look about you.

The effects of light may be the determining factors in the charm — or lack of it — of a given view. If you take a certain sequence of open spaces, trees, and shrubs and look at them in full noon sunlight with the sun behind you, you'll see a rather undifferentiated mass of green. When the sun comes around to the side, it will lend dramatic highlighting to forms and textures, besides casting fine shadows. Backlighting the same scene makes the foliage seem to glow from within with an ethereal quality.

Keeping in mind the changing daily patterns of sunlight, you can shape the views around your house to make the most of them. Bright morning sun, for example, is ideal for backlighting foliage near an eastern window or illuminating morning fog or dew rising in a hollow. Views to the north and south are generally best at midmorning and midafternoon, since the sunlight slanting in from the side creates the maximum visual contrast. In early morning and late afternoon, long shadows lie across lawns and pavements at every point of the compass — and the sky itself is full of color and drama. And don't forget the totally different nighttime views you can create with electric light. Done selectively, night lighting outdoors carries the eye beyond the reflective surface of a window and makes for a stunning theatrical effect.

Much of the impact of any view (or any other facet of landscape design, when you come down to it) has to do with the human eye and mind more than with trees, rocks, grass, or even sunlight. I know a wide hillside that slopes down to a bay of the sea, and scattered over the hillside are a dozen houses. Each house has its own view of the water. One view is Olympian: the land and water lie spread out below like a dream, seeming to have almost no connection to the life of the house or its occupants. Another view is pictorial to the nth degree, cherry trees, sumacs, and bayberry framing an enchanting curve of beach and expanse of blue ocean. My own favorite isn't really a big panoramic view at all, but one

In a small city garden, a raised vantage point gives a delightful view from above. In every kind of setting, keep in mind views from upstairs windows.

with great sensual appeal: it's just a peek at the water over some rocks and grasses outside a house that is practically at sea level. Somehow the sound of lapping waves, the feel of the wind, and the smell of salt give this place a special magic.

**Entries**  A landscape is for people, and considering how people move from place to place is crucial to a landscape design. You could almost describe circulation as a series of entries, of moves from outside to inside. In one sense, of course, all landscape spaces are "outside" because they're outdoors. But you really do enter one space from another, even if both are in the open air. It is a psychological fact that moving onto a new turf generates a tiny primitive anxiety in a person. For that reason alone, every entry should be simple, uncluttered, and enticingly designed.

Every gateway, every flight of steps, every place where you round a corner of the house or come to an opening in a hedge or fence is a form of entry. Think of what you can do to make each one enjoyable.

A major part of every landscaping project is to give a pleasurable quality to the sequence of entries involved in approaching and going into a house. At the first entry, the property line, you move from the public domain into the private, often in an automobile. There should be a generous turning radius to let the car move easily from street to drive, and the drive should begin, at least, on a fairly level grade. A driveway of any length should offer some attractive view along the way, such as a glimpse of a garden or the front door of the house.

The next entry occurs when you get out of the car. Space allowing, there should be a clearly defined parking place, ideally with its own landscaping detail. Stepping onto the walk that leads to the front door is another entry, and it calls for a comfortable transition from the pavement of the parking area to the surface of the walk — the transition itself forming a kind of gateway to the space immediately surrounding the house.

**An entry with a subtle air of mystery. Grade changes prolong the approach to the house, and a sense of ascending adds to expectation.**

**All arrival elements are clearly defined: stone gateway with built-in lighting, visitors' parking, and walk leading to the door. (Note hidden residents' parking beyond.)**

Finally you come to the house. At the doorway you expect people to use most, you should plan for a stoop or other greeting platform generous enough to let at least two people stand simultaneously, with room for screen or storm doors to open or close at the same time. The doors should be hung so that they can swing all the way open until they're flat against the house wall — not come up short against a railing or other obstacle. If possible, an overhang for inclement weather is a nice detail; so is a bell or knocker that's handy, not concealed behind a locked screen door.

There are many houses where the "back" door is in fact the door that is used by family and friends alike as the main entry into the house. In such cases, these guidelines for planning and landscaping of the path, stoop, and so on apply to the back door — which should also be designed to retain its practical functions as chief access route for groceries, packages, children, or whatever. Meanwhile the front door might be played down, concealed, turned into a window, or allowed to serve simply as access to a terrace or porch.

Here I'm really getting into details of the architecture of the house; but it is important to coordinate these with the design of the landscape. Overhangs, steps, retaining walls, railings, or other landscape construction around the entry to the house should be in keeping with the style and building materials of the house proper. If they aren't, they inevitably look tacked on.

In thinking about landscape composition, and structure, always consider compatibility with — and utilization of — nature's own designs as a basic criterion. After all, nature was creating landscapes long before people got into the business. That beautifully proportioned patio won't get much summer use if it is airless and baking hot (you need to know the sun and wind patterns around your house). That bank of forsythia won't provide the desired splash of springtime yellow if it's overshadowed by trees or buildings (it needs sun for good bloom). Climate, soil, and the natural characteristics and needs of plants are central to both the appearance and the usefulness of your landscape.

# 4 A NATURAL ORIENTATION

This chapter has to do with some of the basic facts of the science, as opposed to the art, of landscape design: facts about the natural environment.

Unlike our farming forebears of even a couple of generations ago, we Americans tend to take our physical surroundings very much for granted. But the more time you spend working outdoors, the more you will come to marvel at the natural elements that sustain life on this planet. Being close to nature, being able to study it day by day, is one of the things I enjoy most about being a landscape architect. In a sense it's a luxury — which I cherish. Yet it is absolutely crucial that anyone contemplating a landscape design project pay attention to the natural environment and apply its lessons, whether it be on open farmland, in a suburban backyard, or on a city balcony. Ignore nature or try to fight it, and you cannot win. Let nature inspire and guide you, and you cannot go too far wrong.

Using nature to best advantage means orienting your landscape — both organic and inorganic — to the sun, wind, rain, and soil. Energy efficiency will be one important result. Equally important will be the good health of plants and the comfort of people in and around your house.

**Climate**   It is no accident that the weather is one of the commonest topics of everyday discourse. "Where are my sunglasses?" "This humidity really gets me down." "Looks like snow." Climate pervades our lives in more ways than we often realize. It affects our moods, our habitual routines, our attitudes and ambitions, not to mention our specific plans on any given day.

**Winter and summer effects of this beech grove are dramatically different. Every landscape plan should allow for seasonal weather changes.**

Early colonists and pioneers in this country had no trouble staying in touch with climate. To them, energy-efficient orientation was a matter of common sense combined with age-old skills. In the North, they knew how to back their houses up to shelter (often the barn) and how to

turn the faces of their houses to the south or southwest. Winter was the big threat, not just to comfort but to survival. They also knew, however, what a blessing a deciduous shade tree outside the front door could be in summer. In the South, earlier Americans used deep porches and shady groves to keep sun at bay throughout the year.

In a more sophisticated way, but using the identical basic knowledge, Frank Lloyd Wright designed the famous Taliesin West to use climate to advantage. Built of stone in the Arizona desert, Taliesin West is oriented so that winds blow through the structure much of the time. A central water fountain cools the breezes by evaporation — an ancient form of natural air conditioning.

If you orient your indoor and outdoor spaces sensibly and in concert with climate, you can extend the livability of outdoor spaces by several months and improve the quality of life indoors as well. You can have pockets of sun for winter warmth and early spring bloom; cool spots on sultry days; shelter from wind all year long.

**The sun** The patterns of sunlight and shade on your property have everything to do with what you can grow and where you can grow it. In addition, the sun is the central factor in energy-efficient landscape design. The initial source of all energy on Earth, the sun is the most predictable energy source we have. We know precisely what it will be doing at any given time. It is that reliability that makes the daily path of the sun a major component of every landscaping plan.

The simple diagrams on page 42 illustrate the sunrise-to-sunset patterns as they change from solstice to solstice throughout the northern hemisphere, and the changing angles at which the sunlight strikes the Earth's surface at different seasons. The lessons to be learned here are clear. For warmth in winter, a sensible design will allow the maximum possible amount of sunlight to strike the south-facing walls and windows of the house at that season.

**The sun's path changes throughout the year, causing wide variations in the length of day, direction of the sun's rays, and the angle of the sun in the sky.**

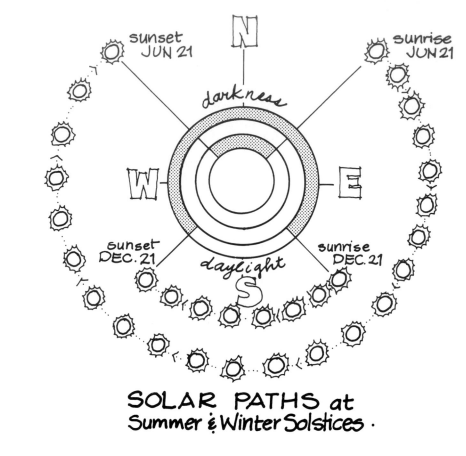

SOLAR PATHS at
Summer & Winter Solstices .

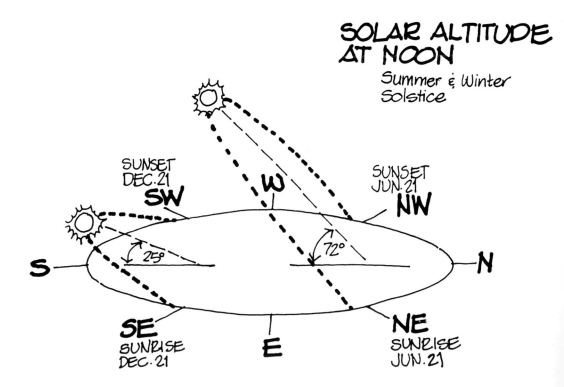

SOLAR ALTITUDE AT NOON

Summer & Winter Solstice

In summer the sun's rays are much closer to the vertical than in winter — so that a fairly narrow overhang or trellis can afford all the protection the south side of a house may need. Windows and walls facing west, where hot afternoon sun slants in, may need a deeper screen or shade. Here's where deciduous foliage can come in. A trellis vine or a shade tree that blocks summer sun will let it come right in once the days are cold again.

Every individual plant has its preferences as to amount and intensity of sunlight. Some shrubs and ground covers are happy in deep day-long shade, while others require at least a dappled sun-shade mixture or sun for part of the day. Some trees and shrubs cannot survive in a place that's both sunny and windy. Many trees and shrubs will tend to lean or reach toward the sun if they are partly shaded, which will affect their form. Keep all these things in mind as you plan; and for specifics of the sunlight needs of any given plant, see the plant descriptions in Part III.

**The wind** A good deal less predictable than the sun, the wind nevertheless plays an important part in landscape design. You can control or even harness its impact to a degree that may surprise you.

Every section of the United States has its own prevailing winds. In much of the Northeast, for instance, the prevailing fair-weather winds (the winds we're most apt to be outdoors in) are westerlies. In summer they swing around to the southwest, in winter to the northwest. Determine your prevailing wind direction(s) and you can use structures or plantings to create wind channels for evaporational cooling in summer — and windbreaks to reduce winter wind velocities by up to 50 percent. (More on this in the section on energy-efficient landscaping in November.) You can also use your knowledge of wind patterns to assess the ideal or less-than-ideal location for any given plant.

Topography also has an impact on wind and on the temperature of the spaces where you live and garden. Cold air sinks and warm air rises. Masses of cool or warm air, seeking their natural levels, actually create thermal air currents — in other words, wind. Cold air settles in valleys; and because of condensation in cooling moist air, fog pockets in low-lying areas are a familiar phenomenon. So are cooling breezes that flow down the sides of hills or ravines.

These thermal effects of topography may sound as though they'd operate only on a very large scale. But in fact, if your property has any topographical variety, you will find that the varying elevations of your land create their own miniature climates. A friend of mine plants annual flowers in two beds, one next to her house, the other about 80 yards away and 8 feet lower down. Every fall, the lower bed suffers a killing frost days or even weeks earlier than the higher one. Every spring, the earth in the uphill bed thaws out sooner. So if you are seeking a way to cool an area, think about trapping downflowing cool air. If warmth is your goal, blocking the cold air flow is one way to attain it.

**Soil** Nearly everything we grow and everything we build is in contact with the soil. Interestingly enough, however, the prerequisites for good growing soil and good building soil are very different. Good growing soil would not serve at all well as the base for a wall, a potting shed, a driveway, or a deck. The reasons for this are buried in the structure of soil.

Structure? you may ask. But soil does have structure: it consists of solids and voids. The best growing soil is about half solids (mineral and organic matter) and half voids (air and water). As you walk through a garden, across a meadow, or among the trees of a forest, you're walking on something that is only about half solid.

It is the presence of water and air, which swell and shrink with changes in temperature, that causes soil to rise and fall with the seasons. All that activity can cause cracks in foundation walls, open canyons in paved drives or terraces, or lead to strange tiltings in structures whose underpinnings have unexpectedly settled. If, however, you compress or compact the soil — so as to drive out the air and water — and if in addition you remove or greatly reduce the organic matter, you have the perfect substrate to support a structure or pavement.

**Soil for growing**  Soils are formed during thousands of years of decomposition of underlying bedrock, acted upon by glaciers, air, and water; and by hundreds of years of decomposition of organic materials — that is, plants. It takes millennia for nature to make topsoil, but only a few decades for human activity to sap it of its nutrients and let it waste. This was the unhappy discovery of settlers on the deforested, used-up soils of New England; and of families faced with the Great Plains dust bowl of the 1930s. It was also a discovery of the ancient Greeks and other ancient peoples, who stripped their land and found that it never recovered. Every age seems to have to make the same "discovery" over again.

Most plant growth takes place in topsoil. Large plants' roots penetrate to the underlying subsoil mainly for purposes of extracting water, and for mechanical support. But even big trees' feeder roots seldom go much beyond 1 foot down — as you realize when you see a tree uprooted. There's many a tree native to North America that can thrive with practically no depth of soil at all.

What is this thing called soil, that in such a thin layer nourishes such infinite variety of life? Apart from air and water, the solid components of a good growing soil are about 10 to 20 percent organic matter (decayed plant life) and 80 to 90 percent mineral matter (rocks, sand, silt, clay).

The larger mineral fragments, from sand to rocks, serve mainly as a skeleton or framework. They provide spaces for air, water, silt, and organic matter to fill in — porosity. The smaller mineral fragments are

**The topmost 12 inches of soil contain the majority of plants' roots. Handle topsoil with care during landscape construction.**

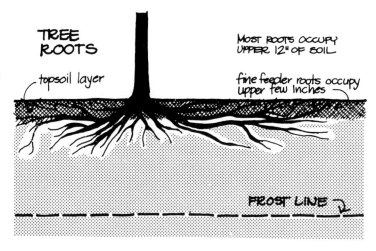

TREE ROOTS

topsoil layer

MOST ROOTS OCCUPY UPPER 12" OF SOIL

fine feeder roots occupy upper few inches

FROST LINE

silt and clay. They, together with the organic matter, provide the essential nutrients that make plant life possible. Of the "N, P, K" triad in every fertilizer mix, silts and clays are important providers of both P (phosphorus or phosphate) and K (potassium or potash). They also yield calcium, magnesium, iron, and a dozen other nutrients plants need, some of which we probably don't even know about yet.

As for the organic matter, it too has both structural and nutritional roles to play. It holds air and water; it contains many nutrients, most notably the essential fertilizer nitrogen (N); it's also responsible for about half the beneficial chemical reactions that make soil soil. In woods and other wild places, organic matter is kept in its necessary proportion by the constantly renewed supply of decomposing vegetation. Organic matter in soil is rapidly broken down by chemical and bacterial action, however. And in cities and suburbs, the soil-renewing cycle of organic growth and decay often gets interrupted by human activities. That is why it's vital that we keep checking and replenishing the organic content of any soil where we hope to grow anything.

Another aspect of the makeup of soil is its pH value. The pH scale indicates the acidity or alkalinity of soil in numbers from 0 to 14. A pH of 7 means the soil is neutral; higher numbers are alkaline; lower ones are acid. Knowing the soil's pH is important because soil nutrients are most available to a given plant when the soil's degree of acidity is proper for that plant. (I've included plants' specific pH needs in their descriptions in Part III.)

To sum up, the ideal soil for growing things will be a fertile, friable loam made up of half solids and half voids. The solid half will include about 40 percent sand, 40 percent silt, 10 percent clay, and 10 percent organic matter. The other half will be equally divided between air and water. This soil will contain the right amount of air spaces for the circulation of gases; allow water to percolate but hold enough to meet plants' needs; and, of course, provide plants with enough of the essential water-soluble nutrients.

**Soil for building** Obviously, pavements, foundations, and other rigid construction can't be built directly on topsoil. A firm building base means either well-compacted subsoil or a bed of sand or rock that will absorb the heavings and shrinkings of underlying soil without transmit-

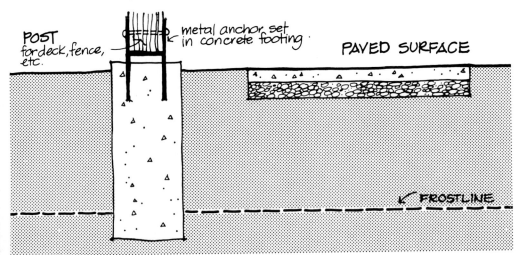

Footings for above-ground landscape structures must extend to solid subsoil below the frost line, while paved areas require only a granular bed to absorb the soil's movement.

ting them to the construction above. Clearly, proper soil for building doesn't just lie around the landscape.

Well-compacted subsoil is what's called for if you are planning major above-the-ground construction such as a deck or gazebo. You have to dig down below frost level, to subsoil that is so hard-packed and so lacking in air and water spaces that — unlike the spongy upper soil — it simply doesn't move around much. There you can rest your footings or foundation, secure in the knowledge that they'll stay where you put them.

For in-the-ground construction like masonry walks or paved patios, you use another approach: digging just deep enough to install a shock-absorbing layer of sand or crushed stone sufficiently coarse and well-drained so that it won't hold water. Everyone has seen the bed of gravel that highway construction crews lay down before they spread the asphalt. A small-scale project works the same.

**Drainage** There is an old rule of thumb to the effect that of all the rainwater that falls on earth, one-third evaporates; one-third runs off (into storm drains, streams, ponds); and one-third percolates into the soil. Although these proportions can vary hugely according to the locality, the time of year, the type of soil, or a hundred other factors, the point is clear. How well we plan for the drainage of our soil will have a lot to do with how well our soil works for us — whether for growing or for building.

Plants cannot survive in waterlogged soil. They suffocate unless their roots have access to both water and air. And there's another hazard to poorly drained soil: excessive runoff, which leads to erosion. The U.S. loses 4 billion tons of irreplaceable topsoil to erosion by water alone every year. But if you cultivate a porous, well-drained soil and fill it with roots, you don't need to lose an ounce.

Proper drainage is as important to the maintenance of structures as it is to the well-being of plants. Seepage in your cellar, standing water

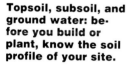

**Topsoil, subsoil, and ground water: before you build or plant, know the soil profile of your site.**

all over your driveway, puddles in the middle of the terrace — any water where you don't want it is at best a nuisance, at worst a destructive menace. Planning for drainage is fundamental to landscape design, and I'll talk about it in detail in Part II.

**Plants and Their Habitats**    The plants that grow around you are part of the natural environment in more ways than one. They depend for survival on soil, sun, and rain. They also make a big difference to microclimates around a house — by casting shade, blocking noise or wind, absorbing heat, generating oxygen, competing or coexisting with other plantings in their neighborhood. Every growing thing is linked with everything else.

Getting to know plants in their natural state is vital to your success in choosing new plants for your property. Once again, it works far better to cooperate with nature than to try to outsmart it. Be observant; look around you and see how both native and imported plant types in your area have adapted to their natural surroundings. They'll give you many ideas about what might work in your own situation.

**Native plants**    A native plant is so completely adapted to its locale that it is self-sustaining to the point of reproducing itself. Throughout this book, "native" means indigenous, not imported, to North America. Native plants' reproductive capacity makes them essential food suppliers for birds and wildlife. Their seeds — berries, nuts, and fruits — are all highly edible. Also, native plants colonize. A typical native is found in the midst of its relatives, the oldest plants surrounded by their offspring and the offspring in turn surrounded by theirs. The result is often dense growth, providing excellent cover and nesting areas as well as food.

You may have seen the colonizing abilities of native plants at work if you've ever had the opportunity to observe the "plant succession" in an open area or vacant lot that has gone to seed over a number of years. First come low-growing weeds; then taller grasses; then, within a couple of years, young shrubs and the seedlings of trees. Each stage makes possible the one that succeeds it. After fifty years there will be woodland where the open ground used to be.

And there are both rhyme and reason to the ways native plants interact with each other and their setting. Plants, like everything else, have an incredibly subtle and complex system of shared and competing needs, mutual support, and mutual dependency. When they coexist happily in the wild it's no accident; it's the result of a perfect equilibrium having been reached.

**Imported plants**    Throughout history, horticulturists have been fascinated with foreign forms of plant life. In America since colonial times, plant explorers and gardening enthusiasts have introduced thousands of foreign plant species and varieties to this continent.

There are some introduced plants that — though exquisite in many ways — are terribly fussy to maintain. Almost every gardener has (knowingly or not) been exposed to the finicky tastes and fragile health of certain nonnative lawn grasses and flowering shrubs. What with elaborate fertilizing, frequent watering, and periodic applications of pesticides, fungicides, and even herbicides, it's a real chore to keep these invalids going. (Needless to say, you won't find any of these plants listed in the following chapters.)

Ferns and native shrubs are perfectly adapted to life along a streambed in the dappled shade of beeches on ascending slopes.

Many imports, however, thrive here and have contributed immeasurably to our landscaping palette — with their blooms, their foliage, their tolerance of difficult growing conditions, and their resistance to disease. Japanese maple, Oriental cherries, boxwood, Norway spruce . . . the list is endless.

Some imported varieties have become basic staples of the American scene. What would spring be without forsythia and lilacs, or summer without the common orange daylily? Yet none of these old friends is native to this continent.

Other introduced plants have flourished just a little too well. Purple loosestrife, while some people are fond of it, is viewed by many as a mortal threat to wetlands plants and wildlife. Bittersweet, Japanese honeysuckle, multiflora rose, and the notorious kudzu vine are other examples of invaders with a habit of taking over any landscape where they're allowed a foothold. This is not to say that there aren't some equally noxious American natives, with poison ivy heading the list. But the imports have a big advantage: their own natural enemies (pests or blights) often don't follow them to their adopted land, so here they can rampage unchecked.

**Plant habitats**   Whether your local plant community is native, imported, or both, its character will be tied to the kind of soil (acid, sandy, humusy, etc.) and the growing conditions (bright or dark, sheltered or windy, wet or dry) in the area. And these conditions in turn should govern your selection of trees, shrubs, or ground covers for your property.

A million variables go into a plant habitat, but for simplicity's sake I'll choose four broad categories. Almost every plant will be at home in at least one of the following:

- Wet meadow habitats are open and unshaded, often low-lying, with normally damp or even swampy soil.
- Dry meadow habitats, often upland, may have rich or rocky soil; they may be protected or windswept; but they are unshaded and dry most of the time.
- Wet woodland habitats, characteristically shady and damp with humus-rich soil, are often protected from wind by virtue of being both low-lying and wooded.
- Dry woodland habitats are often wooded slopes or plateaus — any places where shade and dry (or at least well-drained) soil conditions predominate most of the year.

Within any one of these categories, the possible subcategories and combined or crossover categories are endless. They'll depend on degree or frequency of wetness; density or constancy of shade; wind direction and velocity; acidity or alkalinity of soil; and so on. A low boggy spot, shaded by big oaks much of the summer and yet well protected from winter winds, will support its own range of plant life. A south-facing gravelly slope, dry much of the year and completely lacking in shade, will foster a completely different pattern of growth.

The important point is that your particular set of circumstances is bound to appeal to a certain set of plants. Stick to them, and you can't help but generate a healthy plant community. And plant health is key to a landscape that is good-looking and readily maintainable.

As you use the plant lists throughout Part II and the detailed descriptions in Part III, you'll find that each description mentions the plant's preferred habitat. With natives, this means the habitats that plants most promptly colonize in the wild in North America; with imports, the habitats they choose in their native Europe or Asia. But many plants are flexible. Moisture-loving plants like red maple, for instance, will survive or even prosper in relatively dry conditions. The reverse does not apply, however: a plant adapted to dryness, like honeysuckle, will usually not endure transplanting into wet conditions. Some plants like gray birch

**Another kind of habitat: a thin mantle of soil over and among rock outcroppings supports varied plant life despite dryness and exposure.**

and paxistima, which tolerate sterile or rocky soils in the wild, actually prefer good soil and adequate moisture in cultivation. And every plant does best with its own optimum amount of sunlight or shade — although here again, some are more flexible than others.

As you familiarize yourself with your soil, your prevailing winds, the patterns of sunlight around your house, and the kinds of plant life that flourish in your vicinity, you'll learn a lot — and you'll begin to see things in new ways. Seeing is the essence of design, and everything I've been discussing in these chapters is aimed at helping you to see. Chapter 5 continues that effort by taking you outdoors to evaluate, map, and plan.

# 5   SIZING UP: THE BASE PLAN

I strongly recommend that you make a "base plan" of your place on paper. This educational and constructive first step need not be difficult or expensive; on the contrary, it's usually an eye-opening, exciting, and enjoyable experience.

When you are in the early, pipe-dreaming stages of considering an improvement to your landscape, it's natural to be vague and general. "How about a lovely curving front walk, brick maybe?" "What if we put a cluster of laurels over there and some big viburnums behind them?" "I'd like a tall wood fence here to screen the view of the neighbors' parked car."

If you are serious about going forward, however, it is vital that you come to grips with your site's dimensions, topography, drainage, access routes, sun and shade patterns, and so on. The best way I know to get all the details under control is to go outdoors and measure and make lists, with the goal of producing an annotated map — a base plan.

Making a base plan will give you a boost in many ways. First, planning on paper will force you to see — to assess, make judgments, contemplate alternatives — with more precision and concreteness than any amount of standing around brainstorming. Also, I've found that ideas and solutions begin to speak out for themselves as the paper planning goes on.

Another argument for careful planning is that it's efficient. By the time you have drawn your final sketch and written your final list, you will be in far less danger of making mistakes than if you just plunge in impulsively. At the very least disappointing, mistakes can also be wasteful of time, material, and money. At worst they can actually be destructive. Examples of avoidable mistakes could include planning a pool where ledge is directly below the surface; or planting a deep-rooted tree over a leaching field; or constructing a fence so oriented as to create a tunnel for the prevailing wind. By all means, go ahead and make mistakes; but make them on paper, not in soil or greenery or stone.

The base plan is an elementary diagram or map of your property showing all features of house, grounds, outbuildings, walks, and so on. It will become the foundation for later drawings and elevations (views of things in the vertical plane, like the front facade of a house), if needed. You'll return to the base plan over and over as you tackle problems or indulge in flights of imagination. Using the base plan, you'll be able to make various alternative designs on tracing-paper overlays. So the base plan should be as accurate as you can make it.

Incidentally, there are two possible shortcuts to making the base plan. The first is to transpose onto graph paper (see Equipment, page 52) the plot plan of your property that accompanies the title deed. If you have recently bought the property, putting your hands on the plot plan may be easy. A plot plan usually has been done by a surveyor, which might lead you to assume that it would be one hundred percent accurate. That's not necessarily so, however, especially if yours is very old or if it has been reproduced over and over. Plot plans can also be difficult to use because they tend to be drawn to a very small scale. Nevertheless, a plot plan is often good enough for you to transfer the bare outlines of the house, the property lines, and the driveway (if any) to your base plan.

A second possible shortcut — or a help if you have a really complicated site — can be to hire a surveyor to draw the base plan for you from scratch. Surveyors do get accurate results, which can be essential in some circumstances: for instance, where property lines are in question, or where other structures or features of the landscape could be affected by errors in measurement, or where topography is complex. Against the accuracy you can obtain by having a professional survey done, you have to weigh the fact that surveyors charge a minimum of several hundred dollars a day for the work of the survey crew. On top of that there's the cost of the time it takes the surveyor's office to draw up the plan.

(This last expense — the cost of drafting up the plan based on the surveyor's measurements — may be one corner you can cut. Find out if your surveyor will make you a "field annotated plan." This is just what it sounds like: an accurate but roughly drawn plan, with all information in place but without the refinements of finished drafting.)

For the sake of the argument, let's assume that your situation is not too complicated and you have decided to draw your own base plan. No matter how little experience you have, you can do it. No artistic talent is required. The steps I recommend you take are exactly those I follow myself before I begin preparing a design plan.

**Equipment**   Your first move is a trip to an art or drafting supply store for a few pieces of equipment. Use the following as a checklist.

- Several large (18 by 24 inches) sheets of translucent graph paper, lined at either 8 or 10 squares to the inch so that you can work at scales of either ⅛ inch to the foot or ¹⁄₁₀ inch to the foot. If you're working on only a small piece of land, perhaps a scale of ¼ inch to the foot will be easier to use.
- A piece of plywood, masonite, or heavy-weight Bristol board at least as large as your graph paper, to use as a backup board while you are outdoors making measurements.
- A 12-inch ruler and/or an architect's or engineer's scale — the architect's if you are working at ⅛ inch to the foot, the engineer's if you are working at ¹⁄₁₀ inch to the foot.
- Several HB soft lead pencils, which are somewhat smeary but which give you a dark line.
- A white artgum eraser to clean up mistakes (and the pencil smears).
- A 24-inch roll of tracing paper (sometimes called "flimsy"), which comes in either white or yellow. This paper will be used for later studies, once the base plan is done, but you may as well buy it now.

The only other trip you will have to make is to the hardware store, to obtain:

- A measuring tape; I recommend at least a 50-footer, if not a 100-footer, for more accurate and more efficient measuring.
- A standard 10-foot or 12-foot retractable carpenter's tape. (If you don't mind making successive tapings, you could use this instead of the long tape mentioned above.)
- A hand level or line level for measuring vertical relief (see Vertical Relief, page 55). It's possible that you may have to go to a drafting supply store or blueprint shop for this.

**Basic Measurements**   Clip or tape your graph paper to its backup board, gather up your tape measures, and head outside. A helper is a good idea; but if you don't have anyone to hold the end of the tape for you, use an ice pick, screwdriver, or shish-kabob skewer to anchor the end of the tape to the ground, and you're off. Here is the procedure, step by step.

**1.** Measure the distance from the center of a wall of the house to the nearest property line. Record these two points on the graph paper. If your paper is ruled to ⅛-inch scale, a 50-foot distance will be 50 spaces, or 6¼ inches. Make sure that you choose points on the paper that will allow enough room in all directions for all the other measurements of house and lot to come. This may involve a little trial and error.

**2.** Measure carefully all the walls of the house where they meet the ground, and record their dimensions as a series of points on the graph paper, as shown here. Double check all your measurements; there's no hurry, and accuracy now can save a lot of grief later.

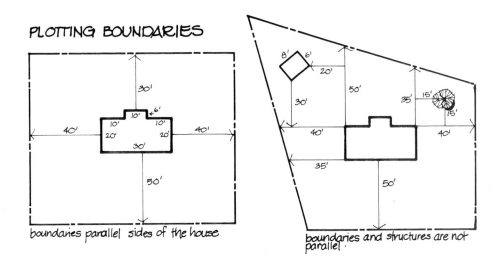

## PLOTTING BOUNDARIES

boundaries parallel sides of the house

boundaries and structures are not parallel.

Measuring and plotting property lines is a simple task. Trees, buildings, etc. can be located by means of coordinate offsets as illustrated.

3. Measure the distance from the center point of each remaining house wall to its nearest property line, and record these points. If by any chance you have a perfectly rectangular house situated parallel to the boundaries of a perfectly rectangular property, you are now home free: all you have to do is extend the property lines from the points you've located, and where they intersect are the corners of your lot.

4. In the more common situation, where the walls of the house are far from symmetrical and where the property lines are not parallel to anything at all, even each other, you will need to locate the corners of the lot and measure their distances from each other and from the house in order to arrive at a diagram of the lot. This is where the architect's rule to ⅛-inch scale (or the engineer's to ⅒) can come in handy, for measuring diagonal distances. If you get frustrated pinpointing boundary lines that run at odd angles, try this. Pace out or measure an imaginary line that extends some fixed straight line, such as a house wall, garage wall, or front walk. Mark it with string or tape. Then go back to (say) the corner of the house and mark out another line at right angles to the first. Then pick a series of points along the troublesome boundary; measure the distances between each of these points and the nearest points on the two right-angled lines; and record the measurements. After doing this just a few times, you'll find that you can plot a pretty accurate location for the boundary. You can also use this method for locating objects such as those listed under Other Information, page 54.

5. At this point you may want to go indoors again, to sit down and use your ruler to draw neat lines between the various points you have so conscientiously measured. You will end up with a schematic rendering of the locations, dimensions, and relative positions of your site and your house.

6. Ascertain which direction is north, and turn your paper so that that direction is roughly at either the top or the right-hand side. (This is the convention.) Draw an N with an arrow, and you have established which end of your base plan is up; needless to say, the way you annotate the plan will depend on this.

7. For future reference, make a note of the scale of your plan in some corner of the graph paper — "¼-inch scale," "⅛-inch scale," "⅒-inch scale," or whatever.

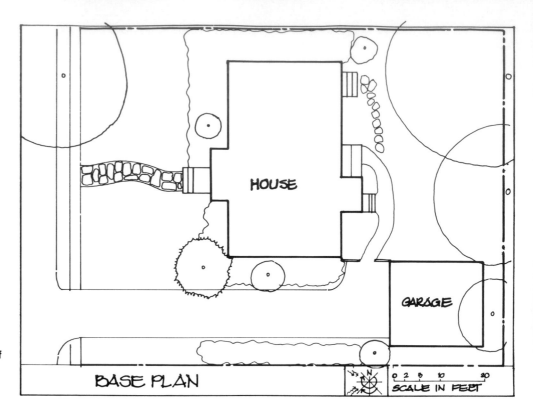

BASE PLAN

HOUSE

GARAGE

N

SCALE IN FEET
0 2 8 10 20

A base plan, clear and uncluttered, shows the edges of all elements that have been measured and located.

**Other Information**   The next move is to decide what other features to include in the base plan. You'll probably want to go outdoors again as you consider these questions. Here is another checklist to guide you; but with this list (unlike the equipment list) I recommend that you pick and choose. Don't get bogged down putting in every little thing at this stage; limit your selections to things that will clearly affect what you are thinking of doing. The base plan is by definition minimal. You can always add details later. Some candidates for inclusion:

- Additional details of the house itself
  General layout of ground-floor rooms
  Roof overhangs
  Windows and doors
  Downspouts
  Water spigots
  Oil fill pipe
  Meter locations
  Window wells
  Doorsteps
- Driveway
- Walks
- Terraces
- Outlines of existing gardens, shrubbery masses, flower beds
- Walls or fences
- Significant shrubs or trees
- Utilities: gas, water, sewer, or septic lines; telephone and electric poles and overhead or underground wires; oil tanks; etc.
- Lampposts and other lighting
- Drainage channels
- Steeply sloping areas

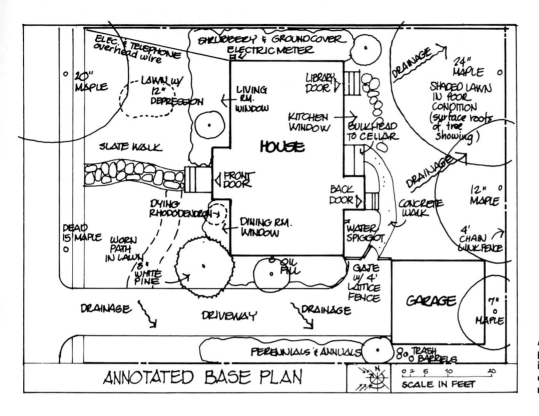

ELEC. & TELEPHONE
overhead wire

SHRUBBERY & GROUNDCOVER
ELECTRIC METER

DRAINAGE

24"
MAPLE °

20"
° MAPLE

LOW 4/
12"
DEPRESSION

LIVING
RM.
WINDOW

LIBRARY
DOOR ▷

SHADED LAWN
IN POOR
CONDITION
(surface roots
of tree
showing)

KITCHEN
WINDOW

BULKHEAD
TO CELLAR

HOUSE

SLATE WALK

DRAINAGE

FRONT
DOOR

12" °
MAPLE

DYING
RHODODENDRON →

BACK
DOOR ▷

CONCRETE
WALK

4'
CHAIN
LINK FENCE

DEAD
15 MAPLE
°

DINING RM.
WINDOW

WORN
PATH
IN LAWN

WATER
SPIGGOT

8"
WHITE
PINE

8 OIL
FILL

GATE
w/ 4'
LATTICE
FENCE

GARAGE

7"
°
MAPLE

DRAINAGE

DRIVEWAY

DRAINAGE

PERENNIALS & ANNUALS

8"
° TRASH
BARRELS

ANNOTATED BASE PLAN

N

0 2 5    10        20
SCALE IN FEET

An annotated base plan helps you keep important existing considerations in mind.

- Areas with poor drainage
- Areas with other significance, such as rock outcroppings, old foundations, level areas, etc.

Many of the features listed above can be indicated on your plan simply with a dot and a brief annotation. Do write small, so as not to crowd the plan excessively. Shown here is the plan at this stage; you can see that trees are simply circles (with "deciduous" or "evergreen" noted); walls are heavy lines; pathways and drives are parallel straight or curving lines. Once again, keep it spare and keep it simple, for clarity's sake.

**Vertical Relief**   While you are wandering around with measuring tape in hand, it makes sense to determine the varying elevations of your plot of land — the vertical, as opposed to the horizontal, distances between points. I find that vertical relief often makes a significant difference to my approach to a given landscape, both because of its visual impact and because of functional concerns (how to separate or connect different levels, for example). Very few properties are perfectly flat, but those that are can often be enhanced by the addition of some ups and downs. On the other hand, a plot with drastic variations in vertical relief presents its own set of landscaping challenges (and pleasures).

Here's a very simple way to measure vertical distances. This system uses equipment that you can make and buy at little expense, and it's fine for most residential landscape situations. If, however, you are going to be undertaking complicated grading or construction, or if your site is very large or very difficult topographically, you may want even greater precision than this method can give you. In that case you can rent a surveyor's level or transit. Or, of course, you can get a surveyor to do the job for you.

**1.** Make a measuring stick 10 to 12 feet long. You can use a two-by-four, a piece of lattice, or any piece of lumber that's long enough and not too unwieldly. If it is not light colored, paint it for visibility. Measure it out into 1-inch sections and paint the foot numbers — 1, 2, 3, etc. — as large and black as possible. Or if you prefer meters and decimeters, use them. You are now ready to use your hand level (the final item in the equipment list on page 52) to start measuring.

**2.** First, a word about the level. Either a hand level or a line level will do; but I find the hand level a little easier and more flexible to work with, so the instructions that follow are geared to it. A line level consists of a spirit level with hooks by which you attach it to a line that has been stretched between two points at different elevations. This necessitates a firm anchor at point A to keep the line taut while you hold the other end at point B. A hand level, however, you just carry around with you. It has a built-in telescope. You stand at one elevation, adjust the position of the instrument until it is level, and see instantly what the difference in elevation is between where you are standing and where the measuring stick is propped.

**3.** Choose a low point against which you will measure all succeeding points. Commonly this is the lowest point of your property. Prop your measuring stick upright in a convenient and visible spot, or get a helper to hold it for you. Looking at the stick through the hand level, make a note of the exact height of your eye — 60 inches, for an easy example.

**4.** Take with you the hand level and perhaps a pad and pencil for noting measurements. Walk to the first higher point that you wish to locate. Since your eye has to be on a plane no higher than the highest mark on the measuring stick, the rise can't be more than 5 feet or so. For greater heights, see step 8 below.

**5.** Sight through the hand level at the measuring stick. The height you see, minus your original eye-level height, will give the difference in elevation at the point where you're standing. For instance, if your level is aimed at the 94-inch mark, but your eye level on the stick was 60

## USING A HAND LEVEL

what you see through the hand level

reading A.  94"
B.  – 60"
difference in elevation  34"

94"

60"

B.

A.

inches, you are standing at a spot 34 inches higher than the place where you propped the stick.

**6.** Repeat steps 4 and 5 until you have located all the different elevations you want to.

**7.** Now for registering your measurements on the base plan. Call the low point zero, and record all measurements of higher points (such as +24″ or +40″). Important elevations to note are those where a change in grade may call for landscaping work — such as a spot that may need a retaining wall, steps, terracing, or antierosion planting.

**8.** If there are differences in elevation greater than five feet, you'll need to "back sight." To do this, take the first measurement as outlined in steps 4 through 6 and jot down your results. Repeat the measuring procedure, but use the previously established high point as the new location for your measuring stick; I recommend that you get a helper to follow along after you with the measuring stick. Do this as many times as you need to get to the highest spot you want to locate, each time making a note of the vertical rise you have measured. Finally, add up your accumulated figures, and you have the total difference between the original low point and the final high point. This last number, the total, is the one you enter in the appropriate place on the base plan.

**9.** There is one kind of circumstance where I often find I can do nicely without the measuring stick. When I'm figuring out the various elevations of a terrain that slopes up and away from the side of a house, I use chalk, charcoal, or tape to mark intervals all the way up the side of the house. The marking operation involves a ladder, needless to say. Then I establish my eye level and walk up the slope, level in hand. It's easy to ascertain the various elevations by taking sights on the marked scale on the side of the house and subtracting my eye-level height from the height I see. I'll go all over the landscape until I've located a good number of different points. A fringe benefit of this system is that you end up relating points in the landscape to the levels of the doors, windows, eaves, porches, or dormers of the house — which is something you ought to do sometime anyway.

**Sun and Wind Diagram**   I spoke in Chapter 4 of the sun and the wind and of some of the ways in which they shape and color our landscapes, our houses, our ways of life. Right at this very basic stage of planning, diagrams of seasonal angles of sun and direction of prevailing winds belong on your base plan. A typical sun diagram and wind arrow are shown here; you can use a compass and a protractor, a drafting compass, or even just a jar lid to make a neat version of a sun diagram in an uncrowded corner of your base plan. It may seem academic as you look at it now, but as you develop your ideas further you'll refer to the sun diagram constantly.

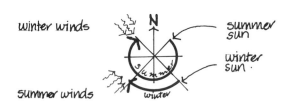

**A simplified version of a sun diagram is accompanied by arrows showing the directions of prevailing summer and winter winds. Put these on a corner of the base plan.**

**Analysis**  You are now the proud owner of a base plan. When you are ready to get it printed, go to a blueprint shop (see your Yellow Pages) and get several prints made, the same size as your original plan. Black line prints are my preference, since they look more like the original drawing; but blue line prints work perfectly well too. Now you can write and sketch all over the prints without ruining your original base plan; and that's the object of reproducing the plan: to allow you to think freely and flexibly on paper.

You probably have been thinking in a general way about your landscaping needs and desires, as you went through the routine of preparing the base plan. Now is the moment to get down to cases and start annotating one of the prints. The problems and opportunities you will want to address usually fall into three general categories: your house, your site, and the people involved. The lists below should get you started — but don't feel limited by them. Trust your judgment, your experience, and your imagination.

**Site**  Under the site category, the important things to note at this stage have to do with the existing situation. It isn't yet time to put in specifics of possible future plantings or construction. Do, however, focus on such considerations as the following:

- Views, good and bad; particularly ones you want to emphasize or to screen or block out completely.
- Vegetation that needs attention. This could include trees or shrubs that should be cut back, or even removed, to open up a view or let in more light; or merely areas that call for thinning, pruning, or a cleanup of deadwood and broken limbs.
- Climatic variations, such as areas that are shady, too sunny (in summer), or too windy (in winter). Every site has its microclimates, as you'll already know if you are a gardener; become conscious of these.
- Seasonally wet or dry areas, or other areas with unusual soil conditions.

**House**  As you look at your house, you can be thinking not only about what exists now, but about changes you may want to incorporate into the landscaping plan. Make notes on the plan of such things as:

- Elements of the exterior of the house (forms, angles, textures, colors, building materials) that you may want to duplicate or echo in the landscape, to provide continuity and cohesiveness between the old and the new.
- Alterations to the house that could make for a more attractive and more comfortable relationship between exterior and interior. You may want to think about adding, subtracting, moving, or enlarging windows or doors; or giving rooms more logical uses.

**People**  Again, this category of considerations includes both what is happening now and what you see coming in the future. Some examples:

- Specific uses of parts of the site, such as areas for parking cars, hanging laundry, collecting trash, raising vegetables, entertaining, or engaging in building projects or other hobbies.

- Children's needs. If there's a sandbox or a swing set now, what will you do with that area later on?
- Requirements for pets (doghouse, fenced yard, etc.) if applicable.

**Regulations**   You have almost finished the sizing-up phase of your landscaping project. You've done a lot of careful hands-on work, as well as a lot of daydreaming, introspection, and practical study of what you have to work with and what you want to make of it. Your final move in this first phase is to stand back a bit from the house and the lot that have absorbed your attention so far, and take a look at your plans from a community perspective.

Be sure to do some research into your city's or town's zoning bylaws and building code. Check for any regulations that might affect your plans, particularly those involving setbacks and height restrictions. Watch out for any easements that may have been granted in past years. Read through the rules governing structures, such as fencing, pools, garages, or gazebos; and be aware early on of the requirements you may have to meet. It's generally easy to comply with the rules and regulations, so long as they don't come as a surprise at too late a stage.

Also speak to your neighbors to make sure that they are in sympathy with your plans. I've heard of families who started joyfully building something as apparently harmless as a tree house — only to have the neighbors object and the town planning board force the destruction of the children's leafy hideaway.

If you find that you will need a zoning variance in order to build some structure on your property, your neighbors' cooperation and support can make the difference between victory and defeat. In many cases, an improvement to one piece of property turns out to benefit all adjoining ones and even the whole neighborhood. But even if it doesn't, an atmosphere of friendly communication is important to any project.

This chapter has concentrated on detailed, mechanical procedures involving lots of work with pencils and paper. Now it's time to look up from the graph paper, to stop focusing on what you have and start picturing what you hope to do. Chapter 6 explores the essential qualities of a landscape that is both functional and beautiful.

---

# 6   DESIGNING YOUR LANDSCAPE

Imagine that your landscape is a series of outdoor rooms. I've already spoken of landscape spaces in architectural terms: "walls," "entries," "ceilings," and so forth. In a very real sense, when you design an exterior space — a landscape — you are doing many of the same kinds of things you do when designing an interior room. You take stock of existing conditions (the size and shape and materials at hand); determine what you'd like to add and subtract; and arrive at a scheme that incorporates spaces, structures, colors, and textures that will suit your taste and serve your purposes.

Every combination of site, house, and family is unique. So I won't attempt here to offer a catalogue of ready-made landscaping styles or prototypes. Not one of them would really fit your needs. Anyway, the delight of designing a landscape lies as much in the process as in the finished product. Very often, a design evolves as you go along. Questions lead to their own answers, problems to their own solutions.

Nevertheless, I can emphasize a few basic precepts about how you go about this process. The first was covered in Chapter 5: make a plan. The second precept: take your time, as much time as possible. Landscaping is a long-term project, and there's no sense in being hasty in the design phase. Spend some time just thinking, looking around you, leafing through gardening magazines, visiting parks and garden centers and other people's houses. You will find that you begin to see landscapes (your own and others) more accurately. You will gradually develop a sensitivity to what pleases you and what might be practical for you — as well as an awareness of what's not your style or is out of your league.

The third golden rule: whenever you make an estimate of a cost, double it. For good measure, also double the time that you allow for any operation to be completed. This realistic word of warning is fundamental to success and happiness in landscape design, especially for the beginner or the do-it-yourself landscaper.

The twin goals of landscape design, as of interior design, are to enhance beauty and to attain a desired level of usefulness, livability, and ease of maintenance. If you had acres and acres to play with, you could consign one area to functional uses and another to visual elegance. But few residential landscapes (or residences) afford that kind of square footage. With space at a premium, your mission is to create a setting that is both a practical living environment and a joy to the eye. Even in very limited space, you can have it all.

I'll focus on the utilitarian aspects of landscape design later in this chapter. For now, however, here are a few guidelines for you in your role as an artist of the beautiful.

**Designing for Beauty**   Ideas and ideals of beauty are as various as people. Once again, I won't try to prescribe, because a landscape that might suit me perfectly might not be your cup of tea. But there are some reliable basic qualities that will improve just about any design.

**Back to basics**   First of all, pay attention to the principles of composition outlined in Chapter 2. Scale, balance, rhythm, emphasis, and simplicity: if your design embodies these five it cannot go far wrong.

Keep in the forefront of your thinking the five elements of design. Masses, forms, and lines make up the basic picture; colors and textures enrich it. Choose them all with an eye to an overall mood or tone that's in keeping with your way of life, the appearance of your house, and your personality.

**Appealing to the senses**   Although I often urge restraint (in the mixing of colors or forms, for instance), when you design with the five senses in mind you can let yourself go. This is one of the particularly exciting things about landscape design. The more senses a landscape appeals to, the better. Sight and touch — the opportunities are obvious and limitless. Hearing — don't discount the importance of the sounds of foliage, water, wind, birds, even the human voice. The sense of smell — at every moment and at every season, you are smelling the world around

A feast for the senses in an English garden: massed shrubs, ground covers, perennials, and herbs are redolent with spring fragrance.

you, however unaware you may be. The fragrance of roses and the heady sweetness of honeysuckle come readily to mind; but the smells of pine trees, newly turned earth, a pile of wet leaves in the fall, or a warm wind are equally important to the nose. The sense of taste might seem minor in connection with the landscape — but don't forget the taste of a blade of grass or of homegrown blueberries, or the way a picnic or even a drink of water outdoors somehow tastes better than it ever does indoors. Even the smallest garden can appeal to all five senses, and it should.

Developing character: the addition of trickling water points up the dramatic beauty of this massive rock outcropping and adds sensory appeal.

**Developing character**  How often we think of or describe someone as having "character," a distinctive quality of personality. To be memorable, a landscape too must possess character, a set of images and associations that identify it and set it apart.

The character of a landscape derives partly from regional climate and geography. It partakes of the nature of local materials, the topography of the land, the native vegetation. And a good landscape design will recognize this. It is as risky for a landscape designer to strive for a lush effect in an open rocky setting, or a desert effect in a woodland, as it is for an architect to create a building without reference to or respect for its surroundings. Neither effort will be successful in the long run. In fact, such strained contrivances look more dated and more absurd with every passing season.

Partly, however, the character of a landscape can be the product of your planning and taste. It can come from your choice of focus or emphasis, such as a notable site feature (a rock ledge or the bank of a stream, for instance) or a particular planting or piece of construction. Or it can come from the success of your composition as a whole: the unique way in which you have put together all the elements that make up your landscape.

**Designing for Use**  Beauty is all very well; but as I have already suggested a number of times, a landscape that is beautiful to the eye can lose all its appeal if it's not fitted to the practical needs of its inhabitants.

Instances of beauty without usefulness aren't hard to come by. I think, for example, of a lawn that looks lush and enticing — but which you sink into up to your ankles if you make the mistake of stepping on it at certain seasons. Or a flight of steps whose treads and/or risers are the wrong dimensions, so that they're uncomfortable or even treacherous to

**Fencing and trellis serve two functions, creating a private outdoor living area and at the same time directing visitors to the doorway.**

walk on. Or plantings that are too fragile or formal for a young family, or too difficult for an older person to maintain. Or a wall or deck, handsome in itself, that reflects blinding light and baking heat into the windows of the house.

All these are minor errors but irritating ones. They can't help but detract from the charm of the overall landscape — and they are avoidable. Avoiding them was one of the main purposes of the careful assessment and mapping that went on in Chapter 5. And it is a primary goal of the more creative planning that is going on in this section. Devote some imaginative thought to the functions of each area of your landscape: what purpose does the area serve, and can you improve it with different kinds of planting or structures? Consider the ways people will move from one area to another: how could circulation be made more comfortable? And ask yourself how much effort you want to put into maintaining the finished landscape: is freedom from (or ease of) upkeep a high priority? Easy maintenance is a prime consideration for many people, and a very feasible goal.

**Function and fit**   The exercise of making the checklist in Chapter 5 should have left you with a fairly good idea of the kinds of activities you want to engage in on your property. Here's where you start figuring out how and where to modify (or design from scratch) the landscape to fit everything in. Working with a copy of your base plan, reconsider the factors raised in Chapter 4 on natural orientation.

Soil conditions, for example, may have an impact on your ideas about where you put what. Suppose you want to have a paved outdoor sitting area, a small wading pool, and a vegetable plot. If you try to grow vegetables where the old driveway used to run, you'll have to excavate the compact earth and create topsoil where none exists. Put the pool where the rock outcropping just shows at the foot of that tree, and you

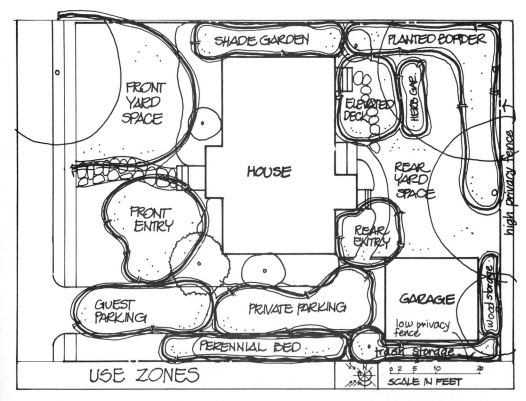

**Indicate use zones on a base-plan overlay to clarify the general types of use of different areas.**

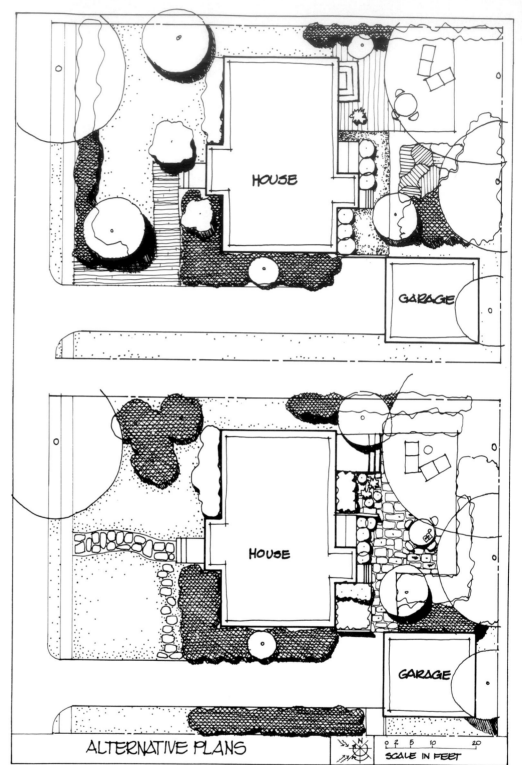

Two alternative plans for the same site. The final plan selected is shown in the hard-lined sketch on p. 71.

HOUSE

GARAGE

HOUSE

GARAGE

ALTERNATIVE PLANS

N

0 2 5 10 20
SCALE IN FEET

won't just be excavating, you'll be blasting. Pave the corner of the lawn where the grass grows tallest and greenest all summer, and you'll have to dig out all the good loam and replace it with a foot-deep bed of gravel.

Climatic factors, too, will have a lot to do with the livability of outdoor spaces and the uses to which you can put them. A windy passage between house and hedge is great for drying laundry, but terrible for sitting with the morning paper. A hot southern exposure next to the house wall is fine for private sunbathing, but not the place to put a sandbox. A deeply shaded spot is perfect for a bed of pachysandra, but a poor choice for a swimming pool.

There is much you can do with plantings and/or construction to modify the effects of sun and wind: tactics like establishing windbreaks, planting (or cutting down) trees, training vines over trellises, or installing ornamental pools or fountains can create whole new microclimates in different areas around your house. Climatic considerations are basic to every move you make in the landscape — from planting a rhododendron to building a brick wall — and they're discussed in detail in the calendar section.

Sort out the different activities that will take place in your landscape, and consider the best amount and location of space for each one. At the outset, segregate public and private space. You might want to take a crayon or colored pencil in some pale tone and cross-hatch one of the copies of your base plan with different tones to indicate public versus private. Or you could lay a sheet of tracing paper over the base plan and color on that. Then break down those two areas more specifically, into living areas, play areas, service areas, and maybe sites for special purposes such as a garden or swimming pool.

One group of functions that will probably fall under the "private space" heading are the strictly utilitarian. Let's face it, everyone has to store trash somewhere. Or possibly you need a tool shed, or a place to split and store firewood, or a location for a cold frame. Think now about how you might dedicate a certain space to these mundane purposes and screen them from the public view — perhaps even from the patio or the windows of the house. Don't forget, as you plan any such working area, the necessity for getting there with whatever vehicles or machines you'll be using, from boat trailer to wheelbarrow.

Think about all other outdoor activities in the same exhaustive way. How will the living area of the landscape be organized? Is the swimming pool the visual focus as well as the focus of activity (if so, attractive fencing will be a high priority) — or should the pool be tucked away around a corner? Is it important to you to be able to keep an eye on the driveway while you're weeding the vegetable patch? Will the prevailing summer breeze waft the fragrance of barbecuing goodies from your outdoor grille into your own or the neighbors' living room — and if so, how will you or they feel about it?

With unlimited space, of course, there would be no problem allocating areas for activities. The less space you have, the more meticulously you need to plan to make everything dovetail. You may even find that you can't do absolutely everything you'd like. But keep juggling spaces and trying new arrangements. You may be surprised at just how much is possible in a very little space.

While you are thinking conceptually about how these areas of activity are going to fit your site and how they are going to be linked and accessed, you should begin to zero in on some approximate dimensions for them. Allowing ample room for each of the uses you envision may call for some ingenuity. Sometimes, if you're in a space bind, the answer is to position two functional areas so that they can be paired up when necessary, to serve one function or the other. For instance, if you plan to do a lot of outdoor entertaining but can't build a terrace broad enough to accommodate the largest crowd you'd like to invite, then you may be able to double the usable space by placing the terrace next to a grassy lawn and providing easy access from terrace to lawn and vice versa. At the other extreme, if you want your terrace just to fit a breakfast table and two people, you might want to consider a balcony with a railing, which wouldn't impinge on the lawn at all. A driveway and turnaround that are used only by family's and friends' cars can be on the small side; but if the same access route has to serve oil trucks, garbage trucks, and delivery trucks, then you'll need a wider drive and a greater depth or diameter to the turnaround.

**Circulation**   Getting cars and oil trucks in and out of your drive is one form of circulation. But every portion of your landscape has its own requirements for access and egress — and planning for them is part of your job at this stage.

For inspiration you can turn first to the things that please and annoy you (respectively) about the way the movement of people and things around your property works now.

Very often, circulation problems have actually been built into a house and site. A typical case is that of the service doorway which leads to the kitchen and laundry, but which catches the eye of visitors before the front door, so that all visitors come barging right into the kitchen. To obviate this problem, there should be a clearly delineated approach to the front entrance to the house: a route that is fairly direct, visible from the visitor's parked car, and so designed as to say, "Welcome — this is the way in."

Another pet peeve of mine is the drive that leads straight to someone's garage door. As a visitor, you have to park in front of the garage, so that you block access to it, which makes you feel like an intruder. And if the garage door is open it's usually to the owner's embarrassment. The best solution, if at all possible, is to allow for a visitors' parking place separate from the place where the family car is kept. If that's not possible, see what other ingenious means you can develop to steer guests' cars away from the garage and screen its cluttered interior. You might build a curve into the driveway, with shrubbery or a fence to shield the offending garage from view.

And then there are the little things. Has the dog worn a bare spot where he rounds the corner of the house on his way from front door to back? Maybe that's the place for some flagstones or a brick walk. Are you always wishing you could go directly from the living room to the corner of the patio that's warm and sunny even in winter? Maybe a door could be opened up. Does the post office van dig at least one rut in the lawn every spring? Maybe the drive should be wider, or a stone curb be placed along the edge of the grass.

While you are pondering these things, review the checklist you made in Chapter 5. Be sure to provide for access to utilities' meters (for reading), to the septic tank (for cleanouts), to the well or to water or sewer lines (for maintenance). The March Materials and Construction section gives dimensional requirements for walks, steps, and drives. Use

**Circulation is especially important around this rambling old house now turned into five condo units. Visitors' parking, service areas, and walkways are carefully planned.**

these as a general guide to how much space to allow for these necessary avenues of circulation.

**Maintenance**   Design and installation, exciting though they may be, are the tip of the landscaping iceberg. The rest of it is upkeep: month in, month out, season after season, year after year. Unlike vegetables or annual flowers, landscape plants often outlive the people who planted them. (Many, if not most, trees and shrubs and vines take several years to attain the size and form for which they were chosen in the first place.) And landscape construction materials are by definition engineered to endure years of sun, rain, and ice.

Since these furnishings (as it were) of the landscape will be with you for such a long time, I urge you to decide at the outset how much time you want to spend grooming and cleaning up around them. Minimum maintenance may be your chief priority; or you may enjoy gardening and welcome seasonal chores as a change of pace and an opportunity to be outdoors. Whichever, this is the time to do a little soul-searching and decide on a general approach.

For ease of care, one basic rule is to keep your design simple in every respect. Lay out the lawn — if any — with gently curving edges, no corners or small areas that are fussy to mow. Keep high-maintenance areas like flower beds and vegetable plots few in number, manageable in size, and easy to get at. Steer clear of trees or shrubs that will demand regular pruning or trimming.

For that matter, avoid any plant that will actually create work. Unless you like raking, don't plant a large-leaved deciduous shade tree where it will dump a mountain of leaves on a lawn or terrace every autumn. Keep fruiting trees like cherries or crabapples away from paved areas where their squashed fruit will be a nuisance. And make sure that all plants you select are healthy and well adapted to the use and location you plan for them.

In Part II, the calendar section, every monthly chapter has a

Landscape Tasks entry dedicated to upkeep and maintenance. For those who are more interested in freedom from upkeep, the February chapter talks about planning an easy-maintenance landscape and gives a list of plants that require minimal care.

By now you have come almost full circle, from a crash course in the basics of landscape design, to the production of the base plan and its accompanying checklists, through some conceptual thinking about how you might add to or alter your landscape for both beauty and use, to the part that is the most fun of all — sketching and finally putting into effect the solution.

# 7  FROM SKETCH TO REALITY

In the preceding chapters I have looked at aspects of landscape design from various angles; and I've tried to encourage you not to make any actual changes in your place until you have thought the project through with great thoroughness. By now, I hope you have done just that. This is the time to settle down in earnest with the base plan and the tracing paper.

**Sketching**  Clip a piece of tracing paper over a clean copy of the base plan and sketch in roughly the various areas and circulation routes you have devised. You will probably want to do this more than once, whether to refine your first thoughts or to try whole different tacks. You may throw out more sketches than you keep. Don't be too compulsive about accuracy or precise dimensions. The idea is to arrive at a design, then pin down the details as needed — much as a fashion designer sketches out a "look" without too much concern for anatomical realism or the exact locations of seams or buttons.

When you have pretty well exhausted your ideas, pick the sketch that you feel will work the best, and start refining it. Check the dimensions of pathways, flights of steps, walls, planting areas; make sure they're going to fit. Think about the kinds of plants, paving, and construction materials you may be using. If you're going to be making any grade changes, review the vertical relief measurements noted on the base plan, and decide whether you will be using masonry retaining walls, wood timbers, sloped banks, or what. And keep looking back at the base plan — to be sure (among other things) that in your enthusiasm you haven't put structures or pavements over septic tanks, utility rights-of-way, town easements, or other hidden pitfalls.

The more details you add, the more jumbled your sketch will look. It's helpful to take some colored pencils or marking pens and color the different surfaces. I make driveways light gray, walks a light tan, decks or terraces the same color as the walks or slightly darker (two layers of the same color), lawns a light green, and planting areas a darker green. Deciduous trees can just be circles with no additional color, so as not to obscure the ground plane. (You may want to fill in the circles that represent evergreens, though, at least if they're the kind of evergreens whose foliage starts right down at ground level.)

At this point the design will begin to look very beautiful and you may be tempted to summon the local brickyard and have the local nursery send over a truckload of shrubs. One more stroke of patience, please — better first to test out your hunches on the ground.

**Layout and Mockup** Take measurements directly from your scaled drawing and measure out each structure, planting, path, wall, etc. on the ground, using the longest tape measure you have. As you get each measurement correct, mark it somehow so that you can begin to see what the finished product will look like. Let your imagination run riot. Here are a few easy marking ideas:

- Garden hoses are handy for laying out curved bed edges, walkways, or other curved linear elements on the ground plane.
- To lay out perfectly straight lines, use stakes and string.
- If you want to get a bird's eye view of a ground-plane layout, mark the beds, shrubs, etc. with agricultural limestone. Then go up to the top floor of your house and look out the window.
- You can mock up fences or walls with cardboard and stakes; or with blankets draped over string, rope, or wire.
- To locate the tops of things (trees, buildings, porch roofs, and such) and see how they'll affect views and where their shadows will fall, prop up bamboo poles or two-by-fours. I have even on occasion sent up helium-filled balloons on premeasured strings; make sure it is a calm day, though.
- To get a sense of the view and other sight lines from a proposed deck, put yourself on a stepladder at the same height you'd be if you were sitting in a chair on the deck. Now try "standing" on the deck. Repeat several times, moving the ladder to different spots on the imaginary deck.

Some of these gimmicks and acrobatics may sound far-fetched, but you really should do all you can to test out your landscaping plan before you take any steps to make it happen. This on-site visualizing phase is harder than it sounds. Imagine the difference between a bare stage and the same rectangular space with props, scenery, and backdrop in place. The difference in apparent size alone — not to mention the totally changed mood and character — is astounding and often difficult to anticipate. Difficult, but not impossible, and approaching possibility is the object of all this measuring and mocking up.

And again, now, not later, is the time to discover your mistakes. Maybe that fence could be slightly lower, that patio two feet wider, or those steps made into a ramp instead. Replacing plants is a nuisance; relocating or rebuilding construction is an expensive nuisance.

Once you have tested your plan until you feel confident that it is as good as you can make it, a sensible move is to take your final sketch to a garden center or nursery that does construction to get their advice. (Naturally, they may be more lavish with advice if it is clear that you'll be buying materials from them.) Sound them out on the construction materials and details of any decks or terraces, pathways, pools, or other structures you have planned. Get their reactions to the plants you've chosen for various locations and functions. No nurseryman or landscape contractor wants to be party to a disappointing outcome; so there's almost a built-in guarantee they will do all they can to steer you right according to their own best judgment. (I'd certainly expect, however, that after all this planning you would not be too far off the track.)

If your design is simple in concept and modest in scale, you may be able to work straight from your sketch. If, on the other hand, there's

For laying out edges of beds, drives, and walks I often use limestone. Viewing from a distance or from an upstairs window shows how the design will look on the ground.

sophisticated construction, grading, or extensive and elaborate planting involved, you may need to go one further step — to "hard-lining."

**Hard-lining**   To compute needed quantities of construction materials (pipe, lumber, stone, concrete) or to pinpoint relationships like those between flights of steps and the floor grade of a house, you'll need a hard-lined drawing instead of a sketch.

For hard-lining you abandon the tracing paper and go back to transparent graph paper. It's best to use the same scale as that of your base plan (unless you have found that scale unworkable in the long run) so as to avoid a lot of extra mathematics. Using T-square and triangle, make a precise version of the base plan and landscaping design, incorporating all the elements of your working sketch, but neatly, with exact measurements shown.

You may also want to draw one or more elevations (side or front views) or sections (cutaway slices to show foundations, drains, or underpinnings). If you do, you'll have to go outside again to measure or estimate the heights of existing elements — such as your house, a tree, a fence, or a hedge — that you want to represent on the elevation or section. It isn't really hard work to make these drawings, although it is time-consuming. If your design calls for much sophisticated plotting and drafting, however, you may decide that this is one time to consult a professional landscape architect.

Still, I'd encourage you to avoid hard-lining at all, even if you are already working with a landscaping professional, unless the magnitude or complexity of the plan positively demands it. The reason is that hard-lining can stifle imagination and limit flexibility. Just as it is human nature not to want to get rid of something once it's in place, it is human nature to resist changing a hard-lined drawing.

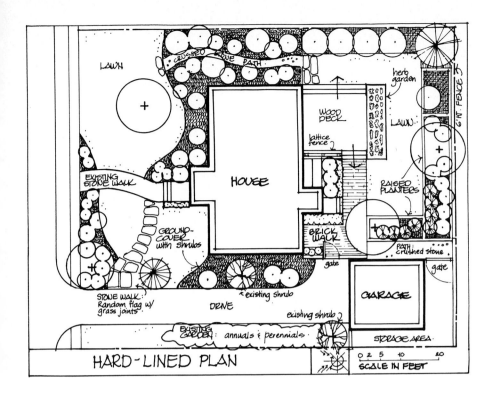

LAWN

CRUSHED STONE PATH

herb garden

6 FT. FENCE

WOOD DECK

LAWN

lattice fence

EXISTING STONE WALK

HOUSE

RAISED PLANTERS

GROUND-COVER with shrubs

BRICK WALK

PATH crushed stone

gate

STONE WALK: Random flag w/ grass joints

DRIVE

existing shrub

GARAGE

gate

EXISTING GARDEN

annuals & perennials

existing shrub

STORAGE AREA

HARD-LINED PLAN

SCALE IN FEET

0 2 5    10                    20

Here, the chosen plan has gone from rough sketch to hard-lined finished drawing.

But in landscaping it is vital that you keep an open mind as you go along. There are always surprises, things you didn't anticipate on paper. Sometimes they are happy surprises, and you find that you end up with a more attractive solution than you thought possible. Sometimes they are unhappy, and you have to have the flexiblity to cope with them. I never design a landscape where the final result matches the paper plan in every detail. And I never tire of making changes and adjustments when I can see there's an improvement to gain.

**Into the Ground**   At last, the fruits of all your careful and creative thought: action! It's time to lay out a schedule, pinpoint costs, and get to work.

**Making a schedule**   In any landscaping job, from the most sweeping transformation to the most minor change, work must progress in sequence — and from the bottom up.

Just like a building, a well-constructed garden almost always has some underpinnings. The schematic drawing here makes the point clear. Is there going to be hard construction, such as a walk, drive, or terrace? Bases must be laid. Will there be a wall, some steps, a deck, or a fence? Footings must be constructed early on. What about drainage — from condition of topsoil to depth of subsoil, from topography to drains, drywells, and gutters? Get the basic groundwork done before anything else. For example, dig trenches for utilities *before* you spread or seed topsoil. Grade soil into the forms and planes desired *before* you put plants into the ground.

Seasonal considerations also enter in. In the Northeast, for instance, most landscaping work occurs during the six or seven months when the earth is unfrozen and most workable — roughly April through

Contemplating an adjustment to a landscape plan.

# UNDERGROUND CONSIDERATIONS·

**Below-ground preparations often take more time and money than anticipated, yet are critical for quality results in the long run.**

October. Whatever area you live in, think ahead realistically about what can be accomplished in the available time. For Hardiness Zones 5 and 6 (see the Zone Map on pages 346–347), a very rough approximation of spring and fall planting seasons might go as follows.

## Planting

|  | Season begins | Season ends |
|---|---|---|
| *Spring Planting* | | |
| Lawns | 1–15 April | 15–30 May |
| Evergreens | 1–15 April | 15–30 May |
| Deciduous plants | 1–15 April | 15–30 May |
| *Fall Planting* | | |
| Lawns | 1–15 August | 15–30 September |
| Evergreens | 1–15 September | 1–15 November |
| Deciduous plants | 1–15 October | 15–30 November |

(If you're at the northern range of your area, you want to take the later dates for beginning and earlier dates for ending each season; if southern, the opposite: earlier dates for beginning and later dates for ending each season. And if you're in Zone 7 or south, everything can begin and end earlier in spring and later in fall.)

If your project calls for time-consuming construction that runs beyond the spring planting dates, it may be sensible to put off planting until later. Traditionally, fall is the preferred time for planting lawns, and many trees and shrubs — although nurseries now have techniques that allow planting right through the summer. If you're stuck in the fall beyond the dates for seeding a lawn, the solution is usually sod. Consider doing major earth-moving — such as excavating, filling, or otherwise disrupting the site — in the fall. Let the whole project settle in over the winter, then complete and refine it and do the planting in the spring.

**Shopping for materials**   If you are going to undertake your project on your own, you'll be buying your own plants and construction materials; and some exploratory shopping (at least) has to take place before you can firm up your budget. This can be tremendous fun, as well as educational. It's no different from shopping for anything you're unfamiliar with at first. Go through the Yellow Pages, then visit materials yards and nurseries. Find a reputable dealer; ask lots of questions; and buy only when you are satisfied with quality, price, and whatever guarantees are available. Used materials and bargain rates may not really save you money if quality is sacrificed, so go carefully.

**Using landscape architects and contractors**   When to call in a landscape architect, and on what basis? If you find yourself totally unable to decide between different design possibilities, or if you feel technically unequipped to organize or execute the work, a word or two of professional advice can be both helpful and reassuring. It needn't necessarily cost a fortune: most landscape architects offer you the option of a one- or two-hour consultation at a flat hourly rate. A more extensive involvement, of course, is a different matter, with lower hourly rate but lots more hours spent in design, detailing, selecting materials, and supervising construction and planting.

If you decide to hire a contractor to do any phase of the job (or all of it), get him to supply you with samples of the materials he intends to use before starting work; or work out an agreement whereby he'll use materials that you choose and purchase. For instance, if you find a source of stone that's just what you want for a patio or walk, talk with the contractor and make sure he approves of it before you pay for it. The reason it's important to have all these things clear is that contractors' standard operating procedure is to buy materials at a discount (anywhere from 5 to 30 percent), then charge you the full retail price to cover their delivery and handling charges and any guarantees they offer.

If you are undertaking a project that involves several different contractors — say, a mason, an electrician, a driveway contractor, and a carpenter — you can serve as your own general contractor. That is, you hire all the individual contractors yourself and you coordinate their respective efforts. Or you can have a general contractor do this for you. You'll probably pay 10 to 20 percent more for the job as a whole if you use a general contractor, but you'll save any number of headaches.

I am a great believer in having the landscape contractor on a job also serve as the general contractor. Of all the people involved, he is apt to have the best sense of what should happen when; and thus he can ensure a proper meshing of all facets of the project. Be certain he has this capability from previous projects that you have seen or that you know to have been successfully completed.

**Budgeting and staging**   I mentioned earlier how important it is to double every cost estimate at the planning stage. When you start shopping and talking with contractors and so forth, you may actually find that you can't do everything you hope to do all at once. In that event, I'd encourage you to do the work in stages.

The best way to approach staging, I think, is to complete one area at a time — and do a good job of it. That will give you the satisfaction of seeing at least one thing finished before you go on to the next. The alternative — trying to skimp overall, installing mere twigs for plantings,

Staging: only the path, fence, and a few shrubs were installed in the first phase here. Phase 2 will add ground covers and additional planting to extend the blooming through the season.

laying temporary surfaces for pavements — may be necessary in some cases; but it can be very discouraging and trying to the patience. All too often, "good enough just for now" becomes "forever, and never really right."

Be sure of your own priorities. If one thing must precede another, should it be the service area? The public view from the street? The private side terrace? Keep both appearance and practicality in mind.

When you're trying to cut back cost overruns, it's natural to look first at the most expensive items and see if they can wait or somehow be modified. Heavy construction projects like drives, walks, walls, and steps often look like the most obvious candidates for postponement. Yet in some instances, postponing one or more of these jobs for reasons of economy can hamper your enjoyment or use of the site or actually create larger costs later on. An exposed, unstabilized bank or steep unpaved drive, for example, can erode so badly that extensive (and expensive) repair work has to be done before the final planting or paving can be installed. In the long run it may be best to have all these big jobs done in one fell swoop, because you save on equipment costs. Once machines or equipment are on-site it's efficient to keep them in use; besides, remobilizing at a later date always costs extra.

**Contracts**   No matter how small the job may seem, you should always have written contracts with all help, from electricians to general contractors to landscape architects. A signed agreement clarifies everyone's expectations as to service or material to be provided, cost, and date of completion or delivery.

Landscape design and construction does take patience, care, and love — but so does any project that's worth doing. All you really need are some ideas to stir your imagination and some practical guidance to keep your feet on the ground. And so on to Part II, where you should find plenty of both.

# PART II THE LANDSCAPING YEAR

The twelve-month structure of Part II has offered me some wonderful opportunities. Many facets of landscaping are indeed seasonal. There are indoor times and outdoor times; planting, pruning, and building times; times for bloom and for fruit and for shade. It's the most natural thing in the world to deal with these subjects in the months appropriate to them.

This calendar format has also, however, presented me with some interesting dilemmas. Many topics simply cannot be restricted to one month or even one season: they're year-round in application. I have made choices, often very personal or arbitrary ones, about where to include what. For instance, I have talked about drives and walks in early spring, a time when it's natural to plan and construct major landscape spaces or to make improvements in anticipation of warmer weather. But paving can be laid in any month from March to October. By the same token, dogwoods crop up all over the place: like many landscape plants they come in many forms and have innumerable useful and ornamental roles to play. That's why I have not detailed the specific characteristics or cultural requirements of individual plants as they appear in the month-by-month chapters here, but have assembled them in Part III. This is a major departure from the other Victory Garden books, but makes good sense in terms of accessibility, I think.

Locating things in Part II is a matter of following the directories. The contents of each month's chapter are listed in the table of contents at the beginning of the book; they're also thumbnailed on the title page of each month; and of course they are exhaustively indexed at the back of the book.

Detailed how-to instructions for all the topics raised in Part II fall under two headings. For inanimate materials and construction projects, I'll introduce each material — its origins, its assets and liabilities, its relative costs, its uses — and show you how I tackle numerous projects from the standpoint of design, utility, and economy. But this isn't a construction manual. There are excellent publications available telling you how to lay a concrete pavement, build a wooden deck, or pipe an artificial water-

Layers of white, pink, and red azalea bloom carpet this woodland floor.

fall. I have listed many of them in Further Reference at the end of this book. Look there if do-it-yourself construction is your interest. Here I'm concerned more with the whys and wherefores than with the how-tos.

For plants, the detailed how-to information can be found in the Part III description of each individual plant. In monthly sections dealing with flowering shrubs, shade trees, ground covers, and so on, I'll generally just remind you to give each plant the kind of soil, amount of sun, and degree of shelter that it likes best.

Nor will I try to write here the ultimate treatise on coping with bugs, viruses, bacteria, fungus diseases, weeds, and other garden nuisances. Both *Crockett's Victory Garden* and *Crockett's Flower Garden* do a good job on many specific ailments and their cures. But the permanent landscape plants I talk about in this book — trees, shrubs, vines, and ground covers — really should be able to endure most of the cyclical pests and blights that come their way. A basically healthy oak tree afflicted with leaf gall (for example) just isn't comparable to a zucchini riddled with borers or a tea rose smothered in powdery mildew. In addition, my overall approach to landscape plants tends toward the Darwinian: I give them an environment suited to their needs, and from there on it's survival of the fittest.

I will, however, indicate in the Landscape Tasks section each month the times of the year when you may want to undertake controls or preventive measures such as dormant oil spraying of fruit trees, fertilizing lawns and beds, or killing poison ivy. For myriad other problems, from Japanese beetles to fire blight, I refer you to the chemical and biological controls available at your garden center or through landscape nurseries or garden centers.

I should mention here that this book carries on the Victory Garden tradition of focusing primarily on the plants, soils, and climate of the region where the Victory Garden is: the Northeast, roughly Zones 5 and 6. The Zone Map on pages 346–347 will enable you to make any necessary adjustments in planting information.

In the interest of breaking the multifarious subject matter of Part II into manageable and findable segments, I've organized each month's material into the following five subject areas.

**Landscaping Opportunities**   This monthly section sets up a seasonal landscape situation or scenario and explores the aspects I've found to be important. Many of these sections offer lists of recommended plants. Some, like the sections on energy-efficient landscaping or on the winter landscape, approach their topics more in terms of general concepts and issues.

**Plants for a Purpose**   Hedging, shading, year-round color or form, ease of care — many Plants for a Purpose sections group plants by their functions. Others represent major, multipurpose horticultural categories, like native plants, broad-leaved evergreens, or small deciduous trees. While these sections are placed in seasonally appropriate months, every plant listed has a part to play all year long.

Every plant mentioned in this book appears in at least one of these Plants for a Purpose lists; many appear on several. Taken all together, the lists make up a complete collection of the trees, shrubs, vines, and ground covers that I recommend most highly for use in our region. But please be aware that I've really had to limit myself. Many personal favorites of mine have had to be excluded because of slow growth, disease problems, or other liabilities. Russian olive, white oak, and black locust are examples.

**Materials and Construction**   Dedicated to the inorganic side of landscaping, these sections introduce the raw materials you'll be working with, and will help you think in terms of design. Sometimes they follow in sequence from month to month. May's section on wood for outdoor construction precedes June's discussion of decks, for instance. In other cases, they're linked to plant-oriented topics covered that month. In November, fences and gates accompany a section on hedges, since all three are useful for screening and protection from wind.

**Plants by Design**   These lists suggest plants purely for visual qualities. In the winter and fall lists I have grouped plants with colorful bark and twigs and interesting bark textures; plants with attractive fruits and with yellow, orange, or red foliage; and plants with notable textures and forms. In March through August I have listed flowering trees and shrubs in order of bloom — so that if your aim is to have at least one plant or group of plants flowering in every month, you can make a selection from these lists.

Two cautions about using the order-of-bloom lists. First, the succession of bloom (what follows what) will be about the same wherever you are — but the absolute dates will vary widely according to your location and the particular nuances of local weather. (Make adjustments according to the Zone Map.) Second, try not to overdo. If you go much beyond one or two varieties in bloom at any one time (unless your place is really huge), your plantings may detract from, rather than complement, each other's beauty.

**Landscape Tasks**   If seasonal projects and annual upkeep are your pleasure, this section should give you plenty to do. It's essentially a checklist, and you are encouraged to pick and choose.

Finally, a word about plant names and the organization of the dozens of plant lists throughout Parts II and III.

In the text, I've used familiar common names of plants. In lists in Part II, the common name comes first, followed by the Latin botanical name. (I have followed *Hortus* as my authority where spellings were in question.) But each list and each section of Part III (where the botanical name precedes the common name) is alphabetical by *botanical* name — because so many plants go by two or more common names that the only firm nomenclatures are the botanical ones. Most plant lists in this book name individual species — as in "weeping birch (*Betula pendula*)." Where I'm talking about a whole genus as a group, however, you'll see entries like "birches (*Betula* spp.)," meaning simply "various species of birch." The abbreviation "spp." stands for "species."

If you're in doubt about where to find any plant, just look in the index. Every plant is thoroughly cross-indexed under all its names.

The calendar year begins with January, and by a happy coincidence that's when many a successful landscaping project also enters the planning stages. It makes a very good month to begin our exploration of the real stuff of landscaping.

# JAN

**Masses and forms of evergreens in a winter silhouette, dramatized by a squall of snow.**

The winter landscape has a profound fascination. Far from dead, it is waiting, full of sleeping life. It abounds with stark contrasts and subtle colors — and often with dramatic lines, forms, and textures. This chapter explores aspects of landscaping appropriate to winter: stratagems for making the most of the latent beauty of the landscape; plantings to provide food and habitats for birds and wildlife; trees and shrubs with colorful bark for bright accents at this time of year. The Materials and Construction section looks at stone and gravel — materials you'd install later, but which you may now want to investigate, price, and contemplate using in projects in the coming months.

### Landscaping Opportunities
# THE WINTER LANDSCAPE

Most of the year we use our landscape, enjoying it, maintaining it, engaging in various activities outdoors. In the winter we tend to be in physical contact with the landscape far less often. In this season *seeing* becomes the main interaction between us and the landscape, and views from windows take on new importance.

**Sleeping Beauty**   Much to the dismay of my family — and often of the professional gardeners or custodians involved — I enjoy visiting gardens and parks in midwinter. Amid cries of "but there's nothing to see," and "you really should come back in June when the azaleas bloom," I can wander happily among bare boughs and frozen soil. What there is to see is the architecture of the landscape, stripped of the summer's concealing green mantle. It is the undulating form of the land itself; the skeletons of the trees and shrubs growing there; the shapes of manmade structures.

Line becomes all-important. The tracery of leafless boughs against the sky; intricate shadow patterns on snow or bare ground; the now visible edges of paths, fences, trellises, walls. Linear elements that were softened by summer growth come into focus now with new clarity.

Light and color have new contexts and new meanings in winter. The rays of winter sunlight strike the earth at a shallower angle, creating longer shadows and lighting objects more from the side than from above. And everyone knows what snow does to a landscape: how it makes the sky seem bluer, and how all those long shadows reflect the sky's deep azure.

Even without snow, winter light unveils new ranges of color: the pinkish tops of long grasses, the purple hue of a hillside covered with second growth, the silvery or red tones of tree trunks we normally assume are brown, or the red-orange glow of shrubs we always think of as green.

Space itself changes (to the eye) in winter. Boundaries and demarcations seem to move. Summer's dense clump of leafy shrubbery or small trees suddenly grows transparent in winter, allowing the view to include a slope, a clearing, or larger trees beyond. A shady planting drops its umbrella of leaves, opening a huge space of sky above. Low-angled the sunlight may be, but in winter there's lots more of it, if you live among deciduous trees.

**Special winter effect: a dusting of snow emphasizes pattern and line. Snow melts off the warmer surfaces of paving stones and remains in the colder joints between.**

**Unlimited Possibilities**   Learning to see the beauty of the winter landscape is your first step. Thinking about ways to shape it to your taste and needs is the second. Now, while everything is open and exposed, look for projects that can be carried out in milder seasons, for your pleasure in winters to come.

The slanting winter light, for example, is ideal for backlighting dramatic elements in the landscape. You need to make sure that those dramatic elements are positioned properly in relation to your house and the sun. Put a picturesque tree such as a Japanese maple, or a wall or fence with interesting spaces built into it, to the south, southeast, or southwest of your house, and it will be backlit for a good part of the day.

Think about bringing things into silhouette, with or without back-lighting. Some silhouettes make themselves, like the graceful curves of birches against a tall hemlock, or the dark forms of smaller evergreens against a pale wall or lawn. Other silhouettes you can create or emphasize through your choice of plantings or by clearing away underbrush or competing growth.

This is the season when evergreens really come into their own — yews, cedars, hemlocks, pines, and other conifers large and small; and broad-leaved evergreens like laurels, hollies, or rhododendrons. These were just part of the general greenery a few months ago, but now they take center stage. They establish boundaries, frame views, add blocks of solid form and color; and they play several parts at once. A clump of red cedars, for instance, affords a perfect haven for birds and small animals. In addition, its individual trees are appealing in shape and send dramatic elongated shadows across a grassy or snowy lawn. Besides, the bluish gray-green foliage of the trees is a perfect foil to the grays, browns, or greener greens around it.

(Be cautious with evergreens, though. Too large or too numerous conifers can create a dark and gloomy effect. Above all, never plant a forest tree like a Canadian hemlock or white pine right next to the house: it will rapidly take over the whole landscape.)

You can use the colors, textures, and densities of your plantings to affect visual perspective and the apparent scale of things, particularly in winter. Formal gardens in the classical mode employed rows of shrubbery to give an impression that long allees were receding into the distance. In an informal way and on a humbler scale, you can team conifers

Even in a newly installed landscape, winter changes are dramatic.

Line, light, and shadow are all-important in this rhythmic winter composition.

and deciduous trees to create vistas with an illusion of depth or distance greater than actually exists. Light-colored (such as autumn olive) or bluish-colored (such as Colorado blue spruce) or fine-textured (such as Thurlow willow) plants, set at the far edge of your field of vision, will help it seem farther away than it really is.

Deciduous trees and shrubs have their own special places in your winter landscape, and the plant lists this month highlight aspects of their seasonal appeal. You can select plants with a view to attracting birds and wildlife from the Plants for a Purpose section. Or think about plants with colored bark or twigs, either as individual accents or in groupings for stronger long-distance effects: this month's Plants by Design list has lots of suggestions. Your job is to achieve the maximum effect with the plantings you choose, and you can do this by arranging them carefully. If you put a beautiful red-stemmed shrub dogwood or gray-barked shadblow against a backdrop of second growth fifty yards from your house, it won't amount to much. But place the same plant northwest of the house and ten feet from a window, and the afternoon sun will illuminate the graceful silvery branches of the shad or set the scarlet branchlets of the dogwood ablaze with color. If you can, group three or five Oriental cherries (for instance) in a well-lit spot, within view of the house and against a light-toned background that will set them off, and they'll really make a statement.

## Plants for a Purpose
# PLANTINGS FOR BIRDS AND WILDLIFE

Birds are the flowers of our winter landscape; and January is a fine time to watch the birds at their busiest. It is also a good time to think about the kinds of trees and shrubs that can make your garden an appealing place for birds and small wildlife. My emphasis here is not on feeding birds at feeding stations (although that's a fine idea too) but on including a variety of food and water sources, cover, and nesting areas in the design of your landscape itself. As a sampler of the kinds of plants we'll be looking at, one study of the wildlife food value of woody plants listed the ten most important as oak, blackberry, cherry, dogwood, grape, pine, blueberry, maple, sumac, and beech.

Why encourage wildlife around your property? The entertainment value and sheer beauty of birds and chipmunks and rabbits can't be denied (even if you are not a rodent fan). And like everything in nature, all these creatures play roles in the ecosystem. A landscape devoid of any wildlife would indeed be sterile.

**Landscaping for Birds and Wildlife**   The basic needs of wild creatures are little different from our own, and even the smallest garden can meet many of them. They include:
- Food such as seeds, nuts, berries, other fruits, flower nectar, insects, grubs, earthworms, etc.
- Cover, from overhanging eaves to dense evergreens to hollow trees, for refuge from predators as well as shelter from weather.
- Water for drinking and bathing throughout the year.
- Nesting areas with shelter and privacy.

A variety of plantings is important. You are aiming for both a diverse assortment of food sources and a year-round sequence of flowering and fruit bearing. This is not to suggest, however, that you should buy one of every kind of plant birds and animals like and sprinkle them indiscriminately around the landscape. You can easily incorporate a healthy variety of plants for wildlife and still follow good principles of design. If you want to use several kinds of small trees and shrubs, plant them in groups. Limit your single specimens to larger trees, and set them behind or beyond the clustered lower plantings.

Many wild animals, including birds, gravitate to "edges" — spots where two habitats meet, such as lawn and flower beds, shrubbery and taller trees, field and woodlot. By staying around the edge area, a creature can have two habitats in the space of one: forage plus shelter, or nesting plus bathing, for instance. A well-planned landscape will offer some edge territory, and the birds will be pleased.

A bit more of a challenge — and what's most appealing to wildlife — is something as close as possible to a natural habitat. It's not that this is hard to do, but it may not be to your taste or feasible in your particular situation. You need two things: native plants (or naturalized plants that have adapted completely to local conditions) and a certain amount of untidiness.

For the first requirement, the plant list in this section offers all kinds of good candidates that meet the needs of wild creatures. These plants also serve many design requirements, from screening and shade to color, texture, and other ornamental interest. After looking at the list you may want to purchase some nursery-grown plants for your wildlife; or you may find that you already possess quite a few. If there are maples, pines, wild berry bushes, or fruiting vines (for instance) on your land, you can just hold on to them and supplement them with a few well-chosen shrubs, small trees, or ground covers.

**Favored customer: birds brings animation and color to the winter landscape.**

The second challenge is providing for some messy areas. It has been said that the gardening slob is the birds' best friend. You don't really have to be a slob, but you will have better luck with birds if you can plan for some areas that are not immaculately groomed. Birds and animals love dead trees and rotting logs, tall grasses, brush piles, brier patches, boggy areas, and flowers gone to seed. With a few unkempt spaces such as these, you will keep — or soon acquire — a fine population of wildlife. But if you just don't have the space, you can still achieve many of the effects of wilderness in microcosm, by using hedges, massed plantings, a compost heap, a few thorny or prickly plants, a water source of some sort, and a couple of plants that provide berries or seeds at different seasons. The drawing on page 86 suggests a range of wildlife habitats; compress or expand them according to the space and the flexibility you have.

As you plan your landscape, keep an eye on the habits of the birds and animals that are already there. It is always simpler to keep existing wildlife happy than to attract them to a place where they've never lived before. I think of a neighbor of mine whose property is bounded by a tumbledown low stone wall. The wall used to house a dozen chipmunk families, and we all enjoyed watching them industriously gathering acorns in fall, or basking in the late-afternoon sun in spring, or coming out to view the world after a summer rain. Then my neighbor built a cedar fence all along the southeast side of the wall — and the chipmunks moved out. I don't really know why, although I have a few

WILDLIFE HABITAT

windbreak

ornamental planting

water

dead trees

unmown area

ideas. The wall is much mossier now, and I think it is probably colder and damper all year. Also, the chipmunks may have resented the loss of their 360-degree view from the top of the wall; perhaps they felt threatened by sneak attack. Or perhaps the air currents along and through the wall have been disrupted. Whatever their reasons for leaving, my neighbor misses the chipmunks. As do I.

I do realize that there are those who don't wholeheartedly adore chipmunks — or, for that matter, rabbits or any small rodents. Would-be growers of vegetables, strawberries, or other berries fall into this category. It is worth noting, though, that if supplies of water and wild berries, nuts, and seeds are abundant, birds and animals seem far less inclined to raid the human beings' food supply. This is just one more argument for landscaping with an eye to the needs of birds and wildlife.

**Specific Plants for Birds and Wildlife**  The list here represents my own favorites among the hardy plants that are attractive to birds and wildlife. It includes many native plants and ranges from very large trees down to ground covers. If you can work into your landscape design a selection of these plants, you can expect within a few seasons to have visits from most of the resident birds.

There are countless other possibilities, of course. Your nurseryman may have good suggestions. Or if you're especially interested in attracting particular kinds of birds, your nearest Audubon Society can recommend plantings that will suit the tastes of your favored customers.

**Winterberry holds its fruit right through till spring, provender for wild birds and color for a winter landscape.**

Another plant for birds is Virginia creeper or woodbine. The vine's dark fruit contrasts with its colorful foliage in the fall.

## Plantings for Birds and Wildlife

### Large Trees

Red maple (*Acer rubrum*)
American beech (*Fagus grandifolia*)
Red cedar (*Juniperus virginiana*)
White pine (*Pinus strobus*)
Red oak (*Quercus rubra*)
Canadian hemlock (*Tsuga canadensis*)

### Small Trees and Tall Shrubs (fruiting in summer; good for keeping wildlife out of crops)

Shadblow, juneberry, or serviceberry (*Amelanchier canadensis*)
Flowering dogwood (*Cornus florida*)
Black or rum cherry (*Prunus serotina*)
Elderberry (*Sambucus canadensis*)

### Small Trees and Tall Shrubs (holding fruit into winter)

Washington hawthorn (*Crataegus phaenopyrum*)
Autumn olive (*Elaeagnus umbellata*)
Winterberry (*Ilex verticillata*)
Flowering crabapple (*Malus floribunda*)
Fragrant sumac (*Rhus aromatica*)
Korean mountain ash (*Sorbus alnifolia*)

Arrowwood (*Viburnum dentatum*)
American cranberrybush (*Viburnum trilobum*)

### Small to Medium Shrubs

Japanese barberry (*Berberis thunbergii*)
Gray dogwood (*Cornus racemosa*)
Regel privet (*Ligustrum obtusifolium regelianum*)
Tatarian honeysuckle (*Lonicera tatarica*)
Bayberry (*Myrica pensylvanica*)
Highbush blueberry (*Vaccinium corymbosum*)

### Ground Covers

Creeping juniper (*Juniperus horizontalis*)
Canada yew (*Taxus canadensis*)
Lowbush blueberry (*Vaccinium angustifolium*)

### Vines

Bittersweet (*Celastrus scandens*)
Virginia creeper or woodbine (*Parthenocissus quinquefolia*)
Grapes (*Vitis* spp.)

Detailed information and recommended varieties can be found in Part III.

## Materials and Construction
# STONE AND GRAVEL

It's still too early in the year to do outdoor construction, for the most part. But that makes this a natural time to lay plans and choose materials for projects to be implemented later.

The longest-lasting material and the material that does most to impart a feeling of permanence to any landscape is stone. That goes both for stone that occurs naturally in the form of outcroppings, rock ledges, or boulders, and for man-made structures. Egyptian tombs and obelisks, Greek statuary and temples, Roman forums and arcades have lasted undamaged for thousands of years. (It took our century's burning of fossil fuels to create the atmospheric pollutants that are now dissolving these ancient works of stone. Even so, their endurance record is pretty good.) Stone's beauty and permanence have made it the material of choice for all sorts of public and monumental construction in every continent, right down to the present. And stone remains the material of choice for many applications today, from pavements, walls, steps, and rock gardens to sculptures, water basins, and light standards.

Stone does have its liabilities as a construction material. It is not notably flexible. In fact it is excruciatingly difficult to work with, from first quarrying through milling, transportation, and installation. Every phase of the handling of stone calls for special equipment and expertise. Therefore it is costly, both in time and in dollars.

Even so, stone has its place. This section deals with the basic facts about stone and gravel and the forms in which they're available to you, the consumer. And it touches upon some of the pleasures and perils of working with stone.

**Stone**    Stone or rock (but in the stone business it's called stone) is bedrock that has been quarried, then cut or milled into any of a multitude of forms and dimensions.

**Properties of stone**    If you think about it, you're probably already aware of many of the natural properties of different kinds of stone,

Huge slabs of granite dwarf quarry workers. The stone will serve many purposes after being cut into dimension stone, flagstones, crushed stone, or stone dust.

**Wide variation in texture and color exists within a single kind of stone. Here, granite paving stones surround a larger bluestone slab.**

just from living with them. There are the workable, crumbly textured sandstones; the smoothly striated slates; the indestructible, quartz-flecked granite; the waxy, fragile, beautifully streaked marble. The table here shows some of the kinds of stone most often used in landscape construction.

## Stone for Landscape Construction

| Type | Relative Cost | Texture and hardness | Color range | Landscape uses |
|------|---------------|----------------------|-------------|----------------|
| Granite | Expensive | Coarse crystals to fine graining; very hard | Wide range, from light gray to black, with intermediate greens, reds, and pinks | Blocks, sets, or cobbles for paving, curbs, or steps; flagstones; irregular rubble or cut stone for walls; crushed for aggregate in concrete |
| Limestone | Moderately expensive | Fine to crystalline; fairly soft | White or light gray to buff | All uses |
| Sandstone (including bluestone) | Least expensive | Granular, with grains cemented together | Light buff to light brown or brick red to blue-gray | Walls, flagstones, copings, steps |
| Slate | Least expensive | Fine crystalline | Gray-green, brick red or dark brown, gray | Flagstone, copings, steps, low walls |
| Marble | Most expensive | Fine granular to coarse crystalline | Highly varied, from white to black, with intermediate greens and pinks | Thresholds, furniture, custom ornamental features, refined paving |

**Commercial forms**   Stone is available commercially (see your Yellow Pages under "stone — crushed" and/or "stone — natural") in six forms, which go under the following designations:

- Fieldstone: irregularly shaped pieces of stone, usually weathered, which have been found lying around in open fields. Hence the name.
- Rubble: irregular, rough-textured fragments of quarried stone with at least one "good" face.

**Cut rubblestone and fieldstone: different approaches convey different feelings. Cut stone is crisper, more architectural (and costly); fieldstone softer and less formal.**

- Dimension stone: pieces cut to given sizes, either left rough or with smoothly ground or polished surfaces.
- Flagstone: flat slabs in asymmetrical shapes, sliced anywhere from 1 to 2 or more inches thick.
- Crushed or broken stone: quarried stone that has been crushed mechanically into sharp-edged fragments anywhere from ¼ inch to 2½ inches across. Not to be confused with "gravel" — see below.
- Stone dust or powder: mechanically crushed fragments sized less than ¼ inch across. Again, this is not the same as what's referred to as "gravel."

**Gravel**  In the terminology of the stone business, "gravel" means a material distinct from small broken-up bits of quarried stone. Gravel comes in small pieces naturally, rather than being quarried and crushed by machines. It is formed when bedrock is fractured or eroded by natural forces such as glaciers, rain, rivers, or the sea. Wear and tear further reduce the sizes of the individual pebbles, and the pieces become worn or even rounded at the edges. Gravel may range in size from very small pebbles (but larger than sand) to biggish chunks that look to the uninitiated a lot like rocks.

**Commercial Forms**  Like stone, gravel acquires a terminology when it becomes a consumer product. The classifications of gravel are:

- Pea gravel: the smallest-sized pieces, ranging from ¼ inch to ½ inch across.
- Small graded gravel: pebbles anywhere from ½ inch to 3½ inches across.
- Cobbles and boulders: worn or rounded chunks, larger than 3½ inches across.
- Pit or bank-run gravel: ungraded material directly from the gravel pit or "bank," containing everything from sand and small pebbles all the way up to large rocks.
- Crushed gravel: coarse gravel that has been machine-crushed into sizes ranging from ⅜ inch to 2½ inches across.

**Designing and Building with Stone and Gravel**  The thumbnail descriptions of stone and gravel types above suggest pretty clearly the ways you might use them in the landscape. Fieldstone and rubble yield very naturalistic or rustic effects. For walls, pavements, or other structures, you'll get a more smooth and civilized look with dimension stone or flagstone. Crushed stone can be compacted into a solid base for pavements of all kinds, and stone dust is a good setting bed for modular pavers like bricks or granite blocks. Gravel is at home in driveways, parking areas, and many kinds of paving uses; or even as a "stone mulch" around plantings. (See the Materials and Construction sections of March, April, and October.)

A few words of inspiration here — and of caution. Stone is a marvelous material. Wherever circumstances and available funds permit, I try to work stone into my landscape designs. One can achieve a vast spectrum of effects, from gutsy rusticity to great refinement or formality, depending on one's choice of texture, color, and joint patterns. Stone also serves as a most satisfactory way to link a man-made construction to the soil and growing things around it — since stone itself is from and of the earth. It ties the parts of a landscape design together.

But a stone masonry project is not to be undertaken lightly or inadvisedly. This is not just a matter of its relatively high price, which I mentioned above. I have built many things out of stone — fireplaces and walls, slate and bluestone pavings, fieldstone and boulder rock gardens — and every one I have finished only with some pain and anguish. Working with stone really hurts. It's as if you had to match your stubbornness and patience against the obduracy of the stone itself.

Yet if you can manage to finish a piece of work in stone, there's absolutely nothing quite so satisfying. You'll need time, patience, willpower — and, unless you do it all yourself, lots of money. Only you can decide if stone is for you.

**Red-stemmed shrub dogwood is one of many plants (listed on next page) whose colorful bark and twigs make striking accents in the winter landscape.**

## Plants by Design
# COLORFUL BARK AND TWIGS

### Gray-Barked Trees and Shrubs

Red maple (*Acer rubrum*)
Shadblow, juneberry, or serviceberry
(*Amelanchier canadensis*)
Allegheny serviceberry (*Amelanchier laevis*)
Yellowwood (*Cladrastis lutea*)
*Summer-sweet clethra (*Clethra alnifolia*)
*Gray dogwood (*Cornus racemosa*)
*Autumn olive (*Elaeagnus umbellata*)
American beech (*Fagus grandifolia*)
European beech (*Fagus sylvatica*)
Rivers beech (*Fagus sylvatica 'Riversii'*)
Tatarian honeysuckle (*Lonicera tatarica*)
Korean mountain ash (*Sorbus alnifolia*)
*European cranberrybush (*Viburnum opulus*)
*American cranberrybush or highbush cranberry (*Viburnum trilobum*)

### Green-Barked Trees and Shrubs

*Bronx forsythia (*Forsythia viridissima 'Bronxensis'*)
*Kerria (*Kerria japonica*)
Thurlow weeping willow (*Salix elegantissima*)
Sassafras (*Sassafras albidum*)
Japanese pagoda tree (*Sophora japonica*)

### Yellow-Barked Trees and Shrubs

*Yellow-twig red-osier dogwood
(*Cornus sericea 'Flaviramea'*)
Golden weeping willow (*Salix alba tristis*)

### Red-Barked Trees and Shrubs

Paperbark maple (*Acer griseum*)
*Japanese maple (*Acer palmatum*)
River birch (*Betula nigra*)
*Siberian dogwood (*Cornus alba 'Sibirica'*)
Red-osier dogwood (*Cornus sericea*)
*Flowering dogwood (*Cornus florida*)
Tanyosho pine (*Pinus densiflora 'Umbraculifera'*)
Oriental cherry (*Prunus serrulata*)
Meadow rose (*Rosa blanda*)
Virginia rose (*Rosa virginiana*)
Japanese stewartia (*Stewartia pseudocamellia*)
Dwarf European cranberrybush
(*Viburnum opulus 'Nanum'*)

### White-Barked Trees

Paper birch (*Betula papyrifera*)
European birch (*Betula pendula*)
Cutleaf European birch (*Betula pendula 'Gracilis'*)

*Indicates a plant whose younger twigs have the desired color, so that regular pruning (to stimulate abundant young growth) is needed for maximum winter color effect.

Detailed information and recommended varieties can be found in Part III.

# LANDSCAPE TASKS FOR JANUARY

**Catalogues**   If you are already on a few mailing lists, you don't need this reminder. If you aren't, let this be your cue to think about your gardening needs for the coming growing season. January is definitely the time to map out your plans and to choose and order what you need from seedsmen's and nurserymen's catalogues.

**Salt**   Salt for melting snow and ice should be used with great discretion. As an alternative, as long as the weather is not too cold, try a light application of commercial fertilizer.

Paperbark maple offers not only rich color but paper-thin peeling strips for textural interest.

The two salts widely available are sodium chloride (effective to 10°F) and the more expensive calcium chloride (effective to −40°F). Often calcium chloride is mixed with sodium chloride to boost its potency. But both salts will damage lawns and many plantings; and they do more insidious and long-lasting damage if they are used where they can percolate through groundwater into wells, streams, or reservoirs. So go easy.

**De-icing** Brush snow from ornamental evergreens before it can melt (or be rained on) and then freeze, resulting in a heavy load of ice.

**Antidesiccants** In a mild spell (when the temperature is above freezing for a day or so) you may want to use an antidesiccant spray on needled and broad-leaved evergreens. Rhododendrons, azaleas, laurels, boxwood, yew, pine, and spruce are among the plants that may "winterburn." The sprays coat the leaves or needles with a plastic film; this slows plants' water loss when the ground is frozen, and thus helps prevent winterburn. Particularly for new plantings whose root systems are still getting established, antidesiccants are sometimes a sensible form of insurance for the first two seasons or so.

**Vines** This leafless season is a good time to cut back overgrown vines, both domestic (English ivy, wisteria, Virginia creeper) and wild (woodbine, wild grape, bittersweet, honeysuckle).

**Mulches** Use evergreen boughs from Christmas or from pruning to mulch over evergreen perennials, bulb beds, and rock gardens — any of the smaller, more shallow-rooted plants in your garden.

**Christmas Trees** Another way to recycle Christmas greens: collect a few neighbors' Christmas trees and stack them together into a teepee for the birds. Birds will appreciate both the dense protective foliage and the resulting bare patch of ground underneath (for foraging and scratching).

## Rooting Hardwood Cuttings

**Rooting Hardwood Cuttings**    An easy way to propagate many garden plants, and a good project for January, is to make hardwood cuttings. This method works well with the plants listed here, among others.

Buttonbush (*Cephalanthus occidentalis*)
Dogwood (shrub types) (*Cornus* spp.)
Forsythia (*Forsythia* spp.)
Kerria (*Kerria japonica*)
Privet (*Ligustrum* spp.)
Honeysuckle (*Lonicera* spp.)
Mock-orange (*Philadelphus* spp.)

Willow (*Salix* spp.)
Elderberry (*Sambucus canadensis*)
Spirea (*Spiraea* spp.)
Stephanandra (*Stephanandra incisa*)
Coralberry (*Symphoricarpos* spp.)
Persian lilac (*Syringa persica*)
Viburnum (*Viburnum* spp.)

You'll get the best stems for hardwood cuttings if you start a year in advance by pruning the plant back hard in the previous dormant season — to encourage vigorous new growth. These fast-sprouting shoots will be the readiest to send out roots when you make them into cuttings the following fall or winter.

To make the cuttings, cut 6- to 8-inch pencil-thick sections with the top end cut at least an inch above the nearest growth bud. Tie the cuttings into bundles you can grasp comfortably in one hand, and tap the bottoms of the bundles to bring all the bottom ends of the cuttings even with each other. Tie the bundles with wire or cord; label them; and bury them in earth, damp sawdust, or dampened peat moss, to keep them from drying out. Store them for three to four weeks at 50° to 55°F; after that, reduce the temperature to 32° to 40°F so that the tops won't start to grow too soon.

After six to eight weeks of storage, hardwood cuttings can be set in the ground to grow, preferably in full sun, as soon as the ground can be worked.

**Cutting, bundling, and storing hardwood cuttings: a winter project for new plants in spring.**

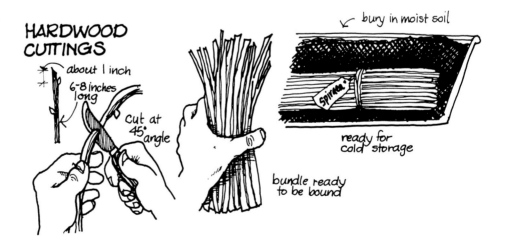

HARDWOOD CUTTINGS

about 1 inch
6-8 inches long
cut at 45° angle
bundle ready to be bound
bury in moist soil
*Spirea*
ready for cold storage

### Rooting Evergreen Cuttings

**Rooting Evergreen Cuttings**   Another, slightly trickier, propagation project for midwinter is rooting cuttings of broad-leaved evergreens and conifers. Some particularly good candidates for rooting at this season are shown below.

Box (*Buxus* spp.)
False cypress (*Chamaecyparis* spp.)
Euonymus (*Euonymus* spp.)
English ivy (*Hedera* spp.)
Holly (*Ilex* spp.)
Juniper (*Juniperus* spp.)

Japanese spurge or pachysandra
   (*Pachysandra* spp.)
Firethorn (*Pyracantha* spp.)
Yew (*Taxus* spp.)
Arborvitae (*Thuja* spp.)

(Also see June for softwood cuttings to be taken in spring.)

Take cuttings in early morning. Using a sharp knife or a razor blade, make a cut at about a 45-degree angle, and about ¼ inch below a node (where leaf joins stem) if possible. The best cuttings come from the terminal sections of stems, but a long growth can be cut into several sections. The cuttings should be 2 to 6 inches long, depending on how husky the stems and leaves are.

Remove the bottom third of the leaves or needles on each cutting; then immediately dip the base of the stem into rooting hormone and set the cutting into a moist, well-drained rooting medium. (If there will be any delay, store cuttings in a plastic bag in the refrigerator.) They should be inserted to about one-third of their total length in the medium.

For the first week or so, keep the cuttings protected in a glass or plastic container (to hold moist air in) and lightly shaded from direct sunlight. Once roots have formed and grown at least ½ inch long, you can carefully transplant the cuttings to pots for the greenhouse or windowsill, where they can stay until spring.

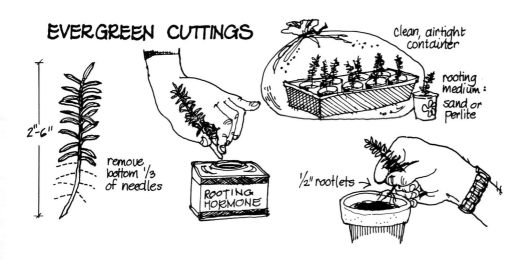

**EVERGREEN CUTTINGS**

2"-6"

remove bottom ⅓ of needles

ROOTING HORMONE

clean, airtight container

rooting medium: sand or perlite

½" rootlets →

Many evergreen shrubs and trees can also be propagated by cuttings taken now.

# FEB

**A colorful variety of evergreen foliage in a dwarf conifer nursery.**

**Lacebark pine: outer plates peel off to reveal multicolored inner bark layers.**

In February the days are lengthening perceptibly but winter has by no means relaxed its grip on the landscape. Much of our appreciating of the outdoors is still being done from indoors, through windows. For close-range viewing, the Plants by Design list this month features interesting bark textures. There are plants with silky or velvety bark (like beeches or yellowwood); plants with "exfoliating" bark that peels off in strips or flakes, often revealing contrasting colors below (like red cedar or lacebark pine); and plants with deeply fissured barks, for a rugged look (like white ash or shagbark hickory).

Indoor activities are already beginning now for vegetable and flower gardeners, whose seeds go into flats starting around Washington's Birthday. But aspirations for the landscape are still primarily restricted to planning. Major paving projects are one excellent subject for early planning; continuing from last month's section on stone, I'll introduce concrete and asphalt here. Another good thing to plan for is ease of — or freedom from — upkeep. (Concrete and asphalt certainly qualify in that department.) And the Landscaping Opportunities and Plants for a Purpose sections this month are devoted to the maintenance-free theme.

## Landscaping Opportunities
# EASY-MAINTENANCE LANDSCAPING

Every landscape requires some maintenance. How much or how little depends on many different factors. The most significant of these are the kind of landscape you start with (whether intensive or extensive, simple or complex, wild or cultivated); the standards you set for your landscape and yourself; and the kinds of landscape furnishings you use, from plants to inanimate materials.

Many people derive great joy from puttering in the garden, and seek out projects and plantings that will offer creative challenges in the puttering department. But what if your goal is to do as little maintenance as possible? You can reduce to a minimum upkeep time, energy, and expense without sacrificing either the beauty or the well-being of a landscape.

Simplicity of design is central. Obviously, you may not have complete control over the basic nature of your landscape: topography, older plantings, and layout of spaces may have been determined before you moved in. But if you have the luxury of starting from scratch, you can build into your planning the various suggestions listed here and vastly lighten your maintenance burdens in years to come.

Another form of luxury is owning a woodland property. There you can simply let nature happen around you, carving out a few finite open spaces for lawn, vegetable or flower beds, or shrubbery as desired.

A far more typical situation, though, is the moderately open property with a few scattered mature trees and some lawn and planting areas that you're hoping to keep looking respectable with as little effort as possible. Or you may be retaining some sections of an established landscape and redoing others to suit your tastes or your budget of time.

Whatever your circumstances, I can offer the following ideas. Many of my suggestions come under the heading of avoiding tasks to start with by designing with forethought. Beyond that, I'll suggest ways to streamline tasks if you do undertake them.

## Space Planning

**Space Planning**   Make certain that each use you plan for your landscape will happen in the most appropriate part of the site. There's a best place for everything. Making the logical choices can avert a lot of extra effort directed at forcing success, rather than letting it come naturally. Put a parking area in a flat place, a vegetable patch where the soil and sun are best, and so on.

At the initial planning stage, or when redesigning, make high-maintenance areas small. (Obvious though this sounds, it's a precept honored more in the breach than in the observance.)

Group together types of planting that require similar kinds of maintenance — watering, weeding, feeding, pruning, etc.

Avoid planting anything in deep shade, particularly lawn grasses.

Around driveways and walks, leave sufficient unobstructed space to cope with mounds of snow at snow-shoveling time.

**Lawns**   Lay out lawns for ease of mowing. That means no sharp corners where you'll have to stop or turn around, and no nooks or crannies.

Rule out the necessity of hand trimming. Put "mowing edges" alongside all planting beds, structures, and grade changes. Install sand pits around tree-trunks.

Establish gentle grades. Banks with slopes steeper than 1:3 (33 percent) are too hard to mow.

For an instant lawn, use sod rather than seeding. (Keep in mind that this is a more expensive method.)

To eliminate lawn damage (and dirt splashing on foundations or siding), install gravel strips under drip lines of roof edges without gutters.

**In this easily maintained yard, planted and paved areas are edged, beds are raised and narrow, and shrubs are selected for minimum care.**

Although it takes a few years to establish, a no-lawn approach like this bed of evergreen pachysandra totally eliminates lawn maintenance chores.

**Trees and Shrubs**   Use the best possible soil for all growing areas. Again, this may seem obvious, but it's terribly important. Any plant is more trouble-free if it's truly healthy and well-nourished; any plant will behave like an invalid in soil unsuited to its needs.

Select the best-quality disease- and pest-resistant plants available. Look around you to see what types of plants are thriving in your area, and follow the clues they provide. I have avoided listing excessively fussy plants throughout this book; but for a list of notably unfussy ones, see the Plants for a Purpose section this month. Your local nursery is also an invaluable source of local information.

Slow-growing and dwarf varieties will keep pruning to a minimum. Your initial cost will probably be higher, however, because greater numbers of small plants are required to fill a given area; besides, these little gems are expensive, since they take so long to grow in the nursery.

For sturdy growth, space trees and shrubs sufficiently far apart so they'll be exposed to sun and good circulation of air on all sides.

Avoid planting trees that litter — like fruit trees or others known for heavy seed drop — adjacent to paved surfaces. Their fruits tend to get squashed underfoot or their litter accumulates and becomes a nuisance to clean up.

Prune trees for open branching, to let the wind blow through harmlessly and forestall breakage.

**Irrigation**   When planting trees and shrubs, build a mulched reservoir to hold water around each plant. Or group plantings, consolidating them into a single mulched bed.

Space water faucets no less than 100 feet apart, so every area can be reached with 50 feet of hose.

If absolutely necessary (although generally I try to avoid this), take the plunge and install underground irrigation piping. It will free you from dragging hoses and sprinklers around your property day after day.

**Flower and Vegetable Beds**  Make sure the soil is the best and most fertile you can provide.

For the sake of your back, where weeding or other hand work will be needed in a planted bed, consider raising the bed above grade level. Also make sure that every spot in the bed is within reach from the edge — or at least within reach when you've got one foot in the bed.

Use some form of edging to keep grass rhizomes out of beds, and mulch in.

**Preventing migration of mulch or granular paving, a steel edge cleanly separates this pea-stone path from the planting bed.**

Vegetable gardens should be either very small or very large. That is, plant them compact, with raised beds and intensive cropping (foliage shades out weeds and no ground lies fallow); or plant them roomy, spaced out sufficiently so that you can use a power tiller or push cultivator for cultivating between rows.

Separate beds of different kinds of plants; keep those with similar cultural needs together.

For flowers, choose perennials over annuals. Perennials bloom for a shorter period each year, but they do it all by themselves. With some planning you can have an assortment of perennials blooming in any given week all summer long.

When you're picking out ground covers, perennials, bulbs, etc., select the varieties that are easiest to care for once established. Eschew those that call for regular or annual digging, dividing, pruning, fertilizing, or pest-control spraying.

**Equipment**   Organize your tools and maintenance equipment in one convenient location, preferably a shed or ell with its own entrance.

Make certain that wheeled vehicles (lawn mowers, grass-seed spreaders, wheelbarrows, leaf carts, etc.) can get around your entire property without having to double back or detour because of steps, walls, steep banks, or narrow passageways.

Keep pavements flush with lawn areas to avoid obstructing lawn mowers or other wheeled vehicles.

Provide electrical outlets in convenient locations for hedge shears and other electric-powered gadgets.

**Structures and Furnishings**   For permanent landscape fixtures, select materials for longevity. Good candidates include stone, concrete, and pressure-treated or naturally rot-resistant woods. Watch out for any material that's going to need to be replaced in a short time. Stay away from woods that will demand painting, varnishing, or staining.

Wherever possible, build in. Walls can incorporate seats; fences and rails can incorporate benches; trellises can take the place of umbrellas; and so on.

Fences can be used rather than shrubbery for privacy. A fence takes a lot less work than a hedge or shrub screen, particularly a hedge or screen that requires regular clipping or pruning. If you want a green wall, you can always plant vines to curtain the fence.

---

### Plants for a Purpose
# TREES AND SHRUBS REQUIRING MINIMUM CARE

If your resolve is to plant only trees and shrubs that can virtually be forgotten once established, then the list here is for you. You may have to do without some of the shrubs with the most exciting flowering or fruiting characteristics, or some of the grandest foliage trees; but even so, here is a wide choice of plants that includes good candidates for almost any situation you may have.

My criteria are simple: plants included here are subject to few pests or diseases, and/or tolerant of those that do come along; they call for limited, if any, pruning; they drop minimal quantities of needles or leaves (which is why there are few large deciduous shade trees on the list); they are adaptable to most soils and conditions. And although some of the big evergreens are indeed large, you can obtain smaller sizes and slower growth of these durable favorites if you select compact or dwarf varieties.

You'll notice that native plants are well represented in this list — a testimony to their crusty perseverance once established in compatible surroundings.

In addition to the plants offered here, many of the ground covers and vines that appear in the June Plants for a Purpose section call for very little maintenance once established. Some of them, of course, need more care than others. And some of them — particularly among the vines — are such vigorous growers that they require restraining. But they are a group well worth your attention as you consider low-maintenance plantings for your garden.

Three times I have used the phrase "once established." By that I mean "after fully recovering from transplanting and pursuing vigorous unimpeded growth." To recapitulate once more my familiar theme, it is up to you to provide proper soil and sufficient light; to plant these trees and shrubs with care; and to water them as needed until they get settled. Any plant, no matter how stalwart, has certain minimum requirements for survival. And any plant in a weakened state (whether from transplanting shock or from inadequate basic conditions) is vulnerable to attack by insects and diseases that would not normally bother it.

**Katsura tree is one of those plants with minimal insect or disease problems. As shown in autumn here, the foliage remains clean and undamaged throughout the season.**

## Minimum-Care Trees and Shrubs

### Small to Medium Deciduous Trees

Shadblow, juneberry, or serviceberry (*Amelanchier* spp.)

River birch (*Betula nigra*)

European hornbeam (*Carpinus betulus*)

Katsura tree (*Cercidiphyllum japonicum*)

Yellowwood (*Cladrastis lutea*)

Kousa or Japanese dogwood (*Cornus kousa*)

Cornelian cherry dogwood (*Cornus mas*)

Smoke tree (*Cotinus coggygria*)

Washington hawthorn (*Crataegus phaenopyrum*)

Autumn olive (*Elaeagnus umbellata*)

Golden-rain tree (*Koelreuteria paniculata*)

Star magnolia (*Magnolia stellata*)

Crabapples (*Malus* spp.)

Sorrel tree or sourwood (*Oxydendrum arboreum*)

Amur cork tree (*Phellodendron amurense*)

Sassafras (*Sassafras albidum*)

Japanese pagoda tree (*Sophora japonica*)

Japanese stewartia (*Stewartia pseudocamellia*)

Bradford pear (*Pyrus calleryana* 'Bradford')

Fragrant sumac (*Rhus aromatica*)

Korean mountain ash (*Sorbus alnifolia*)

Korean stewartia (*Stewartia koreana*)

### Large Deciduous Trees

Red maple (*Acer rubrum*)

Beeches (*Fagus* spp.)

Ginkgo or maidenhair tree (*Ginkgo biloba*)

Thornless honey locust (*Gleditsia triacanthos inermis* and vars.)

Sweet gum tree (*Liquidambar styraciflua*)

Dawn redwood (*Metasequoia glyptostroboides*)

Black gum or black tupelo (*Nyssa sylvatica*)

Zelkova (*Zelkova serrata*)

### Deciduous Shrubs

Korean white forsythia (*Abeliophyllum distichum*)

Chokeberries (*Aronia* spp.)

Detailed information and recommended varieties can be found in Part III.

## Materials and Construction
# CONCRETE AND ASPHALT

Preparing for the active months to come, last month's Materials and Construction section talked about stone and gravel — the most basic and most permanent of landscape construction materials, and strictly natural in origin. Now for some man-made products that share some of the attributes and uses of stone: concrete and asphalt. Both are in fact made partly of stone. Both are, like stone, hard and durable and easy on upkeep. Both work together with (or in place of) stone in paved areas, from walks and drives to patios and terraces. And concrete finds still further uses in nonpaving construction such as steps, walls, planters, and pools.

Almost anywhere you go, you will walk, drive, park, shop, play, or work on asphalt or concrete or both. These materials are so widely used in public places that the response they elicit in many people is a definite ho-hum. Yet there are good reasons for their ubiquitous presence. Besides being durable, they are versatile; they are readily available; and

## Minimum-Care Trees and Shrubs (*continued*)

Japanese barberry (*Berberis thunbergii*)
Summer-sweet clethra (*Clethra alnifolia*)
Sweet fern (*Comptonia peregrina*)
Gray dogwood (*Cornus racemosa*)
Red-osier dogwood (*Cornus sericea* vars.)
Fragrant winter hazel (*Corylopsis glabrescens*)
Redvein enkianthus (*Enkianthus campanulatus*)
Winged euonymus (*Euonymus alata* vars.)
Forsythias (*Forsythia* spp.)
Fothergillas or witch alders (*Fothergilla* spp.)
Witch hazels (*Hamamelis* spp.)
Rose-of-Sharon or shrub althea (*Hibiscus syriacus*)
Hydrangeas (*Hydrangea* spp.)
Regel privet (*Ligustrum obtusifolium regelianum*)
Honeysuckles (*Lonicera* spp.)
Bayberry (*Myrica pensylvanica*)
Bush or shrubby cinquefoil (*Potentilla fruticosa*)
Shining sumac (*Rhus copallina*)
Rugosa rose (*Rosa rugosa*)

Spireas (*Spiraea* spp.)
Crispa cutleaf stephanandra (*Stephanandra incisa* 'Crispa')
Coralberries (*Symphoricarpos* spp.)
Viburnums (*Viburnum* spp.)

### Evergreen Trees

White fir (*Abies concolor*)
Hinoki false cypress (*Chamaecyparis obtusa* vars.)
Thread false cypress (*Chamaecyparis pisifera* 'Filifera' and vars.)
Norway spruce (*Picea abies* vars.)
Pines (*Pinus* spp.)
Douglas fir (*Pseudotsuga menziesii*)
Umbrella pine (*Sciadopytis verticillata*)
Canadian hemlock (*Tsuga canadensis* vars.)

### Evergreen Shrubs

Japanese or boxleaf holly (*Ilex crenata* vars.)
Inkberry (*Ilex glabra*)
Winterberry (*Ilex verticillata*)
Junipers (*Juniperus* spp.)
Canby paxistima (*Paxistima canbyi*)
Rhododendrons (*Rhododendron* spp.)
Yews (*Taxus* spp.)

---

they are relatively inexpensive, which is often the primary reason for their use.

In designing for your home landscape, however, you have a chance to use concrete and asphalt with far greater care and imagination than are feasible in large-scale public construction. You can take advantage not only of their utilitarian virtues but of their other essential qualities — including, of all things, beauty.

With every plant or construction material I use, I try to think first about the intrinsic nature of the material itself, so I can bring out its full potential. The one thing asphalt and concrete have in common is that each consists of a form of glue binding together loose granular material to make a monolithic mass. That's where the similarity of the two materials ends. Their components and chemistry are completely unrelated. Once hardened, concrete is rigid and rocklike; it can be used for three-dimensional construction as well as for paving. Asphalt, on the other hand, always retains some degree of flexibility.

I won't attempt here to make you an instant concrete or asphalt expert. But I will give you enough basic information to be an informed consumer of both products.

**Concrete**  The three components of concrete have changed very little since the days of the Roman Empire. First, there's cement, now a patented formula called Portland cement. Second, there's the "aggregate" of granular materials the cement binds together: sand and gravel or crushed stone. It is the nature of the gravel in the aggregate that provides much of the color, texture, and specific character of a given concrete mix. Finally, there's water, which sets off a chain of chemical reactions in the cement. These reactions cause the concrete to set within the first 45 minutes or so after pouring; to harden within the first 10 hours; to cure within the first 7 days; and to reach its final maximum strength at the end of 28 days.

The compressive strength (resistance to crushing) of concrete is measured in pounds per square inch, or psi. Concrete formulated for landscape work should range from 2000 to 3500 psi, depending on its intended use.

**Buying concrete**  You can buy concrete in any of three forms. If you're going to need more than 1 cubic yard (27 cubic feet) of concrete, the most prudent way is often to buy it completely mixed and ready to pour. This form is called transit-mix and is delivered in the familiar trucks with the rolling barrels that mix the concrete en route. With transit-mix your big job is to measure your needed quantity correctly, prepare the site carefully, and have all systems go for delivery on the appointed day. Transit-mix company drivers do not have time or flexibility to wait around while you get organized. If they do have to wait, you usually have to pay them extra.

Transit-mix companies generally will not deliver amounts smaller than one cubic yard. For these small jobs, you may decide to buy ready-mix concrete. This is a bagged mixture of all the dry ingredients (cement, sand, and gravel), to which you just add water. Like prepared food mixes, this product saves time but is frequently more expensive than the raw materials if you buy them separately and put them together yourself.

Mixing your own concrete from scratch has its drawbacks (hard work) and its pleasures. In the long run, the advantages are in cost — compared to ready-mix or transit — and in the freedom this method gives you. You can spread the mixing and pouring over several work periods rather than doing it all at once, if you want; and you can experiment and perfect just the texture and color you desire. (More on texture and color under Variations, below.)

To compute how much concrete you are going to need (and therefore, possibly, what form you will buy it in) measure all dimensions of whatever you plan to construct. Use this formula:

$$\frac{\text{width (feet)} \times \text{length (feet)} \times \text{thickness (inches)}}{12} = \text{cubic feet}$$

For instance, suppose you are building a concrete pad 10 feet square and 4 inches thick. That's $10 \times 10 \times 4 = 400 \div 12 = 33\frac{1}{3}$ cubic feet, or somewhat more than 1 cubic yard. If you are working with larger amounts, dividing your cubic-foot amount by 27 will give you the number of cubic yards. Now you can start considering whether to order transit-mix, buy the bagged ready-mix, or mix your own.

**Variations on the concrete theme**  A wonderful variety of colors and textural effects can be given to concrete with a little extra thought and effort. All these variations are ways to liberate concrete from its pallid gray public image.

You've probably seen textured concrete surfaces created by wood or steel floats or brooms. Another standard finish, "exposed aggregate," results when the cement paste is washed and scrubbed away from the uncured concrete to reveal a pebbly layer of aggregate at the surface. Other ways to expose the aggregate include sandblasting, bush hammering, or grinding the concrete. Hammering and grinding are best left to experienced masons; sandblasting you may decide to do yourself with rented equipment.

Exposed aggregate is all the more colorful and appealing if ornamental stones or gravel have been incorporated in it. They can also be embedded in the top layer of concrete after spreading, but it is better to have them mixed right in if you can. If this makes the aggregate just too expensive, some masons pour a base slab of standard concrete, but leave the surface unfinished. Then, at the point when the base is still "green" but its surface water is gone, they make up a mixture with the more fancy aggregate and apply it 1 inch thick.

A particularly nice exposed-aggregate concrete. Pebbles were thoughtfully selected for color and texture and are smooth enough for bare feet to walk on.

Another way to color concrete is with pigments. Pigment can constitute up to 10 percent of the weight of the cement in the mix. For colors other than grays and browns, however — even with white cement — I find that pigmented concrete colors are pretty much limited to pastel tones. If I am looking for a really strong color, I often end up using brick or stone instead, or go to an exposed aggregate with naturally colored gravel to add the color. A pigment, like an ornamental aggregate, can either be mixed in with the concrete or sprinkled on top after pouring. (In this case it's called "shake.") I prefer to mix pigment into the concrete itself, which seems to me to give better durability and greater uniformity of color.

**Asphalt**  Asphalt, certainly one of the least glamorous of landscape construction materials, has a few undeniable virtues. For large, hard-working pavements like drives and turnarounds, it is tough, easy to come by, and relatively cheap. And although its spectrum of colors and textures is narrower than that of concrete, asphalt is still a lot more versatile than you might imagine if your main exposure to it has been on highways and sidewalks.

This sticky blackish substance has an ancient pedigree. As early as 3000 B.C., people in Mesopotamia and the Indus Valley were using asphalt in masonry, street construction, and waterproofing. The Egyptians employed it in mummification. They recognized that it was resilient, waterproof, and permanent; our word *asphalt* comes from the Greek for "safe, secure, and steadfast."

The earliest users of asphalt found it in the form of partly evaporated petroleum deposits, or "lakes." Since 1865, when petroleum drilling began, we've relied on asphalt created as a byproduct of the petroleum refining process. Mixed with sand or stone, it becomes the basic binding ingredient of asphalt paving, and that is its chief role in landscape construction.

**How asphalt paving is made**   Asphalt paving consists of a mixture of about 10 percent asphalt (by weight) with stone aggregate. Both the mixing and the spreading of asphalt are generally jobs for a contractor. Your responsibility is to seek out a reliable contractor who will work with you to achieve the texture and color you want. Particularly if you're hoping for special textures or colors (see below), you should ask to see some successful installations the contractor has done in the past. A good contractor will be pleased to show off his work.

The most common and most commonly recommended mixing procedure involves heating the asphalt and mixing it with the aggregate at a temperature of 275°F in a hot-mix plant. Transported rapidly to the site, this mixture is laid and compacted before it can cool beyond 185°F. With hot mixes, as you can see, a short distance between site and mixing plant is desirable, so it is generally mandatory that your contractor be a local one.

Cold-mix asphalt contractors are fewer and farther between, but when you can find it, cold mix can be less expensive. The problem with cold mix is that it takes many months to reach its final hardness, and in the meantime all traffic has to be kept religiously off it or you end up with dents and scars in the finish. But if you can postpone using your new asphalt for the requisite amount of time, and if you can find a contractor who has good experience using cold-mix asphalt, I recommend considering it for economy's sake.

There's also the old form of asphalt paving called macadam, after the man who invented the process. In macadam the stone is laid and compacted in place, then sprayed with controlled quantities of emulsion or hot asphalt. Then fine aggregates are spread over the whole thing and rolled in to fill the chinks. Time and wear expose the surfaces of the stones, and the resulting colors and textures are very attractive, especially if large stones were used at the beginning. Macadam installation today is a specialty operation, however, and expensive.

**Textures**   All asphalt mixes are put together according to formulas or recipes calling for the specific proportions of various sizes of aggregate that will create the proper texture for the job. The terminology for these mixes varies from place to place; you'll run into names such as "sand mix," "rice mix," "binder," and so on, denoting coarser- and finer-textured formulas. Nomenclature aside, the standard numerical designations in the industry are as follows:

| Designation | Maximum stone size |
|---|---|
| 2A | 1½ inches |
| 3A | 1 inch |
| 4A | ¾ inch |
| 5A | ½ inch |
| 6A | ⅜ inch |
| 7A | #4 (± ¼ inch) |
| 8A | #16 (± 1/16 inch) |

If a pavement of very fine-textured asphalt is desired (say 7A or 8A), it's common practice to lay a "base course" or "binder course" of coarser mixture such as 3A or 4A, followed by a 1-inch "wearing course" of 7A or 8A. The reason for this is that a full 3-inch thickness of the finest-textured mixture might soften and suffer damage in very hot weather.

Most widely used for walks and drives are types 5A, 6A, or 7A. Ask your contractor what degree of fineness he likes to work with and why, and go take a look at installations of the type he suggests in situations comparable to yours. There's no significant difference in price or durability from one type to another, so your choice is a matter of taste; but contractors sometimes have preferences based on habit or convenience.

**Colors** Newly laid asphalt paving is always blackish, the color of the asphalt emulsion itself. The eventual color usually comes from the stones in the aggregate: time and traffic wear away the asphalt from the surface of the pavement, and the stones' own color comes through.

This asphalt base layer has coarse-textured stones. In the top layer, the oil mix will slowly wear off and reveal the color and texture of the pebbles.

They are most often gray, so that weathered asphalt is usually gray too. But other colors can be attained. If the aggregate in the mix incorporates white, green, brown, or red stones, these colors will emerge very gradually. (There are some beautiful slate-red roads I know of in Massachusetts and Pennsylvania.) The larger the stones in the aggregate, the greater the amount of surface and the more color will eventually be revealed. That's probably the best and surest route to colored asphalt, but it is slow. Besides, you may have trouble prevailing on an asphalt mix plant to use special colored aggregate for a small batch of mix such as you're apt to need for a residential installation — so don't get your hopes up.

Several possible methods for achieving a colored asphalt surface have been suggested in the literature, although I have yet to meet a contractor who has actually tested them out. One is to roll a layer of crushed stone into the surface of newly laid hot asphalt. Another involves spreading stone dust and cement on hot asphalt before rolling. Another calls for sandblasting the surface of cured asphalt for an instant weathered look.

When you investigate these specialized forms of asphalt installation you'll meet with considerable diversity of regional practice and individual opinion. The secret is to find a reputable specialty contractor who can show you installations that have stood the test of time. You should be prepared for specially mixed or laid paving to cost more than standard paving — although with a little creative prodding you may be able to pay only slightly more than for a quality standard job.

Finally, consider practicality versus eye appeal and make sure that what you're getting is worth the investment. The most decorative surfaces are not necessarily the most practical. Rough textures can be annoying to walk or ride bikes on; light-colored surfaces will show oil and grease stains, and won't heat up to melt ice and snow as fast as dark ones. If a pavement leads right to your front door or is part of the view from some important windows, then a pleasing appearance may be worth a little impracticality — not to mention extra effort and cash. If not, perhaps a well-installed standard black asphalt walk or drive will answer your needs very well.

**Peeling bark strips and checkered patches are among the many landscape contributions of mature paper birch. See the list on the next page for other textured barks.**

## Plants by Design
# TEXTURED BARK

### Smooth Barks (Silky or Velvety)

Shadblow, juneberry, or serviceberry (*Amelanchier canadensis*)

Allegheny serviceberry (*Amelanchier laevis*)

Gray birch (*Betula populifolia*)

Yellowwood (*Cladrastis lutea*)

American beech (*Fagus grandifolia*)

European beech (*Fagus sylvatica*)

Paperbark cherry (*Prunus serrula*)

### Exfoliating Barks (Peeling in Strips or Flakes)

Paperbark maple (*Acer griseum*)

River birch (*Betula nigra*)

Paper birch (*Betula papyrifera*)

Shagbark hickory (*Carya ovata*)

Kousa or Japanese dogwood (*Cornus kousa*)

Red cedar (*Juniperus virginiana*)

Lacebark pine (*Pinus bungeana*)

Japanese stewartia (*Stewartia pseudocamellia*)

American arborvitae (*Thuja occidentalis*)

### Coarse or Deeply Fissured Barks

Norway maple (*Acer platanoides*)

Shagbark hickory (*Carya ovata*)

White ash (*Fraxinus americana*)

Detailed information and recommended varieties can be found in Part III.

# LANDSCAPE TASKS FOR FEBRUARY

**Lawn Furniture and Tool Maintenance**   Before the first warm spell, get your outdoor furniture and gardening tools in shape. Oil wooden surfaces, or apply preservative if needed; apply rust inhibitors to metal surfaces.

**Catalogues**   Last chance to order new plants and seeds from mail-order suppliers for planting in the coming season.

**Bird Feeding**   Just when the days are lengthening and you can see spring around the corner, the supply of food for birds is at its lowest. Your bird population needs not only seeds but water and grit. In addition, suet helps keep birds warm; but beware of peanut butter or soft fats. Their gluelike consistency can actually be dangerous.

**Dormant Oil Spraying**   Peaches (right now) and apples, pears, and cherries (when their buds show a tip of green) may benefit from a spraying with viscous oil. Harmless to birds and bees, this coats and smothers the egg masses of damaging insects; it can make a big difference to the fruit crop later on.

**Antidesiccants**   Broad-leaved and needled evergreens that have been exposed to strong sun and/or drying winds over the winter may need to be sprayed with an antidesiccant again (see January). Pick a day when the temperature can be expected to stay above freezing.

**Tree Guards**   Roving rodents can kill a fruit tree by girdling it — that is, by chewing off a belt or "girdle" of bark and cambium all the

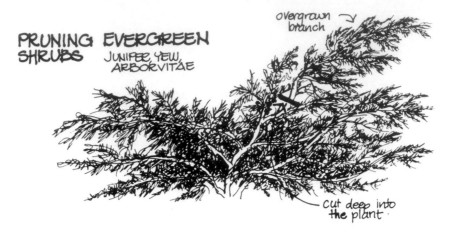

PRUNING EVERGREEN
SHRUBS   JUNIPER, YEW,
ARBORVITAE

*overgrown branch*

*cut deep into the plant*

**Give evergreen shrubs like juniper, yew, or arborvitae minor trimming now; or cut overgrown shoots back deep into the plant.**

way around the trunk, which interrupts the circulation of water and nutrients to the upper trunk and branches. If you've set up tree guards (see November) to protect your trees, check them now and make sure they're intact and doing their job. If not, trample down snow around the bases of the trunks to keep rodents from reaching the tender bark higher up.

**Mulches**   Check mulches over perennials or rock garden plants and replace any that have become dislodged. When and if the soil thaws this month, tamp back into place any small perennial plantings that have been heaved up by frost; then mulch to protect for the duration of the early spring.

**Tree Transport**   If you are planning on removing a large tree or having one installed, either of which is a job for a professional and requires the use of heavy equipment (trucks, cherry pickers, backhoes), this may be the time to do it. Machinery that would plow deep ruts in your lawn during the spring or fall will do far less damage when the ground is frozen solid. Talk to your landscape contractor or tree man, and be certain he's had experience planting big trees in frozen soil.

**Dormant Pruning**   February is the time for dormant pruning of fruit trees, evergreens, and any ornamental trees and shrubs that bloom from the end of June onwards.

**Fruit trees**   Apple, pear, and peach trees benefit from careful pruning now if they are overgrown, with limbs tangling or competing for sun. Consider pruning them if they have damaged limbs; or if heavy lateral limbs are distorting the trees' shapes or weakening their crotches; or if there are vertical shoots springing skywards parallel to the main trunk or leader. Cut any offending branches cleanly, leaving no stumps. Always use clean, sharp shears and saw. As a further hygienic measure, get rid of old dried-up fruits and cut off and burn any cankered growth, to eliminate the canker-causing fungi or bacteria.

**Narrow-leaved evergreens** including arborvitaes, junipers, and yews may call for one of two kinds of pruning at this season: elimination of dead or unwanted boughs, and trimming of tips for shape or neatness. I don't recommend shearing them into rigid shapes, but merely guiding their growth and keeping their size within bounds, if needed. (Pines, firs, spruces, and hemlocks are best done later on.)

**Ornamental trees and shrubs** that bloom in late June or after can be pruned now as needed — from minor shaping to drastic surgery of old overgrown limbs or thinning of multiple bushy shoots. These plants form flower buds on this spring's growth, so pruning will only encourage more lavish bloom. Often improved by more or less severe pruning at this season are such shrubs as butterfly bush, rose-of-Sharon, and shrub hydrangeas.

Another group of plants you can prune hard now are kerria and the shrub dogwoods grown mainly for the red or yellow winter color of their young stems. If you cut them back to stumps now, they'll be a mass of color next winter.

Many spireas, even though they bloom in June, do well if their oldest stems and small weak shoots are cut back to the ground now — much like the treatment prescribed for lilacs later on (see May).

*Do not*, however, do heavy pruning now on early-spring-flowering plants if you want to see any bloom this year. Their buds are already set on last year's stems. These include flowering quince, forsythia, honeysuckle, mock-orange, andromeda or pieris, flowering cherries, azaleas and rhododendrons, some spireas, and lilacs.

There are some small trees that — although they bloom in spring — can be discreetly thinned now for better form or overall size. Cut away sucker growth, overgrown limbs, or branches that rub against each other. You can guide new growth to some extent by cutting back just to a bud that is pointed in the general direction you want the branch to go. Shadblow, redbud, white fringe tree, flowering and Kousa dogwoods, hawthorns, golden-rain tree, magnolias, crabapples, sorrel tree, and mountain ash all can be given this kind of pruning in dormancy.

Other candidates for the most cautious of thinning now are the spring-blooming shrubs and small trees whose fruit has ornamental value. Obviously, if you prune them all over now they won't flower much — and no flowers means no fruit. On the other hand, if you prune all over after they bloom, you'll get the flowers but still no fruit. Therefore, limit pruning to cutting out only the most disorderly or leggy stems or suckers in the dormant season. Among this group: barberries, smoke tree, Cornelian cherry dogwood, gray dogwood, cotoneaster, autumn olive, winged euonymus, shrub honeysuckles, bayberry, firethorn, some shrub roses, snowberry, and viburnums.

# MAR

**Early spring sunlight floods through leafless branches, and naturalized squill (scilla) makes a blanket of glorious blue.**

**Fuzzy harbingers of spring.**

This is an exciting month: we're at the beginning of the landscape planting season.

The technical arrival of spring is the vernal equinox on March 21. In much of the Northeast, admittedly, spring may still seem a distant prospect as gusty March winds pile last fall's dead leaves in new and unwelcome places and mud reigns supreme. But even in this climate there are signs that the season is changing. The weather is somewhat milder, all in all. And whenever the clouds lift, this is a beautifully bright time of year — the days are as long as they were in October, but because there are no leaves on the trees there is actually far more light. And the first flowers appear on trees and shrubs: witch hazels, red maples, pussy willows, forsythia.

With the excitement of spring in the air, I'd like to take this month to consider one of my favorite kinds of landscape: the "wild" garden. Native plants, appropriate in wild gardens (and everywhere else), are my topic in Plants for a Purpose. In the Materials and Construction section, I'll look at some uses of stone, concrete, and asphalt: drives, walks, steps, and walls. And the very first flowering trees and shrubs of spring appear in Plants by Design this month, beginning a sequence of bloom that will go on through August.

## Landscaping Opportunities
# THE WILD GARDEN

There are two ways to create a wild garden. The first is the laissez-faire, let-it-happen method. The second is the management or cultivation method. The two are not necessarily mutually exclusive — although if you carry them to extremes they will produce very different end results.

Under a total laissez-faire approach, all you do is let your land go back to nature. You'll get tall grasses; weeds (burdocks, milkweed); vines (wild morning-glory, wild grape, woodbine); and in a short time, young shrubs (gray dogwood, sweet fern) and the saplings of what will some day be tall trees. The precise species that move in will depend largely on your climatic and soil conditions. If you try this, you may like what you get or you may not. At any rate, in a mere twenty years or so, if the neighbors let you live that long, your back-to-nature corner will be quite a little jungle.

There are not, however, very many residential settings where you would want — or be able — to let the land return to the wild, whole hog. A far more attractive and more feasible approach is a variation on this theme: a modified or partial laissez-faire attitude.

Modified laissez-faire is a convenient and appropriate choice, for instance, for a wooded corner or overgrown edge of your property. You can let the native trees and underbrush take over. Your only mandatory chore is to repel pernicious invaders (such as nettles, poison ivy, or wild grape) that threaten the well-being of your family or your other plantings. Beyond that, you can do as much or as little as you like.

Another possible, though sometimes controversial, candidate for modified laissez-faire is the lawn. Many people find they can live very happily with a meadow instead. For some thoughts on meadows see next month's Plants for a Purpose section on lawns.

**Cultivating Your Wild Garden**   The managed or cultivated wild landscape is only distantly related to the let-it-happen scene. Here we're talking about two things: deliberately concentrating on native plants, and using those plants to enhance or even to create from scratch a "natural" or wild-seeming landscape. Basic to the whole idea, of course, is the goal of capitalizing on the assets of the native plants themselves. The choice of plants and the design of the wild landscape should reinforce each other. And the whole arrangement should be as maintenance-free (as in nature) as possible.

**Habitats for native plants**   As with every planting project, deciding on natives to be kept in or introduced into a wild garden is a matter of matching the plant to the habitat. And as usual, the first step is some thoughtful observation. Consider the soil type and degree of wetness, the exposure to wind and sun, the rainfall and extremes of temperature. Study the plants that are already flourishing in or near the location you have in mind.

Chapter 4 in Part I of this book describes the range of typical plant habitats; and each plant description in Part III indicates that plant's preferred setting. Here are just a few examples of plants you might consider (a lot more are in Plants for a Purpose this month):

Often-used plants for open, low-lying "wet meadow" situations are shadblow, arrowwood, summer-sweet clethra, and of course willows.

Open, upland "dry meadow" habitats attract plants like Washington hawthorn, red cedar, sumac, and black haw.

If yours is a sheltered, shady "wet woodland" site, it is suited to all sorts of large forest trees, from beeches to oaks to shagbark hickory; and shrubs like mountain laurel, elderberry, and drooping leucothoe.

For shady, well-drained "dry woodland" habitats consider trees like red oaks and hemlocks, together with acid-loving shrubs like azaleas, rhododendrons, and highbush blueberries.

**Designing a Wilderness**   Having determined the characteristics of and the plants suited to your wild habitat, you can think about the visual effects you'd like to achieve. In some ways, a pleasing "wild" design has to work like any other kind of design. The principles of scale, balance, rhythm, emphasis, simplicity, and so on apply here as anywhere. As in any composition, you'll need to establish background, middle ground, and foreground. For backdrop, you could use larger conifers or densely branching trees and large shrubs. In the middle ground you might group smaller trees with display interest, such as showy flowers, fruits, or colored branches. The shrubs or trees in the foreground could be planted singly or in small clusters to complete the composition.

In other ways, designing a wild garden presents a special set of challenges and opportunities. Since you're aiming to create (or emphasize) an effect of naturalness, you need to be attentive to the ways plants actually do arrange themselves in the wild. An obvious instance is natives' colonizing habit. You should imitate it, and plan on small colonies of at least 3 or 5 plants.

Always keep in mind, too, that you're shooting for a self-maintaining habitat. So try to anticipate how your wilderness will do after a few years of benign neglect. Will that tree create a thicket of saplings around itself? Will this vine smother the nearby shrubs to death?

The plants in your wild garden should also be adapted to harmonious coexistence with each other. Group them according to their mutual

**This man-made "wild" garden, photographed in late summer, brings nature almost into the house. Plantings (many native) surround the small pool at the base of a rock outcropping.**

needs (such as acid soil, shade, or moisture) and according to their ability to promote each other's welfare. Under a shade tree whose roots are going to drain the soil of its nutrients, plant a ground cover that likes poor soil — and that can tolerate heavy annual mulchings of fallen leaves. On a steep bank where erosion prevention is a priority, be sure not to give your bank-dwelling plants more (or less) shade than they want.

A simple wild garden design might include the following steps. First, the determination to leave a few large existing native trees in place to form a partial canopy of shade. Second, the choice of "understory" material to be clustered around and under the trees. Third, the addition of a few specimen middle-sized trees or larger shrubs for accent use (spring bloom, fall foliage, textured bark, etc.). And finally, but perhaps most important of all, the establishment of dense ground covers adapted to the setting, to prevent unwanted plants from springing up and to provide food and cover for small wildlife.

One of the joys of the wild garden is that space — or lack of it — is no object. Maybe all you have is a patch about 12 feet square. Right there you have room for a hollowed-out boulder (to hold water) with a clump of gray birch behind it, some low-growing blueberries around it, and a group of red-osier dogwoods at one side. It will be lovely.

Nor is a rural location in any way a requirement. You could have a wild garden on a city rooftop, if it came to that. One of my favorite "wild" gardens is a tiny plot about 30 feet square, in the shadow of Boston's tallest skyscraper. It's planted with several black cherries in the rear, a large group of tall viburnums in the middle, and spreading juniper in the front. In and among the branches birds flute and chirp, in casual disregard of the busy hotel traffic across the street and the construction of another tower less than a hundred feet away.

## Plants for a Purpose
# NATIVE PLANTS

Native plants are the obvious choice for a "wild" garden, but I'm certainly not advocating that you limit your use of natives to wild-seeming landscapes. Whatever your landscaping need — color, shade, hedging, attractive form, texture, or fruit — a native plant will very often meet it in fine style. Each time I reach the stage of deciding on plant materials for a design (and particularly for a more-or-less "natural" design), I look to natives first; then to "naturalized" imports that perform just as if they belong here.

Interestingly enough, however, the landscape design and horticultural professions of any given geographical region traditionally haven't paid much attention to their native vegetation. The emphasis has usually been on importing, studying, and cultivating "exotic" or "ornamental" plants — plants native to anywhere except the area in question. For that reason (and especially if you live in the Northeast, to which this list is specifically tailored), you may be startled when you read the list of native plants that follows. Like the man in the Moliere play who was enchanted to learn that he was speaking prose every time he opened his mouth, you may be pleased to discover that you're already quite an expert on native plants.

A composition of native broad-leaved and needled evergreens and deciduous trees and shrubs in driveway planting: bayberry, dogwood, spreading juniper, holly, white pine.

### Choosing Natives for Landscape Use

Native plants, in addition to all their other fine qualities, are practical: often the hardiest and easiest-to-care-for candidates for any given situation. They have adapted over millions of years to coexistence with each other and with their environment. They've developed hereditary defenses against, or tolerance of, many native bugs, weeds, fungi, and diseases.

Why consider nonnatives at all? Well, there are an awful lot of beautiful and useful plants that have been introduced from other parts of the world. I think it's a mistake to be too dogmatic on the question of natives versus nonnatives. Some gardeners do feel that natives should be given total free rein to take over the landscape, with only minimal help or control. Others are willing to help nature to a greater degree, by introducing into their locality native plants that haven't existed there before. Others use natives mixed with nonnatives to achieve just the landscape look they want. And there are plenty of people who don't know or particularly care what's native and what isn't, just so it grows.

I certainly can't dictate what you may want to do. But if you are interested in giving native plants a boost in your landscape, here are a few tips.

### Buying Native Plants

First, look around you and see what's already growing happily in your immediate neighborhood. Next, decide on how you'll be using natives.

If you're hoping to find native plants through commercial sources, prepare yourself to hunt around a bit — for two reasons. The first is one of attitude. A plant that is native to an area is often perceived by people as a weed; or at best, as just part of the background, nothing to seek out or make a fuss over. The second reason for the spotty availability of native plants in nurseries is that they are often tricky, sometimes virtually impossible, to transplant once they've grown to a decent size. Most of them are no trouble to move when they're tiny. But when you start with a plant that's scarcely more than a seedling, it takes years to achieve the

landscape effect you're after. This state of affairs does have its silver lining, however: when you can find them, native plants are often very young and small and therefore inexpensive.

Recently, too, the advent of containerized growing has brought more and bigger natives to the marketplace. Containers, together with the new awareness of and interest in native plants, may make a tremendous difference to the native-plant scene within the next few years. One sign that things are changing is the experience of a friend of mine in New Jersey — who founded his very successful nursery business on nothing other than native plants. Around 1960, he started contracting with local farmers to clean out their drainage ditches. He dug out saplings of native red maple, black gum, and shadblow (among others); trucked them to his place; set them out in nursery rows; nurtured and pruned them carefully; and marketed them as "specimens," which in the nursery trade means plants of the highest quality. It still prospers, marketing native trees as well as nonnatives.

So if you're shopping for native plants, my best advice is to take a list of alternative choices with you, and look around. You may well be lucky. As a jumping-off place, here is a list of my own favorites.

**Native red maples grow along highways and make a welcome splash of color in the earliest spring (despite litter around their feet).**

# Native Plants for Many Landscape Uses

## Small Deciduous Trees

Shadblow, juneberry, or serviceberry
(*Amelanchier canadensis*)
Redbud (*Cercis canadensis*)
Flowering dogwood (*Cornus florida*)
Washington hawthorn (*Crataegus phaenopyrum*)
Sorrel tree or sourwood
(*Oxydendrum arboreum*)
Black haw (*Viburnum prunifolium*)

## Medium and Large Deciduous Trees

Red maple (*Acer rubrum*)
Sugar maple (*Acer saccharum*)
River birch (*Betula nigra*)
Shagbark hickory (*Carya ovata*)
Yellowwood (*Cladrastis lutea*)
American beech (*Fagus grandifolia*)
White ash (*Fraxinus americana*)
Thornless honey locust (*Gleditsia triacanthos inermis*)
Sweet gum (*Liquidambar styraciflua*)
Black gum or black tupelo (*Nyssa sylvatica*)
Black cherry or rum cherry (*Prunus serotina*)
Scarlet oak (*Quercus coccinea*)
Sassafras (*Sassafras albidum*)

## Deciduous Shrubs

Red chokeberry (*Aronia arbutifolia*)
Summer-sweet clethra (*Clethra alnifolia*)
Sweet fern (*Comptonia peregrina*)
Red-osier dogwood (*Cornus sericea*)
Fothergillas or witch alders
(*Fothergilla* spp.)
Witch hazel (*Hamamelis virginiana*)
Bayberry (*Myrica pensylvanica*)
Bush or shrubby cinquefoil (*Potentilla fruticosa*)
Pink pinxter azalea or pinxterbloom
(*Rhododendron nudiflorum*)
Rose-shell, early, or honeysuckle
azalea (*Rhododendron roseum*)
Swamp azalea (*Rhododendron viscosum*)
Shining sumac (*Rhus copallina*)
Highbush blueberry (*Vaccinium corymbosum*)
Arrowwood (*Viburnum dentatum*)
American cranberrybush or highbush
cranberry (*Viburnum trilobum*)

## Evergreen Trees

American holly (*Ilex opaca*)
Red cedar (*Juniperus virginiana*)
White pine (*Pinus strobus*)
Canadian hemlock (*Tsuga canadensis*)

## Evergreen Shrubs

Inkberry (*Ilex glabra*)
Mountain laurel (*Kalmia latifolia*)
Drooping leucothoe (*Leucothoe fontanesiana*)
Mountain andromeda or pieris (*Pieris floribunda*)
Carolina rhododendron
(*Rhododendron carolinianum*)
Catawba rhododendron
(*Rhododendron catawbiense*)
Rosebay rhododendron or great laurel
(*Rhododendron maximum*)
Canadian yew (*Taxus canadensis*)

## Ground Covers

Bearberry (*Arctostaphylos uva-ursi*)
Black chokeberry (*Aronia melanocarpa*)
Bunchberry (*Cornus canadensis*)
Wintergreen (*Gaultheria procumbens*)
Creeping juniper (*Juniperus horizontalis*)
Partridgeberry (*Mitchella repens*)
Canby paxistima (*Paxistima canbyi*)
Lowbush blueberry (*Vaccinium angustifolium*)
Yellowroot (*Xanthorhiza simplicissima*)

## Vines

Trumpet vine or common trumpet
creeper (*Campsis radicans*)
Bittersweet (*Celastrus scandens*)
Virginia creeper or woodbine
(*Parthenocissus quinquefolia*)

Detailed information and recommended varieties can be found in Part III.

## Materials and Construction
# DRIVES, WALKS, STEPS, AND WALLS

March is not only the beginning of the planting season but the beginning of the season for landscape construction. And whether you are designing a whole new landscape or doing a major or minor overhaul, you are very likely to be altering or adding a drive, a walk, some steps, or a wall. The first three — drives, walks, and steps — are essential components of your landscape's circulation system. Their design and layout, dimensions, and constituent materials will have great impact on the overall feeling and workability of your landscape. Walls are included here because they have a close family relationship to steps. They're made of many of the same materials and in much the same manner as steps, and the two often go together where changes in grade are involved.

Every situation demands a unique solution, so I won't attempt to offer blueprints here, just broadly applicable specifications for proper construction and comfortable dimensions. The creativity has to come from you. There's at least some degree of flexibility in all the minimums and maximums and ideal ratios I'll outline here: my guidelines are intended to help you, not stump you.

**Drives and Walks**   I feel strongly about the comfort and safety of people as they arrive at your home (see Chapter 6 in Part I, on design). The entry drive, parking area, front walk, and main entry into the house should be clearly visible and easy to negotiate.

Without a doubt the shortest distance between two points is a straight line, but that does not mean that the ideal walk or drive should be laid out perfectly straight. Even with very little space, there's almost always a more exciting (and often more practical) solution. A drive or walk with a gentle curve or sequence of curves, or a pathway with an

**Opposite: this door in the wall enframes a curvilinear walkway, making a pleasant and inviting entry.**

**Changing orientations along walks and drives add interest to the views both entering and leaving the house.**

specimen tree

earth mound

increase width at changes in direction.

planting

ENTRY

ALIGNING WALKS FOR CHANGING VIEWS in both directions.

**Lay out intersecting curves without straight stretches: straight lines spoil the effects of smoothly flowing walks, drives, or planting-bed edges.**

# LAYING OUT CURVES

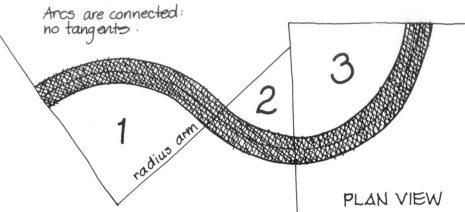

Arcs are connected: no tangents.

radius arm

1    2    3

PLAN VIEW

offset or jog part way along can afford a pleasant series of changing views. You can tailor your design to existing views, create new spots of interest with plantings or structures, or open up sightlines by removing old trees or shrubbery. It's exciting to explore the possibilities, and there's usually more than one good option. Keep in mind that with front walks it's reassuring always to have a glimpse of the front door visible along the way — although it certainly doesn't have to be in full view all the time.

As you begin to envision your new or revamped drive or walk, there are some design and structural criteria that you should be aware of.

**Curves**   For visual interest always give sequential curves arcs of different radii. Connecting tangents (straight stretches) should be short or, preferably, nonexistent. For ease of layout, sketch the radius point or center of each curve on the radius arm of the last preceding curve. These rules apply to all curves in the landscape: walks, drives, walls, or edges of plantings or beds.

The one generic drawback of a drive or walk that is curved or offset purely for visual appeal is that it will be longer, will take more time and more materials to build, and therefore will cost more than a straight one. But the smaller the project, the less the difference in cost; and conversely, the larger the project, the greater the gain in interest and satisfaction. Either way, I think it is almost always worth it.

**Slopes**   A practical reason for lengthening a drive or walk by curving it is to reduce the steepness of its slope. On uphill terrain, the more winding a path, the less abrupt its angle of rise.

The ideal slope for a walk is between 1 and 5 percent (see April Materials and Construction on earthwork and drainage). It should never exceed 10 percent — so if the immediate approach to your house is steeper than that, some curving or zigzagging of the walk or use of steps or ramps will be mandatory. As for drives, the optimum grade is 1 to 7 percent; they should never exceed 20 percent, and that only for short distances. Parking areas should not be sloped more than 5 percent, and preferably 2 to 3 percent.

Knowing the total rise of the area in question and the desired percentage of slope for the walk, drive, or parking area, you can easily determine the proper length for the pavement with this formula:

$$S = \frac{R}{D}$$

where

S = slope as a percentage (for instance, 5 percent, or .05)
R = rise in feet and
D = distance in feet.

If you have to join two slopes (one down, one up), allow for a gradual, smooth transition — or vertical curve, as engineers call it — at bottom or top. Avoid sharp intersecting peaks or valleys. Finally, if you're curving a drive or walk so as to ease travel up a grade, avoid tight curves. Snow or ice can turn a narrow curve into a treacherous trap for pedestrians or cars.

**Drainage**   In a landscape where topography is varied and runoff occurs, drives and walks will have a tendency to become drainage reservoirs — and in winter, ice-skating rinks — unless you take steps to drain them properly at or before the time of their construction.

For a flat paved surface running cross-slope, the best approach is to build a catchment uphill to trap rainwater and melting snow, then channel it along the slope parallel to the pavement until it can be directed into a storm drain. Sometimes this isn't possible, and in such cases a second alternative is to angle the paved surface itself slightly downhill, to force water to drain across it and away.

Another solution works well but is expensive: you can "crown" a walk or drive, giving it a smooth convex curve from side to side with the crest running down the middle of the pavement for all of its length. Even in the heaviest rains, there will be a dry spot along the crest of a well-

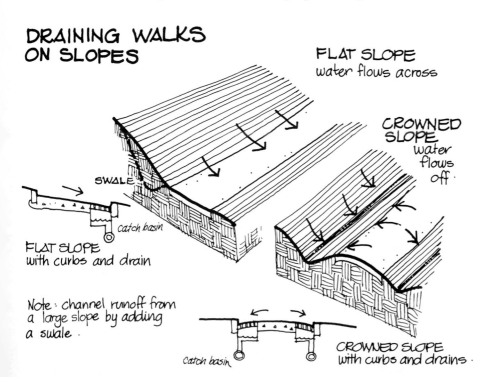

DRAINING WALKS ON SLOPES

FLAT SLOPE
water flows across

CROWNED SLOPE
water flows off

SWALE

catch basin

FLAT SLOPE
with curbs and drain

Note: channel runoff from a large slope by adding a swale.

catch basin

CROWNED SLOPE
with curbs and drains.

Two approaches to draining pavements are shown here. If runoff is a problem, intercept and channel rainwater uphill of the pavements.

crowned pavement. With good soil drainage, the runoff from a crowned drive can be allowed to percolate by itself; you may need cobbled or graveled gutters at the edges to channel the water, however. A softly crowned drive is handsome, but in view of the complexity and cost of building it I am usually more inclined to settle for a shallow, flat slope that lets water flow off to one side rather than both.

**Dimensions** Standard dimensions for walks and drives are based upon the dimensions and speed of movement of the people and vehicles (respectively) that are expected to be using them. Comfort, ease, and safety are the common goals.

Walks in gardens or lawns should be at least 3 feet (36 inches) wide; better still, 42, 48, or 54 inches, if the scale of the setting permits, to let two people walk easily side by side. For a flowing, fluid look you can vary the width of a walk along its length or flare it at either end. For an illusion of greater or lesser distance, you can make a walk narrower at one end or the other. Or for comfort at bends or corners, try adding extra latitude, just as a river carves out space for itself at its bends.

Whenever a fence, hedge, or other object beside a path is higher than 2 feet — an average minimum height for the hands of adults walking along swinging their arms — there should be a buffer strip at least 2 feet wide between the object and the path. The buffer strip can be grass, flowers, a ground cover, stones, gravel, you name it. By the same token,

**Widen walks at curves, and flare at the ends for ease of transition.**

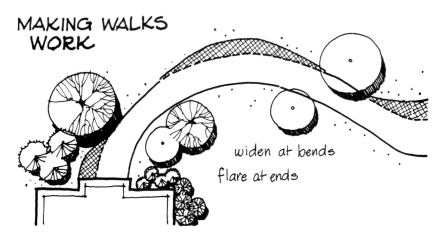

MAKING WALKS WORK

widen at bends

flare at ends

**For a comfortable feeling, make a wall next to a walk no higher than 24 inches; or maintain a border strip next to a higher wall.**

WALLS & BORDER DIMENSIONS

24" max.

24" min. border

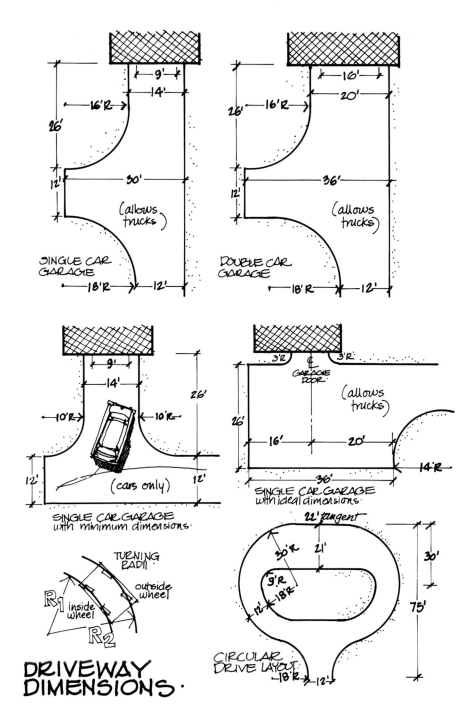

SINGLE CAR GARAGE

DOUBLE CAR GARAGE

(allows trucks)

(allows trucks)

SINGLE CAR GARAGE with minimum dimensions

(cars only)

SINGLE CAR GARAGE with ideal dimensions

(allows trucks)

GARAGE DOOR

TURNING RADII

outside wheel

R₁ inside wheel

R₂

DRIVEWAY DIMENSIONS·

CIRCULAR DRIVE LAYOUT

21' tangent

if a wall is to run right along one side of a walkway, its height should be kept to 2 feet or less so that you won't brush your hand against it or feel crowded.

Drives should never be less than 10 feet wide. Preferably they should measure 11 or 12 feet for straight runs or gradual curves, and 12 to 14 feet at corners or sharp curves. Radii for driveways and parking areas are based on the turning radii of the vehicles for which they're designed.

**Steps and Walls**  Both steps and retaining walls signal grade changes, and as such they have major impact where they appear. Free-standing walls are equally important in the landscape because they are so solid and opaque; they define or divide space emphatically.

Since steps and walls are made of building construction materials, they can be closely tied to the house or other structures in style and degree of formality. Or if they're at a distance, they can be very much a part of the garden or open landscape, and appropriately informal or rustic. In any setting and whatever the style, the design and building of steps and walls offer great scope for creativity. There's always a way to make them gracious and attractive, and it is fun to do.

**Steps**  Steps are for people, and must be designed to fit the average comfortable pace. A hundred years ago the great landscape architect Frederick Law Olmsted worked out a formula for the proper relationship of riser height to tread depth, and his rule still stands. It states: $2R + T = 27$, where R = riser height in inches and T = tread depth in inches.

**For safe and comfortable outdoor steps and ramps, stay as close as possible to these established guidelines.**

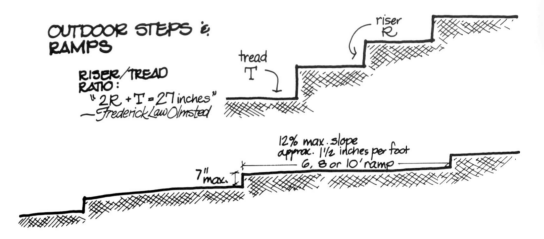

OUTDOOR STEPS & RAMPS

RISER/TREAD RATIO:
" $2R + T = 27$ inches"
—Frederick Law Olmsted

tread T

riser R

7" max.

12% max. slope approx. 1½ inches per foot
6, 8 or 10' ramp

For outdoor steps, risers should be not less than 4 inches or more than 7 inches high. The accompanying tread depths are shown in the table here. I like best to build outdoor steps with risers of 5 to 6 inches, treads of 17 to 15 inches. These proportions are visually satisfying and physically comfortable. You can actually cheat on tread depths by an inch one way or the other, if space or design demands. What you must never do, however, is vary the riser and/or tread dimensions within a single flight of steps. That throws people off balance and constitutes a real safety hazard.

### Riser and Tread Dimensions for Outdoor Steps

| Risers | Treads |
| --- | --- |
| 4 inches | 19 inches |
| 4½ | 18 |
| 5 | 17 |
| 5½ | 16 |
| 6 | 15 |
| 6½ | 14 |
| 7 | 13 |

The soft, flowing contour of a field-stone retaining wall is punctuated by the crisp lines of a flight of granite steps.

Some other guidelines on steps:

- In general, steps should not be narrower than the walks they connect (if any), and preferably not narrower than 42 inches anyway. There are occasional exceptions, such as with a miniature garden path or where there's a space bind.
- Never use just one step — it's a tripper. If you've got only one step's worth of rise, figure out an alternative. You could build a gradual ramp instead; or raise the upper grade or depress the lower grade to use more than one step. Three steps is the desirable minimum, although two is acceptable.
- Always construct the top tread flush with the upper surface, as warning for those about to descend the steps. A change of texture or material — from gravel path to stone step, from brick to bluestone, from bark chips to timbers, or whatever — serves as additional warning.
- For drainage, slope the treads slightly forward. Minimum slant is 1 percent, maximum 2 percent.
- Use a railing on at least one side if you have more than four steps.
- For large grade changes, say more than 5 feet or more than you can handle with 10 risers, you should plan to incorporate landings. Landings allow both visual and physical refreshment. A change in direction in a long flight of stairs is also a good idea, to lessen the daunting impression of a lengthy climb and provide the added attraction of changing views at turning points. To permit one pace between the end of one flight and the beginning of the next, a landing should be at least 4 feet long; to permit two paces, 6 feet.
- A long shallow slope is best negotiated with ramp-steps: a combination of single risers set at even intervals of 6, 8, or 10 feet with intervening ramps angled upwards not more than 12 percent.

Informal ramp-steps: timbers form steps and contain the loose gravel on the sloped ramps.

Walls or steps of
pressure-treated
timbers are often a
feasible do-it-your-
self project.

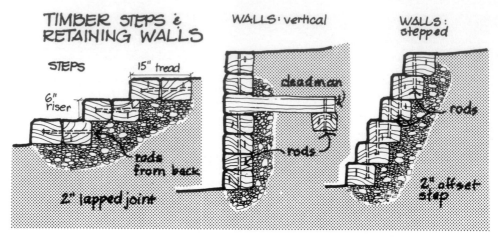

TIMBER STEPS &
RETAINING WALLS

STEPS

15" tread

6" riser

rods from back

2" lapped joint

WALLS: vertical

deadman

rods

WALLS: stepped

rods

2" offset step

**Retaining walls**   The primary function of a retaining wall is to hold back the soil behind it, permitting an abrupt change in grade without an erosion disaster. A retaining wall can be of any height from 1 foot up; a wall a foot or less in height is called a curb. I always try to engineer things so I can make a retaining wall 18 to 24 inches high that will serve for sitting as well as retaining.

Often, however, it's necessary to hold back more soil than a 2-foot wall can handle, and this is where retaining-wall construction gets tricky. The weight of soil and water and disruptive activities of frost necessitate both strong construction and sophisticated drainage. You have to avoid water buildup behind the wall by providing for water to drain down to and through the base of the wall.

The figures here indicate the kinds of footings and dimensions that will make for sturdy retaining walls constructed of commonly available materials like timber, stone, or brick in a climate where water and frost do their best to knock down whatever you put up.

One of the most elementary forms of retaining wall is a dry-laid stone wall. Its great advantage is that it is automatically self-draining and needs no separate concrete footing: you just dig down and begin laying the stones a foot or so below ground level. If you can find a skilled dry-wall mason to lay one up for you, or if you're patient enough to learn to do it yourself, this can be an attractive and practical way to hold back soil. But if you are contemplating a retaining wall 3 feet or more in height, I do recommend that you at least consult with a stone mason to ensure that you will be using the proper materials and methods. It's too arduous a task not to do it right the first time.

You can also build a mixture of dry-laid and mortared wall, using some mortar within the wall to hold it together. This compromise approach is useful for the less patient or experienced among us and works very well.

It's important to find the right kind of stone for the kind and size of retaining wall you want. Rubblestone or fieldstone will give a rough, informal look. A more formal or architectural appearance is created by cut stone or by stones with naturally flat cleavage planes that fit together neatly — such as slate, some sandstones, or some limestones.

**Freestanding walls**   Freestanding walls lend a sense of solid permanence to a landscape. They define or segregate spaces with absolute finality. Whether formal or informal, unrelated, related, or even connected to buildings, they are almost always very architectural in feeling.

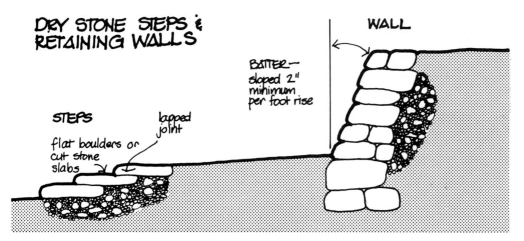

## DRY STONE STEPS & RETAINING WALLS

WALL

BATTER — sloped 2" minimum per foot rise

STEPS

lapped joint

flat boulders or cut stone slabs

Dry-laid stone steps and retaining walls are other possibilities for the home owner, but entail somewhat more effort and skill.

They are also expensive — particularly tall freestanding walls, which present some specialized architectural and engineering challenges and are really beyond the scope of this discussion.

If you are inclined to build a low seat wall and can afford it, I think it's the way to go. A low masonry wall is the perfect border, never needing trimming, fertilizing, or replacement. It provides attractive built-in seating. And it can afford shelter and privacy, too, if you back it or top it with an open fence or plantings.

In a climate where winter freeze-thaw cycles are a way of life, two all-important precautions must be taken with any freestanding masonry wall. First, always build a solid foundation below frost level. And second, always provide the wall with a water-tight coping along the top, to prevent water from seeping into joints, freezing, and causing the joints to crack. Such a coping can be made of brick, stone, concrete, shingles, or even painted boards; but it is crucial to the durability of the wall.

The construction of walls is not an easy undertaking or one for the total novice. Just moving the materials from place to place — be they bricks, stone, concrete, or concrete block — is a staggering job. Specialized skills are required if you want to achieve a professional-looking product; and you really do, since you're building for posterity. If at all possible, I'd recommend that you find a contractor who will work with you and be guided by you in a spirit of teamwork.

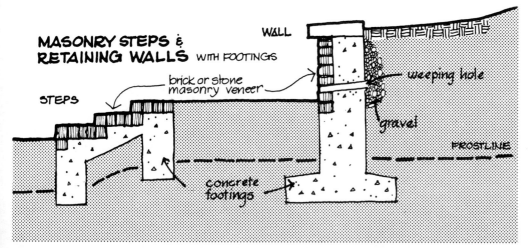

## MASONRY STEPS & RETAINING WALLS WITH FOOTINGS

WALL

STEPS

brick or stone masonry veneer

weeping hole

gravel

FROSTLINE

concrete footings

Masonry steps and retaining walls (or freestanding walls) with concrete footings involve greater skill and more time, equipment, and expense.

## Plants by Design
# MARCH BLOOMERS

**For earliest flowering in Zones 5 and 6.**

Red maple (*Acer rubrum*)
Cornelian cherry dogwood (*Cornus mas*)
Showy border forsythia (*Forsythia intermedia* 'Spectabilis')
Chinese witch hazel (*Hamamelis mollis*)
Vernal witch hazel (*Hamamelis vernalis*)
Goat willow (*Salix caprea*)

Detailed information and recommended varieties can be found in Part III.

# LANDSCAPE TASKS FOR MARCH

**Uncoverings**  Choose an overcast day (to avoid a sudden shock of bright sun) and remove protective winter windscreens from boxwoods or other evergreens around the house. This should be accomplished by the end of the month.

**Last Call for Dormant Pruning**  Even though their buds may no longer be dormant, strictly speaking, you can do some last-minute dormant pruning (see February) of fruit trees and late-flowering shrubs if you haven't done so already. But the sooner the better. And you can still trim shade trees and flowering trees, except dogwood. Dogwood and the early-spring-flowering shrubs — that is, flowering before June — should not be pruned until after they bloom.

**Pest Control**  March is also the last call for dormant oil spraying of apple and pear trees (see February).

**Transplanting**  As soon as the soil becomes workable after frost is gone, you can plant orchard and ornamental trees purchased from a nursery — or transplant your own to different locations. In particular, trees that do not take kindly to fall transplanting should be installed as soon as possible. This means birches, magnolias, dogwoods, and fruit trees. Rhododendrons and azaleas should ideally go into the ground in spring, too. (See September and April Landscape Tasks sections for planting/transplanting details.)

**Repair and Rehabilitation**  Hedges or shrubs that have suffered bad breakage in winter storms should be pruned out, to encourage healing and healthy new growth. Damaged privet, for instance, can be cut back to stumps only a few inches high and it will stage a rapid and abundant resurgence.

In bloom this month, delicate yellow flowers of Cornelian cherry dogwood mark the advent of early spring.

**Root-Pruning in Advance**   If you are planning to move an established tree or shrub from one place to another, I recommend that you root-prune it at least one full growing season (or up to a year) in advance. And this is the month to do it, since active root growth is starting now.

This is a trick many nurseries use with their field-grown (as opposed to container) stock. It's particularly helpful with trees or larger shrubs that are difficult to move, such as oak or magnolia; and with wild-growing natives like flowering dogwood or cherry.

With shrubs and very small trees, just chop the roots with vertical spade-cuts in a circle around the plant. The diameter of the circle should be roughly 10 inches for every 1 inch of diameter of the plant's stem.

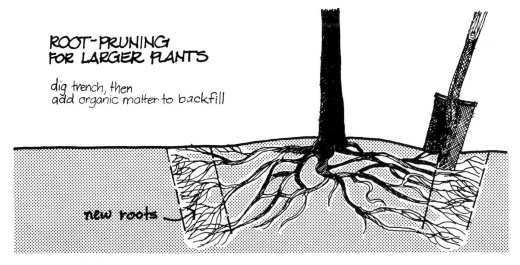

ROOT-PRUNING FOR LARGER PLANTS

dig trench, then add organic matter to backfill

new roots

Root-pruning now will concentrate the feeder roots within a limited area. This helps the plant recover from digging and transplanting in the fall or in the following spring.

For larger shrubs and trees, use the same diameter rule but dig down deeper, making a trench all around the plant and cutting each exposed root with sharp clippers. When you backfill the trench, amend the soil with organic matter and fertilizer; and in a dry season, water regularly.

The result of root-pruning will be the development of a dense bundle of new roots close to the base of the stem. When you dig up the tree in the fall (or a year from now), its feeding system will be in place for rapid recovery from transplanting.

**Soil Testing**   Soil acidity, or pH level (see page 45), has a bearing on the success of your landscape — because the wrong pH for a plant, whether too low (acid) or too high (alkaline), will bind up soil nutrients so the plant can't get at them. With the growing season getting under way this month, this is the time to find out whether your soil is right for your chosen plants. Most landscape and garden plants appreciate a slightly acid pH of about 6 to 6.5; but there are many exceptions, such as azaleas and blueberries. The descriptions in Part III should be your guide.

### Amounts of Agricultural Limestone to Bring Soil pH to 6.5

| | *Pounds of limestone per hundred square feet* | | |
|------|------------|------|-----------|
| pH | Sandy loam | Loam | Clay loam |
| 4.0 | 11.5 | 16 | 23 |
| 4.5 | 9.5 | 13.5 | 19.5 |
| 5.0 | 8 | 10.5 | 15 |
| 5.5 | 6 | 8 | 10.5 |
| 6.0 | 3 | 4 | 5.5 |

Note: Hydrated limestone is more expensive but works more quickly, and you use only three-fourths as much as indicated above.

In general, soils west of the Mississippi tend to be somewhat alkaline; that is why it's such hard work to succeed with azaleas in parts of the Midwest. Western gardeners can and do boost the acidity of their soil by adding agricultural sulfur.

Soils east of the Mississippi tend to be somewhat acid, largely as a result of the leaching effect of thousands of years of water runoff — not to mention the more recent phenomenon of acid rain. Because of both these factors, eastern soils move gradually toward greater acidity as time passes. The addition of limestone will bring the soil back closer to neutral, and a limestone treatment every three to five years is generally advisable.

Before you add limestone or anything else to your soil, however, run a soil test. I recommend sending a soil sample or samples to your state university extension service. They can provide you with not only a pH reading but a nutrient analysis indicating what — if anything — should be done to improve the fertility of your soil. You can also purchase home soil test kits and run the test yourself; but the extension service route is often free for the asking or available at only nominal cost, and I think it gives fuller and more precise information.

With either method, your main job is to get a good soil sample. At several evenly spaced locations in the testing area, take small samples — about a cup each — every 2 inches from the surface to 8 inches down.

Spread all the samples to dry on newspaper in some conveniently out-of-the-way spot. When the soil is completely dried out, mix and pulverize it well, and pack up a sample of no less than a pint for the laboratory.

If your landscape conditions or the uses you plan for your soil vary greatly, then separate samples should be prepared for the different conditions or intended uses. Label the samples and have them tested individually. An example of this kind of circumstance would be a site where part of the land was dry and part very wet. Or a site where part of the land had been pine woods for many years, part open field — but all was intended to be turned into lawn. Or a site where a former lawn was to be converted to part evergreen shrubbery, part perennial bed.

The table here is a quick guide to the correct amounts of limestone to use to modifiy the pH of your soil. The results of your soil test will show you just where you stand on the pH scale, as well as what other improvements you will want to make to tailor each area of soil to the needs of its specific crop.

# APR

**Magnolias' blossoms are a billow of white, and their gray bark adds highlights among the muted tones of April woods.**

April is an unpredictable month. Sometimes it's showery, sometimes freezing, sometimes too hot too soon. Two things you can usually count on, however: greenery and water. There's a haze of green in woods and shrubberies. And all around you the ground plane is turning green — from hills and fields to playgrounds, parks, and lawns. This seems a good month to think about plantings and configurations for the ground plane: banks and slopes and the plants for them, the handling of soil drainage, and lawns.

---

### Landscaping Opportunities
# BANKS AND SLOPES

Steep man-made banks occur inevitably wherever people construct level living spaces in sloping terrain. Cutting into a hillside to level an area for a terrace, for instance, or building up from grade to enlarge a backyard, will disturb topsoil, subsoil, and often even underlying rock. If your landscape includes any such artificially banked areas, this section is for you.

Naturally formed slopes like hillsides, riverbanks, or glacial moraines are usually no problem. Nor should there be any difficulty with topographical variations you add to your place for design purposes, such as a gentle contouring of the lawn or a berm (a ridge with plantings) to baffle traffic noise. Angling such surfaces to forestall erosion is part of correct construction procedure.

But the banks created by the leveling of sloped areas do present a challenge: how to establish plantings or build retaining structures to prevent the big enemy of man-made banks, erosion.

**Banks and Erosion**   Erosion is influenced by a complex of causes that range from chemical to mechanical; but the three central factors are soil quality, type of bank construction, and location.

**Soil**   Every soil has its own "angle of repose": the steepest angle at which that soil can rest without the force of gravity causing its particles to roll downhill. The angle of repose for a moist, heavily organic loam is very different from that of a light, dry, sandy or pebbly soil. The kind of soil a bank consists of will have a lot to do with its ability to stay put.

**Construction**   In terms of origin, there are two kinds of man-made banks: "cut" and "fill." Often, when a slope is terraced to obtain a level area, both kinds of banks are constructed, one above the level, one below. But sometimes you'll be working with just one or the other.

When you cut into a slope, making a *cut bank*, you remove the topsoil and expose the vulnerable subsoil. It's vulnerable because it lacks the organic "glue" and web of plant roots to bind its mineral components together. Under the onslaught of rain and weather, the tendency of exposed subsoil is to run in rivulets downhill. You have surely seen this along fresh highway cuts, if not on your own property.

When you build out from a slope, making a *fill bank*, you have a somewhat different and often more serious erosion problem. No matter how high quality the soil you add on to the existing slope, it has been profoundly disturbed by excavation, transportation, and reinstallation. And the more disturbed soil is, the more swift it is to wash away under the further disruptions of frost, wind, and rain.

**Location**   The tendency of a bank to erode is also partly a function of where it is situated in relation to the rest of the landscape. With a cut bank — whose soil is likely to lack organic matter, fertility, or other redeeming qualities — a dry uphill location is one more hazard to overcome. If there is a large runoff area above the bank in question, whether a cut or a fill bank, you'll face a constant threat of erosion; but at least you'll have a built-in water supply for any plantings you establish to hold the soil in place.

**Coping with Banks**   Once you become bank-conscious, you'll begin noticing all around you the various approaches to the engineering and landscaping of banks. Highway and other construction sites are sources of endless examples, good and bad, even though their scale sets them apart from anything you'll be dealing with in a residential situation.

The first thing to ask yourself about the treatment of any bank is how the bank fits into the overall design of your place. Do you look at it or over it? If a bank is the main view from your living-room windows, you'll want to dedicate considerable care and imagination to making it a thing of beauty (as well as restraining it from disintegrating in the first heavy rain). If it's the boundary strip at the far side of the children's play area, your chief concerns are soil retention and safety. If it's a transitional area between the driveway and the front lawn, perhaps it should be decorative in an unobtrusive way; or perhaps you'll want it to support some screening plantings.

Other than walls, you have two broad groups of materials with which to shape and control your banked areas. Plantings are usually the easiest and least expensive, and you'll probably want to use some plantings even if you introduce other structures too. But you may also have access to terracing helpers in the form of stone or wood.

**Stone and wood**   Stones, large and small, can be great for informal terracing — in part because they're often conveniently present in or around the same bank you're hoping to terrace. You can use a riprap of small, medium, and medium-large stones to enclose earth pockets, which in turn will support shrubs, vines, or ground covers. For boulder terracing, you can move larger rocks into place to create topsoil terraces where shrubbery or grass could be planted.

Or you can use wood: boards, logs, railroad ties, or other heavy timbers, appropriately pressure-treated for rot resistance. Any of these will break the sloping angle of the bank just enough to hold vegetation and keep the soil where you want it.

The ultimate structural retention for a steep bank is, of course, a retaining wall. But since the construction of a wall is as much an architectural or design decision as an engineering one, I discussed and diagrammed retaining walls in last month's Materials and Construction section.

**The terms "cut" and "fill" refer to ways banks are created as a result of leveling operations. Boulders, timbers, and plantings aid in stabilizing soil at man-made banks.**

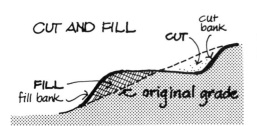

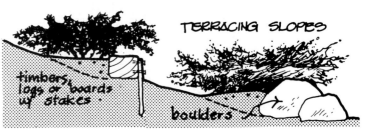

**Above left: a six-foot bank is held in place by a combination of evergreen ground covers and boulders nestled into the soil. Above right: cut stone, hand set into the bank, retains soil and forms a clean-edged surface.**

**Plantings**   Unless you are privy to some source of free boulders, pressure-treated timbers, or modular stone for retaining walls, the first choice for banks is generally planting. Whether grass, shrub, vine, or ground cover, you are looking for plants that will rapidly develop fibrous root systems to enmesh the soil — as well as anchor the plants themselves. They should also tolerate low soil fertility (especially with cut banks), low moisture, and/or heavy shade or exposure to strong sun, depending on the orientation of the bank.

Because of the tough, fast-growing network of roots they develop, sod-forming or bunch-forming grasses are often the best plants for banks. (If you're planning to mow your grassed bank, however, it must not have a slope greater than 1 foot rise for every 3 feet horizontal distance.) Many varieties are available at nurseries or garden centers. There are good sod-forming mixtures of Kentucky bluegrass and creeping red fescue; or a type known as K-31 fescue, which is so cohesive it is often used in athletic fields. Or if your bank is large enough to handle the tall, tufty, bunch-forming ornamental grasses — many of which grow to be 3 to 5 feet tall — consider native grasses like switchgrass or panicgrass, or handsome imports such as ribbongrass or a South African variety called weeping love grass. All these grasses, besides keeping the earth from eroding, will supply cover for small wildlife and attractive seed heads for dried flower arrangements.

Shrubs and other nongrass plantings for banks should be of kinds that propagate readily from rhizomes or from branches that root spontaneously when they touch the ground. The whole idea is to establish a close-knit, tenacious community of plant life as fast as possible. The following are a few excellent candidates for the job.

## Plants for Banks and Slopes

### Shrubs and Small Trees
Sweet fern (*Comptonia peregrina*)
Siebold forsythia (*Forsythia suspensa sieboldii*)
Creeping juniper (*Juniperus horizontalis*)
Fragrant sumac (*Rhus aromatica*)
Memorial rose (*Rosa wichuraiana*)
Coralberry or Indian currant (*Symphoricarpos orbiculatus*)
Lowbush blueberry (*Vaccinium angustifolium*)
Yellowroot (*Xanthorhiza simplicissima*)

### Vines
Bittersweet (*Celastrus scandens*)
Wintercreeper (*Euonymus fortunei*)

Henry honeysuckle (*Lonicera henryi*)
Hall's honeysuckle (*Lonicera japonica* 'Halliana')

### Ground Covers
Bearberry (*Arctostaphylos uva-ursi*)
English ivy (*Hedera helix*)
Japanese spurge or pachysandra (*Pachysandra terminalis*)
Ribbon grass (*Phalaris arundinacea picta*)
Vinca, periwinkle or myrtle (*Vinca minor*)

Detailed information and recommended varieties can be found in Part III.

**Hall's honeysuckle grows vigorously on a steep, sunny bank. But don't let it escape its bounds or it will smother everything in sight!**

## Plants for a Purpose
# LAWNS AND LAWN GRASSES

With everything starting to grow and turn green, April is one of the best times to plant, feed, and generally refurbish your lawn. (August/September is also an ideal time to start a lawn.)

Lawn grass, hard-working ground cover for large areas, can also be treated sculpturally as in this landscape composition.

There's no denying the beauty of a clipped green lawn. It finishes off an outdoor space, satisfying the eye's need for a landscape floor that is restful and inviting in texture and color. Lawns have become part of the American vernacular; and although they're not for everyone (I encourage no-lawn solutions for small properties and wooded properties, for instance) they do find a place in a great many settings, even if only in the form of a small green terrace in an otherwise natural or wild landscape.

Lawns also have their utilitarian functions. For one thing, they can be beneficial to their natural environment. They do a superb job of erosion prevention. They contribute massive amounts of organic matter to the soil in the form of clippings and dead roots. (Fifty percent of all grass roots die each year and are replaced with new ones.) And think of the volume of oxygen returned to the air by the constant "breathing" of lawn grasses.

Lawns serve their human proprietors in countless ways as well, undergoing incredible abuse in the process. We're apt to take lawn grasses too much for granted. They go through life tightly crowded, continually pruned, repeatedly crushed; few other plants could endure such treatment.

Yet lawn grasses are plants too, and plants that form a permanent part of almost every home landscape. Because we demand so much from them — in beauty and in hard service — their selection and care call for as much attention as we give any other plant.

**What Kind of Lawn Is for You?**   Before you plant a new lawn or set to work to improve an old one, think about what kind of lawn you really want. The types of grass you plant will depend not only on soil, exposure, and climate but on the effect you want to achieve and the amount of annual upkeep you want to devote to the finished lawn.

Conventional lawn-grass mixtures are blended of assorted grasses such as fescues, bluegrasses, bent grasses, and others, including many nonnatives. The goal of conventional lawn care is to prevent the growth of other types of plants by promoting thick growth of the approved grasses and keeping them short.

Decide at the outset just how fussy you want to be. At one extreme, perhaps nothing less than a showpiece of close-cropped green will satisfy you. If so, you should plant by the book and plan on intensive fertilization, weed and disease control, watering, and spot reseeding.

Or you may be of my general school of thought. For my lawn, I provide excellent soil and I seed or overseed with the best obtainable mix of grass seed for my location. After that, I pretty much let the lawn cope on its own. I mow, but I'm not a heavy waterer or constant weeder.

Possibly you'll find that you can be happy with a rough lawn that is really just a clipped pasture, full of clover and plantains and other visiting vegetation. If so, you can seed on a casual basis, ignore the feeding and watering guidelines offered below, and mow when needed to keep it looking reasonably neat.

Or perhaps you're the type for a meadow rather than a lawn. A meadow is not seeded with conventional lawn grasses. For a meadow, native grasses that reproduce themselves by seeds or rhizomes are permitted to grow relatively long and tufty. And among and between the tufts you will soon have a vast diversity of plant and animal life: clovers; thistles; wildflowers like daisies, goldenrod, buttercups, or Queen Anne's lace; all sorts of small creeping plants and infant shrubs, like wild strawberries, wild roses, and blackberries; and birds and other small creatures attracted by this bounty. If you mow once a year in late fall you can maintain a good stand of wildflowers; or if you prefer a neater summer look, also mow in early summer.

Right now, around my own house, much of the open space is kept as lawn. I am fond of its conventional crisp neatness and its lovely color. Still, the mown lawn is a fairly recent tradition, having begun around the mid-1800s among affluent landowners who were able to pay gardeners to cut the grass by hand. Before gardeners it was grazing animals that fertilized and cropped the grass, and what they produced was far from velvety greensward. Nowadays, few of us can hire gardeners — and still fewer possess grazing animals — and keeping that turf in good repair can be a big job. I am not sure I'd be quite so devoted to my lawn if my children didn't mow it so as to be able to play ball games on it. Once the kids leave home, I just may let some of the lawn-grass carpet grow into a meadow-grass shag.

One good answer to the lawn question is a combination of styles. You might settle for a small area of fine-quality turf right next to the house, where you look at it or use it often, with an expanse of rougher and less demanding grass around the fringes, maybe 10 yards out or so — a kind of adaptation of the golf course "green" and "rough."

**Lawn Soils and Slopes**   For every kind of lawn, good soil is a must. You can't expect miracles from a few grass seeds scattered on infertile subsoil, particularly if the soil is steeply pitched, hard-packed clay, or badly drained. The grass will fail and the soil will either wash away or sprout weeds, or both.

Good lawn soil should be loose, not compacted. It should contain lots of organic matter (peat moss, compost, composted manure, or humus); if it doesn't, spread a layer a couple of inches thick over the top of

**Soil preparation is indispensable for lawns (and all other plantings). Piles of loam, manure, and sand are ready to be mixed and spread before seeding, sodding, or planting.**

the soil and work it in. The soil's pH should be about 6.5. If it is lower than 6.0, add limestone to raise the pH (see Soil Testing in the March Landscape Tasks).

As for the slope, a lawn should always be graded *away* from the house, at least 2 percent (for drainage). Rarely should it be graded more than 33 percent, or 1:3. A slope of more than 1:3 is too hard to mow. I like to blend a lawn's contours into the existing terrain as much as possible, using broad but subtle bowls (properly drained, of course) and roundish hills. I do this for two reasons. First, the effects of sunlight and shadows — especially in early morning and late afternoon — are far more dramatic on slightly undulating terrain. Second, it's very difficult to create a lawn that is perfectly flat. Rather than trying to obliterate unevenness, it makes sense to exploit it, even accentuate it. Leave the flat planes to decks and patios, and treat the soil in a more sculptural way.

**Choosing Lawn Grasses**   Whether you are seeding from scratch or overseeding or patching an established lawn, the correct choice of lawn grass seeds is crucial to success. See if your garden center has a mix that is recommended for your climate, soil type, exposure (sun or shade), and planned use (from purely ornamental to heavy wear and tear). Some other dos and don'ts:

- Don't use a single variety of a single species of seed. It's too easy for a single infestation of insects (like chinch bugs) or fungi (like snow mold or fusarium blight) to wipe it out.
- Don't use the very fine bent grasses that are intended for putting greens; the care and feeding of these is a job for professional turf-tenders.
- Do read the label on any seed mix carefully. Look for more than one variety of one species, plus at least one other species. Make sure that the seed is fresh, dated the current year. Look for at least 50 percent combined bluegrasses and fine fescues, and not more than 25 percent of the turf-type perennial ryegrasses. Check to see that the germination rate is 80 to 90 percent (or higher) and that "weed" and "crop" seeds add up to less than 1 percent.

The table on page 146 shows in a nutshell the salient characteristics of bluegrasses and fescues, which are the top choices for lawns in the Northeast. It's easy to see why these two types complement each other so well, and why they do such a good job in our climate.

Creeping red fescue, once it is established, can be left unmowed for a "meadow look" and cut just three or four times a year. Tall fescue varieties are the most durable for athletic fields or other areas subject to hard use, but they are very coarse textured. Another grass you may encounter in your label-reading is redtop; but redtop should not constitute more than 10 percent of any mix. It is a short-lived "nurse grass" that germinates in several days, gives a green appearance to an area while the slower varieties are germinating, then disappears as the prime grasses starve it out.

**Lawn Grass Care**   Like all growing plants, lawn grasses respond to attention — but more dramatically than most, because they are so small and their roots are superficial. You've probably seen a lawn turn two shades greener overnight after its fall or spring feeding, or watched a brown dormant lawn miraculously grow green within days following a

## Grass Types

| Grass species | Advantages | Disadvantages |
|---|---|---|
| Kentucky bluegrass (*Poa pratensis*) | Best all-around color and texture | Dislikes shade<br>Poor in sandy soils<br>Requires abundant moisture<br>Browns out at 80°F (revives with irrigation)<br>Requires 6.0–7.0 pH — more lime applications |
| Fescues (*Festuca* spp.), including chewings fescue, creeping red fescue | Tolerate sun or shade<br>Tolerate low fertility<br>Will accept 5.5–6.5 pH — fewer lime applications<br>Tolerate drought | Stiff and wiry; do not form superior quality turf |

late-summer rainfall. Having provided the right soil and proper drainage, and having seeded your lawn with the right grasses for its location and use, you have three main responsibilities in the maintenance department: mowing, watering, and feeding.

**Mowing**  Turf grasses thrive best when no more than one-third of their total height is removed at a mowing. If you let the grass grow to a straggly 6 inches, then hack it down to 3 inches, you'll remove 50 percent of the grass plants' leaves, which weakens the plants and thus the turf as a whole. The point of this is that your mowing schedule has to adjust itself to grasses' seasonal rhythms of growth. Frequent spring mowings give way to more widely spaced mowings as summer advances — even no mowings at all if you let your lawn go dormant (see Watering, below). Things speed up again in fall, until cold weather brings growth to a halt once more.

As a general rule, I recommend keeping grass cut to a height of not less than 2½ inches. USDA studies have demonstrated that bluegrass cut to 1 inch contains 10 times as many weeds as the same grass cut to 2 inches. The longer grass simply shades out the weeds. The best crabgrass control I know of is to feed the lawn in the fall, then keep it cut to 3 inches in the spring until the germination of crabgrass slows down. When crabgrass no longer threatens, you can lower the blade to 2½ inches.

**Watering**  Most lawn grasses flourish best when they are supplied with the equivalent of at least 1 inch of water per week. If this amount does not come consistently from rainfall, and it rarely does, you can supplement it with a sprinkler or automatic irrigation system.

On the subject of irrigation systems, my general rule is the more manual the better. If a built-in system is truly necessary in your particular circumstances, I recommend that you go to a thoroughly reputable local contractor for advice and installation. But even for a large and demanding lawn, I feel that a preferable solution is to install a few quick-coupling valves at strategic locations and move hoses and sprinklers to where they're needed. My reasoning is that each patch of lawn, with its particular sun, shade, and soil conditions, has its own irrigation needs — as do the trees, shrubs, and other plantings in and around the lawn. An automatic system generally over- or underwaters some of the landscape all of the time. Besides, drainage and runoff are problems; and really good materials, fittings, and hardware for lawn systems are hard to find.

The grass is genuinely wilted and in need of a drink when it turns a light blue-green and visible footprints remain after it's been walked on. At this point a deep soaking is in order. You want the soil to be moist 6 or 8 inches down; this can take several hours with the sprinkler.

After the spring burst of growth is over, it's not harmful to let established, well-rooted lawn grasses go into summer dormancy. The leaves will turn dull-colored or brown, but the crowns will stay alive until cooler weather and fall rains bring forth new green growth.

**Feeding**   Most lawns stay healthiest with one or two feedings per year, 1 pound of nitrogen per 1000 square feet per feeding. For all lawns, September to October is the best time to feed; the next best is April. Your garden center can supply you with good fertilizers and directions for application. I use organic fertilizers like manure, cottonseed meal, or Milorganite (dried sewage sludge) myself, but just so there's plenty of nitrogen your lawn won't care where it comes from.

Finally, keep an eye on your soil's pH or acidity (see Soil Testing in the March Landscape Tasks). If you need to spread lime, fall and early spring are best; but if you don't get around to it in fall, you can apply lime at any time in the winter.

## Materials and Construction
# EARTHWORK AND DRAINAGE

In Chapter 4 of Part I, I pointed out the differences between soil for growing plants and soil for supporting structures. There's one respect in which plants and structures share the same need, however. They both

**Drainage at dripline below eaves: instead of a gutter and downspouts, decorative stones have wood edging and the drain pipe is buried underneath.**

require soil that is properly drained. Excess water can suffocate the roots of plants; and when it freezes it will cause the soil and anything constructed on top of it to heave, tip, settle, or crack.

Handling the soil and planning the final configuration of a piece of property so as to provide for satisfactory drainage needn't necessarily be difficult. And yet I find that I run into at least the potential for drainage problems on almost every project in which I'm involved.

The origins of these problems are many. When I am working on rehabilitation of a tired landscape in an older neighborhood, the challenge often boils down to worn-out, badly compacted soil. With a new house, the configuration of the land may have been well enough thought out; but the ravages of excavation, backfilling with poor soil, compaction by heavy machinery, and/or a too-hasty spreading of topsoil have often left an erosive and infertile wasteland.

There are also those instances where land previously considered "marginal" and left undeveloped is now being converted to residential use. Under the pressure of demand for housing in already overpopulated suburbs, house lots are being laid out in former wetlands, on steep slopes, or on top of or adjacent to major masses of bedrock. These sites present a special set of serious problems to contractor, landscape designer, and homeowner alike. Without sophisticated engineering of a kind that's beyond the budget of most developers, many of these lots are just drainage disasters waiting to happen.

So if yours is a new landscape — or an old one ripe for revitalization — you may have drainage on your agenda. Proper drainage is basically a matter of two things: the structure of the soil, and the surface configuration of the land and its pavements.

**Handling the Soil**   Most soils in metropolitan areas have been mapped and identified as to physical characteristics, limitations, and potential uses. Begin by checking with your county cooperative extension or U.S. soil conservation service; they should be able to provide you with soil characteristics for your property.

**The right soil profile for drainage**   The natural "profile" of soil — that is, the positions and thicknesses of its various layers in a natural state — is the ideal you are striving for. The topsoil should be several inches to 1 foot deep, and should be high in humus, fertile, and crumbly or "friable." Below that, the subsoil should be 2 to 3 feet thick and capable of being spaded without superhuman effort. The transition from topsoil to subsoil should be gradual, not abrupt. And the two layers should consist of "compatible" soils: their textures (loamy, sandy, or clayey) should be closely enough related so that water that drains through the topsoil will also be able to percolate through the subsoil.

This profile will allow rainwater to move slowly but steadily down through the upper 3 feet or so of earth, where most growth occurs, before joining the groundwater. And it will keep the groundwater or water table down where it belongs, not too close to the surface.

**The wrong soil profile and how to fix it**   Soil that is too thin or too compacted will let excessive amounts of rainwater run off. A disturbed soil with inadequate organic matter for cohesion may permit percolation at first, but it will rapidly erode and eventually settle into a muddy sump.

The typical new home construction site often combines all these problems. There may be assorted excavations that have been backfilled with construction debris; a layer of subsoil from the basement excavation, now bulldozed over the surface of the landscape; an extremely thin coating of old topsoil right around the house; or possibly some imported topsoil (which may or may not be compatible with the site's subsoil) spread just barely thick enough to support newly seeded grass or a carpet of newly laid sod. And the machines that have accomplished all this will probably have packed the subsoil to a degree where a shovel thrust into the ground meets rocklike resistance 3 inches down.

Certainly not an ideal situation. But time and natural forces will be on your side, and you can do a lot to help. Nature's biggest contribution is the annual series of freeze-thaw cycles, which heave, shatter, ventilate, and loosen compacted soil. Your contribution is to add organic matter — peat moss or compost, at least 3 inches thick before you fork it in — and to fertilize, cultivate, and irrigate where necessary. The purpose of all this is to make it possible to develop a lively community of plant growth. That done, the roots and leaves of the plants will aerate and add compost to the soil mix — and a better-draining profile will result.

You still may find that you have to add topsoil. If so, remember that when soils are excavated they get shaken up and loosened, and their volume increases by almost 25 percent. But once installed, they settle down to their original volume. So order at least 25 percent more cubic footage than you need for the area to be covered.

When adding topsoil, be sure to scratch up the surface of the subsoil so that the two soils will blend somewhat where they meet. This will avert what's known as an "interface" problem, where roots encounter a dramatically alien subsoil and react by stopping dead, just as though they'd met the inside of a pot or container.

For the same reason, if you are replacing topsoil in a pit that was dug for a new plant, backfill the pit with the same soil that was taken out of it (after enriching it with manure and peat moss or compost), rather than dumping in topsoil from a different source.

**Surface Configurations**   Well-constructed and -cultivated soil will permit maximum percolation of rainwater into the subsoil. For the excess water that just won't percolate even in the best of soil, the surface configuration of the land is critical. Practically every surface should have some degree of slope or pitch, however minute, so that it will shed rainwater and allow you to channel it where you want it. That is, away from buildings, off patios, to the edges of grassy lawn areas, across walks, and off driveways.

**Water table maintenance**   One of the goals of good drainage is to keep the soil's water table, or level of groundwater, as stable as possible and at the level to which existing plants and structures are adjusted. In many urban and suburban situations a low water table is a problem. (Large quantities of pavement direct rainfall right into storm drains — and from there into rivers and the sea. The groundwater and the overall structure and quality of the soil suffer as a result.) So avoid funneling all rainwater off your property. Try to find some spot where you can allow water to collect and leach back into the soil. This could be a drywell or "French drain" (a pit filled with gravel); an out-of-the-way corner of a lawn; or a dip in a gravel drive or cobbled walk.

Or you may have the opposite problem, a water table that's elevated seasonally (or permanently) to the point where it will drown the roots of trees or shrubs in your yard. You can handle this in two ways, as

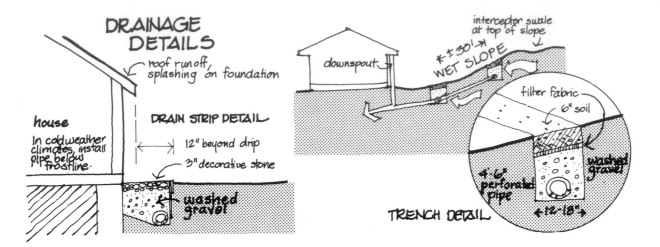

DRAINAGE DETAILS

roof runoff, splashing on foundation

house

In cold weather climates, install pipe below frostline.

DRAIN STRIP DETAIL

12" beyond drip

3" decorative stone

washed gravel

downspout

interceptor saddle at top of slope

± 30'

WET SLOPE

filter fabric

6" soil

4-6" perforated pipe

washed gravel

12-18"

TRENCH DETAIL

**Some ways of handling typical drainage problems right around the house.**

shown in the diagrams here: install drain tile to lower the groundwater, or build raised beds to keep the roots of your plants above the water table.

**Slopes for landscape surfaces** There are some well-established guidelines for the best angles of slope for different kinds of landscape space. These angles are expressed as ratios of rise to distance. An example: a slope that rises 1 foot over a distance of 4 feet is called a 1:4 ("one to four") or 25 percent slope.

Slopes from 10 to 100 percent are normally referred to in terms of ratios, rather than percentages. Slopes from 1 to 10 percent — the most minimal, gentle slopes — are usually expressed in percentages. For instance, a walk that rises 5 feet over a distance of 100 feet has a 5 percent slope.

### Slope Ratios and Percentages

| Ratio | Percentage |
|-------|------------|
| 1:1 | 100 |
| 1:2 | 50 |
| 1:3 | 33 |
| 1:4 | 25 |
| 1:5 | 20 |
| 1:10 | 10 |

The following table, showing the minimum, maximum, and optimum slope angles for landscape surfaces, should come in handy if you're in the position of grading your property (or part of it) from scratch. In that case you may well be able to build in the best possible surface drainage. But if that is not your situation, these figures may offer some helpful clues to the causes of unsatisfactory drainage. Often, correcting a drainage problem is a matter of making only a small adjustment.

Making adjustments in grade can, of course, give rise to a common dilemma: what will the grade change do to an existing tree in its path? If the change is more than a couple of inches, the effects on many trees could be fatal. An established root system is where it is because it gets just the right amounts of water, oxygen, and nutrients from its par-

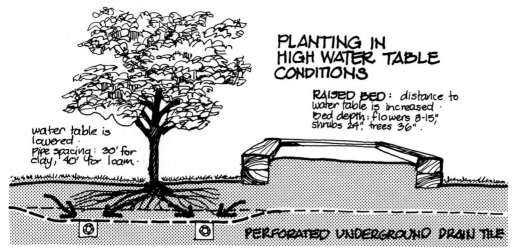

## PLANTING IN HIGH WATER TABLE CONDITIONS

RAISED BED: distance to water table is increased. bed depth: flowers 8-15", shrubs 24", trees 36".

water table is lowered. pipe spacing: 30' for clay, 40' for loam.

PERFORATED UNDERGROUND DRAIN TILE

In places where water accumulates or where the water table is too high, you can install drainage tiles or raise the planting beds.

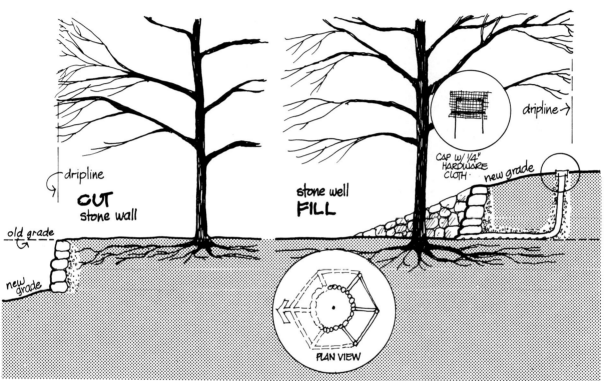

dripline

CUT
stone wall

old grade

new grade

stone well
FILL

CAP w/ 1/4" HARDWARE CLOTH.

dripline →

new grade

PLAN VIEW

ticular type and depth of soil. Add to — or subtract from — the grade level and you'll alter this whole picture. Not to mention the fact that a quick way to kill any established tree is to pile soil up around, or scrape it away from, the base of its trunk.

Whether filling or cutting away grade around an established tree, the dripline of the tree is a critical dimension. The detail shows a plan view of ventilation pipes if the tree is surrounded by fill on all sides.

## Slopes for Landscape Surfaces

| Type of surface | Maximum | Minimum | Optimum |
|---|---|---|---|
| Lawns/grass areas | 1:4 | 1% | 1½% to 10% |
| Berms/mounds | 2% | .5% | 1% |
| Mowed slopes | 1:4 | — | 1:5 |
| Planted slopes | 10% | .5% | 3% to 5% |
| Unmowed banks | Angle of repose | — | 1:4 |

The solution is to make for the plant an island of the same grade it has been used to: a pit or platform of soil, as shown on page 151. This will probably require some retaining structure to support the terrace of higher ground around the tree (if you've lowered the grade) or the higher surrounding level below which the tree's roots are established (if you've raised it). Again, this need not be an expensive or difficult piece of construction, but it is a necessary one if you want to maintain the health of that heirloom tree.

**Cascading sprays of Japanese andromeda (pieris) blossoms delight the eye in April.**

## Plants by Design
# APRIL BLOOMERS

### Trees
Norway maple (*Acer platanoides*)
Red maple (*Acer rubrum*)
Birches (*Betula* spp.)
Cornelian cherry dogwood (*Cornus mas*)
Magnolias (*Magnolia* spp.)
Sargent cherry (*Prunus sargentii*)
Higan cherry (*Prunus subhirtella*)
Yoshino cherry (*Prunus yedoensis*)

### Shrubs
Korean white forsythia (*Abeliophyllum distichum*)
Shadblow, juneberry, or serviceberry (*Amelanchier* spp.)

Littleleaf box (*Buxus microphylla*)
Forsythias (*Forsythia* spp.)
Winter honeysuckle (*Lonicera fragrantissima*)
Mountain andromeda or pieris (*Pieris floribunda*)
Japanese andromeda or pieris (*Pieris japonica*)
Korean azalea (*Rhododendron mucronulatum*)
Bridal-wreath spirea (*Spiraea prunifolia*)

### Ground Cover
Vinca, periwinkle, or myrtle (*Vinca minor*)

Detailed information and recommended varieties can be found in Part III.

**Forsythia's sunny yellow gives a sense of warmth on a brisk spring day. Pruning back shoots after flowering will improve the form of this particular hedge.**

# LANDSCAPE TASKS FOR APRIL

**Lawn Care**  April is one of the best times to start a new lawn from seed (see September Landscape Tasks); and if your lawn is ready for seeding now, it's all to the good.

This is also a good month to feed an established lawn with a high-nitrogen fertilizer, both to encourage it as it revives from winter dormancy and to fortify it for the summer ahead (see September Landscape Tasks).

**Vine Pruning**  Prune vines growing on trellises or against the house. With vines around the house, inspect them carefully to make sure they're not invading window frames or working their way under gutters or shingles. Vines will bounce back from fairly heavy cutting, so don't be shy.

**Lily Planting**  April is the month to set out lily-of-the-valley pips, water-lily bulbs, and daylily (*Hemerocallis*) plants.

**Spring Planting Tips**  Fall (see September) is a fine time to plant many trees and shrubs; but if your plant list includes any of the following, get them into the ground now:

Red maple (*Acer rubrum*)
Birch (*Betula* spp.)
Dogwood (*Cornus* spp.)
Cotoneaster (*Cotoneaster* spp.)
Hawthorn (*Crataegus* spp.)
European beech (*Fagus sylvatica*)
English ivy (*Hedera helix*)
Rose-of-Sharon (*Hibiscus syriacus*)
Mountain laurel (*Kalmia latifolia*)

Sweet gum (*Liquidambar styraciflua*)
Tulip tree (*Liriodendron tulipifera*)
Magnolias (*Magnolia* spp.)
Andromeda or pieris (*Pieris* spp.)
Rugosa rose (*Rosa rugosa*)
Azalea and rhododendron (*Rhododendron* spp.)
Yew (*Taxus* spp.)

Many nurseries do manage to install these plants in the fall — very carefully — with considerable success. Many others, however, attempt it only with some rate of failure. In my experience it is best to stay with spring planting of these species.

**Heeling in: a temporary measure for holding bareroot plants if circumstances prevent immediate planting.**

## HEELING IN

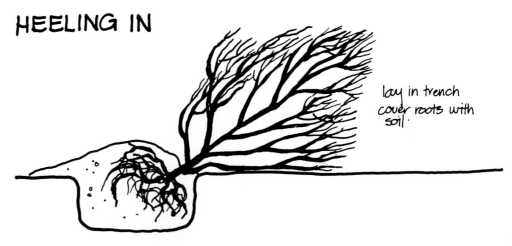

lay in trench
cover roots with
soil.

You can find the main rundown of planting procedures in the September Landscape Tasks section. But there are a few special points about spring planting that I'd like to make here.

First, although the soil doesn't have to be warm, it must be workable. It should crumble readily in your hand. Never plant in mud.

Second, if you are planting or transplanting bareroot, it's vital that you prevent the roots from drying out. At this season there can be interruptions before you can get a plant in the ground — sudden snowstorms, frozen or waterlogged soil, and so on. If there's going to be a substantial wait, dig a trench and heel the plant(s) in. That is, lay the roots into the trench so that the stem emerges at an angle to the ground, cover the roots with soil, and water well. For a shorter wait, such as overnight, some gardeners stir up a slurry of soil and water and set the roots in it. My preference is simply to cover the roots with moistened spaghnum moss or burlap and keep the plants out of the sun.

Finally, don't forget your plants once they're in place. If the spring season is dry, water faithfully.

# MAY

**Fragrance and the hum of honeybees fill the air along this pathway through a flowering crabapple grove.**

687

With the beauty of flowering plants, fresh green foliage unfolding everywhere, and the sounds and scents of spring, May beckons you outdoors to enjoy the landscape. And the long days combined with temperate weather make this also an ideal month to go outdoors and build things. This month I'll focus on some of the loveliest elements of the landscape: fragrant plants; deciduous shrubs (many of them flowering); and wood as a material for structures like decks and trellises to ease and enhance your hours outdoors.

## Landscaping Opportunities
# THE FRAGRANT GARDEN

Perhaps more than any other single sensory quality, the fragrance of a place leaves an indelible impression in the mind. If you think for a minute about your memories of places, you'll realize that all memories involve smells. "Scents more than sounds or sights make the heartstrings crack," said Rudyard Kipling; and it's true that a scent can call up instantly a complex of memories and emotions.

When you are on vacation or visiting a new spot, you're especially open and awake to your surroundings; and some of your liveliest scent-associations come from these moments. It takes no more than the mingled smells of snow and conifers to lift a mountain lover's spirits. As for me, the scent of Hall's honeysuckle always takes me back to a friend's swimming pool in the Massachusetts woods: in summer the air is filled with sweetness from the honeysuckle vines that curtain the fence around the pool area. I also remember with pleasure the fragrance of silver lindens in the Brooklyn Botanic Garden; the redolence of boxwood in the sun at Mount Vernon; and the heady scent of rugosa roses along the Nantucket shoreline.

But fragrances and their happy associations belong in your workaday life as well. Every house has its own characteristic, unmistakable smell; so should every garden. With a little planning, you can enhance the beauty and the personality of your place through fragrance.

Fragrant sweet alyssum is planted in front of a bed of thyme and sage.

**Planning a Fragrant Landscape**   The ancient Greeks cultivated their best-smelling plants near their windows, and medieval monasteries had beds of fragrant herbs near their infirmaries to soothe and to cure the ill. Essentially, you want to put the fragrant plants within close range of the places where people live, work, and play — maybe even within touching distance. Here are some examples to start you off:

**Doors**   Try putting near doorways plants that will give off scent when people brush their foliage in passing. These could be permanent plantings, or movable. In summer, for instance, I always crowd our back door with large pots of rosemary.

**Windows** to the south and/or west, where summer breezes will draw through, are wonderful locations for sweet-smelling flowering plants. Ground-floor windows are easy; for second-floor windows use tall shrubs (like mock-orange, elaeagnus, or lilac) or small trees (like crabapple, magnolia, or linden).

**Fragrant perennial herbs**   If you grow these herbs near where you walk or sit outdoors, their aromas are released when you touch them or crush their foliage. Put low-growing thyme among stepping stones;

mint (with a good deep edging to contain it) in a shady spot; lavender in a protected corner. By the way, chives among your roses are handsome in bloom, handy for cooking, and repellent to the roses' insect pests.

**Vines**  Honeysuckle or wisteria or other vines can be trained over arbors or on fences, or on supports around windows or entryways.

**Massed shrubs** yield a bonus of fragrance by virtue of sheer strength of numbers. Consider borders or screens of fragrant flowering shrubs like summer-sweet, lilac, mock-orange, honeysuckle, or viburnum.

**Lilacs, age-old favorites, evoke nostalgia as they saturate the air with delightful scent.**

**Trees**  Crabapples, magnolias, or lindens planted in clusters (a minimum of three) are extra-splendid if you can prune their lower branches to allow you to walk or sit under them. They make a bower of bloom that is a feast for the senses, delightfully fragrant and delightful to look at as well.

**Evening fragrance** adds enchantment to the spring and summer landscape. Plants that continue to perfume the air even in darkness are good choices for areas where you'll be sitting outdoors after sundown, or for south-facing windows that stay open at night. There are many trees and shrubs in this category, and some particularly attractive ones are marked with asterisks in the plant list that follows.

As you select fragrant plants, keep in mind the successive seasons for bloom, and try for a plant or two to highlight each one. Coming with the first thawing of the earth in late winter, witch hazels' blossoms are harbingers of the general reawakening. Magnolias, crabapples, fothergilla, viburnum, and early honeysuckle drench the spring air with fragrance; bulbs like hyacinths and narcissus do their part as well. Lilacs, native and hybrid azaleas, mock-orange, fringe tree, and later honeysuckles usher in the summer. Roses are a world of fragrance unto themselves. Then come lindens and summer-sweet. In fall there's the fragrant foliage of bayberry and sweet fern; and the autumnal blossoms of native witch hazel are the year's last hurrah.

Rugosa or saltspray rose is one of the sweetest-smelling roses and a wonderful shrub for many settings.

## Fragrant Plants

Orange-eye butterfly bush (*Buddleia davidii*)
Boxwood (*Buxus* spp.)
*White fringe tree (*Chionanthus virginicus*)
Summer-sweet clethra (*Clethra alnifolia*)
Sweet fern (*Comptonia peregrina*)
Chinese witch hazel (*Hamamelis mollis*)
Common witch hazel (*Hamamelis virginiana*)
*Regel privet (*Ligustrum obtusifolium regelianum*)
Winter honeysuckle (*Lonicera fragrantissima*)
*Hall's honeysuckle (*Lonicera japonica* 'Halliana')
Magnolia (*Magnolia* spp.)
*Crabapple (*Malus* spp.)

Bayberry (*Myrica pensylvanica*)
Mock-orange (*Philadelphus virginalis*)
*Rose-shell azalea, or early or honeysuckle azalea (*Rhododendron roseum*)
Pinxterbloom or pinxter azalea (*Rhododendron nudiflorum*)
Swamp azalea (*Rhododendron viscosum*)
Azalea and rhododendron hybrids (*Rhododendron* spp.)
Roses (*Rosa* spp.)
Sassafras (*Sassafras albidum*)
*Persian lilac (*Syringa persica*)
Common lilac (*Syringa vulgaris*)
*Lindens (*Tilia* spp.)
Korean spice viburnum (*Viburnum carlesii*)
*Japanese wisteria (*Wisteria floribunda*)

*indicates plants fragrant after dark.
Detailed information and recommended varieties can be found in Part III.

## Plants for a Purpose
# DECIDUOUS SHRUBS FOR SEASONAL DISPLAY

This month, deciduous ornamental shrubs are in their glory. Azaleas, lilacs, viburnums, spireas — they flower in a rainbow of colors and a bright bouquet of fragrances.

Yet flowers are not all that this vast and varied group of plants has to offer. Of all landscape plants, to my mind, deciduous shrubs give you the most for the least. Among them you can find plants that are gorgeous in spring or summer bloom or fall foliage color; plants adapted to every conceivable kind of growing condition, soil, or exposure; plants that resist every pest or disease known to horticulture; plants that grow fast (or slow); plants you can propagate easily without a greenhouse; and even plants that are comparatively cheap.

The sizes, forms, and textures of deciduous shrubs are wonderfully various. As a result, you can use them in many different ways in the landscape. Grow them singly or massed; up close or at a distance; neatly clipped or running wild; as borders, hedges, specimens, or background planting. The individual descriptions in Part III suggest uses for each shrub.

Always think about the nature of a shrub as you decide where and how to use it. Consider not only its likes and dislikes as to soil, sun, moisture, and so on, but its natural ultimate size. All too often an appealing nursery-size plant grows rapidly into a monster 12 to 18 feet tall and equally broad. A shrub like that is not a wise choice for a spot next to a walk or up against a foundation, where it will have to be repressed mercilessly on an annual basis.

If yours is a small property, do investigate small or slow-growing varieties of the shrubs that appeal to you. Breeders are constantly developing new selections with smaller gardens in mind. Some of the plants listed below are naturally small. Others have dwarf cultivars mentioned

Korean white forsythia, not a true forsythia, deserves wider use. Sprays of April blossoms add a dash of white, nice in companionship with its yellow-flowering namesake.

here or elsewhere in this book. Many others, however, are available in dwarf forms if you ask around.

This list of deciduous ornamental shrubs represents a careful culling of my own favorites. There are many, many additional plants that could have been included if I'd had a whole book to devote to the subject. The ones selected here, however, should give you a fine palette of possibilities to meet almost any landscaping need. *Please note* that the size ranges suggested are very variable, according to growing conditions; they're intended only as the most general guide.

**Redvein enkianthus: spring flowers (here topped with late-season snow) and fall foliage color are among many assets of this upright shrub or small tree.**

## Deciduous Ornamental Shrubs

### Small Shrubs (up to 5 feet mature height, approximately)

Korean white forsythia
 (*Abeliophyllum distichum*)

AZALEAS

Korean azalea (*Rhododendron mucronulatum*)

Pinxterbloom or pinxter azalea (*Rhododendron nudiflorum*)

Japanese barberry (*Berberis thunbergii*)

Sweet fern (*Comptonia peregrina*)

Dwarf red-osier dogwood (*Cornus sericea* 'Kelseyi')

Yellow-twig red-osier dogwood (*Cornus sericea* 'Flaviramea')

Cranberry cotoneaster (*Cotoneaster apiculatus*)

Skogsholmen bearberry cotoneaster (*Cotoneaster dammeri* 'Skogsholmen')

Dwarf winged euonymus (*Euonymus alata* 'Compacta')

Bronx forsythia (*Forsythia viridissima* 'Bronxensis')

Dwarf fothergilla or witch alder (*Fothergilla gardenii*)

Annabelle hydrangea (*Hydrangea arborescens* 'Annabelle')

Kerria (*Kerria japonica* 'Pleniflora')

Regel privet (*Ligustrum obtusifolium regelianum*)

Bush or shrubby cinquefoil (*Potentilla fruticosa*)

Fragrant sumac (*Rhus aromatica*)

Rugosa rose (*Rosa rugosa*)

Virginia rose (*Rosa virginiana*)

Anthony Waterer spirea (*Spiraea bumalda* 'Anthony Waterer')

Daphne spirea (*Spiraea japonica* 'Alpina')

Snowmound Nippon spirea (*Spiraea nipponica* 'Snowmound')

Crispa cutleaf stephanandra (*Stephanandra incisa* 'Crispa')

Chenault coralberry (*Symphoricarpos chenaultii*)

Coralberry or Indian currant (*Symphoricarpos orbiculatus*)

Dwarf Korean lilac (*Syringa palibiniana*)

Dwarf European cranberrybush (*Viburnum opulus* 'Nanum')

Yellowroot (*Xanthorhiza simplicissima*)

### Medium-Size Shrubs (5 to 10 feet mature height, approximately)

Red chokeberry (*Aronia arbutifolia*)

AZALEAS

Flame azalea (*Rhododendron calendulaceum*)

Exbury hybrid azaleas (*Rhododendron* 'Exbury Hybrids')

Ghent azaleas (*Rhododendron gandavense*)

Jane Abbott hybrid azaleas (*Rhododendron* 'Jane Abbott Hybrids')

Rose-shell, early or honeysuckle azalea (*Rhododendron roseum*)

Royal azalea (*Rhododendron schlippenbachii*)

Pink-shell azalea (*Rhododendron vaseyi*)

Swamp azalea (*Rhododendron viscosum*)

Buttonbush (*Cephalanthus occidentalis*)

Flowering quince (*Chaenomeles speciosa*)

Summer-sweet clethra (*Clethra alnifolia*)

Siberian dogwood (*Cornus alba* 'Sibirica')

Red-osier dogwood (*Cornus sericea*)

Showy border forsythia (*Forsythia intermedia* 'Spectabilis')

Siebold weeping forsythia (*Forsythia suspensa sieboldii*)

Large fothergilla or witch alder (*Fothergilla major*)

Vernal witch hazel (*Hamamelis vernalis*)

Winterberry (*Ilex verticillata*)

Winter honeysuckle (*Lonicera fragrantissima*)

Tatarian honeysuckle (*Lonicera tatarica*)

Bayberry (*Myrica pensylvanica*)

Virginal mock-orange (*Philadelphus virginalis*)

Beach plum (*Prunus maritima*)

Meadow rose (*Rosa blanda*)

Father Hugo rose (*Rosa hugonis*)

Elderberry or American elder (*Sambucus canadensis*)

Bridal-wreath spirea (*Spiraea prunifolia*)

Vanhoutte spirea (*Spiraea vanhouttei*)

Persian lilac (*Syringa persica*)

Potanin or daphne lilac (*Syringa potaninii*)

Late lilac (*Syringa villosa*)

Highbush blueberry (*Vaccinium corymbosum*)

Burkwood viburnum (*Viburnum burkwoodii*)

Korean spice viburnum (*Viburnum carlesii*)

Linden viburnum (*Viburnum dilatatum*)

European snowball viburnum or guelder-rose (*Viburnum opulus* 'Roseum')

Doublefile viburnum (*Viburnum plicatum tomentosum*)

### Large Shrubs (over 10 feet mature height, approximately)

Orange-eye butterfly bush (*Buddleia davidii*)

Cornelian cherry dogwood (*Cornus mas*)

Gray dogwood (*Cornus racemosa*)

Fragrant winter hazel (*Corylopsis glabrescens*)

Autumn olive (*Elaeagnus umbellata*)

Redvein enkianthus (*Enkianthus campanulatus*)

Winged euonymus (*Euonymus alata*)

Chinese witch hazel (*Hamamelis mollis*)

Common witch hazel (*Hamamelis virginiana*)

Rose-of-Sharon or shrub althea (*Hibiscus syriacus*)

Peegee hydrangea (*Hydrangea paniculata* 'Grandiflora')

Spicebush (*Lindera benzoin*)

Amur honeysuckle (*Lonicera maackii*)

Shining sumac (*Rhus copallina*)

Goat willow or French pussy willow (*Salix caprea*)

Chinese lilac (*Syringa chinensis*)

Common lilac (*Syringa vulgaris*)

Arrowwood (*Viburnum dentatum*)

European cranberrybush (*Viburnum opulus*)

Black haw (*Viburnum prunifolium*)

Siebold viburnum (*Viburnum sieboldii*)

American cranberrybush or highbush cranberry (*Viburnum trilobum*)

Detailed information and recommended varieties can be found in Part III.

**A May-blooming variety of spirea, an old-fashioned and well-loved flowering shrub.**

## Materials and Construction
# WOOD

Everyone feels at home with wood. From the soft and silvery touch of a weathered shingle, to the warm glow of a hardwood floor, to the comfortable creak of an old rocking chair, the qualities of wood are part of our American experience.

Beyond its familiarity and sensory appeal, wood is a practical and popular choice for a multitude of landscaping uses. It is versatile, workable, relatively economical, and available almost everywhere. You can make anything with wood: decks, steps, or bridges; fences, railings, trellises, or shelters; planters, light standards, edging, or garden furniture.

The more you know about wood — as with any material — the better able you will be to choose and use wood properly. And that's important, because with proper selection and construction, wood will provide years of trouble-free use and pleasure. Used incorrectly — years of trouble. Let's look at wood from three vantages: wood as a raw material, wood as a commercial product, and wood as it enters into design and construction.

**Wood in the Raw**   All wood is divided into two categories: "hardwood" and "softwood." Hardwood comes from deciduous trees, softwood from coniferous trees. Many hardwoods are in fact very soft (such as basswood or balsa); and many softwoods are among the hardest available woods (such as yellow pine or Douglas fir). Whether hardwood or softwood, all woods consist of hollow cellulose tubes (about 70 percent) and of lignin, the adhesive that gives wood its strength or rigidity (about 30 percent).

Hardwoods are rarely used for landscape construction. They are tough to work with; besides that, they tend to split, check, and/or discolor, and they will rot faster outdoors than softwoods will, because of their lower levels of natural preservatives (oils and resins). The exceptions are isolated species such as teak or black locust; and railroad ties, usually made of oak treated with creosote as a preservative.

**Wood for outdoor use comes in a wide range of colors, textures, grains, and hardnesses. Here, left to right, are cedar, fir, and redwood.**

## Softwood Types

| Wood | Hardness/softness | Strength | Workability | Weathering capability and rot resistance | Availability | Cost |
|------|-------------------|----------|-------------|-------------------------------------------|--------------|------|
| Cedars (northern white, western red) | soft; low density | weakest | easy to work but won't hold nails well; paintable | rot resistant; weathers to silver gray | readily available as stringers and fencing | moderately expensive |
| Cypress | tough; medium density | strong | holds paint well | rot resistant; weathers to black, then gray | hard to find | expensive |
| Douglas fir (includes Sitka spruce, Engelmann spruce, white fir, etc.) | moderately hard; dense | strong | does not hold paint well; difficult to work; splinters | moderate resistance to rotting (requires preserving and stain) | available as timbers for structure | moderately expensive |
| Pine (southern yellow) | hard; dense | strongest | shrinks and warps; does not hold paint well, but does stain well; hard to work | treated for resistance to decay; requires stain | widely available | least expensive |
| Redwood | moderately dense | strong | most versatile; easy to work, paint, and stain | rot resistant; weathers to uniform gray | hard to find in all grades | expensive |

The softwoods used in outdoor construction are generally cedar, cypress, Douglas fir, southern yellow pine, and redwood. This table gives a condensed breakdown of these woods' salient natural characteristics, their assets and liabilities, and their relative availability and cost.

**Wood in the Lumber Yard**   When you begin looking for wood for your project, find out first what is conveniently available. Be as flexible as you can as to type of wood, grain, grade, and dimensions of boards, and you'll give yourself a wider selection to choose from. Don't be shy about telling your supplier what you are planning to do and asking for his advice. There are often two or three different (and differently priced) solutions to a given problem. Pick the one that makes sense for you.

Do, however, always use seasoned wood. "Green" wood, being about 50 percent water, is weaker, more likely to warp, and more apt to rot. Seasoned wood is 2½ times stronger. Air-dried wood has a moisture content of 15 percent, which is ideal for outside construction as this is the equilibrium moisture content that is reached naturally out of doors. Kiln-dried wood has the lowest moisture content of all, 7 to 10 percent, and is best used for interior woodwork only. If you do use it for outdoor work, make sure it is well fastened; when it absorbs moisture to attain that 15 percent equilibrium level, it will probably warp.

**Standard dimensions** are traditionally cited in even inches. As you know if you've ever built anything, however, boards' nominal sizes are not their actual measurements but their measurements before the shrinkage that comes with drying. The table here shows how shrinkage affects measurements; to take an example, a "1 by 8 inch" board is actually ¾ inch by 7¼ inches.

In the lumber business, "boards" are anything under 2 inches thick; "lumber," 2 to 5 inches thick; and "timber," 5 or more inches thick. Standard sizes of boards, lumber, and timber are listed below. Be warned, however, that not all sizes are always available at every lumberyard.

## Lumber Dimensions

| Nominal | Actual |
|---|---|
| 1 inch | ¾ inch |
| 2 | 1½ |
| 4 | 3½ |
| 6 | 5½ |
| 8 | 7¼ |
| 10 | 9¼ |
| 12 | 11¼ |

## Standard Dimensions

| | Thickness | Width | All available in these lengths |
|---|---|---|---|
| Boards: | 1 inch | 2, 3, 4, 5, 6, 8, 10, 12 inches | 8 feet |
| Lumber: | 2 inches | 2, 3, 4, 6, 8, 10, 12 inches | 10 feet |
| | 4 inches | 4, 6, 8, 10, 12 inches | 12 feet |
| Timber: | 6 inches | 6, 8 inches | 14 feet |
| | 8 inches | 8 inches | 16 feet |
| | | | 18 feet |
| | | | 20 feet |

**Grain** means the visible pattern on the surfaces of a board, created by the exposure of the tree's growth rings when the saw cuts through the trunk. The most common method of making logs into wood is "plainsawing," where the log is simply sliced into parallel boards from end to end. As the diagram on page 168 suggests, this procedure results in boards whose grains vary from "vertical grain" (or "edge grain") to "flat grain." An older method of sawing logs was "quarter sawing," where the log was sliced so as to produce all vertical-grained boards. You can see from the diagram on page 168 that quarter sawing generates a lot of waste wood and therefore is expensive — and seldom used today for construction lumber. (It is still used with fine hardwoods for furniture, cabinetry, boatbuilding, or other specialized applications.)

The reason for quarter sawing, however, remains valid: vertical-grained boards are subject to minimal distortion, and distortion can be a major hazard in construction projects. Cupping, shrinkage, or diamonding of boards all result from the grain of the boards involved.

The lesson to be learned here is the importance of checking the end graining of all wood you select — provided, of course, that the lumberyard will let you. Choose vertical-grained boards if you can; if you can't, at least be conscious of the grain in each board so that you can position it properly once you start building. Always put the bark side downward when building anything outdoors.

**Grades** are designations of levels of quality in seasoned softwoods — softwoods other than redwood, that is, which has its own grading system (page 169). Essentially, the top grade is all "clear" (no knotholes), vertical-grained, blemish-free stock. The lowest grade may have holes, bark, or other scars or blemishes, and will be suitable only for the roughest uses (crates, pallets, etc.).

My personal choice for landscape construction is common number 1 or 2, whose defects are not particularly noticeable outdoors. Number 3 is fine for rustic effects.

# WOOD GRAIN

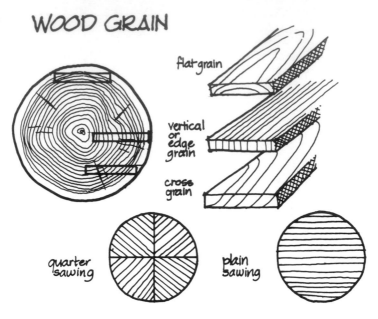

flat grain

vertical or edge grain

cross grain

quarter sawing

plain sawing

Redwood, usually my first choice for outdoor construction, has its own separate system of grades. Redwood suppliers recommend that heartwood Grade D or sapwood Grades D and E be used outdoors; they refer to these as the "garden grades." You may find, however, that Grade D heartwood, "construction heart," contains too great a mixture of heartwood and sapwood and is too streaky to give you the advantages you seek when you use redwood — namely, even color, consistent weathering, and uniform resistance to rot. Grade C "select" all heart is preferable for finish surfaces and for surfaces exposed to dampness.

## Lumber Grades

SELECT: Good appearance for finish; no or small knots

| | | |
|---|---|---|
| Grade A | (best) — clear | } suitable for natural |
| Grade B | (or "B and better") — blemish-free | finishes |
| Grade C | small defects | } suitable for paint |
| Grade D | (utility) — knots under ½ inch | finishes |

COMMON

| | | |
|---|---|---|
| No. 1 | sound knots | |
| No. 2 | loose knots | } little waste |
| No. 3 | larger knots, bark edges | |
| No. 4 } No. 5 } | poorest | considerable waste |

**Preservatives** are necessary with some woods whose own natural rot resistance isn't adequate for the job they are being asked to do. Every wood preservative is either petroleum based (these include creosote and pentachlorophenol, known as "penta") or water based (compounds of copper, zinc, arsenic, chrome, or chloride). There are any number of different brands and processes utilizing these two families of preservatives, and your lumber supplier should be able to give you informative literature on the particular product and process you are considering.

Do be sure, if you buy preservative-treated wood, that it is pressure treated rather than surface treated. Surface-treated wood has merely been dipped or painted with preservative, which affords at best only the most temporary protection against decay. Surface treatment will weather away; it is useless wherever the wood is in contact with soil, and it's equally useless above ground wherever the wood is not also stained or painted.

Pressure treatment, on the other hand, comes in two degrees, depending on your requirements. For applications above ground, preservative is pressure-pumped into the microscopic interstices between the cells of the wood. For below ground, the cells themselves are permeated with the preservative solution.

A few words of caution if you are working with preservative-treated wood. First, do not use wood treated with a petroleum-based compound for any construction that will come in contact with human skin: these compounds burn (and they also smell, particularly when heated by the sun). This goes for benches, decks, garden furniture of all kinds. Petroleum-based preservatives work well, however, for fences, sills, underpinnings, and stringers.

Second, be aware that cutting or drilling will violate the pressure-treated member by exposing untreated inner portions to air and water and therefore rot. If you do have to cut into treated wood, apply to the cut or drilled surfaces a liberal dose of whatever liquid preservative your supplier recommends. And remember to wear gloves and to avoid breathing in the sawdust. You may want to use a disposable dust mask. Some of the preservative solutions are definitely toxic.

**Designing and Building with Wood**  I've already touched on the important elements in your decisions about what kinds of wood to use: availability and common sense. For special situations where dimensional precision and finished appearance are critical, such as a trellis over a formal patio, the better grades of the best available woods will give you the most satisfactory results. Conversely, the "utility" grades aren't really suitable for much but the roughest or temporary construction work.

For most outdoor construction, redwood is my first choice. It is easy to work with; it lasts practically forever with little care; it always looks attractive, both new and weathered. It is, however, expensive. You can often find an economical alternative in a fir or pressure-treated pine; but bear in mind that both of these woods have to be stained rather than painted. If painting is essential in your situation, you should use cypress or, once again, redwood. It's ironic that the same woods that do best when left to weather naturally are also the ones that take paint the best.

Many of the same elementary rules that apply to landscape design in general also apply to designing with wood. Proper scale, simplicity, and compatibility with existing structures all are important.

**Redwood Grades**

| All Heartwood | Containing Sapwood |
|---|---|
| Grade A  (clear, all heart, vertical grain) | Grade A  (clear, vertical grain) |
| B  (clear, all heart) | B  (clear) |
| C  (select, all heart) | C  (select) |
| D  (construction heart)* | D  (construction)* |
| | E  (merchantable)* |

*Grades suitable for landscape construction, known as "garden grades."

**All-important in wood construction: strong joints where wood members meet.**

**A wood deck set on the ground needs a well-drained base.**

**Wood building tips** All the rules for outdoor wood construction share one overriding goal: to keep water out. Any piece of wood that contains or absorbs more than 20 percent moisture will rot sooner or later. Do whatever you can to prevent moisture from coming or staying in contact with wood.

Take special care at joints; use flashing or tarpaper, and don't leave endgrains exposed (they act as wicks for water).

The hardware for outdoor joining and fastening work should always be galvanized or an aluminum alloy. Any metal that will oxidize (rust) will rot the wood directly around it. Rot will allow the fastener to loosen and eventually pull out, and that's the end of that joint.

Avoid putting wood into direct contact with soil. Use concrete footings, beds of stones, or a sand base, if possible.

Ventilate. Space joints instead of butting them; leave an air space wherever a structure meets another structure; use washers with bolts, and so on.

Avoid concave warping of horizontal boards (which will trap water) by laying the boards with the convex side of the grain (the bark side) down. This way, if the boards do warp they will tend to shed rather than accumulate water.

And finally, use standard lumber sizes. It's far easier and cheaper to tailor your construction project to available lengths and widths of lumber than the other way around.

I enjoy working with wood — the activity itself, as well as the finished products. Wood is a very forgiving material. Whatever you build, however, don't be tempted to try shortcuts or substitute inferior types or grades of wood. Stick to approved materials and methods and your wood construction will be a source of lasting pleasure.

In bloom in May are spirea (above left) and pink flowering dogwood (above right).

## Plants by Design
# MAY BLOOMERS

### Early May

Sugar maple (*Acer saccharum*)

Flowering quince (*Chaenomeles speciosa*)

Saucer magnolia (*Magnolia soulangiana*)

Japanese flowering crabapple (*Malus floribunda*)

Tea crabapple (*Malus hupehensis*)

Zumi crabapple (*Malus zumi calocarpa*)

Beach plum (*Prunus maritima*)

Oriental cherry (*Prunus serrulata*)

Callery pear (*Pyrus calleryana*)

### Mid-May

Horse chestnut (*Aesculus hippocastanum*)

Redbud (*Cercis canadensis*)

Flowering dogwood (*Cornus florida*)

Redvein enkianthus (*Enkianthus campanulatus*)

Large fothergilla (*Fothergilla major*)

Kerria (*Kerria japonica* 'Pleniflora')

Sargent crabapple (*Malus sargentii*)

Carolina rhododendron (*Rhododendron carolinianum*)

Royal azalea (*Rhododendron schlippenbachii*)

Bridal-wreath spirea (*Spiraea prunifolia*)

Common lilac (*Syringa vulgaris*)

Korean spice viburnum (*Viburnum carlesii*)

### Late May

Amur honeysuckle (*Lonicera maackii*)

Tatarian honeysuckle (*Lonicera tatarica*)

Bush or shrubby cinquefoil (*Potentilla fruticosa*)

Black or rum cherry (*Prunus serotina*)

Catawba rhododendron (*Rhododendron catawbiense*)

Boule de Neige rhododendron (*Rhododendron catawbiense* 'Boule de Neige')

Ghent azaleas (*Rhododendron gandavense* vars.)

Pinxterbloom or pinxter azalea (*Rhododendron nudiflorum*)

Snowmound Nippon spirea (*Spiraea nipponica* 'Snowmound')

Vanhoutte spirea (*Spiraea vanhouttei*)

Chinese lilac (*Syringa chinensis*)

Persian lilac (*Syringa persica*)

European cranberrybush (*Viburnum opulus*)

Black haw (*Viburnum prunifolium*)

Siebold viburnum (*Viburnum sieboldii*)

Japanese wisteria (*Wisteria floribunda*)

Detailed information and recommended varieties can be found in Part III.

# LANDSCAPE TASKS FOR MAY

**Garden Visitations**  This is the best time of year to visit gardens in bloom — not only private gardens but public arboretums, botanical gardens, and parks, as well as commercial nurseries. You can visit just for pleasure; or you can take notes and photos of plants you particularly like, then look them up in this book to see how and where they might fit into your own landscape design.

**Spent Flower Removal**  Now and throughout June, pinch off or cut off the spent blooms of lilacs, rhododendrons, and mountain laurel. This may sound like a nuisance, but it doesn't take that much time and it will definitely boost flower production in the following year. The reason is that throughout the summer the shrub will put its energies into forming new flower buds rather than ripening seeds where the old flowers bloomed. Besides, this pinching is often all you need to do by way of "pruning" to keep rhododendrons, azaleas, and mountain laurel neat and compact.

**Removing spent blooms from rhododendrons, laurels, and lilacs helps insure better flowering next year.**

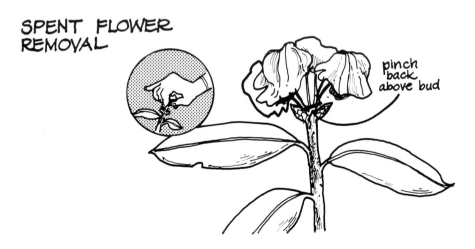

SPENT FLOWER REMOVAL

pinch back above bud

**Cutting and Pruning**  The dormant pruning season (see January and February) is long past. Now and next month are the time to prune plants that have finished blooming so that their postpruning growth can include formation of new flower buds for next spring — and to prune evergreens that are putting out new bright green growth. Every family of trees and shrubs has its own timetable for pruning.

**Cherries and magnolias** should be cut back this month after their blossoms fall, but only very sparingly. Both these plants recover slowly from pruning, and extremely slowly from severe pruning.

**Spireas and lilacs** in flowering hedges will stay in good condition if you cut them back quite strongly after they finish flowering. A good approach to lilacs is to cut down all of the small shoots or suckers every year; to trim back the longer young growth (for shape) every year; and to cut at least one-third of the largest, oldest stems to the ground every two or three years. Spireas can be pruned even more drastically: remove most of their oldest stems every spring to encourage sturdy new growth.

**Needled evergreens** such as yew, hemlock, pine, and arborvitae are eligible for trimming and shaping now. Snip off the tips of the soft

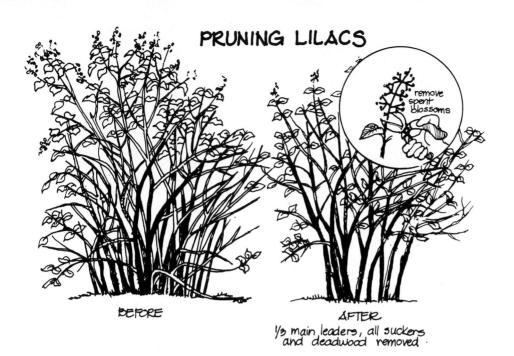

# PRUNING LILACS

BEFORE

AFTER

remove spent blossoms

⅓ main leaders, all suckers and deadwood removed.

Lilacs respond wonderfully to this kind of attention.

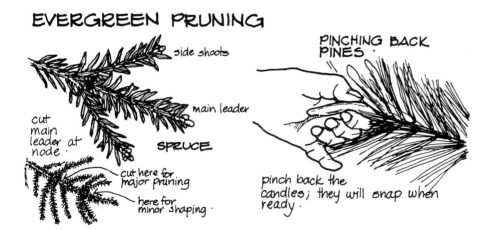

## EVERGREEN PRUNING

side shoots

main leader

SPRUCE

cut main leader at node.

cut here for major pruning

here for minor shaping.

PINCHING BACK PINES.

pinch back the candles; they will snap when ready.

Pinching and pruning as appropriate keep evergreen trees' sizes within bounds.

new growth; this will promote compact, bushy growth without deforming the plant.

**Propagation by Simple Layering** Simple layering means reproducing plants by fastening a portion of a branch (or branches) to the earth and keeping it in position until it roots. This form of propagation — unlike propagation by cuttings (January and June Landscape Tasks) — often occurs spontaneously in nature and is therefore very easy to do successfully. Azaleas and rhododendrons are among the plant types easiest to reproduce this way; others (see the list on page 175) include many shrubs and even trees whose lower branches naturally bend close to, or touch, the soil.

For simple layering, all you need is patience. It can take as long as 18 or 24 months for a layered stem to acquire a root system ample enough to withstand transplanting. And successful transplanting and es-

Judicious removal of branches helps enhance the shape of weeping white pine.

tablishment of the new plant is (as with softwood cuttings) often the trickiest phase of the whole project.

**Ahead of time** With simple layering as with hardwood and softwood cuttings, you'll have the best results if you prepare the plant ahead. In this case, prune the desired branch or branches severely the preceding spring to encourage fast-growing new shoots. These artificially promoted shoots will root far more readily than shoots of the same age produced by the plant in its normal course of growth.

**When to layer** Rooting capacity is at its peak during the peak growth period: that is, early spring. It's worth trying from spring into midsummer, however.

**Preparing the soil** Choose a location with a good amount of sun, since warmth hastens rooting. Cultivate the soil well; it should be friable, with good moisture-retaining capability, but never soggy. If necessary, lighten it with sand, peat moss, or compost. Then firm it gently.

**Preparing the stem** Choose a flexible shoot of the previous year's growth. Remove leaves and side shoots from 4 to 24 inches back from the tip. Layers usually root best if the stem is wounded or girdled at a spot about 9 inches behind the tip. To girdle it, wrap a piece of copper wire around it and twist it snug; or peel off a 1-inch ring of bark. To wound it, you can make a diagonal cut about ½ inch long, reaching halfway through the stem, and prop the cut open with a pebble or piece of wood. Or some gardeners prefer to take the shoot in both hands and give it a sharp twist; or simply to shave a ¼-inch slice off the underside of the stem.

**Pegging down the layer** Make a 6-inch-deep trench in the earth. Secure the wounded or girdled portion of the stem in it with a stake, forked stick, wire hoop, rock, or anything that will hold the stem firmly in place. For more vertical growth, you can also prop the end of the layer upright by driving a dowel into the soil and tying the tip to it with soft garden twine. Finally, fill in the trench with soil, firm the soil gently, and water well.

**Layer care** For the rest of the season and possibly the next season too, keep an eye on the layer. You are waiting for the layer's tip to put up vigorous new growth, showing that it has rooted. See that the soil is kept moist, since drying out sets back or even kills the new roots. Weed the area. If the layer looks as if it will be ready to transplant in the fall, you can cut it back in late summer to encourage still more root production.

**Layering: many plants can be reproduced by this simple method of vegetative propagation.**

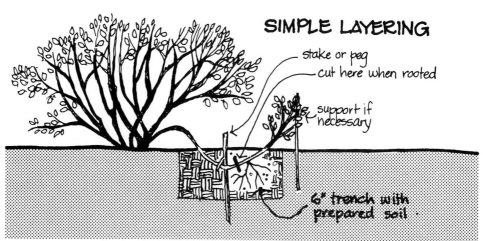

SIMPLE LAYERING

stake or peg
cut here when rooted
support if necessary
6" trench with prepared soil

**Transplanting**   The best time to lift and transplant a layer is in fall (if the roots are well established by then) or in the following early spring. Failing that, wait until the next fall. Begin by severing the stem that connects the layer to the parent plant. Then lift the new plant, using a spading fork and disturbing the roots as little as possible. Set it immediately in its new location; if for some reason it must wait, it should be heeled in. After transplanting, tend the layered shoot as you would any new plant. Cut back its top growth, give it light shade, and watch its water supply.

**Other layering techniques**   Variations on the simple-layering theme are many, and you may enjoy exploring the literature and trying some of them. They include compound or serpentine layering (pegging down several sections of a long shoot or vine); tip layering; dropping; mound or stool layering; French layering; and air layering.

**What to layer**   Very many vines naturally reproduce themselves by layering, so if you want to increase anything from akebia to wisteria I'd suggest trying simple layering first. Also, low-growing ground covers with creeping stems are excellent layering candidates by nature. As for trees and shrubs, I've listed here some popular types that lend themselves beautifully to layering.

## Trees and Shrubs to Propagate by Layering

Shadblow, juneberry, or serviceberry (*Amelanchier* spp.)
Katsura tree (*Cercidiphyllum japonicum*)
Quince (*Chaenomeles speciosa*)
White fringe tree (*Chionanthus virginicus*)
Dogwood (shrub types) (*Cornus* spp.)
Smoke tree (*Cotinus coggygria*)
Cotoneaster (*Cotoneaster* spp.)
Hawthorn (*Crataegus* spp.)
Redvein enkianthus (*Enkianthus campanulatus*)
Euonymus (*Euonymus* spp.)
Beech (*Fagus* spp.)
Forsythia (*Forsythia* spp.)

Fothergilla or witch alder (*Fothergilla* spp.)
Witch hazel (*Hamamelis* spp.)
Rose-of-Sharon or shrub althea (*Hibiscus syriacus*)
Holly (shrub types) (*Ilex* spp.)
Juniper (*Juniperus* spp.)
Kerria (*Kerria japonica*)
Leucothoe (*Leucothoe* spp.)
Privet (*Ligustrum* spp.)
Honeysuckle (*Lonicera* spp.)
Andromeda or pieris (*Pieris* spp.)
Azalea and rhododendron (*Rhododendron* spp.)
Lilac (*Syringa* spp.)
Viburnum (*Viburnum* spp.)

Detailed information and recommended varieties can be found in Part III.

**Watering and Mulching**   The month of May is sometimes quite dry, so keep an eye on any newly planted shrubs or trees, and water them if there's an extended drought. By way of prevention, mulches around the bases of plants help conserve moisture in the soil. You can use shredded pine bark, bark nuggets, wood chips, pine straw, stones, or gravel. As a fringe benefit, a good thick mulch will stop many weeds from growing. The weeds that do make it through to daylight will be leggy and easy to pull out by the roots.

*June*

# JUN

**Layers of white, pink, and red azalea bloom carpet this woodland floor.**

June is the month when the hours of daylight are longest and the sun rides highest in the sky. Sunny gardens are a mass of brilliant color now. Yet as the days grow hotter, it's also a pleasure to turn to the cooler, shadier areas of the landscape. Gardening in full shade is my first topic this month, followed by ground covers and vines — often among the top choices for shady locations. For outdoor leisure on long June days I'll consider decks and trellises in the Materials and Construction section; and I'll recommend June-blooming trees and shrubs to keep your yard in flower throughout the month.

## Landscaping Opportunities
# PLANTING IN WOODLAND SHADE

Even with homesites on generally open land, there are areas of shade: day-long "open shade" along the north side of a house, a wall, or a stand of evergreens; the filtered "light shade" under fine-foliaged trees or under trellises or other open canopies; or the "half shade" or "partial shade" of an area that's in sun half the day, shadow the other half, like a yard at the east side of a house.

The plant lists throughout this book contain many good candidates for open shade, light shade, and partial shade situations. But what about the day-long unbroken shade under a canopy of mature woodland trees? That is what's known as "full shade under trees," and it is a special case.

Every plant needs some light. The question is how little you can get away with. Let me start with one warning: if the woods in question are low-branched, closely planted evergreens (like hemlocks, firs, or immature pine forest) you can probably forget about growing anything under them. You should also keep your ambitions firmly in check if you're working under large deciduous trees with wide-sprawling, shallow root systems: maples and beeches are the worst.

But if the woodland consists of tall, open deciduous trees or conifers that have lost a lot of their lower branches and are beginning to permit the growth of an understory of vines, shrubs, and ground covers, there's a lot you can do.

A clump of fern and a large group of laurels thrive in this shady woodland setting.

**Planning a Woodland Garden**   One of my favorite places to visit is the Garden in the Woods in Framingham, Massachusetts, which was started many years ago by a landscape architect and gardener and is now headquarters for the New England Wildflower Society. The feeling of the place is that of a natural woodland; yet the understory trees, shrubs, and ground covers have been planned and shaped to blend into the most marvelous composition of colors, textures, and forms. It is breathtaking. And if you have some time to dedicate to the project, you can achieve the same kind of rich yet natural effect (on a more modest scale) in your own woodland setting.

Before you begin, take a look at what you have. If nothing at all is growing under the trees, you may be faced with one of those worst-case scenarios I mentioned above. More typically, however, you'll find an interesting tangle of low-growing ground plants, high-growing briers, shrubs, small trees, and vines. Even with a good handbook, some of these may be tough to identify. But don't just rip everything out wholesale.

Take photos and cut leaf samples of a good number of varieties, and send these materials to your state university extension specialist for identification.

Believe it or not, you'll find this exercise enormously helpful. Knowing the likes and dislikes of the plants already thriving in your potential woodland garden, you'll have a huge head start on finding plants that are equally well adapted to the site but more to your personal taste.

Also, you could well discover that one or two of the components of your existing jungle are plants recommended in the woodland plant list that follows. If so, you may want to build them into your design — which gives you a head start of another kind.

A second thing not to do at the outset is to clean up all the mess of leaves, rotted branches, and nameless organic matter that carpets the woodland floor. That litter, as it decays, is an important moisture-retaining, weed-suppressing mulch and a source of nutrients for the trees and shrubs growing in it. Since competition for nutrients is right up there with absence of light as a liability of woodland life, you want to do all you can to sustain and even augment the bacterial and chemical processes that are already in action. Depending on what plants you will be installing, you may need to add extra mulch, peat moss, compost, or fertilizer to the soil under the trees.

Approach the woods with respect; the indigenous communities of plants and wildlife have formed a network of interdependencies, and you want to beware of disrupting things. Be conservative.

You should also approach a woodland setting with patience — and with a certain philosophical attitude. Plants adapted to woodlands are usually (by nature) very slow-growing: expect to wait several years for the effects of your design to be apparent. And all that shade and competi-

**Play of contrasting textures in a Washington, D.C., woodland garden: large shiny leaves of hosta (above) and fine-foliaged ground covers (below) capture light in distinctive ways.**

tion with large trees for light, water, and nutrients is a strain on even the best adapted plant, so prepare yourself for a few failures along the way.

### Selecting, Planting, and Maintaining Woodland Plants

Beyond conservatism, patience, and resignation to the inevitability of occasional setbacks, I can offer a few concrete guidelines.

**Emphasize native plants**   The majority of plants I'll suggest for shaded woodland locations are natives. Many of these can survive with as little as one-tenth the light demanded by sun-loving species. In addition, they are equipped to hold their own in their ongoing competition with the larger plants whose roots, trunks, and foliage will be above, below, and all around them. Many natives among the plants listed here can be collected from fields and woods near you; or buy them at a good nursery. (For more discussion on choosing and using native plants, see March.)

**Establish colonies**   Most native plants tend to grow in colonies anyway, and you want to capitalize on their self-propagating tendency, not fight it. And if some members of a colony fail to thrive, their neighbors can fill in for them. Also, in terms of scale and balance, the sheer size and strong forms of the trees in a wooded environment really call for underplantings with a good deal of substance — and colonies of growth can provide that where single specimens might not. Finally, as a bonus, the bird and wildlife population will flock to enjoy the cover, nesting areas, and food supplied by densely clustered growth.

**Mix generations**   If a garden is flourishing in full shade, the corollary is that it will fail in full sun (or, often enough, even in half shade/half sun). I've seen beautiful woodland plantings suffer terribly from

**The bright yellow-green color and dainty texture of sweet woodruff make it a perfect choice for heavily shaded spots.**

shade deprivation when a great old tree died and had to be removed. So endeavor to keep a cross-section of young, old, and middle-aged trees growing together. That way, when old cover is damaged or destroyed, new cover can fill the gap.

**Irrigate and mulch**   Particularly for the first two years, and particularly with nonnatives or with the less determined natives, a boost from you in the form of mulch and water can make or break a woodland planting. Plants respond heartwarmingly to this kind of attention while they're getting established.

A shaded landscape is always a challenge, but it's a cornucopia of possibilities as well. At every season, and especially at midsummer, it can be a place of pure delight.

## Plants for Shady Woods

### Trees and Shrubs

Shadblow, juneberry, or serviceberry (*Amelanchier* spp.)
Red chokeberry (*Aronia arbutifolia*)
Black chokeberry (*Aronia melanocarpa*)
Barberry (*Berberis* spp.)
Redbud (*Cercis canadensis*)
Summer-sweet clethra (*Clethra alnifolia*)
Flowering dogwood (*Cornus florida*)
Redvein enkianthus (*Enkianthus campanulatus*)
Fothergilla or witch alder (*Fothergilla* spp.)
Witch hazel (*Hamamelis virginiana*)
Inkberry (*Ilex glabra*)
Winterberry (*Ilex verticillata*)
Mountain laurel (*Kalmia latifolia*)
Drooping leucothoe (*Leucothoe fontanesiana*)
Regel privet (*Ligustrum obtusifolium regelianum*)
Spicebush (*Lindera benzoin*)
Native azaleas (*Rhododendron calendulaceum, R. nudiflorum, R. visocosum*)
Native rhododendrons (*Rhododendron carolinianum, R. maximum*)
Chenault coralberry (*Symphoricarpos chenaultii*)
Coralberry or Indian currant (*Symphoricarpos orbiculatus*)
Canadian yew (*Taxus canadensis*)
American arborvitae (*Thuja occidentalis*)

Canadian hemlock (*Tsuga canadensis*)

### Ground Covers

Bugleweed (*Ajuga* spp.)
Bearberry (*Arctostaphylos uva-ursi*)
Sweet woodruff (*Asperula odorata*)
Lily-of-the-valley (*Convallaria majalis*)
Bunchberry (*Cornus canadensis*)
Ferns (many genera and species)
Daylilies (*Hemerocallis* spp.)
Plantain lilies (*Hosta* spp.)
Evergreen candytuft (*Iberis sempervirens*)
Partridgeberry (*Mitchella repens*)
Japanese spurge or pachysandra (*Pachysandra terminalis*)
Canby paxistima (*Paxistima canbyi*)
Bloodroot (*Sanguinaria canadensis*)
Stonecrop (*Sedum* spp.)
Blueberry (*Vaccinium* spp.)
Vinca, periwinkle, or myrtle (*Vinca minor*)
Violets (*Viola* spp.)
Yellowroot (*Xanthorhiza simplicissima*)

### Vines

Wintercreeper (*Euonymus fortunei* vars.)
English ivy (*Hedera helix*)
Climbing hydrangea (*Hydrangea anomala petiolaris*)
Virginia creeper (*Parthenocissus quinquefolia*)

**Vinca, a wonderful standby ground cover for shady places, will also flourish in sun.**

Detailed information and recommended varieties can be found in Part III.

# GROUND COVERS AND VINES

Not only in shady spots (although they are wonderful there) but throughout the landscape, ground covers and vines have important parts to play. In fact I often allocate 10 to 15 percent (or more) of a total planting budget to these hardworking plants. Some ground covers and vines are unobtrusive mats of green; others have gorgeous flowers or dramatically textured or variegated foliage. Whatever their texture or color, they give definition, character, and life to large forms and spaces. They contribute the final brushstrokes to the landscape picture.

Vines and ground covers also have very practical uses. They are frequently the only way to cover an arid bank or shady woodland floor. They're wonderful for shading out weeds at ground level among larger plantings of shrubs or trees. Growing over trellises or arbors, vines provide welcome summer shade to houses and grounds. Growing over fences, they curtain out unwanted views.

Almost every plant listed here is very easy to propagate and, given soil and conditions that are to its liking, virtually maintenance-free. The one exception I would make to that statement is that many of this group are by definition vigorous spreaders — or, in the case of vines, rampant climbers and twiners. Containment of spreading rhizomes, or annual or biennial prunings, may be called for. If you want to avoid that kind of chore, just stay away from the most eager growers among the lists that follow.

Ground covers and vines are a hugely wide-ranging assortment of plants, spanning succulents, grasses, perennial flowers, herbs, low-growing shrubby plants, and large climbing vines; and including both woody plants (evergreen and deciduous) and herbaceous perennials. That's why there are five lists here: evergreen and deciduous nonherbaceous (woody) ground covers, herbaceous perennials, and evergreen and deciduous vines. The woody ground covers are basically low-growing, spreading shrubs. The herbaceous ground covers and the vines, however, call for a little explanation here.

**Herbaceous Perennials**   Unlike every other kind of plant listed in this book, most of these ground covers are not visible in winter, dying back completely and then reemerging with new growth in spring. (There are some evergreens among them, however, as noted in their descriptions.) Many of these plants are covered with flowers for short periods; in fact that is sometimes a problem, if their vivid yellows or pinks or reds compete with flowering shrubs just when you want to give the shrubs priority. My solution to this (although many fine gardeners do not share my view) is to use the bright-flowering herbaceous ground covers as color features in nonflowering settings, such as gardens consisting mainly of grass and conifers. Where there are flowering trees and shrubs, I tend to choose ground covers more for foliage than for flowers.

**Vines**   Many vines make excellent ground covers — but they also tend to scramble up any and all upright objects they encounter. This makes them great for shading, draping, curtaining, and screening purposes. It also means that they can kill trees and shrubs by slow strangulation; so if you're using vines in the same area with other plantings, you have to give them their own supports and keep an eye on them.

Some vines, such as wisteria, twine themselves bodily up and around in a spiraling pattern. Others, like grapes, send out little tendrils to hold onto whatever they're climbing. Still others have tiny rootlets at intervals along the stems (like English ivy) or put out little adhesive holdfasts (like Boston ivy).

These varying means of support determine where and how you can use different vines. Ivies, for instance, should never be grown against a wooden structure because the rootlets or holdfasts damage the wood. A big vine like grape or wisteria needs a wire, pipe, or wood support of its own. If you're growing a twining or tendril-twisting vine — like five-leaf akebia or pink anemone clematis — against your house, you should provide support other than the house itself. And if the outside of your house is painted, it would be smart to make the vine's support system removable so that you can hinge it away from the house at painting time.

## HOW VINES CLIMB

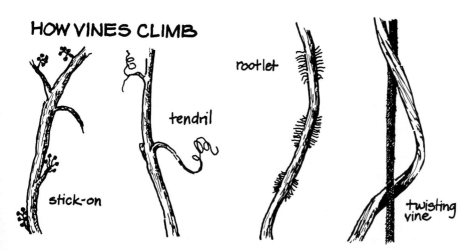

rootlet

tendril

stick-on

twisting vine

A vine's individual personality results partly from the way it attaches itself to its substrate as it climbs.

**Above left, common Boston ivy and a small-leaved variety grow together on a wall for a pleasant interplanted effect. Above right: delicate-leaved ferns are perfect for a moist niche, and this variety has lively fall color too.**

The sampling of vines listed here is drawn from among innumerable possibilities.

## Ground Covers and Vines

### Nonherbaceous Deciduous Ground Covers

Black chokeberry (*Aronia melanocarpa*)
Sweet fern (*Comptonia peregrina*)
Bunchberry (*Cornus canadensis*)
Crown vetch (*Coronilla varia*)
Bronx forsythia (*Forsythia viridissima* 'Bronxensis')
Virginia rose (*Rosa virginiana*)
Memorial rose (*Rosa wichuraiana*)
Daphne spirea (*Spiraea japonica* 'Alpina')
Lowbush blueberry (*Vaccinium angustifolium*)
Yellowroot (*Xanthorhiza simplicissima*)

### Evergreen Ground Covers

Bearberry (*Arctostaphylos uva-ursi*)
Skogsholmen bearberry cotoneaster (*Cotoneaster dammeri* 'Skogsholmen')
Purple wintercreeper (*Euonymus fortunei* 'Colorata')
Wintergreen (*Gaultheria procumbens*)
Candytuft (*Iberis sempervirens*)
Japanese garden juniper (*Juniperus chinensis procumbens*)
Sargent juniper (*Juniperus chinensis sargentii*)
Creeping juniper (*Juniperus horizontalis*)
Drooping leucothoe (*Leucothoe fontanesiana*)
Partridgeberry (*Mitchella repens*)
Japanese spurge or pachysandra (*Pachysandra terminalis*)
Canby paxistima (*Paxistima canbyi*)
Goldmoss stonecrop (*Sedum spurium*)
Houseleeks or hens-and-chickens (*Sempervivum tectorum*)
Canadian yew (*Taxus canadensis*)
Vinca, periwinkle, or myrtle (*Vinca minor*)

### Herbaceous Perennial Ground Covers

Pink yarrow (*Achillea millefolium* 'Rosea')
Goutweed or bishop's weed (*Aegopodium podagraria*)
Bugleweed or carpet bugle (*Ajuga reptans*)
Rockcress (*Arabis procurrens*)
Moss sandwort (*Arenaria verna*)
European ginger (*Asarum europaeum*)
Lily-of-the-valley (*Convallaria majalis*)
Dwarf eared coreopsis (*Coreopsis auriculata* 'Nana')
Pinks (*Dianthus* spp.)
Siberian draba (*Draba sibirica* 'Repens')
Mock strawberry (*Duchesnea indica*)
Epimediums (*Epimedium* spp.)

## Ground Covers and Vines (*continued*)

Ferns (many genera)
Sweet woodruff (*Galium odoratum*)
Prostrate baby's breath (*Gypsophila repens* 'Rosea')
Daylilies (*Hemerocallis* spp.)
Plaintain lilies (*Hosta* spp.)
Creeping jenny or moneywort (*Lysimachia nummularia*)
Creeping mint (*Mentha requienii*)
Persian ground-ivy (*Nepeta faassenii*)
Ribbongrass (*Phalaris arundinacea picta*)
Moss pinks or ground pinks (*Phlox subulata*)
Solomon's-seal (*Polygonatum biflorum*)
Pearlwort (*Sagina subulata*)
Bloodroot (*Sanguinaria canadensis*)
Ground bamboo (*Sasa pumila*)
Thymes (*Thymus* spp.)
Allegheny foam-flower (*Tiarella cordifolia*)
Violets (*Viola* spp.)
Barren strawberry (*Waldsteinia fragarioides*)

### Deciduous Vines

Five-leaf akebia (*Akebia quinata*)
Porcelainberry or porcelain ampelopsis (*Ampelopsis brevipedunculata*)

Trumpet vine or common trumpet creeper (*Campsis radicans*)
Bittersweet (*Celastrus scandens*)
Sweet autumn clematis (*Clematis dioscoreifolia robusta*)
Pink anemone clematis (*Clematis montana rubens*)
Climbing hydrangea (*Hydrangea anomala petiolaris*)
Henry honeysuckle (*Lonicera henryi*)
Hall's honeysuckle (*Lonicera japonica* 'Halliana')
Virginia creeper or woodbine (*Parthenocissus quinquefolia*)
Boston ivy (*Parthenocissus tricuspidata*)
Chinese or silver fleece vine (*Polygonum aubertii*)
Grapes (*Vitis* spp.)
Japanese wisteria (*Wisteria floribunda*)

### Evergreen Vines

Wintercreeper (*Euonymus fortunei* vars.)
English ivy (*Hedera helix*)

Detailed information and recommended varieties can be found in Part III.

**Climbing hydrangea is splendid topping a fence or a masonry wall.**

## Materials and Construction
# DECKS AND TRELLISES

Enjoying the outdoors is high on June's agenda. A natural setting such as a woodland garden is one fine place to do that; another is an outdoor deck.

Wood (see May Materials and Construction) is the primary material for both decks and trellises, and primarily the softwoods that do such a good job in outdoor use: redwood, cedar, cypress, spruce, or white pine.

If you want a high and dry raised terrace or patio, but can't or don't want to build on grade because of a problem like sloping topography, you're talking about a deck: an elevated wooden platform.

And if you wish to provide some sun screening, an arbor for vines, or just an ornamental overhead structure, whether related to a deck or elsewhere, you're talking about a trellis: an open-air overhead structure.

### The Architecture of Decks and Trellises
Decks and trellises are often thought of and referred to as part of the landscape — yet I feel they're more aptly considered architecture. They are usually closely related to the house in location, style, materials, or all three. Also, they definitely function as outdoor rooms. A deck is a floor, a trellis a ceiling. Add a few vertical elements such as hanging or potted plants, a railing, some trees, or the side of the house — and presto, a well-defined space, or "room."

### Uses and locations
First, consider how you are going to use the spaces you create. Will you be relaxing, dining, sunning, swimming, partying, viewing, or all of the above? Plan for comfortable circulation between and within these outdoor spaces. Let the purposes you have in mind determine their location and orientation, just as the purposes of an indoor room would determine its position in the house.

**Modular deck sections — versatile, easy to install, and practical — require good drainage and good wood. Here, redwood decking atop a gravel bed makes a handsome parquet.**

Most people put decks immediately outside the house, an inch below floor level, and with sliding doors connecting to the interior of the house — usually to the living room, dining room, or family room. Such a deck directly extends and opens up the living area. It's easily accessible and welcoming to visitors.

But sometimes a "floating" deck is the answer, away from the house, perhaps with a bridge or path connecting it to one or more convenient entrances. With a floating deck, you can often design in some grade variations or even different levels for the deck itself. This treatment can open up new and more enticing views and better separate the various landscape spaces. Also, when the deck in question is to be on a level with an upper floor of the house, the space beneath it is apt to be dark and uninviting; but a separated deck allows light to penetrate both beneath it and through to the windows of the house. A freestanding deck will, however, require more elaborate bracing than one connected to the house.

**Materials**  As always, try to integrate and coordinate as best you can with the architecture of the house. Too many decks convey a tacked-on feeling. Even if your deck is a late addition, it does not have to look that way. Many neutral styles and finishes will blend with almost any architecture. Just stay away from violent contrasts like a heavy, timbered rustic deck up against a white clapboard Colonial.

Before you get into detailed design or construction, stand back one last time and make sure that a deck is really the best answer. Sometimes a hasty decision results in a deck being built where a stone or brick terrace on grade would have been a more natural choice, and a forced look is the outcome.

**Decks**  You build a deck or a trellis from the bottom up (footings, post anchors, posts, beams, joists, finally decking) — but you design a deck from the top down. First you determine the size and shape of deck surface that will meet your needs and fit your location. Then you select the decking material and decide which direction you want the decking boards to run. All other structural specifications follow from these initial decisions. (Shown on page 188 is a schematic representation of decks' and trellises' structural parts.)

Angled decking boards lend extra structural strength and can be exciting to look at, but they do entail waste and thus extra expense. In general, for a deck adjoining a house, I prefer decking boards parallel to

**Above left: a "floating" deck allows an unobstructed view from within the house and draws people out for a new perspective. Above right: an attached deck makes a graceful transition from the first floor of the house to the lawn two feet lower down.**

**Nomenclature and basic components of deck and trellis structures.**

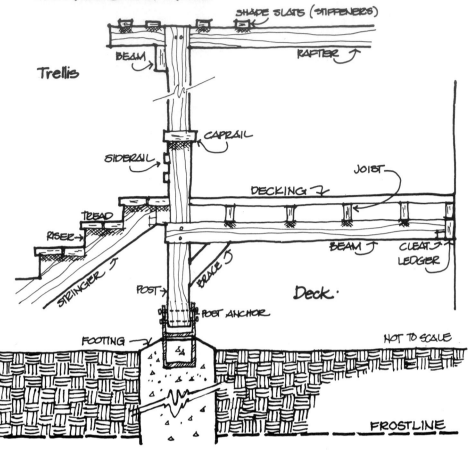

DECK & TRELLIS NOMENCLATURE

SHAPE SLATS (STIFFENERS)

BEAM

RAFTER

Trellis

CAPRAIL

SIDERAIL

JOIST

DECKING

TREAD

RISER

BEAM

CLEAT

LEDGER

STRINGER

BRACE

POST

Deck.

POST ANCHOR

FOOTING

NOT TO SCALE

FROSTLINE

**This low railing is simply an extension of the deck's main support posts: an easy and sturdy approach to railing construction. (Use higher railing in dangerous conditions.)**

the house wall, since a more restful or harmonious feeling results. The exceptions are cases where you want to direct the view outwards by using deck flooring perpendicular or at an angle to the house.

My first and last word of advice on designing these structures is to keep them extremely simple — or consult a professional. A good carpenter may be your best bet for advice (and help, if needed) on the job, if you can find one who's willing. Or talk over your plans with a landscape architect, an architect, or a structural engineer. If your design is really complex, the structural engineer may be brought into the picture anyway. The point is that if it's not designed and built for decades of use and weather resistance, a deck can turn into a serious safety hazard. It must be not only attractive and useful, but strong and durable.

**Railings** Railings may be built on extensions of the deck's support posts or attached separately to joists, beams, or fascia boards. Benches or wide rails are often attractive, provided a fall over the edge would not be hazardous: the deck should not be at too great a height, and there should be grass or shrubbery underneath, not sharp rocks. The railing requirements in local building codes vary greatly, so before you plan your deck's railing, check the codes for your area. That goes for both basic railing structures and benches or low, wide rails suitable for sitting.

# RAILING EXAMPLES

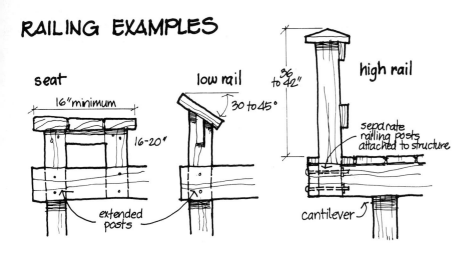

seat

16" minimum

16-20"

extended posts

low rail

30 to 45°

high rail

36 to 42"

separate railing posts attached to structure

cantilever

Railings: always check local building codes. If the view through is important, use a transparent type; and if young children may climb, use vertical balusters.

Vertical balusters work well with post-and-beam construction. And since railings are a key safety factor, vertical balusters — which are tough to climb — are my choice if young children will be using the deck. I use balusters no more than 6 inches apart (between edges) and no less than 40 inches high: an unclimbable height for small children.

**Stairs**   With all wood stairs, follow the formula $2R + T = 27$ for proper riser and tread proportions, where $R$ = riser height in inches and $T$ = tread depth in inches. Using this formula and the standard lumber sizes available, you can determine the most comfortable and economical dimensions for your deck's stairs.

For treads, use lumber to match the decking; for risers (if any) lumber should match joists or fascia boards; and stair railings should match deck rails.

This simple arbor, in Ann Hathaway's cottage garden in England, is made from peeled branches.

**Trellises**   With a trellis, you may want to design as much from the bottom up as from the top down. The size and spacing of the posts supporting the overhead structure may be as important to you as the size and spacing of the horizontal members above.

The enormous latitude of possible dimensions, densities, and designs for trellises makes it hard for me to give you firm guidelines — beyond strongly encouraging you to give any trellis a clear 8- to 8½-foot height to its underside. A lower ceiling feels cramped and tight outdoors, unless it is very small.

Trellises are perfect for hanging things: furniture, lights, plants, hammocks. Take advantage of the opportunities a trellis offers — but as always, don't let the hanging motif become too much of a good thing.

One good choice for a trellis structure is an egg-crate system with square or rectangular openings. This kind of arrangement gives you great flexibility: you can insert mats or louvers in openings as you wish, moving them around seasonally for varying areas of shade. You can obtain still further shading with roll-down screening between the posts, either along the outside edge or inside the line of the "roof" of the trellis.

Before you translate your ideas into wood, make a reasonably accurate mockup of the trellis you plan to build and test it out at different times of day to see the approximate quality of the shade it will cast.

## Plants by Design

# JUNE BLOOMERS

### Early June

White fringe tree (*Chionanthus virginicus*)
Yellowwood (*Cladrastis lutea*)
Siberian dogwood (*Cornus alba* 'Sibirica')
Kousa or Japanese dogwood (*Cornus kousa*)
Drooping leucothoe (*Leucothoe fontanesiana*)
Flame azalea (*Rhododendron calendulaceum*)
Catawba rhododendrons (*Rhododendron catawbiense* vars.)
Rugosa rose (*Rosa rugosa*)
Late lilac (*Syringa villosa*)
Arrowwood (*Viburnum dentatum*)
Linden viburnum (*Viburnum dilatatum*)
Black haw (*Viburnum prunifolium*)

### Mid-June

Washington hawthorn (*Crataegus phaenopyrum*)
Mountain laurel (*Kalmia latifolia*)
Privet (*Ligustrum* spp.)
Tulip tree (*Liriodendron tulipifera*)
Hall's honeysuckle (*Lonicera japonica* 'Halliana')
Roses (*Rosa* — many spp.)
Tree lilac (*Syringa amurensis*)

### Late June

Virginal mock-orange (*Philadelphus virginalis*)
Rosebay rhododendron or great laurel (*Rhododendron maximum*)
Anthony Waterer spirea (*Spiraea bumalda* 'Anthony Waterer')

Detailed information and recommended varieties can be found in Part III.

# LANDSCAPE TASKS FOR JUNE

**Lawn Maintenance**   For weed control and a healthy lawn, it's best to mow your lawn no shorter than 2 or 2½ inches. The shade cast by the blades of grass serves to prevent broad-leaved weeds' seeds from sprouting: it's too dark down there. It also keeps moisture in the earth, thereby cutting down on your watering time and expense.

**Crabgrass Control**   If you have problems with crabgrass, postemergent weed controls will kill the seedlings as they appear. The packages of the various weed-killing chemicals provide instructions for their use. Be sure to follow the instructions carefully if you go this route. I'd recommend using these herbicides only as a last resort, however. By far the best way to suppress weeds is to promote a sturdy, dense growth of grass (see the April and September sections on lawns and their installation and maintenance) and cut it at the appropriate length.

### June Pruning

**Spireas, forsythia, lilac, and quince** that finish blooming in June should be pruned as soon as their flowering season ends. Pruning procedures for lilacs and spireas are detailed in the May chapter; forsythia and quince can be rejuvenated either by removing their oldest stems or by cutting the whole shrubs back to 6 inches from the ground. A more moderate trimming is also acceptable if you want to avoid the crew-cut look.

**Low-growing perennials** like rock cress, evergreen candytuft, or moss pink should be cut back severely once they finish flowering, to encourage compact, sturdy growth for next year.

**Shade trees** are often best pruned in full foliage — that is, now. You may be thinning them in order to open up a summer view or increase light filtration to the ground level; if so, doing the job now enables you to tell exactly what results you are getting. Or you may want to remove lower branches to accentuate the lines of a tree's trunk, or to clear space for people and air circulation beneath. Or you may simply be keeping the tree healthy, by lopping crossing branches or dead or diseased limbs (which can harbor rot and insects), or by preventing it from shading its own foliage too densely.

For any of these purposes, there's a right way to prune a shade tree. Use clean, sharp equipment; a pole pruner with a saw on the end is

**A professional tree man works at pruning a big shade tree.**

# PRUNING TREES

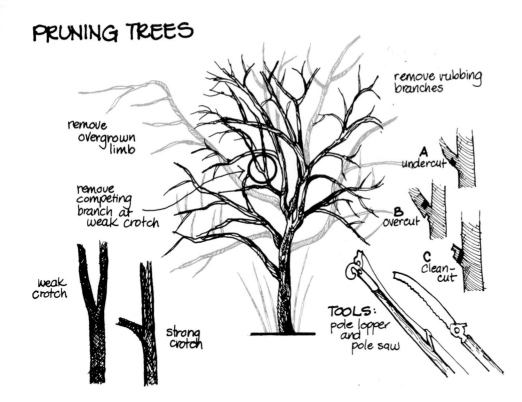

remove rubbing branches

remove overgrown limb

remove competing branch at weak crotch

A undercut

B overcut

C Clean-cut

weak crotch

strong crotch

TOOLS: pole lopper and pole saw

**When pruning a tree of any size, consider the overall form and balance of branches in the crown as well as the tree's health and well-being.**

a good multipurpose tool, but for more maneuverability I prefer two poles, one with a saw and another with a pruner. Start from the top, thinning judiciously and checking often to make sure you're not distorting the shape of the tree or creating unsightly gaps. With each branch, first make a cut into the underside of the branch several inches from the crotch (see figure A, above), to forestall the bark's tearing all the way to the trunk. Cut off the limb several inches farther out (figure B), then cut off the remaining stump as close as possible to the trunk (figure C). Leave no crotch to trap moisture (which causes rot) and slope the cut surface down, away from the trunk, so as to shed rain.

For large trees beyond the reach of the pole pruner, it may be best to hire a professional tree man — both to ensure the job's done right and to avoid the dangers involved in climbing and felling big limbs.

At this season the wounds heal rapidly, which is good for the tree. Even so, it's a good idea to paint or spray all cuts 2 inches or more in diameter with antiseptic tree paint, to prevent excessive loss of sap and to deter insects and fungus. Smaller cuts, less than 2 inches across, don't need to be painted.

**Broad-leaved Evergreens** If you haven't done it already (see May), give your rhododendrons, azaleas, andromedas, or laurels a thick acid mulch now (like pine needles, oak-leaf compost, or wood chips) to help keep their roots cool and their soil moist in the hot weather to come.

Continue breaking or cutting off the spent flower heads on late-blooming azaleas, andromedas, and mountain laurel. Be sure not to harm the new buds for next year, which will be coming along just below the remains of the old flowers.

**Irrigation**  Deep watering of lawns and gardens is critical in June. Surface sprinkling, on the other hand, is worse than useless. Water early in the morning, before the heat of the day, and give each area of your grounds the equivalent of 1 inch of water per week, unless rainfall provides it. (Leave an empty straight-sided container outdoors to check.)

**Propagation Project: Rooting Softwood Cuttings**  This method of propagation is a good deal trickier than rooting hardwood cuttings (see January), since every phase of the procedure is fraught with hazards to tender young shoots; but success is definitely feasible with several popular landscape plants, so you may enjoy giving it a try.

This method of propagation, like others involving rooting sections of stems, works much better if you prepare a young plant with a rigorous pruning ahead of time. For softwood cuttings, cut back during the dormant season — any time from late fall through winter — to promote a surge of new growth in spring.

Some trees, shrubs, ground covers, and vines that often root successfully from softwood cuttings taken at this season are listed here. The starred plants can often be propagated from cuttings — which become known as "semiripe," then "hardwood," as the season advances — throughout the summer, fall, and early winter.

English ivy, shown growing companionably with sweet woodruff, can be propagated practically any time.

### Plants for Propagating from Softwood Cuttings

Barberry (*Berberis*)
Butterfly bush (*Buddleia*)
*Boxwood (*Buxus*)
Cotoneaster (*Cotoneaster*)
Dogwood, shrub types (*Cornus*)
*Euonymus (*Euonymus*)
Forsythia (*Forsythia*)
Ginkgo (*Ginkgo*)
*English ivy (*Hedera*)
Hydrangea (*Hydrangea*)
*Holly (*Ilex*)
*Juniper, creeping (*Juniperus*)
Kerria (*Kerria*)
Privet (*Ligustrum*)
Honeysuckle (*Lonicera*)
Magnolia (*Magnolia*)

Dawn redwood (*Metasequoia*)
*Japanese spurge (*Pachysandra*)
Boston ivy (*Parthenocissus*)
Mock-orange (*Philadelphus*)
Andromeda (*Pieris*)
*Firethorn (*Pyracantha*)
Azalea and rhododendron
(*Rhododendron*)
Rose (*Rosa*)
Willow (*Salix*)
Spirea (*Spiraea*)
Stewartia (*Stewartia*)
Lilac (*Syringa*)
*Yew (*Taxus*)
Viburnum (*Viburnum*)
Wisteria (*Wisteria*)

*Can often be propagated from cuttings throughout summer and fall and into early winter.
Detailed information and recommended varieties can be found in Part III.

**When to cut**  Softwood is the plant's new spring growth, and it is ready for cutting when its leaves are fully out and fully colored. If it bends but won't break, or if new leaves are still emerging at the tip, it's too young. If it is too stiff to snap readily, it's too old. If it snaps crisply, it should be about right. Choose healthy-looking normal growth from the outside of the plant, not outsized shoots or spindly growth.

**Advance preparation**  Before you cut, have a container of powdered rooting hormone on hand and prepare the sterile rooting medium.

# SOFTWOOD CUTTINGS

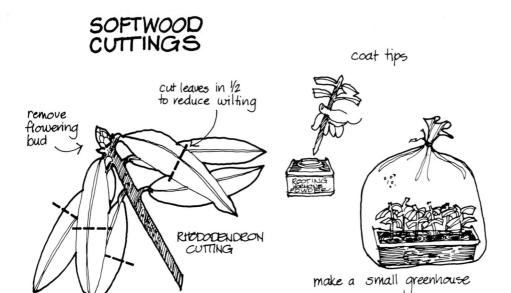

remove flowering bud

cut leaves in ½ to reduce wilting

RHODODENDRON CUTTING

coat tips

ROOTING HORMONE POWDER

make a small greenhouse

**Try your luck with softwood cuttings. Many desirable landscape plants can be reproduced this way throughout spring, summer, and even fall.**

You can use sterile sand, vermiculite, perlite, or a mixture of sand and peat moss. Whichever medium you use should be kept moist but not soggy. Flower pots, flats, or boxes make fine containers.

**Making cuttings**   Choose a cool early morning to start. Using a very sharp, thin-bladed knife, take cuttings of terminal growth about 2 to 6 inches long. Make the cuts at about a 45-degree angle. Large-leaved plants like rhododendrons require longer cuttings; small-leaved ones like privet, shorter cuttings. Remove the leaves from the bottom third of each stem. If the cutting has large leaves, cutting off the outer half of each leaf will diminish transpiration and make the cutting less apt to wilt. As you make each cutting, immediately put it between damp sheets of paper or cloth. Drying out at this stage is fatal.

**Cuttings into medium**   Once your collection is complete, use a pencil to make a hole in the rooting medium where each cutting is to go. Dip the tip of each cutting in the rooting hormone powder (see instructions on the hormone container) and insert the bottom third of the cutting in the medium. Gently firm the medium around it. Keep the cuttings in a warm place — ideally 70° to 80°F — and protected from direct sunlight. To keep both the medium and the atmosphere around the cuttings humid, cover them with a plastic cover, put them in a plastic bag, or place a glass jar over them.

**Rooting and hardening off**   Some cuttings will send out roots in a couple of weeks; others may take as long as 3 months. Keep the medium moist, watch, and be patient. Once they have roots about 1 inch long (pull them out to check) you can start hardening them off by removing their coverings for longer and longer periods each day. After a week or so you can carefully transfer them to potting soil in pots in a bright window or greenhouse.

Once new top growth has started, the cuttings can be treated like any young plants: they can move outdoors if the weather is still mild, or wait in the greenhouse or cold frame to be planted outdoors next spring.

# JUL

Flowering perennials and annuals come into their own in my herb garden in midsummer, stealing the scene from the trees and shrubs.

The longest day of the year was the June 21 summer solstice, so midsummer has officially passed by the time July begins. July *feels* like midsummer, though, and keeping cool is a high priority. This month I'll consider some cooling topics: plants to grow in and around water; pools and other water displays to delight the eye and ear and freshen the air around you; and big shade trees to relax beneath.

## Landscaping Opportunities
# PLANTING IN AND AROUND WATER

There is no limit to the kinds of plants you can use around water. While potted flowers are pretty beside a pool, this section will focus on water plants as such, from plants that actually live in water to plants for edges and backgrounds of still or moving water.

Examples of the affinity between water and vegetation abound in nature. Think of a stream in the woods: hemlock and beech tower overhead and the rocks along the water's edge are covered with mosses, while ferns and bunchberry grow in the crevices. In the shallows of every pond or lake are rushes, sedges, and grasses; trees and shrubs like willow, birch, swamp oak, alder, and viburnum — to mention just a few — thrive on sloping banks nearby.

And the relationship is not just biological but visual. Reeds and water lilies need water, of course — yet in a sense the water needs the reeds and lilies too. They complement and enhance each other.

**Water-loving plants such as willows, cattails, and red maples have a natural rightness around a pond, as in this autumn landscape.**

**In the Water**   Water lilies are the plant of choice for midpond or midpool growing. There are two categories: tropical and hardy. *Hardy water lilies* are day bloomers and carry their flowers just above the surface of the water. *Tropical water lilies* have larger leaves and flowers; they hold their blossoms on tall stalks, well above the water (good for cutting); and some of them bloom at night. Many of them are fragrant. Both tropical and hardy types have been extensively hybridized and are available in a wide range of sizes and colors from suppliers who specialize in water plants. Be sure to select lilies in scale with your setting — some of the larger-leafed tropical varieties are really huge and demand large ponds to hold them.

**Growing water lilies**   Among the hardy lilies, some are sufficiently tough to survive year-round in ponds and streams in the north, provided their roots are below the frost line. They die back to their roots under the ice, then reemerge in all their glory in June. If you have a natural pond that you can allow to freeze and thaw all winter, you're all set.

Artificial pools, however, present a different challenge. Usually they're drained for winter; if not, they often freeze solid. To avoid winterkill, take up hardy water lilies in fall after the first frost. Store them in a box of damp sand in a cool place (about 50°F) until early May, then replant them.

Tropical lilies really have to be considered annuals unless you have a greenhouse where you can overwinter and propagate them. Lacking a greenhouse, you should resign yourself to buying a fresh supply of tubers each spring. Set them out when your pond water is well warmed up, in June.

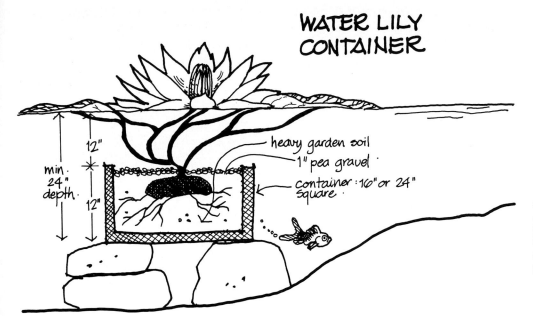

## WATER LILY CONTAINER

min. 24" depth

12"

12"

heavy garden soil
1" pea gravel
container: 16" or 24" square

**Water lilies need water at least 24 inches deep. Containers are readily available, or build your own.**

Both types (except hardy lilies living in a natural pond) require a separate underwater container for each plant. This diagram shows the minimum dimensions. Fill the container with heavy garden soil mixed with well-rotted manure — no peat or compost, which would be too light. Top the soil with 1 inch of pea gravel to keep the water clean. The best material for the container (though the most expensive) would be redwood or cedar; pine or fir, while acceptable, will rot eventually. Steer clear of wood that has been treated with preservatives, which can be toxic to plants and/or fish.

**Water-lily environments**   Water lilies need three things for their well-being: four to six hours of direct sunlight each day, ample space, and adequate oxygen.

Both for good design and for good plant culture, it's important not to have more than *half* your total water surface covered with plants. In addition, each individual water lily has its own territorial requirements. A large one needs 12 square feet of water surface; a medium one 10 square feet; small ones 4 square feet each. As you can see, one large lily or three small ones will demand a pool surface area of at least 24 square feet — that is, double the area required by the lilies themselves. Three large lilies will need a pool with not less than 72 square feet of surface area. Do your computations before you order your lilies.

There are two ways to ensure that your pool water contains ample oxygen for the support of water lilies. First, control algae, which tend to proliferate in still water and consume more than their share of the water's oxygen. A small recirculating pump will both aerate and move the water, which will discourage algae. You can also install floating plants to shade out sunlight and thereby prevent the growth of algae (they need light too). Choose floating sunshades (such as water chestnuts, water hyacinths, water lettuce, or water fern) whose size, character, and growing habits are in keeping with the overall effect you're after — be it bold and vivid or small-scale and restrained. If the floating plants become too nu-

**Strong horizontal lines of water-lily pads and stiffly upright stalks of irises are in counterpoint, heightening each other's effects.**

merous and start to take over the pond or pool, they're easy to control: just scoop them out.

The second approach to oxygen maintenance is to add oxygenating plants to your pool colony. Available from those same water-lily suppliers, they include eel grass, arrowheads, elodea (sometimes called anacharis), and water milfoil.

**Plants for boggy edges**   There are many lovely plants that won't live in deep water but flourish at the shallow edges where only their roots are submerged. If yours is a natural or naturalistic pond or pool, and if you can arrange a trickle of water to prevent stagnation, you can cultivate varied and fascinating bog plants like baby's-tears, papyrus, arrowhead, horsetail, umbrella plant, water canna, water iris or flag, or water poppy.

**Around the Edge**   Many kinds of herbaceous foliage and flowering plants lend themselves to planting around the edges of water displays. You can set these plants in pockets of soil between paving stones or rocks; use them as ground covers; or plant them in larger free-standing groups. For plantings near still water, I particularly like upright-growing plants like loosestrifes or ferns, which contrast with the horizontal surface of the water and make great reflections. Around falling water or fountains, cascading and spreading plant forms are appealing to echo the water's effect.

Among my favorite water's-edge plants are primroses; irises; orchids; buttercups; daisies; lilies, including garden lilies (*Lilium*), daylilies (*Hemerocallis*), and plantain lilies (*Hosta*); loosestrifes, ferns, grasses, rushes, sedges, and reeds. In addition, many ground cover plants grow beautifully in rock crevices and on banks. (For a selection of these plants, see June Plants for a Purpose.)

**In the Background**   If you have the space to create a complete water garden setting, a progression from smaller herbaceous plants to shrubs and then trees will round out the picture. A word of warning, however: don't plant trees close to the water on any side, and don't plant them anywhere except to the north. Otherwise they will cast shade and inhibit the growth of all your other lovely water plantings. If they are too near the water (the distance depends on size and type of tree and force of prevailing wind), they will drop leaves and debris into the pool. Besides, their roots will be apt to invade piping and rock masonry or even crack the pool itself.

The plants listed below are all adapted to watery surroundings, and therefore have an air of rightness as background plantings for a pool or pond. Incidentally, many of these trees and shrubs are also fine candidates for any spot where wet soil is a problem, even without a pool, pond, or waterfall.

Plants with soft weeping and cascading forms make lovely reflections.

## Background Plants for Pools and Ponds

### Medium and Large Trees
Red maple (*Acer rubrum*)
River birch (*Betula nigra*)
Weeping European birch (*Betula pendula*)
Gray birch (*Betula populifolia*)
Sweet gum (*Liquidambar styraciflua*)
Weeping willow (*Salix alba tristis* or *Salix elegantissima*)
American arborvitae (*Thuja occidentalis*)

### Small Trees
Cutleaf Japanese maple (*Acer palmatum dissectum*)
Allegheny serviceberry (*Amelanchier laevis*)
Redbud (*Cercis canadensis*)
Thread cypress (*Chamaecyparis pisifera* 'Filifera')
Kousa or Japanese dogwood (*Cornus kousa*)
Cornelian cherry dogwood (*Cornus mas*)

### Shrubs
Buttonbush (*Cephalanthus occidentalis*)

Siberian dogwood (*Cornus alba* 'Sibirica')
Red-osier dogwood (*Cornus sericea*)
Japanese garden juniper (*Juniperus chinensis procumbens*)
Spicebush (*Lindera benzoin*)
Japanese andromeda or pieris (*Pieris japonica*)
Flame azalea (*Rhododendron calendulaceum*)
Pinxterbloom or pinxter azalea (*Rhododendron nudiflorum*)
Swamp azalea (*Rhododendron viscosum*)
Carolina rhododendron (*Rhododendron carolinianum*)
Goat willow or French pussy willow (*Salix caprea*)
Blueberries (*Vaccinium* spp.)
Viburnums (*Viburnum* spp.)

### Vine
Japanese wisteria (*Wisteria floribunda*)

Detailed information and recommended varieties can be found in Part III.

## Plants for a Purpose
# SHADE TREES

In the full heat of summer there's nothing more delicious than the green shade under a big tree. But like the decision to get married, the choice of a shade tree involves a major long-term commitment. So approach it thoughtfully. Look beyond quick inducements and superficial charm, and consider the needs the tree will have and the contributions it will make ten, twenty, or fifty years in the future.

Without a doubt there's a tree to meet every individual landscaping requirement. It would be great if there were some one tree that combined all the most sought-after characteristics. It would have lovely foliage, flowers, fruit, form, and bark; its flowers would be fragrant and its fruit tasty but not messy; the fall foliage would look sublime but never demand raking; and the tree would be long-lived, hardy under every duress, stately, yet small enough to have charm as well. . . .

But there's no such thing around — at least not yet. Since the late 1960s the federal government has run an "urban forestry" program aimed at discovering and propagating the plant strains most perfectly suited to the city or suburban landscape; and several state universities are also working in this area. By the early years of the next century you may well be able to find trees that will meet a broad range of criteria without any of the drawbacks or weaknesses their species now possess.

Meanwhile, the first guideline for the selection of large trees is: restrain yourself. It's natural to yearn for the flowers of one tree, the fall color of another, the fast growth of a third. It's also natural to yield to the siren song of nurseries with bargain rates and bonus collections — "five trees for the price of two" and so on. But that way clutter lies. Before you know it you'll have a mini-arboretum in your front yard, like one family I know whose yard started as a naked expanse of earth when they first moved in: now, ten years later, it's a jungle of wildly various vegetation.

Another guideline: be brave enough to let a tree go if it's not right for your place. Very often, good landscape gardening consists of elimination as much as any other single activity. A frequent trap for the unwary is the tree that's already growing on your property, whether it's a volunteer seedling struggling up through the forsythia, or a sickly middle-sized shade tree, or a huge monster. For many people it's all but impossible to say good-bye to the seedling, the sickly, or the monstrous. But sometimes it has to be done. A weed is a plant out of place, and that applies equally to the grass in the flower bed, the lilies-of-the-valley sprouting between the bricks of the front walk, and the ancient Norway maple that's shading out or starving out every other plant you possess. Get rid of trees that are unhealthy, crowded, past their prime, out of keeping, or out of proportion, and you can often do more for your landscape than you could accomplish by installing a dozen new specimens.

That said, you may still be in the market for a new tree. Here are some general considerations and a few recommended candidates.

**Choosing a Shade Tree** The smaller your grounds and the fewer trees you need, the more of a challenge the decision-making process. The range of possibilities is vast. Your first job is to isolate the qualities most important to you: color of foliage, density of shade, fragrance of flower, appeal to birds, etc. The list on page 204 includes some exceptionally fine all-around trees; but if you're looking for some specific attribute such as fall foliage, form, texture, or bark color, you will find other ideas in the Plants by Design sections of October through February.

Remember the rule of proper scale. Be alert to the ultimate size of the tree you select and how it will relate to the scale of its surroundings. All the trees listed on page 204 are over 30 feet tall in maturity (trees for smaller spaces are listed in May). But there's wide variation even among these larger trees: a 40-foot yellowwood plays a very different part from an 80-foot beech.

Trees' fall foliage color often varies depending on location, climate, etc. Sassafras leaves can be yellow or red.

The old rule of simplicity also applies. Hard though it may be to restrict yourself to one or two types of trees, it's usually better to do so unless you have a very expansive territory to cover. If you plan to install three trees in one spot, it's better to plant three of one variety than one each of three types.

Keep in mind the branching habits of trees when they are mature. Do you want upswept branches, horizontal, or drooping; dense and twiggy or open and graceful? Sometimes this is hard to discern in a nursery sapling, so check Part III (or a nursery catalogue) when in doubt. Most trees do not assume a real individual character until they reach a trunk diameter of 4 to 6 inches.

Where fall foliage color is a factor in your choice, here are a few hints. It's the combination of cool nights and warm sun that brings out the most vivid oranges, reds, and red-purples; so trees in that color range will do best in a location with ample sun. Yet there is considerable variation in color from one plant to another within the same species, from one spot to another in the same neighborhood, and even from one year to another in the same plant. Some of these variations depend on the genetic makeup of the individual plant, others on annual vagaries of weather, others on topography and microclimates. For all these reasons, I always pick out red maples, sugar maples, and oaks in nurseries in fall so that I can be confident of at least their potential for color. Another trick is to take into account the angles of sun and sources of shade on your property. Often only the sides of plants exposed to southern and western sun will color up fully. (Similarly, shrubs or small trees in open or partial shade will not color like those in full sunlight.) So choose and position all your plants with this in mind.

Finally, some trees lend themselves especially well to grouping, and actually take on a stronger, richer appearance than if they were planted alone. Often these are trees that grow in clusters or colonies in natural situations, such as oak, American beech, ash, maple, hickory, or birch. Other trees, because of strong individuality or massive size, tend to be most effective as single, isolated specimens — like sugar maple, linden, or honey locust. But no tree can or should be pigeonholed strictly as a "grouping" rather than a "specimen" tree. Any big tree, growing by itself with no competition for sun, water, or soil nutrients, will mature into a specimen with character and stature it wouldn't ever have attained as part of a cluster or grove. The choice of handling depends on the effect you want.

Above, honey locust (left) and Amur cork tree (right) are shade trees with fine-textured summer foliage. The photo of the honey locust shows the delicacy of its branches and twigs in winter silhouette.

## A Selection of Shade Trees

*Norway maple (*Acer platanoides*)
Red maple (*Acer rubrum*)
Sugar maple (*Acer saccharum*)
*Red horse chestnut (*Aesculus carnea*)
Horse chestnut (*Aesculus hippocastanum*)
Paper birch or canoe birch (*Betula papyrifera*)
*Cutleaf weeping birch (*Betula pendula* 'Gracilis')
*Katsura tree (*Cercidiphyllum japonicum*)
*Yellowwood (*Cladrastis lutea*)
American beech (*Fagus grandifolia*)
European beech (*Fagus sylvatica*)
White ash (*Fraxinus americana*)
Ginkgo or maidenhair tree (*Ginkgo biloba*)
Thornless honey locust (*Gleditsia triacanthos inermis*)

Tulip tree (*Liriodendron tulipifera*)
Black gum or black tupelo (*Nyssa sylvatica*)
*Amur cork tree (*Phellodendron amurense*)
Scarlet oak (*Quercus coccinea*)
Red oak (*Quercus rubra*)
Golden weeping willow (*Salix alba tristis*)
*Thurlow weeping willow (*Salix elegantissima*)
*Sassafras (*Sassafras albidum*)
Japanese pagoda tree (*Sophora japonica*)
Littleleaf linden (*Tilia cordata*)
*Crimean linden (*Tilia euchlora*)
Silver linden (*Tilia tomentosa*)
Zelkova (*Zelkova serrata*)

*Indicates trees that are medium-sized, with mature heights of approximately 30 to 50 feet. Other trees listed will reach 50 to 100 feet or more.

Detailed information and recommended varieties can be found in Part III.

## Materials and Construction
# WATER IN THE LANDSCAPE

Water is cooling to look at, to wade or swim in, and to listen to. It can also actually cool the air around you — both because of the refrigerating effect of evaporation, and because water retains coolness longer than air.

In the natural landscape there is no element more captivating, more irresistibly attractive than water. It speaks to every physical sense — and to our inner beings as well. Water is, after all, the primary component of every living thing on this planet.

From the simplest reflection mirrored in a quiet pool to the thunderous resonance of a mountain cataract, the spectrum of effects water creates in nature is nearly infinite. Man-made gardens have always celebrated water. Pools and fountains were the focal points of Roman atria, Moorish courtyards in Spain, Moghul palace grounds in India, palace gardens in China and Japan. All of these — and the extravagant water vistas of Italian villas, the artificial lakes of French châteaux, the ponds and lakes of the English country tradition — have their descendants in public and private gardens in this country. Still or flowing, falling or leaping, bubbling or misting, water in the landscape is a source of charm, mystery, an almost hypnotic fascination.

If you're lucky enough to have a wet lowland or a spring or stream on your property, use this section primarily as a source of design ideas. The construction end of things will really consist of adapting the natural topography and vegetation to suit your utilitarian and/or decorative ends. Consult your state university extension service or soil conservation service for guidelines on handling ponds or streambeds in your specific area. If necessary, you may want to introduce or recirculate water to supplement the natural supply during the dryest season.

Few homesites are blessed with existing water supplies, however. Nor do most people even have the kind of topography that will

Natural effects of water, from falls (below, left) to smooth sheets (below, right), suggest varieties of water display that can be adapted for the home landscape.

make falls or basins for water once it is brought in. So this section focuses on uses of water that include both importing water and constructing environments for it.

**Water as Ornament**   As with so many facets of landscape design and construction, the first step in working with water is to look and think. Look at the forms and manifestations of water in nature, and think about how they work. How does water move along a steep or irregular bank, against a shallow beach, around rocks in a stream? What shapes does it take in open ponds or narrow channels? What land forms cause it to lie glassy smooth, to trickle quietly, or to splash energetically? With an awareness of natural forms of water activity (or inactivity), you can channel, direct, or contain water in effective and pleasing ways.

**Forms of water display**   Ornamental water effects can be grouped into three categories, to be used singly or in combination:

- Piped water is pumped and propelled through nozzles or jets to form sprays, squirts, gurgles, splashes, or drips, as in all kinds of fountains.
- Falling water is pulled by gravity over drops in elevation, resulting in falls, spills, rapids, or eddies.
- Still water lies at rest, as in a lily pond, fishpond, reflecting pool, or birdbath.

You must decide what effect or combination of effects is appropriate for the scale and character of your setting. A quiet trickle into a sunken birdbath? A decorative spray that can be illuminated at night? A simulated streambed ending in a reflecting pool next to a terrace? You can let the water display blend with its environment, or design it to enhance the theme or overall motif you have chosen for the space.

**Mechanisms for water display**   Both the location and the purpose of the water display will affect the details of its construction. A lily pond for a large sunny lawn will be designed differently, and have different mechanical requirements, from a naturalized pond in a shady low spot.

But a few basic items are common to all water displays from birdbaths to swimming pools. At the very least, you'll require a basin to contain water and a source of water to fill it. And, of course, if there is to be moving water, then a pump is needed to recirculate it. There should also be a bottom drain to permit cleaning the basin from time to time, and an overflow drain in case heavy rains or snow melt fill it beyond its capacity. If there's a pump, you'll need electricity to power it. And while you're installing electricity, you may want to consider installing lighting as well: the combination of water and illumination can produce wonderful effects at night.

One measure of good design and construction of any landscape fixture is that it should look as attractive in winter (five to six months of the year) as in summer. Therefore, no pipes, pumps, electrical cords, or lamps should be visible. They spoil the effect at any time, and they look particularly sad and out of place in winter when the pool or other display is drained.

**Swimming Pools**   By far the most widespread use of water in the American landscape is the swimming pool. If you ever fly into or out of a metropolitan airport, look at the suburbs spread out beneath you: the turquoise rectangles, ovals, and circles dot the landscape with incredible density and regularity.

Swimming pools, dedicated to pleasing the sense of touch, can and should (though they seldom do) appeal to the eye and the ear as well. Unlike a lily pond, a reflecting pool, or a miniature waterfall, however, a swimming pool in a residential landscape is something of a bull in a china shop. It can't help but make a major impact on everything within range. Because a swimming pool is so cumbersome, so big, so visually potent, there is often a tendency for homeowners and contractors alike to put aside their good taste and training and just build the thing willy-nilly.

The rectilinear design of the swimming pool is integrated with that of the house close by, and the bottom of the pool is painted gray for an elegant subdued color of water.

But you can have the sensual delight of a cool dip on a sultry day and still create a pool habitat that is harmoniously integrated with its surroundings and a thing of beauty in itself. This doesn't necessarily involve great added cost. It's more a matter of thoughtfully taking stock of where and how you will build the pool, and of coordinating line, form, and materials with the existing setting. As with ornamental pools, an attentive eye is your most valuable tool.

I'll give you here what I consider the most important rules of thumb for designing swimming pools, based on my own experience with a large number of them.

**Location**   If your pool is near your house (either because that's all the space you have or because you want the pool to be part of the view from your windows), I suggest that you put it very close to the house and key its size, shape, construction materials, furnishings, and plantings to those of and around the house. If you live in the North, however, and if you have enough space to let the pool occupy a separate self-contained area, I'd encourage you to go this route — primarily because in this climate, swimming pools are not very agreeable to look at for most of the year. And whether near or far from the house, a pool should not be under trees or downwind of them. Trees' falling leaves and detritus make a terrible mess of a pool.

**Type**   I do not recommend an aboveground pool under any normal circumstances. It may be cheaper than an inground one, but it is bound to be an eyesore from at least one vantage point.

**Shape**   Take your cues from the house, the space available, and the setting. Free-form pools are tricky to work with if they're right up against the straight lines of house, patio, and so on; they're easier if somewhat removed from the house in a natural area. Rectangular pools can work well anywhere. And keep practical considerations in mind when you choose the pool's shape: try to balance cut and fill, making use somehow of the material excavated from the pool.

**Deck**   My own preference is for an exposed-aggregate concrete with round pebbles in a good range of colors — provided the job is expertly done. You can also build pool decks of wood; or of modular paving tiles, blocks, or bricks. Or stone: bluestone, granite, slate, limestone. Of all materials the least expensive is concrete, the most expensive stone.

A coping (a rounded, slightly protruding edge) offers an element of comfort and practicality. I do feel, however, that the standard foot-wide precast coping makes an extremely strong linear statement. Particularly near the house, it's sometimes preferable to let the edge of the deck be the edge of the pool.

Drainage is a major issue with decks. Slope all deck surfaces away from the pool, and arrange carefully for drainage of any planting areas around the deck. If water seeps below a concrete deck it will freeze and cause heaving and cracking.

**Equipment**  As with ornamental pools, concealment of plumbing is mandatory. It sometimes comes as a shock to discover the amount of plumbing, power machinery, and other apparatus and chemical input a simple swimming pool involves. The minimum will be pump, filter, supply of chlorine, and algae control. If you're going to heat the pool you'll need heating units, fuel storage capacity, and so on. Plan for an enclosure for all this gear before the pool is built, not as an afterthought.

**Fencing**  Fortunately (since town ordinances require it anyway), fencing affords great scope for ingenuity and creativity. How to make the pool secure, yet allow for air circulation and nice views while at the same time avoiding a fenced-in feeling — this challenge can be fun to meet. Wrought iron is costly but elegant for formal garden settings. The least expensive and most transparent fencing (in fact it's almost invisible) is a black-vinyl-coated wire mesh with rectangular openings, stretched between posts of wood or black-painted steel. I am not partial to chain-link fence, but if for some reason you are stuck with it you can soften the effect with shrubbery or vines. Other than metal, the best choice will be one of the almost unlimited forms of wood fencing. Depending on style and finish, wood fits into any design and blends with any surroundings.

## Plants by Design
# JULY BLOOMERS

### Flowering trees and shrubs for summer color

### Early July
Swamp azalea (*Rhododendron viscosum*)
Korean stewartia (*Stewartia koreana*)
Japanese stewartia (*Stewartia pseudocamelliia*)
Littleleaf linden (*Tilia cordata*)
Crimean linden (*Tilia euchlora*)
Silver linden (*Tilia tomentosa*)

### Mid-July
Common trumpet creeper (*Campsis radicans*)

Golden-rain tree (*Koelreuteria paniculata*)
Sorrel tree or sourwood (*Oxydendrum arboreum*)
Memorial rose (*Rosa wichuraiana*)

### Late July
Buttonbush (*Cephalanthus occidentalis*)
Summer-sweet clethra (*Clethra alnifolia*)
Rose-of-Sharon or shrub althea (*Hibiscus syriacus*)

Detailed information and recommended varieties can be found in Part III.

# LANDSCAPE TASKS FOR JULY

**Irrigation**   Keeping up the water supply of lawns, flowers, and shrubs — particularly evergreens — is a major July responsibility. Give each garden area an occasional deep watering, not frequent sprinklings (which really do more harm than good).

Newly transplanted trees and shrubs are particularly vulnerable to drought, and need watching. If you have a great many plants to attend to, a moisture-meter probe can be a help. This instrument consists of a thin probe with a meter on the end: you plunge the probe a foot deep in the soil, and the meter tells you the status of the soil moisture.

**Wisteria Pruning**   After wisteria blooms it should be radically pruned. This promotes flower production and prevents the vines from getting too heavy and unruly — which can be a major threat when a vine is on a wooden porch, trellis, or arbor. I let each vine develop just a few main trunks, and cut back all lateral branches to 10 to 12 inches from the main stem.

Left to itself, wisteria will tear apart almost any trellis. Prune hard after bloom; the more you prune, the better for the vine (and the trellis).

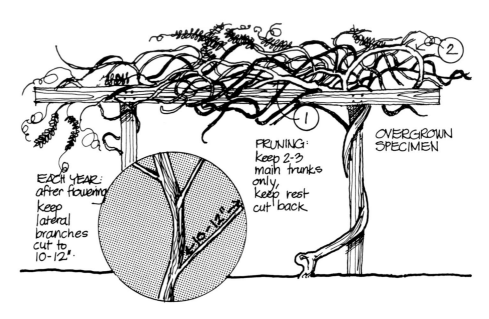

**Hedge Pruning**   Keep up the trimming of deciduous hedges as needed (see November Plants for a Purpose for some guidelines). Many deciduous hedge plants call for several shapings a year.

Be sure to prune evergreen hedges by the end of the first week of July. Their annual growth period is ending then anyway, so a good shaping will last until the following spring. More important, you want to give any tender new growth that does come after pruning a chance to harden off before cold weather.

**Pest Control**
**Red spider mites**   Watch for red spider mite damage to evergreens, particularly the close-needled dwarf varieties. These mites are most apt to invade in dry weather. If necessary, spray with a miticide

such as malathion; two applications are usually needed. As always with poisons, follow the label directions to the letter.

**Poison ivy**   This noxious and invasive plant definitely qualifies as a pest. If any poison ivy grows on your property you should stop it before it multiplies. If you catch it early, you can pull it out by the roots. Or there are a number of liquid and granular compounds on the market you can mix with water to spray on the plants. Pick a dry spell: if you spray just before a rain, the herbicide will wash off and leave the poison ivy as happy as before. Wear heavy clothing and gloves, and as always, be scrupulous about reading and following the directions for proper use of the spray.

**Nursery Sales**   This is often a month for great markdowns at nurseries. If you're in the market for balled and burlapped or container-grown trees or shrubs, you may be able to get them now at a reduced rate and plant them successfully. Do, however, stick to a supplier you know and have confidence in; a tired or sickly plant is never a bargain.

# AUG

**In sultry August weather, the pool imparts a sense of refreshment and repose to this Japanese garden.**

"The old of the moon in August is the time to cut your brush," goes a true old saying. Brush cut now stays cut — because trees and shrubs have pretty much stopped growing for the year. Everything is slowing down. Nights are longer, lawns are dormant. In suburbs and cities, the cool evenings and gentler sun make outdoor greenery especially welcoming now. I'll look at some special aspects of gardening in the city this month — and at plants for small spaces (city or country); garden furnishings; and the select group of landscape plants that come into bloom in August.

---

### Landscaping Opportunities
# CITY GARDENS

Designing and building a city garden is worth all the ingenuity (and effort) you can put into it. Particularly in the heat of summer, nothing gives such wonderful respite from the clamor and bustle of city life as a garden.

Yet the fact remains that creating a city garden almost seems to define itself as a series of problems. The best way I know of to surmount these obstacles is to recognize and address them at the start. They will probably consist of some or all of the following:

**Soil**   Most urban soils are better described as dirt, and consist of construction debris, gravel, and sand. If you're lucky enough to possess something resembling proper loam, it has probably been beaten down to the consistency of concrete. Porosity, fertility, and drainage capacity are probably going to be up to you.

**Shade**   A city means density of both buildings and people. Even if your garden plot is not deeply shaded by abutting structures, you're likely to want to provide yourself with privacy by means of a wall or fence — and that means shade. Plants that require a lot of sun will stretch toward the light, growing leggy and frail. So you're probably going to have to stick to shade-tolerant plants.

**Air**   City air is actually a mixture of air with dust, soot, carbon monoxide, sulfur dioxide, and other particles and gases, none of which are beneficial to plants (or people, for that matter). But for the foreseeable future, air pollution has to be considered a fact of urban life. Some plants and construction materials will suffer badly from the dust, soot, etc., and these you must avoid. Other plants are quite adaptable and, in their quiet way, improve air quality.

**Accessibility**   Most city gardens seem to be relegated to leftover space. You may find that your only access to your city plot is through the laundry-room door, down a narrow alley, or even over a roof and down a fire escape. This will have a lot to do with how ambitious your plans for planting and construction can be.

**Cost**   The cost of improving your soil, providing for drainage, installing some greenery, and possibly doing a little paving or construction may be somewhat daunting. But at least, since a city garden is almost always very small, its cost is finite. To do an equally good job on a suburban site would probably cost quite a lot more — without yielding such positively dramatic results.

**Designing a City Garden**   The great opportunity and first priority in a city garden is to bring a bit of nature into an unnatural

The skillful use of shade-tolerant vines and broad-leaved evergreens creates a haven of beauty in a tiny walled city garden.

setting. Japanese bonsai, the art of cultivating individual specimens or groves of dwarfed trees in containers, can put a miniature living forest on a windowsill. You can think of a city garden as a larger kind of bonsai — a microcosm you can shape to evoke all the wonder of the natural world. The smallest, simplest things will do the trick: a tree with berries to attract birds, a source of running water, or a little patch of green where the sunlight falls.

The basic design guidelines I follow for a city garden are the same as those for any landscape (see Part I). But a few watchwords are in order here.

First, let simplicity be your guiding principle. It is often hard for the zealous gardener to resist cramming too lavish a variety of forms, colors, or textures into too small a space. But the effect can't help but be distracting and cluttered. In a city garden restfulness is the goal.

Second, think small, particularly when you select plants. Most plants that are well adapted to the shady, constricted, and polluted environs of a city garden are in fact modest in size. Don't be tempted by big forest trees or by the kinds of shrubs that send up hundreds of shoots every year so that they sprawl over the countryside. You won't be happy with the burgeoning habits of these plants for long, and they won't be happy with you.

Third, put practicality foremost, both in the construction stage and as you plan for future maintenance. For instance, if you're going to be hand-carrying paving material from the street, through the kitchen, and out into the garden, your paved area had better be small; and big stone slabs are not recommended. Or if you have no outdoor water source, keep your planting ambitions modest. In other words, think through not only what you're going to do but how you're going to do it. You may well find that the means dictate the ends, rather than the other way around.

**Building a City Garden**    It should be all too clear by now that in a city situation, both the designing phase and the building phase will be as much a matter of coping with difficulties as anything else. I'll take the building process in the same order as the difficulties I listed at the beginning of this section.

I am assuming here that your garden is at ground level. (For a balcony, window-box, or rooftop garden, you'll be working primarily with containers — see the October Landscaping Opportunities section.) At ground level, your biggest chore and most important contribution will be to improve the soil. First, get a soil test (see March Landscape Tasks). "Proceeding without a soil test," an old-time gardener said to me, "is like building a house without a blueprint." A good way to tackle soil and drainage problems is to construct raised beds. If you can till the soil mechanically or by hand and bring in additional topsoil and organic matter (compost, manure, and/or peat moss), great. If you can't do that, you can still avail yourself of the benefits of raised beds by digging soil out of one place and piling it in another. Add peat moss and perlite, which both come cleanly bagged and are light to carry, to improve tilth (texture and porosity) and fertility. Install curbs of wood, stone, or brick; if you have raised your bed(s) only 6 inches, you'll have gained deeper and more friable soil. And if it's deep and friable, that is half the battle. Limestone, fertilizers, whatever you add now will have a proper matrix to be added to.

What to do about the place where you removed soil? Perhaps pave it, cobble it, or put a sandbox or a small pool in it; or install footings and a small deck over it. This is the sort of issue that makes practicality such a vital consideration at the design stage.

One way to deal with poor drainage is to build a drainage gutter or conduit that connects to a downspout from the roof. The downspout presumably leads to a drain, which leads to a storm sewer somewhere. If this is not feasible, you should consider a drywell or "French drain": a hole or trench filled with gravel, where water can collect and leach off slowly into the subsoil. (A drywell might be one good use for that spot where you excavated soil for your raised bed.) There's one possible hitch, however. Your subsoil may be so densely compacted, rocky, or clayey that it won't permit leaching. Check by digging a hole a foot across and several feet deep and filling it with water. If the water disappears overnight, your subsoil is probably in good shape for leaching. But if after 24 hours some of the water is still there, you are going to have to find another way to collect and dispose of excess rainwater.

You can't do much about the problem of shade from neighboring buildings, except to make allowance for it in your choice of plants and construction materials. But if part of your shade is going to result from your own construction of, say, a screening fence, you can have some impact. Try to pick a design that is at least partly open to sunlight (the November Materials and Construction section has some good suggestions).

The air-polluting particles and gases that will be the daily diet of your city garden also fall into the category of things you cannot change and will have to live with. The plants listed at the end of this section are all resilient and well adapted to survival in city air. If you decide to go beyond this list for some favorite of your own, do talk over your selection with a knowledgeable nurseryman to be sure your choices will be successful. Similarly, some garden construction materials will work better in polluted circumstances than others. Obviously, you should steer clear of white paint, pale masonry, and pale stones like limestone or marble. Choose wall and seating materials that show dirt as little as possible. For paving materials think in terms of surfaces that can be swept or hosed down with ease. And keep the questions of accessibility and cost always in mind.

**Choosing Plants for the City Garden**  The plants listed here are chosen mainly for their ability to put up with city conditions, from shade to poor soil to dirty air; so this is a very strictly limited group. There are countless other good possibilities in this month's Plants

A narrow raised planting bed is easy to maintain and holds precious soil for ground covers and vines. (The newly repointed wall will look better when the mortar darkens.)

for a Purpose section and in the lists of ground covers and vines in June. Just be sure not to pick anything that's specifically described as intolerant of urban life, and you may have good luck. A little adventurous experimentation is not out of line, when a green oasis is the goal.

## Plants for the City Garden

### Shade Trees

European hornbeam (*Carpinus betulus*)
Katsura tree (*Cercidiphyllum japonicum*)
Ginkgo or maidenhair tree (*Ginkgo biloba*)
Thornless honey locust (*Gleditsia triacanthos inermis*)
Japanese pagoda tree (*Sophora japonica*)
Littleleaf linden (*Tilia cordata*)

### Smaller Deciduous Trees

Japanese maple (*Acer palmatum*)
Weeping European birch (*Betula pendula*)
White fringe tree (*Chionanthus virginicus*)
Flowering dogwood (*Cornus florida*)
Washington hawthorn (*Crataegus phaenopyrum*)
Star magnolia (*Magnolia stellata*)
Sorrel tree or sourwood (*Oxydendrum arboreum*)
Amur cork tree (*Phellodendron amurense*)
Bradford callery pear (*Pyrus calleryana* 'Bradford')

### Evergreen Trees and Shrubs

White fir (*Abies concolor*)
Douglas fir (*Pseudotsuga menziesii*)
Umbrella pine (*Sciadopitys verticillata*)
Yews (*Taxus* spp.)
Canadian hemlock (*Tsuga canadensis* — dwarf vars.)

### Deciduous Shrubs

Japanese barberry (*Berberis thunbergii*)
Flowering quince (*Chaenomeles speciosa*)
Summer-sweet clethra (*Clethra alnifolia*)
Cotoneasters (*Cotoneaster* spp.)
Redvein enkianthus (*Enkianthus campanulatus*)
Winged euonymus (*Euonymus alata*)
Showy border forsythia (*Forsythia intermedia* 'Spectabilis')
Rose-of-Sharon or shrub althea (*Hibiscus syriacus*)
Peegee hydrangea (*Hydrangea paniculata* 'Grandiflora')
Regel privet (*Ligustrum obtusifolium regelianum*)
Winter honeysuckle (*Lonicera fragrantissima*)
Vanhoutte spirea (*Spiraea vanhouttei*)
Black haw (*Viburnum prunifolium*)

### Broad-leaved Evergreens

Boxwoods (*Buxus* spp.)
Boxleaf holly (*Ilex crenata* 'Convexa')
Inkberry (*Ilex glabra*)
American holly (*Ilex opaca*)
Mountain laurel (*Kalmia latifolia*)
Drooping leucothoe ((*Leucothoe fontanesiana*)
Japanese andromeda or pieris (*Pieris japonica*)
Laland firethorn (*Pyracantha coccinea* 'Lalandei')
Rhododendrons and azaleas (*Rhododendron* spp.)

### Vines

Boston ivy (*Parthenocissus tricuspidata*)
Virginia creeper (*Parthenocissus quinquefolia*)
Japanese wisteria (*Wisteria floribunda*)

### Ground Covers

Wintercreeper (*Euonymus fortunei* vars.)
English ivy (*Hedera helix* vars.)
Japanese spurge or pachysandra (*Pachysandra terminalis*)

Detailed information and recommended varieties can be found in Part III.

# PLANTS FOR SMALL SPACES

How small is small? City gardens are small, of course, but in this section I am also considering everything from balcony or rooftop gardens to side yards in the suburbs and enclosed nooks next to houses or along walls in larger properties.

Not all small-scale situations require small plants, to be sure. If you have an old shade tree or a tall pine growing happily up and out of a narrow passageway or in the corner of a small yard, and if its location, condition, and appearance please you and create a pleasant canopy, by all means keep it.

But for the most part, gardens in circumscribed settings work best with modest-sized plantings. A big tree or large mass of shrubbery is apt to dominate everything else visually and give you a cramped, hemmed-in feeling. Big trees cast a lot of shade, making it hard for you to grow anything else under them, even grass. The roots of larger trees and shrubs take so much of the soil's moisture and nutrients that it is a constant battle for any other plant to survive near by. Besides, in their efforts to work their way out of confinement these hungry root systems will also tend to heave pavements or clog drains.

**Japanese maple varieties offer many textures, from this fine cutleaf type to coarser lobed-leaved selections.**

The plants listed on page 220, by contrast, make docile and cheerful citizens in close quarters. They're well suited to raised beds or containers, as well as to planting in the earth. They'll provide you with beauty of flower, texture, or form, as you choose, but without growing you out of house and home.

### Designing a Small Garden

The basic precepts of small-garden design are identical to those for the design of more roomy landscapes. First, it's important to plan. Sketch your design on paper; then measure it out and test it with mockups to see how it will work. Pay extra attention to proper scale, because it's extra important here.

Perhaps most important of all is simplicity. If ever there's a risk of developing a claustrophobic clutter, it is when space is limited. So restrain yourself. Tempting though it may be to try one of everything, you'll achieve a far happier effect if you stick to a few varieties. If necessary, group them for more mass or coverage.

### Choosing Trees and Shrubs

There are two large groups of plants not listed here that are in fact ideal for small spaces: ground covers and vines. (See the June Plants for a Purpose section.) Any number of ground covers can also be grown as container plants or in a rock-garden arrangement or as miniature shrubbery. And very often a vine can give you all the benefits of a tree or flowering shrub — but take up no more horizontal space then it needs for a foothold at the base of a wall or trellis.

Also, consider using shrubs as trees. Quite a few varieties in the June list of deciduous ornamental shrubs can be pruned to one to three stems and treated like small trees in a small garden, and they are lovely this way. Some that you might consider using are autumn olive, redvein enkianthus, shining sumac, or Siebold viburnum.

Finally, bear in mind that many deciduous and evergreen shrubs, broad-leaved evergreens, and small trees are now available in dwarf forms. Small cultivars of rhododendrons, azaleas, andromeda (pieris), lilacs, even hemlocks can be found. If your heart is set on a tree or shrub you've discovered elsewhere in this book, do ask your nursery if they have a reliable dwarf variety to fit your small plot.

That said, here is a selection of my own favorites for planting where space is at a premium.

## Trees and Shrubs for Small Spaces

### Deciduous Trees

Japanese maple (*Acer palmatum*)
Shadblow, juneberry, or serviceberry (*Amelanchier canadensis*)
Weeping European birch (*Betula pendula*)
Gray birch (*Betula populifolia*)
Redbud (*Cercis canadensis*)
White fringe tree (*Chionanthus virginicus*)
Flowering dogwood (*Cornus florida*)
Kousa or Japanese dogwood (*Cornus kousa*)
Cornelian cherry dogwood (*Cornus mas*)
Washington hawthorn (*Crataegus phaenopyrum*)
Star magnolia (*Magnolia stellata*)
Crabapples (*Malus* spp.)
Sargent crabapple (*Malus sargentii*)
Sorrel tree or sourwood (*Oxydendrum arboreum*)
Weeping cherry (*Prunus subhirtella* 'Pendula')
Bradford callery pear (*Pyrus calleryana* 'Bradford')
Korean stewartia (*Stewartia koreana*)

### Deciduous Shrubs

Crimson pygmy Japanese barberry (*Berberis thunbergii* 'Crimson Pygmy')
Cranberry cotoneaster (*Cotoneaster apiculatus*)
Skogsholm bearberry cotoneaster (*Cotoneaster dammeri* 'Skogsholmen')
Compact winged euonymus (*Euonymus alata* 'Compacta')
Bronx forsythia (*Forsythia viridissima* 'Bronxensis')
Dwarf fothergilla or witch alder (*Fothergilla gardenii*)
Bush or shrubby cinquefoil, or potentilla (*Potentilla fruticosa*)
Korean azalea (*Rhododendron mucronulatum*)
Daphne spirea (*Spiraea japonica* 'Alpina')
Compact Korean spice viburnum (*Viburnum carlesii* 'Compactum')
Compact or dwarf cranberrybush viburnum (*Viburnum opulus* 'Compactum' or 'Nanum')

### Evergreen Trees and Shrubs

Dwarf or pyramidal hinoki false cypress (*Chamaecyparis obtusa* 'Nana' or 'Nana Gracilis')
Dwarf golden thread false cypress (*Chamaecyparis pisifera* 'Filifera Golden Mop')
Dwarf Chinese garden juniper (*Juniperus chinensis procumbens* 'Nana')
Nest spruce (*Picea abies* 'Nidiformis')
Dwarf white pine (*Pinus strobus* 'Nana')
Dwarf Japanese yew (*Taxus cuspidata* 'Nana')
Hetz Midget arborvitae (*Thuja occidentalis* 'Hetz Midget')
Dwarf or weeping hemlock (*Tsuga canadensis* 'Bennett' or 'Coles Prostrate')

### Broad-Leaved Evergreens

Littleleaf box (*Buxus microphylla* vars.)
Boxwood (*Buxus sempervirens* 'Vardar Valley' or 'Green Gem')
Hellers Japanese holly (*Ilex crenata* 'Helleri')
Dwarf inkberry (*Ilex glabra* 'Compacta')
Dwarf drooping leucothoe (*Leucothoe fontanesiana* 'Nana')
Canby paxistima (*Paxistima canbyi*)
Compact Japanese andromeda or pieris (*Pieris japonica* 'Compacta')
Carolina rhododendron (*Rhododendron carolinianum*)
Evergreen azaleas (*Rhododendron* 'Delaware Valley White,' *kaempferi*, 'Herbert,' 'Hinocrimson,' 'Hinodegiri')
Wilson rhododendron (*Rhododendron laetivirens*)
Purple gem rhododendron (*Rhododendron* 'Purple Gem')

Detailed information and recommended varieties can be found in Part III.

## Materials and Construction
# OUTDOOR FURNITURE

A beautiful landscape can be both enjoyed from a distance and cherished from within. Outdoor furniture lets you observe, participate, recreate, and relax in your landscape. This is just as true of furnishings in a spacious place as of seating and eating places in a tiny city patio. And a few hints may be helpful for both situations.

First, although you want to assemble furnishings that will comfortably meet your family's needs, you do not want to crowd your place with a hodgepodge of furniture and equipment — or break the bank, for that matter. Where should you start? What should you select? How much should you spend?

Begin by making list of all the areas you have available and of the activities requiring furniture that go on in each. It might look something like this:

### Furniture Needs by Area and Activity

| Place | Activities | Furniture |
| --- | --- | --- |
| Under shade trees | Family and party dining, cocktails, conversation, resting | Picnic table, chairs, small tables, hammock? |
| Terrace next to a window | Breakfast, lunch, supper, sitting | Table and chairs; trellis for shade? |
| Barbecue | Cooking | Grille, utility table, bench for cook or guests |
| Flower garden | Sitting, viewing | Ornamental bench |
| Children's play area | Climbing, swinging, jumping, sliding, building, digging, acting, etc. | Play equipment |

As you consider what to buy to fulfill the requirements of your own list, bear in mind the following ground rules.

- Don't try to stuff furniture for every conceivable purpose onto a small terrace or patio. If you have a little additional space, you can find separate homes for some activities and liberate the patio from clutter; if not, you'll need to make compromises, or perhaps include a small storage shed in your plans.
- Select good-quality furniture that combines sturdy construction and durable materials with restraint of design. In general, furniture should not dominate the landscape but blend into it. The possible exception might be a special piece or group of pieces that are intentionally chosen as an ornamental feature — such as a custom-made wooden settee, painted white, in an herb or flower garden.
- Try to avoid putting outdoor furniture directly in the line of a prime view.
- If you're working on furniture at the base plan stage of a landscape design, you can experiment with paper templates cut to scale. You'll probably discover that you want to make your ter-

**Urban and suburban settings with similar background colors show the range of choices in outdoor furnishings. Formal wrought iron suits the city garden, above left. Above right, aluminum-framed furniture with white cushions contrasts starkly with the house.**

race larger, or to put some of the furniture away from the house, or even to buy less furniture. That can be all to the good if it lets you invest in better quality in the items you do buy.

- If you aren't able to use a plan and templates (or indeed, even if you are), make a deal with the supplier to allow you to return your garden furniture if you are not happy with it once you see it in place. This is one component of the landscape that you can easily take back if it's not the way you pictured it, and you should.

Now for a few ideas on furniture to meet the needs suggested in the areas-and-activities list above.

**Under shade trees (away from house)**   Here's the perfect place for a good big redwood or cedar table, benches, chairs, and maybe a small table or two. I prefer movable benches, since the fixed ones are hard for older people to get in and out of, and uncomfortable for small children. If you want to get fancy, you can add cushions; but they cannot stay out in the weather, so you need a place to store them and the patience to haul them out and back every time you use them.

A shady spot — ideally, under evergreens — is also lovely for a hammock. Children can't resist hammocks, though, so be sure to have a soft surface underneath, such as grass, shredded bark, or any soft mulch.

**Terrace next to a window**   Since an area like this constitutes a view from inside the house as well as a comfortable, enticing outdoor living space, I'd choose chairs and tables that are modest-scaled, unobtrusive, more delicate than the rustic cedar type. There's furniture of thin steel with wire mesh fabric, all painted black, that practically disappears, so that it doesn't impinge on your view of your plantings. Or you can get furniture with aluminum or vinyl-coated parts and open fabric webbing; again, for easy maintenance and an inconspicuous quality, I recommend dark colors or neutrals if possible. Save lightweight aluminum furniture with multicolored webbing for the beach.

**Barbecue**   There are many eminently satisfactory kinds of grilles, from the smallest hibachi to the most imposing masonry edifice. Whatever kind you prefer, I like to have a small table (about 2 by 3 feet) near by, where you can organize food supplies. Another amenity is a place where you can sit while the food sizzles, or where friends or family members can perch and keep the cook company.

**Flower garden**   By "flower garden" here I'm suggesting any place designed primarily for viewing but where you'd like to set aside a spot to relax. Some unusual and beautiful form of seating, such as an English teak bench or a cast-iron Victorian grapevine settee, would be appropriate in such a place; and there are many less costly but well-designed and comfortable alternatives.

**Children's play area**   Children do grow up. Play yards are temporary and should be designed accordingly; have in mind a second or ultimate role for the space once it's no longer used for children's play.

Furnishings for play areas should be sturdy and minimal. They can range from the standard sandbox, jungle gym, and swing set (wooden ones preferred: they're softer and warmer to the touch) to complex and expensive play systems. In my experience, however, children rapidly tire of most of this equipment and have far more fun inventing their own games wherever you least anticipated it. Besides, you get a much better ride on a long rope hung from a tree limb than on a swing set. There's no substitute, however, for the sandbox. All the kids love it. So do all the neighborhood cats. Put it in a place where you can grow flowers, herbs, or vegetables afterwards; my sandbox herbs are flourishing.

A decorative stone bench at Dumbarton Oaks in Washington, D.C.: more pleasant to look at than to sit on.

## Plants by Design
# AUGUST BLOOMERS
## A few standouts in the later-summer landscape

### Trees and Shrubs
Orange-eye butterfly bush (*Buddleia davidii*)

Summer-sweet clethra (*Clethra alnifolia*)

Rose-of-Sharon or shrub althea (*Hibiscus syriacus*)

Peegee hydrangea (*Hydrangea paniculata* 'Grandiflora')

Sorrel tree or sourwood (*Oxydendrum arboreum*)

Japanese pagoda tree (*Sophora japonica*)

### Vines
Clematis (*Clematis* spp.)

Chinese fleece vine (*Polygonum aubertii*)

### Ground Cover
Plantain lilies (*Hosta* spp.)

Detailed information and recommended varieties can be found in Part III.

**Rose-of-Sharon or shrub althea (below left) and fragrant summer-sweet clethra (below right) are two of the relatively small group of trees and shrubs blooming in August.**

# LANDSCAPE TASKS FOR AUGUST

**Lawn Upkeep**   You can, if you wish, allow your lawn grass to go dormant now. Growth will tend to slow down naturally, toward the end of July; and if you stop watering, it will come to a halt almost completely. It doesn't hurt lawn grasses to rest awhile before reviving with cooler weather and autumn rainfall. Besides, dormant grass doesn't take much mowing, so you get a rest too.

You may decide to keep up the watering, however, if you dislike the dull, dry appearance of a dormant lawn, or if your lawn gets the kind of strenuous wear (such as badminton or softball games) that would damage brittle grass.

**Evergreen Pruning**   Firs and spruces have to be treated a little differently from pines and hemlocks and other needled evergreens, because they form new buds along the sides (not at the outer ends) of their twigs. Now through late fall, you can see where the new growth will come; so this is the time to cut back selectively and judiciously, saving some buds for next spring. (For pruning of other needled evergreens, see May Landscape Tasks.)

**Trimming Deciduous Hedges**   In late August, you can give a final trimming to most deciduous hedge plants and they'll be all set until next spring. The prunings of this past spring and summer will have promoted dense growth of new shoots from the sides of cut twigs, but at this season the plants have pretty much finished growing for the year.

**Euonymus Scale**   It's at this time of year that scale insects really do a job on evergreen euonymus (wintercreeper and similar types). The leaves and stems of the plant will be covered with white insects. Scale can do real damage to euonymus if you let it go unchecked. Spray with oil emulsion, summer strength.

**Tools and Equipment**   As gardening chores slow down, go over all your gardening tools and get them into good condition. Clean, sharpen, and oil as appropriate, both for winter rustproofing and for the sake of a good start next spring.

# SEP

**A sweep of meadow grass just beginning to turn golden speaks of the end of summer.**

The golden days of September are a time of ripening and harvest — and of new beginnings. This month I'll touch upon some of the glories and the liabilities of fruits and berries grown in the home landscape. I'll discuss small trees that are superb for foliage and fruit at this time of year, and plants noted for ornamental (as opposed to edible) fruit display. I'll introduce brick as a paving and building material, since this is a great month for building. And since September begins the fall planting season, when you can put new trees into the ground while you enjoy the fruits of the old ones, I'll delve into the procedure for planting trees and shrubs.

## Landscaping Opportunities
# THE FRUITING GARDEN

Not only do fruit-bearing plants produce delectable yields, many of them also hold their own as decorative members of the landscape plant community. As a group, fruiting trees, shrubs, and vines are probably the most maintenance-intensive plants you'll ever have to deal with. They seem to keep you busy with spraying, pruning, fertilizing, weeding, cleanup at every month of the year. In this necessarily brief section, I won't try to give you all the cultural specifications (the Further Reference offers some good sources) but will outline a general philosophy and some design tips for using fruit-bearing plants in your landscape.

**Fruits for the Eating**  I have suffered some resounding defeats in my ventures with tree fruits, particularly with plums and cherries — and a few gratifying triumphs with peaches and apples. I've also met varying results with bush and vine fruits: fantastic raspberries and good grapes year after year, but only moderate success with blueberries. Despite all my tribulations, however, I firmly believe that fruiting plants are worth the struggle; because the kinds of fruits and berries you grow in your own yard are so good. They are completely unlike supermarket fruit. Commercial growers are forced to concentrate on specially bred types that can be picked unripe and that will keep their color and soundness throughout shipping and storage and on market shelves. They can't afford to grow the same mouth-watering varieties the home gardener can indulge in.

My own approach is to keep the plants I grow as healthy as possible. The most pest-resistant crop is one that grows vigorously and ripens fast. This means full sun, ample moisture, proper soil, and plenty of mulch where required. It also means clean growing practices, including regular removal of dead fruit and damaged branches in and around productive trees and shrubs. I do use a dormant oil spray as a preventive measure on peach, apple, and pear trees (see February and March Landscape Tasks). And finally, I try to temper with realism my expectations of the more difficult crops. Good years and bad years come and go, but there are some crops that seem to have nothing but bad years; and those I do without.

**Landscaping with Productive Plants**   Many fruit-bearing plants, especially the trees, are beautiful in bloom and attractive throughout much of the rest of the year. They can play as big a part in your landscape as you want; they don't have to be relegated to far corners or tucked behind the garage. Apples, cherries, or pears can stand on their own as specimen trees or can be part of shrub borders. Highbush blueberries are handsome shrubs by any standard, fine for borders or grouped plantings. Lowbush blueberries are second to none as a ground cover for thin, acid soil, perhaps among oak trees or pines. A little ingenuity will suggest uses even for the more challenging plants. Grapevines are lovely growing across a trellis for shade, or along an open fence for added summer screening. A mass of raspberries or blackberries can be worked into a shrub border or used as an informal barrier or hedgerow.

What plants to grow and how to fit them in? A lot depends on the amount of space and sun you can provide. Soil type, exposure, drainage, and other growing conditions are important too. As a quick guide, this table indicates the basic space, soil, and time requirements of the various fruiting plant groups. When you've arrived at a preliminary list of the plants you'd like to try, talk to a dependable nursery or garden center in your area to determine what specific varieties will be best adapted to the conditions you have to offer and the time you'd like to put in.

## Fruit-Bearing Plants

| Fruit | Spacing* | Soil preference | Years until bears | Years bearing |
|---|---|---|---|---|
| Raspberry | 3–4 feet, with 6 feet between rows | Deep loam | 2 | 8–10 |
| Blackberry | 3–4 feet, in a block or in rows 8 feet apart | Any fertile soil | 2 | Indefinite |
| Blueberry (highbush) | 4 feet, with 6–8 feet between rows | Well-drained acid soil, not too fertile | 3–4 | Indefinite |
| Peach | 16–20 feet | Sandy or stony loam | 2–3 | 10–15 |
| Plum | 20 feet | Heavy silt or clay loam | 3–4 | 20–30 |
| Cherry: | | | | |
| Sweet | 25–30 feet | Sandy loam | 3–5 | 40 |
| Sour | 20 feet | Clay loam | 3–5 | 25 |
| Apple | 30–40 feet | Loam | 6–8 | 40–50 |
| Pear | 30 feet | Clay loam | 3–6 | 30–40 |
| Grape | 8–10 feet | Any fertile soil | 2 | 50 |

*Spacing for dwarf and semidwarf trees (see discussion on page 230) can vary from 12 to 18 feet; consult nursery for instructions.

Above left: an apple tree provides both bounteous fruit at arm's reach and a foliar archway over the house entrance. Above right: a pear espaliered against a wall takes an enormous amount of care to grow and maintain.

## Space Savers: Dwarf and Semidwarf Fruit Trees

If your space is limited or if you crave fruit trees that are docile and easy to maintain, dwarf or semidwarf apples, pears, plums, or cherries may be for you. Dwarf fruit trees reach a top size of about 10 to 12 feet, semidwarfs 12 to 18 feet, with cherries slightly larger than other types in both categories.

Essentially these are trees of different desirable varieties that have been grafted onto slow-growing rootstocks. (There are also some genetic dwarfs, a new development.) The grafted rootstocks hold back the trees' annual growth rate, but otherwise the dwarfed trees are identical to their full-size counterparts. All you sacrifice is quantity of fruit, not quality or size of individual fruits.

You'll find that these trees not only save space but tend to begin fruiting at a younger age. Being modest in size they also ease the tasks of pruning, thinning, picking, and upkeep in general. Because the grafting of these plants requires experts — and because they take a longer time to train and grow to the size at which you buy them — you should be prepared to pay more for these trees.

**Special training methods** There are some specialized pruning and training systems to which dwarf and semidwarf trees are ideally

Save space, create decorative patterns, and (against a wall) have earlier fruit with plants trained in espalier forms. Here are some sample designs.

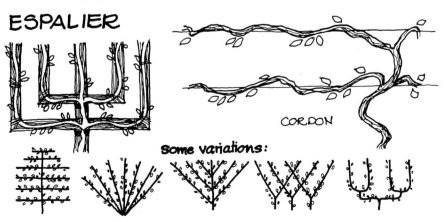

ESPALIER

CORDON

some variations:

suited. These methods go back many centuries in European gardening, and the terms we use for them come from the French: *espalier* and *cordon*. Both systems involve training plants to grow against south-facing walls, trellises, or fences. They're a wonderful way to have the beauty and productivity of fruit trees in an absolute minimum of space, which was one of the reasons for their original development. In addition, you can often grow as espaliers varieties that would not necessarily be hardy as freestanding specimens, because of the shelter and extra warmth provided by the supporting wall. For the same reason, an espaliered plant usually bears fruit earlier than it would elsewhere.

Beyond all these practical arguments, espaliers make fascinating decorative plantings to soften or screen a bare wall. They're often the perfect answer in a city garden or small patio.

Creating and maintaining espalier fruit trees is a project, however. The steps involved include training from purchase to maturity, then annual maintenance for optimum bearing. Of all the fruits I've mentioned, dwarf apples and pears take best to this treatment. Peaches come next, then plums. For all of them, be prepared to spend plenty of time clipping, tying, coaxing, and cajoling to achieve the final artistic — and productive — result.

---

**Plants for a Purpose**
# SMALL TREES FOR FLOWERS, FOLIAGE, AND FRUIT

There's no one month that I can single out as tailored to a discussion of small trees — because they do so much all year round. But the fruits of many of these plants definitely add to their appeal, so I have picked September.

Large trees offer big masses of shade or color, big architectural effects. For smaller-scale but no less important effects, small trees play a vital part in the landscape. What a small tree may lack in size it very often makes up many times over in a profusion of beauty.

Yet the appeal of small trees also stems partly from the very fact of their size. They're on a human scale. In a garden of limited size, such as a city or suburban plot, the large tree is a monster, the small tree a model resident. Small trees add more delicate textures, more encompassable forms to the landscape. They're ideal for locations close to houses and outdoor living areas, where the many charms of their flowers, foliage, fruits, bark, and branches are most visible and immediate.

What constitutes "small"? There's no clear demarcation line. Some "small" trees are also perfectly fine shade trees despite a mere 20 feet of overall height. Some "small" trees, supposed to top out at 30 feet, can fool you if conditions are perfect by growing on to 50 or 60 feet. For purposes of this section of this book, I'll arbitrarily put the bottom size limit of a mature small tree, as opposed to a shrub, at around 12 feet; the top at around 30 feet. (For deciduous shrubs see May, and for taller deciduous shade trees see July.)

You can use small trees in an almost infinite number of ways. They make fine isolated specimen plants for display on their own; they're good fillers in shrub borders; they provide summer shade near windows,

**Weeping flowering cherry and magnolia, enchanting in spring bloom (as here), are small trees with much to offer in the landscape throughout the year.**

Golden-rain tree really catches the eye when it's in flower. Bursts of yellow bloom cover the tree in late summer.

on lawns, or in patios. Whatever their functional role, their changing colors, forms, and lines are lovely throughout the year.

**Flowers** Perhaps the moment of greatest glory for many of the small trees listed in this section is the season of bloom: spring. The blossoms — often fragrant — are mostly in shades of white, pink, or yellow. Some of my favorite moments have been spent wandering through groves of blooming magnolias, crabapples, and cherries. It is a sensation you simply never forget.

There are also several small trees that bloom in mid- to late summer, so that you can spread your trees' blooming season throughout much of the year (as shown in the Plants by Design lists of March through August) — provided you have enough room. Room is a criterion because in a small property, as I've said elsewhere, too many different varieties can make for confusion. If you are working with limited space, try to limit yourself to just a few kinds of flowering trees.

**Summer Foliage** Spectacular though the blooming season is, the season of foliage is equally important and lasts a great deal longer. Some small trees' leaves are compound (sets of small leaves arranged on a stem); some are heart-shaped, star-shaped, or oval; most are somewhat smaller and finer in overall texture than those of bigger trees, so that they contribute variety to a landscape's patchwork of colors and textures. And in autumn, small-sized leaves tend to blow around and vanish into crevices and corners, not blanket the countryside with heavy accumulations demanding raking. For many people that's a very good thing.

**Fruit and Fall Foliage** Many ornamental trees produce fruit — in a spectrum of colors from yellow to red to blue-black. Some fruits, like red maple's, appear in spring and keep the tree's glow of color alight for weeks. Most, however, ripen in September and October (and this month's Plants by Design list includes many of the best). At this time of

Even without leaves, many small trees have distinctive forms. This group includes representative favorites chosen for form.

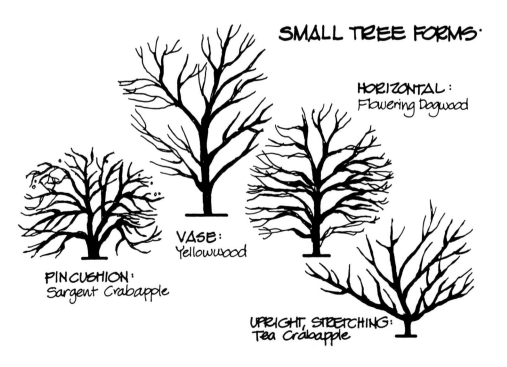

SMALL TREE FORMS·

HORIZONTAL:
Flowering Dogwood

VASE:
Yellowwood

PINCUSHION·
Sargent Crabapple

UPRIGHT, STRETCHING:
Tea Crabapple

year, the dried fruits, seeds, and pods of many small trees make wonderful accents for dried flower arrangements.

Some of the most cherished fruiting trees are those — like hawthorn and many viburnums — whose fruits hang on long into the cold season. The trees and the flocks of birds that visit them provide winterlong live entertainment.

(Be aware, though, that some fruiting trees can make quite a mess. Some drop their fruits en masse after the first few frosts; with others it is the feasting of birds and wildlife that generates the litter. In either case, if the plant in question is next to a paved area or refined lawn, cleanup can be a tiresome chore. Place your fruiting trees accordingly.)

The autumn leaf color of small trees can be every bit as vivid as that of large ones. You can choose colors ranging from the sunny yellows of birches to the deep scarlet of Japanese maple, with every hue in between.

**Color, Form, and Line in Winter**   For locations around your house, where you'll be viewing them at close range throughout the long leafless season, consider the color and texture of bark and twigs as well as the overall branching habit, density, and form of the plant. There's a multitude of possibilities. The smallest Sargent crabapple has a low pincushion shape, much wider than it is tall. A yellowwood grows into a vase shape, up to 30 feet tall and equally broad at its top. The fine branches of flowering dogwoods or black haw take on striking horizontal lines. Kousa dogwood and tea crabapple seem to surge upward.

The trees listed here will afford beauty at every season of the year. If you have a specialized interest — such as in native plants, shade-loving plants, or fruit, fragrance, or bark color — you can find specialized lists in other sections of this book.

## A Selection of Small Trees

Paperbark maple (*Acer griseum*)
Japanese maple (*Acer palmatum*)
Bloodleaf Japanese maple (*Acer palmatum* 'Atropurpureum')
Red cutleaf Japanese maple (*Acer palmatum* 'Atropurpureum Dissectum')
Green cutleaf or threadleaf Japanese maple (*Acer palmatum* 'Dissectum')
Shadblow, juneberry, or serviceberry (*Amelanchier canadensis*)
Allegheny shadblow or serviceberry (*Amelanchier laevis*)
Gray birch (*Betula populifolia*)
Redbud (*Cercis canadensis*)
White fringe tree (*Chionanthus virginicus*)
Yellowwood (*Cladrastis lutea*)
White flowering dogwood (*Cornus florida*)

Pink flowering dogwood (*Cornus florida rubra*)
Kousa or Japanese dogwood (*Cornus kousa*)
Cornelian cherry dogwood (*Cornus mas*)
Smoke tree (*Cotinus coggygria*)
Washington hawthorn (*Crataegus phaenopyrum*)
Chinese witch hazel (*Hamamelis mollis*)
Golden-rain tree (*Koelreuteria paniculata*)
Merrill magnolia (*Magnolia loebneri* 'Merrill')
Saucer magnolia (*Magnolia soulangiana*)
Star magnolia (*Magnolia stellata*)
Adams crabapple (*Malus* 'Adams')

Dogwoods head the list of small trees, and juxtaposing pink and white varieties brings out the best of each in the blooming season.

## A Selection of Small Trees *(continued)*

Donald Wyman crabapple (*Malus* 'Donald Wyman')

Japanese flowering crabapple (*Malus floribunda*)

Tea crabapple (*Malus hupehensis*)

Mary Potter crabapple (*Malus* 'Mary Potter')

Red jade crabapple (*Malus* 'Red Jade')

Sargent crabapple (*Malus sargentii*)

Winter gold crabapple (*Malus* 'Winter Gold')

Zumi crabapple (*Malus zumi calocarpa*)

Sorrel tree or sourwood (*Oxydendrum arboreum*)

Sargent cherry (*Prunus sargentii*)

Paperbark cherry (*Prunus serrula*)

Oriental cherry (*Prunus serrulata*)

Autumn-flowering cherry (*Prunus subhirtella* 'Autumnalis')

Hally Jolivette cherry (*Prunus subhirtella* 'Hally Jolivette')

Weeping Higan cherry (*Prunus subhirtella* 'Pendula')

Yoshino cherry (*Prunus yedoensis*)

Bradford callery pear (*Pyrus calleryana* 'Bradford')

Korean mountain ash (*Sorbus alnifolia*)

Korean stewartia (*Stewartia koreana*)

Japanese stewartia (*Stewartia pseudocamellia*)

Japanese tree lilac (*Syringa reticulata*)

Black haw (*Viburnum prunifolium*)

Detailed information and recommended varieties can be found in Part III.

## Materials and Construction
# BRICK AND PAVERS

September and October are the last two months when the weather allows much outdoor construction work, if you live in a northern climate. So this month I'll look at one of my favorite construction materials, brick; and next month at terraces and patios, for which brick is one ideal choice.

Bricks are made of baked clay, one of the three time-honored building materials provided by nature and used by human beings since prehistoric times. (The other two, of course, are stone and wood.) To this day, brick finds almost limitless uses. In the landscape, it's perfect for walks, boundary walls, screening walls, posts, planters, steps, and pavements.

The color and texture of brick have a lot to do with its popularity. The natural earth tones of baked clay, in shades of red, brown, and yellow, fit perfectly into any outdoor setting and add warmth to the most bleak urban surroundings. The regular patterns in which bricks are laid, and the small sizes and matte surfaces of the individual bricks themselves, are easy on the eye.

Besides, in the United States, so much historic construction of the Colonial and Revolutionary periods was of brick that there's a faint nostalgic air about it. Brick evokes the heritage of the past.

Brick also possesses plenty of practical virtues as a material, particularly for the novice or do-it-yourself builder. For one thing, bricks are widely available in a good selection of types, sizes, and colors. For another, brick is relatively easy to work with and far more forgiving of trial and error than many materials. This is especially true of dry-laid brick used as a paving material. As for expense, even though the cost of anything whose manufacture uses fuel (as brick kilns do) continues to spiral, brick is still less expensive than most forms of stone.

**Buying Brick**   As a general rule, the harder the brick, the better it will serve you in outdoor use. Hardness is arrived at by longer firing at higher temperatures. This causes the grains of the clay to fuse and the pores to close, making the brick impenetrable by water; and as with so many things in outdoor construction, water and ice are the big enemies of brick. If a brick is capable of absorbing more than 8 percent of its weight in water, it will crack or spall (chip) or flake apart when the absorbed water freezes. So impermeability by water is critical.

A visit to a brickyard may dazzle you (or daunt you) at first with the huge assortment of types, sizes, colors, and costs. But when you zero in on the kinds that are actually suited to landscape construction, your range of choices becomes more manageable. They include two basic types:

**Building bricks** come in many grades, depending on whether they are intended for indoor or outdoor use. For outdoor walls, the best bricks are the ones sold as "building brick type SW" — that is, building brick that will stand up to severe weathering.

**Bricks, old and new. Below left: moss softens the running-bond pattern of old red bricks. Below right: brick soldiers are set flush with grade as edging for newly laid pavement.**

**Pavers** are manufactured expressly for use in paving, and if paving is your goal you should stick to them. Very dense and hard, pavers are designed for extra-low water absorption and extra-high compressive strength: i.e., resistance to crushing.

Whether you are working with building bricks or pavers, you'll probably find a rich selection of colors and textures available. Your choice will be dictated partly by your own likes and dislikes; partly by the materials and colors with which you want to harmonize, such as those of your house or drive or other existing landscape structures; and partly by the functions the bricks are to fulfill. You'll see colors varying from pale cream, through golden yellows, to oranges, reds, and browns that range from russet to deep purplish hues. I prefer the middle to darker range in the red to brown hues. The many textures of brick include smooth, scored, combed or roughened, sandy or slick. All these textures result from the machinery used in the manufacturing process, where mold surfaces, extruding machines, or cutting devices leave their imprints on the wet clay before the bricks are fired. For outdoor use, I tend to favor a sand mold finish. This is produced when sand is sprinkled in the mold as butter is spread in a baking pan, to make the mold release the brick easily when it's overturned after baking. The grains of sand give the brick a slightly softened, worn appearance, unlike the more crisp surfaces obtained by other cutting or molding methods.

Although colors and finishes are a matter of your own taste and judgment, I will give you one firm word of advice about brick: don't buy salvaged brick for outdoor use. Old bricks may look charming, with their subtly toned colors and battered shapes. They may even be cheap, although that is by no means the rule. But they come from unpredictable or unknown sources and may be of many different degrees of hardness. If they're really old, they are almost certain not to be as hard-fired as bricks must be to endure the weather.

I learned this lesson the hard way. Every spring my patio is a shambles of cracked and flaking bricks — because I paved it with lovely old bricks that were never intended to stand up to rain, snow, ice, and the deep freezes of winter. That was before I knew better.

**Designing with Brick**   As I've already said, there is an almost limitless variety of types of brick — and that goes for dimensions as well as colors and textures. The most common, however, are two standardized sets of measurements.

**Brick sizes**   Bricks sized 4 by 8 by 1⅝ to 2¼ inches are often dry-laid and tightly fitted. Their 4 by 8–inch dimensions are the basis for the sizing of the other standard type, "modular" bricks.

Modular bricks measure 3⅝ by 7⅝ by 2¼ inches. With a little arithmetic you can see that a modular brick laid with ⅜-inch mortar joints or grouts will fit the 4 by 8–inch module.

The reason that standard sizes come under the heading of designing is that whatever you build, you'll have to compute quite carefully the dimensions and construction method before you can decide on what kind of bricks to get and how many of them. The numbers of bricks *without* mortar joints to make up one square foot of paved surface are:

| Brick size | Bricks per sq. ft. |
|---|---|
| 4 × 8 inches (flat) | 4.5 |
| 3⅝ × 7⅝ inches (flat) | 5.2 |
| 2¼ × 7⅝ inches (on edge) | 8.4 |

**Bricklaying patterns**   There are many, many patterns you can follow when you lay out brick. Sometimes the most delightful effects are created by a combination of patterns; sometimes a single traditional pattern is the best. It depends on the context. The most familiar and widely used patterns are the classic running bond, stacked (or jack-on-jack), herringbone, and basketweave. These and some less traditional patterns and combinations are shown in the illustrations on page 238.

All these patterns can be accomplished with either standard 4 by 8–inch pavers dry-laid with butted joints, or modular bricks using ⅜-inch mortar joints. But if you use the smaller modular bricks dry-laid, only the running, stacked, and herringbone patterns are feasible, since the other patterns require that the width of each brick be exactly half its length. To make matters a little more complicated, if you use mortar joints with the full-size 4 by 8–inch pavers, forget the basketweave patterns: the width of the joints will throw off the overall fit.

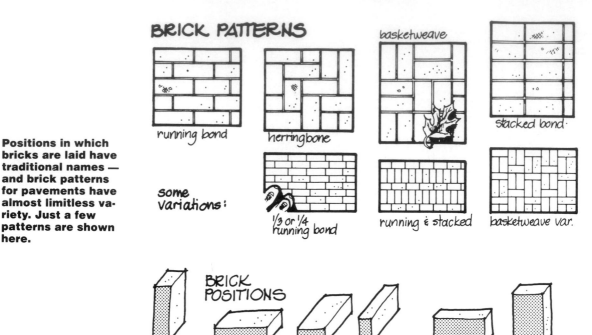

**BRICK PATTERNS**

running bond · herringbone · basketweave · stacked bond

some variations: · 1/3 or 1/4 running bond · running & stacked · basketweave var.

**BRICK POSITIONS**

soldier · stretcher · header · rowlock · shiner · sailor

Positions in which bricks are laid have traditional names — and brick patterns for pavements have almost limitless variety. Just a few patterns are shown here.

Bricks can be laid up in walls, edgings, or pavements in different positions, called soldier, stretcher, header, and rowlock. Each has its uses and advantages depending on the situation, and playing around with alternatives is another pleasant facet of working with brick.

**Brick Substitutes**  Your researches in your local brickyard will also introduce you to at least some of the many bricklike modular materials that are on the market. Asphalt and concrete "bricks" and blocks come in a wide variety of shapes and sizes. I have seldom found these very satisfactory for residential landscape use, however. Their prevalent colors are somewhat synthetic-looking grays, greens, and reds that (for me) do not coexist happily with natural landscape surroundings. And their textures are apt to be equally unappealing. But as you shop around you may just discover some locally available concrete or asphalt block that will suit your taste and pocketbook. So don't write these products off entirely until you have spent some time looking.

## Plants by Design
# NOTABLE FRUIT DISPLAY

### Fruit with Unusual Form or Size
Honey locust (*Gleditsia triacanthos*)
Sweet gum (*Liquidambar styraciflua*)
Tulip tree (*Liriodendron tulipifera*)

### Fruit with Notable Color
Red maple (*Acer rubrum*)
Barberries (*Berberis* spp.)
Bittersweet (*Celastrus scandens*)

White fringe tree (*Chionanthus virginicus*)
Dogwoods (*Cornus* spp.)
Cotoneasters (*Cotoneaster* spp.)
Hawthorns (*Crataegus* spp.)
Winged euonymus (*Euonymus alata*)
Winterberry (*Ilex verticillata*)
Hollies (*Ilex* spp.)
Privet (*Ligustrum* spp.)

The color of viburnums' fall fruit often makes as great a contribution as that of their spring bloom.

## Notable Fruit Display (continued)

Honeysuckle (*Lonicera* spp.)
Crabapples (*Malus* spp.)
Bayberry (*Myrica pensylvanica*)
Firethorns (*Pyracantha* spp.)
Sumac (*Rhus* spp.)
Roses (*Rosa* spp.)
Elderberry (*Sambucus canadensis*)
Korean mountain ash (*Sorbus alnifolia*)
Blueberry (*Vaccinium* spp.)
Viburnum (*Viburnum* spp.)

Bittersweet (*Celastrus scandens*)
Hawthorns (*Crataegus* spp.)
Winterberry (*Ilex verticillata*)
Bayberry (*Myrica pensylvanica*)
Scarlet firethorn (*Pyracantha coccinea*)
Meadow rose (*Rosa blanda*)
Rugosa rose (*Rosa rugosa*)
Coralberry (*Symphoricarpos orbiculatus*)
European cranberrybush viburnum (*Viburnum opulus*)
American cranberrybush viburnum (*Viburnum trilobum*)

### Fruit Remaining into Winter

Red chokeberry (*Aronia arbutifolia*)
Barberries (*Berberis* spp.)

Detailed information and recommended varieties can be found in Part III.

# LANDSCAPE TASKS FOR SEPTEMBER

**Starting New Lawns**   What with cool weather, plenty of rain, and the fact that grasses are entering a natural growth surge now, this is the best time of the year to get new grass started. (Another good time is the April growth period.) Whether a whole new lawn or a patch here and there, the basic procedures are the same. Cultivate the top 6 or 8 inches of soil. Work in lime and peat moss if needed (see Soil Testing in March). Add a high-nitrogen complete fertilizer like 10-6-4 or 20-15-10, or an organic fertilizer such as manure or cottonseed meal. Rake the soil smooth, roll it, then sow a good mixture of bluegrass and fescues that are adapted to your climate. A grass-seed spreader does the most even job of distribution. Rake lightly to cover the seeds with a little soil, then roll the area again.

For a week or so, sprinkle the newly seeded grass as often as necessary to keep it evenly moist until it sprouts. If traffic is a problem, protect the new lawn from dogs and passersby by spreading light brush, bramble cuttings, netting, or other barriers over it.

**September Lawn Feeding**   If your lawn is already in place, this fall growing season is the proper time to feed and lime it. The April Plants for a Purpose section mentioned the fertilizing requirements of lawn grasses, but here's a reminder to keep you on schedule.

In the Northeast, where soil pH tends to drift lower (more acid) year by year, it's a good idea to apply 50 pounds of ground limestone per 1000 square feet of lawn in early spring every three or four years. (For your lawn's measurements, the base plan made in Part I is a helpful reference.) Lawn grasses like a minimum pH of 6.0, preferably 6.5.

As for feeding, there are many commercial forms of slow-release, high-nitrogen synthetic fertilizer available, and they carry their own instructions as to quantities per square footage of lawn. I tend to prefer cottonseed meal (although it's more expensive than the man-made products), which is very slow releasing and contains goodly amounts of phosphorus and potash as well as nitrogen. Fifteen pounds per 1000 square feet is ample. For an extra boost, you can also spread 5 pounds of bonemeal per 1000 square feet, to add extra phosphorus for strong stiff growth. Or alternatively, you can forget all the above and use dried or well-rotted cow manure at the rate of 100 pounds per 1000 square feet. My wife's grandmother always relied on manure from the local dairy farm, and she had the best lawn in her neighborhood.

**Lawn Mowing**   Keep mowing, but now you can lower the height of the blade to 1½ inches if you want. Annual weed seeds are no longer sprouting; burning sun is no longer such a threat; and it will be easier to rake leaves off short grass as the fall wears on.

**Lily-of-the-Valley Division**   Lily-of-the-valley will grow more thickly and bloom more lavishly if you divide the pips every three or four years — and now is the moment to do it. Dig everything up; choose the huskiest-looking pips; and replant them 6 inches apart from each other, just below the soil's surface. Enrich the soil with bonemeal and some well-rotted manure.

**Wisteria**   If your wisteria failed to bloom, root-prune it (see March Landscape Tasks) this month. Then give it a high-phosphate feeding such as bonemeal, rock phosphate, superphosphate, or a commercial mix like 6-18-6. Leave it alone over the winter, then prune it drastically in February or March. The results will amaze you.

**Ripening Harvests**   Each September-ripening garden fruit has its own set of needs.
   **Grapes** ripen well in the heavy shade of their foliage, but do not ripen further after picking — so leave them on the vine until they're practically bursting.
   **Apples** need bright sun to ripen. You may actually want to thin the foliage of the trees to let the sunlight get at the fruit. Apples should not be picked until they're ripe: that moment comes when there's no green color left (except with green apples, of course) and when a quick turn of the wrist pulls the apple loose.
   **Pears,** by contrast, want to be picked while they are still firm, a week or so before they would have softened. Ripen them indoors in a cool, dark place.

**Planting Trees and Shrubs**
   **Deciduous ornamental trees and shrubs**   Most kinds can be planted in the fall. (For a list of exceptions, see the April Landscape Tasks.)
   **Evergreens**   Early this month is the optimum time to plant narrow-leaved evergreen trees or shrubs, or to move them from one place to another.
   **Broad-leaved evergreens**   Although early spring is by far the season of choice, broad-leaved evergreens such as mountain laurel, boxwood, rhododendrons, some evergreen azaleas, hollies, and so on can be planted in early fall if you are careful. Once in place they should be given a deep watering and a thick acid mulch such as pine needles, oak leaves,

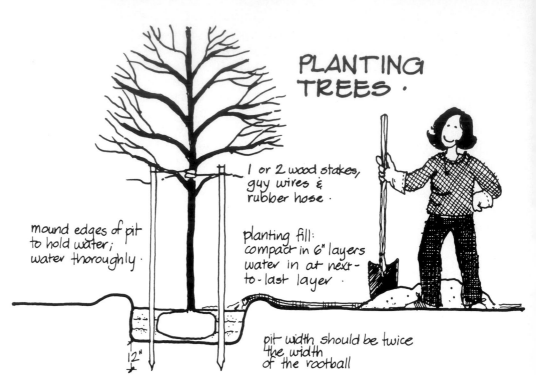

PLANTING
TREES.

1 or 2 wood stakes,
guy wires &
rubber hose.

mound edges of pit
to hold water;
water thoroughly.

planting fill:
compact in 6" layers
water in at next-
to-last layer.

pit width should be twice
the width
of the rootball

12"

**Planting a tree: be
certain the pit is big
enough and the soil
is good enough.**

or wood chips; and in a windy or sunny location they will benefit from an antidesiccant spray.

For all of the above, prepare in advance the place where the plant is to go. You want to be able to install it promptly after you bring it home or remove it from its present location. Make a planting hole twice the diameter of the root ball or container and about the same depth. For a bareroot plant, the hole should be about a foot wider than the spread of the roots, and just a bit deeper than they reach.

Enrich the soil you've excavated from the hole with manure and compost or peat moss, about one-fifth to one-quarter the volume of the soil, to have it ready for backfilling. Roughen and loosen up the soil around the sides and especially at the bottom of the hole: you want a gradual transition between existing topsoil (and/or subsoil) and the enriched mixture you'll be putting back in.

If you are putting in a tree bareroot, take care not to let its roots dry out while it awaits planting (see April for some suggestions on keeping roots moist).

If the plant is balled-and-burlapped, you can leave the burlap on (provided it's not plastic; in that event remove it). Real burlap will rot away in the ground and the roots will grow right through. If the plant is in a container, you may possibly be able to tap it out; more probably, you'll have to cut the container off with heavy shears or metal cutters.

Set the root ball or roots into the hole so that the plant's stem emerges from the ground at the same level as it did in the nursery. Work earth gently but thoroughly in among the roots of a bareroot plant. Fill in the earth in 6-inch layers, firming down each layer. Once the plant is settled, remove the cords that bound the burlap, if it was wrapped, and loosen the burlap around the top. With some extra soil, build a saucer around the plant to act as a reservoir for water. Then water thoroughly.

With a balled-and-burlapped deciduous tree, I usually cut out about a third of the branches after planting, so as not to overburden the already stressed root system. The tree recovers rapidly.

In fall planting, you should usually stake young trees with trunks 1 inch or more in diameter. A sturdy stake driven into the soil, plus a rope or guy wire run through a section of rubber hose (so as not to scrape the bark off), will keep the tree from swaying in autumn and winter gales and exposing its roots to the air. A single stake should be placed at the side from which the prevailing winter wind blows; or double stakes, for a tree with a trunk over 2 inches thick, on both sides. Stakes should stay in place for the first two years.

Another winter precaution: mulch or mound soil around the bases of plants newly installed at this season.

During the first few months especially, and throughout its first two years, make sure the newly installed tree or shrub is regularly watered, either by rainfall or by you. Getting it well established now will make all the difference to its long-term health and beauty.

**Review and Planning**   While the successes and failures of the past growing season are fresh in your mind, make a map, list, or chart to remind yourself what to change and what new things to try next year.

*October*

# OCT

**Foliage begins to turn color sooner in low-lying places.**

This month I'm looking in two directions: outdoors, and ahead into winter. This is the season for really splendid fall color. The autumn foliage in the northeastern United States is about as spectacular as any in the world (only parts of our West Coast, northern Japan, and southwestern Europe have anything to rival it); and the trees and shrubs that produce this brilliant show should be a part of every planned landscape in this area.

October is the last dependable month for major outdoor construction, and the terrace and patio section here will give you ideas for an enjoyable outdoor living space for next spring, summer, and fall. Container plants, ideal for patios, are portable and versatile enough to contribute to every part of the landscape in every season, and that's the subject I'll talk about first.

Also, casting an eye ahead to the coming months, I'll introduce some of the handsomest plants of the winter landscape (and all year round): broad-leaved evergreens.

### Landscaping Opportunities
# CONTAINER LANDSCAPING

**This rooftop garden shows the amazingly lush effects possible with containers. Baskets and pots of all sizes work together wonderfully here.**

Containers add another dimension to a landscape even if you have plenty of ground space for planting — and in some places where the ground just won't do, they alone can make planting possible. They are the only answer to gardening on rooftops, stoops, or balconies. They are a wonderful solution to the problem of putting greenery or flowers in paved areas. They're just the thing if you want to break up an expanse of terrace and lawn but don't want to dig a bed. And they are mobile, so you can shift them to different locations as the spirit moves, or take them indoors for special occasions. Besides, many plants really show themselves off best of all in a pot or box or urn that brings them closer to eye level and gives them something from which their lower fronds or branches can gracefully hang down.

There's just one drawback to container gardening in any northern climate — winter. The cold does a job on many container plantings, for two reasons. First, few normal landscape plants can tolerate root temperatures below 20°F; but in a container outdoors, a plant will be exposed to cold far greater than that — usually with fatal results. Second, when soil freezes it expands, and a rigid container (earthenware, metal, plastic, even concrete) will crack.

So if you want to use containers for permanent plantings like shrubbery or perennials, you must have a winter plan. Here are a few ideas:

- Hardy yews and junipers in good big wooden planters will usually survive.
- Hollies, hardy azaleas, and broad-leaved evergreens will need shelter and a site chosen for minimal temperature extremes.
- For smaller shrubs, a greenhouse or coldframe is great for overwintering. Or you can remove hardy shrubs from their containers and bury them in the ground in an out-of-the-way spot for the winter.
- Nonhardy shrubs and some flowers can even be brought indoors to a cool, bright window.

- If the plants are neither hardy nor transportable, you'll have to discard them, store the containers in a dry place, and start again next year.

**Designing with Containers**   Here you are bounded only by the limits of your imagination (and possibly your budget). There are scads of options both in plant materials and in container materials, designs, and arrangements. I won't attempt to cover them all, but again, here are the general guidelines I follow:

- I like to use groups of containers of different sizes, with the largest to the rear so I can build an ascending foliage mass. It often makes sense to use larger plants in the larger containers, as background for the whole arrangement.
- For a look of restraint combined with fullness, stick to one or perhaps two kinds of plants in the same grouping or large container.
- For a more lively or splashy effect, you can combine several varieties of plants in a grouping or a large container. If they're together in one container just make sure that it is big enough to house everything comfortably; see container dimensions below.
- Not all your pots need be ornamental in themselves. It's nice to have handsome wooden tubs, Italian ceramics, or elaborately molded concrete planters; but camouflage can give you flexibility, save weight, and save lots of money. For instance, a really big tub or sawed-off barrel can be given a homemade facelift. Or a cheap metal or plastic container looks fine inside an attractive woven basket.

**Container Specifications**   Whether you build your own (see below) or choose from the enormous range of ready-made containers on the market — glazed or plain terra cotta, concrete, Plexiglas, plastic, cast iron, metal, wood, or stone — the basic criteria for their design are the same. Size, weight, and (as usual) drainage are the major issues.

**Size**   Allow the right cubic footage of soil for the plant(s) you plan to grow. Too large a container will look ungainly in relation to the plant, will be unnecessarily heavy, and may present drainage problems. But too small a container is a more common and more serious problem. A container too small for its plant will cause the plant to become root-bound. This will make the plant look sickly, stunt its growth, and possibly kill it. Ascertain first what kind of plant you're going to put in a container; find out from the plant's supplier what its required volume of soil will be; then choose a generous-sized container to house it.

Shallow soil dries out quickly, so as a general rule I never use a soil depth of less than 10 inches; I prefer 12 inches as a minimum. A window-box-type planter should be at least 10 by 10 by 36 or 42 inches. Beware of bowl- or dish-shaped containers where the top flares outwards. The thin soil around the circumference will dry out much faster than the rest and will be useless for growing anything except perhaps succulents that tolerate near-arid conditions.

**Weight**   If portability is a goal, consider both the weight of the container itself and the weight of the volume of soil it is designed to hold. Soil (including its moisture) weighs about 100 pounds per cubic foot. Lightweight planting mixes containing perlite as well as lots of peat moss weigh much less: 50 to 80 pounds per cubic foot when wet. All the same, you can see that a container a foot and a half square, with a plant growing in it, will be no picnic to move. Large planters, if they have to be moved, can be transferred on dollies. You can improvise with rollers and boards, or drag the container on a burlap bag or toboggan.

**Drainage**   Water must not be allowed to accumulate in the bottom of a container, where it will cut off the oxygen supply to the roots and discourage or even kill the plant. Every planter should have plentiful drainage holes in its base. I don't recommend putting shards or pebbles in the bottom of containers for outdoor plants, however. This can cause too-swift drainage and drying out of the lower roots, particularly in hot weather. Instead, I put small pieces of screening over the drain holes.

In addition, a well-drained soil mix is a must for healthy plants. My favorite mix consists of one-third good garden loam, one-third sharp builder's sand, and one-third sphagnum peat moss. To lighten this soil, I'll often make up the basic mix, then add another one-third perlite (by volume). For acid-loving plants I reduce the loam and increase the peat moss by 10 percent each.

### Build-It-Yourself Containers

**Build-It-Yourself Containers**   If you are feeling ambitious you may enjoy designing and building planters tailored to your particular landscape needs. The materials of choice for home-built containers are wood and concrete.

**Often an old artifact makes a good container, as with this copper receptacle from England.**

The best woods to use are the naturally rot-resistant cedar, redwood, or cypress. Or you can use wood that has been pressure-treated with preservative. Marine or exterior-grade plywood will also perform fairly well, although you have to cover up the raw edges to prevent water from seeping in. Alternatively you can have a galvanized metal liner made to fit your wooden container, which will make any kind of wood last much longer. Be sure that all metal hardware (nails, bolts, etc.) is galvanized; plain steel will rust out, and cause unsightly stains in the process.

Large molded concrete containers are generally beyond the scope of a home construction project. Small concrete troughs are certainly feasible, however. They can serve as beautiful settings for miniature plantings; or hold low-growing perennials or dwarf conifers or herbs; or even make excellent birdbaths.

**Plants for Containers**   For many gardeners, the ultimate in container gardening is bonsai: the Japanese art of dwarfing large trees by pruning their roots and foliage and training them into carefully predetermined shapes. These miniature plantings make a fascinating and very time-consuming horticultural hobby; but they are not especially useful for the average patio or front stoop, since bonsai trees have to be studied up close in a properly scaled setting. They also need winter protection and careful monitoring of light and water. If bonsai is your interest, some good sources of further information are listed in the Further Reference.

Apart from bonsai, however, it's the smaller and slower-growing trees and shrubs that are best suited to growing in planters. When they become root-bound you can root-prune them (shave off the outermost 2 inches of roots all around), then replant in the same pot with new soil. Or repot them in a bigger container if you want them to continue growing.

The best adapted of all are dwarf and very slow-growing varieties — evergreen or deciduous, flowering or not — and small plants like ground covers. (The August Plants for a Purpose list focuses on trees and shrubs for small spaces, many well suited to containers; and the June list includes ground-cover plants.) With these you won't face frequent repottings, and the plants themselves will be contented rather than permanently thwarted in their natural growth patterns. A contented container plant is easy to maintain, so that with a minimum of annual upkeep you will have a charming decorative element for your landscape.

## Plants for a Purpose
# BROAD-LEAVED EVERGREENS

With winter around the corner, this is an appropriate time to start thinking about winter greenery — and broad-leaved evergreens' unique contribution.

When I think of broad-leaved evergreens in their full glory, I must admit it is the southern landscape that comes to mind. Southern hollies and magnolias, among others, are magnificent full-sized trees that stay green all year. The magnolia is surely the queen of broad-leaved evergreens.

Yet in the Northeast, those broad-leaved evergreens that will stand up to the climate are especially precious. They afford color and a sense of life even in the bleakest winter weather. Their textures and forms are utterly different from those of other northern winter greenery — the conifers, or "narrow-leaved" evergreens. Used as hedge plants, broad-leaved evergreens like boxwood or boxleaf holly do just as great a job in the winter as in the summer. And when spring comes, the flowering broad-leaved shrubs — azaleas, laurels, andromedas, rhododendrons — burst forth with blossoms in the most luscious array of colors. They are breathtaking. With all the varieties and cultivars that are available, you can plan for a sequence of bloom that will last from April into July, in as wide a spectrum of colors as you like, from white to blue-violet to pink to yellow.

Rich varieties of forms and foliar textures are available in rhododendrons.

In the North, however, there are no broad-leaved trees, as such, that will survive the winter except one or two species of hollies. So for Zones 4, 5, and 6, we're really talking about shrubs. For the most part they belong to a small group of genera: *Rhododendron* (which includes what we call azaleas as well as rhododendrons), *Ilex* (hollies), *Buxus* (boxwoods), and *Pieris* (andromedas or pieris).

**Designing with Broad-leaved Evergreens**   There are some people who dislike rhododendrons and some of the other broad-leaved evergreens because they look so wizened in winter. A friend once said, "Rhododendrons make me feel cold just looking at them." I see what she meant — rhododendron leaves do curl up in self-defense against mid-winter's dry cold. It is also true that in severe winters some boxleaf hollies and boxwoods have a tendency to turn a sickly yellow-brown, making you wonder if they will ever return to green again. American holly and the various types of mahonia are susceptible to a depressing brownish-gray tipburn. As for some of the evergreen azaleas, they simply drop their leaves altogether if things get too cold for them, and grow a new crop the following spring.

Yet these drawbacks have never bothered me particularly. It seems to me that the many assets of broad-leaved evergreens more than compensate for their one flaw of looking pinched in cold weather. Often, too, I believe that people's aversion to broad-leaved evergreens stems from unfortunate choices of location, which are by no means the plants' fault. It used to be very common for rhododendrons, laurels, and others of the larger broad-leaved shrubs to be promoted as "foundation plantings." So when people looked out their windows in winter the first thing they saw was a dismal mass of curled, leathery-looking, dark-green leaves. In fact it might be the only thing they saw, in older houses where the shrubbery had been allowed to get somewhat overgrown. No wonder that rhododendron phobia became a common malady.

There's a simple solution to this complaint  Don't use rhododendrons or other large broad-leaved evergreens right around the house. (They don't do their best in hot south- or west-facing locations anyway. If you want them around the house, stick to the north or east sides for the best results.) Instead, think of broad-leaved evergreens as wonderful plants for the long view. They're great at the edge of a lawn under tall trees, for instance, where they'll get slightly filtered sun in summer and a modicum of shelter in winter. Not to mention the possibility of a nice acid mulch in the form of falling leaves or needles every autumn. Even if you don't have many tall trees, any reasonably distant location will do fine. Just so that you don't have to stare at forlorn curled-up or tipburned leaves right outside your window all winter long.

I have to confess to a partiality to broad-leaved evergreens in the wild. If you've ever been lucky enough to come upon a mass of native rosebay rhododendrons or mountain laurel flourishing by a streambed in the woods, you may agree. There is nothing quite so majestic, so completely and prosperously at home as these plants. They grow to a size and stature that make them more like trees than shrubs.

Even if you can't provide a wilderness, keep in mind how happy these plants are in a roomy setting, and avoid placing them in very tight arrangements or in very rigidly structured surroundings. Try to plan for a variety of textures. Combine smaller-leaved plants with the larger-leaved ones, and work into your design some deciduous shrubs — which could be deciduous azaleas — to add lighter summer color and provide airy breathing spaces in the winter composition. Provide for well-spaced blooming times and a variety of colors, too. See if you can combine some very early plants like andromeda and the earliest rhododendrons, some middle-blooming azaleas, and some late-blooming laurel, azaleas, and rhododendrons. Think about a palette of colors, perhaps from white to rose to red, or from lavender to deep blue-violet.

**Buying Broad-leaved Evergreens**   The first thing you will learn when you start shopping for broad-leaved evergreens is that the range of choices is vast. There are always new cultivars being introduced and newly fashionable varieties being promoted. My best advice: seek out tried and true varieties whose virtues are well proven and whose needs you can easily determine. There's generally nothing like a plant that has stood the test of generations of gardeners and thousands of geographical locations.

**Inkberry is good for informal hedges, and its black fruits are true to its name.**

**Different hollies have different fruit habits and leaf forms, as in long-stalk holly (above left) and American holly variety (above right).**

The broad-leaved evergreens listed here are all good and hardy in the north. They all will do their best, however, if you can give them at least some degree of protection from the bitterest winter wind. Some like full sun; others will prosper in filtered shade. The rhododendrons, azaleas, laurel, and andromeda will bloom approximately in the time periods indicated in their descriptions in Part III, so that you can decide on a rough calendar of bloom for your garden. But don't try to calculate this too precisely. Every plant has its vagaries, and all plants' blooming schedules are contingent on the weather of seasons past as well as present.

## Broad-leaved Evergreens for Year-round Appeal

AZALEAS (EVERGREEN)
  Herbert azalea (*Rhododendron kaempferi* 'Herbert')
  Hinocrimson azalea (*Rhododendron obtusum* 'Hinocrimson')
  Hinodegiri azalea (*Rhododendron obtusum* 'Hinodegiri')
  Delaware Valley White azalea (*Rhododendron* 'Delaware Valley White')
Littleleaf boxwood (*Buxus microphylla* vars.)
Common boxwood (*Buxus sempervirens* vars.)
Boxleaf holly (*Ilex crenata convexa* vars.)
Inkberry (*Ilex glabra* vars.)
Blue holly (*Ilex meserveae* vars.)
American holly (*Ilex opaca*)
Longstalk holly (*Ilex pedunculosa*)
Mountain laurel (*Kalmia latifolia* vars.)
Coast leucothoe (*Leucothoe axillaris*)
Drooping leucothoe (*Leucothoe fontanesiana*)

Oregon holly-grape (*Mahonia aquifolium*)
Canby paxistima (*Paxistima canbyi*)
Mountain andromeda or pieris (*Pieris floribunda*)
Japanese andromeda or pieris (*Pieris japonica* vars.)
Laland firethorn (*Pyracantha coccinea* 'Lalandei')

RHODODENDRONS
  Boule de Neige rhododendron (*Rhododendron* 'Boule de Neige')
  Carolina rhododendron (*Rhododendron carolinianum*)
  Catawba rhododendron (*Rhododendron catawbiense* vars.)
  Chionoides rhododendron (*Rhododendron* 'Chionoides')
  Scintillation rhododendron (*Rhododendron fortunei* 'Scintillation')
  Wilson rhododendron (*Rhododendron laetivirens*)

Rosebay rhododendron or great
  laurel (*Rhododendron
  maximum*)
Nova Zembla rhododendron
  (*Rhododendron* 'Nova Zembla')

P.J.M. hybrid rhododendrons
  (*Rhododendron* 'P.J.M.
  Hybrids')
Purple gem rhododendron
  (*Rhododendron* 'Purple Gem')

Detailed information and recommended varieties can be found in Part III.

## Materials and Construction
# TERRACES AND PATIOS

October may have its frosty nights, but much of this month is truly delightful outdoors, just right for sunning on the patio. The joy of a terrace or patio is that it extends your daily living space. It's a cleaner, cozier, usually more private place than the rest of your landscape. A terrace or patio makes an enticing adjunct to the house for many months of the year, and I highly recommend that you have at least one — or more than one, if possible.

**Planning and Design**    The best place for a terrace or patio is on the south side of the house. There you'll get the most use out of it spring, summer, and fall. The west side is a good second choice, although it misses the morning sun. Both south- and west-facing terraces need at least partial summer shading. Terraces facing east or north will be cool in summer, but less welcoming in spring and fall.

As with any outdoor construction, allow plenty of room. One of the most common failings of terraces and patios is being built too small. Start by thinking about an area double the size of your living room. You may find, when you stake it out on the ground, that that's really too big or impractical in your setting; if so, at least try to provide access to an adjoining lawn area that will take care of overflowing people and furniture when needed.

Overflow areas don't have to be on the same level as the basic

For entertaining on a small raised terrace or patio, it's important to plan an adjacent area where people can overflow.

783

terrace or patio. In fact there's no law that says the terrace or patio itself has to be on a single, continuous, level plane. That approach often works fine; but in many cases it works equally well to break spaces up with changes in elevation — with a broad flight of steps, for instance, or a planting bed or a pocket of trees.

The essential difference between a terrace and a patio is the amount of enclosure. A terrace is a generally level space abutting or nearby the house, but open to views both to and from the surrounding landscape. In addition to being an outdoor living room, a terrace often serves as the visual transition between the house and its larger environment. Therefore it is important that the terrace's location, size, proportions, materials, edge treatments, and so forth be in keeping with the landscape as a whole — as well as with the house to which it is linked.

A patio is also a level outdoor space, but by definition it is enclosed on at least three sides, either by the house or partly by house, partly by walls or other structures. Patios trace their ancestry to European courtyards and cloisters; they migrated to this country with the Spanish settlers of the Southwest. They carry on a tradition where a central garden was embraced and sheltered by living quarters. A patio is thus more closely related to the interior functions of the house and somewhat less involved with the surrounding landscape than a terrace. Often a patio can be relatively small in scale. The intimacy of its connection with the house means that details of its design and construction should be thought out with great care. Should there be a fence enclosing it, or a solid or perforated wall? How about a vine-grown trellis for shade over part of the area? How much privacy, how much shelter from wind? How much square footage for children's play or for plantings or for entertaining? The responses to these kinds of questions depend on the character of your house and its surroundings, the needs of the people who'll use the patio, the available space, and of course the available budget.

**Paving Materials**   If walls — or absence of them — define the difference between a patio and a terrace, floors define the similarity. Both patios and terraces are floored, or paved, usually with something other than grass. That's what gives them their delightfully livable quality. The focus of this section is on the floors themselves.

Should your patio or terrace pavement be warm-colored or cool, fine-textured or coarse? The first thing to consider is the relationship between the color and texture of the paving material and those of the house: the two should make sense together. Also think about practical effects. A dark color in a sunny exposure will absorb heat and be scorching on a hot summer day. A very pale color in a south-facing spot will reflect a lot of light, sometimes blindingly so.

Then there's the question of formality or informality. For a tidy, formal appearance, the components of a pavement should be regular and repetitive, like brick, modular stone, or tiles. The joints between paving modules should be tight and evenly spaced. If a casual or countrified air is your goal, use irregularly shaped and sized paving materials like slate or bluestone slabs and lay them in random patterns.

After you've dealt with these preliminary issues, consider availability and cost — both the cost of the materials and the cost (in dollars or in time) of installing them. Your choices of design and materials will have a lot to do with the degree to which you're going to do the work yourself.

Time and money sometimes become tradeoffs, particularly where skills like stonecutting or bricklaying are concerned.

For instance, giant granite slabs are murder to handle. Modular brick is comparatively easy. Or you can order concrete delivered and lay it yourself without too much difficulty. If price is no object, or if do-it-yourself time is nonexistent, then you'll be thinking in terms of hiring the whole project out to a contractor. That opens up a great latitude of possible materials, approaches, and costs.

Again, beware of fantastic bargains on used materials. What looks like a bargain now may be a big liability in the long run. A friend of mine built his front walk out of irregularly shaped salvaged cobblestones; they didn't cost anything at the outset, but the cracks between them never fail to throw visitors off balance, particularly those wearing high-heeled shoes or no shoes at all. And he wrecks at least one snow shovel every year.

Modular paving materials include brick, cement blocks, bluestone, slate, and granite (among others). Each comes in the form of regularly sized and shaped blocks, usually rectangular or square, and well adapted to an infinite variety of patterns and designs. Irregularly sized and shaped stone pieces are also widely used to create informal or artistic effects.

Modular pavings can be wet-laid (cemented together with mortar) or dry-laid. Always use an edging with dry-laid modular paving, to prevent creep. For brick pavements, an attractive and easy edging is a row of brick "soldiers" set on end in the earth. Or use rot-resistant wood like cypress, heart redwood, or heart cedar; or pressure-treated fir or pine. Granite cobblestones or modular masonry blocks also serve well.

**Stone**   I recommend that you have all stone cut for you by your supplier, particularly if you're planning on an irregular or random pattern. The supplier should also provide you with a joint pattern for a random design, because these are very hard to work out until you've had a good deal of training or experience. A rule of thumb for a good random pattern is that the same joint line should run along no more than 3 stones' sides before changing direction.

## IRREGULAR STONE PATTERNS ·

**Never let a joint run along the sides of more than three paving stones in a row.**

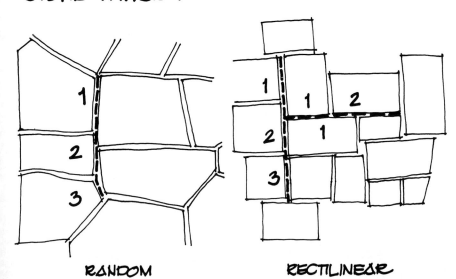

RANDOM          RECTILINEAR

Take with you to the supplier a cardboard cutout representing any curved or unusually shaped objects around which the stone pavement will have to fit. The supplier can use your cutout as a template.

There are some bluestones and slates you can cut yourself, and you may enjoy trying it, particularly if just a few cuts are called for. I always make sure to buy at least 10 percent more stone than the job calls for if I'm going to be cutting it, to make up for disasters and ordinary waste. Use a masonry blade in a skill saw to score the stone; then break it off the rest of the way with a rubber or wooden mallet. Or for really professional cuts, you can rent a water-cooled, table-mounted masonry saw.

**Brick**   Unfortunately, the hard-baked pavers that are best suited to outdoor use are also very hard to cut. The best approach to cutting brick is to work out a pattern that cleverly incorporates all whole bricks with no ragged edges or gaps, so that you don't have to do any cutting at all. If you do have to cut a few, you can mark them with pencil and take them to your supplier to be trimmed down to size. To cut your own bricks, first practice on some waste samples until you feel competent. Use a mallet and "brick set," or brick chisel. Score the brick all the way around, then break it off with a sharp blow; or lay the brick on hard-packed wet sand and slice it in two with the chisel.

**Granular paving** Gravel, crushed stone or stone dust, crushed brick, ornamental stones such as river or beach pebbles, bark nuggets, or bark shreds: all these are what I call granular paving. They all make attractive surfaces, and they are all easy to install dry-laid. They do have certain liabilities, however. They're not suitable for use on sloped areas, where storms will wash them away, but only on level surfaces with good drainage. They're less easy to keep clean than harder surfaces, and weeds and grass invade them more swiftly. And they will "creep" unless you give them an edging to hold them in place. For edgings you can get specially made metal strips (Ryerson Steel) in ³⁄₁₆ by 4–inch or ¼ by 5–inch sizes. There are also several plastic edgings available, but in my opinion these are often too conspicuous. Most of them have a tube along the top edge that makes them feel and look bulky. They also tend to be so flexible that it's difficult to achieve a clean, unwavering line. But often the best solution to edging granular pavements is the same as for brick or stone: wood, cobblestones or masonry blocks, or bricks. These materials do the job they're intended for and enhance the overall appearance of the patio or terrace as well. With all materials, that final overall effect is something always to keep in mind.

**Drainage** As with every other phase of landscape construction, good surface and subsurface drainage is imperative for paved patios and terraces. Slope everything away from the house. Smooth-textured pavements — like concrete, or smooth stones or bricks laid in mortar over concrete — should be sloped at least 1 percent, or ⅛ inch per foot. More irregular surfaces, such as granular pavings, dry-laid brick or stone, or rough stone set in mortar, should be sloped at least 2 percent, i.e., ¼ inch per foot.

If the surrounding soil offers plenty of absorption for runoff, simply sloping the pavement will be adequate. But if you have poorly drained soil, a high water table, or shallow soil over ledge, you should also provide drainage in the form of a drywell or a pipe to a storm drain.

**Base Preparation** You can't just slap paving down on unprepared earth. Thorough preparation of the underlying grade, as well as of the pavement's supporting and/or setting materials, is crucial to the finished appearance and durability of the pavement. The key word here is consistency. Beneath any kind of paving material there must be consistency of grades, of drainage, of compaction of soil. Otherwise you are bound to end up with uneven settling and cracking in due course.

A very common hazard is a site that is wholly or partly filled. Usually, the soil in the area of deepest fill is the most disturbed and the least compacted, and will therefore settle noticeably in the seasons after it's paved over. Make sure that fill goes in in 6-inch layers, with each layer watered and compacted evenly.

All pavements require some substrata under the surface material — usually well-tamped crusher-run (crushed stone and stone dust) or bank-run gravel. This table gives the requirements in a nutshell. There are, however, occasional situations where much of this preparation can be omitted, particularly for dry-laid pavements (brick, stone, or granular materials laid without cement). If you are lucky enough to have a porous sandy or gravelly soil and to live in an area where frost does not penetrate more than about a foot down, you can skip the base course of gravel or stone. Just prepare and compact the underlying surface evenly.

### Base Preparations for Landscape Pavements

| Paving Material | Base |
| --- | --- |
| Concrete | 6 inches well-compacted gravel or crushed stone; base should extend 1 foot in all directions beyond edge of area to be paved. |
| Modular materials (stone, brick, concrete blocks, etc.) | *Wet-laid:* 6 inches well-compacted bank-run gravel or crushed stone, topped by 3- to 4-inch concrete base slab (reinforced with wire fabric mesh if necessary) and ¾-inch mortar setting bed. |
| | *Dry-laid:* 6 inches well-compacted gravel or crushed stone plus 1½-inch bed of sand or stone dust; edging to prevent creep. |
| Granular materials (gravel, crushed stone, ornamental stones, bark nuggets, etc.) | *Dry-laid:* 6 inches well-compacted crusher-run or bank-run gravel; edging to prevent creep. |

## Plants by Design
# COLORFUL FALL FOLIAGE

Plants appearing in both yellow and red categories can have predominantly yellow, red, or purple coloration according to soil, sunlight, temperature, or a combination of variables.

### YELLOW FOLIAGE

### Small Trees

Shadblow, juneberry, or serviceberry (*Amelanchier* spp.)
Redbud (*Cercis canadensis*)
White fringe tree (*Chionanthus virginicus*)
Golden-rain tree (*Koelreuteria paniculata*)
Star magnolia (*Magnolia stellata*)

### Medium to Large Trees

Norway maple (*Acer platanoides*)
River birch (*Betula nigra*)
Paper birch or canoe birch (*Betula papyrifera*)
European white birch (*Betula pendula*)
Cutleaf European birch (*Betula pendula* 'Gracilis')
Gray birch (*Betula populifolia*)
European hornbeam (*Carpinus betulus*)
Shagbark hickory (*Carya ovata*)
Katsura tree (*Cercidiphyllum japonicum*)
American yellowwood (*Cladrastis lutea*)
American beech (*Fagus grandifolia*)
European beech (*Fagus sylvatica*)
White ash (*Fraxinus americana*)
Ginkgo or maidenhair tree (*Ginkgo biloba*)
Honey locust (*Gleditsia triacanthos*)
Sweet gum tree (*Liquidambar styraciflua*)
Tulip tree (*Liriodendron tulipifera*)

## Colorful Fall Foliage  (*continued*)

Amur cork tree (*Phellodendron
  amurense*)
Black or rum cherry (*Prunus
  serotina*)
Littleleaf linden (*Tilia cordata*)

### Shrubs

Summer-sweet clethra (*Clethra
  alnifolia*)
Witch hazel (*Hamamelis* spp.)
Spicebush (*Lindera benzoin*)

### Vine

Bittersweet (*Celastrus scandens*)

## RED, PINK, AND ORANGE-RED FOLIAGE

### Small Trees

Japanese maple (*Acer palmatum*)
Shadblow, serviceberry, or juneberry
  (*Amelanchier canadensis*)
Allegheny serviceberry (*Amelanchier
  laevis*)
Flowering dogwood (*Cornus florida*)
Kousa or Japanese dogwood (*Cornus
  kousa*)
Cornelian cherry dogwood (*Cornus
  mas*)
Smoke tree (*Cotinus coggygria*)
Washington hawthorn (*Crataegus
  phaenopyrum*)
Sorrel tree or sourwood
  (*Oxydendrum arboreum*)
Callery pear (*Pyrus calleryana*)
Shining sumac (*Rhus copallina*)
Korean stewartia (*Stewartia koreana*)

### Medium to Large Trees

Red maple (*Acer rubrum*)
Sugar maple (*Acer saccharum*)
Katsura tree (*Cercidiphyllum
  japonicum*)
American beech (*Fagus grandifolia*)
Sweet gum tree (*Liquidambar
  styraciflua*)
Black gum or black tupelo (*Nyssa
  sylvatica*)
Sargent cherry (*Prunus sargentii*)
Scarlet oak (*Quercus coccinea*)
Red oak (*Quercus rubra*)
Sassafras (*Sassafras albidum*)

### Shrubs

AZALEAS
  Flame azalea (*Rhododendron
    calendulaceum*)
  Royal azalea (*Rhododendron
    schlippenbachii*)
  Pink-shell azalea (*Rhododendron
    vaseyi*)
Japanese barberry (*Berberis
  thunbergii*)
Siberian dogwood (*Cornus alba
  'Sibirica'*)
Red-osier dogwood (*Cornus sericea*)
Redvein enkianthus (*Enkianthus
  campanulatus*)
Winged euonymus or burning bush
  (*Euonymus alata*)
Dwarf winged euonymus (*Euonymus
  alata* 'Compacta')
Fothergilla or witch alder (*Fothergilla*
  spp.)
Fragrant sumac (*Rhus aromatica*)
Rugosa rose (*Rosa rugosa*)
Virginia rose (*Rosa virginiana*)
Bridal-wreath spirea (*Spiraea
  prunifolia*)
Blueberry (*Vaccinium* spp.)
Arrowwood (*Viburnum dentatum*)
European cranberrybush (*Viburnum
  opulus*)
Black haw (*Viburnum prunifolium*)

### Vines

Virginia creeper or woodbine
  (*Parthenocissus quinquefolia*)
Boston ivy (*Parthenocissus
  tricuspidata*)

## PURPLE TO PURPLISH-RED FOLIAGE

### Small Tree

Japanese stewartia (*Stewartia
  pseudocamellia*)

### Medium to Large Trees

White ash (*Fraxinus americana*)
Red cedar (*Juniperus virginiana*)

### Shrubs

Gray dogwood (*Cornus racemosa*)

Katsura tree foliage is yellow or multi-colored in fall, but the tree is valuable in the landscape all year round.

## Colorful Fall Foliage  *(continued)*

Cranberry cotoneaster (*Cotoneaster apiculatus*)

Drooping leucothoe (*Leucothoe fontanesiana*)

Regel privet (*Ligustrum obtusifolium regelianum*)

Bayberry (*Myrica pensylvanica*)

Canby paxistima (*Paxistima canbyi*)

Beach plum (*Prunus maritima*)

Chenault coralberry (*Symphoricarpos chenaultii*)

Korean spice viburnum (*Viburnum carlesii*)

Linden viburnum (*Viburnum dilatatum*)

Doublefile viburnum (*Viburnum plicatum tomentosum*)

### Ground Covers

Purple wintercreeper (*Euonymus fortunei colorata*)

Andorra juniper (*Juniperus horizontalis plumosa*)

*Opposite: The red-orange foliage of red maple glows in the autumn sunlight and the satiny blackness of pond water makes a dramatic contrast.*

Detailed information and recommended varieties can be found in Part III.

# LANDSCAPE TASKS FOR OCTOBER

**Fall Planting Continued**   You can still plant many trees and shrubs this month. In fact, the preferred planting season for deciduous trees and shrubs (as opposed to lawns, broad-leaved evergreens, and needled evergreens) extends from now through the end of November. (See September Landscape Tasks for planting instructions for all trees and shrubs.)

**Lawns and Leaves**   Keep the lawn mowed (see September) and rake leaves reasonably often to prevent them from matting and smothering the grass.

Your leaves are valuable. Don't bag them up and throw them away: pile them in the compost heap along with all the rest of your clean, disease-free garden refuse. Add limestone to speed the composting process come spring. Oak-leaf compost is particularly precious, being acid and therefore a great soil additive or mulch for azaleas, rhododendrons, and other broad-leaved evergreens.

**Watering**   Azaleas and rhododendrons, evergreen trees and shrubs, newly planted trees, and newly installed perennials should all be kept watered. (Lawns, however, don't need it.) Monitor rainfall and irrigate accordingly.

**Cleanup**   Hard though it is to get around to it, this is the time to clean, repair, and store garden furniture and equipment. Also clean up and compost all dead leaves and other garden debris, except material that harbors insects, weed seeds, or fungi. Get rid of this material; burn it if your local statutes permit, or send it to the dump if not.

# NOV

**Sugar maples cast dense shade for summer comfort and have unforgettable autumn color — but in November they are notable for vast leaf piles.**

With shortening days, cold nights, early frosts, perhaps even a snow flurry, November is a chilly month. And for people in cold climates, the November fuel bill is almost as chilling as the weather. The hottest days of summer may have been uncomfortable, but they were nowhere near as expensive as winter promises to be.

This month, energy-efficient landscaping becomes a concern: planning your structures and plantings to maximize shelter from wind and retention of the sun's warmth in winter — and the opposite in summer. (It wouldn't make sense to try to plan for either season in isolation, since the structures and plantings stay in place all year.) Hedges and fences are important for both winter wind protection and summer shade, so they're included here too. And I'll provide some ideas on plantings for textural highlights — a year-round subject, but well suited to this month, whether you are actually installing trees now or just contemplating plans for next spring.

---

### Landscaping Opportunities
# ENERGY-EFFICIENT LANDSCAPING

Human beings have always tried to keep warm in winter, and in climates like that of the Northeast it has always been a dirty, time-consuming, and/or expensive job to do that — with the exception of the brief but luxurious period between 1900 and 1973.

Similarly, people have always tried to keep cool in summer, but with far less success, until air conditioning really took hold around 1960. Up until then it was a matter of staying in the shade and moving slowly.

For many people it was a rude shock to learn in 1973 that energy for heating and cooling would never again be both cheap and effortless to come by. Conservation of heat — and natural cooling techniques — were rediscovered as a top priority of architecture and landscape design. Energy-saving tactics that had been forgotten came to light once more.

Most of these tactics have a lot to do with simple common sense. But what's exciting about them is the very considerable difference they can actually make. A landscape designed to block summer sun and winter wind — and to capture winter sun and summer breezes — can reduce energy costs for a centrally heated, air-conditioned house by 30 percent or more per year. Consider the following facts and figures.

**Warmth in Winter**   In winter sun is a friend, wind an enemy.
- Increase in heat loss from building surfaces is directly proportional to the square of increase in wind speed. That is, if wind speed increases from 10 to 20 mph (doubles), the heat loss will be 4 times as great.
- Wind velocity can be reduced by as much as 80 percent by a properly designed windbreak. I'm told that that amount of reduction in wind will cut heating bills by about 30 percent.
- If window overhangs and plantings let sun flow unobstructed into the windows of a house, the shortwave radiation of the sun's rays will warm up objects within the house; the objects will store the heat and help keep the house warm. The darker the color of the floors, furnishings, or walls where sunlight falls, the more heat will be retained. This is what's known as "passive solar" design and it involves no esoteric gear, just a little forethought.

**Summer Cooling**   Shading trellises or shade trees, vegetative ground covers, and wind tunnels in the form of hedges or structures can actually cool your house as well as its surrounding land.

- An unshaded asphalt pavement in summer can be 25°F hotter than the air above it.
- A structure such as a garage will be as much as 20° cooler in summer if shaded on the south and west by deciduous trees. (Deciduous because you don't want the shade in winter, of course.)
- Air temperature above a lawn is 15° cooler than above exposed earth. In the woods, it's 25° cooler than above exposed earth. And air temperature above a lawn mowed at a 3-inch height is 10° cooler than above one closely cropped to ½ inch. (As for astroturf, it heats the air up 50° hotter than above the close-cropped lawn.)
- The wind-chill created by air drawing through an evergreen tunnel on an 80° summer day makes the air feel as though it were 70°.

**Designing for Comfort**   Your first move in planning an energy-saving landscape is to determine where the sun and the wind are coming from, winter and summer. Sun angles and directions vary continually and from place to place. Some seasonal observation and recordkeeping (perhaps in the form of notes on your base plan) will give you the data you need. Prevailing wind directions are also various, and for total accuracy they should ideally be measured by you (since local topography has a lot to do with wind flow). To determine prevailing winter and summer winds in your area, put up 6-foot posts or stakes here and there on your property; attach to the tops pieces of ribbon about 1 inch wide and 1 foot long; and record the wind directions daily for a couple of weeks in each season.

**Sun**   In much of the United States we have sun for about half of all daylight hours, year round; in summer more, in winter less.

For winter, the diagrams on page 266 should suggest how to trap sun in and around your house. Eighty-five percent of the total energy from the sun flows our way between 9 A.M. and 3 P.M., and in winter the angle of the sun's rays between those hours varies from 10 to 30 degrees in this area. So try to orient living areas with lots of windows to the southeast. And avoid putting evergreens or other plantings where they'll shade windows, walls, or roofs in that southerly facing crescent during the peak sunlight hours.

On the south and west sides of the house, where you want the sun's warmth but where blinding reflected light from the snow may be a problem, you can plant a visual buffer of low evergreens. Or short deciduous trees will filter the light effectively, and give you a bonus of some shade in summer.

For summer, deciduous vines on upright screens or trellises do a great job of absorbing the sunlight, preventing it from turning a south-facing wall into a giant radiator.

On the east or southeast side of the house, small deciduous trees to screen windows from the potent late-morning sun are helpful. And on the south and west, overhangs and trellises to keep the sun out of the windows in summer can let it shine right in in winter, thanks to the different angles of the rays at different seasons.

Deciduous shade trees can cool your entire property as well as your house itself. Some cast deep, opaque shade; others a broken or filtered shade. The table here compares the percentages of visible sunlight blocked by various popular shade-tree species. I like different kinds of shade for different effects and purposes: heavy shade for a more intimate grotto or dense forestlike feeling; open, airy shade for simply breaking the direct sunlight with patterns of branching and foliage on the ground. Select your trees carefully for the quality of shade you have in mind.

## Percentages of Sun Blocked by Various Shade Trees

### 85 to 90% blocked
Norway maple (*Acer platanoides*)
European beech (*Fagus sylvatica*)
Silver linden (*Tilia petiolaris*)

### 80 to 85% blocked
Red maple (*Acer rubrum*)
Sugar maple (*Acer saccharum*)
Red oak (*Quercus rubra*)
Weeping willow (*Salix* spp.)
Littleleaf linden (*Tilia cordata*)

### 75 to 80% blocked
Shadblow or serviceberry (*Amelanchier* spp.)
Shagbark hickory (*Carya ovata*)
Katsura tree (*Cercidiphyllum japonicum*)
Japanese pagoda tree (*Sophoria japonica*)

### 60 to 70% blocked
Honey locust (*Gleditsia triacanthos*)
White pine (*Pinus strobus*)

**Shade out summer sun and introduce warming rays in the winter by adjusting the height and dimensions of a trellis or overhang. (Don't let evergreens block winter sun.)**

**Wind** For winter, windbreaks are the name of the game. They are most effective if they're solid masses of evergreens positioned perpendicular to the flow of the prevailing wind — because evergreen trees will grow taller than any wall. A good solid windbreak should be planted as broad as it is tall. It will reduce wind velocity up to 80 percent for a distance of 3 to 5 times its height. This should help you figure out how tall a windbreak you want and how close to the house (or other area to be sheltered) it will need to be.

Another way to insulate the house in winter is to plant low evergreen or deciduous shrubs against the foundation or walls of the house on the sides facing the winter wind. These plants will trap snow and create pockets of dead air: both effective forms of insulation.

For summer, trapping and funneling the wind to ventilate both outdoor and indoor living spaces is your goal. The increased wind velocity caused when a broad flow of air is channeled through a narrow opening, called the Venturi effect, is shown here. The wind-trapping barriers can be hedges, walls, shrub masses, even other buildings. A breezeway does a terrific job if you orient it right.

All in all, the arrangement of your landscape can make a tremendous difference to your comfort, not to mention your expenditures on heating fuel or air-conditioning electricity. It's fun to see it happen.

An evergreen arborvitae hedge forms a year-round visual screen and muffles sound from the adjacent roadway.

Reduce or increase velocity of seasonal winds by manipulating the air flow as suggested here.

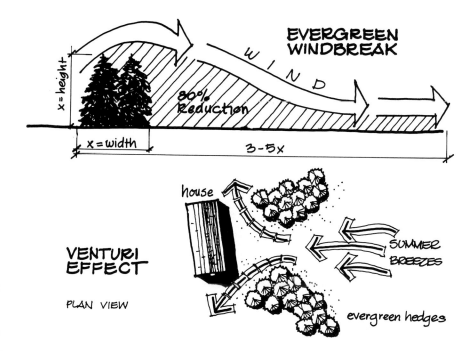

EVERGREEN WINDBREAK

x = height

80% Reduction

WIND

x = width

3-5x

VENTURI EFFECT

PLAN VIEW

house

SUMMER BREEZES

evergreen hedges

## Plants for a Purpose
# HEDGES

Arranging plants together to form rows or walls of green is a practice as old as landscape gardening itself. For thousands of years, people have used hedges as barriers, privacy screens, backgrounds for other types of planting, or ornamental borders or edgings. They've also used them to block cold winter winds or to funnel breezes for summer cooling or provide summer shade, as detailed in the preceding section.

In this section I'll look at some uses of hedges and some essentials of hedge care and maintenance. And I'll list some of the plants best suited for use in hedges, either because of their own natural sizes and shapes or because of their tendency to respond to pruning with vigorous bushy growth.

**Hedges for Screening**   Hedges can be massive or diminutive, evergreen or deciduous, transparent or opaque. Let me say right here that if complete privacy is the goal in your situation, you should probably invest in a fence or wall instead of a hedge. There are environmental hazards that can and do open gaps in even the sturdiest of hedges — ice storm damage, falling branches, or excessive zeal on the part of the end on the local touch football team.

Next to a wall or fence, the most effective year-round screen is an evergreen hedge, with the individual plants set in at least two staggered rows, so that if one is lost the others will fill in and the green wall will remain opaque. Many narrow-leaved evergreens like yews, juniper, or arborvitae do well. So do broad-leaved evergreens like inkberry, boxwood, or boxleaf holly — but be cautious with these last plants if the hedge's functions include winter wind protection, because many of them are subject to winterburn.

Even for purposes of privacy or visual screening, you may find that a deciduous hedge will serve your needs perfectly. If the hedge is used for summer shade but the shade is no longer wanted in winter — and/or if the hedge screens an area where you don't spend much time in cold weather — perhaps you can let the leaves go for the sake of the added light and sense of space. Again, the plants in a deciduous hedge

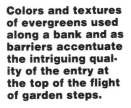

**Colors and textures of evergreens used along a bank and as barriers accentuate the intriguing quality of the entry at the top of the flight of garden steps.**

should be staggered, for summer privacy and for an air of fullness in winter. The range of deciduous hedge plants is vast — from shrubs like lilacs, honeysuckle, and privet, to trees like hawthorn and even lindens and beeches.

The height of a screening hedge depends on its location and function. Usually, hedges for privacy are taller than eye level; but if all you want to do is screen a view seen from a sitting position, you may not need such a tall hedge.

**Hedges for Borders**   Low hedges make elegant edging or borders, and very effective physical barriers as well. They can be evergreen or deciduous, formal or informal. As backgrounds, they set off other plants through contrasting color and texture. As boundaries, they contain and define spaces. They can also be transitional elements, where they ease the eye from the softness of the natural landscape to the hard-edged forms of buildings or other structures.

In these more decorative roles, the best hedge plants are usually smaller or dwarf plants with finer textures, to fit their uses in smaller-scale or more structured surroundings. If you want an ornamental hedge to keep out unwanted visitors as well, choose a particularly dense or even a prickly plant, like a hedge yew, barberry, or rugosa rose.

**Some Hedge How-Tos**   Think carefully at the outset about what you want from the plants you choose. The maintenance of a hedge doesn't have to be a major project, if you choose dwarf plants or plants with naturally compact forms. But if — for whatever reasons — you want to use bigger, more aggressive plants, then plan realistically on spending some time keeping them under control, one to three times a year.

Be conscious of the growing conditions of the area where you contemplate installing your hedge. Imagine what will happen if the hedge is in full sun for half its length, in dense shade for the other half; or if part of the hedge has its roots in well-drained soil, part in a soggy low spot. If you want a consistent hedge, you'll have to find or develop consistent conditions.

When you prune and shape your hedge, there's a right way and a wrong way to do it. Whether squared-off or rounded in form, all hedges should be allowed to grow wider at the base than at the top. Wider top growth — or even equal widths at top and bottom — will shade the bases of the hedge plants, often causing loss of lower foliage and an open, scrawny look along the bottom of the hedge.

What if your hedge is scrawny all over? It is sometimes best to start anew: dig the whole thing up and replant, perhaps with a different kind of shrub. With a deciduous hedge, however, you may be able to stop short of total demolition. Many an old and sad deciduous hedge can be restored to youthful exuberance by being cut right back to 6-inch stumps in early spring. If they're sufficiently vigorous, the plants will send out

**HEDGE PRUNING**

light can reach all foliage

yes

top foliage shades out bottom

no

**Basic rule of hedge pruning: shape the hedge to allow as much light as possible to reach all foliage, top and bottom.**

multiple shoots of new growth to compensate for their loss. To test whether the plants do possess the needed degree of vigor, experiment on an inconspicuous part before attacking the whole hedge.

Evergreen hedges, however, don't respond to this kind of treatment. In fact they may die if you try it. But regular annual trimmings will keep them thick and bushy without any trouble. Prune evergreens just after their spring growing season, but no later than the Fourth of July. If you wait longer, the new growth that comes after pruning may not have time to harden off before cold weather, and the plants may suffer needless winter damage.

A hedge that is to serve purposes other than hedging has some special care requirements. Many people like to make hedges of plants that will bloom in spring, and perhaps also produce edible seeds or fruits. But productive plants usually can't undergo the kind of regular trimming that hedges receive and still produce. The trimming removes flower buds and throws off the plants' blooming and fruiting schedule. So if you do want to establish a multipurpose hedge, allow it plenty of room. You won't be able to repress it with any severity. Prune discreetly right after flowering, and leave much of the current year's flowering growth intact if you want to have seeds or fruits later on.

**Plants for Hedges**  You can make a hedge out of virtually any tree or shrub that will grow in your climate (although some will work a lot better than others). In some gardening traditions, the creation of hedges out of unlikely material represents the ultimate in hedge culture. European hedges sometimes consist of old beech trees, dwarfed to 6-foot size by pruning since they were saplings — while their unpruned brothers stand 100 feet tall near by. Wandering across the English rural landscape there are 3-foot hedges of hawthorn trees, which if left to themselves would grow 30 feet tall. At Dumbarton Oaks in Washington, D.C., you can see an enclosure of hornbeams that are kept in shape by dint of weeklong clipping sessions several times a year. These, however, are heroic measures, and not really pertinent to the common or garden residential hedge.

Whether hedges are made of artificially dwarfed forest trees or of naturally compact shrubs, we usually think of them as consisting of a single variety of plant. But even that isn't necessarily the rule. In Japan it's typical to have several different kinds of plant in the same clipped hedge, making a tapestry of foliage and branch textures. It can be a fascinating effect. My only word of warning, if you are considering trying the Japanese approach, is that such a hedge should stand pretty much alone. With other plants around it, a multiplant hedge can give a somewhat busy feeling, particularly in surroundings where space is limited.

The raison d'être of all hedge plants is dense growth and finite size. If you choose trees or shrubs that are innately large, you'll have to keep them in fairly strict bondage by cutting and shaping; and your efforts will inevitably prevent the plants from fulfilling their natural cycles of blooming and fruiting. Some people feel uncomfortable with plants forced into artificial shapes and sizes. If you are of that school of thought, or if you simply haven't a great amount of time, interest, or equipment to dedicate to hedge care, your best choices will be self-limiting smaller shrubs of naturally bushy character. There are plenty of those in the list that follows, small plants that can go a year or three without any pruning at all.

If you are considering a more ambitious hedge, look to the larger evergreen and deciduous shrubs and trees listed here. It will take more work on your part to keep them within bounds, but they'll lend themselves to effects of great substance and even grandeur.

## Plants for Hedges

### Large Evergreen Tree Forms (look for compact or dwarf varieties in your nursery)

Norway spruce (*Picea abies*)
Austrian pine (*Pinus nigra*)
Douglas fir (*Pseudotsuga menziesii*)
Douglas arborvitae (*Thuja occidentalis* 'Douglas Pyramidal')
Canadian hemlock (*Tsuga canadensis*)

### Large Evergreen Shrubs

Common box (*Buxus sempervirens*)
Intermediate yew (*Taxus media* 'Densiformis')
Hatfield yew (*Taxus media* 'Hatfieldii')
Hicks yew (*Taxus media* 'Hicksii')
Hetz Wintergreen arborvitae (*Thuja occidentalis* 'Hetz Wintergreen')

### Medium Evergreen Shrubs

Japanese box (*Buxus microphylla japonica*)
Dwarf Japanese yew (*Taxus cuspidata* 'Nana')

### Small Evergreen Shrubs

Hellers Japanese holly (*Ilex crenata* 'Helleri')
Nest spruce (*Picea abies* 'Nidiformis')
Dwarf Canadian hedge yew (*Taxus canadensis* 'Stricta')
Hetz Midget arborvitae (*Thuja occidentalis* 'Hetz Midget')

### Large Deciduous Trees

European hornbeam (*Carpinus betulus*)
American beech (*Fagus grandifolia*)
European beech (*Fagus sylvatica*)
Littleleaf linden (*Tilia cordata*)

### Small Deciduous Trees/Large Deciduous Shrubs

Cornelian cherry dogwood (*Cornus mas*)

Washington hawthorn (*Crataegus phaenopyrum*)
Winged euonymus (*Euonymus alata*)
Rose-of-Sharon or shrub althea (*Hibiscus syriacus*)
Amur honeysuckle (*Lonicera maackii*)
Sargent crabapple (*Malus sargentii*)
Chinese lilac (*Syringa chinensis*)
Arrowwood (*Viburnum dentatum*)
European cranberrybush (*Viburnum opulus*)
Black haw (*Viburnum prunifolium*)

### Medium Deciduous Shrubs

Japanese barberry (*Berberis thunbergii*)
Dwarf winged euonymus (*Euonymus alata* 'Compacta')
Showy border forsythia (*Forsythia intermedia* 'Spectabilis')
Tatarian honeysuckle (*Lonicera tatarica*)
Vanhoutte spirea (*Spiraea vanhouttei*)
Dwarf Korean lilac (*Syringa palibiniana*)
Persian lilac (*Syringa persica*)
Doublefile viburnum (*Viburnum plicatum tomentosum*)

### Small Deciduous Shrubs

Red-leaved Japanese barberry (*Berberis thunbergii* 'Atropurpurea')
Regel privet (*Ligustrum obtusifolium regelianum*)
Rugosa rose (*Rosa rugosa*)
Anthony Waterer spirea (*Spiraea bumalda* 'Anthony Waterer')
Dwarf European cranberrybush (*Viburnum opulus* 'Nanum')

**Inkberry is used effectively as a screening hedge; vinca planted along the base is very similar in texture.**

Detailed information and recommended varieties can be found in Part III.

## Materials and Construction
# FENCES AND GATES

When you're looking for an energy-efficient landscape, security, or privacy immediately — and you want it to last a good long time — a fence is often the way to go. And this month you can still build fences, even the concrete footings, if you pick your time astutely. Well-built fencing may represent a substantial investment compared to a planted border or hedge, but over the long haul it also represents a quick, enduring, and maintenance-free answer to your needs.

With maximum longevity the goal, it is important that fences and gates be not only well built but thoughtfully selected. A stopgap solution generally turns out to be unsatisfactory in one way or another. But (possibly for the very reason that fences can be put up relatively swiftly) mistakes are often made with fences, to their owners' lasting chagrin. To help you make a choice you'll live with happily, I'll start by outlining a few of the most common errors made in fence design and construction.

**Fencing Pitfalls**   Other than exercising excessive haste, people usually go astray in deciding on the size and type of the fence, its fit and relationship to its environment, or the amount of fencing used for the job at hand.

**Wrong size or type**   You've probably seen plenty of ill-considered fences. A chain-link security fence usually imparts a feeling of being imprisoned rather than protected. A one-sided fence may look great in one family's yard but be a horrendous eyesore from the neighbors' vantage. An opaque fence designed for privacy can cut off light and ventilation as well as views in and out. Too tall a fence can make you feel more isolated than separated; this is particularly likely to happen in a small-scale place with a fence 6 feet or more high.

**All fences fall into three groups: transparent, semitransparent, and opaque. On a slope, architectural fences should be stepped; informal ones can follow the topography.**

FENCE TYPES:

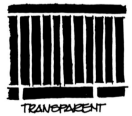
TRANSPARENT

SEMI-TRANSPARENT

OPAQUE

FENCES ON SLOPES

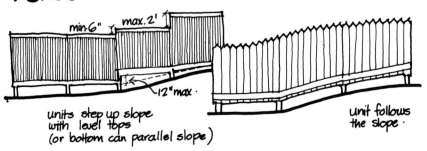

min. 6"   max. 2'   12" max.

units step up slope
with level tops
(or bottom can parallel slope)

unit follows
the slope.

**Faulty relationship to surroundings**   The materials, style, and finish of fencing should be in harmony with those of the house and other structures near it. Solid or semitransparent fences that are attached to the house or very close to it should be treated architecturally. That means that if the land slopes up or down, the fence should be stepped and the top of each segment kept level.

Transparent fences, on the other hand, can be allowed to follow the lines of the topography. So can fences (even solid ones) that are at a distance from the house. Let them be related primarily to the landscape rather than the house itself.

**Too much fencing**   The most common mistake of all may be to use too much fencing, or at least too much of one type. It's rare indeed that fencing is needed around an entire property. But in cases where a complete surrounding fence is called for, it usually works best to use one major type with perhaps a compatible variation to meet the needs of some specific area (privacy, screening, security, traffic control, or whatever) or to afford visual relief, rather than one homogeneous type all the way around.

**Planning Fences and Gates**   Let's look at the main considerations that enter into a wise choice of fencing for your property. Before you begin, check into your town's published zoning regulations to see if there are limitations on fence height, setback from property lines, direction of best face, etc. You want to do fencing only once and do it right.

**Location**   This is the most important issue to resolve. Think about fences as walls or dividers that separate and define outdoor spaces or landscape "rooms," and you're 90 percent of the way towards a satisfying and functional fencing plan. Before you start building you need to be able to visualize very concretely what the finished effect will be. Test out the proposed placement of your fence by stringing clothesline where the fence is to run; drape sheets or blankets over it if necessary for an even greater sense of the visual effect. This will also help you decide two other important questions: what type of fence to build and how high it should be.

**Type of fence**   The location and purpose will determine the overall type of the fence: opaque, semitransparent, or transparent.

Opaque fencing offers complete privacy but will cut off light, air

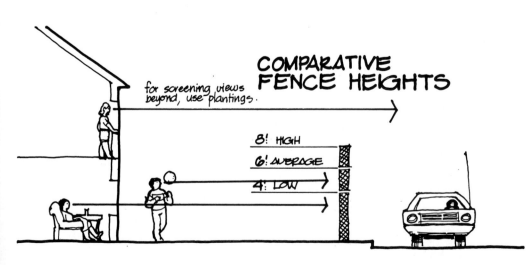

for screening views beyond, use plantings.

COMPARATIVE FENCE HEIGHTS

8' HIGH
6' AVERAGE
4' LOW

Fences are effective screens at lower levels, but they have their limitations. For screening second-story views, use plantings.

**Fence types: a custom-made redwood fence (above left) is close to the house and architectural in feeling, while this stockade-type border fence at the property line (above right) has plantings at its foot and overflowing its top that integrate it with the natural surroundings.**

**Below, a decorative lattice, scalloped gate, and scrolled steel arch welcome visitors.**

circulation, and views to the outside. You have to weigh your need for privacy against your desire for summer breezes or a feeling of openness.

Semitransparent fencing permits a good deal of air and light to pass through; it allows you glimpses or an impressionistic sense of views beyond; and it affords considerable privacy from passing cars, although not from the view of people on foot outside. This is the kind of fence I use most often. Very often, too, I combine opaque and semitransparent types in one fence. Semitransparent and opaque sections one above the other, for instance, can give complete privacy to a sitting area while allowing views and air circulation through the upper part of the fence. Vertical louvers can be angled to permit views in one direction only and yet let air circulate. I think that the ideal semitransparent fence would be one with movable vertical louvers that you could adjust to changing wind and sun directions and differing needs for privacy, like a vertical venetian blind. It would be expensive to build, although you could probably do it with simple hardware like that used in the old wooden shutters. I've never yet had a chance to try one.

Transparent fences often perform utilitarian roles, such as restricting children or animals, or surrounding swimming pools. A secure fence that allows unobstructed views is the wrought-iron type. (For complete transparency it should be painted a dark color.) Or transparent fences can be used as purely visual or decorative borders, like rail fences or traditional picket fences.

**Size of fence**   Keep fencing as low as possible for the effect or purpose intended — provided that you also keep it in scale with surrounding structures and plantings. Here again, your clothesline-and-blanket rig is an invaluable aid to planning. You can determine whether the height you have in mind will just screen the view you want to screen or whether you're in danger of overfencing. The diagram on page 273 gives you the accepted maximum and minimum heights for various purposes.

**Style of gate**   Where a space is enclosed with fencing, a gate is sometimes also needed. A gate can be a functional and pleasant part of the entry experience — or it can be merely exasperating.

Make sure your gate is big enough for the traffic it will have to bear, including lawn mowers, leaf carts, or other vehicles. And above all, a gate should work. Gates are as fussy to hang as doors, and there's the added dimension of the weather to contend with: wetting and drying and freezing and thawing play havoc with moving parts. Be sure your gate is built with appropriate hardware and sturdily braced against sagging.

Fencing affords scope for whimsy (left) — but be careful. At right, the sturdy service gate is well braced, not designed as an invitation for use by visitors.

Like other parts of a fence, a gate should be stylistically in keeping with the rest of the landscape. Usually this means using the same materials as the fence proper. But I don't recommend making a gate identical (except for its hinges) to the fence. A gate should convey a greeting and a sense of welcome. Try to give it some special quality: change the spacing or size of its members, or express its supporting structure, or give it a different height or outline.

**Finishes for Fences and Gates**   You may choose to let wooden fences weather naturally. But if a fence abuts or runs very close to your house, particularly if you have wood trim or siding, it should be the same or a complementary color; and this may mean paint or stain. For long life and ease of maintenance I'd usually recommend wood-preservative stain rather than paint on wooden fences and gates. Paint tends to capture moisture in joints so that the wood rots underneath — but the object of finishing the wood in the first place is to keep moisture away from end grains and joints.

Foliage textures are used for landscape effect. Highlighting this textural tapestry are white birchbark and variegated hosta.

For this same reason, and whether you paint or stain, it's best to treat all members before you assemble them and touch them up afterwards. It is very difficult to get into all the nooks and crannies, and impossible to get into the joints, once the fence is built.

**After the finish**   Very often the real finishing touch for a fence consists of the plantings along it. A fence can be an ideal backdrop for flowers, shrubs, or trees. Or you can design it specifically to serve as a framework for vines or espaliers. Foliage and flowers are the perfect camouflage for any little flaws or awkward corners in a fence; they soften stark lines and rough edges; and they complement the colors and textures of fencing materials.

---

Plants by Design

# FOLIAGE TEXTURE

---

**Textural high spots for the landscape: plants with very coarse and very fine foliage textures**

---

### COARSE-TEXTURED PLANTS

### Deciduous Trees
Horse chestnut (*Aesculus hippocastanum*)
Sweet gum tree (*Liquidambar styraciflua*)
Tulip tree (*Liriodendron tulipifera*)
Saucer magnolia (*Magnolia soulangiana*)
Red oak (*Quercus rubra*)

The softness of white pine foliage texture is especially appreciated against a contrasting wall.

### Deciduous Shrubs
Fothergilla or witch alders (*Fothergilla* spp.)
Witch hazels (*Hamamelis* spp.)
Hydrangeas (*Hydrangea* spp.)

### Needled Evergreens
White fir (*Abies concolor*)
Hinoki false cypress (*Chamaecyparis obtusa*)
Norway spruce (*Picea abies*)
Japanese black pine (*Pinus thunbergiana*)

### Broad-leaved Evergreens
Rhododendrons, large-leaved (*Rhododendron* spp.)

### Vines
Bittersweet (*Celastrus scandens*)

English ivy (*Hedera helix*)
Boston ivy (*Parthenocissus tricuspidata*)
Grapes (*Vitis* spp.)

### Ground Covers
European ginger (*Asarum europaeum*)
Drooping leucothoe (*Leucothoe fontanesiana*)

### FINE-TEXTURED PLANTS

### Deciduous Trees
Japanese maple (*Acer palmatum*)
Birches (*Betula* spp.)
Hornbeams (*Carpinus* spp.)
Beeches (*Fagus* spp.)
Honey locust (*Gleditsia triacanthos*)
Golden larch (*Pseudolarix amabilis*)
Weeping willow (*Salix* spp.)

### Deciduous Shrubs
Barberries (*Berberis* spp.)
Cotoneasters (*Cotoneaster* spp.)
Privet (*Ligustrum* spp.)
Azaleas, small-leaved (*Rhododendron* spp.)
Spireas (*Spiraea* spp.)
Blueberries (*Vaccinium* spp.)

### Needled Evergreens
Junipers (*Juniperus* spp.)

## Foliage Texture *(continued)*

White pine (*Pinus strobus*)
Hemlock (*Tsuga canadensis* vars.)

### Broad-leaved Evergreens

Boxwood (*Buxus* spp.)
Japanese holly (*Ilex crenata*)

### Vine

Common trumpet creeper (*Campsis radicans*)

### Evergreen Ground Covers

Bearberry (*Arctostaphylos uva-ursi*)
Japanese garden juniper (*Juniperus chinensis procumbens*)
Canby paxistima (*Paxistima canbyi*)
Vinca, periwinkle, or myrtle (*Vinca minor*)

Detailed information and recommended varieties can be found in Part III.

# LANDSCAPE TASKS FOR NOVEMBER

**Last Call**   Many trees and shrubs can still go into the ground now — but this is it. You can also dig, divide, and replant lily-of-the-valley if you haven't gotten around to it before. (See September for both procedures.)

**Pools and Ponds**   Drain and clean artificial pools; remove and store hardy water lilies, or discard tropical ones. You can cover your pool with boards or a tarpaulin or other covering, or fill it with leaves and lay branches over the top. The protection will reduce the stress of winter's repeated wettings, freezings, and thawings.

**Lawn Mower**   Send the lawn into winter at a height of no more than 2 inches. Then clean the lawn-mower blades, and have them sharpened and adjusted if necessary. Don't procrastinate; in spring every lawn-mower shop will be inundated with urgent business.

**Leaves and More Leaves**   When the last of the leaves have fallen, give a final raking and mulching all around. You can let leaves remain around the edges of shrubbery, perennial beds, and so forth as an informal mulch; or if that looks too untidy to you, put all leaves on the compost heap and mulch your plants and beds with straw, bark chips, salt-marsh hay, pine straw, or any mulch of your choosing.

**Tree Guards**   It's wise to protect young fruit trees, ornamental cherries, or crabapples with wire netting, wood, plastic coil wraps, or heavy paper if there are any rabbits, mice, or deer in your neighborhood. These animals like to chew on tender bark in the lean winter months, and their "girdling" can kill a young tree.

**Lilacs**   Cut away all the suckers at the bases of lilacs. Spread manure around them, leave it over the winter, and work it in in spring, to nourish new growth and promote bloom.

**Hardwood Cuttings**   Take hardwood cuttings now from forsythia, privet, or mock-orange. Bundle them up and store them buried in damp sand in a cold place (a cellar or cold frame is good) during the winter. They'll root swiftly if you plant them in the earth in spring.

# DEC

*Landscaping Opportunities*
**Night Lighting Outdoors**

*Plants for a Purpose*
**Needled Evergreens**

*Materials and Construction*
**Metal**

*Plants by Design*
**Form**

*Landscape Tasks for December*

**This lake in Callaway Gardens, Georgia, mirrors the splendor of a December sunset.**

This wintry month it's natural to think about light. The winter solstice and the holidays arrive simultaneously — the former bringing the longest night of the year, the latter all kinds of festivities and the man-made illuminations to go with them. Evergreens are a natural topic here too, December being practically synonymous with the rich greens and woodsy scents of pine, spruce, and fir. Along with evergreens let's look at the forms of trees that make distinctive statements in a landscape composition — since one of the great contributions of evergreens is that their forms stay the same through every season. And for the concluding Materials and Construction section, metal seems a resoundingly good choice: a material as cold and crisp as this season, and more important in the landscape than you might suppose.

### Landscaping Opportunities
# NIGHT LIGHTING OUTDOORS

Most houses are built with a bare minimum of outdoor lighting: a floodlight or two, perhaps, and a lamp beside the front door. But floodlights are essentially security lighting. Designed to repel burglars or illuminate the area in emergencies, they glare or even blind you. They're far from welcoming. The same wattage can be put to work in other, far more attractive ways. Consider reserving your floodlight for real emergencies and installing other forms of outdoor lighting for beauty and safety combined.

Some of the most stunning effects of outdoor lighting occur when there's snow on the ground and on the branches of trees, and December often obliges with a light fall of snow. Yet at every season, well-designed lighting can create beauty or excitement around your house at night.

**Outdoor lighting takes many forms. A simple homemade fixture (left) is a safety factor on a sloping walk with steps. A sophisticated arrangement (right) is built into a trellis.**

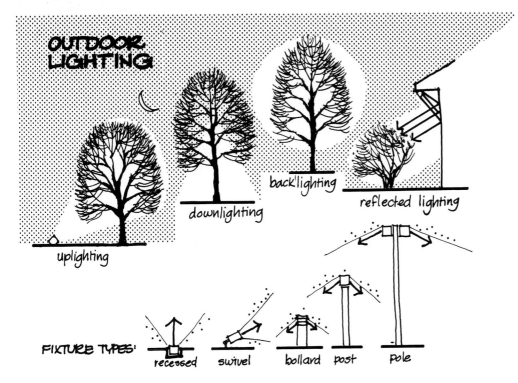

**OUTDOOR LIGHTING**

uplighting

downlighting

back lighting

reflected lighting

FIXTURE TYPES: recessed  swivel  bollard  post  pole

Sketched here are some often-used ways to create appealing effects with outdoor lighting, and some typical outdoor fixtures.

**Lighting for Safety**   Lighting belongs first and foremost where hazards exist. A hazard is anything that might cause you or your guests to slip, stumble, or fall in the dark: steps, abrupt changes in grade, or changes in the material you walk on (pavement to grass, for instance).

The figures here show some of the types of fixture that you can use to make your property a safe and hospitable place after dark. There are posts with lamps mounted at or above eye level, to give off a gentle area light. Or there are lamps on shorter posts, which direct illumination onto the ground in a clear-cut pattern. Some short, fat "bollard" fixtures — 2 to 3 feet tall and 6 or 8 inches in diameter — contain lamps within the post itself. Other fixtures are boxes with lamps recessed to cast a soft glow, like the lights in movie-theater aisles.

As you look at these fixtures in a store or catalogue, you'll see that some cast light from a concealed or cutoff source while others are designed so that the bulb itself, as well as the light it casts, can be seen. If you don't want any visible bright spots of light, but you like a feeling of restrained elegance or a mysterious quality, concealed-source lighting may be the best approach for you. I must admit that in some instances I like to see lamps sparkling along a long path or driveway, or a handsome fixture atop a post at the beginning of a front walk. This approach is more animated and exciting. The lights seem like a greeting from the house and the people within. But it is important to make sure that the fixtures and their bulbs don't generate annoying glare.

**Lighting for Effect**   Outdoor lighting can also be used chiefly for effect. In many cases lighting for visual interest can satisfy utilitarian purposes too, and that is always my goal.

A couple of examples: a spotlight in a cylindrical fixture high in a tree can cast wonderful shadows on the ground and still illuminate the path to the front door. Or a lamp attached to a roof soffit to create a wash of light down a textured stone wall can also make the adjacent steps negotiable. In the first example the light is direct; in the second the light is reflected, or indirect. Both forms of lighting are designed for appearance, but they also enable people to move safely around the landscape at night.

Lighting to enhance the beauty of the night landscape usually takes one or more of the forms shown on page 281: uplighting, downlighting, backlighting for silhouettes, reflected lighting, lighting for shadows or textures, and moonlighting (using lamps positioned to simulate moonlight). Some of these give a simple, straightforward look; others create an air of mystery or a theatrical mood.

**Installing Outdoor Lighting**   It's not hard to install a low-voltage system yourself, if your house boasts a waterproof outdoor electrical outlet. You just purchase a 12-volt transformer, some wire (up to about 100 feet), and the fixtures you need; plug the transformer into the outlet; and arrange the lights where you want them. You can bury the wire in the ground or conceal it under mulch or thick shrubbery. You can even build fixtures to your own design, using materials suited to the setting.

There are some major drawbacks to a low-voltage system like this, however. You are limited to 5 or 6 fixtures on the circuit, and the bulbs can be no brighter than 75 watts. The longer the run of the wire, the dimmer the lights will be. And the standard plastic fixtures available are seldom attractive in themselves.

But if you can get around these disadvantages, there are two main arguments for using this kind of system. It is absolutely harmless because of its low voltage; and it is comparatively very economical to install and operate.

If the minuses of the 12-volt system outweigh its pluses for you, then a standard 120-volt system will be the solution. This will cost more to install and run, and its high voltage makes it more dangerous; but it will give you far more flexibility — and more light.

I would recommend that you have an electrician do all the wiring from the service panel to the switches to an outdoor junction box or panel. Then you can put in as many cables and fixtures as you like, provided you do not exceed the amperage limit for each circuit.

Be sure to use 3-wire direct burial cable and bury it far enough below ground so that a sharp shovel will not cut it. Be cautious about the locations of all buried fixtures: most "waterproof" fixtures leak, and a leaking fixture is dangerous.

I can't really recommend any standard line of outdoor lighting fixtures on the market. For some reason, good design and good materials are very hard to find; perhaps because the demand for outdoor fixtures is not great. The best insurance is to arrange ahead of time with your supplier to allow you to return any fixture that doesn't look right when you see it in place.

---

### Plants for a Purpose
# NEEDLED EVERGREENS

I usually think of needled evergreen trees and shrubs as background and frame for a landscape. Very often, though, they serve as important foreground plants. And sometimes they steal the entire scene.

They are necessary in every landscape — and so versatile that you can use them for any purpose at all.

Evergreens are such a mainstay because practically all of them retain their foliage, and therefore their mass, form, color, and texture, all year long. (The exceptions are interesting for reasons of their own.) Their forms run the gamut from prostrate creepers that carpet the ground to towering specimens with their heads in the clouds. As for their colors, the palette encompasses steely blues, bright to blackish greens, and greens variegated with white or yellow. Their textures are equally varied: some evergreens have flat frondlike scales, some short bristles, some long stiff needles, some short silky ones.

The big four among needled evergreens are pine, spruce, fir, and hemlock. These trees forest vast areas of the United States and yield much of the lumber used in building construction. Both the native species and the hundreds of introduced and cultivated varieties of these trees can make wonderful landscape plants — but most of the native species are basically large forest trees, and will grow into huge, overpowering specimens. Use these giants only on very large properties. For other settings, choose varieties bred for small size and/or slow growth. They'll give you equal drama without that looming effect.

More modest-sized evergreens are the junipers, yews, and arborvitae. Many of these plants will grow into small trees if you let them, but they're easy to restrain to shrub size and that is how they are most often used. Nestling near the house or at the edge of the lawn, they are companionable human-scaled plants.

Among the evergreens listed on page 284 are plants to serve all kinds of landscape functions. Some provide food and habitats for wildlife; some are natives, suitable for wild or naturalistic landscapes; some make great hedges; and there are ground covers, shade trees, specimens, and trees and shrubs for borders and screens.

**Umbrella pine holds its needles in a unique whorled pattern.**

**Gold-tipped variegated false cypress catches the sun and helps warm the winter landscape.**

## Needled Evergreen Trees and Shrubs

White fir (*Abies concolor*)

Hinoki false cypress (*Chamaecyparis obtusa* vars.)

Thread false cypress (*Chamaecyparis pisifera* 'Filifera' and vars.)

Chinese juniper (*Juniperus chinensis* vars.)

Creeping juniper (*Juniperus horizontalis* vars.)

Red cedar (*Juniperus virginiana* vars.)

Dawn redwood (*Metasequoia glyptostroboides*)

Norway spruce (*Picea abies* vars.)

Jack pine (*Pinus banksiana*)

Lacebark pine (*Pinus bungeana*)

Swiss stone pine (*Pinus cembra*)

Tanyosho pine (*Pinus densiflora* 'Umbraculifera')

Dwarf mugho pine (*Pinus mugo pumilio*)

Austrian pine (*Pinus nigra*)

White pine (*Pinus strobus* vars.)

Japanese black pine (*Pinus thunbergiana*)

Golden larch (*Pseudolarix kaempferi*)

Douglas fir (*Pseudotsuga menziesii*)

Umbrella pine (*Sciadopitys verticillata*)

Canada yew (*Taxus canadensis* vars.)

Dwarf Japanese yew (*Taxus cuspidata* 'Nana')

Intermediate yew (*Taxus media* vars.)

American arborvitae (*Thuja occidentalis* vars.)

Canadian hemlock (*Tsuga canadensis* vars.)

Detailed information and recommended varieties can be found in Part III.

## Materials and Construction
# METAL

Metals are not exactly the materials most prevalent in the landscape. Even so, they have quite a few uses: you'll find metals in fencing and railings, lighting fixtures and posts, drain frames and grates, bed edgings, and furniture — and in myriad forms of hardware and fastenings.

Most often you will be buying metal items ready-made. And for the most part you'll be dealing with ferrous (iron-containing) products, although you will probably also encounter nonferrous metals such as copper and aluminum and alloys such as brass and bronze.

Metal is capable of being bent, and as such is used to full advantage in this curved railing.

This section is by way of an introduction to the metals around you: their makeup, their properties, and some roles they play in the landscape.

**Iron and Steel** Steel as we know it has been around only since the 1850s. Before then, cast iron and wrought iron were manufactured by processes unchanged for 500 years.

Carbon content defines the differences between various types of iron and steel. Wrought iron is almost pure iron, containing less than 1/10 of 1 percent carbon. It is soft and malleable; when forged (heated to workable softness) it can be hammered into any shape required. Craftsmen in Colonial America and up to the early 1900s made wrought-iron tools, utensils, and furnishings a true art form.

Cast iron has a very high carbon content, 2 to 6 percent, almost the same as pig iron (unrefined iron smelted from crude ore). Iron of this type is brittle and nonmalleable. Melted and poured into forms or molds, it is the material of ornamental ironwork, rigid heavy objects like manhole covers, furniture, and hardware.

Steel comes in many categories for many purposes, and the carbon content of the different types varies from a mere trace (.05 percent) to a relatively high 1.5 percent. "Soft steel" is reserved for uses where strength and stiffness are unimportant, such as wire or pipe. "Mild steel" offers both strength and machinability and is used in everything from bolts to bridges to building construction. "Spring steel" is resilient enough for use in springs; "tool steel" is tough and high in carbon and is used for making precision instruments with close tolerances.

Stainless steel is an alloy that incorporates any of a number of other metals to provide rust-resistance and sheen. Added to stainless steel may be chromium, magnesium, or nickel in various proportions.

"Bright steel" means chrome-plated steel (commonly found in the form of nuts and bolts) and should never be used outdoors, as it will rust.

**Weathering steel** A special steel with a high phosphorus content, weathering steel rusts rapidly to a rich chocolate brown. It reaches its full color in about three years, then stops, having given itself a permanent finish that will never need attention. This material can be extremely handsome in the landscape, provided it's used in the right place. During the weathering process, large amounts of rust accumulate, wash off, and stain all surrounding surfaces; so you should never use this steel against any wall or on any pavement that will show the stains. Stone pebbles are an ideal edging or ground cover beneath a fence, gate, arbor, or lamppost made of weathering steel, because you can stir them around and somewhat conceal the staining.

**Galvanized steel**  All steels except stainless steel need some form of protective finish or coating to prevent corrosion. Exposed nongalvanized steel of any kind should always be painted with a primer and rust-inhibiting paint. For longevity in outdoor use, the best treatment for plain steel is galvanizing, or coating with zinc. Most galvanized products you buy should be hot-dip galvanized. Electroplating results in a more uniform but thinner and less durable zinc coating; so ask for hot-dipped stock.

(Beware, however, of using galvanized nails or bolts or other connectors in visible spots on redwood or red cedar construction. Both these woods contain an acid that makes the zinc corrode and stain. Use aluminum or aluminum-coated steel nails and fasteners instead.)

In order to paint galvanized steel, you have to roughen its surface. You can do this by letting it weather a year until it "pickles" (turns a chalky gray). Or you can etch it with a 5 percent solution of hydrochloric, phosphoric, or acetic acid in water. After weathering or etching, use a zinc chromate primer before applying finish coats of paint. A far easier approach, and my own preference in most situations, is to leave galvanized steel alone. The color of the weathered zinc coating blends pleasantly with woods that have also been left to weather to a silvery gray.

A few words of warning about corrosion of unlike metals are in order here. When different metals are in contact in a moist environment, one will corrode the other. This phenomenon is called galvanic action; it results from warring between the metals' electrons, and will wreak havoc where it occurs. (It is a problem well known to anyone familiar with boats.) The solution is never to mix metals. Don't use brass, bright steel, or plain steel bolts or screws with zinc-coated hinges, for example. Never combine bright steel nuts with galvanized bolts.

**Old iron**  Antique (or used) artifacts of wrought or cast iron make wonderful garden features. I am always searching for old ornamental grilles, gates, posts, and newels, as well as old garden furniture. Often I'll design an entire outdoor setting around one or two of these pieces. If you are lucky enough to have access to old ironwork, just be sure to use it with restraint and incorporate it carefully into surroundings of fitting character.

**Aluminum**  Steels are capable of being cast, forged, wrought, rolled, and welded; but they cannot be extruded (forced under pressure through a die), and that is where aluminum comes in. Aluminum is easily extruded into complicated fluted, grooved, or ridged shapes, so that it is the material of choice for many a handrail, screen, and window or door frame. Once exposed to the weather it forms its own protective coating, aluminum oxide, an inert grayish film. It needs no other other protection — although you can buy it painted, vinyl-coated, or "anodized" in various colors. Anodizing is a form of electroplating. I find that under heavy traffic it tends to scratch and wear off, so I don't advise it for uses such as doorsills or handrails where deteriorating appearance will be a problem.

Antique cast-iron fence sections can often be incorporated in designs for small gardens.

You can use aluminum as a structural material in applications where light weight is a key criterion, such as large gates or movable planters. It's made in many of the same forms and dimensions as steel. Aluminum chairs and tables are often marketed as patio furniture: they are reasonable and portable, but not very stable, permanent, or (in my opinion) attractive.

If you are putting in or replacing screening in windows, doors, or porches, I strongly recommend black aluminum mesh, which is darkened by a process called "alodizing." It does not reflect indoor light as does shiny aluminum, and therefore it yields a wonderfully clear view. (Old-fashioned copper screening, now too expensive to use, darkened naturally over time with the same satisfactory result.) I stumbled upon this fact by accident when replacing one of two screens in a door. Oblivious to what the hardware store was cutting for me, I took the screen home to find that the old mesh was shiny, the new one black. The contrast was remarkable.

**Copper**   Copper makes a wonderful roofing material for a small garden structure. Its velvety jade-green patina "sets" in eight to ten years and forms a permanent, insoluble protective coating. Or if you prefer to keep the original warm reddish color alive, you can do so with a yearly application of linseed oil.

Copper also, needless to say, finds uses in flashing, drain pipes, and fountains and their plumbing.

This decorative copper water fountain accents a city garden. Copper and water have visual (and practical) affinity.

**Brass and Bronze**   These two alloys of copper are probably the most esoteric and expensive of landscape metals, but I mention them because they definitely have their places as architectural highlights. A shiny brass name or number plate adds an accent of charm and dignity to a front door. A rich golden-brown bronze railing or banister is elegant in its own right.

Brass is a blend of copper and zinc in variable proportions; the more zinc, the more silvery and bright the brass. Bronze combines copper and about 10 percent tin. Tin is much in demand for other commercial uses, and as it becomes more rare and costly, so does bronze.

From fencing to plumbing to railings to statuary, metal plays many parts as no other material possibly could. If you have a place for metal in your landscape you'll find there is excitement in shopping for it, designing with it, and enjoying it over the years.

## Plants by Design

# FORM

### Large and small trees for character and emphasis

**Above, the dogwood's rounded shape breaks the line of a fence. Opposite, the lofty pyramidal form of a dawn redwood is echoed where the trunk widens at its base.**

### Vase/Fan-Shaped Forms

Yellowwood (*Cladrastis lutea*)
Kousa or Japanese dogwood (*Cornus kousa*)
Tea crabapple (*Malus hupehensis*)
Japanese pagoda tree (*Sophora japonica*)
Zelkova (*Zelkova serrata*)

### Pyramidal Forms

White fir (*Abies concolor*)
Sweet gum (*Liquidambar styraciflua*)
Dawn redwood (*Metasequoia glyptostrobides*)
Spruce (*Picea* spp.)
Korean mountain ash (*Sorbus alnifolia*)
Korean stewartia (*Stewartia koreana*)
Japanese stewartia (*Stewartia pseudocamellia*)
Littleleaf linden (*Tilia cordata*)
Hemlock (*Tsuga canadensis*)

### Oval to Round Forms

Japanese maple (*Acer palmatum*)
Norway maple (*Acer platanoides*)
Sugar maple (*Acer saccharum*)
Horse chestnut (*Aesculus hippocastanum*)
Redbud (*Cercis canadensis*)
White fringe tree (*Chionanthus virginicus*)

Flowering dogwood (*Cornus florida*)
Cornelian cherry dogwood (*Cornus mas*)
Washington hawthorn (*Crataegus phaenopyrum*)
Beeches (*Fagus* spp.)
White ash (*Fraxinus americana*)
Saucer magnolia (*Magnolia soulangiana*)
Crabapples (*Malus* spp.)
Red oaks (*Quercus rubra*)
Willows (*Salix* spp.)
Lindens (*Tilia* spp.)

### Weeping Forms

Weeping European beech (*Fagus sylvatica* 'Pendula')
Weeping cherry (*Prunus subhirtella* 'Pendula')
Weeping willows (*Salix* spp.)
Sargent weeping hemlock (*Tsuga canadensis* 'Pendula')

### Columnar or Fastigiate Forms

Paper birch (*Betula papyrifera*)
Gray birch (*Betula populifolia*)
Pyramidal hornbeam (*Carpinus betulus* 'Columnaris')
Red cedar (*Juniperus virginiana*)
Hicks yew (*Taxus media* 'Hicksii')
American arborvitae (*Thuja occidentalis*)

Detailed information and recommended varieties can be found in Part III.

# LANDSCAPE TASKS FOR DECEMBER

**Bird Feeding**   If your yard is abundant in plants with seeds and fruits for birds, you may not need to supplement their diet with store-bought seeds. If not, now is the time to set up a feeding station or three. Warning: this is a winter-long commitment. It is not fair to accustom wildlife to feeding, then withdraw the supply. If you start now, plan to continue putting out provender until April.

**Snow Stamping**   After a heavy snowfall, trample down circles around young fruit trees. This will protect them from tunneling rodents; the packed snow is hard to dig.

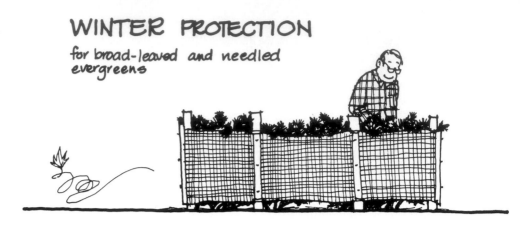

# WINTER PROTECTION

*for broad-leaved and needled evergreens*

Protect tender plants from the full brunt of winter wind. This is one method; battens nailed outside burlap will keep the fabric from tearing loose from the stakes.

**Needled and Broad-leaved Evergreens** Until the ground freezes, water newly planted needled evergreen trees and shrubs. Once the ground is frozen, give them a thick mulch of straw or matted leaves to reduce damage from freeze-thaw cycles. Burlap windscreens to shelter evergreen shrubs from the prevailing winter wind are a good idea, too. Don't wrap the plants tightly, just create a barricade by driving stakes around them, then stretching the fabric around the stakes. Or build an informal A-frame of scrap lumber.

If you have boxwood or boxleaf holly plants in an exposed location, they too will benefit from burlap windbreaks.

Rhododendrons, azaleas, mountain laurel, and andromeda (pieris) will endure the coming months better if you can give them a few final waterings before the ground freezes solid. If they're not already well mulched, do it now. Antidesiccant spray can be applied to newly planted broad-leaves during a mild spell (40°F or up), to forestall damage from severe winter drying.

The flattened oval of a Japanese maple on an upper terrace stands out against an evergreen backdrop, especially in fall when the foliage turns scarlet.

**Salt Advice**   Some gardeners find that a light application of commercial fertilizer melts ice from walks as effectively as salt — at least, as long as the cold is not too intense. If you must salt, keep the stuff away from lawns, shrubs, and all garden plantings. It is harmful to plants. It's also harmful to groundwater and aquifers, and should be used only when ice endangers life and limb.

**One More Chance**   Here are a few samples of things you can still do if you've missed getting around to them before. It may be late, but it's still definitely beneficial to:

- Mulch perennials, shrubs, and all fruit-bearing garden plants with materials like oak leaves, pine straw, straw, bark chips, or evergreen boughs (except hemlocks, which rapidly lose their needles).
- Protect fruit trees, particularly young ones, with collars to fend off hungry animals.
- Clean up the dead remains of last summer's vegetation.
- Stake newly planted trees for support.
- Clean and oil those garden tools.
- Make lists of good ideas for next year.

**Advance Notice**   At the other extreme, some tasks usually reserved for early in the new year can just as well be done now. For more details on all of these, see January:

- Send for seed catalogues and get your orders in early.
- Take hardwood cuttings of trees and shrubs.

December may seem a quiet month in the landscape. Summer's flowers and fruits have long since died or been harvested. Trees and shrubs and lawns are dormant. It's too cold to build anything. People are busy with other things; they haven't time even to page through the garden and nursery catalogues, much less make ambitious plans for redesigning the front entry area or planting dogwoods under the oaks. But don't let December fool you. This is really the upturn, the beginning of the great rebirth. The pace has been slowing; now it's about to speed up. As the days begin almost imperceptibly to lengthen at the end of this month, I like to look ahead to the new year, the coming spring, and everything starting anew once more.

# PART III PLANT DESCRIPTIONS

Every plant recommended in this book is described here. This selection is by no means exhaustive; it represents many tough choices, for there are thousands of wonderful plants available. But at the least it should give you a good head start on deciding what plants will work for your landscape.

Opposite: forms, colors, and textures of conifers bring a winter landscape alive.

**Type/Size Groupings**  For easy reference the descriptions are grouped according to type and approximate mature height of plant:
- Deciduous trees — small, medium, large
- Deciduous shrubs — small, medium, large
- Needled evergreen trees and shrubs
- Broad-leaved evergreens
- Deciduous ground covers
- Herbaceous perennial ground covers
- Evergreen ground covers
- Deciduous vines

These groupings are intended only as the most general guide. The maximum heights of trees and shrubs are very difficult to pinpoint; depending on genetic heritage and growing conditions, what looks like a big plant in the description may actually stay very modest in size, or vice versa. So don't let the size categories discourage you or tie you down.

Needled evergreen trees and shrubs are a somewhat special case. Many needled evergreen "shrubs" used in the landscape are actually dwarf or compact varieties of huge evergreen trees. But multiple descriptions would have required excessive repetition; so the small needled evergreens are included in descriptions with their large-sized ancestors. Be sure to glance through the descriptions to see what compact and dwarf plants are available.

**Alphabetization**  Within each grouping, plants are almost always organized alphabetically according to botanical (Latin) name. Shadblow, for instance — whose other common names include Juneberry and serviceberry — appears under A for *Amelanchier*, its genus. The names of the two species I've described, *canadensis* and *laevis*, determine the order of appearance of the two plants within the *Amelanchier* genus.

There is an exception to this alphabetization system, however. Azaleas, which are of the *Rhododendron* genus, can be found under A for

Azalea in the Medium Deciduous Shrubs and Broad-leaved Evergreens sections.

**Varieties and Cultivars**  A variety of a species is given as an extension of the italicized Latin name — such as *Salix alba tristis* for golden weeping willow. A cultivar — short for "cultivated variety" — is given as a capitalized name in single quotes, such as *Salix alba* 'Tristis', another frequently used form of the botanical name of golden weeping willow. In this instance I use the first form. But they're both the same plant, and you'll see both forms of the name in the literature and in your visits to nurseries. There are many discrepancies in writers' and nurserymen's handling of botanical names, so don't be alarmed if you encounter them with or without italic, quotes, capitals, or whatever.

The varieties and cultivars I offer here are by way of a guide to some of the most popular and time-tested plants, and/or to those that I have had happy experience with. Again, however, my suggestions should by no means dictate or limit your choice. Nurseries make new introductions all the time; besides, regional availability is widely diverse.

**Cross-references**  You'll often find a plant named in one section with a cross-reference to a description appearing in another. This happens because a given vine (for instance) can also serve as a ground cover, or because a given small shrub is actually a cultivar of a large shrub or tree species. I've tried to be very thorough in cross-referencing; but if you're interested in a certain type of plant — say, maples or viburnums — please check in all the size groupings as well as the index so as not to overlook the very plant you want.

**Cultural Specifications**  Where appropriate, I've spelled out plants' needs for sun, soil, shelter, etc. Where these are not mentioned, you can assume the plant is adaptable — but always consult your nurseryman about the particular variety you're considering.

**Zone/Origin/Height Lines**  With each description (usually at the end) I've given the plant's northernmost hardiness zone, using the USDA zones shown on the map on pages 346–347. These zones reflect minimum winter temperatures, the lowest the plant will tolerate. The plant's origin, whether native to North America or imported from Europe or Asia, is shown next, followed by the *approximate* maximum mature size of the species named at the start of the description. Needless to say, many trees (particularly) take 20 or 50 or 100 years to reach the size indicated. And in many instances, compact or dwarf varieties suggested within the description are far smaller than the species height at maturity.

# SMALL DECIDUOUS TREES

**Approximately 12 to 30 feet mature height.**

***Acer griseum*** (paperbark maple) is named for its delicately peeling cinnamon-brown bark, and the bark is one of its great landscaping assets. Its other contributions are dainty three-part compound leaves, whose summer green changes to rich russet and red in fall; and a compact, upright, oval shape that makes this a good specimen plant for even a small garden. It tolerates soil of almost any type, including clay soils, although it prefers well-drained moist soil and a location in full sun.

Zone 6 / China / 20 to 30 feet

***Acer palmatum*** (Japanese maple): The deeply lobed, star-shaped leaves of this small tree are a familiar sight in home landscapes — and no wonder. The Japanese maple is a picturesque plant, with pale gray branches that spread horizontally to create layers of light and color among the foliage and a low, rounded overall shape. You can grow it as an accent or specimen tree, or encourage multistemmed growth in a shrub border. Japanese maple prefers a moist, well-drained, slightly acid soil and a location where there is some protection from strong sun and drying winds. There are countless cultivars. Many have foliage in shades of red all season long, like bloodleaf Japanese maple (*Acer palmatum* 'Atropurpureum'), which like the species can grow into a sizable small tree up to 30 feet tall. Others have leaves that are cut between the lobes, like green cutleaf or threadleaf Japanese maple (*Acer palmatum* 'Dissectum') and red cutleaf Japanese maple (*Acer palmatum* 'Atropurpureum Dissectum'), which are smaller, more umbrella-shaped trees seen in Japanese gardens. Look for these and other time-tested cultivars at a reliable local nursery, since some of the newer or more esoteric cultivated varieties can be unpredictable.

Zone 6 / China, Korea, Japan / 30 feet

***Amelanchier canadensis*** (shadblow) is so named because it blooms when the shad run upriver, in parts of the country where they have shad. It also goes by the names shadbush, downy serviceberry, juneberry, and service-tree — among others. This tall shrub or small tree is valuable for its white flowers in early spring, its streaky gray bark year-round, its brilliant yellow to red autumn color, and its berries, which are appetizing to birds. Its many stems and fine branches can form a rounded crown in an open sunny spot, although in the woods shadblow is more leggy. It thrives in moist or even wet acid soil and will tolerate full sun or partial shade. I like to use it in naturalistic plantings, woodland edges, or shrub borders.

Zone 5 / Native / 6 to 20 feet

***Amelanchier laevis*** (Allegheny serviceberry) is very similar to its close relative, shadblow (*Amelanchier canadensis*). It's a lovely tree, with white flowers that bloom briefly in early spring, purplish young leaves that mature to green, then turn yellow or red in the fall; and sweet black berries that are great bait for birds and wildlife. It does well in acid soils and is ideal for naturalistic or woodland plantings. It is not temperamentally suited (or sufficiently pollution-tolerant) for urban settings. This is one *Amelanchier* that looks best as a single-stemmed tree, whereas the others lend themselves to growing with multiple stems or trunks.

Zone 5 / Native / 20 feet

***Betula populifolia*** (gray birch) does have its liabilities — chiefly, a tendency to be fragile, with weak crotches, and to perish at the early age of fifteen or twenty years — but it is still a valuable plant for naturalistic landscapes where the more imposing native or European birches might be out of keeping, or (because of its size) for smaller properties. The gray birch has, despite its name, white bark. It usually grows multistemmed, and its delicate beauty derives both from that clustering effect and from the fine, dark green foliage that turns a glittering yellow in autumn. Given conditions to its liking, gray birch will colonize itself by seed or create thickets of suckers. It tolerates almost any soil: wet, dry, poor, rocky, even sterile burnt-over soil. (Maybe that's why it is sometimes called "poverty birch.") It will put up with full sun or partial shade, although it does not thrive if there's much competition from larger, hungrier plants.

Zone 4 / Native / 20 to 40 feet

**Cercis canadensis** (redbud): Also called eastern redbud or Judas tree, redbud has large, lustrous, heart-shaped leaves. Its trunk usually divides near the ground into several stems, and its ascending branches form a broad, spreading, flat-topped to rounded crown. Redbud is a member of the pea family; it bears pinkish-purple flowers in spring before its leaves emerge, making it a wonderful candidate for flower displays, and it produces pealike pods in fall. It does well in deep, well-drained, moist but not wet soils. Cuttings can be taken in midsummer if you want to propagate this tree. It's an all-purpose plant, attractive in woodland or wild landscapes, in group plantings, in shrub borders, or even as a specimen plant.

Zone 5 / Native / 20 to 30 feet

**Chionanthus virginicus** (white fringe tree): This small, spreading tree (or large shrub) blooms in June and looks like a snowstorm, covered with very pungently fragrant tassels of white. The male plants are more showy in flower than the females, but if you have a female fringe tree it will reward you in September with dark blue fruits that are a major attraction to birds. The leaves come out very late in the spring; they are lustrous and quite large, giving the fringe tree a relatively coarse foliage texture. In the right spot and with harmonious surrounding plantings, this is a wonderful specimen plant or candidate for grouped plantings or borders. It's especially valuable in city gardens or around large buildings, since it stands up to pollution and will tolerate a good deal of shade (although it will do best in full sun). Plant it in spring in moist, deep, somewhat acid soil. It almost never needs pruning.

Zone 5 / Native / 10 feet (30 in wild)

**Cornus florida** (flowering dogwood): This small tree is justly known as the best ornamental of all trees native to the northern United States. It holds its branches horizontally, and its spreading form is often wider than it is tall at maturity. Its beautiful white spring "flowers" are, like poinsettia "flowers," actually bracts, and they appear before the leaves. Flowering at the same time, pink flowering dogwood (*Cornus florida rubra*) makes a splash of clear, rosy coral. On both varietes, summer foliage is dark green and turns to purplish red in the autumn. The red berries of the flowering dogwood are loved by birds, and in winter its reddish young twigs add color to the landscape. Flowering dogwoods should be moved balled and burlapped, and need a well-drained, moist, acid soil. They thrive in partial shade although full sun will do. The only conditions they cannot survive are poorly drained soils or protracted drought. They will be beautiful wherever you put them, whether in groups or as specimen trees, near or at a distance from the house. A backdrop of dark color will show off the white-flowering ones especially well.

Zone 5 / Native / 20 to 40 feet

**Cornus kousa** (Kousa dogwood or Japanese dogwood) blooms about three weeks later than flowering dogwood (*Cornus florida*) and is a fuller, more densely branched tree. Its abundant white bracts — what we usually think of as its flowers — are pointed at the tip in contrast to the notched petals of the flowering dogwood. They are best viewed from above, since they are borne upward. Kousa dogwood not only blooms in spring, but it produces red fruits that look like raspberries in early fall, and scarlet to purple fall foliage; and its attractive exfoliating bark peels off to show cream and reddish patches that are a note of warmth in the winter landscape. This is a marvelous all-around tree for every kind of use — as a specimen, in grouped plantings, around buildings, in shrub borders. Its horizontally layered branches make a crisp counterpoint to the dominant vertical lines of buildings or other trees. It does demand a well-drained, moist, acid soil that is high in organic matter, and plenty of sun.

Zone 6 / Japan / 20 feet

**Cornus mas** (Cornelian cherry dogwood): See Large Deciduous Shrubs.

**Cotinus coggygria** (smoke tree): Among the virtues of this small tree (sometimes considered a large shrub) are its adaptability and ease of transplanting. You can move smoke tree bareroot or balled and burlapped, and it will survive in almost any well-drained soil. Once established, it demands almost no upkeep. It has a loose, open habit of growth — you might even say unkempt — so I plant several together for a better overall effect. Smoke tree has medium-textured blue-green foliage. It gets its name from the long, drooping, pinkish-grayish clusters of flowers it bears in midsummer, which do give the whole tree a smoky, cloudy appearance. A perfectly beautiful variety that is a favorite of mine is purple smoke tree, *Cotinus coggygria* 'Purpureus'.

Zone 6 / Southern Europe to China / 15 feet

**Crataegus phaenopyrum** (Washington hawthorn): This small tree, with its picturesque thorny branches and beautiful, jagged-edged leaves, has something to offer in every department. Its clusters of dainty white flowers come in June; its fall foliage is a handsome red-orange; its glossy red fruits ripen in autumn but remain on the tree all winter, which contributes color to the landscape and appeals to the bird population. Washington hawthorn is great for hedges and screens, since it does not mind being clipped or pruned, but it also makes an attractive accent plant. It does have a couple of liabilities, however. Its thorny twigs can be treacherous to the uninitiated; so put it in a place where traffic is infrequent. Also, some people dislike the smell of the flowers — another reason

for putting the tree a distance from the house, preferably in a spot with full sun.

Zone 5 / Native / 25 to 30 feet

**Enkianthus campanulatus** (redvein enkianthus): See Large Deciduous Shrubs.

**Hamamelis mollis** (Chinese witch hazel): See Large Deciduous Shrubs.

**Koelreuteria paniculata** (goldenrain tree): In mid-July this small shade tree produces a glorious show of large, drooping clusters of yellow flowers — "very lovely to look upon and lie under," one writer says, and I agree. The many-lobed leaves are almost fernlike in complexity, and they make a dense, neatly rounded mass in summer; the slightly ascending branches are not dense, however, and in winter they are a delicate fan against the sky. Goldenrain tree will prosper in a sunny location with any kind of soil. Another big point in its favor is that it will survive drought, heat, wind, alkaline soils, and polluted air. Prune it for shape or size during winter; its flower buds will form on the spring's new growth.

Zone 6 / China, Korea, Japan / 30 feet (equally wide)

## MAGNOLIA SPP.

Magnolias should be planted in early spring only. They need deep, moist, acid soil with ample organic matter. Give them full sun, or at most some light shade. Although these are small trees above ground, they need ample room for their roots to develop. Avoid putting magnolias against south-facing walls, where the sun's heat will bring their buds out early, only to be nipped by the year's last spring frosts.

**Magnolia loebneri 'Merrill'** (Merrill magnolia): The notable attribute of this hybrid is that it grows much faster and flowers younger than most other magnolias — even younger than star magnolia. It is a vigorous, spreading, sturdy tree. If you have the patience, it can easily be propagated by softwood cuttings.

**Magnolia soulangiana** (saucer magnolia): If you appreciate the flowers of this tree you will forgive them their habit of dropping messy brown petals all over the lawn after they bloom. The blossoms are as much as 10 inches across and shaped more like cups or goblets than "saucers." They range in color from lavender to deep magenta-purple. Emerging in April before the leaves, they make a stunning display. This tree is slow-growing (although it blooms at a very young age) and as wide-spreading as it is high. It often produces multiple stems like a shrub.

**Magnolia stellata** (star magnolia) is one of the earliest magnolias to bloom; one of the hardiest of the Asiatic varieties; and a much-loved, much-used specimen flowering tree that never wears out its welcome. The fuzzy, silky buds and lavish white April flowers with their 12 to 15 floppy petals give this tree a special place in people's hearts. They make a stunning contrast to city walls — or to the browns of rural landscapes where few other trees or shrubs have come alive yet.

Zones 5 to 6 / Japan, China / 15 to 30 feet

**Malus (flowering crabapple) variety.**

## MALUS SPP.

Flowering crabapple (or crab, for short) varieties, clones, and cultivars are so numerous that I can't even tell you how many there are. New ones are being discovered or developed as you read this, because crabapples hybridize themselves with reckless abandon. A good nursery, however, will offer a few fine proven varieties. You can choose the particular size of tree, overall branching form, shade of blossom, and color and size of fruit that appeal to you. Do be sure to pick varieties known to be resistant to fire blight and apple scab, two scourges of crabapples. All types mentioned below are resistant, with the possible exceptions of *Malus hupehensis* and *Malus* 'Red Jade' — but these two are great favorites with which I've always had good luck, so I include them for your consideration.

Give any flowering crabapple a moist, well-drained, acid loam and plenty of sun. If pruning is necessary, do it very discreetly right after flowering in early June. Most flowering crabs will be hardy in Zone 5. In height most of these trees range from 15 to perhaps 30 feet, but their different shapes and branching habits are as numerous as their varieties.

**Malus floribunda** (Japanese flowering crabapple) is one of the choicest of all. Clothed in fragrant white blossoms in early May, it is a miraculous sight. It's hard to overuse a tree like this. Plant it as a single specimen, in a cluster, at the edge of woodland, next to a house, in a patio, in a shrub border, or wherever. Japanese flowering crab offers a neat rounded form and fine foliage texture all summer — and its small red fruits give it particular appeal to birds in the autumn.

**Malus hupehensis** (tea crabapple) is one great favorite for its vase-shaped form. Its branches spread out and upward to give it a shape like a fan or inverted triangle. In spring, pink buds open to fragrant white flowers all along its branches and twigs; and in fall the fruits are greenish-yellow to red.

**Malus 'Mary Potter'** (Mary Potter crab) is another type with pink buds and white blossoms, but with profuse red fruits, a wide, upright form, and picturesquely curved branches.

**Malus sargentii** (Sargent crabapple): See Large Deciduous Shrubs.

Other good varieties are 'Adams', for pink flowers and long-lasting, cherry-sized fruit; 'Donald Wyman', whose low, broad, mounded shape is a mass of white bloom in spring; 'Red Jade', which is named for its abundant and enduring bright-red fruit, and which boasts gracefully weeping branches and white flowers; 'Winter Gold', another white-flowered type with beautiful yellow fruits in the fall (but they darken after frost); and the hybrid *zumi calocarpa*, most noted for its glowing red fruits that hang on the tree — for color and for bird appeal — all the way into February.

## Oxydendrum arboreum (sorrel tree or sourwood)

**Oxydendrum arboreum** (sorrel tree or sourwood) is sometimes called lily-of-the-valley tree for the clusters of sweet-smelling flowers, similar to lilies-of-the-valley, that it bears in August to September. But its flowers are just one of its fine attributes. The leaves are a lustrous dark green and shaped like the leaves of laurel (to which sorrel tree is related); but in fall, unlike laurel leaves, they turn a gorgeous scarlet. The bark is gray, deeply furrowed, with scaly ridges. The overall shape is a tidy round-topped pyramid, with drooping branches. All in all, this is a born specimen tree: a star at every season, not a plant to be relegated to a background role. Move it balled and burlapped into a good location in full sun (where its flowering and fall color will be at their best) or in partial shade. Sorrel tree should have an acid, peaty, moist, well-drained soil.

Zone 5 / Native / 25 to 30 feet (75 in wild)

## PRUNUS SPP.

Flowering cherry: Many of these beautiful ornamental trees come to this country from the Orient, bringing with them the elegant decorative quality that we associate with classical Chinese or Japanese design. The *Prunus* genus includes a vast and complex diversity of species, natural varieties, and cultivars and hybrids — among them all the cherries, native and imported, as well as all the apricot, plum, prune, peach, nectarine, and almond species. (Think of their stone pits and you'll see the family resemblance.) All I'll do here, however, is touch upon a selection of the most tried and true flowering cherries for spring display.

Cherries are very flexible as to soil, provided it is well drained. They need full sun for good flowering, which at best lasts no longer than 10 days. They do not do well in badly polluted circumstances. Cherries are relatively short-lived plants — many varieties live only about 20 years. But these few drawbacks should not deter anyone from enjoying their extraordinary loveliness while they last.

**Prunus sargentii** (Sargent cherry): See Medium Deciduous Trees.

**Prunus serotina** (black or rum cherry): See Large Deciduous Trees.

**Prunus serrula** (paperbark cherry) comes from China, and although it can be hard to find in nurseries it is worth the search. Its bark is a beautiful, lustrous, dark mahogany-red, a wonderful asset in winter. The May flowers are white and pleasant, although not as spectacular as the bark. This is a small, vigorous tree that reaches a top height of 30 feet and is hardy in Zone 6.

**Prunus serrulata** (Oriental cherry): Oriental cherries are mainly available in the form of cultivars — of which there are about 120 in existence, with at least 50 sold in the United States. Every good nursery will offer a few. Oriental cherries are usually upright or vase-shaped, with white, pale pink, or deep pink blooms, many double. The 'Kwanzan' cherry, one of this group, is a highly popular and hardy double-flowering type. It has deep-pink blossoms and heavy vase-shaped branching with glossy bark. Another popular form is 'Amanogawa', which grows narrow and tall and makes a good hedge or barrier. It has large double light pink flowers. Oriental cherries grow to 20 feet or so; they are indigenous to China, Korea, and Japan and are hardy in Zone 6 or Zone 7, depending on the variety.

**Prunus subhirtella** (Higan cherry) from Japan, is another plant seen mostly in the form of specific varieties and cultivars. And they are remarkable. In height they range from 15 to 30 feet. One is the weeping cherry (*Prunus subhirtella* 'Pendula'), with pink flowers that bloom in April on slender, gracefully weeping branches — the tree looks like a fountain of pale pink. Another cultivar, autumn-flowering cherry (*Prunus subhirtella* 'Autumnalis'), produces pink flower buds in summer that will open in a mild autumn, then bloom fully again the following spring. A popular cultivar is Hally Jolivette cherry (*Prunus subhirtella* 'Hally Jolivette'), a small plant with delicate pink blooms and multiple slender stems. As a group, Higan cherries are hardy in Zone 6.

**Prunus yedoensis** (Yoshino cherry) is also Japanese. It is one of the taller cherries, at 40 feet, and its spreading tiers of fragrant white to pale pink blossoms are a beautiful sight in May. This variety makes up the majority of the Washington, D.C., tidal basin cherry-blossom display. It is hardy in Zone 6.

---

**Rhus copallina** (shining sumac): See Large Deciduous Shrubs.

**Syringa reticulata** (Japanese tree lilac): Unlike the better-known shrubby forms of lilac, this is a true tree, with bark like a cherry's. Its stiff, spreading branches make a rounded umbrellalike crown. The large, pyramidal, creamy-white flower clusters bloom in mid-June. Their scent is heavy, almost annoying to some people. You can use Japanese tree lilac as a specimen tree, or in groups, or even as a street tree — it's very pest-free and easy to care for. Give it rich soil, an airy location, and full sun for best flowering.

Zone 5 / Japan / 20 to 30 feet

**Viburnum prunifolium** (black haw): Although it's a member of the viburnum group, black haw is often seen not as a shrub (like many viburnums) but as a small tree. It's very adaptable as to soil and sun. It resembles a hawthorn in habit: stiffly branched and twiggy, upright and round-headed overall. You can encourage multi-stemmed growth and use it as a hedge plant, or train a single stem and let it develop as a specimen or as a component in a shrub border or massed planting. Its dark green foliage turns red to bronze in the autumn. Its large, creamy-white flat-topped flower clusters appear in mid-May. The clustered fruits are interesting: as they ripen they pass from yellow to rose to blue-black, and often you'll find all hues represented in one cluster. Birds eat them up. People relish them too, and have used them for preserves since Colonial times.

Zone 4 / Native / 12 to 20 feet

**Viburnum sieboldii** (Siebold viburnum): See Large Deciduous Shrubs.

---

# MEDIUM DECIDUOUS TREES

**Approximately 30 to 50 feet mature height.**

**Acer platanoides** (Norway maple): I recommend using one of the reliable cultivars (see below) of this tough and versatile shade tree. Unlike some other maples, Norway maple will tolerate street fumes and city pollution, and it will get along in hot, dry conditions and poor soils, even sand or clay. With all these sterling qualifications it's easy to see why Norway maple is sometimes considered overused. It casts a thick shade in summer. In fall its big star-shaped leaves are bright golden yellow; and there are tons of them, so be prepared to rake. Give this tree plenty of room, both for its rounded, densely branched crown and for its shallow but spreading root system (which makes growing anything under it, including grass, nearly impossible). Two excellent cultivars are 'Emerald Queen', a rapid grower with great resistance to pests and diseases and an upright oval form; and 'Summer Shade', a similar tree but with leathery dark green leaves.

Zone 4 / Europe / 40 to 50 feet (90 in wild)

**Aesculus carnea** (red horse chestnut) a hybrid with deep-pink flowers and far darker green leaves than the common horse chestnut, is valued both for its mid-May blooms and for its dense, rounded form. It shares many of the liabilities as well as the assets of other horse chestnuts (see horse chestnut, *Aesculus hippocastanum*, in Large Deciduous Trees, below) and should be used only if you have plenty of space so that its untidiness won't be a problem. It likes well-drained soil in light shade or full sun. A strikingly handsome variety in bloom is the ruby horse chestnut (*Aesculus carnea* 'Briotii'), with extra-large clusters of deep rose to red flowers.

Zone 4 / Hybrid (Europe) / 30 to 40 feet

**Betula nigra** (river birch, also called red birch) is one birch that thrives in wet acid soils. And in fact its fondness for wet feet is one of its main claims to fame. It also, however, has fine-textured foliage and russet-tinged exfoliating bark, so that it lends a lively accent of texture and color to the landscape. It is an excellent specimen tree for wild or wide-open landscapes. The trunk often divides near the ground, so that each tree looks like two or more trees growing together. The overall form of the tree is pyramidal to oval-headed, but growing more rounded in maturity.

Zone 5 / Native / 40 to 90 feet

**Betula pendula** (weeping birch or European white birch) has white bark at an earlier age than paper birch (see *Betula papyrifera* in Large Deciduous Trees), and is a very graceful, very popular tree for the residential landscape. Its fine, slightly drooping branches and delicate twigs form a symmetrical pyramid. Its leaves are glossy and even smaller and more triangular than those of the paper birch; they stay green relatively late in the fall, then turn yellow-green or yellow. Weeping birch is fast-growing and hardy, although like many birches it tends to die young. It's easy to transplant and tolerant of many soils. If it needs pruning, do it in summer or fall, since late-winter or early-spring pruning will cause copious "bleeding." Cut-leaf weeping birch (*Betula pendula* 'Gracilis') is another vigorous, rapid grower, with an elegant upright form, pendulous branches, and deeply cut leaves that grow on clustered stems, giving the foliage a fine lacy texture.

Zone 3 / Europe / 40 to 50 feet

**Cercidiphyllum japonicum** (Katsura tree) has leaves much like those of redbud (*Cercis canadensis*, in Small Deciduous Trees) — shaped like plump, rounded hearts — but smaller, and slightly scalloped all around. In fall the foliage is yellow-orange to scarlet. The bark is brown and rather shaggy in maturity. This makes a lovely, fine-textured specimen tree for shade. It's untroubled by pests and diseases and very adaptable as to soil, provided it gets enough moisture. It prefers to be planted in early spring. You can let Katsura tree develop with multiple stems, or limit it to one. If kept to one central trunk, it will be a slim upright oval for its first 20 years or so, then grow more massive and spreading in old age.

Zone 5 / China, Japan / 40 to 60 feet

**Cladrastis lutea** (American yellowwood) is a small shade tree that grows as broad as it is tall, with a rounded crown of delicate branches. Its extremely smooth gray bark makes a handsome winter accent; its white early-June flowers are abundant and popular with bees; and its bright yellowish-green foliage is another asset. Yellowwood can be transplanted balled and burlapped into well-drained soil, and it is not particular as to alkalinity or acidity. Prune yellowwood only in summer — it will "bleed" profusely at other seasons. It is lovely as a specimen or in groupings.

Zone 4 / Native / 30 to 50 feet

**Phellodendron amurense** (Amur cork tree): The short, stout trunk of the cork tree separates just a few feet from the ground into several large, outspread branches that grow up and out to give the tree a low, spreading, open-topped shape. Its small, yellow-green compound leaflets cast a light, open shade. When amur cork tree is old (but not until then) the bark forms the beautiful corklike ridges for which the tree is named, and the overall form is extremely picturesque. This is an unusual and decorative plant for large properties, but both its branches and its shallow, fibrous roots are too wide reaching for any spot where space is at a premium. It will thrive in any soil and happily endures both drought and pollution. It does best in ample sun.

Zone 4 / China / 30 to 45 feet (equally wide)

**Prunus sargentii (Sargent cherry).**

**Prunus sargentii** (Sargent cherry) is a big tree as cherries go, occasionally reaching a height of 50 feet or more, and spreading to be as broad as it is tall. Its pink flowers are the earliest to bloom of all cherries, coming in late April to early May; its leaves are a shiny dark green, changing to deep red-bronze in fall; and its berries, ripening in midsummer, are black and elongated.

Zone 5 / Japan / 50 feet

**Pyrus calleryana 'Bradford'** (Bradford callery pear) is one of the very few pears sufficiently resistant to pear trees' many blights and pests to qualify as a top-notch ornamental tree. Its uplifted branches form a tidy pyramid, and in spring the tree is a cloud of purest white bloom. The leaves are a glossy, deep green and change to rich red or purple late in the autumn. Don't

expect a harvest from this tree, however: there aren't any fruits. Bradford callery pear is wonderful for a suburban street or city tree, since it tolerates pollution, dryness, poor soils, and cramped quarters (although it is subject to damage from ice storms). Try to give it full sun for the best bloom and leaf color. Try not to prune it, since its tightly branched limbs help support each other.

Zone 5 / China (clone) / 30 to 50 feet

**Salix elegantissima** (Thurlow weeping willow): The leaves of this elegant tree are narrow slivers of dark green, hanging on long, graceful branches that sweep down all the way to the ground. The younger twigs are also green. As a whole the Thurlow willow is upright and moderate in size, not built on so grand a scale as the golden weeping willow (*Salix alba tristis*, in Large Deciduous Trees). It is perfectly hardy as far north as Zone 5. Beautiful near water, where reflections enhance the effect of weeping, this willow will grow in any damp or moist soil. Give it full sun, and prune in summer or fall if necessary.

Zone 5 / Hybrid (China) / 40 feet

**Sassafras albidum** (sassafras): Although this tree can be tricky to transplant (having a deep taproot), once established it thrives in poor, gravelly soil. It will generate multiple shoots around its base — gradually turning its trunk into a wonderful free-form sculpture. Its form is pyramidal at first, then irregularly flat-topped, with short, stout, contorted branches. Sassafras leaves come in all shapes, from elliptical to mitten-shaped or three-lobed; in autumn they change to yellow, orange, deep scarlet, or purple. The fall foliage alone makes this an outstanding ornamental tree. The roots and the corky, dark reddish-brown bark contain an aromatic oil and were used by early settlers to make sassafras tea. Sassafras is usually found as a container plant in the nursery. Give it a well-drained, loamy, acid soil with full sun or light shade. It's a good specimen tree, or attractive in small groups or naturalistic plantings.

Zone 5 / Native / 30 to 60 feet

**Sophora japonica** (Japanese pagoda tree): See Large Deciduous Trees.

**Sorbus alnifolia** (Korean mountain ash) is a modest-sized but upright tree, with smooth, dark gray bark and bright green leaves that bear a strong resemblance to beech leaves. Its white flowers form large, flat-topped clusters in May. The September fruits are handsome red-orange berries, also appearing in clusters, and the fall foliage turns orange and scarlet to match. This is a great all-around specimen tree for lawns in country or suburban areas, but it will not stand city pollution. Other than that it is most flexible and undemanding and will perform well in just about any well-drained soil. (I would not recommend other species of mountain ash, however. They are seriously disease-prone.)

Zone 6 / China, Korea, Japan / 40 to 50 feet

**Stewartia koreana** (Korean stewartia): Like all stewartias, this tree can be hard to find commercially and is relatively fussy to transplant (in spring only, please). Yet in every way and at every season, Korean stewartia is a real star in the landscape. Its form is a dense, upright pyramid. In July it bears large, cup-shaped, white flowers with prominent yellow stamens. The camellia-like leaves are a glossy deep green; in fall they turn brilliant orange or scarlet. The bark is a dark brown that flakes like a sycamore's to reveal patches of green beneath. Give this tree a moist, acid soil with plenty of peat moss or compost added, and try to provide a sheltered location with sun most of the day, but not during the hottest hours.

Zone 6 / Korea / 35 to 45 feet

**Stewartia pseudocamellia** (Japanese stewartia), another member of this elegant genus, can grow considerably taller than Korean stewartia. Its form is pyramidal; its bark is a strong red-brown, peeling in long plates; and its fall foliage is purplish-red. The white camellia-like flowers, somewhat smaller than those of Korean stewartia, are a lovely sight blooming in July against the dark green foliage. Move this tree with tender loving care (see Korean stewartia) and only in spring. Give it moist, acid, humusy soil and protection from burning sun.

Zone 6 / Japan / 60 feet

**Tilia euchlora** (Crimean linden): This lovely hybrid linden forms an upright, symmetrical pyramid, its branches extending outward or drooping slightly from its straight trunk. The glossy bright green leaves are heart-shaped, and the small yellow flowers contribute a delightful fragrance in late June or early July. A vigorous grower, Crimean linden does a great job as a shade tree and tolerates street and city circumstances well. It requires a good deal of sun and a good, moist soil. (For larger lindens, see Large Deciduous Trees.)

Zone 5 / Hybrid (Europe) / 40 to 60 feet

# LARGE DECIDUOUS TREES

**Approximately 50 to over 100 feet mature height.**

**Acer rubrum** (red maple): The branches of this tall shade tree form a pyramidal or elliptical shape in maturity. The bark is a light gray that stands out in winter woodlands; the trunk grows more and more rough and scaly in old age, while the branches stay a smooth gray. The red maple is named not for its foliage (as is sometimes said) but for its small spring flowers. They are so profuse that they give the woods a red haze in early April, and they're followed by fruits that continue the color. The fall foliage ranges from yellow to crimson. Also called swamp maple, this tree is a fast grower, tolerates damp conditions, and prefers an acid soil. Red maple is beloved of birds for both food and cover. One cultivar that's particularly glorious in its fall foliage is the aptly named 'October Glory'.

Zone 4 / Native / 60 feet (120 in wild)

**Acer saccharum** (sugar maple), often called rock maple or hard maple, is another wonderful shade tree for large lawns or wild landscapes. It does poorly, however, in crowded circumstances, it can't handle pollution, and de-icing salts kill it; so it is not a city tree. Its fall foliage is chiefly brilliant yellow to burnt orange or reddish — the mainstay of New England's fall color extravaganza. Sugar maples tolerate some shade, and like a well-drained, fairly moist, fertile soil. 'Green Mountain' is a cultivar that withstands dry conditions well and has the added virtue of vibrant orange to scarlet fall foliage. Unless you have an awful lot of sugar maples, a lot of space, and a lot of time, I don't recommend that you try to make maple syrup. You have to boil down over 4 gallons of sap for every pint of syrup you get.

Zone 4 / Native / 60 feet (120 in wild)

**Aesculus hippocastanum** (horse chestnut): This is one of those trees that used to be fashionable and therefore widely planted, but now have fallen out of style. Yet there are those who love it, for three reasons. The first is its white mid-May flowers, which resemble little Christmas trees or candelabra all over the tree, each 10-inch cone of blossoms held upright atop a platter of outspread leaves. The second is its silken-skinned brown nuts, nested singly or in pairs inside their spiky hulls, which plop to the ground in September to delight the squirrels and schoolchildren. The third reason derives from its former popularity: the horse chestnut was part of many people's youth and evokes a nostalgic warmth in their hearts. If you want to have horse chestnuts, a roomy property is the best. They're too messy for use on small lawns or along streets, since they're always dropping leaves, twigs, or fruits. Plant horse chestnuts in well-drained soil in light shade or full sun. 'Baumannii' is a good choice; its flowers are long-lasting and it doesn't produce any of those prickly chestnuts. (For the smaller red horse chestnut, see Medium Deciduous Trees.)

Zone 4 / Southern Europe / 50 to 75 feet

**Betula papyrifera** (paper birch or canoe birch) starts out in life with brown bark, and its younger branches stay reddish-brown; but by the time the tree is about 15 feet tall the trunk turns a chalky white with faint horizontal black markings. The bark peels in thin layers: this is the stuff of birchbark scrolls and birchbark canoes. A much-loved tree and a native fixture of the American landscape, paper birch can have multiple stems or a single sturdy trunk, and either way it is a beautiful tree for larger lawns or large area plantings. Its youthful pyramidal form gives way to an irregular, more or less oval form in older age. The leaves are small and pointed, almost wedge-shaped. The foliage, when stippled with sunlight, makes glittering patterns in the wind — the more so when autumn turns it bright yellow. Give paper birch ample sun and a well-drained soil; it does best in an acid, moist, sandy or silty loam.

Zone 3 / Native / 50 to 70 feet (90 to 120 in wild)

**Carpinus betulus** (European hornbeam): This elegant tree has striated gray bark and graceful slender branches. Its dense foliage is dark green in summer, yellow or yellowish-green in fall, and virtually pest-free. The European hornbeam is also wonderfully adaptable: it will grow in almost any well-drained soil; it will tolerate light shade or prosper in full sun; it does fine around large buildings, along streets, in paved areas, and in landscape groupings; and it puts up with shearing to the extent that it can even be used as a hedge plant.

Zone 5 / Europe / 40 to 60 feet

**Carya ovata** (shagbark hickory): This large, beautiful tree is named for its dark gray, deeply fissured, shaggy bark. It usually develops a straight, cylindrical trunk and tall crown. The fragrance of hickory smoke is familiar to everyone, if only in the form of smoked ham — and all hickories have edible nuts, some more edible than others. A cousin of the shagbark hickory, for instance, is the pecan tree. There are just a few drawbacks to hickories as landscape plants. For one thing, they are almost impossible to transplant because of their very deep taproots. For another, they have a tendency to drop bits and pieces all year long: leaves, stems, fruit, or all three. They are also very tall when they reach their growth; they're not for the small yard. But if you have an open or wooded area with hickories in it, by all means keep them (or plant new ones). They are lovely to have.

Zone 5 / Native / 60 to 120 feet

**Fagus grandifolia** (American beech) is a magnificent forest or parkland tree, although not at all a tree for a small yard or urban setting. On top of that, it grows quite slowly (if you plant a young beech it will attain its mature glory in your great-grandchildren's time) — so I don't recommend that you go shopping for beeches unless you're adding native trees to your woodland setting. If you have an American beech on your property, you are lucky. The smooth, silvery bark is elegant all year round. The tall, straight trunk supports many horizontally spreading branches with delicate twigs, and the bright foliage captures sunlight all summer and turns a beautiful golden bronze in fall. Sometimes the dry leaves hang on through the winter. The shallow roots spread picturesquely around the base of the tree, stopping growth of anything else there except moss; and the prickly nuts attract many of the most appealing wild birds and small animals. Beeches prefer acid soil, full sun, and plenty of room.

Zone 4 / Native / 70 to 120 feet

**Fagus sylvatica** (European beech) has been loved and cultivated for centuries, here and in Europe. It is a gorgeous, symmetrical tree that grows almost as broad as it is tall, with light gray bark that takes on a sculptural quality. Its shimmering deep green foliage often sweeps the ground, and the branches spread out and upwards from a base low on the trunk. It is not for small properties. Left to grow unimpeded as a specimen tree, European beech will attain a huge height and girth (there's one in England with a trunk 21 feet around); but it also takes to pruning and shaping, to the degree that it can be used as a hedge plant. Like the American beech, it has bronze fall foliage and seeds that are much appreciated by wildlife. It is almost as hardy as American beech, and prefers moist, well-drained soil with plenty of sun. One of the most famous cultivars of European beech is the copper beech (*Fagus sylvatica* 'Atropunicea' or 'Cuprea'); another fine purple-leaved cultivar is the Rivers beech (*Fagus sylvatica* 'Riversii'). Weeping beech (*Fagus sylvatica* 'Pendula') has gracefully drooping branches that give it a special gravity and elegance in winter.

Zone 5 / Europe / 50 to 100 feet

***Fraxinus americana*** (white ash) is a big, rangy, fast-growing tree. In the wild its seeds rapidly create thickets of young trees, and these can be a nuisance if they get out of control. If you can contain it, however, white ash makes a handsome shade tree, with dense summer foliage, good fall color (anything from yellow to red to purple), and impressive overall size. Besides, it is very flexible as to soil type and other growing conditions — although it prefers full sun. The best white ashes for residential landscapes are cultivars, which tend to be more modest in size and less vulnerable to blights and pests than the basic species. One excellent type is 'Rosehill', which has reddish-bronze fall foliage; tolerates poor, alkaline soils; and won't produce seeds, so that you won't be overrun by ash seedlings.

Zone 4 / Native / 50 to 80 feet (120 in wild)

***Ginkgo biloba*** (ginkgo or maidenhair tree): This prehistoric plant has survived virtually unchanged for 150 million years. Its leaves are unique and unmistakable: small green fans that shed a dappled, open shade and turn a buttery yellow in fall. The dark, rigid branches with their many short twigs are as distinctive in winter as the whole tree is year round. Ginkgo is very adaptable and immune to insects and blights. It prefers a sandy, deep, moist soil but will grow almost anywhere and in soil of any acidity or alkalinity; it's a fine tree for difficult situations, including city conditions, as long as there's ample sun. Generally, male ginkgos are the only ones offered for sale, since the females' seeds create a messy maintenance job and have a foul smell too.

Zone 5 / China / 50 to 80 feet

***Gleditsia triacanthos*** (honey locust) has wicked thorns all over its trunk and branches, so that it's not really a tree for the domestic landscape; but its thornless varieties (*Gleditsia triacanthos inermis*, available in many cultivars) are very popular for their delicate pealike foliage and outstanding adaptability. They are tolerant of salt, drought, alkaline soils, and pollution, so they're much loved by city dwellers and people with seaside gardens. Besides, their roots run deep and won't heave sidewalks, and their small leaves require no raking to speak of. As with a few other trees and shrubs I'll mention, the honey locust has suffered somewhat from overuse by urban landscape architects and highway planners — but it can still be a lovely solution for a difficult site where very light, dappled shade is the goal. Consider the cultivars 'Halka', 'Shademaster', and 'Skyline', which offer steeply uplifted branches and symmetrical forms.

Zone 5 / Native / 30 to 100 feet

***Liquidambar styraciflua*** (sweet gum tree), named for its fragrant, sticky sap, needs plenty of space around it for its wide-reaching roots, so that it's not a tree for a city garden. But given room enough, this is a most elegant, symmetrical specimen tree. Its serrated star-shaped leaves are an exceptionally beautiful green in summer and turn anything from yellow to scarlet to purple in the fall. Its fall fruits are round, spiky brown clusters of seed capsules, popular for Christmas decorations although somewhat messy under foot. Plant sweet gum in the spring, in deep, moist, slightly acid soil. Give it full sun. It takes a while to settle down, but once established it is no trouble to maintain.

Zone 6 / Native / 60 to 75 feet (120 in wild)

***Liriodendron tulipifera*** (tulip tree) is one of those plants that people persist in loving even despite a few rather serious liabilities. It is very large in maturity; it is somewhat weak-wooded; and it suffers dreadfully from scale and aphid infestations and related fungus diseases. Nevertheless, its large, cup-shaped greenish-yellow-orange June blossoms, bright yellow autumn color, and handsome pyramidal form have earned it a place in the landscape. It is definitely a specimen tree for roomy locations. Its large leaves cast a dense shade. There are some 100-foot-tall tulip trees on the lawn at Mount Vernon, with trunks 6 feet in diameter. As a child I dug a small tulip tree out of the woods and transplanted it; at first the leaves withered and dropped, but an old gardener friend cut it back and it survived. Now, thirty years later, it stands 70 feet tall and has a trunk 2 feet across. Plant tulip tree in early spring, and give it full sun and a deep, moist, well-drained loam.

Zone 5 / Native / 70 to 150 feet

### Metasequoia glyptostroboides

(dawn redwood): This tree is something of a curiosity in the average landscape, but a very handsome one that deserves your consideration. It needs a sunny, large-scale setting. It is a deciduous conifer of very ancient pedigree (50 million years old, a survivor from the earth's prehistoric forests and thought to be extinct until found in China in 1944). Both its overall form and its trunk are conical: the trunk is fluted or buttressed at the bottom and dwindles upwards to its straight, slender top, so that it has a unique appearance in winter. The bark is reddish and exfoliates in long strips. The branches are held outwards horizontally or droop slightly, and the twigs are very fine. The fronds of bright green hemlocklike needles give a soft texture to the tree in summer. Dawn redwood likes moist (or even damp), slightly acid soils. It is easy to establish and grows rapidly into a very large specimen.

Zone 6 / China / 100 feet

### Nyssa sylvatica

(black gum or black tupelo) grows wild on hillsides and in swampy places throughout the eastern United States. This can be a superb ornamental tree — the only difficulty being that it is somewhat tricky to transplant because of its deep taproot. But plant it with care into deep, moist, acid soil, and you will have a specimen plant of singular beauty. The form of black gum is pyramidal in youth but more round-topped in maturity, with close-set, horizontal or slightly pendulous branches. Its bark is almost black and eventually grows cracked and ridged into an alligator texture. The lustrous dark green leaves change to vibrant, glowing yellows, oranges, and scarlets in fall. Black gum prefers sun or semishade; it is not tolerant of air pollution, so it grows best in open areas or in naturalized or woodland plantings.

Zone 5 / Native / 90 feet

### Prunus serotina

(black cherry or rum cherry) can grow to be a very big tree with dark brown bark, drooping branches, and graceful, lustrous dark green leaves. Its branches are covered with pendulous clusters of white blossoms in May; the blossoms are succeeded by fruits that ripen from colorful red to black in August and September. This hardy native grows wild almost everywhere, from moist, fertile soils to gravelly uplands to dry, sandy locations. Too often passed up (both by nurserymen and by consumers) in favor of less sturdy imported plants, black cherry is a fine tree. It has been valued since earliest Colonial times for its lumber — and since long before that for its fruits, which make fine wine and jelly as well as fine provender for birds. (Also see Small Deciduous Trees for a group of lovely Oriental flowering cherries.)

Zone 4 / Native / 50 to 60 feet (100 in wild)

### Pseudolarix kaempferi

(golden larch), also called *Pseudolarix amabilis*, is a rare member of the select group of deciduous conifers. Its cones are striking (although borne high in the tree so that they can be hard to see): they are a handsome reddish-brown and shaped like roses in full bloom. In the fall the long, soft, light green needles of golden larch turn a bright yellow. Its winter skeleton is a broad pyramid of fine brown twigs. With its open texture and wide-spreading, horizontal branches, this tree has a lovely profile in the landscape year-round. It can eventually reach a great height, but it is so slow growing that it will fit comfortably in modest-scaled surroundings for many human generations. It needs a deep, moist, acid, well-drained soil, and it is happiest if afforded some shelter from wind.

Zone 6 / China / 50 to 120 feet

### Quercus coccinea

(scarlet oak) has glossy, deeply cut leaves that turn a striking deep scarlet in the fall, and the acorns and furrowed bark typical of oaks. This is not the most massive of the oaks; even so, it is a big, stately tree with a wide-open habit of growth and does best in large-scale naturalistic landscapes. It is often found growing wild in dry, sandy soils. Not always available through nurseries, scarlet oak is nevertheless a tree to cherish if you can find it or if you have it growing on your land. I prefer it to pin oak (*Quercus palustris*), which has much the same habit and leaf except that its lower branches tend always to bend toward the ground.

Zone 5 / Native / 75 feet (100 in wild)

**Quercus rubra** (red oak): The many fine qualities of this oak make it one of the best choices as a lawn tree, for large open areas, or for wild landscapes. Red oak grows quite fast; it has a handsome round-topped form; it's easy to transplant and widely available; it withstands city pollution; and, like all the native oaks, it is a great haven and source of food for birds, squirrels, and other small wildlife. The bark is rough, ridged, and gray-brown. The leaves, deeply cut although not as fine-textured as those of scarlet oak, turn russet-red in fall. Their one flaw is a tendency to hang onto the tree for a good part of the winter; this can be annoying to people who like their landscapes tidied up in due season. Give red oak a well-drained, acid, sandy loam, and full sun.

Zone 5 / Native / 60 to 75 feet (100 in wild)

**Salix alba tristis** (golden weeping willow) is a tree that needs no introduction. It's one of the hardiest and most beautiful of all willows, with golden-brown bark and golden twigs and narrow, silvery-green leaves. Wonderfully adapted to wet ground, it will grow rapidly in almost any adequately moist soil. It is fibrous-rooted and no problem to transplant. Willows as a group are quite subject to disease and insect damage, but this is one of the toughest available. Pruning it (in summer or fall) and fertilizing it will lengthen its lifespan. If you're shopping for golden weeping willow through commercial suppliers, you may find it listed as *Salix alba* 'Niobe' or *Salix vitellina* 'Pendula' or even just *Salix niobe*. They all mean golden weeping willow.

Zone 3 / Europe, Northern Africa, Western Asia / 75 to 100 feet

**Stewartia spp.** (stewartias): See Medium Deciduous Trees.

**Sophora japonica** (Japanese pagoda tree) does not bloom until late July or August; then it produces long clusters of creamy-white pealike blooms. This is a graceful, round-headed tree, extremely tough, and disease and pest resistant. It will survive in poor soils, shade, drought, heat, even city pollution. Its compound leaves cast a finely dappled shade. Its younger branches and twigs are green (a pleasant touch in winter in the city) and its bark is a pale grayish-brown, deeply ridged. A good cultivated variety is the regent scholar tree (*Sophora japonica* 'Regent'), which is faster- and straighter-growing and which flowers at only 6 or 8 years of age, as opposed to 10 or 15 for the basic species.

Zone 5 / China, Korea / 50 to 75 feet

**Tilia cordata** (littleleaf linden) is a wonderfully tidy, organized tree to look at. Its form is a tight, regular pyramid of small, leathery, heart-shaped leaves. The neat shape (and pollution tolerance) of littleleaf linden has given it great popularity as a street tree — but it's a lovely shade tree for a lawn or patio, too. Its flowers appear in late June or early July, small and inconspicuous but very sweetly scented and enticing to bees (linden-flower honey is delicious). Plant it into any moist, well-drained, fertile soil; it's not particular about pH. Give it full sun if possible. Often used in Europe as a hedge plant, this linden responds well to severe pruning or even shearing. The cultivar 'Greenspire' is relatively fast-growing; and its trunk does not divide but heads skyward in a perfectly straight line, proving the aptness of its name.

Zone 4 / Europe / 60 to 70 feet

**Tilia tomentosa** (silver linden) takes its name from the white undersides of its leaves; they create a soft shimmering effect when stirred by the wind. This is an exquisite tree for lawns and other residential areas. It has smooth, light gray bark when young (although the bark darkens and furrows somewhat in the older tree), and the bark color is particularly handsome if you grow it as a multistemmed specimen. Silver linden has a regular pyramidal to oval habit, and its late-blooming flowers are sweetly fragrant. It has the added virtue of tolerating heat and drought better than many other lindens. It likes a moist, fertile, well-drained soil and ample sun. In its native Europe it has been planted and admired as a shade tree for thousands of years. (For a somewhat smaller linden, see Crimean linden — *Tilia euchlora* — in Medium Deciduous Trees.)

Zone 5 / Europe / 50 to 70 feet

***Zelkova serrata*** (zelkova, or Japanese zelkova) is a member of the elm family and shares some of the grace and grandeur of the American elm — but not, luckily, its susceptibility to Dutch elm disease. It is vase-shaped in youth and retains that form in old age. Its leaves are small, very similar to elm leaves. A handsome shade tree for lawns, streets, or any area with plenty of room, it prefers deep soil and tolerates drought well. An extra-hardy and rapid-growing zelkova cultivar is 'Village Green', whose foliage turns russet-red in fall and whose trunk is straight and smooth.

Zone 6 / Japan, Korea / 50 to 80 feet (equally wide)

# SMALL DECIDUOUS SHRUBS

**Approximately 5 feet and under mature height.**

***Abeliophyllum distichum*** (Korean white forsythia) is not really a forsythia, although it looks like one in some ways. This is an unassuming small shrub, multistemmed and rounded in habit, with medium-textured foliage. In early spring it comes into its own with pretty and extremely fragrant white flowers. The flowers are borne all along the leafless stems in April (or earlier, depending on the location) and look very handsome in company with the yellow true forsythias. Korean white forsythia is tough and adapted to many soils. It likes full sun or light shade. It can be renewed by being cut back severely after flowering. In severe winter climates, give it protection from wind and cold.

Zone 6 / Korea / 3 to 5 feet

**Azaleas:** See Medium Deciduous Shrubs.

***Berberis thunbergii*** (Japanese barberry): Valuable for hedges and groupings and for its appeal to birds and wildlife, the Japanese barberry is a low-growing, dense, prickly shrub. Its small oval light green leaves turn orange to scarlet in the fall, and its bright red berries hang on most of the winter. Japanese barberry does best in full sun but will tolerate some shade; it is easily transplanted bareroot, and will survive in just about any kind of soil, even dry. It does have a couple of drawbacks, however. If you ever have occasion to prune it (for shape or size), you'll need thick gloves and a lot of fortitude: the thorns are terrible. Also, its fine tangled thorny stems have a habit of trapping dry leaves and other unsightly debris all winter. Still, Japanese barberry is a good old landscaping standby — and it makes a great hedge if you want to keep dogs or other visitors off your property. To add a dash of color to your landscape, try red-leaved Japanese barberry (*Berberis thunbergii* 'Atropurpurea'), which has reddish-purple leaves all summer and abundant red berries in fall and winter — or the red-leaved dwarf 'Crimson Pygmy', another good one. These varieties do require full sun for full color.

Zone 5 / Southern Europe to China / 3 to 6 feet

***Cephalanthus occidentalis*** (buttonbush): See Medium Deciduous Shrubs.

**Comptonia peregrina** (sweet fern): See Deciduous Ground Covers.

**Cornus sericea** (red-osier dogwood): See Medium Deciduous Shrubs.

**Cotoneaster apiculatus** (cranberry cotoneaster) grows low and dense. It is popular as a ground cover, a facer plant for shrub borders, or even a bank cover plant. Its only liability is that its stiff, tangled stems clamber over each other to form an impenetrable mound that snags all manner of dead leaves and other debris, often creating an unsightly mess in winter. At other times of year this is a beautiful shrub. Its glossy little dark green leaves turn bronze-red or purplish in autumn and hold their color for a long time. Its crimson berries, ripening in August through September, are enormously decorative. You can grow cranberry cotoneaster in practically any fertile, friable, well-drained soil in full sun. It will tolerate dry soils and seaside locations. Prune it any time at all.

Zone 5 / China / 3 feet

**Cotoneaster dammeri 'Skogsholmen'** (Skogsholmen bearberry cotoneaster): See Evergreen Ground Covers.

**Euonymus alata 'Compacta'** (dwarf winged euonymus): See Large Deciduous Shrubs.

**Forsythia viridissima 'Bronxensis'** (Bronx forsythia): See Deciduous Ground Covers.

**Fothergilla gardenii** (dwarf fothergilla): See Medium Deciduous Shrubs.

**Hydrangea arborescens 'Annabelle'** (Annabelle hydrangea) is a cultivar of the native smooth hydrangea (*Hydrangea arborescens*), a round, mounded shrub with big leaves and many fast-growing stalks. It boasts huge, symmetrical spheres of white blossoms, and it holds its flowers nicely erect on their stems. Annabelle hydrangea starts flowering in July and goes on into late summer. To encourage sturdy growth and bounteous bloom, cut this hydrangea to the ground in late fall or early spring, and

let it grow back like a peony or other herbaceous perennial. It flowers on the spring's new growth. It does best in rich, moist, well-drained soil in partial shade; in prolonged dry spells, water thoroughly.

Zone 5 / Native / 3 feet

**Kerria japonica 'Pleniflora'** (kerria or globe flower): This shrub offers green twigs in winter plus pretty yellow flowers in May. The weight of the round, buttonlike flowers actually bends the slender branches down, giving them a graceful arching line. The overall form of the shrub is rounded and its foliage and twig textures are fine. Give kerria partial or full shade and a well-drained, only moderately fertile loam. It needs frequent removal of dead wood. This makes a good massed planting for a shady, sheltered spot; or use it as a facer plant in front of leggy taller specimens.

Zone 5 / China / 4 to 6 feet

**Ligustrum obtusifolium regelianum** (Regel privet): For deciduous hedges, you can't go wrong with privet. A mass of fine-textured green in summer, a privet hedge is a haze of slender grayish twigs in winter. In between, in September, the plants bear blue-black berries that persist into the winter and are well liked by birds. And the June flowers, although some don't like the smell, are rather pretty to look at: small and pure white against the dark green foliage. A variety of border privet, Regel privet is extremely hardy. It grows low and spreads its branches horizontally, making a strongly horizontal form. Plant privet bareroot — it can handle just about any soil except an extremely wet one, and will survive city soot and smoke, full sun, or half shade. After it has flowered it can be pruned as drastically as you like. To rejuvenate old plants, just cut them back to stumps.

Zone 4 / Japan / 4 to 5 feet, spreading

**Potentilla fruticosa** (bush cinquefoil): Also known as shrubby cinquefoil or potentilla, this plant has a dainty air at every season. Its unique claim to fame is the length of its blooming period: from late spring until the first fall frost it is dotted with neat yellow blossoms the color and size of buttercups. Setting off the flowers, its leaves are fine-textured, deep green, and pest-free. In winter the shrub is a rounded mass of wispy upright stems. Bush cinquefoil grows very slowly and never gets much more than 4 feet tall and wide; it's an ideal plant for small gardens or for borders or massed plantings. It transplants with the greatest of ease and will grow in poor, dry soils and extreme cold; the one thing it demands is plenty of sun. You can find several good varieties of bush cinquefoil, some larger in size or with larger leaves, some with white, creamy, or orange flowers.

Zone 3 / Native / 1 to 4 feet (equally wide)

**Rhus aromatica** (fragrant sumac), unlike the more leggy tree sumacs, is a low-growing shrubby plant with a definite tendency to march across the landscape. Its roots send up suckers, and its stems take root where they touch the ground. As a result, fragrant sumac can do a great job of covering sunny banks or other problem bare spots with dense growth. It has rather nice yellow flowers in March. Its aromatic leaves are jagged-edged and glossy; they grow in clusters of three; and they turn vivid orange, red, or purple in fall. The furry red fruits ripen in August and September. Fragrant sumac is easy to transplant and happy in most soils, although it prefers light well-drained ones.

Zone 4 / Native / 2 to 6 feet (6 to 10 wide)

**Rosa spp.** (rose): See Medium Deciduous Shrubs.

**Spiraea spp.** (spirea): See Medium Deciduous Shrubs.

**Stephanandra incisa 'Crispa'** (Crispa cutleaf stephanandra) is a very small and dense cultivar of cutleaf stephanandra that's ideal for use as a ground cover, bank cover, facer plant, or low hedge or border. It has finely cut leaves that give it a lacy summer texture, and in fall its foliage turns deep red or purple. The slender stems spread gracefully outwards. This shrub grows happily in full sun or light shade, and although it prefers a moist, highly organic soil, it will tolerate almost any soil that is well drained. It's easy to propagate by cuttings or by lifting and dividing older clumps.

Zone 5 / Japan, Korea / 1½ to 3 feet (equally wide or wider)

**Symphoricarpos chenaultii** (Chenault coralberry) will grow in almost any soil, including clays and alkaline soils. It thrives in shade, so it's useful in woodland settings. Its abundant berries ripen in fall, sometimes in such numbers that they bend the slender branches to the ground under their weight. The berries are pink, or pink shading to white where they're out of the sun. The very low-growing, arching habit and densely massed fine twigs of Chenault coralberry make it a good woodland understory plant or even ground cover. It spreads vigorously by suckering around its base, and it demands little in the way of upkeep.

Zone 5 / Hybrid (native) / 3 feet

**Symphoricarpos orbiculatus** (coralberry or Indian currant) is a hardy native and thrives in just about any soil in sun or shade. It spreads like wildfire, so it works well as a holding plant for shaded banks, cuts, or fills. Low, arching, and fine-twigged, coralberry needs no upkeep and has no pests. Its chief ornamental asset is its fall crop of smooth, round, fleshy purplish-red berries. They are very striking and they persist long into the winter.

Zone 3 / Native / 2 to 5 feet

**Syringa spp.** (lilac): See Medium Deciduous Shrubs.

**Viburnum spp.** (viburnum): See Medium and Large Deciduous Shrubs.

**Xanthorhiza simplicissima** (yellowroot): See Deciduous Ground Covers.

# MEDIUM DECIDUOUS SHRUBS

**Approximately 5 to 10 feet mature height.**

*Aronia arbutifolia* (red chokeberry) has berries so sour, as its name suggests, that even the birds won't eat them. The masses of glowing crimson berries stay right on the shrub all winter long, making a cloud of color. Red chokeberry is an upright, open, multi-stemmed plant. Its fall foliage is red to purplish. It tolerates almost any type or condition of soil, though it does its best in good soil with full sun. Unlike many native shrubs, it is not an overly aggressive spreader. Thanks to that fact and to its adaptable nature, you may like to use red chokeberry in borders, grouped plantings, or any spot where a dash of red is called for.

Zone 6 / Native / 6 to 10 feet

## AZALEAS

Azaleas are so widely known and so much loved that there's little I can say to promote their fame any further. They are some of the most beautiful shrubs known to man, that's all. I will confine myself here to summarizing the basic facts of azalea culture and to listing and describing a few hardy deciduous azaleas, several of them natives, that are sure to be star performers — even in our northern climate. (There are also some evergreen varieties described under Broad-leaved Evergreens.)

All azaleas share with other members of the *Rhododendron* genus a need for acid soil. If you live in the Northeast, your soil is probably already somewhat acid. Amend it with acid organic matter such as peat moss or oak-leaf compost, and there you are. The plants will also benefit from fertilizer (manure or other balanced fertilizer) and from mulching year-round with leaves, bark chips, pine needles, or any good acid mulch. Thicken the mulch in winter, after the ground freezes solid.

Azaleas are happiest in a humid environment, and they require some degree of shelter from the hottest summer sun and the most biting winds of winter. Surrounding trees and shrubs can provide such shelter; or plant azaleas near a rise in ground level, or along a fence, building wall, or woodland edge.

Plant azaleas in the late fall or early spring. You may also enjoy propagating them by simple layering (see May) or by softwood or semiripe cuttings (see June).

*Rhododendron calendulaceum* (flame azalea) is the most vivid and showy of native American azaleas. It bears its yellow, orange, or scarlet blooms in loose clusters in early June. It is an open shrub, growing as broad as it is tall, anywhere from 4 to 10 feet. Flame azalea is perhaps most beautiful in naturalistic plantings where it can be massed for maximum impact. It is hardy in Zone 6.

*Rhododendron 'Exbury Hybrids'* (Exbury hybrid azaleas) include a large group — also sometimes called Knap Hill or de Rothschild hybrids — with upright forms, bright green foliage, and large, luxuriant blossoms in many shades of white, yellow, orange, pink, and red. They bloom in mid- to late May, and they are hardy in Zone 6. For an orange azalea that's hard to beat, try the Exbury clone 'Gibraltar'.

*Rhododendron gandavense* (Ghent azaleas) are even hardier than the Exbury hybrids, surviving nicely as far north as Zone 5. They grow 6 to 10 feet tall, and their late May flowers come in pure white, pure yellow, and numerous shades and combinations of pink, orange, and scarlet. Some of the flowers are double, with ruffly overlapping petals. 'Narcissiflora' is one of these: a lovely, fragrant double-flowered yellow variety.

*Rhododendron 'Jane Abbott Hybrids'* (Jane Abbott hybrid azaleas) are an introduction of Weston Nurseries in Massachusetts. They are outstanding for large, fragrant, true-pink flowers in late May. They are robust growers and hardy in Zone 5.

**Rhododendron mucronulatum** (Korean azalea): The specialty of this species is its very early bloom. It bears its rosy-lavender blossoms before its leaves appear, in March or early April. Because of this it requires protection from the southern or southwestern sun. Strong sun will open the flower buds prematurely and expose them to fatal frostbite. Korean azalea grows 4 to 8 feet high and equally wide. It's hardy in Zone 5. Its fall foliage is colorful, turning yellow or russet-red.

**Rhododendron nudiflorum** (pinxterbloom, pink pinxter azalea, or downy pinxterbloom) is the hardiest of all the native azaleas (Zone 4). In May, before its leaves come out, it bears fragrant blossoms that range (depending on variety) from almost white to pale pink to deep rose-violet. The summer foliage is a bright green. Pinxterbloom grows low, densely branched, and shrubby, reaching a top height of 4 to 6 feet. It has a tendency to spread by shoots, so it's a fine plant for naturalizing. It is well adapted to dry, rocky, sandy soil.

**Rhododendron roseum** (rose-shell azalea, or early or honeysuckle azalea) is another hardy (Zone 4) and beautiful native shrub. Its bright pink flowers have a sweet, clovelike scent and bloom in May, just as or before the leaves emerge. The dense, spreading branches of rose-shell azalea make it as wide as it is tall — and in the wild it can grow as tall as 15 feet, although it's usually found in more modest sizes ranging from 2 to 8 feet. It will tolerate neutral or even alkaline soils.

**Rhododendron schlippenbachii** (royal azalea): This import from the Orient is a true aristocrat in the garden. It has handsome foliage, dark green above and pale beneath, that turns yellow, orange, or crimson in the fall. But its flowers are its real claim to fame. Exquisite pale-pink to rose single blossoms grouped together in clusters of three to six, they bloom in May just as the leaves begin to emerge. Royal azalea grows 6 to 8 feet high and is upright and rounded. It is hardy in Zone 5.

**Rhododendron vaseyi** (pink-shell azalea), a native of North Carolina, does fine as far north as Zone 5. Its clear rose flowers bloom before the leaves appear, in mid-May; and its foliage puts on an autumn display of rosy red. It will reach a height of 5 to 10 feet, and has an irregular upright form. As a bonus attraction, pink-shell azalea tolerates moist soil conditions exceptionally well.

**Rhododendron viscosum** (swamp azalea) is the most fragrant of native azaleas, bearing its spicy-smelling snowy-white flowers in June or July after the leaves are fully out. It is open and spreading in habit, and can range from 2 to 9 feet in height (and breadth) — or even, rarely, to 15 feet. As its name suggests, swamp azalea will flourish in amply moist soils. There are some cultivars and naturally occurring varieties that have pink flowers, and these too are particularly lovely, hardy shrubs, fine in Zone 4.

---

**Buddleia davidii** (orange-eye butterfly bush) usually dies back to the ground over the winter and blooms the following August on the current year's growth; so treat it like a large herbaceous perennial. This vigorous multistemmed shrub is widely available in many varieties, boasting showy flower spikes in assorted shades of white, pink, red, purple, and blue. Many of the flowers have orange "eyes." All hues and varieties are immensely attractive to butterflies, which flock around the plant and add to its lively effect. Orange-eye butterfly bush has coarse-textured foliage. It will thrive in any soil, without any attention to speak of; and it's simple to propagate from softwood or hardwood cuttings.

Zone 6 / China / 8 feet

**Cephalanthus occidentalis** (buttonbush) loves wet soil and can often be seen growing wild by ponds and streams or in soggy ditches. Its chief attraction is its creamy-white rounded flower clusters (like buttons), which bloom in August at a time when little else is in flower. The sweet, privetlike fragrance of the flowers gives this shrub its other familiar name, "honey-balls." The foliage of buttonbush is rather glossy and appealing, although coarse; and the compound nutlets hang on all winter. This shrub has a loose, gangly form, and isn't really a distinguished landscape plant except for wet or waterside locations. It's easy to divide, transplant, or propagate from cuttings.

Zone 5 / Native / 3 to 15 feet

**Chaenomeles speciosa** (flowering quince): Considered by some to be an undistinguished shrub 50 weeks out of the year and a winter trash-trapper to boot, the common flowering quince is nevertheless an old favorite and truly lovely in its brief season of bloom. The orange-pink, rose, red, or white blossoms on their stiff, spiky twigs make lovely Oriental-style flower arrangements for the house, too. With bees in the neighborhood you may even have a few sour yellow fruits for quince jelly. You can use flowering quince for massed plantings, shrub borders, or barrier hedges. Give it full sun for best flowering; it will grow in almost any kind of soil. Keep it vigorous by pruning out older stems in late spring. You can also renew it by cutting it back to 6-inch stumps after it finishes flowering.

Zone 5 / China / 6 to 10 feet (equally wide)

**Clethra alnifolia** (summer-sweet clethra) is sometimes called summer-sweet, sometimes clethra, and sometimes both. It is a great shrub for massed plantings or borders, almost completely pest-free, and a perfect solution to the problem of what to put in wet ground, shady areas, places with particularly acid soil, or even salty seashore environments. Besides having dense, deep green summer foliage and attractive gray stems for winter color, summer-sweet clethra bears small, pretty, deliciously fragrant white flowers in midsummer (July to August). The bees love it. Plant summer-sweet clethra in moist soil with plenty of organic matter. Or it's quite easy to propagate from cuttings taken in summer. It should be pruned in spring.

Zone 4 / Native / 3 to 8 feet

**Cornus alba 'Sibirica'** (Siberian dogwood), one of the colored-stemmed shrub forms of dogwood, makes its main splash in winter with its loose, upright stems of vivid coral-red. In a roomy situation Siberian dogwood is wonderful for display in a large mass, especially beside water. Its fall foliage is a good reddish-purple. It is not such an enthusiastic colonizer as the native red-osier dogwood (*Cornus sericea*), which makes it a good alternative for locations where excessive spreading would be a problem. It's a hearty grower that will take hold in sun or partial shade in any well-drained soil. Remove its oldest stems regularly, since the younger growth has the color. Siberian dogwood cuttings taken at any time of year root with the greatest of ease.

Zone 3 / Siberia to Northern Korea / 8 to 10 feet

**Cornus sericea** (red-osier dogwood) is most dramatic in winter, when the glowing red color of its stems shines out against dull grasses or white snow. This is a many-stemmed, medium-sized shrub, rounded in overall shape; it spreads rapidly by means of shoots from the base of the plant. The leaves are dark green in summer, purplish-red in fall. Red-osier dogwood grows wild in open, swampy areas and is well suited to damp soils; it's adaptable and easy to transplant either bareroot or balled and burlapped. I like best to use it in massed plantings in spacious settings, where it can spread more or less to its heart's content; but it is also good for shrub borders. A compact dwarf variety is 'Kelseyi', which reaches only 2 feet or so in height. You can use it as a ground cover or as a facer plant for more leggy shrubs in borders. Another variety, yellow-twig red-osier dogwood (*Cornus sericea* 'Flaviramea'), has stems of a potent sulfurous yellow that makes a very strong statement. For the most intense color, cut it back heavily every other spring.

Zone 3 / Native / 7 to 9 feet

**Corylopsis glabrescens** (fragrant winter hazel): See Large Deciduous Shrubs.

**Forsythia intermedia 'Spectabilis'** (showy border forsythia) is an old favorite among the several varieties of border forsythia. This shrub can stand almost any growing conditions, so it's a good choice for city gardens or difficult soils. It puts up with rigorous pruning; and if it's pruned at the correct season (spring, right after blooming) it comes back the next year with an undaunted display of big, bright yellow flowers in earliest spring. It flowers most abundantly in full sun but will tolerate partial shade. Showy border forsythia is upright and bushy (not droopy, like some of its species) and fine for hedges, shrub borders, massed plantings, or planting on banks.

Zone 5 / Asia; European hybrid / 8 to 10 feet

**Forsythia suspensa sieboldii** (Siebold weeping forsythia) is a very slender-branched form of weeping forsythia, with arching, trailing branches that gracefully sweep the ground. Its small golden-yellow flowers appear all along the branches in April, before the leaves emerge. This shrub has long been popular for growing over rocky banks or walls or beside water. It will endure city conditions, although it should have full sun for the best flowering. Plant it in just about any loose, well-drained soil. Or propagate it by cuttings taken at any time of year; June and July softwood or semiripe cuttings root especially easily. Siebold weeping forsythia will also propagate itself if you allow it — the tips of its branches send out roots and start new plants wherever they are in contact with moist soil.

Zone 6 / China / 8 to 10 feet (10 to 15 wide)

**Fothergilla spp.** (fothergilla species or witch alders) really come into their own in autumn, when the glorious colors of their foliage range from bright yellow to vivid scarlet. But they're useful and attractive in shrub borders and other grouped plantings throughout the year, being compact shrubs with spiky white flowers in spring, dense dark green summer foliage, and a neat low form. Dwarf fothergilla (*Fothergilla gardenii*) is the smallest; large fothergilla (*Fothergilla major*) has a more pyramidal form and a top height of 9 or 10 feet. All fothergillas require acid, peaty loam with good drainage. Plant in sunny or partially shaded spots, although they'll have the best flowers and fall color in full sun. Or you can try propagating them from softwood cuttings taken in late spring.

Zone 6 / Native / 2 to 10 feet

**Hamamelis vernalis** (vernal witch hazel): This is the smallest of the witch-hazel group and has the smallest flowers, tiny yellow or reddish blooms with ribbonlike petals. The flowers are very fragrant. They bloom in February or March, and on very cold days the petals roll themselves up tightly to protect themselves from frost. Vernal witch hazel is a dense multistemmed shrub, not open and gangly like its larger relatives. Its stems are an appealing grayish-brown; its dark green summer foliage gives way to brilliant yellow fall color. This is a resilient and useful shrub for massed plantings, screens, or borders — or for any soil where wetness is a problem. It will grow on stream banks and in clay soils. It blooms well in either full sun or shade. For other witch hazels, see Large Deciduous Shrubs.

Zone 5 / Native / 10 feet

**Hibiscus syriacus** (rose-of-Sharon or shrub althea): See Large Deciduous Shrubs.

**Ilex verticillata** (winterberry) is an appealing shrub, a member of the holly family but not evergreen like many others of its species. Given a male winterberry somewhere in the neighborhood, a female winterberry will produce lovely red berries that stay on the plant into late December or even January, providing a feast for birds. Winterberry grows densely, with many fine twiggy branches, so it's good for massed effects or for single specimens in shrub borders. Its foliage, deep green in summer, turns black after frost, which is why one familiar name for the plant is black alder. Winterberry does best in an acid, moist soil; in the wild it colonizes swampy areas. It will prosper in full sun or partial shade.

Zone 4 / Native / 9 feet

**Kerria japonica** (kerria): See Small Deciduous Shrubs.

**Lonicera fragrantissima** (winter honeysuckle) produces its delightfully lemon-scented white flowers in early April, and follows up in May with translucent red fruits that the birds enthusiastically eat. This is a wide-spreading, irregularly shaped shrub whose branches form a tangled mass. The small blue-green leaves hang on well into late fall; in fact this honeysuckle is considered semievergreen in the South. It's a good component of a shrub border or hedge, or in any spot where you can enjoy the fragrance of the flowers. Plant winter honeysuckle in any well-drained loamy soil. It likes full sun and won't stand for wet feet. Prune it after it flowers; or to renew it completely, cut it to the ground and let it develop new shoots from scratch. (For other honeysuckles see Vines and Large Deciduous Shrubs, as well as tatarian honeysuckle, below.)

Zone 6 / China / 6 to 10 feet

**Lonicera tatarica** (tatarian honeysuckle) is often thought of as the best of the honeysuckles for all-around use, very hardy, vigorous, prolific of flower, dense of foliage, with attractive red berries in summer, and with tangled gray stems that make a nice contribution to the palette of winter color. This shrub has been much cultivated, and varieties are available with flowers that range from white to pink, rose, even rosy-red. All bloom in mid-May; and all the flowers are almost intoxicatingly fragrant. There's nothing like a honeysuckle growing in the warm sun near a western wall of a house, where the fair-weather breeze carries the scent through the windows and throughout the house. It will adapt to most soils except waterlogged ones and likes full sun. If you want to prune it, cut it back after it finishes blooming; if it grows tangled or overlarge, you can cut it all the way back to low stumps, and it will bounce back with aplomb.

Zone 4 / Central Asia to Southern Russia / 10 to 12 feet

**Myrica pensylvanica** (bayberry) is a shrub that's easily remembered if you have seen it — and smelled it — once. Low-growing and apt to spread by shoots into thickets of shiny green, bayberry has small, gray, waxy berries that are the basis for perfumed wax candles. You can enjoy the same spicy, aromatic scent by rubbing a leaf between your fingers, or just by standing in the middle of a clump of bayberry on a hot day and inhaling. This plant is a familiar occupant of sand dunes and sandy seashore locations, and it's excellent for massed plantings in any sunny spot where dry, sterile soil or salty surroundings present a challenge. If the winter is mild enough, bayberry will hold on to its leaves; if not, it is deciduous. In summer the branches make attractive greens for indoor arrangements.

Zone 3 / Native / 9 feet

**Philadelphus virginalis** (virginal mock-orange), a hybrid with many fine cultivars, is cherished for its sweet-smelling June flowers. Except when it is in bloom there's little remarkable about this shrub — but to many people the scent of the blossoms during their 2-week peak is enough. Multistemmed, rounded, with arching or upright branches, virginal mock-oranges have extra-large white flowers, often double (depending on variety). They are easy to establish and to maintain; impartial as to sun, shade, and soil type; and extremely tolerant of drought. They'll do their best, however, in good, highly organic soil. They are a breeze to propagate by cuttings taken almost anytime. I'm especially partial to the double-flowering cultivar 'Virginal'.

Zone 6 / Hybrid (Europe) / 4 to 9 feet

**Prunus maritima** (beach plum) is really a shrub for seashore gardens. It thrives in light, sandy soil and is undaunted by heavy doses of salt spray, although it cannot cope with pollution. Given conditions it likes, it grows dense, rounded, and compact. The white flowers bloom in May, followed by bluish or reddish fruits that ripen in late summer and make wonderful jams and jellies. Birds like them, too. Beach plum does best in full sun, and it needs well-drained soil.

Zone 4 / Native / 6 feet

## ROSA SPP.

Rose: The subject of roses fills many a volume, and the cultivation of roses amounts to a consuming passion for many a gardener. Symbols of love, life, truth, and beauty, roses have held a special place in the heart of humankind since time immemorial. There just aren't words in the lexicon that can capture the qualities of this "best and sweetest flower that grows."

For purposes of this book, however, a rose is a rose is a deciduous shrub. I certainly encourage you to study, plant, and enjoy the glorious hybrid tea roses, grandifloras, floribundas, or climbing roses that are the pride of the flower garden; and some good reference works on roses are listed in Further Reference. But in this section I'll focus on just a few of the "species" roses that qualify as shrubs with year-round value in the landscape.

**Rosa blanda** (meadow rose) is a native rose that contributes red twigs to the winter landscape as well as lovely spring and summer bloom and dense masses of summer foliage. It's a broad and spreading shrub, reaching a height of about 6 feet, and hardy even in Zone 3's coldest winters. Its single pink flowers are up to 2½ inches across and very fragrant.

**Rosa hugonis** (Father Hugo rose) has arching canes and a broad, rounded overall habit; it will grow 6 to 8 feet tall and equally wide, or wider. A native of China, it is hardy in Zone 6. It has exquisite single canary-yellow flowers that bloom abundantly all over it in May and June. Its leaves are small. Its dark red to black fruits ripen in August. Like all roses it needs ample sun and well-drained soil; but unlike most roses it flourishes best without fertilization, even in poor soil.

**Rosa rugosa** (rugosa rose), sometimes called saltspray rose, is native to the Orient but grows up and down the Eastern Seaboard wild among dunes and along rocky shores. It perfumes the air with the sweetness of its purplish pink or white blossoms in late June, and provides a dazzling display of orange foliage and large red rose-hips in the late summer and fall. But you don't have to live by the ocean to make use of this sturdy, vigorous rose. It is fine for massed plantings, and being very prickly it makes an impenetrable hedge. It is spreading in habit and reaches a top height of 4 to 6 feet. Hardy in Zone 3, it's a good solution for problem areas like banks, cuts, sandy soils, or salty environments. Give rugosa rose a sunny, open location and well-drained soil with plenty of organic matter worked in.

**Rosa virginiana** (Virginia rose) bears its profuse single pink flowers in June, then yields shiny red fruits that persist on the plant into the winter. The foliage puts on a fiery display of autumn color, and the prickly canes are bright red. Virginia rose makes an impassable hedge or barrier; it grows well in sandy soils; and it's happy by the seashore as well as inland. This robust native is hardy in Zone 4. It's naturally low (with a maximum height of 6 feet) and is apt to form a dense mass of upright stems. Prune it as you wish, or cut it to the ground in early spring for overall renewal.

**Sambucus canadensis** (elderberry or American elder): The heavy clusters of blue-black fruit borne by this shrub are great bait for birds; they're definitely edible by human beings, too, in the forms of jellies, preserves, and even elderberry wine. Elderberry is a hard plant to fit comfortably into the average residential landscape, however. It is a multistemmed, round-topped, sprawling shrub, with medium-textured compound leaves and a very coarse texture of branches and twigs in winter. It produces large, saucer-shaped clusters of small white flowers in June. It is easily established and adaptable as to soils. The best uses for elderberry are in wild landscapes, near wet areas, for roadside plantings or other wide-open areas, or at the edges of woodlands. It also prospers next to a compost pile.

Zone 4 / Native / 5 to 12 feet

## SPIRAEA SPP.

Spirea comes in many varieties and cultivars — a large and well-loved family of useful shrubs originating in the Orient. Most spireas grow dense, rounded, multistemmed, and reasonably low. They like full or partial sun and make great hedges, shrub masses, borders, or facer plants for groups of taller, leggy plants. Spireas' flowers range from white to red and bloom any time from April to August, depending on the variety. They are hardy in Zone 5. Most spireas flower on the current year's new growth, so that you can prune them in very early spring, before growth begins — or right after they finish blooming. They grow well in any well-drained soil. Softwood cuttings taken in June or July will readily take root.

**Spiraea bumalda 'Anthony Waterer'** (Anthony Waterer spirea) is very low-growing (2 feet), bears deep pink flowers in late June, has dark bluish-green foliage, and will grow practically anywhere. It is an excellent spirea for hedges.

**Spiraea japonica 'Alpina'** (daphne spirea), a variety of pink-flowering Japanese spirea, blooms in June and July. This is a very dainty little shrub, only about a foot high at maturity, with small flat-topped clusters of flowerets and fine-textured blue-green foliage. It's useful for low borders or edgings, or for grouping in small gardens or even rock gardens.

**Spiraea nipponica 'Snowmound'** (Snowmound Nippon spirea): Growing rounded and dense, as broad as it is tall, this is a tidy and adaptable shrub with a top height of 3 to 5 feet. The snow-white flower clusters appear in late May or June. The small, oval leaves are a cool blue-green; their denseness and fine texture are reminiscent of boxwood, and in fact this is sometimes called boxwood spirea. Prune it before it blooms for larger and splashier flowers; or to renew it from the ground up, cut it back to short stumps in early spring.

**Spiraea prunifolia** (bridal-wreath spirea), an old-fashioned shrub that some plantsmen consider positively out of date, remains popular for its button-like double white flowers that bloom in May. It can grow to a height of 4 to 9 feet, with a loose and open habit. Its small leaves are a glossy dark green in summer, its fall foliage reddish to orange, in contrast to the total lack of fall color of most other spireas.

**Spiraea vanhouttei** (Vanhoutte spirea) is a fine hybrid, perhaps the toughest of all spireas. This shrub tolerates urban pollution as well as most other hardships. Vanhoutte is a relatively tall member of the spirea group (8 to 10 feet), with leaves of a soft blue-green and graceful, arching branches that form a broad mound. Its showy white flowers appear in late April to May.

## SYRINGA SPP.

Lilacs first came to this country from Europe around 300 years ago, and they've become part and parcel of the American scene. Dozens of species and hundreds of varieties, all stemming from European and Asian ancestors, are now grown and widely sold. The enchanting fragrance of their blossoms — which come in shades of lavender, purple, white, or pink — draws crowds to parks and public gardens for "lilac days" in May and June; but lilacs are equally desirable in your yard or outside your window. Their lovely color and perfume will pervade your life for many weeks.

Like many flowering trees and shrubs, lilacs put on their most spectacular show every other year, with lean years in between. That's to be expected; but you can boost their performance in all years by keeping them properly pruned (see May Landscape Tasks) and properly fed. They appreciate a friable, well-drained soil that is only slightly acid (limestone may sometimes be called for), plus plenty of sun and an occasional fertilizing. Cut out most of the suckers that appear around the base, cut out dead wood promptly, and remove spent flower heads. If you're pruning for shape, do it right after lilacs finish flowering, since next year's flowers will come on this year's growth.

Many lilacs fall victim to powdery mildew in late summer. This gives the leaves a dirty, whitish, dusty look that is unappealing but not really threatening to the plant or to its blooming capacity for the following spring. If powdery mildew bothers you, there are fungicides that can help control it if you follow the instructions religiously.

**Syringa chinensis** (Chinese lilac), a hybrid, blooms in mid-May like its parent, common lilac (*Syringa vulgaris*). Its flowers are a rich lilac-purple, slightly more delicate than those of common lilac, and deliciously fragrant. The arching branches of this fine shrub give it a broad, round-topped form 8 to 15 feet high. This is an adaptable plant and not fussy. Do prune it regularly, removing old stems and thinning shoots, to keep it in good form. (This is sometimes found listed as *Syringa rothomagensis*: same thing.) Zone 6.

**Syringa palibiniana** (dwarf Korean lilac) is one of the smallest lilacs around, and a favorite of mine. With a top height of 6 feet, it is compact but broad, with small, dark green leaves that turn a coppery color in autumn. Its dainty flowers are pinkish lavender. Because of its dense foliage and restrained size, I often choose this lovely shrub for screens, hedges, and borders. Zone 6.

**Syringa persica** (Persian lilac) is small-leaved and modest-sized, with profuse, delicate, sweet-smelling lavender flowers that come in late May. Its foliage is a bluish green and very pretty. Persian lilac has upright, arching branches and grows dense and spreading; it can reach 4 to 8 feet in height, 5 to 10 in breadth, so that it makes a fine flowering hedge or shrub border. Zone 6.

**Syringa potaninii** (Potanin or daphne lilac): Blooming in mid-May along with the many varieties and cultivars of the common lilac, this is prized for the color of its flowers: a clear pink. In addition it is very fragrant. With ample sun it will continue to produce occasional blooms throughout the late spring and summer. It has a graceful upright form and can be as tall as 9 feet. Zone 6.

**Syringa villosa** (late lilac) blooms in June, after most of the other popular lilacs, and as such it plays a distinctive role in the landscape. It is compact and tidy (6 to 10 feet), with very prolific, lightly fragrant pinkish-lilac to white blooms. This makes a good plant for the shrub border; it's dense and bushy, with many stout stems and a moderate overall size. For best bloom, remove suckers and cut down old stems periodically; and pinch off spent flower clusters every year, as with other lilacs. Zone 3.

**Syringa vulgaris** (common lilac) is the oldest lilac to be grown in this country and the parent species of anywhere from 400 to 900 named varieties. It's the archetypal pale-lavender-flowering shrub, tall and leggy (up to 15 feet) in maturity, eventually forming a spreading rounded head, and found in thousands of overgrown hedges and borders or even growing wild across the landscape. Kept properly thinned and pruned, however, it makes a reliable hedge or border plant; and its flowers smell as sweet as any exotic variety. It is easy to plant balled and burlapped, or try propagating it by softwood or hardwood cuttings — or better yet, simply dig up and replant any of the abundant crop of suckers that appear annually around its base. Zone 4.

**Vaccinium corymbosum** (highbush blueberry): This open, small-leaved shrub has small white flowers, tasty berries, and dark blue-green foliage that turns crimson in the autumn. With its many spreading stems it's a little tall and loose for formal settings, but looks attractive in massed plantings or borders, in naturalistic landscapes, or as part of a productive garden planting. For the best berry yield, check with your local agricultural agent or extension service for the cultivar(s) best adapted to conditions in your area. Plant highbush blueberries in acid, highly organic, moist but well-drained soil in full sun or partial shade. Or propagate them by means of softwood cuttings taken in June; these will often root successfully. Highbush blueberries appreciate a good acid mulch. Prune them as soon as the fruiting season is over.

Zone 4 / Native / 6 to 12 feet (equally wide)

**Viburnum burkwoodii** (Burkwood viburnum) is a hybrid that offers sturdy growth and good blight resistance together with wonderful spring fragrance and handsome summer foliage. The pink flower buds open to rounded clusters of waxy white bloom in May, filling the air with spicy-sweet scent. The leaves are a dark, lustrous green above and lighter beneath; they hold their green color late into the fall. Use Burkwood viburnum in borders or massed plantings. It is attractive combined with broad-leaved evergreens. It will flourish in any well-drained soil, but prefers a slightly acid environment.

Zone 6 / Hybrid (Asian) / 6 to 10 feet

**Viburnum carlesii** (Korean spice viburnum): This is one of those beloved shrubs that many experts feel should be replaced by newer, superior strains — but that keeps its loyal following among the gardeners of the world. I think the reason is its fragrance. Nevertheless, I should point out that there are numerous good cultivars and related hybrids, many offering resistance to the troublesome blight that afflicts this plant in maturity. Find out what your nursery recommends. The basic species is a modest-sized shrub with dense upward-spreading branches and crisp, dark foliage that turns winered in autumn. The flowers open in April or May; although the buds are pink the blooms are pure white "semisnowballs" of close-packed flowerets, each a perfect little four-pointed star. As with other viburnums, plant Korean spice viburnum in any moist, well-drained soil; it will bloom best with plenty of sun, but it tolerates some shade. Prune it for size or shape immediately after flowering. If you need a smaller, more dense plant, try the variety 'Compacta', which grows only two-thirds as tall. (For other viburnums see Large Deciduous Shrubs.)

Zone 5 / Korea / 4 to 8 feet (equally wide)

**Viburnum dilatatum** (linden viburnum): Wide, flat-topped clusters of white bloom practically blanket this shrub in May to June; but it's not so much the flowers as the fruits and fall foliage that set the linden viburnum apart. It is dense-growing, broad, and rounded in habit. The cherry-red fruits ripen in showy clusters in September and often persist on the plant into December. Meanwhile the foliage turns a lively russet-red, adding to the overall effect. Linden viburnum yields the best fruit in full sun, but it has no other special requirements.

Zone 6 / Asia / 8 to 10 feet

**Viburnum opulus 'Roseum'** (European snowball viburnum or guelder-rose): See Large Deciduous Shrubs.

**Viburnum plicatum tomentosum** (doublefile viburnum) has been described as "the most elegant of flowering shrubs," and this is indeed a dramatically lovely plant in bloom. The mid-May flowers are of the lace cap type, with tiny flowers at the center of a ring of larger, more showy ones, the whole cluster forming a flat saucer 3 to 4 inches across. In the case of doublefile viburnum these saucers are arrayed in two rows along the top of each branch — hence "doublefile." Since the branches are long and very horizontal, this creates broad, spreading layers of pure white among the green leaves. Come fall, the tiers of foliage turn reddish-purple, also very handsome. The cherry-red fruits borne in clusters along the branches are pretty, but quickly eaten by birds. Like other viburnums, the doublefile viburnum is adaptable and sturdy; it will bloom and thrive in sun or shade, and it's very easy to propagate from cuttings. It is wonderful for massing, screening, or border plantings, or for use near a house where its horizontal lines set off the verticals of the building. A larger-flowering cultivar, and probably the best one for fruiting, is 'Mariesii', which you'll find widely available.

Zone 5 / China, Japan / 8 to 10 feet (wider than tall)

# LARGE DECIDUOUS SHRUBS

**Approximately 10 feet and over mature height.**

**Amelanchier canadensis** (shadblow): See Small Deciduous Trees.

**Cephalanthus occidentalis** (buttonbush): See Medium Deciduous Shrubs.

**Chionanthus virginicus** (white fringe tree): See Small Deciduous Trees.

**Cornus mas** (Cornelian cherry dogwood) could be treated as a large shrub or as a small tree; either way, it grows dense, multistemmed, and rounded. It is a fine plant for hedges, borders, all sorts of grouped plantings around buildings. Its yellow flowers (really bracts) bloom in very early spring; they are small but so profuse that they completely clothe the tree or shrub in a cloud of yellow. The foliage is a good dark green, reddish in the fall. The cherry-red fruits are good for syrups and preserves, as well as appealing to birds and wildlife. Cornelian cherry dogwood adapts to most soil and light conditions, short of dense shade, although it flourishes best in rich, well-drained soil.

Zone 5 / Europe, Western Asia / 25 feet

**Cornus racemosa** (gray dogwood) is a shrub with a slight tendency to walk across the landscape: it sends up fast-growing new shoots from its roots. These newer stems are reddish brown, while the older growth is silvery gray, so that the overall appearance in winter is particularly lively. Gray dogwood boasts white spring flowers, white berries in summer, and dense, purplish fall foliage. Because it grows so thick naturally it is well suited for use in borders, particularly at the edge of woodland, or in massed plantings or naturalistic plantings; and cutting it back in early spring will make it grow all the thicker. It sprawls a little too much, however, to be the ideal hedge plant. It seems to be able to stand poor soil conditions and all kinds of other hardships.

Zone 5 / Europe and Western Asia / 15 to 20 feet

**Corylopsis glabrescens** (fragrant winter hazel), given a dark backdrop of evergreens to show off its drooping sprays of dainty yellow blossoms, makes an enchanting harbinger of spring. The fragrant bell-shaped flowers appear before the leaves in early April, earlier than those of any other flowering shrubs except witch hazels — to which it is related. Fragrant winter hazel is a dense, multistemmed, spreading shrub with a flat-topped to rounded form. Its flowers are vulnerable to late frosts, so provide it with shelter from southern sun (which will hasten its bloom) as well as from cold winds. It prefers a moist, acid, peaty, well-drained soil.

Zone 6 / Japan / 8 to 15 feet (equally wide)

**Elaeagnus umbellata** (autumn olive) is best known as a plant for saltwater locations, where it does exceptionally well. This shrub (or small tree) has lovely gray-green foliage and rather leggy, twisted stems whose bark is silver-gray. The berries, silvery deepening to red in color, are most appetizing to birds. Autumn olive is hardy and adaptable. The cultivar 'Cardinal' is very fast growing and naturalizes easily; it makes a wonderful wildlife planting for larger properties.

Zone 4 / Southern Europe to Central Asia and Japan / 12 to 18 feet

**Enkianthus campanulatus** (redvein enkianthus) can take the form of a narrow, upright shrub or of a small tree. It holds its branches in stratified tiers and its bright green foliage in tufts. Its May flowers are small, pale yellow bells with delicate red veins. At first they hang downward in clusters, then (when spent) turn upward like little chandeliers. They're best appreciated at close range, which is one reason to use enkianthus as a patio or terrace plant. It also makes a sprightly companion to rhododendrons or other broad-leaved evergreens. Its autumn foliage is a brilliant orange to red. Like rhododendrons, it demands a cool, moist, acid soil with plenty of peat moss or compost worked in, and preferably some shelter from intense heat and cold.

Zone 5 / Japan / 6 to 30 feet

**Euonymus alata** (winged euonymus), sometimes called burning bush, is the shrub you notice along roadways and in suburban yards in October, covered with glorious, medium-fine-textured, rose-red foliage. It is a wonderful shrub, broadly vase-shaped in its natural form, but well adapted to heavy clipping and shaping for use in screens and hedges. It's also distinguished enough to serve as a specimen plant, as well as in all kinds of group plantings. In addition to its brilliant autumn color, its bristling, ridged (or "winged") branches and twigs are a spirited note in winter — and especially lovely when frosted with snow. Winged euonymus is very hardy and tough, and tolerates almost any soil and light conditions. If this plant has any flaw, it is that it has been overused in some areas; but that shouldn't deter you from choosing it for your landscape.

If you want a smaller version with many of the same splendid qualities, the dwarf cultivar *Euonymus alata* 'Compacta' is widely available. This is not a tiny plant, but smaller, denser, more rounded, and extremely well suited for use in hedges. It'll scarcely need any pruning at all.

Zone 4 / Northeastern Asia / 9 to 20 feet

**Hamamelis mollis** (Chinese witch hazel): Growing happily in full sun or shade, this tall, open shrub or small tree produces sweetly fragrant yellow blossoms in earliest spring, February through March. It does best in a sheltered location that will protect its flowers from freezing in bud or after they bloom. The foliage turns a clear yellow in fall. Plant Chinese witch hazel in any moist soil, even stream banks or wet

gravelly soil. It's a good shrub for open landscapes, naturalistic settings, shrub borders, or plantings in open shade. One cultivar is 'Brevipetala', whose abundant butter-yellow blooms have petals like ribbons. They look like miniature cheerleaders' pompoms and they smell wonderful.

Zone 6 / China / 30 feet

**Hamamelis virginiana** (common witch hazel) is the only one of the *Hamamelis* species to bloom in the fall. Its small yellow flowers appear in October, November, or even December — while at the same time its foliage also turns bright yellow. This tall shrub is best for wild or naturalistic plantings. The large, crooked branches of common witch hazel form an irregular vase shape in maturity. It grows in most soils, but it does best with plenty of moisture. In full sun it attains its fullest, most shapely growth, but it will manage perfectly well in shady locations.

Zone 5 / Native / 15 to 20 feet

**Hibiscus syriacus** (rose-of-Sharon or shrub althea) is an old American favorite for its showy, roselike blossoms. This is definitely a shrub for borders or hedges, not for a specimen role. The three-lobed leaves emerge late in spring, and the branches are dense and upright. The blossoms form on the current year's growth: you prune rose-of-Sharon in early spring, and it blooms in late summer. Without pruning, the individual flowers will be plentiful but small. Depending on the variety (there are hundreds in cultivation) the flowers may be anything from white to pink to crimson, or from lavender to deep purple. Rose-of-Sharon tolerates any kind of soil, provided it's not too dry or too wet; it thrives in highly organic soil; and it will grow in full sun or partial shade.

Zone 6 / China and Northern India / 8 to 12 feet

**Hydrangea paniculata 'Grandiflora'** (Peegee hydrangea): Named for the *"paniculata* 'Grandiflora'" in its botanical name, this spectacular late-blooming shrub bears wonderful long-lasting flower clusters. Peegee hydrangea grows upright and round-topped, with arching branches and coarse foliage. It is best planted as a group of specimens in the lawn. Its great pyramidal flower clusters appear in July and stay in place long into the fall, changing from white to pinkish-purple, then brown, as the season advances. It will bloom in sun or partial shade, but it wants a rich, loamy, well-fertilized and mulched soil (it is a heavy feeder). Do not trim it but cut out its oldest stems completely in early March: this will help it renew itself.

Zone 5 / China, Japan / 20 to 30 feet

**Lindera benzoin** (spicebush): The small, fragrant yellow flowers of this shrub appear in April, before its leaves are out, making it very pretty in shrub borders or naturalized landscapes — particularly along stream beds. It does well in wet soil and in partial shade, since it's native to woodlands. Its foliage turns bright yellow in autumn. The other assets of spicebush include its very aromatic leaves, twigs, and stems; and (on fertile plants) its scarlet fruits. All of these can be used to make tea. For a fruiting spicebush, make sure you get a pistillate (fertile) specimen.

Zone 5 / Native / 15 feet

**Lonicera maackii** (Amur honeysuckle) can be something of a threat if it is not in a controlled landscape, because the birds enjoy its berries and scatter its seeds around the countryside — and rapid propagation is the result. But if you can restrict it to its proper home, this is a great shrub for hedges and screening plantings. Its white flowers bloom from May into June, deliciously sweet-smelling and ambrosial to bees. Amur honeysuckle grows quite tall and upright for one of its family, and its dense dark green foliage stays on the plant well into late autumn, making a handsome backdrop for the glassy red berries. It's very hardy, and adaptable to most soils and growing conditions (but not very wet situations). It prefers full sun. After it flowers, prune it as severely as you need; cutting it back to the ground will encourage it to grow more dense clumps of stems. Rem Red

honeysuckle (*Lonicera maackii* 'Rem Red') is a USDA introduction that I particularly like. (For other honeysuckles, see Vines and Medium Deciduous Shrubs.)

Zone 3 / China / 12 to 15 feet

**Malus sargentii** (Sargent crabapple): There are literally countless exquisite varieties of crabapple tree (see Small Deciduous Trees) — but Sargent crab is the only one you can really think of as a plant or a flowering screen or hedge. It is shrublike in its low, spreading, multistemmed habit of growth. Apart from that special characteristic, it's a typical crabapple: that is, a wonderful plant that will add beauty and charm to any landscape at any time of year. Its masses of fragrant, pure white flowers appear in spring, followed by very dense apple-green foliage, then abundant dark red fruits that last long into the winter, to the pleasure of the birds. Give Sargent crab a well-drained, moist, acid loam and full sunlight if possible. It should be pruned by early June — immediately after flowering — although you can do some careful removal of suckers or thinning of old growth later in the season.

Zone 5 / Japan / 10 feet (spreading)

**Rhus copallina** (shining sumac): Of all the sumacs, this is the most desirable garden plant — but even this is best for banks, open spaces, naturalistic plantings, or wild landscapes rather than disciplined residential backyards. It can grow into a small tree, but it's usually used as a shrub. The pointed compound leaves are a glossy deep green. In autumn they turn fiery tones of red, so that both in shape and in color they resemble flames; and in fact this tree is sometimes called flameleaf sumac. It has fuzzy red fruits that also ripen in autumn. As a young plant shining sumac is compact and dense; as it ages its branches spread up and outward and it becomes more open and picturesque. The great asset of shining sumac is that it is easily transplanted and will thrive in poor, dry, rocky soil and full sun.

Zone 5 / Native / 20 to 30 feet

**Salix caprea** (goat willow, or French pussy willow): This large shrub or small tree is usually the source of the "pussy willows" sold in florists' shops in March and April, since its silken gray catkins are larger and more showy than those of the true pussy willow (*Salix discolor*). Apart from the catkins, goat willow has limited landscape use. It's susceptible to the splitting, breakage, blights, and pests that beset many willows. It will, however, live cheerfully in soggy conditions; it's easy to propagate and an irrepressible grower. Goat willow can be renewed by being cut back to a stump in early spring. It will send up a forest of long shoots the minute your back is turned.

Zone 5 / Europe to Northeastern Asia / 15 to 25 feet

**Sambucus canadensis** (elderberry): See Medium Deciduous Shrubs.

**Spiraea spp.** (spirea): See Medium Deciduous Shrubs.

**Syringa spp.** (lilac): See Medium Deciduous Shrubs.

**Viburnum dentatum** (arrowwood): This hardy native is named for the strong, straight shoots that grow from its base, which the Indians used to make arrows. It grows into a dense, multistemmed, delicately branched shrub. Its flowers are borne in creamy-white flat-topped clusters in late May to early June, and give way to blue-black October fruits that are much relished by birds. The jagged-edged leaves are lustrous in summer and turn yellow, orange, red, or purplish-red in autumn. Arrowwood makes a marvelous screen, hedge, or filler in a shrub border. It grows quickly in any kind of soil, even in wet locations; and it tolerates shade well. You can propagate it from softwood cuttings taken in June, but you may find that repressing its natural self-propagating tendencies is your primary chore.

Zone 3 / Native / 6 to 15 feet (equally wide)

**Viburnum dilatatum** (linden viburnum): See Medium Deciduous Shrubs.

**Viburnum opulus** (European cranberrybush): This viburnum has three-lobed leaves like maple leaves and contributes a dash of purplish-red color to the autumn landscape. Its chief assets, however, are its showy mid-May flowers and its long-lasting berries. The blossoms are flat-topped clusters of white flowerets, arranged in a pinwheel pattern with small flowers at the center, larger ones around them. The clustered berries are translucent and bright red, persisting well into late fall or winter. European cranberrybush is upright and multistemmed; its form grows more rounded with age as the branches lengthen and arch over toward the ground. It is happy in many different soils and conditions, and makes a distinctive component of shrub borders or massed plantings.

A beautiful cultivar of this shrub is the European snowball viburnum or guelder-rose (*Viburnum opulus* 'Roseum'). Its spheres of white flowerets — "snowballs" — bloom in May; but they are sterile, so there's no fruit to follow. Another nonfruiting variety is a dwarf that's excellent in hedges, the small-leaved, dense *Viburnum opulus* 'Nanum'. Compact European cranberrybush viburnum (*Viburnum opulus* 'Compactum') is a great choice for small gardens or massed plantings; its flowers are lovely and it puts on a glorious display of crimson fruit, but it's only half the size of the species.

Zone 4 / Europe / 8 to 12 feet (equally wide)

**Viburnum plicatum tomentosum** (doublefile viburnum): See Medium Deciduous Shrubs.

**Viburnum prunifolium** (black haw): See Small Deciduous Trees.

**Viburnum sieboldii** (Siebold viburnum) in maturity looks more like a small tree than a shrub: it is sturdy, open, and upright in habit. It can stand alone as a specimen plant or can be used in taller grouped plantings. Its flowers are abundant saucer-shaped clusters of creamy white, practically smothering the plant in late May. The leaves are a crisp deep green. The spectacular fruits ripen from rose-red to black in September to October. Birds devour the fruits themselves, leaving behind the red stems — which give the plant a glow of rosy color for another few weeks. Siebold viburnum is tough and trouble-free, but it does demand adequate moisture. It will tolerate light or partial shade. (For another tree-sized viburnum, see black haw in Small Deciduous Trees.)

Zone 5 / Japan / 15 to 30 feet

*Viburnum trilobum* (American cranberrybush or highbush cranberry) isn't a cranberry at all. But its fruits resemble cranberries — shining red berries growing in clusters, ripening as early as July and persisting on the shrub throughout the late summer, fall, and most of the winter. These fruits are edible both by wildlife and by people; they make excellent jam. American cranberrybush also has handsome foliage and flowers: the leaves are large and three-pointed, similar to maple or ivy leaves in shape; and the flat "lace cap" clusters of showy white flowers, appearing in mid-May, alone could justify this as a plant for anyone's garden. The dense, round-topped form of this shrub makes it well suited for borders or massed plantings. Like all viburnums it is simple to propagate from softwood cuttings. It will bloom in sun or partial shade, suffers few pests or diseases, and is generally unfusy and a pleasure to have around.

Zone 3 / Native / 8 to 12 feet (equally wide)

# NEEDLED EVERGREEN TREES AND SHRUBS

*Abies concolor* (white fir, or Colorado fir) has stiff upright clusters of 2-inch gray-green and bluish-green needles and a bristly, almost furry overall texture. It makes a very dense, sturdy cone of green at every age — although when the species is old, it can be a very large cone indeed. While this fir does best in full sun and rich, well-drained soils, it will tolerate thin rocky soils as well. It will also endure heat, cold, strong winds, partial shade, and even city conditions. Transplant it balled and burlapped. It's normally free of pests and diseases. Unlike some other firs, especially in less than ideal circumstances, it holds its needles well. A reliable standby for any spot that calls for an opaque evergreen tree.

Zone 5 / Native / 50 to 120 feet

*Chamaecyparis obtusa* (Hinoki false cypress) is often called just Hinoki cypress. It is most often seen in the form of its small cultivars; but the basic species is a very tall, slender, round-topped pyramidal tree. With its reddish-brown shredding bark and its picturesquely fanned, waxy, scalelike foliage, this evergreen makes a beautiful specimen or accent plant. Some varieties have blue-green foliage, some dark green, a few yellow-green. Dwarf Hinoki false cypresses are fine in city gardens, containers, or rock gardens, where you can appreciate the beauty of the coral-formed foliage at close range. Hinoki false cypresses prefer well-drained moist soil, plenty of sun, and shelter from drying winds — a humid atmosphere is best of all. Soils should be neutral to acid. Among the many cultivars are 'Gracilis', a dark-foliaged, compact pyramidal form; 'Nana', a tiny and very slow-growing dwarf that may reach a height or 2 or 3 feet; and 'Nana Gracilis', topping out at 4 feet, with foliage of a lustrous deep green.

Zone 5 / Japan / 50 to 75 feet (species; vars. much smaller)

*Chamaecyparis pisifera 'Filifera'* (thread false cypress): Beautiful for its lacy-textured, light green foliage and for the slender, open branches that form an upright pyramid, this variety of Sawara false cypress makes a dramatic specimen plant. Like other false cypresses it prefers a rich, moist, well-drained, neutral-to-acid soil, in full sun or partial shade. It does best in a damp climate. You can install it in fall or early spring; and you can prune it in spring, or remove branches at any season. Compact thread cypress (*Chamaecyparis pisifera* 'Filifera Nana') has drooping frondlike branches that create a dense mound 6 to 8 feet high. The yellow-foliaged dwarf cultivar 'Golden Mop' looks, oddly enough, just like a small golden mop, and is a pleasant accent in a coniferous evergreen grouping.

Zone 4 / Hybrid (Japan) / 50 to 75 feet (species; vars. much smaller)

**Juniperus virginiana** (red cedar): Eastern red cedar, as it's also known, may be known best for its beautifully streaked, spicy-smelling wood, which is much used in storage chests for clothes and blankets (since the aroma is as repellent to moths as it is attractive to humans). But this hardy tree has plenty of landscape value, too. The erect, pointed forms of cedars are a familiar and appealing sight in overgrown pastures in New England, particularly near the sea — proof of this tree's affinity for poor, rocky, and even alkaline soils. The reddish bark that peels in long papery shreds is another asset. Still another is the dense evergreen foliage, which makes for excellent windbreaks or sheltering hedges. Plant red cedar ideally in a sunny, airy location with good moist soil. The variety 'Canaertii', which has a compact form, dark green foliage, and abundant blue berries, is smaller overall than the species. (For other junipers, see Evergreen Ground Covers.)

Zone 3 / Native / 40 to 50 feet (species; vars. much smaller)

**Metasequoia glyptostroboides** (dawn redwood): See Large Deciduous Trees.

**Picea abies** (Norway spruce): Because it grows very fast when it is young, Norway spruce has long been popular for shelter or screening uses. As a specimen tree it reaches a great height, and I admire it in wide-open spaces or large suburban properties where the sweeping branches with

their pendulous branchlets lend a graceful note to the landscape. I would not recommend it as a plant for a small yard, however. There are several smaller cultivars of Norway spruce, many of which demand almost no pruning to stay within bounds, so that they are suitable for an opaque hedge all year long. A particularly low-growing, flat-topped one is nest spruce (*Picea abies* 'Nidiformis') — but your nursery can show you a selection to choose from. Norway spruce is easy to move because of its shallow root system, and thrives in a sandy, moderately moist, well-drained soil. It does best in a cold climate.

Zone 3 / Northern and Central Europe / 60 to 100 feet (species; vars. much smaller)

## PINUS SPP.

Pine: These beautiful trees, a mainstay of the modern lumber industry and the source of wood products from paper to turpentine, are also a mainstay of the American landscape. Of all the many sizes and shapes of pines, only a small selection are described here; but even among these few you'll find plants to meet a great range of requirements.

Pines are generally tougher and more adaptable than spruces or firs. Their one important demand is to be either moved very young or carefully root-pruned in the nursery. The reason is that pines often develop a taproot that makes transplanting more and more difficult as they mature. Pines can also be pruned for thick, compact growth in hedges or screens: if you remove one-half of each "candle" of new growth in late spring, multiple buds will form below the cut.

All pines fall into three categories according to the number of needles grouped in each sheath. The 5-needle pines, like white pine and Swiss stone pine, have the softest texture because of their soft, feathery, densely grouped needles. Next come the 3-needle types, such as lacebark pine. The 2-needle types include mugho pine, Austrian pine, Jack pine, and Japanese black pine, all of which have a coarser, more bristly texture because of their more widely spaced, relatively rigid, sharp-pointed needles.

Many of these are large trees, reaching a mature height of 35 to 75 feet or more. A few, as noted below, are small or even shrubby.

**Pinus banksiana** (jack pine) is a utility tree for difficult situations. It will cling stubbornly to life in wretched soil where better-quality pines or deciduous trees won't grow. In maturity it spreads into a shrubby, flat-topped shape, perhaps 35 to 50 feet tall. Its mature bark furrows into thick plates, and its shortish, stiff, paired needles are dark green. This hardy native flourishes on dry banks, in full sun, and in sandy, gravelly, and/or acid soil; and it can take intense cold. Zone 3.

**Pinus bungeana** (lacebark pine) has beautiful red-brown bark that exfoliates like that of a sycamore, showing creamy-white patches beneath. Of Chinese origin, this is a specimen tree for viewing at close range, near the house or terrace. It has stiff, dark green needles in sets of three. Pyramidal in youth, often multistemmed, it develops slowly into a 30- to 50-foot-tall and picturesquely spreading tree in old age. Lacebark pine prefers well-drained soil and full sun, and tolerates limestone soils. Zone 5.

**Pinus cembra** (Swiss stone pine) comes from Europe. It requires a loamy, well-drained, slightly acid soil with full sun and very good circulation of air. It transplants more easily than most pines. When young it is a very slender pyramid, almost columnar; it becomes more open and flat-topped in maturity. It is slow-growing and stays a modest size (about 25 feet) for many years. The needles of Swiss stone pine, growing in fives, are quite long and dense, giving it a soft foliage texture. This makes a lovely specimen tree or mass planting. Zone 3.

**Pinus densiflora 'Umbraculifera'** (Tanyosho pine) is a variety of Japanese red pine. Its bark is a striking orange-red. Its long, soft, twisted bluish-green needles, growing in pairs, are uniquely decorative. So is the form of Tanyosho pine: it develops into a small (10 to 12 feet) umbrella-shaped tree, usually with picturesque multiple trunks and dense spreading branches, like a scaled-up bonsai tree. This is a dramatic accent plant. It needs sunny conditions and a well-drained, somewhat acid soil. Zone 5.

**Pinus mugo pumilio** (dwarf mugho pine): This sturdy plant is descended from trees native to Europe's mountain ranges. It is low-growing, spreading, or even prostrate, and can be used in groups or planted as an individual specimen. Very hardy and a slow grower, it can be pruned for thickness and small size. It does best in deep, moist loam; it tolerates partial shade. Its rigid paired needles are a medium green, and its stems are held upright, giving it a bristly, brushlike texture overall. Zone 3.

**Pinus nigra** (Austrian pine) is moderate-sized, with handsome, stiff, shining dark green needles and cinnamon-brown bark, both of which you can appreciate best at close range. It tolerates shade, dirt, and pollutants and is flexible as to soil type and condition, so that it's at home in or out of the city. It does not suffer from alkaline soils, wind, or exposure to salt spray. You can prune its young growth in spring, for screening or hedging purposes; or plant it in groups or as a specimen. Dense and pyramidal when young, a mature Austrian pine — which can reach 50 feet — becomes flat-topped, with a stout trunk and stout, spreading branches. Zone 5.

**Pinus strobus** (white pine) has a windswept look in old age: a tall charcoal-gray trunk and clouds of soft blue-green foliage like feathery plumes against the sky. For its first half-century, however, it has a plump, pyramidal shape most distinguished for the softness of its texture and color. This is a beautiful tree, a basic component of the North American landscape since time immemorial. If you use white pine in a wild landscape it will rapidly colonize from seed. Or if you have plenty of space you can grow it as a specimen or in groupings; or you can shear it into a hedge of whatever dimensions you desire. Left to itself it will grow to 50, 80, even 100 feet or more. White pine will grow in nearly any well-drained soil. It needs plenty of light but will tolerate some shade, although shade will make it grow somewhat spindly. It will not, however, put up with salty conditions or urban air pollution. Zone 4.

**Pinus thunbergiana** (Japanese black pine) can stand large amounts of salt water, even drenchings by winter storms and hurricanes, so it is invaluable as an accent plant for seaside locations. It's a beautiful, picturesque, spreading tree with dense foliage. The needles are twisted, dark green, lustrous, and quite long; they grow in pairs. The mature bark is a blackish gray, fissured into irregular plates. This tree prefers full sun; it makes its best growth in good, moist soil, but it also does well in sandy soils. Its mature height ranges (depending on the circumstances) from 20 to 80 feet. Zone 6.

---

**Pseudolarix kaempferi** (golden larch): See Large Deciduous Trees.

**Pseudotsuga menziesii** (Douglas fir) is a noble forest tree by nature, growing to a height of 200 feet or more in the wild. But in smaller-scaled residential landscapes it contributes a wonderfully dense, regular pyramidal shape. Its needles are short and soft (not stiff like those of spruces), and blue-green or gray-green to green. It will do best in a moist, well-drained, neutral to slightly acid soil. It flourishes in a sunny, open location and prefers a somewhat humid atmosphere. High winds can damage it, the more so the bigger it gets. You can find slow-growing, pendulous-branched, or dwarf varieties of Douglas fir; the dwarf types are naturally the best suited to use in hedges, but bigger varieties also make fine screens and windbreaks as well as specimen plants for large properties.

Zone 5 / Native / 80 to 250 feet (species; vars. much smaller)

**Sciadopitys verticillata** (umbrella pine) is so named because its glossy dark green needles are held in whorls that radiate from the stem like the ribs of an umbrella. The tree is roughly pyramidal, but the foliage is so distinctive that it's the detailed texture rather than the overall form that matters in the landscape. The grayish-brown bark exfoliates in long strips. This is a wonderful specimen plant for use near houses, around rocks, or in small gardens. An extremely slow grower, it does best if sheltered from hot sun and freezing winds. Transplant it balled and burlapped into rich, acid soil with plenty of moisture, plenty of sun, and good ventilation.

Zone 6 / Japan / 30 to 90 feet

**Taxus canadensis** (Canada yew), one of just two yew species native to this country, is primarily of use as a ground cover or understory planting in shady naturalized or woodland situations. The hardiest of all yews, Canada yew is a low, sprawling plant with leaders that often root where they encounter the ground. Like other yews it has flat, shiny, dark-green evergreen needles and pretty (but mildly poisonous) red fruits. It likes a fertile sandy loam with top-notch drainage: it won't survive heat, drought, or bad drainage. Dwarf Canadian hedge yew (*Taxus canadensis* 'Stricta') is less sprawling, with more upright branches and a tighter general habit — but it shares the shade tolerance and great hardiness of the basic species, for people with shady or very cold locations. As its name implies, it is tailor-made for evergreen hedges.

Zone 3 / Native / 3 to 6 feet (6 to 8 wide)

**Taxus cuspidata 'Nana'** (dwarf Japanese yew): This yew will perform well in sun or in shade, in city or in country, heavily pruned or not at all. It is also adaptable as to soil, although (like all yews) it does demand excellent drainage. This is a tidy, compact, slow-growing variety of Japanese yew, with spreading branches that give it a broad, low form. Its foliage is a lustrous dark green and somewhat tufted, making attractive patterns of light and shadow. The new spring growth is a very pretty bright yellow-green. You can prune dwarf Japanese yew just about any time, but I recommend doing it early in the growing season if possible, so as to allow the new growth that follows pruning to harden off before winter.

Zone 5 / Manchuria, Korea, Japan / 10 feet (20 wide)

**Taxus media** (intermediate yew) is more a group than a single type of plant. You'll find it mainly in the form of its many cultivars, each with its characteristic size and growth habit; each with its special assets; and each deservedly popular as a maintenance-free, symmetrical, slow-growing evergreen shrub. The cultivar 'Densiformis' is particularly dense, ideally suited for use in hedges or borders, and twice as wide as it is high (it can grow to 10 feet or more in height). Hatfield yew (*Taxus media* 'Hatfieldii') has a broad, compact form but holds its branches and branchlets erect; its top height is around 12 feet. Hicks yew (*Taxus media* 'Hicksii') is an upright, columnar variety that can grow 20 feet or more tall, with several stems but not nearly as broad and bushy a habit as many yews. All these yews like moist, sandy loam and will thrive in sun or shade. The female plants bear fleshy, mildly toxic red fruits that can be quite decorative against the dark-green foliage. Intermediate yews are excellent for hedges (pruned, of course), groupings, and massed plantings; or use them as facer plants below taller trees.

Zone 5 / Hybrid (England and Japan) / Various sizes

**Thuja occidentalis** (American arborvitae) is another reliable evergreen tree that's generally available in the form of one or another of its many cultivated varieties. Its lacy, fine-textured foliage makes a pleasant contrast to the foliage of needled or broad-leaved evergreens in winter, and to the leaves of deciduous plants in summer. With the basic species, however, the foliage often suffers from winter browning that spoils its looks; and in severely icy or snowy winters there is a tendency for one of its paired or clustered stems to split and droop sideways, giving the tree a very disheveled appearance. That's why the cultivars are usually recommended. One tall and vigorous type for backgrounds or hedges is 'Douglas Pyramidal'. Its fernlike foliage

can be trusted to stay a good dark green year round. So can the foliage of 'Hetz Midget' arborvitae, a very slow-growing, ball-shaped dwarf plant for borders or low hedges. 'Hetz Wintergreen' is a narrow, upright, fast-growing variety that is ideal for a tall hedge (it can reach 60 feet) and keeps its color beautifully. All American arborvitaes are easy to propagate from softwood cuttings taken in fall or winter. They like full sun and a humid atmosphere as well as abundant moisture in the soil, which should be a deep well-drained loam. They tolerate alkaline soils well.

Zone 3 / Native (hybrids) / Various heights

**Tsuga canadensis** (Canadian hemlock), left to itself, will grow into a towering pyramid whose bottom branches create a cave of darkness 20 or 30 feet across. So this is not a tree for a small property unless you keep it small by regular pruning (as in a border or hedge) or use one of its small cultivated varieties. For larger areas or woodlands, Canadian hemlock is magnificent: rapid-growing, densely branched, with small flat needles of a very deep dark green (but bright yellow-green new growth in May and June). Birds and wildlife cherish its fine twigs and close-set branches for shelter and nesting, and its tiny round cones for food. Canadian hemlock prefers a soil that is acid, with ample moisture and good drainage; but it will do fine in sandy soils or even on rocky ledge. It won't tolerate pollution, drought, or heavy winds, however. It responds nicely to pruning, and makes a graceful evergreen hedge or screen. Among dwarf varieties, *Tsuga canadensis* 'Bennett' is compact and spreading, growing broader than it is high. 'Coles Prostrate' literally crawls over the ground, but can also be trained on stakes in any form you wish until the trunks grow sturdy enough to be self-supporting. Sargent weeping hemlock (*Tsuga canadensis pendula* or *sargentii*), the most beautiful weeping conifer, forms a broad dense mound of fine-textured drooping foliage.

Zone 4 / Native / 40 to 100 feet (species; vars. much smaller)

# BROAD-LEAVED EVERGREENS

## AZALEAS

There are just a few azaleas hardy enough to be considered evergreen in Zone 6 or north; and in a severe winter, even these selections should be expected to lose a good many leaves. Deciduous azaleas, described under Medium Deciduous Shrubs, are a much larger group. Like all members of the *Rhododendron* genus, azaleas need humidity and acid soil. In the north, shelter from hot summer sun and drying winds is beneficial; and azaleas like a thick acid mulch to keep their roots moist and cool in summer. Given these conditions, they'll afford matchless spring beauty, fine-textured summer foliage, and color and mass for the winter landscape. The choices listed here are all low-growing, almost dwarf plants, which is characteristic of azaleas that are evergreen in the north. For more impressive dimensions combined with small leaf texture, some of the small-leaved rhododendrons may be good alternatives.

**Rhododendron 'Delaware Valley White'** (Delaware Valley white azalea) offers bright-green foliage and clear white blossoms, and reaches a top height of 4 feet. Zone 6.

**Rhododendron kaempferi 'Herbert'** (Herbert azalea) is a hybrid with Japanese ancestry, and produces dark reddish-purple flowers. Zone 6.

**Rhododendron obtusum 'Hinocrimson'** (Hinocrimson azalea) is a spreading, dense shrub with small glossy leaves — a hybrid of a Japanese mountain plant. The flowers are an intense crimson. Zone 6.

**Rhododendron obtusum 'Hinodegiri'** (Hinodegiri azalea) has flowers that are a vivid rose-red; in addition it's especially compact, and can be shaped for a clipped hedge or border. Zone 6.

**Buxus microphylla** (littleleaf box or boxwood) is a dense evergreen shrub with small, glossy leaves — a classic favorite for all sorts of low hedges and borders. You can buy it in containers or balled and burlapped, and it will do fine in most well-drained soils, although it prefers mulching to keep its roots cool. It's also best used in locations where it has some protection from the strongest sun, drying winds, and winter cold. The basic species is only barely hardy in Massachusetts (one plantsman describes littleleaf box as turning a "repulsive yellow-green-brown" in winter); but the variety *japonica* and newer cultivars like 'Green Beauty' and 'Wintergreen' (*Buxus microphylla koreana* 'Wintergreen') have been bred specifically for attractive winter color in this climate. Look for them.

Zones 5 to 7 (according to variety) / Japan / 3 to 4 feet

**Buxus sempervirens** (common box or boxwood): This is much larger than its cousin littleleaf box, so it can be used not only in hedges and borders but as a specimen or in massed plantings. It's another dense, multibranched evergreen shrub, with a medium-fine foliage texture. Like littleleaf box, the basic common box prefers a mild climate and can just barely survive extremes of heat and cold; but many sturdy smaller cultivars have been developed that are tailored to the needs of gardeners in the Northeast. Some that have stood the test of many difficult seasons are 'Vardar Valley', 'Green Gem', 'Green Velvet', and 'Green Mountain'. Many of these are hardy even well into Zone 5.

Zones 5 to 6 / Southern Europe, Northern Africa, Western Asia / 15 feet (species; vars. much smaller)

**Cotoneaster spp.** (cotoneaster): See Small Deciduous Shrubs and Evergreen Ground Covers.

**Ilex crenata 'Convexa'** (boxleaf holly) is also called convex-leaved Japanese holly; by either name, it is one of the most useful and hardy broad-leaved evergreen shrubs available to northern gardeners. It doesn't seem to suffer from crowded, dirty city conditions, and it will endure severe pruning, so it is ideal for hedges. Prune it after its current season's growth has hardened off. Boxleaf holly is dense and low-growing; its small, oval leaves are a glossy dark green like those of most hollies. Its flowers and small black berries are inconspicuous (and anyway it won't bear fruit unless it's a female with a male near by). It prefers a light, acid soil. There are many fine cultivars; a couple of reliable ones are the dwarf 'Compacta' and the even more compact dwarf 'Helleri'.

Zone 6 / Japan / 9 feet (24 wide)

**Ilex glabra** (inkberry) is a popular and adaptable native shrub, a member of the holly family. Its clusters of small, shiny, oval leaves add a sprightly touch to the winter scene. Inkberry (so called for its black berries) will grow happily in wet soil; it prefers acid soil, but also does well in salty (alkaline) surroundings. It is best used in massed plantings. You can prune it as heavily as necessary, or alternatively let it expand into a broad mass, which it does by sending up shoots or suckers from around its base. 'Compacta' is a good dwarf form of inkberry.

Zone 4 / Native / 6 to 8 feet (8 to 10 wide)

**Ilex meserveae** (blue hollies or Meserve hollies) are a fairly recent introduction — a cross between English holly (*Ilex aquifolium*) and prostrate holly (*Ilex rugosa*), with the virtues of both and the failings of neither. These hardy hybrids have a distinctive bluish tinge to their foliage and make striking accent plants. The typical spikiness of the leaves makes blue-holly hedges impervious to man or beast. If there is a male blue holly in the vicinity, the female blue hollies will bear lovely red berries. Blue holly cultivars named 'Blue Angel', 'Blue Princess', 'Blue Prince', and the like come in assorted sizes and growth habits. They are all adaptable as to soil and sun conditions, and maintain their notable color throughout the winter.

Zone 5 / Hybrids / 6 to 20 feet

**Ilex opaca** (American holly), growing in the wild, forms a large and beautifully symmetrical cone of lustrous green. Its brilliant red berries stay on the tree well into the winter, and are much sought after for decorations around Christmastime. As with all hollies, only the female tree bears fruit, and it requires a male nearby for pollination. Holly prefers loose, moist, acid soil; it won't survive in extremely dry locations or in poorly drained soil, and it requires shelter from strong winds. If you're in the market for a specimen holly or for hollies for grouping, shop around a little. There are about 300 cultivars of American holly available. Look for varieties of proven worth that are known to flourish in your particular set of climatic and soil conditions.

Zone 6 / Native / 40 to 70 feet

**Ilex pedunculosa** (longstalk holly): This is a hardy, upright shrub or small tree with handsome, laurellike leaves and bright red berries the size of peas, borne singly on long stalks, not in clusters like those of American holly. This exceptionally resilient member of the holly group will stand up to drying winds, summer heat, and poorly drained soils. Its foliage is very dense, and it makes a strong statement as a specimen plant or in massed plantings. It is a kind of a Cinderella among hollies — a plant that many experts consider too little appreciated and deserving of much wider popularity.

Zone 6 / Japan and China / 20 to 30 feet

**Ilex verticillata** (winterberry): See Medium Deciduous Shrubs.

**Kalmia latifolia** (mountain laurel): This broad-leaved evergreen shrub has been loved by generations of gardeners up and down the East Coast. I mention the east because mountain laurel requires soil acidity; given that and a cool, moist, well-drained loam, it will prosper in considerable shade as well as in full sun. It is marvelous for massed plantings, borders, or even naturalizing on larger properties. Its June flowers are extraordinary: clusters of small 10-sectioned cups that are rosy in bud, white in full bloom, and as crisply perfect as porcelain. The leaves, a deep glossy green, make fine winter arrangements inside the house as well as brightening the outdoor scene. There are several good cultivars and varieties, some more compact, some with red to pink flowers (such as the variety *Kalmia rubra* or the cultivar *Kalmia* 'Fuscata').

Zone 5 / Native / 30 feet

**Leucothoe fontanesiana** (drooping leucothoe) bears sprays of fragrant, white bell-shaped flowers in spring, and its lustrous leaves stay on the plant year round, deep green in summer and bronze-toned throughout the winter. The branches of this graceful shrub curve in fountainlike arches — hence the name. Use drooping leucothoe (pronounced lew-KO-tho-ee) in groupings; as a facer plant to hide bare stems of taller shrubs; as a cover for a shady bank; or as "understory" growth in naturalistic or woodland plantings. Like the better-known azaleas and rhododendrons, to which it is related, drooping leucothoe prefers an acid soil. It is best planted in spring; it needs a moist, well-drained soil high in organic matter, and will tolerate partial to full shade (although it can stand full sun if there's plenty of moisture). It will not tolerate drought or excessive drying. If drooping leucothoe becomes overgrown or leggy, restore bushy growth and vitality by cutting it back to the ground after it flowers. For a lower-growing, more spreading variety, look at coast leucothoe (*Leucothoe axillaris*); or at dwarf leucothoe (*Leucothoe fontanesiana* 'Nana'), which grows 2 feet high but 6 feet across.

Zone 5 / Native / 3 to 6 feet (equally wide)

**Mahonia aquifolium** (Oregon holly-grape or grape-holly) is classified as a broad-leaved "evergreen" shrub even though its leaves are actually a bronzed brown in winter. It is a good border plant for shady locations, with clusters of bright yellow flowers in spring, glossy leaves shaped like holly leaves, and blue-black late-summer fruits that closely resemble Concord grapes. Oregon holly-grape likes a moist, well-drained, acid soil, and at least partial shade. It requires protection from heat and drying.

Zone 6 / Native / 3 to 6 feet

**Paxistima canbyi** (Canby paxistima): Formerly called pachistima, this is a useful low-maintenance evergreen shrub, categorized as a "broad-leaved" evergreen although it's by far the narrowest-leaved plant to come under that heading. For that reason, and because it grows low to the ground and spreads horizontally, and because of its handsome bronze fall color, Canby paxistima is wonderful in combination with other broad-leaved or needled evergreens in grouped plantings or low borders. You can propagate it from cuttings taken in summer. In the wild it colonizes rocky soils, but it prefers a moist, well-drained soil with good organic content.

Zone 5 / Native / 1 to 2 feet (3 to 5 across)

**Pieris floribunda** (mountain andromeda or pieris) gives winter-long promise of spring, because its flower buds are formed in summer and are visible throughout the winter months, a pale greenish white against the plant's dense evergreen foliage. This is a lovely, low, rounded shrub — a perfect choice for grouped plantings of broad-leaved evergreens or for use in woodland borders or naturalistic plantings. In very early spring the fragrant white flowers bloom, held aloft in small spires. Mountain andromeda likes a light, peaty soil, although it's not as demanding of acidity as some other broad-leaved evergreens. Give it a location in partial shade if possible. Keep it away from windy places in full sun, where its leaves are apt to burn in late winter.

Zone 5 / Native / 2 to 6 feet (equally wide)

**Pieris japonica** (Japanese andromeda or pieris) is taller and more upright than the related mountain andromeda. Its flower buds are visible on the shrub all winter long and bloom in earliest spring; they are graceful cascading clusters of fragrant white bells, similar to lilies-of-the-valley. With its lustrous dark green foliage, Japanese andromeda makes a fine specimen plant or combines with other broad-leaved evergreens in massed plantings or shrub borders. Several cultivated varieties have been developed. A compact type (*Pieris japonica* 'Compacta') is smaller-growing and smaller-leaved, for smaller gardens; others offer pink flowers, variegated leaves, or leaves with decorative textures. Give Japanese andromeda a somewhat acid, well-drained, highly organic soil, and partial shade; it will do best if sheltered from strong winds. Prune it in spring, after its flowering.

Zone 6 / Japan / 9 to 12 feet (species; vars. much smaller)

## Pyracantha coccinea 'Lalandei'

(Laland firethorn): One of the hardiest cultivars of scarlet firethorn, this is an outstanding broad-leaved evergreen for informal hedges or barriers or for training as an espalier plant against walls or fences. It's often just the thing for a walled city garden. Its small leaves are a glossy dark green and it bears white flowers in late spring. Its small but very abundant berries, ripening in September, are a brilliant orange-red; they persist on the plant well into the winter, giving it a festive look. The firethorn's thorns are long, straight, and sharp. It is flexible as to soil pH. It prefers a well-drained soil and will tolerate dry soil; and it will produce the best crop of berries if it gets a good amount of sun. Whether you are using firethorn as a free-standing plant or espaliered, you'll need to prune it often to keep it within bounds.

Zone 6 / Italy to Western Asia / 6 to 18 feet

## RHODODENDRON SPP.

The genus *Rhododendron* incorporates all the plants commonly called azaleas as well as all the rhododendrons — but I've listed azaleas under "Azaleas" here and elsewhere in this book. The great majority of rhododendrons (unlike azaleas) really are evergreen in the north.

If you've investigated rhododendrons at all, you already know that this is a huge clan of shrubs. Indeed, a large body of literature and numerous horticultural organizations concern themselves solely with the subject of rhododendrons and their relatives. There are 900 identified *Rhododendron* species and uncountable varieties. What I'll offer here is a small sampling of reliable and widely obtainable varieties. Your nursery will be able to introduce you to other good ones.

All rhododendrons should be planted into acid, moist, highly organic soil. The top of the earth ball should be at the surface of the ground — don't plant them deep. They do best in a humid climate and will prosper in locations where there is shelter from extreme cold as well as from dry heat and drying winds. Prune rhododendrons early in spring, if necessary; and after they bloom, remove spent flower clusters to encourage the formation of abundant new buds for next year.

## Rhododendron 'Boule de Neige'

(Boule de Neige rhododendron), a hybrid of Caucasian origin, is one of the finest white-flowering rhododendrons available, with clear, pure-white blossoms in late May. Zone 6.

## Rhododendron carolinianum (Carolina rhododendron) is one of the best and most popular rhododendron species, with small dark-green leaves and pale rosy-purple flowers in mid-May. It's not a huge plant, but grows to a height of around 6 feet; it generally has a compact, rounded shape. Give Carolina rhododendron sun or partial shade and protection from strong wind and sun. It is a native, and fine for naturalizing. Zone 5.

## Rhododendron catawbiense (Catawba rhododendron), another native species, can grow very large, and has medium-large leathery leaves. It's wonderful growing in large masses at the edge of woodland or in wild landscapes; and it is tough enough for cold or exposed locations. The species flowers around mid- to late May. The best flowering Catawba rhododendrons are its many cultivated varieties. 'Roseum Elegans' is a great standby, long loved

and much used for its reliability in flowering and its ability to withstand extreme temperatures; its flowers are a clear lavender-pink. 'Compactum' also bears rosy-lavender blossoms, but is smaller and more dense and rounded. The variety *album* has large clusters of white bloom with yellow markings. 'Nova Zembla' bears gorgeous red flowers and is another type with exceptional resistance to heat and cold. Zone 5.

### *Rhododendron* 'Chionoides'

(Chionoides rhododendron) is a later-blooming cultivar with long, light green leaves and a compact, wide-growing form. The flowers are white with yellow "eyes," giving the shrub a very crisp, clean, springy look. Zone 6.

### *Rhododendron fortunei* (Fortune

rhododendrons) include many hybrid varieties, all with a common origin in eastern China. They can grow to 12 feet and have large, loosely clustered leaves. The late May blooms are fragrant and very large, and all in pink to red tones. One of my favorite *fortunei* cultivars is a Dexter hybrid called 'Scintillation', with pale pink blooms. Zone 6.

### *Rhododendron laetivirens* (Wilson

rhododendron) is a very hardy and charmingly compact and neat hybrid variety. Growing slowly to a top height of 4 feet or so, it is fine for small-scale gardens, even rock gardens, or for planting close to the house where larger types would be out of place. Its small, rose-colored to purplish flowers appear in early June, but they're almost incidental. The small leaves are glossy and similar in size and shape to those of mountain laurel: I use this

**Rhododendron 'P.J.M. Hybrids'.**

shrub more for its great foliage than for its flowers. Zone 5.

### *Rhododendron maximum* (rosebay

rhododendron, or great laurel), may be the hardiest of all the larger rhododendrons — and it really is large. Under ideal conditions in the wild it can grow into a great spreading mound as much as 30 to 40 feet high at its highest point; but in cultivation it will stop at 10 to 12 feet. Rosebay rhododendron is valued primarily as a background planting, rather than for its flowers. It has large, leathery leaves and bears small, pinkish-purple blossoms in late June. It needs semishade, being a plant that thrives in open woodlands. Use it with caution on small properties. Zone 4.

### *Rhododendron* 'P.J.M. Hybrids'

(P.J.M. hybrid rhododendrons) bloom in late April, and so profusely that they are completely covered with brilliant lavender-pink, not a leaf showing. They make a stunning display, although I find the color somewhat overpowering; I'd recommend using P.J.M. hybrids in front of masses of other bright green foliage. These rhododendrons grow to be 3 to 6 feet tall. Their leaves are small, glossy, and dark green; they turn a rich purple-bronze or dark red in the fall. P.J.M.s are happy in sunny, exposed locations. Zone 4.

### *Rhododendron* 'Purple Gem' (Pur-

ple Gem rhododendrons): These dwarf evergreen rhododendrons are tidy and rounded in form — ideal plants for the smaller garden. Their leaves are very small, and their profuse April flowers are a light bluish purple. They're hardy in Zone 5.

# DECIDUOUS GROUND COVERS

*Aronia melanocarpa* (black chokeberry): This smaller relative of red chokeberry offers an interesting mixture of assets and liabilities. It's a wonderful shrubby ground cover for wet areas and for naturalistic landscapes. It is easy to propagate from cuttings; it tolerates shade; and it thrives in all kinds of soils, from boggy to sandy.

Black chokeberry holds its abundant blackish-purple fruits most of the winter, so that a large mass makes quite an impact. On the other hand, it rapidly spreads across the countryside by sending up forests of suckers, so that you may find it hard to contain; it's not for use in disciplined landscapes.

Zone 6 / Native / 3 to 5 feet

**Comptonia peregrina** (sweet fern) is aptly named, for its aromatic dark green foliage is soft and feathery in appearance, like a bed of forest ferns. Its slender stalks create a broad flat-topped mound and it spreads and colonizes readily from suckers. Sweet fern is happiest in infertile, sandy, acid soils (give it lots of peat) and therefore makes a fine plant for banks and other poor-soil areas, provided they are adequately moist. I enjoy crushing several leaves and indulging in the redolent sweet yet spicy aroma.

Zone 3 / Native / 2 to 4 feet (4 to 8 wide)

**Cornus canadensis** (bunchberry) is one of the most beautiful of ground covers for naturalistic woodland settings. It is a member of the dogwood clan; its exquisite white flowers (actually bracts), blooming in May and June, are reminiscent of those of flowering dogwood. They're followed by clusters of bright red berries that are edible by human beings as well as wildlife. The leaves are carried in whorls like little pinwheels; they are a glossy dark green, changing to wine-red in fall. This plant needs cool, moist, acid soil, rich in humus and somewhat shaded. Probably the best way to get it started is to transfer sections of sod from established plantings. Given conditions it likes, bunchberry is wonderful under pines, broad-leaved evergreens, or other acid-loving plantings.

Zone 3 / Native / 3 to 9 inches

**Coronilla varia** (crown vetch) is chiefly useful for erosion control on steep, rocky banks. Its roots do a great job of holding soil in place, and its thick foliage shades out weeds. Don't try to grow it in a well-kept garden, though. It spreads like wildfire and will rapidly become a pest. Its compound leaves consist of many small oval leaflets, giving it a fine texture; and if you can mow it in spring it will make a dense, brilliant-green mat throughout the summer. It dies back to brown stems in winter.

Zone 4 / Europe / 2 feet

**Forsythia viridissima 'Bronxensis'** (Bronx greenstem forsythia) flowers prolifically at a young age, but never grows more than a foot or so tall and twice as broad. It is very compact and bushy, with green stems and bright-yellow April blossoms. This little plant is at home in small gardens, rock gardens, patios, containers, or any sunny place where the cheerful air of forsythia is wanted but the site's dimensions require a dwarf. It also makes an excellent ground cover, turning a bank into a carpet of yellow. Like all forsythias it's very easy to propagate.

Zone 6 / China / 1 foot (2 wide)

**Rosa wichuraiana** (memorial rose): Easy to grow in poor soils, free from pests or diseases, and covered with fragrant snowy-white flowers in June and July, this rose is an appealing ground cover for banks and other informal open spaces. It has dark green, lustrous compound leaves. It is a fast spreader, growing as much as 10 feet in a season and multiplying itself rapidly. The canes trail along the ground, often rooting where they touch, and forming a tangled mat of foliage; or they will climb if you give them something to climb over.

Zone 6 / China, Korea, Japan / 1 foot

**Spiraea japonica 'Alpina'** (daphne spirea): See Medium Deciduous Shrubs.

**Vaccinium angustifolium** (lowbush blueberry), a native inhabitant of the dry, acid, and infertile soils of former pastures in New England, makes a pretty and indestructible ground cover. The little bell-shaped pinkish-white flowers are followed in July by berries of an intense, dusty blue. These can be unpredictable in quantity, depending on the season; but abundant or not, their flavor is the very essence of summer. (The taste of wild or naturalized blueberries bears only a remote relationship to the blandness of the oversized cultivated berries you find in markets.) Blueberries grow on tiny bushes with woody stems; they're not a plant for walking on. The small leaves turn a rich scarlet in fall. You'll get the best berry crops if you have the plants in full sun, but they will also grow well in light shade or partial sun.

Zone 3 / Native / 2 to 8 inches

***Xanthorhiza simplicissima*** (yellowroot) qualifies as a shrub, since it grows upward from the ground on woody stems to a height of 2 feet — but its great use is as a ground cover, particularly for banks or other challenging situations. It makes a dense mat of roots, stems, and foliage, and spreads rapidly across its allotted territory by means of underground stolons.

It has cutleaf foliage like celery leaves. It will thrive in full sun or partial shade in almost any well-drained, adequately moist soil; it does especially well along stream banks or in other damp, lightly shaded areas. You can transplant it (take divisions of older plants) in spring or fall.

Zone 5 / Native / 2 feet

# HERBACEOUS PERENNIAL GROUND COVERS

***Achillea millefolium* 'Rosea'** (pink yarrow) will tolerate poor, dry soil and likes full sun. With feathery, finely cut leaves and small pink flowers all summer, it grows 6 inches to 2 feet tall. Zone 3.

***Aegopodium podagraria*** (goutweed or bishop's weed): Low-growing (6 to 14 inches), sprawling, speedy to cover good or poor soil, this can be a pest if you don't contain it. It's happy in sun or shade. Especially handsome in shade is the variegated silveredge goutweed (*Aegopodium podagraria* 'Variegatum'). Zone 4.

***Ajuga reptans*** (bugleweed or carpet bugle) makes a flat mass of interestingly creased and dimpled leaves 8 to 12 inches from the ground. It holds its clusters of small white bugle-shaped flowers above the leaves. Zones 3 to 4.

***Arabis procurrens*** (rockcress) quickly creates a dense mat of shiny leaves in sun or light shade. Its white flowers bloom in April or May; it's pretty in rock gardens or as an edging plant. Zone 5.

***Arenaria verna*** (moss sandwort) is great for planting among stepping stones or along pavement edges in sun or shade. It forms a 2-inch-high mat of fine, evergreen, mosslike foliage. It bears small white flowers in May. For contrast, a golden-leaved variety is *Arenaria verna* 'Aurea'. Zones 3 to 4.

***Asarum europaeum*** (European ginger): Five inches tall, the glossy evergreen leaves of this wild ginger are 2 to 3 inches across and shaped somewhat like the foliage of violets. This is an elegant ground cover for shady or wooded situations. Zone 5.

***Convallaria majalis*** (lily-of-the-valley): The sweet-scented bell-shaped white flowers of this plant need no introduction. This is a determined spreader, new plants popping up from rhizomes in the most unlikely places. Contain it with a physical barrier, or be prepared to weed it out of your lawn, walks, or patio. Lily-of-the-valley thrives in shade as well as sun. Zones 3 to 4.

***Coreopsis auriculata* 'Nana'** (dwarf eared coreopsis) is an ideal rock garden plant in full sun. Its blossoms are orange-yellow, 2 inches across, and daisy-shaped; they bloom in June and July. Its overall height is 6 inches. Zone 5.

***Dianthus spp.*** (pinks) have fine, soft, gray-green foliage; and their June flowers come in white, pink, scarlet, or purple tones. Sprawling and fuzzy-textured, they are lovely growing in low mounds over rocks in full sun. Zones 3 to 4.

***Draba sibirica* 'Repens'** (Siberian draba) is a fast-growing, trailing plant, bearing large, open rosettes of leaves. Its dainty yellow flowers bloom in both spring and fall. It's attractive in rock gardens. Zone 4.

**Duchesnea indica** (mock strawberry) looks like a strawberry and spreads like a strawberry. Its runners create a thick mass of jagged-edged compound leaves about 2 inches off the ground, and it bears small yellow flowers. Zone 6.

**Epimedium spp.** (epimediums), otherwise known as barren-wort or bishop's hat, are excellent ground covers for full sun or for shade where the soil is good. Growing 6 to 12 inches high, their leaves are evergreen but turn reddish in winter. *Epimedium alpinum rubrum* has red and yellow flowers; *Epimedium pinnatum*, bright yellow; and *Epimedium youngianum*, white. Zones 4 to 6, depending on variety.

**Ferns** are not one genus but dozens, and I won't attempt to cover them all here. Their graceful, feathery forms and soft textures are familiar to nearly everyone. Suffice it to say that many ferns make fine ground covers for shady places, around water, or in large-scale open settings (depending on type of fern) — and that they are tough and easy to maintain once established in conditions appropriate to their needs. Some of my own favorite types are the following, all hardy in Zone 4. Hay-scented fern (*Dennstaedtia punctilobula*) is easy to grow and reaches a height of 2 to 3 feet, with fronds almost a foot across. It will thrive in most soils and it spreads by rhizomes, so it's great for shaded banks; in·fact it can be somewhat invasive. Cinnamon fern (*Osmunda cinnamomea*) does well in moist soil and partial shade and grows up to 3 feet tall; in spring its curled fiddleheads are charmingly fuzzy. Royal fern (*Osmunda regalis*) is very tall — up to 6 feet — and needs an acid soil. I like to grow it beside water, where it makes sumptuous reflections. Lady fern (*Athyrium filix-femina*) is much smaller, reaching 2 feet or so, with wide, finely cut fronds. It is partial to limestone soils, well adapted to use around rocks, and no trouble to grow. Common polypody (*Polypodium vulgare*) is only about 10 inches tall, with fine-textured, ever-

green fronds about 2 inches across; it's exquisite among rocky crevices and flourishes in shallow, rocky soils. Maidenhair fern (*Adiantum pedatum*) is dainty and delicate, with lacy bright green foliage on wiry stems. It grows up to 2 feet tall, and almost as wide; it likes cool, moist, shady spots, where it spreads slowly by rhizomes.

**Galium odoratum** (sweet woodruff), formerly known as *Asperula odorata*, bears clusters of exquisite, fragrant white flowers in May and June; its whorled leaves are sweet-scented too. Six inches tall, it is fine in texture. It flourishes in shade and does well among rhododendrons or in combination with English ivy. Zone 5.

**Gypsophila repens 'Rosea'** (prostrate baby's-breath) is a charming rock-garden plant with its fine, linear leaves and its low (6 inches) trailing habit. It likes full sun and a more alkaline soil if possible. Its tiny flowers are pale pink and bloom in clouds from June through July. Zone 4.

**Hemerocallis spp.** (daylilies): Most of these are ground covers of the tall persuasion, although there are some dwarf varieties. They grow with great vigor, sending their cheerful blooms to heights of 3 or 4 feet above their 1- or 2-foot foliage. Their flowers come in white, yellows, oranges, pinks, and reds. They don't need any care but they appreciate plenty of sun (although they tolerate partial shade). Zones 3 to 6, depending on variety.

**Hosta spp.** (plantain lilies): The large, glossy leaves of these durable plants come in many shades of green or variegated with white. Hostas are happy in partial shade, and produce spikes of white or purple flowers every summer no matter how resolutely you neglect them. Zone 4.

**Lysimachia nummularia** (creeping jenny or moneywort) is a creeping vine densely covered with small, round, flat leaves. Best suited to wet soils, it's perfect beside a pool or along a stream. It grows 2 inches high and bears abundant yellow flowers all summer. Zone 4.

**Mentha requienii** (creeping mint) has the smallest leaves of any mint (⅛ inch long), and it creeps along the ground, reaching a height of only 3 inches or so. It makes a delightfully scented, fine-textured ground cover for full sun and gives you a bonus of small pale-purple flowers in summer. Zone 6.

**Nepeta faassenii** (Persian ground-ivy): For full sun, this sprawling plant offers gray-green leaves with a wrinkly texture and bears clouds of lavender-blue bloom from May to July. It grows 8 to 12 inches high. (Sometimes offered in the trade under the name *Nepeta mussinii*.) Zone 4.

**Phalaris arundinacea picta** (ribbongrass) is a terrific ground cover for poor, dry soils or ornery banks in full sun. In such conditions it grows low and thick. Its leaves are attractively striped. It can be a pest if allowed to get out of control; keep it away from good moist soil and mow it down a few times a year. Zone 4.

**Phlox subulata** (moss pinks or ground pinks) form a 6-inch-deep mat of stiff, linear leaves. They are semi-evergreen and great for banks or rock gardens. In March they bloom profusely — white, pink, red, or blue according to variety. Zone 4.

**Polygonatum biflorum** (Solomon's-seal) is coarse-textured and too large for small gardens (its arching sprays are 2 to 3 feet tall); but it can be useful in full shade and moist soil. It bears pendant white bell-shaped flowers in May to June, and dark-blue fruits in fall. Zone 4.

**Sagina subulata** (pearlwort) is a mosslike, matted evergreen plant growing only 4 inches tall. It thrives in shade and is ideal for use among stepping stones. In July and August it produces profuse small white flowers. Zone 5.

**Sanguinaria canadensis** (bloodroot), a lovely ground cover for shady wooded settings, is notable not only for its red stems (and roots) but for its star-shaped white flowers, blooming in May, and its deeply cut, wavy-lobed fo-liage. Bloodroot grows 3 to 8 inches tall. It self-sows rapidly in the rich acid soil of its native woodlands; you can propagate it by division in spring or — preferably — fall. Zone 4.

**Sasa pumila** (ground bamboo) should be grown only in sun and restrained from sending out runners and taking over the landscape. Its attractive long narrow leaves reach a height of 12 inches. Zone 6.

**Thymus spp.** (thymes): With their fine-textured evergreen foliage and soft color, often grayish or gray-green, these aromatic plants are lovely along walks, among stepping stones, and in rock gardens in the sun. They grow very low to the ground. Many bear dainty flowers in various colors. Zones 4 to 6, depending on variety.

**Tiarella cordifolia** (Allegheny foam-flower) makes a wonderful ground cover for shady to partially shady places, particularly in wild or woodland gardens with rich, slightly acid soil. Its spires of white flowers bloom in April to July. Its deeply veined, jagged-edged leaves grow 6 to 12 inches from the ground. Zone 4.

**Viola spp.** (violets) grow 6 inches to a foot tall, with colors ranging from white to yellow to blue, violet, or rose. Their pretty heart-shaped leaves sprout in clusters, spreading joyfully in acid soil. Totally undemanding, violets flourish in partial shade. Small types are good in rock gardens; larger ones make attractive borders (if you can keep them from spreading) or wood-land undergrowth. Zones 3 to 7, depending on variety.

**Waldsteinia fragarioides** (barren strawberry) is particularly well adapted to poor, dry soils in full sun, where it makes a flat evergreen bed of glossy strawberrylike leaves just 4 inches off the ground. Its enchanting yellow flowers bloom in May and June. Zone 5.

# EVERGREEN GROUND COVERS

***Arctostaphylos uva-ursi*** (bearberry) is a charming and sturdy fine-textured ground cover. Red berries appear in late summer and are much savored by wildlife. Happy in seaside locations and largely untroubled by pests or diseases, it thrives in poor sandy soils with very high acidity (pH 4.5 to 5.5). Its leaves are oval and a glossy dark green, turning bronze to reddish-purple. Growing under its preferred conditions, a single plant will form a dense mat up to 15 feet across. Plant bearberry on a slope or over a wall in any informal setting, in sun or partial shade.

Zone 3 / Native / 6 to 12 inches

***Cotoneaster dammeri 'Skogsholmen'*** (Skogsholmen bearberry cotoneaster) is an exceptionally vigorous variety of this sturdy semievergreen to evergreen ground cover. Creeping stems grow outward rapidly in all directions, taking root where they touch the soil and carpeting a large area in a short time. Or you can grow it espaliered against a wall, or treat it as a low shrub for banks or borders. The tiny oval leaves are a lustrous dark green, and in mild years stay on the plant (somewhat wizened) all winter. The berries are persistent and a perky bright red, but fairly sparse compared to the massed fruits of many other cotoneasters. Skogsholmen bearberry cotoneaster will put up with dry or rocky ground and even salt spray; but it will flourish and spread most briskly in fertile, peaty soil with adequate moisture.

Zone 6 / China / 1 to 1½ feet (6 or more wide)

***Euonymus fortunei*** (wintercreeper) mutates readily and is available in countless forms. All are tolerant of sun and shade. All are evergreen, with more or less small, slightly serrated, oval or pointed-oval leaves. And all are capable of climbing or sprawling as needed, depending on variety. Wintercreeper is extremely easy to grow and to propagate from softwood cuttings; but you must watch out for and control euonymus scale, a pernicious insect that can really do a job on this plant. You can use wintercreeper as a ground cover, a vine, a low, spreading shrub, a border, or even a hedge plant. The variety *colorata* is a rambling ground cover type whose leaves turn purple in winter. Another variety, *radicans*, trails or climbs, and its glossy leaves have a wavy texture. 'Minima' is low-growing and fine-textured, with ½-inch leaves. 'Kewensis' is the smallest of all, a low-growing miniature with tiny leaves only about ¼ inch long.

Zone 5 / China / Ground cover or clinging vine

***Gaultheria procumbens*** (wintergreen): Sometimes known as checkerberry, this is such an appealing ground cover for cool, moist situations with humusy acid soil that I include it here in case you can provide the conditions it requires. Tolerant of shade, it is lovely as a companion plant for broad-leaved evergreens or in wooded settings. It has glossy dark green leaves that turn reddish in winter, and red berries that ripen in midsummer and stay on the plant until the following spring. The leaves when crushed or chewed yield the delightful oil of wintergreen.

Zone 4 / Native / 6 inches

***Hedera helix*** (English ivy), a familiar house plant, is also one of the most adaptable outdoor plants that exist. Like so many vines, its only failing is a slight tendency to travel where it is not wanted. It has glossy evergreen 3- to 5-lobed leaves (depending on variety), and it climbs by means of rootlets that adhere to rocks, masonry, tree trunks, or wooden structures. It will thrive in dense shade or full sun, and makes few demands except protection from the hottest sun and the coldest winds. You can use it as a vine to curtain any vertical surface, or as a spreading ground cover; or you can grow it in a container, train it as a

**Hedera helix (English ivy).**

shrub, or virtually anything else. A particularly hardy English ivy for northern gardens is the small-leaved variety known as *baltica*.

Zone 6 / Europe / Ground cover or clinging vine

***Iberis sempervirens*** (evergreen candytuft) is charming in edgings, among rocks, or interplanted with flowering bulbs or among evergreen shrubs. Its lacy, fine-textured foliage is dark green, setting off the crisp white flower clusters that bloom in April and May. Candytuft is adaptable as to soil and sun, although it prefers good soil and ample sun. It's easy to propagate by softwood cuttings. It performs best if pruned heavily after flowering. Over time, it will sprawl and propagate itself (by layering) to form broad mats of foliage.

Zone 6 / Europe, Asia / 12 inches

***Juniperus chinensis*** (Chinese juniper) in its native habitat is a slender, pyramidal tree that grows quite tall — but it is hardly ever seen in that form in the United States. Here it is the numerous cultivars that are widely known and very popular. Some are ground covers, some miniatures, some small evergreen shrubs; some make superb specimen plants, some are better suited to borders or massed plantings. The foliage is prickly and usually bluish or gray-green. Chinese junipers prefer well-drained, moist, alkaline soils and will do well in full sun or partial shade. Compact Pfitzer juniper (*Juniperus chinensis* 'Pfitzeriana Compacta') is a bushy, compact, gray-green variety. Chinese garden juniper (*Juniperus chinensis procumbens*) grows low — only up to 2 feet high — and is creeping or broadly mounding in habit. Its dense blue-green foliage makes a very handsome ground cover. A slow-growing dwarf cultivar of this same plant (*Juniperus chinensis procumbens* 'Nana') is rounded and spreading, holding its branches in flat layers; it never grows more than a foot high, and its foliage is blue-green and mosslike in texture. Another low ground cover or rock garden plant, Sargent juniper (*Juniperus chinensis sargentii*), has grass-green to blue-green foliage and is great for poor dry soils or seaside planting.

Zone 5 / China, Mongolia, Japan / All sizes

***Juniperus horizontalis*** (creeping juniper), which comes in a vast assortment of cultivated varieties, is an enormously useful evergreen ground cover for difficult situations. It will happily take command almost anywhere, from an arid, rocky bank to an exposed, wind-chilled city corner lot. It derives its sturdy tenacity from its origins on and around North America's swamps, seaside cliffs, and gravelly slopes. Low-growing, fibrous-rooted, with a strong inclination to take over the landscape, creeping juniper flourishes in any soil. Its fine-textured and somewhat prickly foliage is a bluish gray-green, turning violet in the winter. The variety known as Andorra juniper (*Juniperus horizontalis* 'Plumosa') is a flat-topped and fast-spreading ground cover. 'Bar Harbor' is a ground-hugging creeper with a top height of 1 foot.

Zone 4 / Native / 1 to 2 feet (spreading)

***Leucothoe fontanesiana*** (drooping leucothoe): See Broad-leaved Evergreens.

***Mitchella repens*** (partridgeberry): This is a familiar Christmastime gift plant, sold in florists' shops in decorative glass bowls or rings; but paradoxically it is one of the most difficult ground covers to establish in the residential landscape. It is really at home only in wild woodlands. It needs moist, acid soil with some shade and plenty of humus. If you have the conditions it needs, partridgeberry makes a fine-textured low-growing ground cover. Its glossy white-veined leaves are dainty year round; it has tiny pinkish-white flowers in spring and summer; and in fall it bears sprightly scarlet berries that last into the winter.

Zone 4 / Native / 2 inches

**Pachysandra terminalis** (Japanese spurge or pachysandra:) Almost everyone is familiar with this indomitable, maintenance-free evergreen ground cover. It is happiest in light to deep shade, where it spreads rapidly by means of underground stolons and successfully crowds out all would-be weeds, forming a thick, dark green carpet of lustrous foliage. Japanese spurge tolerates many soils but ideally prefers well-drained acid soils with adequate moisture and lots of organic matter. With good soil, it has no objection to city surroundings.

Zone 5 / Japan / 6 to 12 inches

**Paxistima canbyi** (Canby paxistima): See Broad-leaved Evergreens.

**Sedum acre** (goldmoss stonecrop) is just one of over 300 species of *Sedum*. This is a hardy, tiny-leaved, mat-forming plant for use among rocks or around steps, or in any sunny spot where you want a sprightly ground cover with a soft, mossy texture. Its foliage is light green, and it bears small bright yellow flowers from late May through June. Goldmoss stonecrop is an eager spreader, even in poor soil, and very easy to propagate by division or cuttings.

Zone 4 / Europe, Asia / 2 inches

**Sedum spurium** (two-row stonecrop) creeps along the ground to create a dense mat of stems and foliage. It is one of the hardiest and best all-around ground covers for dry, sunny, exposed locations, being semievergreen and

very pretty to look at in bloom. Its rounded leaves turn red in winter. Its 2-inch clusters of pink flowerets blossom in July to August. It spreads energetically, or you can easily multiply it by cuttings or division.

Zone 4 / Asia Minor / 3 to 6 inches

**Sempervivum tectorum** (houseleeks, or hens-and-chickens) look wonderful growing around steps, among rocks, or as a ground cover in any small-scale situation that lets you enjoy them close up. They are succulents shaped like rose blossoms. Each larger plant or "hen" (they grow up to 4 inches across) surrounds itself with various sizes of small plantlets or "chickens," and they make a tight ground-covering mass. The gray-green leaves are edged with reddish or purplish tones. The pink flowers bloom on tall fuzzy stalks. Given sun and good drainage, houseleeks will happily survive total neglect in the most exposed locations. You can also pot them up in fall to use as houseplants.

Zone 5 / Europe and Asia / 4 to 12 inches

**Vinca minor** (vinca, periwinkle, or myrtle) is another very well-known and long-loved evergreen ground cover. It can be slow to establish, but once settled in conditions to its liking it makes a beautiful carpet of fine-textured, lustrous, dark-green foliage. The dainty late-April flowers of the species are lilac-blue, and there are cultivars available in many shades of white, blue, and purple. Set vinca plants 1 foot apart in light or partial shade; and give them good, humusy, well-drained soil for best results.

Zone 5 / Europe and Western Asia / 3 to 6 inches

# DECIDUOUS VINES

**Akebia quinata** (five-leaf akebia): Hardy, vigorous to the point of aggressiveness, and charming both in foliage and in flower, this twining vine will rapidly cover anything you allow it to: banks, walls, trellises, or even other shrubbery. Keep it within bounds. It has no insect or disease problems. The dainty 2- or 3-inch oval leaves are held in clusters of 5 and are a deep, rich green, keeping their color late into the fall. (In warm climates, in fact, they are evergreen.) Give five-leaf akebia deep, rich soil and room to grow in.

Zone 5 / China, Korea, Japan / Twining vine

**Ampelopsis brevipedunculata** (porcelainberry or porcelain ampelopsis): The great claim to fame of this vine is its fruit, which ripens in September and October. Each cluster may include berries of lavender, yellow, and the final vivid blue. The dark green leaves are 3-lobed like grape leaves. Porcelainberry grows well in any well-drained soil. It should be given something to climb over. It will fruit best in full sun and if the spread of its roots is restricted.

Zone 5 / China, Korea, Japan / Climbing vine

**Campsis radicans** (common trumpet creeper) produces clusters of gorgeous red-orange trumpet-shaped flowers in midsummer. The compound leaves are bright green and relatively fine-textured. If you have wet soil, dry soil, or any other problem conditions and need a durable climbing plant, this vine may be for you. It will grow practically anywhere and is definitely of the rampant persuasion. It grows into such a thick, heavy mass that it requires some support in addition to its own small root-like holdfasts. It's easy to propagate.

Zone 5 / Native / Clinging vine

**Celastrus scandens** (bittersweet, or American bittersweet) is a fast-growing vine about which some people have mixed feelings. (Maybe that's why it is called bittersweet.) For all its virtues, it can be a menace to the landscape: it will swarm over every plant or structure in sight if it's not kept firmly under control. This means cutting it back at least once a year. I grow mine on a 7-foot post to keep it contained. Bittersweet is, however, adaptable to virtually any soil. And birds love it for its berries. The berries are bright yellow, and when fully ripe they split open to reveal a crimson seed inside; they make a popular addition to dried arrangements for the house. If you do decide to acquire some bittersweet, be sure the nursery labels the plants as to sex — because you won't get any berries at all unless you have both a female bittersweet and a male.

Zone 4 / Native / Twining vine

**Clematis dioscoreifolia robusta** (sweet autumn clematis): Formerly known as *Clematis paniculata*, this clematis bears fragrant white flowers in August and September. The cascades of feathery blossoms engulf the vine, and the vine has a habit of engulfing everything else. This is a vigorous grower that forms a lush mass of lustrous semievergreen foliage. If you can keep it from taking over the landscape, sweet autumn clematis is a very easy plant to grow; it positively thrives on neglect.

Zone 6 / Japan / Climbing vine

**Clematis montana rubens** (pink anemone clematis) bears its lavish rosy-red flowers in June, when it is a real showpiece in the landscape. It will grow into a bower of foliage over a trellis, fence, wall, or any structure that affords support for the twining tendrillike leaf stalks. Clematis flourishes best when it is given cool roots (a well-drained soil and ample mulch), and it needs at least some shade during the day. If you have to prune it, keep in mind that it blooms on the previous year's wood.

Zone 6 / Himalayas, China / Climbing vine

**Euonymus fortunei** (wintercreeper): See Evergreen Ground Covers.

**Hedera helix** (English ivy): See Evergreen Ground Covers.

**Hydrangea anomala petiolaris** (climbing hydrangea): This coarse-textured, vigorous climber is marvelous in large-scale settings where the masses and textures can support a hefty vine like this one. The resplendent white flower clusters appear in June. The leaves are an elegant, deep, glossy green. Leaves and flowers are borne on lateral branches that reach out 1 to 3 feet from the main stems. The whole plant can grow upwards as much as 60 or 80 feet; or it will clamber over a wall, trellis, or other free-standing structure. The weight of climbing hydrangea means that it must be given sturdy support if it's to go far. The vine is dramatic even in winter, when you can see its layered meshes of twigs all covered in shaggy exfoliating cinnamon-brown bark. Climbing hydrangea does best in deep, rich, moist, well-drained soil in eastern or northern exposures.

Zone 5 / China, Japan / 60 to 80 feet

**Lonicera henryi** (Henry honeysuckle) is a vine form of honeysuckle that makes an easy-care, sweetly scented ground cover without quite the rampant runaway qualities of some of its relatives. Nevertheless, it is vigorous enough so that you have to watch it and possibly cut it back from time to time. Its small oval leaves and thin, flexible stems develop into a dense tangle on the ground. The flowers are yellow to purplish red and bloom from June to August; the fruits that follow are black and well liked by wildlife. This honeysuckle tolerates some shade and many different soils; it cannot stand boggy situations, however. It is happiest with ample sun and well-drained, loamy soil.

Zone 5 / China / Twining vine

**Lonicera japonica 'Halliana'** (Hall's honeysuckle) can be a menace if it gets out of control, rampaging over the landscape and smothering any tree or shrub it gets a purchase on. But there is just nothing like it for shrouding a fence, bank, or other barrier in dense dark-green foliage — with the added attraction of deliciously fragrant creamy-white flowers that perfume the air and delight the bees all summer long. This vigorous vine likes any loamy, well-drained soil but cannot tolerate wet situations. It is happiest in full sun. If it threatens to outgrow its intended site, cut it back ruthlessly: it can take it.

Zone 5 / Japan / Twining vine

**Parthenocissus quinquefolia** (Virginia creeper or woodbine) This vine is so tough and resilient that one friend of mine complains it's impossible to kill. If you use it appropriately, however, you shouldn't want to kill it. It holds on to any surface (it provides its own cement) so it makes a great "drapery" to add softness and color to walls. Its 5-part leaves are lustrous green in summer and change to rich purple-scarlet in early fall. Often, in fact, that first dab of red at the top of an old oak tree will be Virginia creeper, not oak. After the leaves fall — which they seem to do all at once, making a glowing carpet on the ground — you can see the small, blue-black berries that give the vine such a high rating with birds. The cultivar called Engelmann woodbine (*Parthenocissus quinquefolia* 'Engelmannii') is an attractive smaller-leaved version.

Zone 4 / Native / Climbing vine

**Parthenocissus tricuspidata** (Boston ivy): Neither an ivy nor native to Boston, this handsome clinging vine came to this country from the Orient. It achieved some slight publicity in 1982, when acres of it were stripped from the walls of the buildings of Harvard University so that old bricks could be repointed (the ivy's adhesive rootlets had not done the masonry any good), which deprived the campus of a hundred-year-old leafy look. The large, 3-lobed, glossy leaves of Boston ivy make a richly textured tapestry that undulates in the breeze. The blue fruits are greatly relished by birds. The leaves are most gorgeous in the fall, when they turn a deep ruby red. Then they drop, leaving a flat tracery of slender stems. This is a fine and indestructible plant for trellises where you want light to filter through in winter, as well as for walls or other stone surfaces. It will flourish in any soil and in any exposure at all. For smaller leaves and a finer texture, the cultivar 'Lowii' is a good choice.

Zone 5 / China, Japan / Climbing vine

**Polygonum aubertii** (Chinese fleece vine, or silver fleece vine) will completely blanket an unsightly fence with its bright green foliage in a matter of months. It is an irrepressibly energetic twining vine and can grow as much as 15 feet in one season. It offers the added feature of fragrant greenish-white flowers, borne in dense clusters in August. Chinese fleece vine will grow almost anywhere and in any amount of sun or shade. It spreads so rapidly (by rhizomes) that it can become a pest, but it's a useful workhorse where it can be contained.

Zone 5 / China / Twining vine

**Vitis spp.** (grapes): For ornamental use, grape vines are a long shot in most settings. The hardy native fox grape (*Vitis labrusca*) is a ruthless smotherer that — much though the birds love it — I can't recommend for any landscape. Other species are somewhat more docile, and some gardeners like them for training over trellises, along fences, or over steep banks. Grapes are fast-growing and tough, with dense, coarse-textured foliage, picturesquely twisting stems, and papery reddish-brown bark. They are happy in well-drained or even dry soils and in partial shade to full sun (although for fruit they demand ample sun). The real joy of grapes, to me, is to have a trellis where you can shape and prune a fruiting vine. (See instructions in the January Landscape Tasks.) There are many marvelous strains adapted to Zones 5 and 6, often hybridized with *Vitis labrusca* for hardiness and vigor. Your nursery can suggest possibilities for your soil and exposure. With just a little care you'll have grape leaves for stuffing and a shady bower for sitting in all summer long — and

with a little more care, a mouth-watering crop for juice, jelly, and eating fresh off the vine in September.

Zones 5 to 6 / Native, Oriental, and European / Clinging vine

**Wisteria floribunda** (Japanese wisteria): This magnificent flowering vine makes a potent statement throughout the year. Its twining, twisted trunks are picturesque in winter; they grow very thick and gnarled in old age. Its leaves come out in late spring and are a bright yellowish-green. Its foot-long dangling clusters of purple flowers emerge about the same time as the leaves; they are breathtaking to see and almost overwhelmingly fragrant, although you should not count on them to bloom until the plant is around 7 years old. For best flowering, give wisteria full sun and a soil not too rich in nitrogen, but fertilize occasionally with phosphate. Since this is a fast-growing and eventually a very massive plant, give it a metal-pipe support or trellis: it can destroy wooden structures. It can also be trained (with support) to grow like a tree. Cultivars with different colored flowers include 'Alba' (white) and 'Rosea' (pink).

Zone 5 / Japan / Twining vine

# FURTHER REFERENCE

The brief book list that follows includes some of my favorite standbys as well as books that are periodically updated to provide state-of-the-art information. All the works listed are widely available at bookstores, garden centers, and supply centers, or directly from their publishers. I do encourage you to seek advice from your local nurseryman or garden center; but if you have more questions than they have time to field, you may want to explore the literature.

The best all-around general garden encyclopedia:

Wyman, Donald. *Wyman's Gardening Encyclopedia*. Revised and Expanded Edition. New York: Macmillan, 1977.

Other encyclopedic works that you may want to consult:

Bush-Brown, James and Louise. *America's Garden Book*. Revised by the New York Botanical Garden. New York: Scribner's, 1980. I actually prefer the earlier editions, which are out of print (but available in libraries); but there is more up-to-date information in the recent one. I used to visit the Bush-Browns when I was in college, and they and their book were a wonderful inspiration.

Taylor, Norman, ed. *Taylor's Encyclopedia of Gardening*, Fourth edition. Boston: Houghton Mifflin, 1976.

Simon and Schuster's Step-by-Step Encyclopedia of Practical Gardening. Christopher Brickell, Editor-in-Chief. New York: Simon and Schuster, 1979–1981. Includes *Fruit*; *Gardening Techniques*; *Garden Pests and Diseases*; *Plant Propagation*; and *Lawns, Ground Cover & Weed Control*.

The best sources for specific topics in gardening, design, and construction are series of handbooks to which new titles are frequently added:

*Brooklyn Botanic Garden Record/Plants & Gardens*. Quarterly publication of Brooklyn Botanic Garden, Brooklyn, N.Y. 11225. Scores of these compact, inexpensive, largely black-and-white booklets are in print, ranging from soils and mulches to trees and shrubs to small-space gardens to garden structures to specialties like roses and bonsai. Catalogue available from BBG.

Time-Life Encyclopedia of Gardening. Alexandria, Va.: Time-Life Books, numerous dates. Over thirty titles on every aspect of landscape gardening from ground covers to design.

Ortho Books (San Francisco, Cal. 94119), a division of Chevron Chemical Company, puts out colorful paperback guides. Among the many titles available are *Award-Winning Small-Space Gardens*; *Do-It-Yourself Garden Construction Know-How*; *All About Fertilizers, Soils & Water*; *All About Growing Fruits and Berries*; *All About Roses*; and *Gardening with Color*.

Sunset Magazine has a book series (published by Lane Publishing Co., Menlo Park, Cal. 94025) that includes *Azaleas, Rhododendrons, Camellias*; *Lawns & Ground Covers*; *Gardening in Containers*; *How to Grow Roses*; *Pruning Handbook*; *How to Build Fences & Gates*; *Sunset Ideas for Patios & Decks*; *Bonsai*; and *Swimming Pools*.

U.S. Government Printing Office (Washington, D.C. 20402) offers a huge variety of inexpensive publications. The two best Subject Bibliographies (catalogues) in the landscaping area are SB-301, *Gardening*; and SB-041, *The Home*. You'll find helpful titles on construction, pest control, cultivation of all kinds of plants, choosing ornamental and fruiting trees and shrubs, attracting birds, and a host of other topics.

It goes without saying that your gardening library should include:

Crockett, James Underwood. *Crockett's Flower Garden*. Boston: Little, Brown, 1981.
———. *Crockett's Victory Garden*. Boston: Little, Brown, 1977.

For general reading and inspiration:

Jekyll, Gertrude. *Wood and Garden. Wall and Water Gardens. Color Schemes for the Flower Garden. The Home and the Garden. Roses*. Topsfield, Mass.: Merrimac Book Service/Antique Collectors Club, reissued 1982–1984. These are classics, written at the turn of the century and now reprinted. Gertrude Jekyll's style is endearing and her artistry and botanical expertise are unexcelled.

For the garden design connoisseur with the utmost patience:

Hubbard, Henry V. and Kimball, Theodora. *An Introduction to the Study of Landscape Design*. Revised Edition. Boston: Hubbard Educational Trust, 1959. The first book of required reading I encountered in my training, and still one of my favorites.

# ZONE MAP

The hardiness zones mapped by the U.S. Department of Agriculture (USDA), shown here, are the ones you are most likely to encounter in gardening books and plantsmen's catalogues. (Some sources list plant hardiness according to the slightly different system of the Arnold Arboretum of Harvard University; just be aware of which set of zones you are working with.) The annual minimum temperature ranges of the USDA zones are listed here. These ranges are approximate and subject to many exceptions, however, as are the demarcations between zones.

Not represented on this map are the average dates of first and last frost for different areas. These vary widely from year to year. They also differ from one place to another, even within a single neighborhood. Some very general indications of spring and fall planting seasons for lawns, trees, and shrubs appear on page 72; but for your particular piece of land, you'll do best to rely on your own experience and that of knowledgeable neighbors.

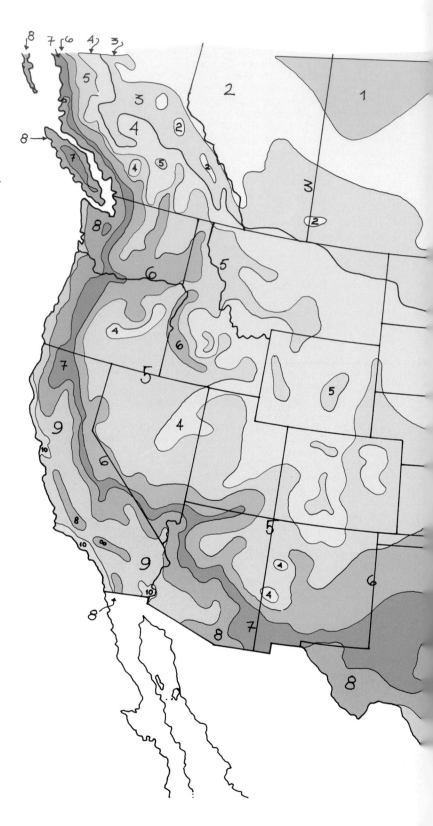

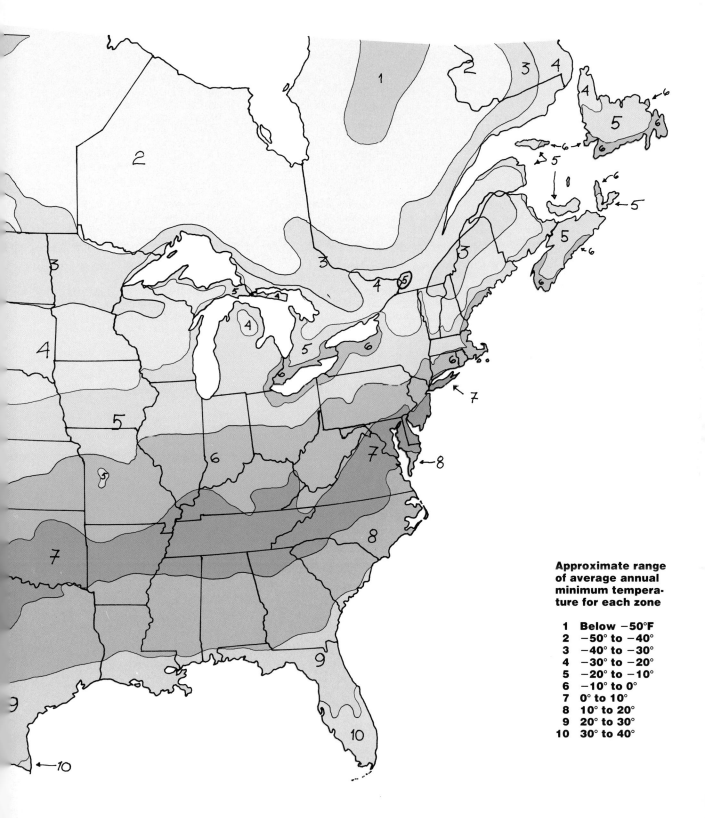

**Approximate range
of average annual
minimum tempera-
ture for each zone**

1   Below −50°F
2   −50° to −40°
3   −40° to −30°
4   −30° to −20°
5   −20° to −10°
6   −10° to 0°
7   0° to 10°
8   10° to 20°
9   20° to 30°
10  30° to 40°

# Index

Page numbers in *italics* refer to illustrations

sassafras albidum, 622, 634, 651, 690, *733*,734, 789, 832–833
sawdust: and nitrogen drawdown, 21, 25, 171; in soil preparation, 24, 46; to improve soil composition, 258; as mulch, 278, 461. *See also* mulching materials
saws: pruning, 642; skill saw, 786
*Saxifraga umbrosa* (London pride), 6
scab, 361. *See also* diseases
*Scabiosa stellata*, 122
scale in design, 555–*556*, 613, 732, 761, 813
scale insects. See pests
scallions, 354, 425. *See also* onions
schedule. *See* garden schedule
scheduling landscape work, 601–602, 609
*Sciadopytis verticillata*, 635, 747, 814, 858
*Scilla* spp., 644–645
screens, 632,; evergreen, 813, fragrant plants, 689; hedge, *797*, 798–799, *801*; trellis, 592, 716; vines, 712, 796
screens, window, 616, 817
scuffle hoe. *See* hoe
Seabrook, Peter, 359
season extenders, 249, 284–285, 500–501; raised beds, 266; cold frame, 266; Wall O' Water, 249, 280–281, 398, 400
seasons: spring and fall planting, 602; and work schedule, 601
security: fences and gates, 802, 804; night lighting for, 810–811
*Sedum* spp., 128, 132, 150, 711, 714, 871
seed catalogs, 268, 292, *293*,521
seed leaves (cotyledons), 273
seedlings: buying, 274–275; fertilizing, 263–264, *271*, 581; hardening off, 275–276, 278; planting outdoors, 275–277; separating, 273; starting, 628; thinning, 283, 286; transplanting, *271*, 273–274, *422*; watering, 310. *See also specific vegetables*
seeds: germination, 270, 272–273, 340–341; pelleted, 340, 341, 378; planting outdoors, 275; sorting, 310; starting indoors, 269–274; storing, 310. *See also specific vegetables*
semi-transparent fences, *802*, 803, 804
*Sempervivum tectorum*, 714, 871
senses, design to appeal to, 590–*591*
septic lines, 584; septic tanks, 596
service areas, 588, 595–596
serviceberry. *See Amelanchier* spp.
sewer lines, 596
shadblow. *See Amelanchier* spp.
shadbush. *See Amelanchier* spp.
shade, 254, 255; artificial, for pepper plants, 231; degrees of, 708, 796; daylilies and, 61, 64; dwarf conifers and, 34; gardening in woodland shade, *708*–711; hostas and, 31, 33, 45–46, 122; and plants for, 629, 711, 712; and plants for drying, 122; peonies and, 172; rhododendrons and, 12, 23, 24; for roses, 78; wildflowers

and, 183, 194; wild garden, 647–648. *See also shade trees*
shade trees, 731–734; for city garden, 747; cooling with, 571, 573, 795; evergreen, 813; pruning, 662, 721, *722–723*; sunblocked by, 796; planting under, 648
shadows: in design, 549, 567; lighting for, 811, 812; on slopes, 675; in winter, 612, *613*
shagbark hickory. *See Carya ovata*
"shake", 637
shallots, 324–325, *428*, 429
shapes: in design, 546–548; pool, 738. *See also* form
shock, in transplanting, 275
shooting star (*Dodecatheon*), 194
shrews, 211. *See also* pests
shrub althea. *See Hibiscus syriacus*
shrubs: for banks and slopes, 671; with colorful bark and twigs, 622; care, 662, 821; with colorful foliage, 789, 791; flowering, 683, 701, 243, 739, 754; fragrant, 689; fruiting, 758–759; planting, 771–773, 791, 807; for pools and ponds, 731; propagating, 703–705; pruning, 642–643, 662, *663–664*, 749; for shady woods, 711; for wildlife, 617. *See also* deciduous shrubs; evergreen shrubs
Siberian carpet cypress, 44
Siberian fig tree, 105
side-dressing, 263. *See also specific vegetables*
silica gel, 120, 129, 131
silky camellia. *See Stewartia malacodendron*
silver fleece vine. See *Polygonum aubertii*
Simmons, Adelma Grenier, 407
simplicity: in design, 560–*561*,566, 597, 628; in paint choices, 733, 745, 749
site, 588; allocating activity areas on, 595–596; construction site, 678–679; on-site visualizing, 599
site selection, 254–255; daylilies, 61; dwarf conifers, 153; hostas, 33–34; lillies, 215; rhododendrons, 23, 24; wildflowers, 182–185, 194
size of garden, 255
sketching designs on base plan, *593*, 598–599
Skogsholm bearberry cotoneaster. *See Cotoneaster dammeri*
sky, in landscape, 564, 567, 612
slate, 619, 621, 660, 739, 785, 786
slope of garden, 254–255
slopes, 584; and banks, 668–669; drainage, *655*, 679, *680*, 681; fences on, *802*, 803; for landscape surfaces, 629, 654–656, 659, 675, 680–681; plants for, 670–671
slow-growing varieties, 630, 691, 778
slow-release fertilizer, 263
slugs and snails, 380, 399, 489–490. See *also* pests
small spaces: designing for, 748–749; plants for, 749–750; small trees for, 761, 763–764

small-space culture, 259, 369–371
*Smilaceae racemosa* (false Solomon seal), 186
smoke tree. *See Cotinus cogygria*
snow: lighting effects with, 810; removal, 622, 623, 629; snow mold, 675; stamping, 819; in winter landscape, *610–611, 612, 613*
snow peas, 323, 426. *See also* peas
snow wreath (*Neviusia Alabamensis*), 190
sod, 259–260, 602, 629; sod-forming grasses, 670
softwood for construction, 695–700; grades, 697–698; types, 696; uses, 716
soil, 573–574; building soil, 575–576; conditions, 588, 593, 595; drainage, 576–577, 678–682; erosion, 660–661, 668–669; preparing for construction, *575–576*, 787–788; profile, 678–679; wet, 731. See also growing soil
soil acidity. *See* pH level
soil alkalinity. *See* pH level
soil preparation, 255–264, 477, 479; adding sand, 46, 81, 153; composition, 256–260; for container gardening, 369; in fall, 258–259, 260, 483, 484, 488, 489, 490, 492–493, 494, 502, 505, 506; fertility, 261–264, 303; fumigating, 68, 192, 193; pH level, 260–261, 502; and purchased topsoil, 21, 34; for raised beds, 263, 267–268; "solarizing", 192, 193; in spring, 259, 260–261; tilling/rototilling, 20–21, 24, 25, 192, 193, 228. *See also* compost; fertilizers; lime/limestone; mulching materials; pH (soil); planting mix; raised beds; *individual plant varieties*
soilless growing medium, 270, *271*, 273, 275, *431*
solar heat, passive, 794–795
solnine, 393
Solomon seal. *See Polygonatum biflora*
sooty blotch, 106. *See also* diseases
*Sophora japonica*, 622, 634, 734, 747, 754, 796, 818, 833, 838
*Sorbus alnifolia*, 617, 622, 634, 643, 764, 770, 818, 356
sorrel. *See Oxydendrum arboreum*
sound, muffling, 668, 797
sourwood. *See Oxydendrum arboreum*
southern red cedar. *See Juniperus*
southern yew (*Podocarpus*), 151
space and mass in design, *544, 545, 546*
space planning, 629
spaces in landscape, *562–563*
spacing: between trees and shrubs, 630; in vegetable beds, 632
spade, 259–260, *326, 328*
spading fork, 260, *326*, 327
spearmint, 405
speciman plants, 614, 615, 648, 733, 761, 813
spicebush, *See Lindera benzoin*
Speedling flats, 297
spider mites. *See* pests
spinach: fertilizing, 263, 325, 474, 493;

(Wildflowers, *continued*)
195; definition of, 176; drying, 121; fertilizing, 192, 194; history of North American, 178; landscaping with, 178, 179, 181, 184–185, 194–195; mulching, 184, 193; pests, 181, 183; planting seeds, 192–193; propagating (vegetative), 178, 181, 187, 191; purchasing, 179, 186, 187, 190–191, 193, 194, 195; seed-grown, 181, 184, 187, 188, 191, 192–193, 195; site selection, 182–185, 194; soil preferences and preparation, 183–184, 192–195; transplanting, 184, 188, 193, 194; watering and drainage, 183, 193, 195; weeds and, 176, 181, 188, 192, 193; as weeds, 187; "wildflower meadows", 186–187

wildlife: landscaping for, 614–616, 673–674; plants for, 577, 617, 670, 710, 813; protecting against, 641–642, 807, 819

willow. *See Salix* spp.

wilting, rhododendron, 27. *See also* rhododendrons

wilts: fusarium, 366, 438; potato, 361; verticillium, 348, 366, 422, 438, 439, 472

wind, 573, 797; and broad-leaved evergreens, 782; determining prevailing directions, 573, 795; protection from: for hostas, 40, 45; for pepper plants, 228, 229, 231, 237; for rhododendrons, 23, 24; and sun diagram, *587*. *See also* windbreaks; windscreens; wind tunnels

wind tunnels, 571, 573; for cooling, 795, *797*

windbreaks, 573, 595, 794, *797–798*

window boxes, 777

windows, 567, 584; fragrant plants for, 688, 689; frames and screening,

816–817; orienting to sun, 795; screening sun, 796

windscreens, 662, 819–*820*

winged euonymus. *See Euonymus* spp.

winter: damage to plants, 623, 641, 662, 779, 782, 798; plants with fruit remaining into winter, 770; sun angles, 795–796; tree planting in, 642; warmth in, 571, 794–795, 796, *797*

winter hazel, fragrant. *See Corylopsis glabrescens*

winter landscape, *570, 610–611, 612, 613–614*, 822; color in, 554; line and form in, 548, 763; plant textures in, 551

winter rye: planting at season end, 471, 472, 483, 488, 489, 490, 492, 493, 494, 510, 511; and soil composition, 258, 259, 261, 263, 264; turning under, *300*, 301, 310, 332

winter squash, 493–494, *507–509*, 518; fertilizing, 262, 263, 401, 431; harvesting, 328, *486–487*, 494, *495*; pests and diseases, 287, 435, 437, 439; planting outdoors, 401, 431; starting indoors, 401; support for, 400; varieties, *269*, 401, 494

winterberry. *See Ilex* spp.

"winterburn", 623, 798

wintercreeper. *See Euonymus* spp.

wintergreen. *See Gaultheria procumbens*

winter-hardy plants: peonies, 162, 167, 170; roses, 86, 87, 89. *See also* frost or cold weather

wintering over: container plants, 776; cuttings, 625, 725; waterlilies, 728

wireworms, 342

Wisley garden (England), 316

*Wisteria* spp., 689, 705, 713, 724; care, 623, 740, 771; *floribunda*, 690, 701, 715, 731, 747, 874

witch alders. *See Fothergilla* spp.

witch hazel. *See Hamamelis* spp.

witches' brooms. *See* dwarf conifers

wood, *695–700*; chips, 705, 723, 772; grain, 697–698; pressure-treated, 632, 669, 698–699; rot-resistant, 632; surface-treated, 699; uses for, 669, 716, 739, 776, 778, 785, 787

wood ashes, 262, 425, 490

wood chips or shavings. *See* mulching materials; wood

woodbine. *See Parthenocissus quinquefolia*

woodchucks, 374, 428

woodland garden, 628, 708–710; plants for, 710–711

woodland habitats, *578*; dry and wet, 579, 647

woodruff, sweet. *See Galium odoratum*

wormwood. *See* artemisia

wreaths/wreathmaking, 403, 513–515. *See also* herbs

Wright, Frank Lloyd, 571

wrought iron, 815, 816; fences, 739, 804; furniture, *752*

yarrow (herb), *128*

yellow root (herb), 100, 651, 671, 693, 711, 714, 841, 866

yellowood. *See Cladrastis lutea*

yew (*Taxus*), 157

Young, Bob, 401

*Zelkova serrata*, 634, 734, 818, 839

zinc, 262

zinnias, 371

zones, hardiness, *876–877*

zoning laws, 589, 803

zucchini, 363, *370*, 398, *456–457*. *See also* summer squash